MILLER COMPREHENSIVE GAAP GUIDE™

1987

A comprehensive restatement of all current promulgated **GENERALLY ACCEPTED ACCOUNTING PRINCIPLES**

MARTIN A. MILLER C.P.A.

HBJ

Harcourt Brace Jovanovich, Publishers
San Diego   New York   London

> This publication is designed to provide accurate and authoritative information in regard to the subject matter covered. It is sold with the understanding that the publisher is not engaged in rendering legal, accounting or other professional service.

The publisher has not sought nor obtained approval of this publication from any other organization, profit or non-profit, and is solely responsible for its contents.

Miller   Comprehensive GAAP Guide
is a trademark of Harcourt Brace Jovanovich, Inc.

Copyright © 1986, 1985, 1984, 1983, 1982, 1981, 1980, 1979, 1978 by Harcourt Brace Jovanovich, Inc.

All rights reserved. No part of this publication may be reproduced or transmitted in any form or by any means, electronic or mechanical, including photocopy, recording, or any information storage and retrieval system, without permission in writing from the publisher.

Requests for permission to make copies of any part of the work should be mailed to: Permissions, Harcourt Brace Jovanovich, Publishers, Orlando, Florida 32887

ISBN: 0-15-601737-7 (hardcover)
ISBN: 0-15-601738-5 (paperback)
ISSN: 0734-8355

Printed in the United States of America

TABLE OF CONTENTS

Foreword   vii
Cross Reference—Original Pronouncements
   to GAAP Guide   ix

Generally Applicable Accounting Principles

Accounting Changes	1.01
Accounting Policies	2.01
Business Combinations	3.01
Changes in Financial Position	4.01
Consolidated Financial Statements	5.01
Contingencies	6.01
Convertible Debt	7.01
Current Assets and Current Liabilities	8.01
Current Value Accounting	9.01
Deferred Compensation Contracts	10.01
Depreciable Assets and Depreciation	11.01
Development Stage Enterprises	12.01
Earnings Per Share	13.01
Equity Method	14.01
Extinguishment of Debt	15.01
Financial Reporting and Changing Prices	15.51
Foreign Operations and Exchange	16.01
General Price-Level Changes	17.01
Government Contracts	18.01
Income Taxes	19.01
Installment Method of Accounting	20.01
Intangible Assets	21.01
Interest on Receivables and Payables	22.01
Interest Costs Capitalized	22.51
Interim Financial Reporting	23.01
Inventory Pricing and Methods	24.01
Investment Tax Credit	25.01
Leases	26.01
Long-Term Construction Contracts	27.01
Long-Term Obligations	27.51
Marketable Securities	28.01

Table of Contents

Nonmonetary Transactions	**29.01**
Pension Plans – Employers	**30.01**
Pension Plans – Settlements and Curtailments	**31.01**
Pension Plan Financial Statements	**31.51**
Product Financing Arrangements	**31.75**
Quasi-Reorganizations	**32.01**
Real and Personal Property Taxes	**33.01**
Related Party Disclosures	**34.01**
Research and Development Costs	**35.01**
Results of Operations	**36.01**
Revenue Recognition	**36.51**
Segmental Reporting	**37.01**
Stockholders' Equity	**38.01**
Stock Issued to Employees	**39.01**
Transfer of Receivables With Recourse	**39.51**
Troubled Debt Restructuring	**40.01**

Specialized Industry Accounting Principles

Banking and Thrift Institutions	**45.01**
Entertainment Industry	
Broadcasters	**50.01**
Cable Television	**51.01**
Motion Picture Films	**52.01**
Record and Music	**53.01**
Franchise Fee Revenue	**60.01**
Insurance Industry	
Insurance Enterprises	**65.01**
Title Plant	**66.01**
Mortgage Banking Industry	**70.01**
Oil and Gas Producing Companies	**75.01**
Real Estate Transactions	
Costs and Rental Operations	**80.01**
Recognition of Sales	**81.01**
Regulated Industries	**85.01**
Disclosure Index	**95.01**
Topical Index	**96.01**

Foreword

This *Comprehensive GAAP Guide* contains all the promulgated and many of the nonpromulgated accounting principles in use today. Each promulgated pronouncement is thoroughly reviewed in a comprehensive format that is easy to assimilate and understand. Many chapters contain in-depth illustrations on the application of the specific accounting principle. Pronouncements covering the same subject matter have been compiled and incorporated in a single chapter regardless of the date of their origin.

Important nonpromulgated accounting principles have been integrated throughout the text in an effort to give the reader a more complete perspective of the specific subject matter.

Perhaps the most important feature of this comprehensive guide to accounting principles is its readability. The utmost care has been exercised to avoid incomprehensible language. Sentence structure has been deliberately simplified as much as possible to foster the maximum comprehension in a minimum period. Illustrations are used generously to demonstrate the applicability of specific concepts and principles, and observation paragraphs are utilized to stress important information.

No attempt is made to resolve apparent errors and conflicts in the promulgated pronouncements. However, these items are objectively brought to the reader's attention.

An innovative Disclosure Index has been provided which contains both required and recommended disclosures currently in use. This index has been designed to assist the preparer or reviewer of financial statements in determining whether necessary disclosures have been made.

Martin A. Miller

Cross-Reference

ORIGINAL PRONOUNCEMENTS TO COMPREHENSIVE GAAP GUIDE CHAPTERS

This locator provides instant cross-reference between an original pronouncement and the chapter(s) in this publication where such pronouncement appears. Original pronouncements are listed chronologically on the left and the chapter(s) in which the pronouncement appears in this GAAP GUIDE on the right. Where an original pronouncement has been superseded, cross-reference is made to the succeeding pronouncement.

ACCOUNTING RESEARCH BULLETINS

(Accounting Research Bulletins (ARB) 1-42 were revised, restated or withdrawn at the time ARB No. 43 was issued.)

ORIGINAL PRONOUNCEMENT	GAAP GUIDE REFERENCE
ARB No. 43 (Restatement and Revision of Accounting Research Bulletins)	
Chapter 1-A:	
Unrealized Profit	Installment Method of Accounting, p. **20.01**
Capital Surplus	Stockholders' Equity, p. **38.01**
Consolidated Statements	Consolidated Financial Statements, p. **5.01**
Treasury Stock	Stockholders' Equity, p. **38.01**
Receivables—Officers & Employees	Current Assets and Current Liabilities, p. **8.01**
Donated Stock	Stockholders' Equity, p. **38.01**
Chapter 1-B:	
Profits or Losses—Treasury Stock	Stockholders' Equity, p. **38.01**
Chapter 2-A:	
Comparative Statements	Consolidated Financial Statements, p. **5.01**
Chapter 2-B:	
Combined Statement—Income & Surplus	Superseded by APB-9
Chapter 3-A:	
Current Assets and Current Liabilities	Current Assets and Current Liabilities, p. **8.01**
Chapter 3-B:	
Application of U.S. Government Securities to Federal Taxes	Superseded by APB-10

GAAP GUIDE / **ix**

Cross-Reference

Chapter 4:
Inventory Pricing

Inventory Pricing and Methods, p. **24.01**

Chapter 5:
Intangible Assets

Superseded by APB-16 and 17

Chapter 6:
Contingency Reserves

Superseded by FASB-5

Chapter 7-A:
Quasi-Reorganizations

Quasi-Reorganizations, p. **32.01**

Chapter 7-B:
Stock Dividends and Splits

Stockholders' Equity, p. **38.01**

Chapter 7-C:
Business Combinations

Superseded by ARB-48

Chapter 8:
Income and Earned Surplus

Superseded by APB-9

Chapter 9-A:
Depreciation and High Costs

Depreciable Assets and Depreciation, p. **11.01**

Chapter 9-B:
Depreciation on Appreciation

Superseded by APB-6

Chapter 9-C:
Emergency Facilities—Depreciation

Depreciable Assets and Depreciation, p. **11.01**

Chapter 10-A:
Accounting for Real and Personal Property Taxes

Real and Personal Property Taxes, p. **33.01**

Chapter 10-B:
Income Taxes

Superseded by APB-11

Chapter 11-A:
Cost-Plus-Fixed-Fee Contracts

Government Contracts, p. **18.01**

Chapter 11-B:
Renegotiations

Government Contracts, p. **18.01**

Chapter 11-C:
Terminated Defense Contracts

Government Contracts, p. **18.01**

Cross-Reference

Chapter 12:
Foreign Operations and Foreign Exchange   Superseded by FASB-52

Chapter 13-A:
Pension Plans—etc.   Superseded by APB-8

Chapter 13-B:
Compensation Involved in Stock Options   Stock Issued to Employees, p. **39.01**

Chapter 14:
Disclosure—Long-Term Leases   Superseded by APB-5

Chapter 15:
Unamortized Discount, Issue Cost, and Redemption Premium Bonds   Superseded by APB-26

ARB No. 44
Declining Balance Depreciation   Superseded by ARB-44 (revised)

ARB No. 44 (revised)
Declining Balance Depreciation   Depreciable Assets and Depreciation, p. **11.01**

ARB No. 45
Long-Term Construction-Type Contracts   Long-Term Construction Contracts, p. **27.01**

ARB No. 46
Discontinuance of Dating Earned Surplus   Quasi-Reorganizations, p. **32.01**

ARB No. 47
Accounting for Costs of Pension Plans   Superseded by APB-8

ARB No. 48
Business Combinations   Superseded by APB-16

ARB No. 49
Earnings Per Share   Superseded by APB-9

ARB No. 50
Contingencies   Superseded by FASB-5

ARB No. 51
Consolidated Financial Statements   Consolidated Financial Statements, p. **5.01**

Cross-Reference

ACCOUNTING PRINCIPLES BOARD OPINIONS

ORIGINAL PRONOUNCEMENT	GAAP GUIDE REFERENCE
APB Opinion No. 1 New Depreciation Guidelines	Depreciable Assets and Depreciation, p. **11.01**
APB Opinion No. 2 Accounting for the Investment Credit	Investment Tax Credit, p. **25.01**
APB Opinion No. 2—Addendum Accounting Principles for Regulated Industries	Superseded by FASB-71
APB Opinion No. 3 The Statement of Source and Application of Funds	Superseded by APB-19
APB Opinion No. 4 Accounting for the Investment Credit	Investment Tax Credit, p. **25.01**
APB Opinion No. 5 Reporting of Leases in Financial Statements of Lessees	Superseded by FASB-13
APB Opinion No. 6 Status of Accounting Research Bulletins	Portions of this Opinion superseded by APB-11, 16, 17, 26 and FASB-8. The balance of this Opinion appears in the following chapters: Stockholders' Equity, p. **38.01** Current Assets and Current Liabilities, p. **8.01** Depreciable Assets and Depreciation, p. **11.01**
APB Opinion No. 7 Accounting for Leases in Financial Statements of Lessors	Superseded by FASB-13
APB Opinion No. 8 Accounting for Costs of a Pension Plan	Superseded by FASB-87
APB Opinion No. 9 Reporting the Results of Operations	Portions of this Opinion superseded by APB-15, 16, 20, 30, and FASB-16. The balance of this Opinion appears in: Results of Operations, p. **36.01**

Cross-Reference

APB Opinion No. 10
Omnibus Opinion—1966

Portions of this Opinion superseded by APB-14, 16, and 18. The balance of this Opinion appears in the following chapters:

Income Taxes, p. **19.01**
Stockholders' Equity, p. **38.01**
Installment Method of Accounting, p. **20.01**

APB Opinion No. 11
Accounting for Income Taxes

Portions of this Opinion superseded by APB-23 and FASB-9. The balance of this Opinion appears in:

Income Taxes, p. **19.01**

APB Opinion No. 12
Omnibus Opinion—1967

Portions of this Opinion superseded by APB-14. The balance of this Opinion appears in the following chapters:

Depreciable Assets and Depreciation, p. **11.01**
Stockholders' Equity, p. **38.01**
Interest on Receivables and Payables, p. **22.01**

APB Opinion No. 13
Amending Paragraph 6 of APB-9, Application to Commercial Banks

Results of Operations, p. **36.01**

APB Opinion No. 14
Accounting for Convertible Debt and Debt Issued with Stock Purchase Warrants

Convertible Debt, p. **7.01**

APB Opinion No. 15
Earnings Per Share

Earnings Per Share, p. **13.01**

APB Opinion No. 16
Business Combinations

Business Combinations, p. **3.01**

APB Opinion No. 17
Intangible Assets

Intangible Assets, p. **21.01**

APB Opinion No. 18
The Equity Method of Accounting for Investments in Common Stock

Equity Method, p. **14.01**

APB Opinion No. 19
Reporting Changes in Financial Position

Changes in Financial Position, p. **4.01**

Cross-Reference

APB Opinion No. 20
Accounting Changes

Accounting Changes, p. **1.01**

APB Opinion No. 21
Interest on Receivables and Payables

Interest on Receivables and Payables, p. **22.01**

APB Opinion No. 22
Disclosure of Accounting Policies

Accounting Policies, p. **2.01**

APB Opinion No. 23
Accounting for Income Taxes—Special Areas

Income Taxes, p. **19.01**

APB Opinion No. 24
Accounting for Income Taxes—Investments in Common Stock Accounted for by the Equity Method

Income Taxes, p. **19.01**

APB Opinion No. 25
Accounting for Stock Issued to Employees

Stock Issued to Employees, p. **39.01**

APB Opinion No. 26
Early Extinguishment of Debt

Extinguishment of Debt, p. **15.01**

APB Opinion No. 27
Accounting for Lease Transaction by Manufacturers or Dealer Lessors

Superseded by FASB-13

APB Opinion No. 28
Interim Financial Reporting

Interim Financial Reporting, p. **23.01**

APB Opinion No. 29
Accounting for Nonmonetary Transactions

Nonmonetary Transactions, p. **29.01**

APB Opinion No. 30
Reporting the Results of Operations

Results of Operations, p. **36.01**

APB Opinion No. 31
Disclosure of Lease Commitments by Lessees

Superseded by FASB-13

FINANCIAL ACCOUNTING STANDARDS BOARD (FASB)-STATEMENTS

ORIGINAL PRONOUNCEMENT GAAP GUIDE REFERENCE

FASB Statement No. 1
Disclosure of Foreign Currency Translation Information

Superseded by FASB-8

Cross-Reference

FASB Statement No. 2
Accounting for Research and Development Costs — Research and Development Costs, p. **35.01**

FASB Statement No. 3
Reporting Accounting Changes in Interim Financial Statements — Accounting Changes, p. **1.01**

FASB Statement No. 4
Reporting Gains and Losses from Extinguishment of Debt — Extinguishment of Debt, p. **15.01**

FASB Statement No. 5
Accounting for Contingencies — Contingencies, p. **6.01**

FASB Statement No. 6
Classification of Short-Term Obligations Expected to be Refinanced — Current Assets and Current Liabilities, p. **8.01**

FASB Statement No. 7
Accounting and Reporting by Development Stage Enterprises — Development Stage Enterprises, p. **12.01**

FASB Statement No. 8
Accounting for the Translation of Foreign Currency Transactions and Foreign Currency Financial Statements — Superseded by FASB-52

FASB Statement No. 9
Accounting for Income Taxes—Oil and Gas Producing Companies — Superseded by FASB-19

FASB Statement No. 10
Extension of "Grandfather" Provisions for Business Combinations — Business Combinations, p. **3.01**

FASB Statement No. 11
Accounting for Contingencies—Transition Method — Contingencies, p. **6.01**

FASB Statement No. 12
Accounting for Certain Marketable Securities — Marketable Securities, p. **28.01**

FASB Statement No. 13
Accounting for Leases — Leases, p. **26.01**

FASB Statement No. 14
Financial Reporting for Segments of a Business Enterprise — Segmental Reporting, p. **37.01**

Cross-Reference

FASB Statement No. 15
Accounting by Debtors and Creditors for Troubled Debt Restructuring

Troubled Debt Restructuring, p. **40.01**

FASB Statement No. 16
Prior Period Adjustments

Results of Operations, p. **36.01**

FASB Statement No. 17
Accounting for Leases—Initial Direct Costs

Leases, p. **26.01**

FASB Statement No. 18
Financial Reporting for Segments of Business Enterprises—Interim Financial Statements

Segmental Reporting, p. **37.01**

FASB Statement No. 19
Financial Accounting and Reporting by Oil and Gas Producing Companies

Oil and Gas Producing Companies, p. **75.01**

FASB Statement No. 20
Accounting for Forward Exchange Contracts

Superseded by FASB-52

FASB Statement No. 21
Suspension of the Reporting of Earnings per Share and Segment Information by Nonpublic Enterprises

Earnings Per Share, p. **13.01**
Segmental Reporting, p. **37.01**

FASB Statement No. 22
Changes in the Provisions of Lease Agreements Resulting from Refunding of Tax-Exempt Debt

Leases, p. **26.01**

FASB Statement No. 23
Inception of the Lease

Leases, p. **26.01**

FASB Statement No. 24
Reporting Segment Information in Financial Statements That Are Presented in Another Enterprise's Financial Report

Segmental Reporting, p. **37.01**

FASB Statement No. 25
Suspension of Certain Accounting Requirements for Oil and Gas Producing Companies

Oil and Gas Producing Companies, p. **75.01**

FASB Statement No. 26
Profit Recognition on Sales-Type Leases of Real Estate

Leases, p. **26.01**

FASB Statement No. 27
Classification of Renewals or Extensions of Existing Sales-Type or Direct Financing Leases — Leases, p. **26.01**

FASB Statement No. 28
Accounting for Sales with Leasebacks — Leases, p. **26.01**

FASB Statement No. 29
Determining Contingent Rentals — Leases, p. **26.01**

FASB Statement No. 30
Disclosure of Information About Major Customers — Segmental Reporting, p. **37.01**

FASB Statement No. 31
Accounting for Tax Benefits Related to U.K. Tax Legislation Concerning Stock Relief — Income Taxes, p. **19.01**

FASB Statement No. 32
Specialized Accounting and Reporting Principles and Practices in AICPA Statements of Position and Guides on Accounting and Auditing Matters — Accounting Changes, p. **1.01**

FASB Statement No. 33
Financial Reporting and Changing Prices — Financial Reporting and Changing Prices, p. **15.51**

FASB Statement No. 34
Capitalization of Interest Cost — Interest Costs Capitalized, p. **22.51**

FASB Statement No. 35
Accounting and Reporting by Defined Benefit Plans — Pension Plan Financial Statements, p. **31.51**

FASB Statement No. 36
Disclosure of Pension Information — Superseded by FASB-87

FASB Statement No. 37
Balance Sheet Classification of Deferred Income Taxes — Income Taxes, p. **19.01**

FASB Statement No. 38
Accounting for Preacquisition Contingencies of Purchased Enterprises — Contingencies, p. **6.01**

FASB Statement No. 39
Financial Reporting and Changing Prices: Specialized Assets—Mining and Oil and Gas — Financial Reporting and Changing Prices, p. **15.51**

Cross-Reference

FASB Statement No. 40

Financial Reporting and Changing Prices: Specialized Assets—Timberlands and Growing Timber

Financial Reporting and Changing Prices, p. **15.51**

FASB Statement No. 41

Financial Reporting and Changing Prices: Specialized Assets—Income-Producing Real Estate

Financial Reporting and Changing Prices, p. **15.51**

FASB Statement No. 42

Determining Materiality for Capitalization of Interest Cost

Interest Costs Capitalized, p. **22.51**

FASB Statement No. 43

Accounting for Compensated Absences

Current Assets and Current Liabilities, p. **8.01**

FASB Statement No. 44

Accounting for Intangible Assets of Motor Carriers

Intangible Assets, p. **21.01**

FASB Statement No. 45

Accounting for Franchise Fee Revenue

Franchise Fee Revenue, p. **60.01**

FASB Statement No. 46

Financial Reporting and Changing Prices: Motion Picture Films

Financial Reporting and Changing Prices, p. **15.51**

FASB Statement No. 47

Disclosure of Long-Term Obligations

Long-Term Obligations, p. **27.51**

FASB Statement No. 48

Revenue Recognition When Right of Return Exists

Revenue Recognition, p. **36.51**

FASB Statement No. 49

Accounting for Product Financing Arrangements

Product Financing Arrangements, p. **31.75**

FASB Statement No. 50

Financial Reporting in the Record and Music Industry

Record and Music, p. **53.01**

FASB Statement No. 51

Financial Reporting by Cable Television Companies

Cable Television, p. **51.01**

Cross-Reference

FASB Statement No. 52
Foreign Currency Translation

Foreign Operations and Exchange, p. **16.01**

FASB Statement No. 53
Financial Reporting by Producers of Motion Picture Films

Motion Picture Films, p. **52.01**

FASB Statement No. 54
Financial Reporting and Changing Prices: Investment Companies

Financial Reporting and Changing Prices, p. **15.51**

FASB Statement No. 55
Determining Whether a Convertible Security Is a Common Stock Equivalent

Earnings Per Share, p. **13.01**

FASB Statement No. 56
Designation of AICPA Guide and Statement of Position (SOP) 81-1 on Contractor Accounting and SOP 81-2 Concerning Hospital-Related Organizations as Preferable for Purposes of Applying APB Opinion 20

Accounting Changes, p. **1.01**

FASB Statement No. 57
Related Party Disclosures

Related Party Disclosures, p. **34.01**

FASB Statement No. 58
Capitalization of Interest Cost in Financial Statements that Include Investments Accounted for by the Equity Method

Interest Costs Capitalized, p. **22.51**
Equity Method, p. **14.01**

FASB Statement No. 59
Deferral of the Effective Date of Certain Accounting Requirements for Pension Plans of State and Local Governmental Units

Superseded by FASB-75

FASB Statement No. 60
Accounting and Reporting by Insurance Enterprises

Insurance Enterprises, p. **65.01**

FASB Statement No. 61
Accounting for Title Plant

Title Plant, p. **66.01**

FASB Statement No. 62
Capitalization of Interest Cost In Situations Involving Certain Tax-Exempt Borrowings and Certain Gifts and Grants

Interest Costs Capitalized, p. **22.51**

Cross-Reference

FASB Statement No. 63
Financial Reporting by Broadcasters

Broadcasters, p. **50.01**

FASB Statement No. 64
Extinguishments of Debt Made to Satisfy Sinking-Fund Requirements

Extinguishment of Debt, p. **15.01**

FASB Statement No. 65
Accounting for Certain Mortgage Banking Activities

Mortgage Banking Industry, p. **70.01**

FASB Statement No. 66
Accounting for Sales of Real Estate

Real Estate-Recognition of Sales, p. **81.01**

FASB Statement No. 67
Accounting for Costs and Initial Rental Operations of Real Estate Projects

Real Estate Costs and Initial Rental Operations, p. **80.01**

FASB Statement No. 68
Research and Development Arrangements

Research and Development Costs, p. **35.01**

FASB Statement No. 69
Disclosures about Oil and Gas Producing Activities

Oil and Gas Producing Companies, p. **75.01**

FASB Statement No. 70
Financial Reporting and Changing Prices: Foreign Currency Translation

Financial Reporting and Changing Prices, p. **15.51**

FASB Statement No. 71
Accounting for the Effects of Certain Types of Regulation

Regulated Industries, p. **85.01**

FASB Statement No. 72
Accounting for Certain Acquisitions of Banking or Thrift Institutions

Intangible Assets, p. **21.01**
Business Combinations, p. **3.01**

FASB Statement No. 73
Reporting a Change in Accounting for Railroad Track Structures

Accounting Changes, p. **1.01**

FASB Statement No. 74
Accounting for Special Termination Benefits Paid to Employees

Superseded by FASB-88

Cross-Reference

FASB Statement No. 75
Deferral of the Effective Date of Certain Accounting Requirements for Pension Plans of State and Local Governmental Units — Pension Plan Financial Statements, p. **31.51**

FASB Statement No. 76
Extinguishment of Debt — Extinguishment of Debt, p. **15.01**

FASB Statement No. 77
Reporting by Transferors for Transfers of Receivables with Recourse — Transfer of Receivables With Recourse, p. **39.51**

FASB Statement No. 78
Classification of Obligations That Are Callable by the Creditor — Current Assets and Current Liabilities, p. **8.01**

FASB Statement No. 79
Elimination of Certain Disclosures for Business Combinations by Nonpublic Enterprises — Business Combinations, p. **3.01**

FASB Statement No. 80
Accounting for Futures Contracts — Marketable Securities, p. **28.01**

FASB Statement No. 81
Disclosure of Postretirement Health Care and Life Insurance Benefits — Deferred Compensation Contracts, p. **10.01**

FASB Statement No. 82
Financial Reporting and Changing Prices: Elimination of Certain Disclosures — Financial Reporting and Changing Prices, p. **15.51**

FASB Statement No. 83
Designation of AICPA Guides and Statement of Position on Accounting by Brokers and Dealers in Securities, by Employee Benefit Plans, and by Banks as Preferable for Purposes of Applying APB Opinion 20 — Accounting Changes, p. **1.01**

FASB Statement No. 84
Induced Conversions of Convertible Debt — Convertible Debt, p. **7.01**

FASB Statement No. 85
Yield Test for Determining whether a Convertible Security Is a Common Stock Equivalent — Earnings Per Share, p. **13.01**

FASB Statement No. 86
Accounting for the Costs of Computer Software to Be Sold, Leased, or Otherwise Marketed — Research and Development Costs, p. **35.01**

Cross-Reference

FASB Statement No. 87
Employers' Accounting for Pensions

Pension Plans - Employers, p. **30.01**

FASB Statement No. 88
Employers' Accounting for Settlements and Curtailments of Defined Benefit Pension Plans and for Termination Benefits

Pension Plans - Settlements and Curtailments, p. **31.01**

FINANCIAL ACCOUNTING STANDARDS BOARD (FASB)-INTERPRETATIONS

ORIGINAL PRONOUNCEMENT | GAAP GUIDE REFERENCE

FASB Interpretation No. 1
Accounting Changes Related to the Cost of Inventory

Accounting Changes, p. **1.01**

FASB Interpretation No. 2
Imputing Interest on Debt Arrangements Made Under the Federal Bankruptcy Act

Superseded by FASB-15

FASB Interpretation No. 3
Accounting for the Cost of Pension Plans Subject to the Employee Retirement Income Security Act of 1974

Superseded by FASB-87

FASB Interpretation No. 4
Applicability of FASB Statement No. 2 to Business Combinations Accounted for by the Purchase Method

Research and Development Costs, p. **35.01**

FASB Interpretation No. 5
Applicability of FASB Statement No. 2 to Development Stage Enterprises

Superseded by FASB-7

FASB Interpretation No. 6
Applicability of FASB Statement No. 2 to Computer Software

Research and Development Costs, p. **35.01**

FASB Interpretation No. 7
Applying FASB Statement No. 7 to Financial Statements of Established Operating Enterprises

Development Stage Enterprises, p. **12.01**

FASB Interpretation No. 8
Classification of a Short-Term Obligation Repaid Prior to Being Replaced by a Long-Term Security

Current Assets and Current Liabilities, p. **8.01**

Cross-Reference

FASB Interpretation No. 9

Applying APB Opinion Nos. 16 and 17 When A Savings and Loan Association or a Similar Institution is Acquired in a Business Combination Accounted for by the Purchase Method — Business Combinations, p. **3.01**

FASB Interpretation No. 10

Application of FASB Statement No. 12 to Personal Financial Statements — Rescinded by FASB-83

FASB Interpretation No. 11

Changes in Market Value After the Balance Sheet Date — Marketable Securities, p. **28.01**

FASB Interpretation No. 12

Accounting for Previously Established Allowance Accounts — Marketable Securities, p. **28.01**

FASB Interpretation No. 13

Consolidation of a Parent and Its Subsidiaries Having Different Balance Sheet Dates — Marketable Securities, p. **28.01**

FASB Interpretation No. 14

Reasonable Estimation of the Amount of a Loss — Contingencies, p. **6.01**

FASB Interpretation No. 15

Translation of Unamortized Policy Acquisition Costs by a Stock Life Insurance Company — Superseded by FASB-52

FASB Interpretation No. 16

Clarification of Definitions and Accounting for Marketable Equity Securities that Become Nonmarketable — Marketable Securities, p. **28.01**

FASB Interpretation No. 17

Applying the Lower of Cost or Market in Translated Financial Statements — Superseded by FASB-52

FASB Interpretation No. 18

Accounting for Income Taxes in Interim Periods — Income Taxes, p. **19.01**

FASB Interpretation No. 19

Lessee Guarantee of the Residual Value of Leased Property — Leases, p. **26.01**

FASB Interpretation No. 20

Reporting Accounting Changes under AICPA Statements of Position — Accounting Changes, p. **1.01**

GAAP GUIDE / xxiii

Cross-Reference

FASB Interpretation No. 21
Accounting for Leases in a Business Combination — Leases, p. **26.01**

FASB Interpretation No. 22
Applicability of Indefinite Reversal Criteria to Timing Differences — Income Taxes, p. **19.01**

FASB Interpretation No. 23
Leases of Certain Property Owned by a Governmental Unit or Authority — Leases, p. **26.01**

FASB Interpretation No. 24
Leases Involving Only a Part of a Building — Leases, p. **26.01**

FASB Interpretation No. 25
Accounting for an Unused Investment Tax Credit — Investment Tax Credit, p. **25.01**

FASB Interpretation No. 26
Accounting for Purchase of a Leased Asset by the Lessee during the Term of the Lease — Leases, p. **26.01**

FASB Interpretation No. 27
Accounting for a Loss On a Sublease — Leases, p. **26.01**

FASB Interpretation No. 28
Accounting for Stock Appreciation Rights and other Variable Stock Option or Award Plans — Stock Issued to Employees, p. **39.01**

FASB Interpretation No. 29
Reporting Tax Benefits Realized on Disposition of Investments in Certain Subsidiaries and Other Investees — Income Taxes, p. **19.01**

FASB Interpretation No. 30
Accounting for Involuntary Conversions of Nonmonetary Assets to Monetary Assets — Nonmonetary Transactions, p. **29.01**

FASB Interpretation No. 31
Treatment of Stock Compensation Plans in EPS Computations — Stock Issued to Employees, p. **39.01**

FASB Interpretation No. 32
Application of Percentage Limitations in Recognizing Investment Tax Credit — Investment Tax Credit, p. **25.01**

FASB Interpretation No. 33

Applying FASB Statement No. 34 to Oil and Gas Producing Operations Accounted for by the Full Cost Method

Oil and Gas Producing Companies, p. **75.01**

FASB Interpretation No. 34

Disclosure of Indirect Guarantees of Indebtedness of Others

Contingencies, p. **6.01**

FASB Interpretation No. 35

Criteria for Applying the Equity Method of Accounting for Investments in Common Stock

Equity Method, p. **14.01**

FASB Interpretation No. 36

Accounting for Exploratory Wells in Progress at the End of a Period

Oil and Gas Producing Companies, p. **75.01**

FASB Interpretation No. 37

Accounting for Translation Adjustments upon Sale of Part of an Investment in a Foreign Entity

Foreign Operations, and Exchange, p. **16.01**

FASB Interpretation No. 38

Determining the Measurement Date for Stock Option, Purchase, and Award Plans Involving Junior Stock

Stock Issued to Employees, p. **39.01**

FINANCIAL ACCOUNTING STANDARDS BOARD-TECHNICAL BULLETINS

FASB Technical Bulletins are issued by the Staff of the Financial Accounting Standards Board to provide timely guidance on specific accounting questions. Technical Bulletins are not approved by the FASB and are not considered promulgated GAAP. However, if a majority of the Board objects to the issuance of a Technical Bulletin, it is not issued.

ORIGINAL PRONOUNCEMENT   GAAP GUIDE REFERENCE

Technical Bulletin 79-1

Purpose and Scope of FASB Technical Bulletins and Procedures for Issuance

No reference

Technical Bulletin 79-2

Computer Software Costs

Superseded by FASB-86

Cross-Reference

Technical Bulletin 79-3

Subjective Acceleration Clauses in Long-Term Debt Agreements — Current Assets and Current Liabilities, p. **8.01**

Technical Bulletin 79-4

Segment Reporting of Puerto Rican Operations — Segmental Reporting, p. **37.01**

Technical Bulletin 79-5

Meaning of the Term "Customer" As It Applies to Health Care Facilities under FASB Statement-14 — Segmental Reporting, p. **37.01**

Technical Bulletin 79-6

Valuation Allowances Following Debt Restructuring — Troubled Debt Restructuring, p. **40.01**

Technical Bulletin 79-7

Recoveries of a Previous Writedown under a Troubled Debt Restructuring Involving a Modification of Terms — Troubled Debt Restructuring, p. **40.01**

Technical Bulletin 79-8

Applicability of FASB Statements 21 and 33 to Certain Brokers and Dealers in Securities — Financial Reporting and Changing Prices, p. **15.51**

Technical Bulletin 79-9

Accounting in Interim Periods for Changes in Income Tax Rates — Income Taxes, p. **19.01**

Technical Bulletin 79-10

Fiscal Funding Clauses in Lease Agreements — Leases, p. **26.01**

Technical Bulletin 79-11

Effect of a Penalty on the Term of a Lease — Leases, p. **26.01**

Technical Bulletin 79-12

Interest Rate Used in Calculating the Present Value of Minimum Lease Payments — Leases, p. **26.01**

Technical Bulletin 79-13

Applicability of FASB Statement-13 to Current Value Financial Statements — Financial Reporting and Changing Prices, p. **15.51**

Technical Bulletin 79-14

Upward Adjustment of Guaranteed Residual Values — Leases, p. **26.01**

Cross-Reference

Technical Bulletin 79-15

Accounting for Loss on a Sublease Not Involving the Disposal of a Segment — Leases, p. **26.01**

Technical Bulletin 79-16

Effect of a Change in Income Tax Rate on the Accounting for Leveraged Leases — Leases, p. **26.01**

Technical Bulletin 79-17

Reporting Cumulative Effect Adjustment from Retroactive Application of FASB Statement-13 — Leases, p. **26.01**

Technical Bulletin 79-18

Transition Requirement of Certain FASB Amendments and Interpretations of FASB Statement-13 — Leases, p. **26.01**

Technical Bulletin 79-19

Investors Accounting for Unrealized Losses on Marketable Securities Owned by an Equity Method Investee — Marketable Securities, p. **28.01**

Technical Bulletin 80-1

Early Extinguishment of Debt through Exchange for Common or Preferred Stock — Extinguishment of Debt, p. **15.01**

Technical Bulletin 80-2

Classification of Debt Restructurings by Debtors and Creditors for Troubled Debt Restructurings — Troubled Debt Restructuring, p. **40.01**

Technical Bulletin 81-1

Disclosure of Interest Rate Futures Contracts and Forward and Standby Contracts — Rescinded by FASB Interpretation - 38

Technical Bulletin 81-2

Accounting for Unused Investment Tax Credits Acquired in a Business Combination Accounted for by the Purchase Method — Investment Tax Credit, p. **25.01**

Technical Bulletin 81-3

Multi-employer Pension Plan Amendments Act of 1980 — Pension Plans—Employers, p. **31.01**

Technical Bulletin 81-4

Classification as Monetary or Nonmonetary Items — Financial Reporting and Changing Prices, p. **15.51**

Technical Bulletin 81-5

Offsetting Interest Cost to Be Capitalized with Interest Income — Superseded by FASB-62

Cross-Reference

Technical Bulletin 81-6

Applicability of Statement 15 to Debtors in Bankruptcy Situations

Troubled Debt Restructuring, p. **40.01**

Technical Bulletin 82-1

Disclosure of the Sale or Purchase of Tax Benefits Through Tax Leases

Accounting Policies, p. **2.01**

Technical Bulletin 82-2

Accounting for the Conversion of Stock Options into Incentive Stock Options as a Result of the Economic Recovery Tax Act of 1981

Stock Issued to Employees, p. **39.01**

Technical Bulletin 83-1

Accounting for the Reduction in the Tax Basis of an Asset Caused by the Investment Tax Credit

Income Taxes, p. **19.01**
Investment Tax Credit, p. **25.01**

Technical Bulletin 84-1

Accounting for Stock Issued to Acquire the Results of a Research and Development Arrangement

Business Combinations, p. **3.01**
Research and Development Costs, p. **35.01**

Technical Bulletin 84-2

Accounting for the Effects of the Tax Reform Act of 1984 on Deferred Income Taxes Relating to Domestic International Sales Corporations

Income Taxes, p. **19.01**

Technical Bulletin 84-3

Accounting for the Effects of the Tax Reform Act of 1984 on Deferred Income Taxes of Stock Life Insurance Enterprises

Insurance Enterprises, p. **65.01**

Technical Bulletin 84-4

In-Substance Defeasance of Debt

Extinguishment of Debt, p. **15.01**

Technical Bulletin 85-1

Accounting for the Receipt of Federal Home Loan Mortgage Corporation Participating Preferred Stock

Nonmonetary Transactions, p. **29.01**

Technical Bulletin 85-2

Accounting for Collateralized Mortgage Obligations (CMOs)

Mortgage Banking Industry, p. **70.01**

Technical Bulletin 85-3

Accounting for Operating Leases with Scheduled Rent Increases

Leases, p. **26.01**

Technical Bulletin 85-4

Accounting for Purchases of Life Insurance Current Assets and Current Liabilities, p. **8.01**

Technical Bulletin 85-5

Issues Relating to Accounting for Business Combinations, Including
- Costs of Closing Duplicate Facilities of an Acquirer
- Stock Transactions between Companies under Common Control
- Downstream Mergers
- Identical Common Shares for a Pooling of Interests
- Pooling of Interests by Mutual and Cooperative Enterprises

Business Combinations, p. **3.01**

Business Combinations, p. **3.01**
Business Combinations, p. **3.01**

Business Combinations, p. **3.01**

Business Combinations, p. **3.01**

Technical Bulletin 85-6

Accounting for a Purchase of Treasury Shares at a Price Significantly in Excess of the Current Market Price of the Shares and the Income Statement Classification of Costs Incurred in Defending against a Takeover Attempt

Stockholders' Equity, p. **38.01**

ACCOUNTING CHANGES

Background

The promulgated GAAP on accounting changes are as follows:

APB-20 – Accounting Changes
FASB-3 – Reporting Accounting Changes in Interim Financial Statements
FASB-32 – Specialized Accounting and Reporting Principles and Practices in AICPA Statements of Position and Guides on Accounting and Auditing Matters
FASB-56 – Designation of AICPA Guide and Statement of Position (SOP) 81-1 on Contractor Accounting and SOP 81-2 Concerning Hospital Related Organizations as Preferable for Purposes of Applying APB-20
FASB-73 – Reporting a Change in Accounting for Railroad Track Structures
FASB-83 – Designation of AICPA Guides and Statement of Position on Accounting by Brokers and Dealers in Securities, by Employee Benefit Plans, and by Banks as Preferable for Purposes of Applying APB Opinion 20
FASB Interpretation-1 – Accounting Changes Related to the Cost of Inventory
FASB Interpretation-20 – Reporting Accounting Changes under AICPA Statements of Position

The promulgated GAAP apply to a full set of financial statements prepared in conformity with GAAP. In addition, the promulgated GAAP specifically do not alter or amend any accounting change made in conformity with industry audit guides issued by the AICPA in the past or in the future.

> **OBSERVATION:** Because the SEC rejected the successful efforts accounting method for oil and gas producing companies which is embodied in FASB-19, FASB-19 was subsequently amended in February 1979 by FASB-25.
> FASB-25 specifically states that for the purposes of the promulgated GAAP on Accounting Changes (APB-20) the provisions of FASB-19 pertaining to the successful efforts method remain in effect. Therefore, since FASB-19 expressses a preference for the suc-

GAAP GUIDE / **1.01**

cessful efforts method of accounting and rejects other methods, an enterprise that changes to any method other than the successful efforts will have the burden of justifying such change (APB-20).

Types of Accounting Changes

Accounting changes are broadly classified as (1) changes in an accounting principle, (2) changes in an accounting estimate, and (3) changes in the reporting entity.

The correction of an error in previously issued financial statements is not an accounting change.

Changes in Accounting Principles

There is a presumption that once adopted, an accounting principle should not be changed in accounting for events or for transactions of a similar nature. The pervasive principle of *consistency* enhances the utility of financial statements.

An accounting principle may be changed if the alternative principle is preferable (rule of preferability).

An accounting change should not be made for a single transaction or for a transaction or event in the past that has been terminated or is nonrecurring.

A change in an accounting principle is the result of changing from one acceptable accounting principle to another acceptable accounting principle. A change in an accounting practice or method is also considered a change in accounting principle. Because the current or future effects of a change in an accounting estimate cannot be separated from an accounting principle, a change in an accounting estimate that is recognized in part or in whole by a change in an accounting principle should be reported as a change in an accounting estimate. For example, a change to expensing from deferring a cost because its future benefits have become doubtful involves both a change in an accounting principle and a change in an estimate, which are inseparable. These types of changes are reported as a change in an accounting estimate.

A change in, or a new, promulgated GAAP or the issuance of an industry audit guide by the AICPA constitutes sufficient support for a change in an accounting principle. Other changes in an accounting principle must be justified by the company making the change.

FASB-32 specifies that the specialized accounting and reporting principles which appear in certain AICPA Statements of Position and Guides on accounting and auditing matters are *preferable accounting principles* for the purposes of justifying a change in accounting principle under APB-20 (Accounting Changes).

The following Industry Audit Guides and one Statement of Position (SOP) were expressly excluded from FASB-32 because they, in the opinion of the FASB, do not contain any specialized accounting and/or reporting principles:

1. SOP 75-4, Presentation of Disclosure of Financial Forecasts
2. The Auditor's Study and Evaluation of Internal Control in EDP Systems
3. Audits of Service-Center-Produced Records
4. Computer Assisted Audit Techniques
5. Medicare Audit Guide

In addition, FASB-32 excludes the industry and audit guide entitled "Audits of State and Local Governmental Units," and SOP 75-3 (Accruals of Revenues and Expenditures by State and Local Governmental Units). The specialized accounting principles and practices for state and local governmental units are promulgated by the Governmental Accounting Standards Board (GASB).

FASB-32 also states that future Statements of Position and Guides on accounting and auditing matters, if acceptable to the FASB and after appropriate due process, may become additional preferable accounting principles (PAP).

FASB-56 and FASB-83 cover the following AICPA publications that contain preferable accounting principles and practices and were issued subsequent to FASB-32:

- Audit and Accounting Guide for Construction Contractors
- Statement of Position 81-1 (Accounting for Performance of Construction-Type and Certain Production-Type Contracts)
- Statement of Position 81-2 (Reporting Practices Concerning Hospital-Related Organizations)
- Statement of Position 83-1 (Reporting by Banks of Investment Securities Gains or Losses)
- Industry Audit Guide (Audits of Banks, 1983)
- Audit and Accounting Guide (Audits of Brokers and Dealers in Securities, 1985)
- Audit and Accounting Guide (Audits of Employee Benefit Plans, 1983)

For the purposes of making an accounting change (APB-20), the specialized accounting principles and practices that appear in the above AICPA publications are designated as "preferable" in accordance with the provisions of FASB-32. In other words, FASB-56 and FASB-83 extend the provisions of FASB-32 to the above AICPA publications.

> **OBSERVATION:** *A clear understanding of PAP is absolutely necessary. Some PAP are merely the application of existing GAAP to specialized circumstances. However, many PAP are clearly new principles that are apparently equivalent to promulgated GAAP. The latter category of PAP are probably the most difficult to comprehend.*
>
> *Since the issuance of FASB-32, the FASB has been extracting the preferable accounting principles and practices from the numerous AICPA publications and has been issuing them in the form of FASB Statements.*

The following borderline areas are not considered a change in an accounting principle:

1. A principle, practice, or method adopted for the first time on new or previously immaterial events or transactions
2. A principle, practice, or method adopted or modified because of events or transactions that are clearly different in substance
3. Changing from an accelerated depreciation method to straight line at a planned point in the life of an asset, provided the plan is made at the time of adoption of the accelerated method and the policy is consistently applied

A change in the composition of the elements of cost (material, labor, and overhead) included in inventory is an accounting change that must be justified on the basis of the rule of preferability (FASB Interpretation-1).

The FASB has delegated to the AICPA the power to issue Statements of Position on how to report accounting changes (FASB Interpretation-20).

The following are the more common changes in accounting principles:

1. A change in the method of pricing inventory, such as LIFO to FIFO or FIFO to LIFO
2. A change in the method of depreciating previously recorded assets, such as from a straight line to an accelerated method or from an accelerated to a straight-line method

3. A change in the method of accounting for long-term construction-type contracts, such as from the percentage-of-completion method to the completed-contract method or from the completed-contract method to the percentage-of-completion method

As mentioned earlier, a change in an accounting principle to effectuate a change in an accounting estimate is not considered a change in an accounting principle. It is considered a change in an accounting estimate.

Reporting a Change in an Accounting Principle

Although the presumption is that once an accounting principle has been adopted it should not be changed, when a change is necessary it should be recognized by including the cumulative effect of the change in the net income of the period of change and not by restating the financial statements of prior periods. The cumulative effect of a change in an accounting principle is equal to the total direct effects (less related taxes) that the change has on prior periods. For example, if the total direct effects of a change in a depreciation method has the effect of increasing prior years' income by $100,000 and if the current year's tax rate is 50%, the cumulative effect of the change in the depreciation method is $50,000. Indirect effects (nondiscretionary effects) are included in the cumulative effect only if they are to be recorded on the books as a result of the change in accounting principle. Direct and indirect effects are discussed more fully later in this chapter.

The effect of a change in an accounting principle for the current period is not included in the cumulative effect, but the net income for the current period is reported by using the newly adopted accounting principle.

Although the cumulative effect is not an extraordinary item, it is shown in the income statement net of related tax effects between extraordinary items and net income, as follows:

Income before extraordinary items (includes the effect of a change in an accounting principle for the current year)	$XX,XXX
Extraordinary items (*Note:* _____)—net of related tax effects	X,XXX

Accounting Changes

Cumulative effect of a change in an accounting principle (includes the effect of a change in an accounting principle for prior years)—net of related tax effects	X,XXX
Net income	$XX,XXX

Earnings per share shown on the face of the income statement should include the per share amount attributable to the cumulative effects of the accounting change (net of related taxes).

At this juncture it may be well to establish the fact that the promulgated GAAP provides some exceptions to the rule of not restating prior-year financial statements in accounting for a change in an accounting principle. The following specific items are exceptions to the general rule, and prior-period financial statements which are presented for comparative purposes must be retroactively restated in reporting a change in an accounting principle:

1. Change from LIFO method of inventory pricing to another method
2. Change in accounting for long-term construction-type contracts
3. Change to or from the "full cost" method of accounting in the extractive industries
4. One-time change for closely held corporations in connection with a public offering of its equity securities, or when such a company first issues financial statements (a) for obtaining additional equity capital from investors, (b) for effecting a business combination, or (c) for registering securities
5. Change from the retirement-replacement-betterment method of accounting for railroad track structures to the depreciation method of accounting (FASB-73)

> **OBSERVATION:** *FASB-73 amends paragraph 27 of APB-20 to specify that a change from the retirement-replacement-betterment method of accounting for railroad track structures to the depreciation method of accounting shall be accounted for by restating all prior-period financial statements that are presented for comparative purposes.*

In computing the cumulative effect of a change in an accounting principle, the *direct effects* of the change are always included, but the *nondiscretionary effects* (indirect effects) are included only if they are being recorded on the books as a result of the change. Direct effects of a change in accounting principle are those adjustments which are necessary to apply the change to all prior periods that are affected. Nondiscretionary effects (indirect) are "secondary effects" that sometimes arise from applying the newly adopted accounting principle to the prior years involved in the change. In other words, nondiscretionary effects are those which are caused by the direct effects. For example, a change from an accelerated depreciation method to the straight-line method will directly affect the net income of the prior periods in which the accelerated method was used. However, profit-sharing expense, incentive compensation costs and royalties based on net income are affected only if the base on which they were computed (net income, income before extraordinary items, etc.) is changed. Therefore, when income of a prior period is changed by a direct effect of a change in an accounting principle, it may result in a nondiscretionary effect. If the nondiscretionary effect is to be recorded on the books as a result of the change in accounting principle, it is included in the cumulative effect. For example, if in prior years a manager had been receiving a bonus of 10% of net income and a change in an accounting principle affects the prior years' bonuses, a nondiscretionary effect results. If an adjustment is to be made to the manager's bonus in the current year (recorded on the books), the nondiscretionary effects, less related taxes, are included in the calculation of the cumulative effect of the change in an accounting principle. However, if the company is owed money by the manager as a result of the bonus adjustment and the company does not intend to collect, the nondiscretionary effect is not included in the cumulative effect, because it is not being recorded on the books.

When a change in an accounting principle involves depreciation, an adjustment must be made to the accumulated depreciation account. Assume that a change in an accounting principle involves a change from an accelerated method to the straight-line method for a particular asset. The direct effect of such a change is the difference in depreciation expense for all prior years in which the particular asset was depreciated. For discussion purposes, let us assume that the difference in the depreciation methods resulted in an increase to prior years' income of $100,000. Thus, the cumulative effect of the change in depreciation methods, before related taxes, is $100,000. If the current year's tax rate is 50%, deferred taxes would have to be adjusted for the tax on the $100,000 cumulative effect. The journal entry to record the cumulative effect of a change in an accounting principle and its related tax effect is as follows:

Accumulated depreciation	$100,000	
Deferred taxes		$50,000
Cumulative effect of a change		
in accounting principle		50,000

The debit to accumulated depreciation increases by $100,000 the net depreciable base of the fixed asset. The credit of $50,000 to the cumulative effect of a change in an accounting principle appears in the current year's income statement between extraordinary items and net income.

When an accounting change from FIFO to LIFO is made in pricing inventory, it may be impossible to compute the cumulative effect. In this and other situations where the cumulative effect cannot be determined, the disclosure of the cumulative effect is omitted. However, the amount of effect in the current year and its per share information should be disclosed in a footnote. The reason for omitting the cumulative effect should also be fully disclosed.

A new depreciation method may be adopted for newly acquired long-lived assets and all future assets of the same class. This does not constitute a change in an accounting principle under the promulgated GAAP. However, if the new depreciation method is applied to previously acquired long-lived assets of the same class, a change in an accounting principle occurs.

A new depreciation method may be adopted for newly acquired long-lived assets and future assets of the same class and at the same time, older long-lived assets of the same class may be depreciated under a different method. This type of change in an accounting principle does not require an adjustment, but APB-20 does require disclosure. A description of the change and its effect on income before extraordinary items and on net income of the period of change, along with related per share data, must be disclosed.

A change in an accounting principle may occur and for some reason only the current year's income statement is presented. In this event, the *regular* and *pro forma* amounts and related per share data for the preceding period must be disclosed in a footnote to the financial statements.

If an accounting change is considered immaterial in the year of change but is reasonably expected to become material in subsequent periods, it should be fully disclosed in the year of change.

In reporting a change in an accounting principle in the income statement, the presentation is broken down into a *regular* portion and a *pro forma* portion. The *regular* portion discloses in total amounts (1) income before extraordinary items and cumulative effect of a change in an accounting principle, (2) extraordinary items, (3) cumulative effect on prior years of the change in accounting principle, and (4) net income, which is the total of the first three items.

For the current year, income before extraordinary items and cumulative effect of a change in an accounting principle are determined by using the newly adopted accounting principle. Extraordinary items are disclosed in the usual manner. The cumulative effect on prior years of the change in accounting principle for the current year must be calculated. For the purposes of APB-20, the cumulative effect consists of the direct effects (less related taxes) that the newly adopted accounting principle has on all prior years and any indirect effects that are actually recorded on the books as a result of the change. Another method of determining the cumulative effect of a change in an accounting principle is the difference between (1) retained earnings at the beginning of the year of change and (2) retained earnings that would have been reported at the beginning of the year if the new accounting principle had been used in prior years.

The last item for the current year (regular portion) is "net income," which is a total of the first three items already discussed. In addition, both primary and fully diluted per share data must be disclosed for (1) income before extraordinary items and cumulative effect of a change in an accounting principle, (2) extraordinary items, (3) cumulative effect on prior years of a change in an accounting principle, and (4) net income.

Any prior years included for comparative purposes in the *regular portion* presentation are disclosed at their previously reported amounts.

The *pro forma* portion of the income statement presentation includes (1) income before extraordinary items, (2) net income, and (3) related per share data for both primary and fully diluted earnings. For comparative purposes *pro forma* information must be disclosed for the current period and all prior periods presented. The *pro forma* portion is presented as if the newly adopted accounting principle had always been used. Thus, the direct effects (less related taxes) of the newly adopted accounting principle and the indirect effects (less related taxes) are used in determining the *pro forma* amounts. However, the indirect effects are used only if they are to be recorded on the books. As discussed previously, indirect effects such as profit sharing, incentive compensation, or royalties arise as a result of a direct effect. Net income is changed by the direct effect, which in turn may create an indirect effect because it is based on the determination of net income. The cumulative effect of a change in an accounting principle does not appear at all in the *pro forma* presentation. The following illustrates the *regular* and *pro forma* presentations required by APB-20:

Accounting Changes

	19X2	19X1
Regular portion:		
Income before extraordinary item(s) and cumulative effect of a change in an accounting principle	$XX,XXX	$XX,XXX
Extraordinary item(s) [describe]	(X,XXX)	X,XXX
Cumulative effect on prior years (to December 31, 19X1) of a change in an accounting principle	X,XXX	–
Net income	$XX,XXX	$XX,XXX
Per share amounts—no dilution:		
Income before extraordinary item(s) and cumulative effect of a change in an accounting principle	$X.XX	$X.XX
Extraordinary item(s)	(.XX)	.XX
Cumulative effect on prior years (to December 31, 19X1) of a change in an accounting principle	.XX	–
Net income per share—primary	$X.XX	$X.XX
Per share amounts—fully diluted:		
Income before extraordinary item(s) and cumulative effect of a change in an accounting principle	$X.XX	$X.XX
Extraordinary item(s)	(.XX)	.XX
Cumulative effect on prior years (to December 31, 19X1) of a change in an accounting principle	.XX	–
Net income per share—fully diluted	$X.XX	$X.XX
Pro forma portion:		
Income before extraordinary item(s), assuming accounting change is applied retroactively	$XX,XXX	$XX,XXX
Earnings per share—no dilution	$X.XX	$X.XX
Earnings per share—fully diluted	$X.XX	$X.XX
Net income	$XX,XXX	$XX,XXX
Earnings per share—no dilution	$X.XX	$X.XX
Earnings per share—fully diluted	$X.XX	$X.XX

Note: As required by GAAP, extraordinary items and the cumulative effect on prior years are both shown on financial statements net of any related tax.

The nature, justification, and preferability (if applicable) of a change in an accounting principle and its effects on income should be clearly disclosed in the financial statements of the period in which the change is made.

For all changes in accounting principles where there is no restatement of prior-period financial statements, the following should be observed:

1. Prior-period comparative financial statements should be presented as previously reported.
2. The cumulative effect of changing to a new accounting principle should be made in net income of the period of the change and should be shown in the income statement between extraordinary items and net income. The effect of the change is *not* an extraordinary item, but should be reported in a similar manner.

    The amount of cumulative effect to be reported is the difference between (a) retained earnings at the beginning of the period of change and (b) retained earnings at the beginning of the period of change adjusted for the retroactive cumulative effect of the new accounting change, including related income tax effect.
3. The earnings per share information on the face of the income statement should include the per share amount of the cumulative effect of the change.
4. The earnings per share (primary and diluted) for income before extraordinary items and net income should be shown on the face of the income statement for all periods presented.

Reporting Accounting Changes—Interim Periods

The cumulative effect of an accounting change is always included in net income of the first interim period, regardless of in which period during the year the accounting change occurs. If the accounting change occurs in other than the first interim period, the current and prior-period interim statements should be restated to include the newly adopted accounting principle. However, the cumulative effect of the change in an accounting principle is included only in the net income of the first interim period.

When the cumulative effects of a change in an accounting principle cannot be determined, the *pro forma* amounts cannot be computed. In this event, as mentioned earlier, the cumulative effect and *pro forma* amounts are omitted. However, the amount of effect of adopting the new accounting principle and its per share data for

Accounting Changes

each interim period and year-to-date amounts must be disclosed in a footnote to the financial statements, along with the reasons for omitting the cumulative effect and *pro forma* information.

Publicly traded companies that do not issue separate fourth-quarter reports must disclose in a note to their annual reports any effect of an accounting change made during the fourth quarter. This is similar to other disclosure requirements of publicly traded companies that do not issue fourth-quarter interim reports.

The following disclosure concerning a cumulative effect type accounting change should be made in interim financial reports:

1. The nature and justification of the change should be made in the interim period in which the new accounting principle is adopted.
2. The effects of the accounting change on income from continuing operations, net income, and related per share data for both, should be made
   a. In the interim period in which the change is made
   b. In each, if any, prior interim period
   c. In each, if any, restated prior interim period
   d. In year-to-date and last twelve-months-to-date financial reports that include the adoption of a new accounting principle
   e. In interim financial reports of the fiscal year, subsequent to the interim period in which the accounting change was adopted
3. The *pro forma* effects of the accounting change on income from continuing operations, net income, and related per share data, should be made:
   a. For the interim period in which the change is made
   b. For any interim period of prior fiscal years for which financial information is presented
   c. In year-to-date and last twelve-months-to-date financial reports that include the adoption of a new accounting principle

If no interim periods of prior fiscal years are presented, footnote disclosure for the corresponding interim period of the immediate fiscal year in which the accounting change occurred should be made for actual and *pro forma* income from continuing operations, net income, and related per share data.

Cumulative Effect vs Retroactive Restatement

An accounting change occurs when an enterprise changes from one acceptable accounting principle or practice to another acceptable accounting principle or practice. For example, a change from the LIFO method of pricing inventory to the FIFO method is an accounting change. However, a change from an unacceptable accounting principle or practice to an acceptable principle or practice is a correction of an error and not an accounting change.

APB-20 (Accounting Changes) requires some types of accounting changes to be reported in comparative financial statements by the "restatement method" and other types to be reported by the "cumulative effect method." Under either method, the most important thing is to communicate to the users of the financial statements that an accounting change has occurred and to disclose the nature and effect of the change in principle or practice.

The "cumulative effect method" and "retroactive restatement method" both require exactly the same information. The total effect (direct and indirect) of the accounting change on all prior periods must be known. This total effect in a "restatement" is charged or credited to beginning retained earnings in the year of change. In the "cumulative effect method" the total effect appears in the income statement of the year of change as a separate item immediately above net income. Under both methods, the newly adopted accounting principle or practice is used in determining net income of the year of change (current period).

In order to "retroactively restate" a particular prior year, the details of any effects of the change in accounting principle on that particular year must be available. If the information is not available, that particular prior year cannot be retroactively restated. In applying the "cumulative effect method," the details of any effects of the change in accounting principle on a particular year must also be available to determine the *pro forma* income statement presentation that is required by APB-20. Thus, if you cannot restate a particular prior year, you cannot determine the *pro forma* presentation required by APB-20.

When using the "cumulative effect method," APB-20 (Accounting Changes) requires a "regular" and *pro forma* presentation of (a) income before extraordinary items, (b) extraordinary items, (c) cumulative effect of a change in accounting principle, and (d) net income. The *pro forma* presentation discloses the above four income statement items and related per-share amounts on the basis that the financial statements presented were retroactively restated.

Accounting Changes

In addition, the "cumulative effect" of a change in an accounting principle may be omitted under APB-20 if it is impossible to compute. In this event, the effects of the change, in the year of change, must be disclosed, along with an explanation as to why the cumulative effect was omitted.

Existing GAAP (APB-9) requires that net income include all items of profit and loss recognized during a period, except prior period adjustments. Prior period adjustments bypass the income statement and are charged or credited directly to retained earnings. Retroactive restatement of a financial statement is accounted for in the same manner as a prior period adjustment. Thus, retroactive restatement bypasses the income statement and retained earnings is charged or credited. However, the restated financial statements reflect all of the details of the revision.

In applying the cumulative effect method, the total effects of the change in accounting principle for all prior periods is reflected in the income statement of the year of change. Thus, under the cumulative effect method the income statement is not bypassed.

The type of modification or modification and qualification that must be made to the opinion paragraph of the standard auditor's report to account for a change in an accounting principle depends upon whether the "cumulative effect" or the "retroactive restatement" method is used to report the change. If the "retroactive restatement" method is used to report the change in accounting principle, the opinion paragraph is modified by including a statement that *consistency has been achieved after giving retroactive effect to the change.* In this event, the modification does not result in a qualification of the auditor's opinion because consistency has been achieved. If the "cumulative effect" method is used to report the change in accounting principle, the opinion paragraph of the auditor's report is modified by including a statement that the *accounting principles have been applied on a consistent basis, except for the specific change which is referred to in the opinion paragraph.* In this event, the modification to the opinion paragraph results in a qualification of the auditor's opinion because consistency has not been achieved. The following examples illustrate the appropriate wording of the opinion paragraph of the auditor's report.

Financial statements restated:

> . . . in conformity with generally accepted accounting principles applied on a consistent basis after giving retroactive effect to the change, with which we concur, in the method of reporting investment values described in Note 1 to the financial statements.

Financial statements not restated:

> ... in conformity with generally accepted accounting principles applied on a consistent basis except for the change, with which we concur, in the method of determining depreciation of plant properties as described in Note C to the financial statements.

Changes in an Accounting Estimate

A change in an accounting estimate is usually the result of new events, changing conditions, more experience, or additional information, any of which requires the revision of previous estimates.

Estimates are necessary in determining uncollectible receivables, salvage values, useful lives, provisions for warranty, and a multitude of other items involved in preparing financial statements.

A change in a depreciation method for a previously recorded asset is a change in accounting principle, but a change in the estimated useful life or in the salvage value of a previously recorded asset is a change in an accounting estimate.

Reporting a Change in an Accounting Estimate

A change in an accounting estimate *should not* be accounted for by restatement of prior years' financial statements. The effect of the change in accounting estimates should be accounted for (1) in the period of change, if the change affects only that period, or (2) in the period of change and future periods, if the change affects both.

A change in an accounting estimate caused in part or in whole by a change in an accounting principle should be reported as a change in an accounting estimate.

Disclosure should be made in current-period financial statements of the effects of a change in an accounting estimate on income before extraordinary items, net income, and related per share data.

If a change in an accounting estimate affects future periods, the effect on income before extraordinary items, net income, and the related per share information should be disclosed in the income statement.

Ordinary accounting estimates for uncollectible accounts or inventory adjustments, made each period, do not have to be disclosed unless they are material.

Reporting a Change in an Entity

Restatement of prior years' financial statements is necessary when an accounting change results in financial statements that are actually statements of a different reporting entity.

All prior and current periods presented should be restated to reflect financial information for the new reporting entity.

Full disclosure should be made describing the nature of the change and the reason for it.

Changes in income before extraordinary items, net income, and related earnings per share should be adequately disclosed.

Reporting Corrections of Errors

Prior-period errors in financial statements discovered subsequently should be reported as prior-period adjustments. Recent promulgated GAAP (FASB-16) limits prior-period adjustments:

1. To corrections of errors in financial statements of prior periods
2. To adjustments resulting from the realization of income tax benefits of preacquisition operating-loss carryforwards of purchased subsidiaries

Errors result from mistakes in mathematics and application of an accounting principle or from misjudgment in the use of facts. A change in an accounting estimate is the result of new information, changing conditions, more experience, or additional information that requires the revision of previous estimates. A change from an unacceptable accounting principle to a generally accepted one is a correction of a prior-period error (APB-20).

The nature of the error and the effect of its correction on income before extraordinary items, net income, and the related per share data must be fully disclosed in the period the error is discovered and corrected.

Financial Summaries

The presentation of accounting changes, including *pro forma* amounts, in financial summaries, including five-year summaries, should be presented in the same way as presented in the primary financial statements (APB-20).

Comprehensive Illustration

The following is a comprehensive illustration of presenting a change in an accounting principle.

At the end of 19X9, a company decides to change from an accelerated method of recording depreciation on plant equipment to the straight-line method. The direct effect of this change is $600,000 (19X9—$100,000; 19X8—$60,000; 19X7—$100,000; 19X6—$140,000; 19X5 and prior—$200,000). The indirect items (nondiscretionary) affected by the change in an accounting principle are an incentive bonus plan and royalties, which are 10% of the annual net income. Any adjustment for indirect effects is to be recorded on the books. Income tax rates are 50%. The company has 1,000,000 shares of common stock outstanding, and the comparative income statements for 19X9 and 19X8 reflect the following without any adjustments for the accounting change:

	19X9	19X8
Income before extraordinary item(s)	$2,400,000	$2,200,000
Less: Extraordinary item(s) (Note: ___)	70,000	–
Net income	$2,330,000	$2,200,000
Primary earnings per share before extraordinary item(s)	$ 2.40	$ 2.20
Extraordinary item(s)	(0.07)	–
Net income	$ 2.33	$ 2.20

The following adjustments are needed in the previous information to account for the change in the accounting principle:

Regular Portion

1. For the current year (19X9), income before extraordinary items and cumulative effect of a change in an accounting principle is calculated as follows:

Before adjustment	$2,400,000
Adjustment for direct effects ($100,000) less taxes (50%)	50,000
Adjustment for indirect effects (10% of $100,000 less 50% taxes)	(5,000)
As adjusted	$2,445,000

GAAP GUIDE / 1.17

Note: Incentive bonuses and royalties of $240,000 had already been recorded on the books (10% of $2,400,000). However, the adjustment for the direct effects results in a net increase of $50,000 to income. Thus, the net indirect effects of $5,000 must be included in the calculation. The net indirect effects of $5,000 reduces income because it is an expense (incentive bonus and royalties).

2. Extraordinary items are presented in the usual manner and require no adjustment.
3. The cumulative effect on prior years of the change in an accounting principle is computed as follows:

Direct effect of the change in accounting principle on all years except the current year	$500,000
Less: 50% taxes	(250,000)
Indirect effect of the change in accounting principle on all years except the current year	(50,000)
Less: 50% taxes	25,000
Net cumulative effect on prior years	$225,000

Note: Both direct and indirect effects are included because indirect effects are to be recorded on the books for the current year.
4. Any prior years presented are disclosed at their previously reported amounts.

Pro Forma Portion

1. The pro forma portion is presented as if the newly adopted accounting principle had always been used. In addition, indirect effects of the change are considered if they are to be recorded on the books.
2. For current year (19X9), income before extraordinary items is calculated as follows:

Before adjustment	$2,400,000
Adjustment for direct effects ($100,000) less taxes (50%)	50,000
Adjustment for indirect effects (10% of $100,000 less 50% taxes)	(5,000)
As adjusted	$2,445,000

Note: Incentive bonuses and royalties of $240,000 had already been recorded on the books (10% of $2,400,000). However, the adjustment for the direct effects results in a net increase of $50,000 to income. Thus, the net indirect effects of $5,000 must be included in the calculation. The net indirect effects of $5,000 reduces income because it is an expense (incentive bonus and royalties).

3. For the prior year presented (19X8), income before extraordinary items is calculated as follows:

Before adjustment	$2,200,000
Adjustment for direct effects ($60,000) less taxes (50%)	30,000
Adjustment for indirect effects (10% of $60,000 less 50% taxes)	(3,000)
As adjusted	$2,227,000

Note: Incentive bonuses and royalties of $220,000 had already been recorded on the books (10% of $2,200,000). However, the adjustment for the direct effects results in a net increase of $30,000 to income. Thus, the net indirect effects of $3,000 must be included in the calculation. The net indirect effects of $3,000 reduces income because it is an expense (incentive bonus and royalties).

The statement presentation for our illustration, taking into consideration the effects of the change in using a different depreciation method, is:

	19X9	19X8
Income before extraordinary item(s) and cumulative effect of a change in accounting principle	$2,445,000	$2,200,000
Extraordinary item (*Note:* ___)	(70,000)	—
Cumulative effect on prior years (to December 31, 19X8) of changing to a different depreciation method (*Note:* ___)	225,000	—
Net income	$2,600,000	$2,200,000
EPS before extraordinary item(s)	$ 2.45	$ 2.20
Extraordinary item	(0.07)	—
Cumulative effect on prior years (to December 31, 19X8) of changing to a different depreciation method	.22	—
Net income	$ 2.60	$ 2.20

Pro forma amounts assuming the new
depreciation method is applied retroactively:

Income before extraordinary item(s)	$2,445,000	$2,227,000
Earnings per share	$ 2.45	$ 2.23
Net income	$2,375,000	$2,227,000
Earnings per share	$ 2.38	$ 2.23

The company in the above illustration had no dilutive securities. Thus, the presentation for fully diluted EPS is omitted.

ACCOUNTING POLICIES

Background

The source of promulgated GAAP for Disclosure of Accounting Policies is APB-22. This promulgated GAAP specifically states that its provisions be followed by nonprofit entities. However, unaudited interim reports for companies which have not changed their accounting policies since the end of the preceding fiscal year need not disclose accounting policies in such interim reports.

> **OBSERVATION:** Unaudited reports issued for internal use only and certain other special reports, apparently would not have to comply with APB-22.
> The promulgated GAAP states that it does not supersede any other promulgated GAAP issued previously.

Overview

All financial statements covered by APB-22 that purport to present financial position, results of operations, and changes in financial position in accordance with GAAP must comply fully with the promulgated GAAP on disclosure of accounting policies.

Significant Accounting Policies

The preferable presentation of disclosing accounting policies is in the first footnote of the financial statements, under the caption Summary of Significant Accounting Policies. The promulgated GAAP (APB-22) specifically states this preference, but mentions the need for flexibility in the matter of formats.

The requirement of the promulgated GAAP is that a description of all significant accounting policies of a reporting entity should be included as an integral part of the financial statements. Basis of consolidation, depreciation methods, amortization of intangibles, inventory pricing, recognition of profit on long-term construction-

Accounting Policies

type contracts, and recognition of revenue from franchising and leasing operations are the examples described in the opinion. However, disclosure of accounting policies should not be duplicated if presented elsewhere as an integral part of the financial statements. In disclosing accounting policies it may become necessary to refer to items presented elsewhere in the report, such as in the case of a change in an accounting principle which requires specific treatment.

> **OBSERVATION:** FASB Technical Bulletin 82-1 requires the disclosure of the sale or purchase of tax benefits through tax leases.

Disclosure

Both the accounting principle and the method of applying such a principle should be disclosed. Informed professional judgment is necessary to select for disclosure those principles which materially affect the financial position, results of operations, and changes in financial position. However, accounting principles and their method of application in the following areas are considered particularly important:

1. A selection from existing acceptable alternatives
2. The areas that are peculiar to a specific industry in which the entity functions
3. Unusual and innovative application of GAAP

Comprehensive Illustration

The following are comprehensive illustrations of the disclosure of significant accounting policies.

Principles of consolidation The consolidated financial statements include the assets, liabilities, revenues, and expenses of all significant subsidiaries. All significant intercompany transactions have been eliminated in consolidation. Investments in significant companies which are 20% to 50% owned are carried at equity in net assets and the corporation's share of earnings is included in income. All other investments are carried at cost or less.

Fixed assets and depreciation Fixed assets are carried at cost. Expenditures for replacements are capitalized, and the replaced items are retired. Maintenance and repairs are charged to operations. Gains and losses from the sale of fixed assets are included in income. Depreciation is calculated on a straight-line basis utilizing U.S. Internal Revenue Service estimated lives. The corporation and its subsidiaries use other depreciation methods (generally accelerated) for tax purposes where appropriate.

Inventories Inventory values are stated at the lower of cost or market using the last-in, first-out (LIFO) method for substantially all qualifying domestic inventories and the average cost method for other inventories.

Income taxes Provision has been made for deferred income taxes where differences exist between the period in which transactions, principally relating to depreciation, affect taxable income and the period in which they enter into the determination of income in the financial statements. The investment tax credit is deferred and amortized over the average life of the fixed assets by reductions in the provision for income taxes.

Pension plan It is the policy of the company and its consolidated subsidiaries to fund pension costs as accrued. Prior service costs are amortized over varying periods not exceeding 40 years.

Patents, trademarks, and goodwill Amounts paid for purchased patents and for securities of newly acquired subsidiaries in excess of the fair value of the net assets of such subsidiaries have been charged to patents, trademarks, and goodwill. The portion of such amounts determined to be attributable to patents is amortized over their remaining lives and the balance is amortized over the estimated period of benefit but not more than 40 years.

Earnings per share Earnings per share is based on the weighted-average number of shares of common stock outstanding in each year. There would have been no material dilutive effect on net income per share for 19X1 or 19X2 if convertible securities had been converted and if outstanding stock options had been exercised.

BUSINESS COMBINATIONS

Background

The promulgated GAAP for business combinations are covered by APB-16, Accounting for Business Combinations, which has been amended by FASB-38, Accounting for Preacquisition Contingencies of Purchased Enterprises, and FASB-79, Elimination of Certain Disclosures for Business Combinations by Nonpublic Enterprises.

Both incorporated and unincorporated entities are covered by APB-16. However, certain types of transactions are not covered by APB-16, as follows:

1. Acquisition of any minority interests in a subsidiary (APB-16 does require the use of the purchase method for this type of transaction)
2. Creation by a corporation of a newly formed corporation for the purpose of transferring the corporation's net assets to the newly formed corporation
3. Transfer of net assets or the exchange of shares of stock between companies under common control

FASB Technical Bulletin 85-5 was issued to provide guidance on the following issues relating to Business Combinations (APB-16):

- Costs of Closing Duplicate Facilities of an Acquirer
- Stock Transactions between Companies under Common Control
- Downstream Mergers
- Identical Common Shares for a Pooling of Interests
- Pooling of Interests by Mutual and Cooperative Enterprises

Each of the above issues relating to business combinations is addressed in this chapter.

Overview

A business combination occurs when one entity acquires part or all of another entity with the object of eliminating any duplication and of combining resources.

The purchase method of accounting for a business combination reflects the acquisition of one company by another. The difference, if any, between the fair value of the identifiable net assets purchased and the amount paid is recorded as goodwill. The acquiring company reports the results of operations of the acquisition from the date it is acquired.

The pooling-of-interests method of accounting for a business combination reflects the union of ownership between the entities involved. The pooling is accomplished primarily by the issuance of common voting stock of the acquiring company. Goodwill is never recorded in a pooling of interests, because the assets and liabilities of the companies involved are carried forward at their recorded amounts. Results of operations are restated for prior periods as if the entities involved had always been combined.

Purchase Method

Business combinations accounted for by the purchase method are recorded at cost. The determination of cost is usually based on the fair value of the property acquired or the fair value of the property given up, whichever is more clearly evident. An asset acquired for cash is recorded at the amount disbursed. In an exchange of assets where no cash is involved, cost is determined by the fair value of the assets given up or received, whichever is more clearly evident. If stock is issued in exchange for assets, cost is determined by the fair value of the assets acquired, which is tantamount to the consideration received for the stock issued.

> **OBSERVATION:** FASB Technical Bulletin 84-1 concludes that the acquisition of the results of an R&D arrangement through the issuance of capital stock should be accounted for at the fair value of the stock issued, or at the fair value of the consideration received, whichever is more clearly evident.

The cost of a liability assumed in a business combination is the present value of the amount that will eventually be paid. The difference between the fixed rate of debt securities assumed and the effective or current yield rate for comparable securities should be recorded as a premium or a discount (APB-21).

The market price of traded securities is usually clear evidence of fair value. However, the market price of a traded security issued in a business combination may have to be adjusted for the quantity issued, price fluctuations, and issue costs. A good barometer for fair value may be the average market price for a period before and after the business combination. In addition, independent appraisals are frequently useful in determining fair value.

Registration and issuing costs of equity securities issued in a business combination accounted for by the purchase method are deducted from the fair value of such securities. All direct costs of the acquisition are included as part of the total cost of the acquisition.

The recorded cost of an acquisition is equal to the determinable amount of cash and other net assets that are unconditionally surrendered at the date of acquisition. Any contingent additional consideration is fully disclosed in the financial statements but is not recorded as a liability. Contingently issuable debt or equity securities are not shown as outstanding until the contingency is definitely resolved. The fact that contingently issuable debt or equity securities are held by an independent escrow agent does not alter the treatment that such securities are not considered outstanding.

Contingent considerations may be based on maintaining or achieving specific earning levels over future periods or may be based on a security's maintaining or achieving a specific market price.

When a contingency consideration based on earnings is achieved, the acquiring company records the current fair value of the additional consideration. At this juncture, it is more than likely that the increase in the cost of the acquisition will be in the form of goodwill. In this event, the goodwill should be amortized over the remaining life of the acquired asset, but in no event more than 40 years (APB-17).

When a contingency consideration based on maintaining or exceeding a specific market price for the securities issued to consummate the acquisition is not achieved, the acquiring company will have to issue additional securities in accordance with the contingency arrangements. The issuance of the additional contingency securities is based on their then-current fair value but does not increase the overall cost of the acquisition, because the recorded cost of the original securities issued is reduced by the same amount. The only item that changes is the total number of shares issued for the acquisition. An example will clarify the situation.

A issues 1,000 shares of its common stock to a seller for an acquisition. The market price of the stock, at the date of the sale, was $12 per share, and A guarantees that, at the end of two years, if the market price is less than $12 per share, it will issue additional shares to make up any difference. Under the agreed-upon conditions A deposits 500 shares of stock with an independent escrow agent.

In accordance with the promulgated GAAP (APB-16), A records the acquisition at $12,000 ($12 per share × 1,000). At the end of the two years the market price of the stock is $10 per share, and the escrow agent delivers 200 shares to the seller in accordance with the seller's instructions. The remainder of the shares is returned to A.

A records the issuance of the 200 additional shares at the current market price of $10 per share for a total of $2,000, and correspondingly reduces the original stock issued to $10 per share, or a total of $10,000. The total acquisition price remains $12,000, and only the number of shares issued changes from 1,000 to 1,200.

In the event that debt securities are issued in an acquisition and that subsequently additional debt securities are issued as contingent consideration, the reduction in the value results in the necessity to record a discount on the debt securities. Discounts arising in this manner are amortized over the life of the securities, commencing from the date the additional securities are issued.

Contingent consideration that provides compensation for services or use of property are accounted for as expenses of the appropriate period on resolution of the contingency.

Interest or dividends paid or accrued on contingent securities during the contingency period are accounted for in the same manner as the underlying security. Therefore, interest expense or dividend distributions on contingent securities are not recorded until the contingency is resolved. In the event a contingency is resolved which results in the payment of an amount for interest or dividends on the contingent securities, that amount is added to the cost of the acquisition at the date of distribution.

When a savings and loan association is acquired in a business combination accounted for by the *purchase* method, the assets and liabilities acquired are recorded at their fair values on the date of acquisition. This is called the *separate valuation* method, as opposed to the *net spread* method, which values the purchase as a whole, based on the spread between interest rates received on the mortgage portfolio and interest rates paid on savings accounts. The net spread method is unacceptable for GAAP purposes.

> **OBSERVATION:** FASB-72 concludes that goodwill arising in the acquisition of a troubled banking or thrift institution should be amortized over a relatively short period because of the uncertainty about the nature and extent of the estimated future benefit related to the goodwill (see Chapter 45.01).

In applying the separate valuation method, receivables are recorded at their present values, using appropriate current interest rates, less allowances for uncollectibility and collection. Payables are recorded at the present values of amounts to be paid, determined at appropriate current interest rates.

Any portion of the purchase price that cannot be assigned to specifically identifiable tangible and intangible assets acquired, less liabilities assumed, shall be recorded as goodwill. Goodwill must be amortized by the straight-line method (APB-17), unless both the following conditions are met:

1. Part or all of the recorded goodwill includes one or more of the following factors which could not be separately determined:
    a. capacity of existing savings accounts and loan accounts to generate future income and/or additional business or new business
    b. nature of territory served

2. The anticipated benefits to be received from the factors in 1 above are expected to decline over their estimated lives.

Only in those cases where both of the above conditions are met can accelerated methods be used to amortize the purchased goodwill (FASB Interpretation-9).

Allocating cost The total cost of an acquisition must be allocated to the individual assets acquired. Each identifiable asset is assigned a cost equal to its fair value. Contingent assets and liabilities are allocated a portion of the total cost of a purchased acquisition, if certain conditions are met (FASB-38). Independent appraisals and/or subsequent sales of acquired assets may provide evidence of fair value. Some methods of determining values are:

1. Inventories—net realizable value less a reasonable profit, except raw material, which should be valued at current replacement cost
2. Receivables—present value of the amount that will be received, less an allowance for uncollectible accounts
3. Marketable securities—net realizable value
4. Plant and equipment—appraised values in accordance with intended use
5. Liabilities—present value of the amount to be paid

An acquiring corporation should allocate costs to assets received and liabilities assumed as follows:

1. All identifiable assets and liabilities should be assigned a portion of the total cost based on fair value at the date of acquisition.

2. Any excess of cost over the amount assigned to identifiable assets less liabilities should be recorded as goodwill.
3. In the event that the assignable fair values of net assets acquired exceed the cost (sometimes referred to as negative goodwill), the noncurrent assets acquired (excluding long-term investments in marketable securities) should be reduced proportionately. Excess of net assets over cost (negative goodwill) should not be recorded unless all the noncurrent assets acquired (excluding long-term investments in marketable securities) have been reduced to zero.

The cost of a business combination accounted for by the purchase method includes the *direct* costs of acquisition (paragraph 76 of APB-16). Liabilities and commitments for expenses of closing a plant that is being acquired in an acquisition are direct costs of the acquisition and are recorded at the present values of amounts to be paid (paragraph 88i of APB-16). However, the cost incurred in closing facilities already owned by the acquiring company, which happens to duplicate other facilities that are being acquired in a business combination accounted for by the purchase method, are not recognized as part of the cost of acquisition (FASB Technical Bulletin 85-5).

Only "out of pocket" or incremental direct costs that are incurred in effecting the business combination are included in the cost of the acquisition (Accounting Interpretation No. 33 of Business Combinations). Direct out of pocket or incremental costs that are capitalized include finders' fees and fees paid to outside consultants for accounting, legal, engineering investigations, and appraisals (Accounting Interpretation No. 33 of Business Combinations). Other direct costs that are incurred in a business combination accounted for by the purchase method that are internal and recurring must be expensed as incurred.

Indirect and general expenses that are related to a business combination accounted for by the purchase method are deducted as incurred in determining net income (paragraph 76 of APB-16). Registration and issuing costs of equity securities issued in a business combination accounted for by the purchase method are deducted from the fair value of such securities (paragraph 76 of APB-16). Costs incurred in unsuccessful business combination negotiations are also deducted as incurred (Accounting Interpretation No. 33 of Business Combinations).

Acquisition of pension plan assets and liabilities FASB-87 (Employers' Accounting for Pensions) amends APB-16 to provide that the assets and liabilities of a pension plan acquired by the purchase method of accounting shall no longer be accounted for in accordance with the provisions of APB-16 (paragraph 88h), but shall be accounted for in accordance with paragraph 74 of FASB-87, which is discussed below.

When a single-employer defined benefit pension plan is acquired as part of a business combination accounted for by the purchase method, an excess of the projected benefit obligation over the plan assets shall be recognized as a liability and an excess of plan assets over the projected benefit obligation shall be recognized as an asset. The recognition of a new liability or new asset by the purchaser, at the date of a business combination accounted for by the purchase method, results in the elimination of any (a) previously existing unrecognized net gain or loss, (b) unrecognized prior service cost, and (c) unrecognized net obligation or net asset that existed at the date of initial application of FASB-87.

In subsequent periods, the differences between the purchaser's net pension cost and contributions will reduce the new liability or new asset recognized at the date of combination to the extent that the previously unrecognized net gain or loss, unrecognized prior service cost, or unrecognized net obligation are considered in determining the amounts of contributions to the plan. In addition, the effects of an expected plan termination or curtailment shall be considered by the purchaser in calculating the amount of the projected benefit obligation at the date of a business combination accounted for by the purchase method.

Contingent assets and liabilities A portion of the total cost of acquiring an enterprise under the purchase method must be allocated to contingent assets, contingent liabilities, and contingent impairments of assets, if any, provided that the following conditions are met:

a. It is probable that the contingent item existed at the consummation date of the business combination accounted for by the purchase method.
b. After the consummation date, but prior to the end of the "allocation period" the facts in a. above are confirmed.
c. The amount of the asset, liability, or impairment can be reasonably estimated.

If the above conditions are met, a portion of the total cost of acquiring an enterprise, under the purchase method, must be allocated to any contingent items (FASB-38).

The "allocation period" is the period that is required by the purchaser to identify and quantify the acquired assets and assumed liabilities for the purposes of allocating the total cost of the acquisition in accordance with APB-16. The "allocation period" will not usually exceed one year from the closing date of the purchase transaction (FASB-38).

After the "allocation period" is over, any subsequent adjustments for contingent items must be included in net income of the period in which the adjustment is recognized. In other words, adjustments for contingent items arising from a purchased acquisition are charged to net income if they occur after the end of the "allocation period." The only exception is for realized tax effects of loss carryforwards of purchased subsidiaries, which are recorded as retroactive adjustments of the purchase transaction (APB-11).

> **OBSERVATION:** FASB Technical Bulletin 81-2 reaffirms that unused investment tax credits acquired by the purchase method should be accounted for in accordance with FASB Interpretation-25. Unused investment tax credits acquired by the purchase method are not considered preacquisition contingencies.

FASB-38 is effective for adjustments that are determined in fiscal years beginning after December 15, 1980.

Disclosure for the Purchase Method

The following disclosures should be made in the period in which a business combination occurs and is accounted for by the purchase method:

1. Name, brief description, and total cost of the acquisition
2. Method of accounting, that is, the purchase method
3. Period for which results of operations of the acquisition are included in the income statement (usually starts from the date of acquisition)
4. Description of the plan for amortization of acquired goodwill
5. Other pertinent information such as contingent payments, options, or other commitments
6. Combining of several minor acquisitions for disclosure purposes is acceptable

The following supplemental information should be disclosed in the notes to the financial statements of an acquiring company in the year of acquisition:

1. Results of operations for the current period combining the acquisition as though it were acquired at the beginning of the period.

2. If comparative statements are presented, results of operations should include the acquisition as though it were acquired at the beginning of the comparative statement period.

> **OBSERVATION:** FASB-79 (Elimination of Certain Disclosures for Business Combinations by Nonpublic Enterprises) provides that the above supplemental information does not have to be disclosed by nonpublic enterprises. For the purposes of FASB-79, a nonpublic enterprise is one (a) whose debt or equity securities are traded in a public market on a stock exchange or in the over-the-counter market or (b) whose financial statements are filed with a regulatory agency in preparation for the sale of any class of securities.

Purchase versus Pooling of Interests

A purchase of assets is accounted for differently from a purchase of a stock interest. In both cases, however, goodwill or negative goodwill can arise. A pooling of interests is accounted for in the same way whether there is an exchange of stock for stock or of stock for net assets. In addition, goodwill or negative goodwill is never recorded in a pooling of interests.

Purchase of assets In the purchase of assets, goodwill is equal to the difference between the purchase price paid and the fair value of the identifiable net assets acquired. If the purchase price paid exceeds the fair value of the identifiable net assets acquired, the goodwill is positive and is recorded on the books as an asset. If the purchase price paid is less than the fair value of the identifiable net assets acquired, the goodwill is negative and it may or may not be recorded on the books as a deferred credit. Identifiable net assets are equal to the fair value of the acquired identifiable assets less the fair value of the assumed liabilities.

On July 1, 19X7, Jones Company sold all its net assets and business to Smith Corporation for $415,000. The following is Jones Company's balance sheet as at July 1, 19X7:

Business Combinations

<u>Balance Sheet</u>

Cash	$ 20,000
Accounts receivable	72,000
Allowance for doubtful accounts	(8,000)
Inventory	120,000
Plant and equipment	260,000
Total assets	$464,000
Accounts payable	$ 60,000
Accrued expenses	5,000
Mortgage payable—plant	120,000
Common stock	200,000
Retained earnings	79,000
Total liabilities and equity	$464,000

Additional Information:

Confirmation of the accounts receivable revealed that $10,000 were uncollectible.

The physical inventory count was $138,000 (fair value).

The fair value of the plant and equipment was $340,000.

The journal entry to record the investment on the books of Smith Corporation is:

Investment in Jones Co. (100%)	$415,000	
Cash		$415,000

The computation of goodwill involved in the transaction is:

<u>Computation of Goodwill</u>

Assets	$464,000
Liabilities ($60,000 + $5,000 + $120,000)	185,000
Total	$279,000
Additional uncollectibles	(2,000)
Increase in inventory	18,000
Increase in plant and equipment	80,000
Adjusted net assets	$375,000
Cost of purchase	415,000
Goodwill	$ 40,000

Assume that the purchase price was $350,000.

Adjusted net assets	$375,000
Cost of purchase	350,000
Negative goodwill	$ 25,000

Negative goodwill does not get recorded, because noncurrent assets (plant and equipment) are reduced to $315,000.

Negative goodwill should never be recorded unless all the noncurrent assets acquired, except long-term investments in marketable securities, have been proportionately reduced to zero.

If after reducing the noncurrent assets (except long-term investment in marketable securities) to zero a credit still remains, it should be classified as a deferred credit—"excess of acquired stock over cost"—and should be amortized to income over the period that is expected to benefit, but not to exceed 40 years (APB-17).

Goodwill may not be written off as a lump sum to capital surplus or retained earnings, nor be reduced to a nominal amount, at or immediately after acquisition.

Purchase of a stock interest The percentage of book value acquired is subtracted from the purchase price, and any residue is goodwill or negative goodwill.

ABC Corporation purchased for $1,500,000 90% of the common stock and 50% of the preferred stock of XYZ Corporation. At the date of acquisition, XYZ Corporation's stockholders' equity was:

Stockholders' Equity

Common stock, 100,000 shares, $5 par, all authorized, issued, and outstanding	$ 500,000
5% preferred stock, 10,000 shares, all authorized, issued, and outstanding	1,000,000
Paid-in capital	200,000
Retained earnings	300,000
Total stockholders' equity	$2,000,000

The computation of the goodwill involved in the transaction is:

Computation of Goodwill

	Minority Interests (10%)	Preferred Stock	ABC Corporation (90%)
Common stock	$ 50,000		$ 450,000
Preferred stock		$500,000	500,000
Paid-in capital	20,000		180,000
Retained earnings	30,000		270,000
Totals	$100,000	$500,000	$1,400,000
Cost of 90% common and 50% preferred			1,500,000
Goodwill			$ 100,000

The journal entry to record the transaction is:

Investment in XYZ Corporation $1,500,000
   Cash $1,500,000

Goodwill of $100,000 was involved.

Goodwill is not necessarily the difference between cost and the book value of an investment, unless the book value is equal to the fair value of the underlying assets. The underlying assets represented by an investment must be individually assigned a fair value at the date of acquisition, and if the assigned fair values are less than the amount of the investment, the difference is goodwill. For consolidation purposes, the acquisition of a stock investment may be considered the purchase price paid for an interest in the underlying net assets of a business.

It must be remembered that if any excess of cost over acquired book value is allocated to depreciable or amortizable assets, the depreciation or amortization expense of subsequent periods must be increased to spread the amount of such excess over the remaining life of the assets.

If after assigning values to the underlying assets of an investment there is resulting goodwill, it must be amortized over a period of 40 years or less, starting from the date of the acquisition of the investment. However, since consolidating adjustments and eliminations are never posted on the books, it is necessary to reduce the beginning consolidated retained earnings, in the years subsequent to the first year, by the amount of depreciation or amortization of prior years.

Assuming that P was amortizing $10,000 of the excess of cost over book value (goodwill) over a 10-year period, the consolidated adjustment for the second full year would be:

Consolidated retained earnings	$1,000	
Amortization, current year	1,000	
Excess of cost over book value		$2,000

Goodwill should not be recorded where it is obvious that the underlying asset in a stock interest purchase or the net assets in a straight asset purchase are undervalued. Any excess cost over book value at the date of acquisition should be assigned specifically to these undervalued assets.

When any excess cost over book value (goodwill) is assigned to specific assets, it must be depreciated or amortized on the consolidated working papers.

Excess cost over book value of $25,000 is assigned (1) $5,000 to a parcel of land and (2) $20,000 to the building located on the land. The building has a 20-year life, and the following adjusting journal entry must be made on the consolidated working papers (assume one full year):

Land	$ 5,000	
Building	20,000	
Investment account		$25,000
Depreciation	$ 1,000	
Accumulated depreciation		$ 1,000

Since consolidated adjusting journal entries are never posted on the books, this journal entry must be repeated each year.

In the final year, when the building is completely depreciated, the following entry is made on the consolidated working papers:

Accumulated depreciation	$20,000	
Fixed asset–building		$20,000

The entry for the land remains and is repeated each year on the consolidated working papers as long as the land is part of the assets of the consolidated group.

All transactions for cash or stock are purchases except the exchange, by the acquirer, of common voting stock for 90% or more of the common voting stock or all of the net assets of the seller (pooling of interests).

In other words all transactions are purchases except those which qualify as a pooling of interests.

In a purchase, operations of the investee are taken into consideration by the investor, from the date of the purchase. There is no retroactive restatement of any financial statements.

Different Classes of Capital Stock

The main point to remember in computing a parent's investment in a subsidiary is to isolate those elements of the subsidiary's stockholders' equity to which the parent company is actually entitled. For instance, if the subsidiary had minority interests, they would have to be excluded in computing the parent's investment. Other items that must be considered are different classes of stock, dividends in arrears, and liquidating dividends. If another class of stock is participating, it must share in the retained earnings of the subsidiary to the extent of its participation. If another class of stock is cumulative as to dividends and dividends are in arrears, the amount of dividends in arrears must be deducted from retained earnings before determining the parent's interest in the subsidiary's stockholders' equity.

The following are guidelines for preferred stock issues:

1. Nonparticipating and noncumulative preferred stocks require no apportionment of retained earnings.
2. Nonparticipating and cumulative preferred stocks require an apportionment only to the extent of any dividends in arrears.
3. Participating preferred stock requires an apportionment of retained earnings, under all circumstances. The apportionment is made on the basis of the total dollar amount of the par or stated values of the securities involved.

On January 1, 19X7, P acquires for $5,200,000 80% of the common stock and 60% of the 5% preferred stock of S. On the date of acquisition the stockholders' equity of S consisted of:

	Shares	Dollars
Common stock ($1 par)	1,000,000	$1,000,000
5% preferred stock ($100 par) nonparticipating and cumulative	50,000	5,000,000
3% preferred stock ($10 par) fully participating and noncumulative	200,000	2,000,000
Retained earnings		2,000,000

The 5% preferred stock has a liquidating preference value of $105 per share and dividends of $350,000 are in arrears. Determine the parent's share of the subsidiary's stockholders' equity as of the date of acquisition.

Apportionment of Retained Earnings

Total retained earnings	$2,000,000
Less: Dividends in arrears–Preferred	350,000
Balance	$1,650,000
Less: Liquidating preference dividend $5	250,000
Balance	$1,400,000
Less: 20% minority interest	280,000
Balance to apportion	$1,120,000
3% preferred, 2/3	746,667
Balance to P Company	$ 373,333

The 3% preferred stock ($10 par) participates fully with the common stock ($1 par) in the earnings of the company. The apportionment is made on the basis of the total par or stated value dollar amounts of the common and 3% preferred, which are $1,000,000 and $2,000,000, respectively. Therefore, the apportionment of retained earnings after all adjustments is 1/3 to common shareholders and 2/3 to the 3% participating preferred shareholders.

Business Combinations

Computation of P's Investment

	Minority Interests 20%	5% Preferred	Participating Preferred	P Company 80%
Common stock	$200,000			$ 800,000
5% preferred		$5,000,000		
3% preferred–participating			$2,000,000	
Retained earnings	280,000		746,667	373,333
Dividend–arrears		350,000		
Liquidating dividend		250,000		
Totals	$480,000	$5,600,000	$2,746,667	$1,173,333
60% of preferred to P		3,360,000		3,360,000
Totals	$480,000	$2,240,000	$2,746,667	$4,533,333
Cost of 80% of common and 60% of preferred				5,200,000
Goodwill				$ 666,667

Acquisition of Stock Directly from Subsidiary

Sometimes a stock interest is acquired directly from the investee. That is, a subsidiary will sell some of its own capital stock to another company. In this event, it must be remembered that the amount paid for capital stock must be added to the stockholders' equity before determining the acquirer's stock interest.

Company S had 100,000 shares of $1 par capital stock outstanding ($100,000) and $60,000 of retained earnings. On January 1, 19X7, Company S authorized an additional 200,000 shares of capital stock ($1 par) and sold them to P Company for $250,000. Determine P Company's stock interest in S Company.

Computation of S Company's Stockholders' Equity

Common stock ($1 par) (300,000 shares)	$300,000
Paid-in capital–common	50,000
Retained earnings	60,000
Total	$410,000

Computation of P's Investment in S

	Minority Interest 33⅓%	P Company 66⅔%
Common stock	$100,000	$200,000
Paid-in capital	16,667	33,333
Retained earnings	20,000	40,000
Totals	$136,667	$273,333
Cost of P's 66⅔%		250,000
Negative goodwill		$ 23,333

Step-by-Step Acquisition

A corporation may acquire a subsidiary in more than one transaction. In this case, any goodwill or negative goodwill involved must be computed at the time of each step-by-step transaction. When control is achieved, it is necessary to adjust to the equity method any earlier step acquisition accounted for by the cost method. The result of this treatment is that the parent's portion of the undistributed earnings of the subsidiary for the period prior to achieving control is added to the investment account of the parent.

Assume that Company P acquired an interest in Company S in two steps: (1) acquired 20% of the outstanding common stock for $200,000; and (2) the following year acquired an additional 60% for $500,000. At the dates of acquisition, the equity book value for Company S was $900,000 and $1,100,000, respectively.

Computation of Excess of Cost over Book Value

First Acquisition
Cost of 20% acquired	$200,000
20% of equity book value of $900,000	180,000
Excess of cost over book value (goodwill)	$ 20,000

Second Acquisition
Cost of 60% acquired	$500,000
60% of equity book value of $1,100,000	660,000
Excess of book value over cost (negative goodwill)	($160,000)

Actually, as of the date of the second acquisition Company P had an investment of $700,000 for 80% of Company S. Company S at the second acquisition date had an equity book value of $1,100,000, and Company P's 80% is $880,000, for which it paid $700,000. If Company P had recorded its first acquisition of 20% by the equity method, it would have recorded its 20% of the $200,000 increase in Company S's book value (assuming that no dividends or other distributions were made to Company P by Company S). Thus the adjusted equity in Company S on the books of Company P would include the original $200,000 purchase price plus 20% of the $200,000 increase in book value (from $900,000 to $1,100,000) or a total of $220,000 ($180,000 + $40,000). The cost of the second acquisition of 60% for $500,000 and the adjusted basis for the 20% at $220,000 equals $720,000, which represents 80% of $1,100,000, or $880,000. The difference of $160,000 is the excess of book value over cost (negative goodwill) indicated by the computation for the second acquisition of 60%.

Stock Exchanges – Companies Under Common Control

In an exchange of stock between two of its subsidiaries, one or both of which is partially owned, a parent company should account for its minority interest at historical cost, if the minority shareholders are not a party to the exchange transaction (FASB Technical Bulletin 85-5). Under this circumstance, the minority interest remains outstanding and is not affected by the transaction. FASB Technical Bulletin 85-5 also reconfirms that the acquisition of all or part of a minority interest between companies under common control, regardless of how acquired, is never considered a transfer or exchange by the companies under common control (Accounting Interpretation No. 39 of APB-16).

The term "business combination" does not apply to the transfer of net assets or the exchange of shares between companies under common control (Paragraph 5 of APB-16). Therefore, the acquisition of some or all of the stock held by minority shareholders of a subsidiary is not a business combination. However, paragraph 43 of APB-16 prescribes exactly how such a transaction should be reported. Under paragraph 43 of APB-16, the acquisition of some or all of the stock held by minority stockholders of a subsidiary, whether acquired by the parent, the subsidiary itself, or another affiliate, should be accounted for by the purchase method (fair value). Under this circumstance, the minority interest is affected by the transaction and the result is that a new minority interest is created in a different subsidiary. Accounting Interpretation No. 26 of APB-16 describes the following transactions in which purchase accounting applies: (a) a parent company exchanges its common stock or assets or debt for common stock held by minority shareholders of its subsidiary, (b) the subsidiary buys as treasury stock the common stock held by minority shareholders, or (c) another subsidiary of the parent exchanges its common stock or assets or debt for common stock held by the minority shareholders of an affiliated subsidiary.

Pooling-of-Interests Method

The purchase method and the pooling-of-interests method are both acceptable in accounting for business combinations, but not as alternatives. A business combination either qualifies for the pooling-of-interests method or is treated as a purchase. *Part-purchase and part-pooling of the same business combination is unacceptable* (APB-16).

> **OBSERVATION:** *The promulgated GAAP requirements for using the pooling-of-interests method are detailed and quite restrictive.*

Conditions for the Pooling-of-Interests Method

1. Each of the combining companies must be autonomous and not have been a subsidiary or division of another corporation within two years before the plan of combination is initiated.

The initiation date is the *earlier:*

a. of the date of public announcement, or notification to the shareholders of any one of the combining companies, the major terms of the plan including the ratio of exchange or a formula which provides for the ratio of exchange, or
b. of the date that shareholders of the company being acquired are notified directly or by newspaper advertisement of the exchange offer (APB Interpretation of APB-16).

A new company, incorporated within the last two years, qualifies unless it was in any way a successor to a company that would not have been considered autonomous.

It is irrelevant whether a parent company or any of its wholly owned subsidiaries distribute voting common stock to effect a combination, as long as the condition of autonomy is met.

> **OBSERVATION:** Although the promulgated GAAP specifically states "wholly owned subsidiary," an APB interpretation (nonpromulgated) suggests that substantially all the subsidiary's outstanding voting stock be owned by the parent and under no circumstances would less than 90% be considered substantially all.

A judicial order to divest is an exception to the rule and both the divesting company and the acquiring company will be considered autonomous.

2. At the date of initiation and at the date of consummation of the plan of combination, each combining company is independent of each other combining company. An intercorporate investment of 10% or less of the total outstanding voting common stock of any combining company is acceptable and will not impair the independence test.

An exchange by a partially owned subsidiary of its common stock for the outstanding voting stock of its parent (a "downstream merger") does not qualify as a pooling of interests, because it fails to meet the independence rule (FASB Technical Bulletin 85-5).

In addition, the term "business combination" does not apply to the transfer of net assets or the exchange of shares between companies under common control (paragraph 5 of APB-16). Therefore, the exchange by a partially owned subsidiary of its common stock for the outstanding voting common stock of its parent (a "downstream merger") cannot be accounted for as a business combination. However, paragraph 43 of APB-16 prescribes exactly how such a transaction should be reported. Under paragraph 43 of APB-16, the acquisition of some or all of the stock held by minority stockholders of a subsidiary, whether acquired by the parent, the subsidiary itself, or another affiliate, should be accounted for by the purchase method (fair value).

Accounting Interpretation No. 26 specifically requires that purchase accounting be applied to downstream mergers. Under Accounting Interpretation No. 26, the exchange by a partially owned subsidiary of its common stock for the outstanding voting stock of its parent should be accounted for as if the parent had exchanged its common stock for common stock held by minority shareholders of its subsidiary. Purchase accounting is applied whether a subsidiary acquires its parent or a parent acquires the minority interest of the subsidiary, because the end result is a single shareholder group. Furthermore, if a new corporation exchanged its common stock for the common stock of the parent and the common stock of the subsidiary held by the minority shareholders, the accounting treatment would be the same.

> **OBSERVATION:** *The promulgated GAAP provides that if a company held as an investment a minority interest of 50% or less on October 31, 1970, and initiates a plan of combination within five years after that date, the resulting combination could be accounted for as a pooling of interests provided all other provisions of the promulgated GAAP were complied with. This section is referred to as the "grandfather clause," and the five-year limitation was deleted by FASB-10.*

3. After a plan is initiated, it must be completed within one year in accordance with a specific plan, or completed in a single transaction.

> **OBSERVATION:** *A pooling of interests is, in essence, a combining of existing shareholders' voting common stock in which the separate shareholder interests lose their identity, resulting in the mutual combination of risks and rights.*
>
> *Any change in the exchange ratio or terms thereof creates a new initiation date for the plan of combination. Any change in the relative voting rights that result in preferential treatment for some common stockholder groups is incompatible to a pooling of interests.*

Litigation or proceedings of a governmental authority that delay the completion of a plan of combination are excepted from the one-year rule, providing they are beyond the control of any of the combining companies.

4. At the consummation date of the plan the acquiring company offers and issues its majority class of stock (voting rights) for no less than 90% of the *voting common stock interests* of the combining

company being acquired. The 90% or more of the voting common stock interests being acquired is determined at the date the plan is consummated.

> **OBSERVATION:** *An APB Interpretation, which is not promulgated GAAP, suggests that the consummation date is the date the assets are transferred to the issuing company.*

This requirement of 90% or more of the voting common stock interests being acquired at consummation date can be related to the requirement that intercorporate investments of 10% or less, in any company being acquired, is acceptable for the independence rule (see condition 2 above).

The determination of whether the acquiring company acquires 90% or more of the outstanding voting common stock interests at the date of consummation excludes the following shares of the company being acquired:

a. any shares acquired for any form of consideration and held at the date of initiation of the plan of combination by the acquiring parent or its subsidiaries
b. any shares acquired, and held, after the date of initiation, by the acquiring parent or its subsidiaries, except those shares acquired by the issuance of the acquiring company's own voting stock

> **OBSERVATION:** *In other words, intercorporate investments in the company being acquired, except those acquired by the issuance of voting common stock after the date of initiation, are excluded in calculating the number of voting common stock interests that are exchanged at the consummation date.*
>
> *The larger the intercorporate investment an acquirer has in an acquisition that was acquired prior to the initiation date, the more difficult the 90% will be to achieve.*

An investment in the voting common stock of the acquiring company held by a company being acquired must be restated in an equivalent number of shares of the company being acquired. The equivalent number of shares is determined by the exchange ratio of the plan of combination and then deducted from the number of voting common shares actually exchanged on the consummation date. The resulting number of shares of the company being acquired must equal 90% or more of its total outstanding voting common shares at the date of consummation.

B has 100,000 shares of voting common stock outstanding and owns an investment in A of 1,000 shares of voting common stock. A initiated a plan of combination to acquire B by offering four shares of its voting common stock (majority class) for each share of B's voting common stock. At the date of consummation, 91,000 shares of B's stock are tendered to A. However, the 1,000 shares of voting common stock of A held by B must be restated into an equivalent amount of B's stock in accordance with the exchange ratio of 4 to 1, which equals 250 shares. In other words, at consummation date B is theoretically the owner of 250 shares of its own stock when restated in terms of the exchange ratio. The 250 shares are deducted from the 91,000 shares tendered, which equals 90,750 shares, and then compared to 90% of the outstanding voting common stock of B at the date of consummation, which in this case is 90,000 shares (90% of 100,000).

As a result, A's acquisition of 91,000 shares is restated to 90,750 shares, which meets the 90% requirement, and the transaction can be accounted for as a pooling of interests.

When two or more companies are being acquired in a plan of combination, each condition necessary for a pooling of interests must be met by each company.

However, 90% of each combining company must be exchanged for voting common stock of the acquiring company and intercompany investments between any of the combining companies are excluded in calculating whether 90% or more of the voting common stock interests are exchanged, but are included in computing the total amount of voting common stock interests outstanding.

A plan of combination may not include a pro rata cash distribution but may within limits include a cash distribution for fractional shares and for shares purchased from dissenting shareholders. Cash may also be used in a plan of combination to retire, or redeem, callable debt and equity securities.

A transfer of *all the net assets* at the date the plan is consummated in exchange for voting common stock (majority class) of the acquiring company qualifies as an exchange of substantially all (90% or more) of the *voting common stock interests*.

Although the requirement is for *all the net assets* of the company being acquired, temporary cash, receivables, and marketable securities may be retained to settle liabilities, disputed items, or contingencies. In a net asset transaction, both voting common stock and

Business Combinations

other stock may be issued by the acquiring company, if the company whose net assets are being acquired has both voting common stock and other stock outstanding. However, the voting common stock and other stock must be issued in proportion to the voting common stock and other stock outstanding, of the company being acquired, at the date of consummation of the plan of combination.

In determining the independence rule (see condition 2 above) in an exchange of voting common stock for net assets, intercorporate investments of 10% or less are evaluated in terms of the issuing company's voting common stock, as follows:

a. The number of voting common shares being issued at the date of consummation for all the net assets is allocated between outstanding voting common stock and other outstanding stock if any. The net assets being acquired should include any intercorporate investment in the acquiring company.

b. A ratio is computed between the number of shares of voting common stock outstanding, at the date of consummation, for the company whose net assets are being acquired, and the number of voting common shares of the acquirer allocated (in a above) to the acquisition of voting common stock interests.

c. An intercorporate investment of the issuer in the voting common stock of the company whose assets are being acquired is restated in equivalent shares of the ratio computed in b above.

d. An intercorporate investment in the issuing company by the company whose net assets are being acquired is not restated, because the number of shares is already stated in terms of the issuing company's stock.

e. In order to meet the 90% test, all intercorporate investments (when restated in terms of the stock of the issuing company) cannot exceed 10% of the number of issued shares of voting common stock allocated and issued for the acquisition of the voting common stock interests being acquired.

P owns 12,000 shares of S's voting common stock that was acquired prior to initiation date. P issues 100,000 shares of its voting common stock to acquire all the net assets of S, which include 1,000 shares of P's voting common stock. The 100,000 shares of P's stock is allocated 70% to outstanding voting common stock and 30% to other outstanding stock. S has 210,000 shares of voting common stock outstanding.

P has allocated 70,000 (70% of 100,000) shares of its stock to acquire the 210,000 shares of S's voting common stock at the consummation date. This results in a ratio of 1 share of P for 3 shares of S.

The 12,000 shares of S that are owned by P are converted to 4,000 shares of P. The 1,000 shares of P that are owned by S are already stated in P's stock. The 4,000 equivalent shares and the 1,000 shares of P equal 5,000 shares and are compared to 10% of the 70,000 shares of P's voting common stock that have been allocated for the acquisition of the voting common stock interests in S. The 5,000 equivalent shares of P are less than the 10% of the 70,000 shares allocated by P for the acquisition and thus the combination qualifies for a pooling of interests.

---

5. No changes in the equity interests of the voting common stock of any combining company may be made in contemplation of a pooling of interests. This restriction is for a period beginning two years prior to the initiation date of the plan of combination and for the period between the initiation date and the consummation date.

Normal distributions based on earnings and/or prior policy are permitted.

The organizational form of a mutual or cooperative enterprise does not have equity interests of voting common stock. The conversion of a mutual or cooperative enterprise to equity interests of voting common stock represents a change in the form of organization, not a change in the equity interests of voting common stock. Therefore, the conversion of a mutual or cooperative enterprise to stock ownership within two years before a plan of combination is initiated or between the dates a combination is initiated and consummated does not preclude accounting for such a combination as a pooling of interests (FASB Technical Bulletin 85-5).

6. The reacquisition of voting common stock by any combining company is allowed except for purposes of business combinations. In addition, any reacquisition of voting common stock between the initiation and the consummation dates must be no more than a normal amount.

A normal amount of reacquired shares is determined by reference to a company's pattern of reacquisition prior to the initiation of a plan of combination.

A systematic pattern of reacquisition of voting common stock established for stock option or compensation plans is permitted.

After a plan is initiated, the acquisition of voting common stock of the issuing company by any combining company is considered the same as if the issuing company reacquired its own shares.

The important point of the provision of GAAP is that shares are not reacquired in substance or form to effectuate a business combination.

7. Each common stockholder to a plan of combination must receive a voting common stock interest exactly in proportion to his voting common stock interest prior to the combination.

A business combination cannot be accounted for as a pooling of interests if the issuer retains a right of first refusal to repurchase the shares issued in certain circumstances, even if the shares issued are identical to other outstanding common shares (FASB Technical Bulletin 85-5).

Generally, restrictions imposed on the sale of stock to the public in compliance with governmental regulations do not violate the provisions of APB-16, providing that subsequent to the combination, the issuer has started the process of registering the stock or had agreed to register the stock (Accounting Interpretation No. 11 of Business Combinations).

8. The common stockholders to a plan of combination must receive the voting rights they are entitled to and must not be deprived or restricted in any way from exercising those rights.

9. The entire plan of combination must be effectuated on the date of consummation.

This provision prohibits contingent shares that are to be issued at a later date, except for contingently issuable shares which will be used to adjust differences in amounts represented at consummation date by management. These differences are recorded as an adjustment to combined stockholders' equity and reflected in net income of the period of resolution or as a prior-period adjustment of the correction of an error of a prior period.

10. After the combination is consummated, any transaction, implied or explicit, that is inconsistent with the combining of the interest of the common stockholders counteracts the effect of combining stockholders' interest.

Application of the Pooling-of-Interests Method

All the conditions for a pooling of interests must be met before a business combination can be accounted for as such. The mechanics of applying the pooling-of-interests method are:

1. At the date the combination is consummated, assets, liabilities, and stockholders' equity are combined and recorded at historical cost, in conformity with GAAP.
2. If an acquiring company issued treasury stock to effectuate part or all of a plan of combination, the treasury stock must first be treated as though it was retired (gain or loss is recorded), and then it is considered the same as any other previously unissued shares.
3. Intercorporate investments in the acquiring company are treated as treasury stock in combined financial statements. Intercorporate investments, other than in the acquiring company stock, are treated as retired stock of the combination.
4. All financial statements for the period in which the combination occurred should be reported as though the combination occurred at the beginning of the period.
5. Prior-year financial statements should be restated on a combined basis.
6. Expenses relating to the combination are expenses of the combined group and should be deducted from combined net income. Examples of such expenses are registration fees, finders' and consultants' fees, and costs and losses resulting from combining the separate companies.
7. If within two years after a combination, a material profit or loss results from the disposal of a significant portion of the assets of the previously separate companies, full disclosure, as an extraordinary item (net of tax effects), should be made in the combined financial statements.
8. Prior to the consummation date of a plan of combination, the investment on the books of the acquiring company (investor) should be accounted for by the equity method, if acquired for voting common stock, and at cost if the investment was acquired for cash.

Under the pooling-of-interests method, the cost of an acquisition is the total par or stated value of the capital stock issued by the acquirer to effectuate the combination. This amount is debited to an investment account and the appropriate capital stock account is credited. Fair values are ignored and goodwill is never recorded in a pooling of interests.

In a consolidated balance sheet the capital stock account will always be equal to the total par or stated value of the outstanding shares of the acquiring company. Therefore, the first adjustment to the investment account on the consolidated working papers is to eliminate the capital stock account of the acquired company. If the capital stock account of the acquired company exceeds the debit in the investment account (not usually likely), any balance is transferred to combined contributed capital by debiting the capital stock account and crediting combined contributed capital.

It is much more likely that the debit in the investment account will exceed the capital stock account of the acquired company. In this event, the excess is debited to any other contributed capital account of the acquired company and if an excess still exists, the balance is debited to consolidated retained earnings. Obviously, no amount should exist in the investment account after these adjustments.

Disclosure for Pooling-of-Interests Combinations

The following disclosures should be made to the financial statements in the period in which the pooling occurs:

1. Brief description of the companies combined
2. Method of accounting for the combination, that is, the pooling-of-interests method
3. Description and amount of shares of stock issued to effect the combination
4. Details of the results of operations for each separate company, prior to the date of combination, that are included in the current combined net income
5. Description of the nature of adjustments in net assets of the combining companies to adopt the same accounting policies
6. If any of the combining companies changed their fiscal year as a result of the combination, full disclosure should be made of any changes in stockholders' equity that were excluded from the reported results of operations.
7. Revenue and earnings previously reported by the acquiring company should be reconciled with the amounts shown in the combined financial statements.
8. Any plan of combination that has been initiated but not consummated at a balance sheet date must be fully disclosed, including the effects of the plan on combined operations and any changes in accounting methods.

In the period that a pooling-of-interests is effectuated, recurring intercompany transactions should be eliminated to the extent possible from the beginning of the period. However, nonrecurring intercompany transactions involving long-term assets and liabilities need not be eliminated, but in that event they should be fully disclosed (APB-16).

CHANGES IN FINANCIAL POSITION

Background

The promulgated GAAP for Reporting Changes in Financial Position is APB-19. This promulgated GAAP applies to all profit-oriented business entities including those with unclassified balance sheets. Financial statements that present financial position and results of operations must include a statement of changes in financial position (hereinafter referred to as the Statement). In some circumstances, such as statements issued for internal use only, the Statement may be omitted.

Overview

The Statement should be prepared on a broad concept and should include all the important changes in financial position. However, book entries such as for stock dividends and splits should not be included.

All important aspects of financing and investing activities, regardless of whether for cash or other elements of working capital, should be disclosed in the Statement.

Objectives of the Statement

The most informative disclosure of the Statement is the funds provided from or used in operations for the period, providing that the effect of extraordinary items is disclosed separately from the effect of normal items.

The objectives of the Statement are:

1. To reflect the amount of funds generated from or used in operations for the period
2. To summarize all the financing and investing activities of an enterprise during the period (whether or not for cash)
3. To disclose appropriately the net changes in each element of funds for at least the current period

Gross Basis

All funds are reported on the Statement at their gross amounts. The only exception to this rule is normal trade-ins to replace equipment, which are shown on a net basis. That is, instead of showing the total equipment traded and the total equipment received, only the difference between the two is shown on the Statement.

> **OBSERVATION:** FASB-12 requires that both the current and noncurrent marketable security portfolios be shown on the balance sheet at their carrying amount, which is the lower of the aggregate cost or market. By doing this, the amount on the balance sheet is a net figure, which includes all debits and credits from sales, purchases, and changes in the valuation account.
>
> FASB-12 contradicts APB-19, because APB-19 requires that outlays for purchases, and proceeds from sales, of long-term investments be separately identified and shown on a "gross basis," whereas FASB-12 requires that both the current and noncurrent marketable security portfolios be shown at their carrying amount, which is the "net basis."
>
> Under FASB-12, it is possible, during a fiscal period, for a company to have in its noncurrent marketable security portfolio sales of $10 million, purchases of $15 million, and an increase in the valuation account of $5 million, and on its balance sheet there would be absolutely no change in carrying value from the preceding fiscal period!

Concept of Funds

Some of the definitions of funds are:

1. Cash
2. Cash and marketable securities
3. Net quick assets
4. Net working capital (excess of current assets over current liabilities)

Regardless of which concept of funds is used, GAAP require the inclusion of "all financial resources" in preparing the Statement.

"All financial resources" include cash, noncash, and nonworking capital transactions that are part of the financing and investing activities of a business, as follows:

1. Funds used for the purchase of, or funds received from the sale of, long-term assets

2. Conversion of preferred stock or long-term debt to common stock
3. Issuance, assumption, redemption, or repayment of long-term debt
4. Issuance, redemption, or purchase of capital stock for cash or noncash assets
5. Distributions to shareholders, including dividends in cash or in property

Some entities do not distinguish between current and noncurrent assets and liabilities and would ordinarily indicate "cash" provided from, or used in, operations, instead of "working capital." Another alternative is the "net monetary concept," or "quick asset" approach, which reflects the changes in all nonquick assets and noncurrent liabilities. However, the preferable concept is the working capital approach, which reflects the changes in the noncurrent accounts that affect the movement of current items.

Each entity has the responsibility of utilizing the "statement format" that is most informative and complies with the objectives of the Statement.

Funds provided or used in operations To arrive at the *funds provided or used in operations* we generally start with net income and adjust it for noncash charges or credits, including:

1. Depreciation expense
2. Amortization expense
3. Extraordinary items
4. Deferred taxes
5. Accrued income or loss from subsidiaries, joint ventures, etc.

If the *fund concept* being used is cash instead of working capital, net income on a cash basis must be adjusted for:

1. Increases or decreases in receivables
2. Increases or decreases in inventories
3. Increases or decreases in accounts payable

Changes in each element of working capital The changes in each element of working capital are the increases or decreases in each current asset and current liability over the amounts in the preceding year, as follows:

Changes in Financial Position

	19X1	19X2	Increase or (Decrease)
Current Assets			
Cash	$10,000	$ 15,000	$ 5,000
Accounts receivable	25,000	35,000	10,000
Inventory	50,000	60,000	10,000
Prepaid expenses	1,000	500	(500)
Total current assets	$86,000	$110,500	$24,500
Current Liabilities			
Accounts payable	$10,000	$ 15,000	$ 5,000
Notes payable-current	20,000	15,000	(5,000)
Accrued expenses	1,000	1,500	500
Total current liabilities	$31,000	$ 31,500	$ 500
Net working capital	$55,000	$ 79,000	
Increase or decrease in working capital			$24,000

Cash Format

The Statement may be prepared on a cash basis. However, the working capital basis is preferred. When preparing the Statement on a cash basis, the increase or decrease in cash during the period is computed instead of the increase or decrease in working capital.

1. The changes in the current accounts are presented in addition to the changes in the noncurrent accounts. (This is because we are starting with cash instead of working capital.)
2. Because all the changes in the current accounts appear on the Statement, there is no need for a separate schedule of changes in the elements of working capital.

Cash provided from (used in) operations should not be used unless all noncash items have been eliminated.

Per Share Amounts

Isolated statistics of working capital, or cash, especially per share information, should not be presented in annual reports to stockholders. If per share information is presented, it should show, as a minimum, amounts of inflow from operations, inflow from other sources, and total outflows, and each per share amount should be clearly identified.

Comprehensive Illustration

The following Consolidated Statement of Changes in Financial Position has been extracted from the Annual Report of Harcourt Brace Jovanovich, Inc.

Consolidated Statement of Changes in Financial Position
FOR THE YEARS ENDED DECEMBER 31, 19X2 and 19X1

	19X2	19X1
Funds provided by:		
Net income	$18,214,173	$16,471,195
Depreciation and amortization	11,390,220	6,143,537
Increase in unearned subscription and other income	1,789,455	3,144,882
Increase in deferred income taxes	1,493,471	37,194
Amortization of publication rights, copyrights, and other intangibles	376,663	229,773
Net income of The Harvest Life Insurance Company	(90,548)	(66,103)
Provided from operations	$33,173,434	$25,960,478
Long-term debt:		
Issued	$21,391,364	$47,472,000
Assumed in purchase of business (Note 2)	–	13,571,333
Deferred income taxes ($2,341,738) less other net noncurrent assets from acquisition of Sea World, Inc.	–	2,221,177
Equity (deficit) of pooled companies at dates of acquisition	844,622	(924,283)
(Decrease) increase in minority interests in subsidiaries (including $2,002,681 applicable to Sea World, Inc. in 19X1)	(121,230)	2,093,536
Proceeds of sale on exercise of stock options	435,659	5,869
	$55,723,849	$90,400,110

Changes in Financial Position

Funds used for:		
Dividends declared	6,158,228	5,542,932
Additions to property and equipment:		
From acquisition of Sea World, Inc.	2,923,992	61,933,978
Other	25,988,856	9,139,148
Contribution to capital of The Harvest Life Insurance Company	500,000	–
Reduction of long-term debt	11,100,557	1,314,049
Purchase of minority interest in Sea World, Inc. (Note 2)	2,002,681	–
Increase in royalty advances to authors	575,730	1,587,681
Decrease (increase) in royalties payable after one year	552,574	(261,622)
Purchase of publication rights, copyrights, and other intangibles	6,314,425	541,803
Increase in other assets	1,855,333	2,365,609
	$57,972,376	$82,163,578
(Decrease) increase in working capital (Note 7)	($ 2,248,527)	$ 8,236,532

Note 7: The increases and (decreases) in the components of working capital are as follows:

	19X2	19X1
Current assets:		
Cash	$ (750,886)	$ 1,178,050
Marketable securities	(2,024,452)	3,013,724
Accounts receivable	13,363,681	8,790,762
Inventories	8,063,212	5,232,263
Prepaid expenses	596,955	512,590
	$19,248,510	$18,727,389
Current liabilities:		
Current portion of long-term debt	8,743,525	578,452
Accounts payable	4,397,579	5,945,871
Accrued liabilities	3,342,639	2,156,224
Royalties payable	697,262	1,860,449
Federal, state, and local income taxes payable	4,316,032	(50,139)
	$21,497,037	$10,490,857
(Decrease) increase in working capital	($ 2,248,527)	$ 8,236,532

The accompanying notes are an integral part of these statements.

CONSOLIDATED FINANCIAL STATEMENTS

Background

The promulgated GAAP for consolidated financial statements, including combined and comparative financial statements, are:

   ARB-43, Chapter 1A—Rules Adopted by Membership
   ARB-43, Chapter 2A—Comparative Financial Statements (as amended)
   ARB-51—Consolidated Financial Statements (as amended)

Considerable nonpromulgated GAAP exists for consolidated financial statements, especially in the area of reporting and types of presentations.

Overview

Consolidated financial statements represent results of operation, changes in financial position, and financial position of a single entity. They are presumed to be more meaningful than separate statements and must be used when the parent controls voting interest of over 50% in a subsidiary. A subsidiary whose main business is leasing property to its parent must be consolidated. Investments of a temporary nature, foreign investments subject to controls and currency restrictions, and investments that are dissimilar and for which separate supplemental information would be more meaningful should not be consolidated.

Accounting and Reporting

Retained earnings of a purchased subsidiary at the date of acquisition are never treated as part of consolidated retained earnings. The retained earnings and capital stock of a purchased subsidiary at the date of acquisition represent the book value that must be eliminated in preparing consolidated statements.

The fact that a subsidiary has a different fiscal year does not justify not preparing consolidated statements. If a subsidiary's fiscal year is within three months or less of its parent's fiscal year, it is acceptable to use those fiscal-year statements for consolidation purposes, providing that disclosure is made of any material events occurring within the intervening period.

A subsidiary or net assets may be purchased (1) for book value, (2) in excess of book value, and (3) for less than book value. If purchased for more than book value, there may be resulting goodwill; if purchased for less than book value, there may be a resulting deferred credit, sometimes referred to as negative goodwill (see Business Combinations).

> **OBSERVATION:** A subsidiary in legal reorganization or bankruptcy is controlled by the receiver or trustee and not by the parent company. Therefore, consolidated financial statements under these conditions would be inappropriate (ARB-43).

There are situations where consolidated statements may be more meaningful if a particular subsidiary is not included. These situations exist where the activity of a particular subsidiary is completely unrelated to the rest of the affiliated group and its inclusion would be meaningless. Banks and insurance companies are examples of subsidiaries that may be excluded in a consolidation of a large group of manufacturing entities.

When a subsidiary is acquired by the purchase method in more than one transaction, each purchase should be determined on a step-by-step basis and consolidation usually not made until control (50%) is achieved. In the year that control is achieved, the percentage amount of net income from the purchased subsidiary will probably vary. For example, if a parent company purchased 25% of a subsidiary at the end of each quarter of a year, the income from the subsidiary that the parent would include in its income would be 0% at the end of the first quarter, 25% at the end of the second quarter, 50% at the end of the third quarter, and 75% at the end of the last quarter. (Income from a purchased acquisition accrues subsequent from the date of acquisition.) The promulgated GAAP suggest two methods for the inclusion of income from a subsidiary in periods where there are several purchases. The preferable method usually is to include the subsidiary in the consolidation as if it had been acquired at the beginning of the period, and to deduct at the bottom of the consolidated income statement the net income of the subsidiary that does not accrue to the parent.

> **OBSERVATION:** Apparently, when using this method, all the revenue and expense accounts of the subsidiary remain in the consolidated income statement, since only the net income that the

parent is not entitled to is deducted from the consolidated net income at the bottom of the statement.

The other method suggested is to include in the parent's consolidated income statement only the subsidiary's revenue and expenses subsequent to the date of acquisition.

In disposal of a subsidiary during the year, the promulgated GAAP suggest that it may be preferable to omit from the consolidated income statement all details of the operation of the subsidiary and to show only the equity of the parent in the earnings of the subsidiary, prior to disposal, as a separate item in the consolidated income statement (the equity method).

Consolidated financial statements are prepared in the same manner for a pooling of interests as they are for a purchase. In the purchase method, fair values are assigned to identifiable assets and any excess cost is recorded as goodwill. In a pooling of interests, the cost of an acquisition is the total par or stated value of the capital stock issued by the acquiring company and goodwill is never recorded. (For further discussion see Business Combinations.)

The equity method (APB-18) should be used for all subsidiaries not consolidated unless the subsidiary is a temporary investment, a foreign investment subject to control and currency restrictions, or where the consolidated statements would be more meaningful if the subsidiary was excluded from consolidation (banks, insurance companies, etc., as members of a large manufacturing group). If the equity method is not used for reasons cited herein, then the cost method should be used. However, when the cost method is used, the consolidated statements should disclose the following:

1. Cost of the investment
2. Underlying equity in the investment
3. Dividends received in the current period
4. Equity of the parent in the net income of the subsidiary for the current period

When the cost method is utilized for unconsolidated subsidiaries, consideration must be given to the other elements of consolidating if it had been used. For example, appropriate recognition should be made of the difference between the cost of the subsidiary and the underlying equity in the net assets at the date of acquisition. As a result, it may be necessary to adjust consolidated depreciation or amortization. Intercompany gains or losses between the consolidating group and the unconsolidated subsidiary must also be reviewed. The intercompany gain or loss on sales made by the unconsolidated subsidiary to members of the consolidated group should be eliminated in determining the equity in the undistributed earnings of the unconsolidated subsidiary. The disclosure requirement of the equity in the undistributed earnings of the unconsolidated subsidiary has been mentioned previously. Intercompany gains or losses on sales to unconsolidated subsidiaries need not be eliminated unless they exceed the unrecorded equity in undistributed earnings of the unconsolidated subsidiary. In any event, if such sales are material, they should be appropriately disclosed. Further disclosure summarizing the assets, liabilities, and operating results is necessary if the total unconsolidated subsidiaries are material in relationship to the consolidated statements.

Combined Financial Statements

Consolidated financial statements are usually justified on the basis that one of the consolidating entities exercises control over the affiliated group. When there is no such control, combined financial statements may be used to accomplish the same results. A commonly controlled group of companies, or a group of unconsolidated subsidiaries that could otherwise not be consolidated, should utilize combined financial statements. Combined financial statements are prepared on the same basis as consolidated financial statements, except that a controlling interest is not included.

Comparative financial statements Comparative financial statements reveal much more information than noncomparative statements and furnish useful data about differences in the results of operations for the periods involved or in the financial position at the comparison dates.

Consistency is a major factor in creating comparability. Prior-year amounts and classifications must be, in fact, comparable with the current period presented, and exceptions must be clearly disclosed.

Consolidation versus Equity Method

The only difference between the equity method of accounting for investments in common stocks and consolidated financial statements is the amount of detail reported. Under both methods all intercompany transactions are eliminated. In consolidated financial statements the details of all entities to the consolidation are reported in full. In the equity method the investment is shown as a single amount in the investor balance sheet, and earnings or losses are generally shown as a single amount in the income statement. This is the reason why the equity method is frequently referred to as "one-line consolidation."

Consolidated Work Papers

The difference between regular work papers for a single business and consolidated work papers is that the adjustments on the regular work papers will be journalized and posted to the books, whereas eliminations and adjustments made on consolidated work papers *are never posted to the books of the individual companies.*

Intercompany Transactions

Sales and purchases The gross amount of intercompany sales and/or purchases is eliminated on the consolidated work papers. When the adjustment has already been made in the trial balance for ending inventory the eliminating entry is made against cost of sales. When the adjustment has not been made for ending inventory the eliminating entry is made against the purchase account.

Receivables and payables Intercompany receivables and payables include:

1. Accounts receivable and accounts payable
2. Advances to and from affiliates
3. Notes receivable and notes payable
4. Interest receivable and interest payable

The gross amount of all intercompany receivables and payables is eliminated on the consolidated work papers. Care must be exercised where a receivable is discounted with one of the consolidated companies (no contingent liability). If the balance sheet reflects a discounted receivable with another affiliate, it must be eliminated by a debit to discounted receivables and a credit to receivables. However, if one affiliate discounts a receivable to another affiliate, who in turn discounts it to an outsider, a real contingent liability exists, which must be shown on the consolidated balance sheet.

Consolidated Financial Statements

Unrealized profits in inventory Regardless of any minority interests, all (100%) of any intercompany profits in inventory must be eliminated on the consolidated work papers if such inventory profits are represented by assets within the group. If the inventory containing intercompany profits has been disposed of to outsiders, no adjustment need be made. If the adjustment for intercompany profits in inventory is not made, consolidated net income is overstated and the consolidated ending inventory is overstated.

P company purchased $200,000 and $250,000 of merchandise in 19X1 and 19X2, respectively, from its subsidiary S at 25% above cost. As of December 31, 19X1 and 19X2, P had on hand $25,000 and $30,000 of merchandise purchased from S. What is the consolidated adjusting entry on December 31, 19X2?

<u>Computation of Intercompany Profits</u>

Beginning inventory	$25,000	=	125%
Cost to S	20,000	=	100%
Intercompany profit	$ 5,000		25%
Ending inventory	$30,000	=	125%
Cost to S	24,000	=	100%
Intercompany profit	$ 6,000		25%

The adjustment is different for a consolidated balance sheet than for a consolidated income statement, because a consolidated balance sheet reflects only the ending inventory, whereas a consolidated income statement usually shows both the beginning and ending inventories. For a consolidated balance sheet only, the consolidated adjusting entry is:

Retained earnings	$ 6,000	
Inventory		$ 6,000

For a consolidated income statement the following adjustments are necessary:

Sales—S Company	$250,000	
Purchases—P Company		$250,000
To eliminate intercompany sales and purchases.		

Consolidated retained earnings	$ 5,000	
Purchases or cost of sales		$ 5,000
To reverse consolidated adjustment of 12/31/X1.		
Purchases or cost of sales	$ 6,000	
Inventory—ending		$ 6,000
To eliminate intercompany profit in ending inventory.		

The adjustment to consolidated retained earnings was necessary because on the prior year's consolidated work papers the intercompany profit was eliminated. Remember, consolidated adjustments and eliminations are never posted to the books of the individual companies. Therefore the beginning inventory for P still reflected the prior year's intercompany inventory profits from S.

If merchandise containing an intercompany inventory profit is reduced from the purchase price to market value and the reduction is equal to, or more than, the actual intercompany inventory profit, no further reduction is made. For example, if merchandise costing one affiliate $10,000 is sold to another affiliate for $12,000, who reduces it to market value of $11,000, the consolidated working paper adjustment for unrealized intercompany inventory profits should be only $1,000.

Minority interests do not affect the adjustment for unrealized intercompany profits in inventories. However, consolidated net income and minority interests in the net income of a subsidiary are affected, because the reduction or increase in beginning or ending inventory of a partially owned subsidiary does affect the determination of net income.

Unrealized intercompany losses in inventory are accounted for in the same manner as unrealized profits, except that they have the opposite effect.

Profits or losses on sales and/or purchases prior to an affiliation are never recognized as a consolidated adjustment.

Unrealized profits in long-lived assets   Regardless of any minority interests, all (100%) of any intercompany profits on the sale and/or purchase of long-lived assets between affiliates is eliminated on the consolidated work papers.

When one affiliate constructs or sells a long-lived asset to another affiliate at a profit, the profit must be eliminated on the consolidated work papers. As with unrealized intercompany profits or losses in inventory, minority interests do not affect any consolidated adjustment for profits in intercompany sales of long-lived assets between affiliates. However, net income of the subsidiary involved in the intercompany profit on a long-lived asset is affected, which in turn affects consolidated net income and minority interests.

In consolidating a subsidiary in a regulated industry, intercompany profits are not eliminated on manufactured or constructed facilities for other members of the consolidated group, to the extent that they are equivalent to a reasonable return on investment as established by industry practice.

If a nondepreciable asset is involved in an intercompany profit on a long-lived asset, the profit is eliminated by a debit to either retained earnings, in the case of an adjusted consolidated balance sheet, or to gain on sale, in the case of a consolidated income statement.

Depreciable assets require the same adjustment for intercompany profit as nondepreciable long-lived assets, and an adjustment must also be made for any depreciation recorded on the intercompany profit.

An 80%-owned subsidiary sells to its parent for $100,000 a piece of machinery that cost $80,000. The sale was made on July 1, 19X1, and consolidated statements are being prepared for December 31, 19X1. The parent depreciates machinery over 10 years on a straight-line basis and recorded one-half a year's depreciation on the purchased machinery.

The first entry eliminates the $20,000 of intercompany profit, as follows:

Gain on sale of machinery	$20,000	
Machinery		$20,000

Since the parent company has recorded one-half a year's depreciation on the machinery, the following additional entry is made:

Accumulated depreciation	$ 1,000	
Depreciation expense		$ 1,000

Because consolidated eliminations and adjustments are never posted to any books, in the second year the following entries are made:

Retained earnings	$20,000	
Machinery		$20,000

To eliminate intercompany profit on prior year's sale of machinery.

Accumulated depreciation	$3,000	
Retained earnings		$1,000
Depreciation expense		2,000

To eliminate the $2,000 depreciation expense on intercompany profit on the sale of machinery and to eliminate the $1,000 depreciation expense for prior year's depreciation.

The process of eliminating the depreciation expense on the intercompany profit on the sale of long-lived assets continues until the asset is fully depreciated, and then thereafter until the asset is disposed of or retired. In our example, the following entry would be made every year on the consolidated work papers after the asset is fully depreciated and before it is disposed of or retired.

Accumulated depreciation	$20,000	
Retained earnings		$20,000

An affiliate that makes an intercompany profit on the sale of long-lived assets to another affiliate may pay income taxes on the gain. This occurs usually when the affiliated group does not file consolidated tax returns and the gain cannot be avoided for tax purposes. In such cases, the intercompany profit on the sale should be reduced by the related tax effects in computing the consolidated adjusting entry.

Intercompany bondholdings Intercompany bonds purchased by an affiliate are treated in the year of acquisition as though they have been retired. Any gain or loss is recognized in the consolidated income statement for the year of acquisition.

The amount of gain or loss on an intercompany bond purchase is the difference between the unamortized bond premium or discount on the books of the issuer and the amount of any purchase discount or premium.

An intercompany gain or loss on bonds cannot occur when an affiliate makes the purchase direct from the affiliated issuer, because the selling price will be exactly equal to the cost.

An affiliate purchases $20,000 face value 6% bonds from an affiliated issuer for $19,500.

On the affiliated investor's books the following entry is made:

Investment in bonds	$19,500	
Cash		$19,500

On the affiliated issuer's books the entry is:

Cash	$19,500	
Discount on bonds payable	500	
Bonds payable		$20,000

The consolidated elimination is:

Bonds payable	$20,000	
Discount on bonds payable		$ 500
Investment in bonds		19,500

An intercompany gain or loss on bonds cannot occur when the purchase price is exactly the same as the carrying value on the books of the affiliated issuer.

The following conditions must exist for an affiliated investor to realize a gain or loss on intercompany bondholdings:

1. The bonds are already outstanding.
2. The bonds are purchased outside the affiliated group.
3. The price paid is different from the carrying value of the affiliated issuer.

Company S acquires $50,000 of face amount 6% bonds from an outsider. These bonds were part of an original issue of $300,000 made by the parent of Company S. The purchase price was $45,000, and the bonds mature in four years and nine months. Interest is payable on June 30 and December 31, and the purchase was made on March 31.

The journal entry on the books of Company S to record the purchase is:

Investment in bonds	$45,000	
Accrued interest receivable	750	
Cash		$45,750

On the consolidated working papers at the end of the year the following entries are made.

Investment in bonds	$ 5,000	
Gain on intercompany bondholdings		$ 5,000
To adjust the investment in bonds to face amount and record the gain.		
Bonds payable—Co. P	$50,000	
Investment in bonds—Co. S		$50,000
To eliminate intercompany bondholdings.		
Interest income—Co. S	$ 2,250	
Interest expense—Co. P		$ 2,250
To eliminate intercompany interest on bonds that was actually earned.		
Interest income—Co. S	$ 788	
Investment in bonds		$ 788
To eliminate amortization of $5,000 discount on bonds recorded on Co. S books. (9/57 of $5,000 = $788)		

Accrued interest payable	$ 1,500	
Accrued interest receivable		$ 1,500

To eliminate accrued interest payable on 12/31/XX by Co. P, and the accrued interest receivable on 12/31/XX by Co. S.

This example contains all the possible adjustments except for an issuer's premium or discount. Assume the following additional information on the original issue:

Face amount	$300,000
Issued at 96	288,000
Date of issue	1/1/70
Maturity date	1/1/80

Company S had purchased its $50,000 face amount when the issue had four years and nine months left to maturity.

On the parent company's books this discount is being amortized over the life of the bond issue at the rate of $1,200 per year ($12,000 discount divided by 10 years).

An adjustment must be made on the consolidated work papers to eliminate the portion of the unamortized bond discount existing at the date of purchase that is applicable to the $50,000 face amount purchased by Company S.

Total discount on issue	$12,000
1/6 applicable to Co. S purchase	$ 2,000
Amount of discount per month ($2,000 divided by 120 months)	$ 16.67
Four years and nine months equal 57 months × $16.67	$ 950

The amount of unamortized bond discount on Co. P books applicable to the $50,000 purchase made by Company S was $950 at the date of purchase. This $950 would have entered into the computation of the gain or loss on intercompany bondholdings. In the example the gain or loss on intercompany bondholdings of $5,000 would have been reduced by $950 ($4,050) and the following additional consolidated elimination would have been made:

Gain or loss on intercompany bondholdings	$950	
Unamortized bond discount		$950

5.12 / GAAP GUIDE

Intercompany dividends Intercompany dividends must be eliminated on the consolidated work papers. Consolidated retained earnings should reflect the accumulated earnings of the consolidated group arising since acquisition which has not been distributed to the shareholders of, or capitalized by, the parent company. In the event that a subsidiary capitalizes earnings arising since acquisition by means of a stock dividend, or otherwise, a transfer to capital surplus is not required in consolidating.

Intercompany stockholdings If a subsidiary holds stock of its parent, it is treated as "treasury stock" on the consolidated balance sheet and subtracted from consolidated stockholders' equity.

Income Tax Considerations

Income taxes must be deferred on any intercompany profits where the asset still exists within the consolidated group. However, if consolidated tax returns are filed, no adjustment need be made for deferred income taxes, because intercompany profits are eliminated in computing the consolidated tax liability.

Minority Interests

Consolidated financial statements are prepared primarily for the benefit of creditors and shareholders.

Minority interests in net income are deducted to arrive at consolidated net income. However, minority interests are theoretically limited to the extent of their equity capital, and losses in excess of minority interest equity capital are charged against the majority interest. Subsequently, when the losses reverse, the majority interests should be credited with the amount of minority interest losses previously absorbed before credit is made to the minority interests.

Computing minority interests in a complex father-son-grandson affiliation may be demonstrated by using the following diagram.

	B		C
A	$40,000	—85%→	$80,000
$100,000 —80%→	SON		GRANDSON
—90%→	$50,000	—75%→	$60,000
	D		E

The computations of minority interests and consolidated net income follow:

	E	D	C	B	A
Net income	$60,000	$50,000	$80,000	$40,000	$100,000
75% to D	(45,000)	45,000			
		$95,000			
90% to A		(85,500)			85,500
85% to B			(68,000)	68,000	
				$108,000	
80% to A				(86,400)	86,400
Minority interests	$15,000	$ 9,500	$12,000	$ 21,600	
Consolidated net income					$271,900

In a situation where a subsidiary owns shares of the parent company, consolidated net income may be found algebraically, as the following illustration depicts:

Company	Unconsolidated income	
A	$40,000	A, the parent, owns 80% of B
B	20,000	B owns 70% of C
C	10,000	C owns 20% of A

$$A \xrightarrow{0.8} B \xrightarrow{0.7} C \xrightarrow{0.2} A$$

Let A = A's *consolidated basis* net income
B = B's *consolidated basis* net income
C = C's *consolidated basis* net income

The figures and relationships can be put into algebraic form so as to compute *consolidated net income*.

$$A = 40{,}000 + 0.8B$$
$$B = 20{,}000 + 0.7C$$
$$C = 10{,}000 + 0.2A$$

Solving for A, we have:

$$A = 40{,}000 + 0.8\,(20{,}000 + 0.7C)$$
$$A = 40{,}000 + 16{,}000 + 0.56C$$
$$A = 56{,}000 + 0.56C$$
$$A = 56{,}000 + 0.56\,(10{,}000 + 0.2A)$$
$$A = 56{,}000 + 5{,}600 + 0.112A$$
$$0.888A = 61{,}600$$
$$A = 69{,}369$$

Since 20% of the parent, A, is owned by an outsider, C, only 80% of A is used as consolidated net income.

$$\$69{,}369 \times 0.8 = \underline{\$55{,}495} = \text{consolidated net income}$$

Disclosure

The consolidation policy should be fully disclosed on the financial statements or in footnotes to the statements.

Disclosure of minority interests The "parent company theory" is used in practice almost exclusively for disclosing minority interests in a consolidated balance sheet. Under the parent company theory, minority interests are *not* considered part of stockholders' equity and are disclosed in the consolidated balance sheet between the liability section and the stockholders' equity section. Where minority interests are insignificant and do not warrant a separate classification in the consolidated balance sheet, some enterprises have seen fit to disclose minority interests among other liabilities. Minority interests in consolidated net income are shown as a deduction of consolidated net income.

Under the "entity theory," minority interests are disclosed within and as part of the consolidated stockholders' equity section of the consolidated balance sheet. Although the entity theory has much more theoretical support, it is seldom used in practice.

CONTINGENCIES

Background

Accounting for contingencies is covered by FASB-5 (Accounting for Contingencies) which amends ARB-50 (Contingencies); FASB Interpretation-14 (Reasonable Estimation of the Amount of a Loss); and FASB Interpretation-34 (Disclosure of Indirect Guarantees of Indebtedness of Others). FASB Technical Bulletin 81-2 has been issued to provide guidance on preacquisition contingencies (FASB-38).

The conditions for accrual of a loss contingency in FASB-5 do not amend any other requirement to accrue a particular type of loss expense in any other existing promulgated GAAP. In particular, the following items are specifically excluded from the scope of FASB-5:

1. APB-12, as it pertains to Deferred Compensation
2. APB-25, Accounting for Stock Issued to Employees
3. Accounting for other employment-related costs, such as group insurance, vacation pay, workmen's compensation, and disability benefits

Overview

A contingency is an existing condition, situation, or set of circumstances involving varying degrees of uncertainty that may, through one or more related future events, result in the acquisition or loss of an asset or the incurrence or avoidance of a liability, usually with the concurrence of a gain or loss. The resulting gain or loss is referred to as a *gain contingency* or a *loss contingency*.

The existence of a loss contingency may be established on or before the date of the financial statements, or after the date of the financial statements but prior to the issuance date of the financial statements. After a loss contingency is established, the probability of its developing into an actual loss must be evaluated. Accounting for a loss contingency is based upon the degree of probability that one or more future events will occur which will result in an actual loss. On the other hand, gain contingencies are never recorded on the books of an entity until they are actually realized, although footnote disclosure in the financial statements may be necessary.

Contingencies

Loss contingencies may arise from the risk of exposure resulting from the following list of items, which is not all-inclusive:

- Collectibility of receivables
- Property loss by fire, explosion, or other hazards
- Expropriation of assets
- Pending or threatened litigation, claims or assessments
- Product warranties or defects
- Catastrophe losses of property

Not all uncertainties in the accounting process are contingencies, as that term is used in FASB-5. Depreciable assets have a reasonably estimated life, and depreciation expense is used to systematically allocate the cost of the asset over its estimated useful life. Estimates, such as depreciation and similar accrued amounts, are not uncertainties as described in FASB-5.

Classification of a Loss Contingency

A loss contingency will develop into an actual loss only upon the occurrence of one or more future events, whose likelihood of occurring may vary significantly. Under the provisions of FASB-5, the likelihood that a loss contingency will develop into an actual loss must be classified as either (a) probable (likely to occur), (b) reasonably possible (halfway between "probable" and "remote"), or (c) remote (slight chance of materializing).

Accounting and Reporting a Loss Contingency

Depending upon whether it is classified as probable, reasonably possible, or remote, a loss contingency may have to be either (a) accrued as a charge to income as of the date of the financial statements, (b) disclosed by footnote in the financial statements, or (c) not disclosed at all.

The following two conditions must be met for a *loss contingency* to be accrued as a charge to income as of the date of the financial statements:

- It is "probable" that as of the date of the financial statements an asset has been impaired or a liability incurred, based on information available before the actual issuance date of the financial statements.

It is implicit in this condition that it must be "probable" that one or more future events will occur to confirm the loss.
- The amount of loss can be reasonably estimated.

> **OBSERVATION:** *If a loss contingency is classified as probable and only a range of possible loss (similar to a minimum-maximum) can be established, then the* minimum *amount in the range should be accrued, unless some other amount within the range appears to be a better estimate (FASB Interpretation-14).*

If an exposure to a loss exists in excess of the amount accrued in accordance with the above provisions of FASB-5, and the amount of the excess exposure is classified as *probable* or *reasonably possible*, financial statement disclosure of the excess loss contingency is required by FASB-5. The disclosure shall contain a description of the nature of the excess loss contingency and the range of possible loss (similar to a minimum-maximum), or include a statement that no estimate of the loss can be made.

If one or both conditions for the accrual of a loss contingency are not met and the loss contingency is classified as *probable* or *reasonably possible*, financial statement disclosure of the loss contingency is required by FASB-5. The disclosure shall contain a description of the nature of the loss contingency and the range of possible loss (similar to a minimum-maximum), or include a statement that no estimate of the loss can be made.

Loss contingencies arising after the date of the financial statements   A loss contingency that is classified as *probable* or *reasonably possible*, which occurs after the balance sheet date but before the issuance date of the financial statements, may have to be disclosed to avoid misleading financial statements. If professional judgment deems this type of disclosure necessary, the disclosure shall contain a description of the nature of the loss contingency and the range of possible loss (similar to a minimum-maximum), or include a statement that no estimate of the loss can be made. On the other hand, it may be desirable to disclose this type of loss contingency by supplementing the historical financial statements with pro forma statements reflecting the loss as if it occurred at the date of the financial statements.

Allowance for uncollectible receivables   For the purposes of GAAP, accounts receivable must be reported at their net realizable value. Net realizable value is equal to the gross amount of the receivables less an estimated allowance for uncollectible accounts.

Contingencies

Under FASB-5 (Contingencies), a contingency exists if, at the date of its financial statements, an enterprise does not expect to collect the full amount of its accounts receivable. Under this circumstance, an accrual for a loss contingency must be charged to income if both of the following conditions are met:

- It is *probable* that as of the date of the financial statements an enterprise does not expect to collect the full amount of its accounts receivable, based on information available before the actual issuance of the financial statements.
- The amount of loss contingency (uncollectible receivables) can be *reasonably estimated*.

If both of the above conditions are met, an accrual for the estimated amount of uncollectible receivables must be made even if the uncollectible receivables cannot be specifically identified. An enterprise may base its estimate of uncollectible receivables on its prior experience, the experience of other enterprises in the same industry, the debtor's ability to pay, and/or an appraisal of current economic conditions. A significant uncertainty exists in the ultimate collection of accounts receivable if an enterprise is unable to reasonably estimate the amount of its uncollectible receivables. If a significant uncertainty does exist in the collection of the receivables, the installment sales method, cost recovery method, or some other method of revenue recognition shall be used (paragraph 12 of APB-10).

In the event that one or both conditions for the accrual of a loss contingency on uncollectible receivables are not met and the loss contingency is classified as *probable* or *reasonably possible*, the nature of the loss contingency and the range of possible loss (similar to a minimum-maximum), or a statement that no estimate of the loss can be made, must be disclosed in the financial statements.

Product or service warranty obligation A product or service warranty obligation is a contingency under the provisions of FASB-5, because of the potential claims which may result from the warranty. If both of the conditions for the accrual of a loss contingency are met, an accrual for the estimated amount of a warranty obligation must be made even if the warranty obligation cannot be specifically identified. An enterprise may base its estimate of a warranty obligation on its prior experience, the experience of other enterprises in the same industry, and/or an appraisal of current economic conditions. If an enterprise is unable to reasonably estimate the amount of its warranty obligation and the range of possible loss is wide, significant uncertainty exists as to whether a sale should be recorded. If a significant uncertainty does exist in estimating a warranty obligation, a sale shall not be recorded and the installment sales method, cost recovery method, or some other method of revenue recognition shall be used (paragraph 12 of APB-10).

In the event that one or both conditions for the accrual of a loss contingency are not met and a loss contingency is classified as *probable* or *reasonably possible*, the nature of the loss contingency and the range of possible loss (similar to a minimum-maximum), or a statement that no estimate of the loss can be made, must be disclosed in the financial statements.

Litigation, claims or assessments If both conditions for the accrual of a loss contingency are met, an accrual for the estimated amount of pending or threatened litigation and actual or possible claims or assessments is required by FASB-5. Some of the factors that should be considered in determining whether the conditions for accrual have been met are the (a) nature of the litigation, claim or assessment, (b) progress of the case, including progress after the date of the financial statements but before the issuance date of the financial statements, (c) opinions of legal counsel, and (d) management's intended response to the litigation, claim or assessment.

In the event that one or both conditions for the accrual of a loss contingency are not met and a loss contingency is classified as *probable* or *reasonably possible*, the nature of the loss contingency and the range of possible loss (similar to a minimum-maximum), or a statement that no estimate of the loss can be made, must be disclosed in the financial statements.

Unasserted Claims or Assessments

An unasserted claim is one which has not been asserted by the claimant because the claimant has no knowledge of the existing claim or does not elect to assert the existing claim. If it is *probable* that an unasserted claim will be asserted by the claimant and it is *probable* or *reasonably possible* that an unfavorable outcome will result, the unasserted claim must be disclosed in the financial statements. However, if these conditions are not met, disclosure is not required for unasserted claims or assessments where apparently the potential claimant has no knowledge of the claim's existence.

Disclosure of Remote Loss Contingencies

As a general rule, financial statement disclosure of loss contingencies that have a *remote* possibility of materializing is not required by

Contingencies

FASB-5. However, loss contingencies that may occur as the result of a *guarantee* must be disclosed in the financial statements, even if they have a *remote* possibility of materializing.

Guarantees to repurchase receivables or related property, obligations of banks under letters of credit or "stand-by" agreements, guarantees of the indebtedness of others, and unconditional obligations to make payments are examples of the types of guarantee contingencies which must be disclosed even if they have a *remote* possibility of materializing. FASB-5 requires that the nature and amount of the guarantee be disclosed in the financial statements. In addition, consideration should be given to disclosing the amount, if estimable, that can be recovered in the event the guarantor is called upon to satisfy the guarantee.

FASB Interpretation-34 (Disclosure of Indirect Guarantees of Indebtedness of Others) was issued to clarify that the term "guarantee of indebtedness of others" (paragraph 12 of FASB-5) includes both direct and indirect guarantees.

In both a direct and indirect guarantee of indebtedness of others, three parties are involved: (1) the debtor, (2) the creditor, and (3) the guarantor. In a direct guarantee, the guarantor agrees to make payment directly to the creditor if the debtor fails to do so. The guarantee runs directly from the guarantor to the creditor. Thus, the creditor has a direct claim against the guarantor if the debtor defaults. In an indirect guarantee, the guarantor agrees to transfer funds to the debtor if a specified event occurs. The guarantee runs directly from the guarantor to the debtor, but the creditor is an indirect beneficiary of the guarantee. Thus, the creditor has an indirect claim against the guarantor because he may exercise the debtor's claim against the guarantor in the event of default. After the guarantor transfers the funds to the debtor, they may become available to the creditor. (The preceding definitions are based on paragraph 2 of FASB Interpretation-34, which is further clarified by paragraph 9, Appendix A, of FASB Interpretation-34.)

> ***OBSERVATION:*** *FASB Interpretation-34 states that the funds transferred to the debtor will become legally available to creditors. However, this does not necessarily mean that any creditor will actually receive the transferred funds. The agreement may specifically require the debtor to use the funds for purposes other than the payment of creditors. For example, the agreement may require that the debtor retain the transferred funds in order to maintain its working capital at or above a specified minimum.*
>
> *Another possibility is that competing creditor claims may be made against the transferred funds, in which event litigation may be the only solution.*

FASB Interpretation-34 describes the following agreements as indirect guarantees of indebtedness of others:

- A guarantor is obligated to transfer funds to a debtor if a specific event occurs. The funds transferred must be legally available to the debtor's creditors, who also expressly have the right to enforce the terms of the agreement in the event of default.
- A guarantor is obligated to transfer funds to a debtor if the debtor's income, working capital, and/or coverage of fixed charges are not maintained at specified amounts.

Thus, one must conclude that an indirect guarantee of the indebtedness of another, for the purposes of FASB Interpretation-34, must involve, among other factors, a transfer of funds from the guarantor to the debtor. However, paragraph 3 of FASB Interpretation-34, further clarifies the situation. Paragraph 3 states that the term "guarantees of indebtedness of others" in paragraph 12 of FASB-5, "includes" those indirect guarantees described in FASB Interpretation-34. The use of the word "includes" in this context may mean "includes, but is not limited to." If this is correct, other types of indirect guarantees of indebtedness of others that do not involve the "transfer of funds" should be disclosed in accordance with FASB-5 when professional judgment warrants such disclosure.

FASB Interpretation-34 makes no mention of who must disclose indirect guarantees of indebtedness of others in accordance with FASB-5. It is obvious that until the indirect guarantee is actually enforced, the guarantor must disclose the *remote* loss contingency that would result from the enforcement of the guarantee. However, there may be circumstances in which professional judgment may require disclosure, by the debtor and/or creditor, of indirect guarantees which have not yet been enforced.

> **OBSERVATION:** *Apparently, the Financial Accounting Standards Board recognized the need for clarification of indirect guarantees of indebtedness of others because some enterprises were interpreting paragraph 12 of FASB-5 to cover only direct guarantees. Thus, indirect guarantees, in some instances, were not being properly disclosed. FASB Interpretation-34 was probably issued to clarify and correct this situation.*

Disclosure of Noninsured Property

An enterprise may be underinsured or not insured at all against the risk of future loss or damage to its property by fire, explosion, or other hazard. The fact that an enterprise's property is underinsured or not insured at all constitutes an existing uncertainty as defined by FASB-5. However, the absence of insurance does not mean that an asset has been impaired or a liability incurred as of the date of the financial statements. Therefore, FASB-5 does not require financial statement disclosure of noninsurance or underinsurance of possible losses, but specifically states that it does not discourage this practice.

Reporting Gain Contingencies

Gain contingencies should be disclosed in the financial statements by footnote, but should not be reflected in income, because to do so might be to recognize revenue prior to its realization. Care should be exercised in disclosing gain contingencies to avoid misleading implications as to the recognition of revenue prior to its realization (ARB-50).

Appropriation of Retained Earnings

FASB-5 does not prohibit an enterprise from appropriating specific amounts of retained earnings for potential loss contingencies. However, the amount of appropriated retained earnings must be reported within the stockholders' equity section of the balance sheet, clearly identified as an appropriation of retained earnings. In addition, the following rules must be observed:

1. No costs or losses shall be charged against the appropriated retained earnings and no part of the appropriated retained earnings may be transferred to income or in any way used to affect the determination of net income for any period.
2. The appropriated retained earnings shall be restored intact to retained earnings when the appropriation is no longer considered necessary.

Preacquisition Contingencies (FASB-38)

A portion of the total cost of acquiring an enterprise under the purchase method (APB-16) must be allocated to contingent assets, contingent liabilities, and contingent impairments of assets, provided that the following conditions are met:

- It is probable that the contingent item existed at the consummation date of the business combination.
- After the consummation date, but prior to the end of the "allocation period" it is confirmed that the contingent item did exist at the consummation date of the business combination.
- The amount of the asset, liability, or impairment can be reasonably estimated.

If the above conditions are met, a portion of the total cost of acquiring an enterprise under the purchase method must be allocated to any contingent items (FASB-38).

The "allocation period" is the period that is required by the purchaser to identify and quantify the acquired assets and assumed liabilities for the purposes of allocating the total cost of the acquisition in accordance with APB-16.

Any adjustment for contingent items arising from a purchase transaction that occurs after the end of the "allocation period" is included in net income of the period in which the adjustment is recognized. An exception occurs for the realized tax effects of loss carryforwards of purchased subsidiaries, which are recorded as retroactive adjustments of the purchase transaction (APB-11).

> **OBSERVATION:** *FASB Technical Bulletin 81-2 reaffirms that unused investment tax credits acquired by the purchase method should be accounted for in accordance with FASB Interpretation-25. Unused investment tax credits acquired by the purchase method are not considered preacquisition contingencies.*

CONVERTIBLE DEBT

Background

APB-14 establishes the promulgated GAAP for reporting the issuance of Convertible Debt and Debt Issued with Stock Purchase Warrants. The issuance of any debt security not explicitly discussed in APB-14 should be accounted for in accordance with the substance of the transaction (APB-14).

For the purpose of applying APB-14, the time of issuance of a debt security is the date on which an agreement as to the terms of the debt security is reached and announced, even though the agreement may be subject to the subsequent approval of the stockholders and/or directors of the enterprise.

FASB-84 establishes the method of accounting and reporting that should be applied to certain conversions of convertible debt that are induced by the debtor. Under FASB-84, an *induced conversion* of convertible debt is one in which the original conversion privileges are changed, or additional consideration is paid, to induce the holder of the convertible debt to convert to the equity securities of the debtor.

FASB-84 amends APB-26 (Early Extinguishment of Debt) to provide that induced conversions of convertible debt that were previously covered by APB-26 are now covered by the provisions of FASB-84.

Overview

Convertible debt is convertible into the common stock of the issuer or an affiliated enterprise, and because of the conversion option, a debtor can generally issue convertible debt at a lower interest rate than comparable nonconvertible debt. Most convertible debt is *callable* at the option of the debtor and is generally subordinated to nonconvertible debt. The characteristics of convertible debt are:

- The issue price is not significantly greater than the face amount.
- The interest rate is lower than the interest rate on an equivalent, but not convertible, security.
- The initial conversion price is greater than the market value of the underlying security.

Convertible Debt

- The conversion price does not change (except pursuant to certain antidilutive considerations).
- The security is usually callable by the issuer.
- The debt is usually subordinate to the nonconvertible debt of the issuer.

Issuance of convertible debt A convertible debt security may be issued with a conversion feature that is physically inseparable from, and part of, the convertible debt security, or with a separate conversion feature, such as a detachable stock purchase warrant.

Under current accounting practice (APB-14), the economic substance of an inseparable conversion option is not recognized at the time the convertible debt is issued, because none of the issuance proceeds from the convertible debt are allocated to the conversion option. APB-14 requires that all of the issuance proceeds be credited to the liability account for the convertible debt after accounting for any related bond discount or premium.

Under current accounting practice (APB-14), the economic substance of a separate conversion option is recognized, because a portion of the issuance proceeds from the debt is allocated to the conversion option. The portion of the issuance proceeds allocated to the separate conversion option is based on the relative fair value of the convertible debt and conversion option on their date of issuance. Thus, the convertible security itself is credited at par or face value, the detachable warrant is credited at market value, and the discount or premium is the residual amount required to balance the cash received.

Xeta Corporation issues $10,000 of 5% convertible preferred stock with a detachable common stock warrant to purchase one share of Xeta's common stock at a specified price. At the time of issuance, the quoted market price of the convertible stock was $97 per share, and the stock warrants were quoted at $2 each. The proceeds of the sale to Xeta Corporation were $9,900. The transaction is accounted for as follows:

Cash	$9,900	
Discount on 5% convertible preferred stock	300	
5% Convertible preferred stock		$10,000
Paid-in capital (stock warrants)		200

Convertible Debt

The difference between the face amount of the 5% convertible preferred stock and the value of the warrants that were recorded on the books ($10,000 + $200 = $10,200) less the amount of cash proceeds received from the sale ($9,900) is equal to the discount ($300).

> **OBSERVATION:** *Proper recognition of the economic substance of the issuance of convertible debt requires that a portion of the proceeds from the issuance of the debt be allocated to the conversion option and credited to paid-in-capital. This is exactly the method of accounting that was required by prior promulgated GAAP (APB-10). However, APB-10 was superseded by APB-14, which does not give recognition to the economic substance of a conversion option that is inseparable from its related convertible security, but does recognize the economic substance of a conversion option that is separable from its related convertible security. Thus, under APB-14, accounting for the issuance of convertible debt with an inseparable conversion option is different than accounting for the issuance of convertible debt with a separate conversion option.*

Conversions of convertible debt Once a separate conversion feature is issued, such as a detachable stock purchase warrant, it is usually separately traded from its related convertible debt security. The separate conversion feature has its own market price, and conversion requires (a) the surrender of the conversion feature, and (b) the payment of any other consideration required by the terms of the warrant.

Under current accounting practice, when a separate conversion feature, such as a detachable stock purchase warrant, is exercised and converted into equity securities of the debtor, in accordance with the original conversion terms, no gain or loss is recognized on the transaction. The amount previously credited to paid-in capital for the conversion feature at issuance is debited, the amount of cash received, if any, is recorded, and the par value of the capital stock issued and the appropriate credit to capital stock in excess of par is recorded. The following is an illustration of such a transaction.

Ace Corporation previously issued convertible debt securities with detachable stock purchase warrants. A credit of $10 for each warrant was recorded in paid-in capital at the date of issuance, representing the relative market value of each warrant. There was no discount or premium on the issuance of the convertible debt with detachable stock purchase warrants. Each stock purchase warrant was con-

Convertible Debt

vertible into 50 shares of Ace Corporation's $1 par value common stock, upon the payment of $200 and the surrender of the warrant. Assuming that one warrant was exercised, the journal entry would be:

Cash	$200	
Paid-in capital (stock warrants)	10	
Capital stock ($1 par value)		$ 50
Capital in excess of par (common stock)		160

Thus, under current accounting practice, the conversion of a separate conversion feature, such as a detachable stock purchase warrant, is accounted for as an equity transaction, and no gain or loss is recorded.

In order to exercise a conversion feature that is physically inseparable from, and part of, a convertible debt security, the entire security must be surrendered, and the debt is retired by the debtor.

Under current accounting practice, when a convertible debt security with an inseparable conversion feature is converted into equity securities of the debtor in accordance with the original conversion terms, no gain or loss is recognized on the transaction. The convertible debt security is surrendered by the holder and the debt is retired by the debtor. The following is an illustration of such a transaction.

Blue Corporation has outstanding $20,000,000 of 14% convertible bonds, with an unamortized bond premium balance of $800,000. Each $1,000 bond is convertible into 10 shares of Blue Corporation's $5 par value common stock. On April 1, 19X1, all of the convertible bonds were converted by the bondholders.

14% Convertible bonds payable	$20,000,000	
Unamortized bond premium	800,000	
Common stock ($5 par × 200,000)		$ 1,000,000
Capital in excess of par (common stock)		19,800,000

Under current accounting practice, no gain or loss is recognized on the conversion of convertible bonds to common stock if the conversion is made in accordance with the original conversion terms.

Extinguishments of debt APB-26 applies to all extinguishments of debt made before or at maturity, except debt that is extinguished through a troubled debt restructuring (FASB-15). APB-26 covers the *extinguishment* of convertible debt but does not cover convertible debt that is *converted* to the equity securities of the debtor in accordance with the original conversion terms in the debt agreement. Thus, it is important to distinguish the difference between an extinguishment of debt and the conversion of debt.

FASB Technical Bulletin 80-1 states that APB-26 applies to all early extinguishments of debt effected by the issuance of common or preferred stock, including redeemable and fixed-maturity preferred stock, unless the extinguishment is a troubled debt restructuring (FASB-15) or a *conversion* by the holder pursuant to conversion privileges contained in the original debt issue.

> **OBSERVATION:** *An accounting interpretation of APB-26 dated March 1973, states that "APB Opinion No. 26 does not apply to a conversion of debt nor does the Opinion specify the accounting for conversion of debt. In practice, however, the carrying amount of the debt, including any unamortized premium or discount, is credited to the capital accounts upon conversion to reflect the stock issued and no gain or loss is recognized."*

An extinguishment of debt is the reacquisition of debt prior to, or at, the maturity date of the debt. Under APB-26, all extinguishments of debt are basically alike, and accounting for such transactions should be the same, regardless of the method used to achieve the extinguishment. Thus, there should be no difference in accounting for an extinguishment of debt by (a) cash purchase, (b) exchange of stock for debt, (c) exchange of debt for debt, and (d) any other method (see paragraph 19 of APB-26).

Gain or loss on the extinguishment of debt is the difference between the total reacquisition cost of the debt and the net carrying amount of the debt on the date of the extinguishment. Under APB-26, gain or loss on the extinguishment of debt is recognized immediately, in the period of extinguishment, and, if material, is reported as an extraordinary item, net of related tax effects (FASB-4). For a more detailed discussion of extinguishment of debt, see chapter entitled "Extinguishment of Debt."

Inducements to convert Generally, convertible debt is issued in anticipation that it will be converted into equity securities, and that the issuer will not have to pay the face amount of the debt at its maturity date. Although most convertible debt issues provide for the issuance of common equity shares upon conversion, the terms of a convertible debt security may provide for the issuance of preferred or other type of equity security upon conversion. When an enterprise converts debt to common equity shares, the liability for the debt is eliminated and the number of common equity shares outstanding is increased, which affects the computation of earnings per share (EPS). When debt is converted to common equity shares, the pretax net income of the enterprise also increases by the amount of interest expense that was previously paid on the convertible debt.

Convertible debt is generally converted by a holder when the market value of its underlying equity securities into which the debt can be converted exceeds the face amount of the debt. If a convertible bondholder does not convert, the issuer may exercise the call provision in the debt to force conversion.

Convertible debt is usually not converted when the market value of its underlying equity securities is less than the face amount of the debt. Under this circumstance, the issuer may either (a) exercise the call provision in the debt and pay the bondholders the face amount of the convertible debt or (b) offer the bondholders an inducement to convert which exceeds the original conversion terms.

Induced Conversions of Convertible Debt

FASB-84 applies to conversions of convertible debt in which the original conversion terms are changed by the debtor to induce the holder of the convertible debt to convert to equity securities of the debtor. Changes in the original conversion terms may include (a) the reduction of the original conversion price to increase the number of shares of equity securities received by the bondholder, (b) the issuance of warrants or other securities, or (c) the payment of cash or some other type of consideration.

FASB-84 applies only to induced conversions that (a) are exercisable for a limited period of time and (b) include the issuance of no less than the number of shares of equity securities required by the original conversion terms for each convertible bond converted. Thus, for each convertible bond that is converted, the debtor must issue, at a minimum, the amount of equity securities required by the original conversion terms.

For the purposes of applying FASB-84, it makes no difference whether the holder of the convertible debt legally exercises, or does not legally exercise, the original contractual conversion privileges.

> **OBSERVATION:** FASB-84 applies only to those induced conversions that are offered for a "limited period of time." Unfortunately, the term "limited period of time" is not explained adequately.

Convertible Debt

Example 1 of Appendix A of FASB-84 appears to indicate that 60 days is considered a limited period of time. Example 2 indicates that 30 days is considered a limited period of time. However, paragraph 32 of FASB-84 seems to indicate that a "limited period of time" may even be longer than 60 days.

In an induced conversion of convertible debt under FASB-84, a debtor does not recognize any gain or loss on the amount of equity securities that are required to be issued under the original conversion terms for each convertible bond converted. However, the fair value of any equity securities or other consideration paid or issued by the debtor, which exceeds the amount of equity securities required to be issued for each convertible bond converted under the original conversion terms, shall be recognized as an ordinary expense on the date the inducement offer is accepted by the bondholder. In other words, the fair value of any incremental consideration that is incurred by the debtor in an induced conversion shall be recognized as an ordinary expense on the date the inducement offer is accepted by a bondholder.

OBSERVATION: *If 500 different bondholders accepted an inducement offer on 40 different days during the "limited period of time" allowed by FASB-84, a separate computation of the fair value of the incremental consideration may be required if the fair value of the debtor's common stock changes from day to day.*

CALCULATION OF INCREMENTAL CONSIDERATION

Black Corporation has outstanding one hundred 10% Convertible Bonds due on December 31, 19X1. Each $1,000 bond is convertible into 20 shares of Black Corporation $1 par value common stock. To induce bondholders to convert to its common stock, Black Corporation increases the conversion rate from 20 shares per $1,000 bond to 25 shares per $1,000 bond. This offer was made by Black Corporation for a limited period of 60 days commencing March 1, 19X2.

On April 1, when the market price of Black's common stock was $60, one bondholder tendered a $1,000 convertible bond for conversion. Under FASB-84, the amount of incremental consideration is equal to the fair value of the additional 5 shares of Black Corporation's common stock on April 1. Thus, the amount of incremental consideration is $300 (5 shares × $60 per share).

Convertible Debt

The journal entry to record the transaction is:

Convertible bonds payable	$1,000	
Debt conversion expense	300	
Common stock ($1 par value)		
($1 × 25 shares)		$ 25
Capital in excess of par		
(common stock)		1,275

The incremental consideration paid or issued by a debtor may also be calculated as the difference between (a) the fair value of the equity securities and/or other consideration required to be issued under the original terms of the conversion privilege and (b) the fair value of the equity securities and/or other consideration that is actually issued.

Market value of securities based on inducement	
(25 × $60)	$1,500
Market value of securities based on original terms	
(20 × $60)	1,200
Fair value of incremental consideration	$ 300

OBSERVATION: *If, on April 2, when the market price of Black's common stock was $62, another bondholder tendered a $1,000 convertible bond for conversion, the amount of incremental consideration, under the provisions of FASB-84, would be $310 (5 shares × $62 per share).*

Effective date and transition FASB-84 is effective for induced conversions of convertible debt that are offered by the debtor on or after April 1, 1985. As with most promulgated GAAP, earlier application of the provisions of FASB-84 is encouraged.

An accounting change which results from the initial application of FASB-84 shall be made by the retroactive restatement of all comparative financial statements presented. In addition, the financial statements of the year of change shall disclose the nature of any restatement and its effect on income before extraordinary items, net income, and related per share amounts, for each year presented.

CRITIQUE OF FASB-84
Induced Conversions of Convertible Debt

There is a significant difference between extinguishment accounting and conversion accounting. As a rule, gain or loss is recognized in extinguishment accounting, while no gain or loss is recognized in conversion accounting. Extinguishment accounting results in the *extinguishment* of a debt, while conversion accounting results in the issuance of equity securities and the *retirement* of a debt. Although FASB-84 refers to both extinguishment and conversion accounting, it does not distinguish between the two methods.

Under FASB-84, the amount of equity securites issued under the original conversion terms is accounted for as a conversion and no gain or loss is recognized, but the market value of any additional conversion inducement is accounted for as an ordinary expense (as opposed to an extraordinary expense). If the additional inducement consists of equity securities, the market value of such securities is credited to capital stock, and if necessary to capital in excess of par, with an offsetting debit to debt conversion expense. If the additional inducement consists of assets other than the debtor's equity securities, the market value of such assets is credited with an offsetting debit to debt conversion expense.

Paragraph 23 of FASB-84, which contains the basis for the above conclusions, is quoted below:

> In a conversion pursuant to original conversion terms, debt is extinguished in exchange for equity pursuant to a preexisting contract that is already recognized in the financial statements and no gain or loss is recognized upon conversion. Unlike a conversion pursuant to original terms, in an induced conversion transaction the enterprise issues shares or pays assets in excess of those provided in the preexisting contract between the parties. The Board believes that the enterprise incurs a cost when it gives up securities or assets pursuant to a previous obligation and that the cost of those securities or assets should be recognized.

When an enterprise gives up *assets* or increases its *liabilities* to induce the conversion of its convertible debt to its equity securities, there is no question that a cost is incurred. However, serious doubt exists whether an enterprise incurs a cost when it gives up its own *equity securities* as an inducement for the conversion of convertible debt.

Paragraph 65 of FASB Concept Statement No. 3 states that expenses represent outflows or other using up of assets or incurrences of

Convertible Debt

liabilities (or a combination of both) during a period. There is no outflow or other using up of assets or incurrence of liabilities when, as a conversion inducement, an enterprise issues its equity securities and records their fair market value as debt conversion expense. The debt conversion expense that is required to be recorded in an induced conversion under FASB-84 does not represent any outflow of assets or the incurrence of any liabilities, unless capital stock is considered an asset. However, since it is widely held that a corporation cannot own part of itself, a corporation's own capital stock should not be considered a corporate asset. Paragraph 43 of FASB Concept Statement No. 3 defines equity, which includes capital stock, as "the residual interest in the assets of an entity that remains after deducting its liabilities." Thus, capital stock cannot be both an asset and part of equity.

Generally, the issuance of capital stock increases an enterprise's assets or decreases its liabilities, and increases the number of capital shares outstanding. The principal amount of a convertible debt issue does not change, regardless of the number of equity shares that are issued in a conversion. When capital stock is issued in a transaction that does not affect the assets or liabilities of an enterprise, only the number of outstanding shares of capital stock is increased, which simply dilutes the equity of the individual shareholders.

FASB-84 also overlooks the fact that the issuance of capital stock is a capital transaction, and under current accounting practice, capital transactions should not enter into the income determination of an enterprise (APB-9). FASB-84 requires that an enterprise record the market value of its capital stock that is issued to induce the conversion of convertible debt, along with an offsetting debit to debt conversion expense. The credit to capital stock increases stockholders' equity, and the debit to debt conversion expense for the same amount is included in determining income for the period. The ultimate effect of the debt conversion expense is to decrease retained earnings (stockholders' equity) in the same amount originally credited to capital stock (stockholders' equity). The net result of this capital transaction is (a) an increase in the number of shares of capital stock outstanding, and (b) the transfer of the fair market value of the capital stock issued to induce the conversion from retained earnings to capital stock, and if necessary, capital in excess of par. Thus, the total assets, total liabilities, and total equity of an enterprise are not changed by the capital transaction required by FASB-84.

> **OBSERVATION:** Ordinarily, a corporation does not recognize a gain or loss when it exchanges its equity securities for property or

money (IRC Sec. 1032). *Thus, it appears that the debt conversion expense created by the capital transaction advocated by FASB-84 would not be tax deductible.*

The debt conversion expense that is recorded under the provisions of FASB-84 does not generate an economic loss to an enterprise, because it does not result in the outflow of any assets or the incurrence of any liabilities. It is the individual stockholders of an enterprise that suffer the economic loss from the accounting required by FASB-84. First, the number of shares issued in a conversion reduces the primary earnings per share of an enterprise which may affect the value of the individual stockholder's investment. Secondly, the debt conversion expense may reduce primary earnings per share even further and, if significant, this reduction in earnings per share may affect the market price of the enterprise's stock. Thus, it is the individual stockholder, not the enterprise, that may suffer economic loss as a result of the provisions of FASB-84.

FASB-84 may encounter some legal problems with the Model Business Corporation Act (MBCA), which has been adopted by many states. Section 19 of the MBCA apparently requires that the consideration for the issuance of capital shares be paid in cash, tangible or intangible property, or in services actually performed for the corporation. It is not clear whether debt conversion expense will qualify as consideration for the issuance of capital stock. In addition, Section 17 of the MBCA appears to require that the consideration for the shares issued in a conversion of debt shall be the principal sum of, and accrued interest on, the debt.

Under current accounting practice, capital transactions are not included in the determination of the income of an enterprise, but are required to be adequately disclosed in the financial statements. Thus, current accounting practices for capital transactions would seem to require that the conversion of debt to equity be accounted for as a conversion, whether or not the original conversion privileges are exercised or additional equity securities are offered by the debtor. In this event, conversion accounting should be applied, and no gain or loss recognized on the capital transaction. Conversion accounting for induced conversions was recommended by some of the respondents to the exposure draft for FASB-84. Paragraph 26 of FASB-84, which reflects this position, is quoted below:

> Some respondents stated that no cost should be recognized on induced conversions of convertible debt instruments. They recommended that the original and incremental consideration be accounted for in the same manner as a conversion pursuant to original conversion terms. They rea-

Convertible Debt

soned that changes in the number of shares issuable to satisfy a preexisting obligation do not change the nature of that obligation and also noted that gains and losses are not recognized by an enterprise in certain types of transactions involving issuance of shares of ownership.

Applying the Provisions of FASB-84

Under FASB-84, if the original conversion terms require the issuance of 50 shares of $1 par value common stock for each $1,000 convertible bond, and the debtor issues, as an additional inducement to convert, five additional shares of its common stock with a total market value of $100 ($20 per share), a loss is recognized on the market value of the additional common stock. The following illustrates the journal entry for such a transaction:

Convertible bond payable	$1,000	
Debt conversion expense ($20 × 5)	100	
Capital stock ($1 par) ($1 × 55 shares)		$ 55
Capital in excess of par (common stock)		1,045

As mentioned previously, the debt conversion expense of $100 creates a loss of $100, which decreases retained earnings (stockholders' equity) by the same amount. The net effect of the transaction is that $100 of retained earnings is converted into $100 of capital stock and capital in excess of par (common stock). If conversion accounting is followed for the same transaction, the results are exactly the same, except there is no loss, and no transfer of retained earnings to capital stock and capital stock in excess of par (common stock). The following illustrates the journal entry for such a transaction:

Convertible bond payable	$1,000	
Capital stock ($1 par) ($1 × 55 shares)		$ 55
Capital in excess of par (common stock)		945

Under conversion accounting, the capital stock issued in the conversion is recorded at the net carrying amount of the debt which is being converted and no gain or loss is recognized on the transaction. The market value of the capital stock is ignored.

If the additional inducement consists of assets other than the debtor's equity securities, the market value of such assets is credited with an offsetting debit to debt conversion expense. Thus, if the original conversion terms require the issuance of 50 shares of $1 par value common stock for each $1,000 convertible bond, and the debtor pays an additional inducement of $100 in cash or $100 in market value of other assets, a loss is recognized in the amount of $100. The following illustrates the journal entry for such a transaction:

Convertible bond payable	$1,000	
Debt conversion expense	100	
Capital stock ($1 par)		$ 50
Capital in excess of par (common stock)		950
Cash or other assets		100

An economic loss occurs when the additional inducement paid by a debtor in an induced conversion is in the form of cash or other assets. The effect of the payment of the $100 cash inducement in the above journal entry (a) decreases cash by $100, (b) creates a loss of $100 (debt conversion expense), and (c) has no effect on the capital stock accounts. The $100 loss results in a $100 decrease in retained earnings (stockholders' equity), which is not offset by any other amount.

CURRENT ASSETS AND CURRENT LIABILITIES

Background

The primary source of promulgated GAAP concerning current assets and current liabilities is ARB-43, Chapter 3A. Other related promulgated GAAP included in this chapter are:

> ARB-43, Chapter 1A—Receivables from Officers, Employees, or Affiliated Companies
> ARB-43, Chapter 3A—Current Assets and Current Liabilities
> FASB-6—Classification of Short-Term Obligations Expected to Be Refinanced
> FASB-43—Accounting for Compensated Absences
> FASB-78—Classification of Obligations That Are Callable by the Creditor
> FASB Interpretation-8—Classification of a Short-Term Obligation Repaid Prior to Being Replaced by a Long-Term Security

FASB Technical Bulletin 79-3 was issued to provide guidance in accounting for long-term obligations that contain subjective acceleration clauses. FASB Technical Bulletin 85-4 provides guidance on accounting for purchases of life insurance.

Operating Cycle

In the ordinary course of business there is a continuing *circulation of capital* within the current assets. For example, with a manufacturer, cash is expended for materials, labor, and factory overhead that are converted into finished inventory. After being sold, the inventory is usually converted into a trade receivable and, on collection of receivable, is converted back to cash. The average time elapsing between expending the cash originally and receiving the cash back from the trade receivable is called an *operating cycle*. One year is used as a basis for segregating current assets when the operating cycle occurs more frequently than once a year. When the operating cycle is *longer than one year*, as with the lumber, tobacco, and distillery businesses, then the longer period should be used as the operating cycle. *In the event that a business clearly has no operating cycle, the one-year rule is used.*

The classification of current assets and current liabilities for a specific company is directly related to the company's operating cycle.

Frequently, businesses have a *natural business year*, at the end of which the company's activity, inventory, and trade receivables are at their lowest point.

Current Assets

Resources that are reasonably expected to be realized in cash, sold, or consumed (prepaid items) during the normal operating cycle of a business are classified as current assets. Current assets are sometimes called circulating or working assets, and cash that is restricted as to withdrawal or use for other than current operations should not be classified as a current asset.

There are several basic categories of current assets:

Cash Includes money in any form, for example, cash on deposit, cash awaiting deposit, and cash funds available for use.

Secondary cash resources The most common type of secondary cash resources are marketable securities..

Inventories Includes all types of inventories including merchandise, raw materials, work in process, finished goods, operating supplies, and ordinary maintenance material and parts.

Receivables Includes accounts receivable, notes receivable, and receivables from officers and employees. To be classified as current assets all these must become due within the current operating cycle.

Prepaid expenses Includes prepaid insurance, interest, rents, taxes, advertising, and operating supplies. Prepaid expenses will not be converted into cash, but if they were not paid in advance, they would require the use of current assets during the operating cycle.

Current assets do not always represent their present realizable cash value. Accounts receivable, net of allowances for uncollectible accounts, are effectively stated at the amount of cash estimated as realizable. Supplementary information should be disclosed that reveals the basis on which current assets are stated and an indication of the method of determining the cost.

Current Liabilities

Current liabilities are obligations whose liquidation is reasonably expected to require the use of current assets or the creation of other current liabilities.

There are several basic types of current liabilities:

Obligations for items that have entered the operating cycle, which include trade payables and accrued liabilities such as wages and taxes.

Other debt that is expected to be liquidated during the current operating cycle, which include short-term notes and the currently maturing portion of long-term debt.

Prepayments that include collections received in advance of services, for example, prepaid subscriptions and other deferred revenues.

Accruals which include estimates of accrued amounts that are expected to be required to cover expenditures within the year for known obligations (1) when the amount can be determined only approximately (provision for accrued bonuses payable) or (2) where the specific person(s) to whom payment will be made is (are) unascertainable (provision for warranty of a product).

Current liabilities should not include a contractual obligation falling due at an early date that is expected to be refinanced or refunded and is not reasonably expected to require the use of current assets or the creation of other current liabilities.

When appropriate, current liabilities should be recorded at their present values of the amounts to be paid.

Working Capital

Working capital is the excess of current assets over current liabilities, and it indicates the relative liquidity of an enterprise.

The statement of changes in financial position is a mandatory part of a complete set of financial statements prepared in conformity with GAAP (APB-19). One of the major purposes of the statement of changes in financial position is to report the increase or decrease in working capital during the period and the changes in each element of working capital.

Changes in each element of working capital The changes in each element of working capital are the increases or decreases in each current asset and current liability over the amounts in the preceding year, as follows:

Current Assets	19X1	19X2	Increase or (Decrease)
Cash	$10,000	$ 15,000	$ 5,000
Accounts receivable	25,000	35,000	10,000
Inventory	50,000	60,000	10,000
Prepaid expenses	1,000	500	(500)
Total current assets	$86,000	$110,500	$24,500
Current Liabilities			
Accounts payable	$10,000	$ 15,000	$ 5,000
Notes payable-current	20,000	15,000	(5,000)
Accrued expenses	1,000	1,500	500
Total current liabilities	$31,000	$ 31,500	$ 500
Net working capital	$55,000	$ 79,000	
Increase or decrease in working capital			$24,000

The *current ratio,* or *working capital ratio,* is a measure of current position and is useful in analyzing short-term credit.

The current ratio is computed by dividing the total current assets by the total current liabilities.

	19X1	19X2
Current assets	$650,000	$525,000
Current liabilities	250,000	225,000
Working capital	$400,000	$300,000
Current ratio	2.6 : 1	2.3 : 1

The *acid-test ratio* is determined by dividing the "cashlike" assets by total current liabilities. The cashlike assets consist of cash, receivables, and marketable securities. Only receivables and securities *convertible into cash* should be included, and restricted cash and securities should be excluded.

	19X1	19X2
Cash	$ 200,000	$ 150,000
Marketable securities	400,000	350,000
Receivables, net	800,000	600,000
Total cashlike assets	$1,400,000	$1,100,000
Total current liabilities	$ 600,000	$ 500,000
Acid-test ratio	2.3 : 1	2.2 : 1

Receivables

For the purposes of GAAP, accounts receivable must be reported in the financial statements at net realizable value. Net realizable value is equal to the gross amount of receivables less an estimated allowance for uncollectible accounts.

Under FASB-5 (Contingencies), a contingency exists if, at the date of its financial statements, an enterprise does not expect to collect the full amount of its accounts receivable. Under this circumstance, an accrual for a loss contingency must be charged to income, if both of the following conditions exist:

- It is *probable* that as of the date of the financial statements an asset has been impaired or a liability incurred, based on subsequent available information prior to the issuance of the financial statements, and
- The amount of the loss can be *reasonably estimated.*

If both of the above conditions are met, an accrual for the estimated amount of uncollectible receivables must be made even if the uncollectible receivables cannot be specifically identified. An enterprise may base its estimate of uncollectible receivables on its prior experience, the experience of other enterprises in the same industry, the debtor's ability to pay, or an appraisal of current economic conditions. A significant uncertainty may exist in the ultimate collection of the receivables if an enterprise is unable to reasonably estimate the amount that is uncollectible. If a significant uncertainty exists in the ultimate collection of the receivables, the installment sales method, cost recovery method, or some other method of revenue recognition should be used (paragraph 12 of APB-10). In the event that both of the above conditions for accrual are not met and a loss contingency is at least *reasonably possible*, certain financial statement disclosures are required by FASB-5.

Two common procedures of accounting for bad debts are (a) the direct write-off method and (b) the allowance method. However, for the reasons discussed below, the direct write-off method is not acceptable for the purposes of GAAP.

Direct write-off method This method recognizes a bad debt expense only when a specific account is determined to be uncollectible. The weaknesses of the direct write-off method are:

1. Bad debt expense is not "matched" with the related sales.
2. Accounts receivable are always overstated, because no attempt is made to account for the unknown bad debts included therein.

Allowance method A percentage of each period's sales or ending accounts receivable is estimated to eventually prove uncollectible. Consequently, the amount determined is charged to bad debts of the period and the credit is made to a valuation account such as allowance for doubtful accounts. When specific accounts are written off, they are debited to the allowance account, which is periodically recomputed.

Bad debts may be estimated as a percentage of sales or of accounts receivable. For financial statement purposes, unearned interest and finance charges are deducted from the related receivable. This is necessary in order to state the receivable at its current realizable value.

Discounted notes receivable arise when the holder endorses the note (with or without recourse) to a third party and receives a sum of cash. The difference between the amount of cash received by the holder and the maturity value of the note is called the discount. If the note is discounted with recourse, the assignor remains contingently liable for the ultimate payment of the note when it becomes due. If the note is discounted without recourse, the assignor assumes no further liability.

The account called discounted notes receivable is a contra account which is deducted from the related receivables for financial statement purposes.

The following is the procedure for computing the proceeds of a discounted note:

1. Compute the total maturity value of the note, including interest due at maturity.
2. Compute the discount amount (the maturity value of the note multiplied by the discount rate for the time involved).
3. The difference between the two amounts (1 minus 2) equals the proceeds of the note.

A $1,000 90-day 10% note is discounted at a bank at 8% when 60 days are remaining to maturity.

Maturity—$1,000 × 102.5% (¼ of 10% plus face)	$1,025.00
Discount—$1,025 × 1.333% (⅙ of 8%)	13.66
Proceeds of note	$1,011.34

Factoring

Factoring is a process by which a company can convert its receivables into cash by assigning them to a factor either with or without recourse. "With recourse" means that the assignee can return the receivable to the company and get back the funds paid if the receivable turns out to be uncollectible. "Without recourse" means that the assignee assumes the risk of any losses on collections. Under factoring arrangements, the customer may or may not be notified.

Pledging

Pledging is the process whereby the company uses existing accounts receivable as collateral for a loan. The company retains title to the receivables but pledges that it will use the proceeds to pay the loan.

Cash Surrender Value of Life Insurance

The proceeds of a life insurance policy usually provide some degree of financial security to one or more beneficiaries named in the policy. Upon death of the insured, the insurance company pays the beneficiary the face amount of the policy, less any outstanding indebtedness.

From an economic standpoint, insurance is a method which is used to spread a specific risk among many individuals. The insurance company assumes the specific risk, such as death, and charges a premium based on actuarial calculations. In the case of death, mortality tables have been established which take into consideration the frequency of deaths among individuals of various age groups. The premiums collected by the insurance company are used to pay current benefits and costs, and the balance is invested to yield investment income. Theoretically, if an individual dies in the year that the mortality tables predict, the accumulated net premiums collected by the insurance company, plus the investment earned on the accumulated premiums, should be sufficient to pay the face amount of the policy and still leave a profit for the insurance company.

Insurable interest An owner of an insurance contract must have an insurable interest in the insured individual in order for the contract to be valid. An insurable interest in life insurance need only exist at the time the policy is issued, while an insurable interest in property insurance must exist at the time of a loss. An insurable interest is a test of financial relationship. A wife may insure the life of her husband, an employer the life of an employee, a creditor the life of his debtor, and a partner the life of a copartner.

A life insurance contract contains the name of the owner of the policy, the name of the insured individual, and the name of the beneficiary who receives the insurance proceeds upon the death of the insured individual. A life insurance contract may have more than one owner and more than one beneficiary. The rights of an owner of a life insurance contract include the right to change the beneficiary, the right to borrow on the policy, and the right to surrender the policy to the insurance company for its cash value. The beneficiary of a life insurance contract has the right to receive the proceeds of the policy upon the death of the individual insured by the contract. An irrevocable beneficiary is one that cannot be changed by the owner of the insurance policy. As a rule, a beneficiary does not have the right to borrow against the insurance policy, change the name of the beneficiary, or surrender the policy to the insurance company for its cash value.

Accounting for purchases of life insurance FASB Technical Bulletin 85-4 provides guidance on accounting for purchases of life insurance. An investment in a life insurance policy should be accounted for at the amount that can be realized by the owner of the policy as of the date of its statement of financial position. Generally, the amount that can be realized from a life insurance policy is the amount of its cash surrender value. The increase in the cash surrender value of an insurance policy for a particular period should be recorded by the owner of the policy as an asset on its statement of financial position. The insurance expense for the same period is the difference between the total amount of premium paid and the amount of increase in the cash surrender value of the policy (FASB:TB 85-4).

> **OBSERVATION:** *Compliance with the provisions of FASB:TB 85-4 is required by all entities that purchase life insurance in which the entity is either the owner or beneficiary of the insurance contract (see Footnote 1 to FASB:TB 85-4). Although they may be the same individual or entity, the owner and the beneficiary of an insurance contract have different contractual rights. As a rule, the beneficiary has only the right to receive the proceeds of the insurance policy upon the death of the insured individual named in the policy. Ownership rights to an insurance contract vest solely with the owner of the policy and include the right to borrow against the policy, the right to surrender the policy for its cash value, and the right to change the beneficiary. Thus, FASB:TB 85-4 is in error by requiring an individual or entity which is solely the beneficiary and not the owner of an insurance policy to report the cash surrender value of the policy as an asset on its statement of financial position. Only an entity that is either the owner or the owner/beneficiary of an insurance policy should comply with the provisions of FASB:TB 85-4.*

An enterprise is the owner and sole beneficiary of a $200,000 life insurance policy on its president. The annual premium is $16,000. The policy is starting its fourth year, and the schedule of cash values indicates that at the end of the fourth year the cash value increases $25 per thousand. The enterprise pays the $16,000 premium, and the journal entry to record the transaction is as follows:

Life insurance expense – officers	$11,000	
Cash surrender value – life insurance policy	5,000	
Cash		$16,000

The cash surrender value of a life insurance policy is classified either as a current or a noncurrent asset in the policy owner's statement of financial position, depending upon the intentions of the policy owner. If the policy owner intends to surrender the policy to the insuror for its cash value within its normal operating cycle, the cash surrender value should be classified as a current asset in the statement of financial position. If there is no intention of cashing in the policy's cash value within the normal operating cycle of the policy owner, the cash surrender value should be classified as a noncurrent asset in the statement of financial position.

Computing Life Insurance Expense

The insurance expense is always the difference between the premium paid (cash) and the increase in the cash surrender value of the policy.

Disclosure

Current assets and current liabilities should be clearly identified in the financial statements, and the basis of determining the amounts stated should be fully disclosed. The following are the more common disclosures that should be made for current assets and current liabilities in the financial statements or in footnotes thereto:

1. Method of valuing current marketable securities (FASB-12)
2. Classification of inventories and the method used (FIFO, LIFO, average cost, etc.)
3. Restrictions on current assets
4. Current portions of long-term obligations
5. Description of accounting policies relating to current assets and current liabilities

Accounts receivable and notes receivable from officers, employees, or affiliated companies, if material, must be reported separately in the financial statements (ARB-43, Chapter 1A).

Current Obligations Expected to Be Refinanced

FASB-6 and FASB Interpretation-8 establish the promulgated GAAP for reclassifying a short-term obligation (current liability) that is expected to be refinanced into a long-term liability, or stockholders' equity. In other words, if a company intends to refinance a short-term obligation into a classification other than current liability, prior to the issuance of the financial statements, it may be allowed to do so at the balance sheet date, even though the refinancing has not occurred. The actual intent to refinance, supported by an agreement which meets certain requirements (discussed below) are prerequisites for the reclassification.

The promulgated GAAP (FASB-6) applies only to those companies that issue classified balance sheets. A classified balance sheet reflects current assets and current liabilities separately for easy determination of working capital and to make the financial presentation more meaningful. Because of the specialized nature of some industries (stock brokers, real estate agents, stock life insurance companies, etc.) unclassified balance sheets are presented and therefore are not affected by the promulgated GAAP.

A short-term obligation should be excluded from current liabilities if the company intends to refinance it on a long-term basis and the intent is supported by either of the following conditions:

1. The actual issuance, after the date of the balance sheet but prior to the issuance of the financial statements, of a long-term obligation or equity security whose proceeds are used to retire the short-term obligation—in essence, the conversion of short-term obligation into a long-term obligation or equity.

    The amount of short-term obligations which can be reclassified cannot exceed the actual proceeds received from the issuance of the new long-term obligation.

    If equity securities are issued, the short-term obligation is excluded from current liabilities but is not included in stockholders' equity.

    OBSERVATION: *The promulgated GAAP (FASB-6) is silent on what classification to use to report the newly issued equity securities on the financial statements.*

2. Prior to the issuance of the financial statements the company has entered into an agreement that enables it to refinance a short-term obligation on a long-term basis. The terms of the agreement must be clear and unambiguous and must contain the following provisions:

    a. The agreement may not be cancelled by the lender or investor (company can cancel), and it must extend beyond the normal operating cycle of the company (if the company has no operating cycle or the operating cycle occurs more than once a year, then the one-year rule is used).

    b. At the balance sheet date and at its issuance, the company was not in violation, nor was there any information that indicated a violation, of the agreement.

    c. The lender or investor is expected to be financially capable of honoring the agreement.

The amount of short-term obligation which can be excluded from the current liabilities cannot exceed the amount of available refinancing covered by the established agreement. The amount must be adjusted for any limitations in the agreement which indicate the full amount obtainable will not be available to retire the short-term obligations. In addition, if the agreement indicates that the amount available for refinancing will fluctuate, then the most conservative estimate must be used. If no reasonable estimate can be made, then the agreement does not fulfill the necessary requirements and the full amount of current liabilities must be presented.

An enterprise may seek alternative financing sources besides those in the established agreements. However, if alternative sources do not materialize, the company must intend to borrow from the source in the agreement.

> **OBSERVATION:** *If the terms of the agreement allow the prospective lender or investor to set interest rates, collateral requirements, or similar conditions that are unreasonable to the company, the intent to refinance may not exist.*

Any "roll over" agreements or "revolving credit agreements" must meet the above provisions to enable a company to classify the related short-term obligations.

> **OBSERVATION:** *Long-term obligations that contain subjective acceleration clauses are not covered by FASB-6. A subjective acceleration clause is one in which the lender can unilaterally accelerate a long-term loan. For example, the loan agreement might state that "if, in the opinion of the lender, the borrower experiences recurring losses or liquidity problems, the lender may accelerate part or all of the loan balance . . . ."*
>
> *FASB Technical Bulletin 79-3 was issued to provide guidance in accounting for long-term obligations that contain subjective acceleration clauses. If it is probable that the subjective acceleration clause will be exercised, the amount of the long-term obligation which is likely to be accelerated should be classified as a current liability. On the other hand, if it is reasonably possible that the subjective acceleration clause will be exercised, footnote disclosure may be all that is necessary. Finally, if the possibility of subjective acceleration is remote, no disclosure may be necessary. Professional judgment is necessary to determine what type of disclosure is required for long-term obligations containing subjective acceleration clauses.*

The financial statements must contain a footnote disclosing the amount excluded from current liabilities and a full description of the financial agreement and new obligations incurred or expected to be incurred or the equity securities issued or expected to be issued.

Classification of Callable Obligations

FASB-78 establishes the promulgated GAAP for the current/noncurrent classification in the debtor's balance sheet of obligations that are payable on demand or callable by the creditor. FASB-78 does not address the creditor's balance sheet classification of demand or callable obligations. FASB-78 is applicable to obligations reported in classified balance sheets and to footnote disclosures of maturities of obligations reported in both classified and unclassified balance sheets. FASB-78 does not alter treatment of *subjective acceleration clauses* in long-term debt arrangements which is presently covered by FASB Technical Bulletin 79-3.

Background Several existing GAAP cover the balance sheet classifications of assets and liabilities into current and noncurrent categories. FASB-6 and FASB Interpretation-8 are concerned with an enterprise's intentions to refinance a current liability into a long-term liability or stockholders' equity. FASB-6 and FASB Interpretation-8 are discussed elsewhere in this chapter.

Chapter 3A of ARB-43 provides that current assets are those that are *reasonably expected* to be realized in cash, sold, or consumed (prepaid items) during the normal operating cycle of an enterprise. Current liabilities are obligations whose liquidation is *reasonably expected* to require the use of current assets, or the creation of other current liabilities during the normal operating cycle of an enterprise. The concept of an enterprise's normal operating cycle is discussed elsewhere in this chapter.

Under the provisions of Chapter 3A of ARB-43, the classification of current assets and current liabilities depends on an enterprise's normal operating cycle, which may be one year or a period longer than one year. Those assets that are reasonably expected to be realized in cash, sold, or consumed during the normal operating cycle of an enterprise are classified as current. Those liabilities whose liquidation is reasonably expected to require the use of current assets, or the creation of other current liabilities, during the normal operating cycle of an enterprise are classified as current. Under Chapter 3A of ARB-43, professional judgment must be used to analyze the substance of the transaction underlying each asset and liability to determine those that shall be classified as current and those that shall be classified as noncurrent.

Long-term obligations that contain subjective acceleration clauses are not covered by FASB-6, FASB Interpretation-8, or Chapter 3A of ARB-43. A subjective acceleration clause is one that permits the lender to unilaterally accelerate part or all of a long-term obligation.

For example, the debt agreement might state that "if, in the opinion of the lender, the borrower experiences recurring losses or liquidity problems, the lender may at its sole discretion accelerate part of all of the loan balance . . ."

FASB Technical Bulletin 79-3 was issued to provide guidance in accounting for long-term obligations that contain subjective acceleration clauses. If it is *probable* that the subjective acceleration clause will be exercised by the creditor, the amount of the long-term obligation which is likely to be accelerated shall be classified as a current liability by the debtor. On the other hand, if it is *reasonably possible* that the subjective acceleration clause will be exercised by the creditor, footnote disclosure may be all that is required. Finally, if the possibility of subjective acceleration is *remote*, no disclosure may be required. Professional judgment is necessary to determine what type of disclosure, if any, is necessary for long-term obligations which contain subjective acceleration clauses.

> **OBSERVATION:** *The probable, reasonably possible, and remote criteria used in FASB Technical Bulletin 79-3 were originally used in FASB-5 (Contingencies). Under FASB-5, probable means that the event is likely to occur and remote means that the event has little chance of occurring. Reasonably possible represents a likelihood that is halfway between probable and remote.*

An *objective acceleration clause* in a long-term debt agreement is one that contains objective criteria that must be used by the creditor as the basis for calling part or all of the loan, such as a specified minimum amount of working capital or net worth requirement. In a long-term debt agreement, it is not unusual to find both objective and subjective acceleration clauses.

In the event of a violation of an objective acceleration clause, most long-term obligations become immediately callable by the creditor, or become callable after a grace period that is specified in the loan agreement. When this occurs, the creditor can demand payment of part or all of the loan balance, in accordance with the terms of the debt agreement.

Classifying callable obligations   The provisions of FASB-78 must be applied by a debtor to all obligations reported in classified balance sheets and to all disclosures concerning maturities of obligations in both classified and unclassified balance sheets. Once the maturity date of an obligation is determined in accordance with the provisions of FASB-78, the debtor shall apply its normal operating cycle to determine whether the obligation shall be classified as current or noncurrent.

FASB-78 is applied to a classified balance sheet to determine whether the obligation should be classified as current or noncurrent for balance sheet purposes. FASB-78 is applied to both classified and unclassified balance sheets to determine the maturity dates of obligations disclosed by footnotes. For example, an unclassified balance sheet may contain footnote disclosures of the maturity dates of obligations, in spite of the fact that the obligations are not classified in the unclassified balance sheet, or may not be separately identified from other obligations in the unclassified balance sheet.

A creditor may have waived the right to demand payment on a specific obligation for a period that extends beyond the debtor's normal operating cycle. In this event, the debtor shall classify the obligation as a noncurrent liability.

> **OBSERVATION:** *FASB-78 does not indicate the form in which the creditor's waiver must appear, or the manner in which an independent auditor should verify the existence of such a waiver. Sound professional judgment will generally require a written waiver by the creditor, supported by appropriate language in the management representation letter. In addition, a written opinion from the client's legal counsel is highly desirable as a means of verifying the existence of any waiver, and is essential if the client wishes to rely on an oral waiver by the creditor.*

At the date of the debtor's balance sheet, an obligation may, by its terms, be payable on demand. In this event, FASB-78 requires that the obligation be classified as a current liability, unless the creditor has waived the right to demand payment for a period that extends beyond the debtor's normal operating cycle. A violation of an objective acceleration clause in a long-term debt agreement may exist at the date of the debtor's balance sheet. FASB-78 requires that such an obligation be classified as a current liability at the debtor's balance sheet date unless:

1. The creditor has waived the right to demand payment for a period that extends beyond the debtor's normal operating cycle, or
2. The debtor has cured the violation after the balance sheet date, but prior to the issuance date of the financial statements, and the obligation is not callable for a period that extends beyond the debtor's normal operating cycle.

> **OBSERVATION:** *FASB-78 appears to offer a debtor an opportunity to delay the issuance of its financial statements long enough to coincide with the date that a violation is cured and thus avoid classifying the obligation as a current liability.*

A long-term debt agreement may provide for a grace period which commences after the occurrence of a violation of an objective acceleration clause. FASB-78 requires that such an obligation be classified as a current liability at the debtor's balance sheet date, unless:

1. The creditor has waived the right to demand payment for a period that extends beyond the debtor's normal operating cycle, or
2. The debtor has cured the violation after the balance sheet date, but prior to the issuance date of its financial statements, and the obligation is not callable by the creditor for a period that extends beyond the debtor's normal operating cycle, or
3. The unexpired grace period extends beyond the debtor's normal operating cycle.

> **OBSERVATION:** Under ARB-43, Chapter 3A, the classification of a long-term obligation that was or became payable on demand depended on whether the debtor reasonably expected the creditor to require payment within the debtor's normal operating cycle. Thus, under ARB-43, Chapter 3A, the pervasive accounting principle of substance over form governed the classification of the long-term obligation. In applying the provisions of ARB-43, Chapter 3A, professional judgment was required to determine the substance of the transaction.
>
> FASB-78, which amends ARB-43, Chapter 3A, requires that an obligation be classified as current or noncurrent, based solely on whether the legal terms of the loan agreement require payment within the debtor's normal operating cycle. Thus, applying FASB-78 should be easy, because no professional judgment is required, and the substance of the transaction can be ignored.

FASB-78 is effective for balance sheet classification of obligations for fiscal and interim periods that begin on or after December 16, 1983. Earlier application of FASB-78 in previously unissued financial statements is encouraged. Retroactive restatement of previously issued financial statements to conform with the provisions of FASB-78 is permitted, but not required.

Compensated Absences

FASB-43 (Accounting for Compensated Absences) is the promulgated GAAP which covers employees' compensated absences and is concerned only with the proper accrual of the liability for compensated absences rather than the allocation of such costs to interim accounting periods. FASB-43 does not apply to the following:

1. Severance or termination pay
2. Stock or stock options issued to employees
3. Deferred compensation
4. Post-retirement benefits
5. Group insurance, disability pay, and other long-term fringe benefits
6. Certain sick pay benefits that accumulate

FASB-43 specifically requires that regulated companies comply with the provisions of FASB-43, in accordance with the Addendum to APB-2.

> **OBSERVATION:** *FASB-43 was adopted by a five to two vote of the Financial Accounting Standards Board.*

Compensated absences arise from employees' absences from employment because of illness, holiday, vacation, or other reasons. When an employer expects to pay an employee for such compensated absences, a liability for the estimated probable future payments must be accrued if all the following conditions are met:

1. The employee's right to receive compensation for the future absences is attributable to services already performed by the employee.
2. The employee's right to receive the compensation for the future absences are vested, or accumulate.
3. It is probable that the compensation will be paid.
4. The amount of compensation is reasonably estimable.

The fact that an employer meets the first three conditions and not the fourth condition must be disclosed in the financial statements.

Vested rights are those which have been earned by the employee for services already performed. Thus, vested rights are not contingent on any future services by the employee and are an obligation of the employer even if the employee quits or is fired. Rights that accumulate are nonvesting rights to compensated absences that are earned and can be carried forward to succeeding years. Rights that accumulate increase an employee's benefits in one or more years subsequent to the year in which they are earned. For the purposes of FASB-43, it makes no difference whether a limit is imposed on the amount of accumulated rights that can be carried forward to future years. For example, if accumulated vacation days can be partially or fully carried forward for use in succeeding years, the employer should accrue a liability equal to the probable number of vacation days the employee will likely use. However, an employer does not have to accrue a liability for nonvesting rights to compensated absences that expire at the end of the year in which they are earned, because they do not accumulate.

Nonvesting sick pay benefits that accumulate and can be carried forward to succeeding years are given special treatment by FASB-43. An employer generally does not have to accrue a liability for such sick pay benefits, as he does for other nonvesting rights that accumulate. This is an exception to the general rule in FASB-43. If payment of nonvesting accumulating sick pay benefits depend on the future illness of the employee, an employer does not have to accrue a liability for such payments. The reasons cited in FASB-43 for this exception are (1) the cost/benefit rule, (2) the materiality rule, and (3) the reliability of estimating the days an employee will be sick in succeeding years. This exception does not apply in circumstances where the employer pays the sick pay benefits even though the employee is not actually sick. Thus, where an employer pays nonvesting accumulated sick pay benefits to employees even though their absences from work are not caused by illness, or if sick pay benefits are allowed to be taken as "terminal leave," the employer should accrue a liability for such payments. Under these circumstances, such payments cannot be considered to be sick pay benefits for the purposes of FASB-43. An employer's general policy for the payment of nonvesting accumulating sick pay benefits should govern the accounting for such payments.

FASB-43 is effective for fiscal years ended on or after December 16, 1981, and earlier application is encouraged.

FASB-43 requires that accounting changes resulting from the adoption of its provisions shall be made retroactively, that financial statements of the year of change shall disclose the nature of any restatement, and that its effect on sales, income before extraordinary items, net income, and related per share amounts for each year shall be restated.

> **OBSERVATION:** *The recognition of a change in an accounting principle, such as FASB-43, through the retroactive restatement of the financial statements violates existing GAAP, because the effects of the change are charged directly to retained earnings and thus bypass the income statement. A change in an accounting principle, such as FASB-43, should be accounted for by including the cumulative effects of the change in net income of the year of change (APB-20). The effects of a retroactive restatement are charged directly*

to retained earnings, as is prior-period adjustment. FASB-16 clearly limits prior-period adjustments to (1) a correction of an error in a prior-period statement or (2) an adjustment for the realization of certain preacquisition tax benefits. Finally, APB-9 requires that net income include all items of income and expense, except (1) prior-period adjustments, (2) dividends, and (3) capital transactions.

If retroactive restatement of the financial statements is not practicable, FASB-43 permits the use of APB-20 in accounting for the effects of the change in accounting principle resulting from the adoption of FASB-43.

CURRENT VALUE ACCOUNTING

Background

There is no promulgated GAAP on current value accounting, and its general use for basic financial statements is prohibited under existing GAAP. However, like general price-level information, current value data may be utilized to supplement the historical cost financial statements required by GAAP.

> **OBSERVATION:** FASB-33 requires the application of some Current Value and General Price-Level Accounting techniques (see Financial Reporting and Changing Prices).

Overview

Current value accounting deals with the measurement of profits, and the valuation of a business entity, during periods of inflation.

In current value accounting, historical costs are replaced by current values that attempt to measure what a company would receive if it disposed of its assets. Thus, current value accounting violates the going-concern concept of GAAP in that it is based on liquidation values.

Current Value Methods

The major problem in current value accounting is the measurement of current values. The two most commonly used methods are the entry value system and the exit value system.

The entry value system is based on cost of replacement or reproduction. Replacement cost is the estimated cost of acquiring new and equivalent property at current prices after adjusting for depreciation, and may be approximated through the use of a specific price index. Reproduction cost is the estimated cost of producing new and equivalent property at current prices after adjusting for depreciation.

The exit value system is usually based on net realizable value in the ordinary course of business or sometimes on discounted future cash flow. Net realizable value is the estimated selling price of the asset less any costs to complete or dispose. Discounted future cash flow is the present value of estimated cash inflows, or cost savings, discounted at an appropriate rate of interest.

Monetary and Nonmonetary Items

To apply current value accounting methods, it is necessary to separate assets and liabilities into monetary and nonmonetary, in the same manner as in general price-level information.

Monetary assets or liabilities are fixed in terms of currency and are usually contractual claims. Since these amounts are fixed, there is usually no need to restate monetary assets and liabilities. Examples of monetary assets and liabilities are cash, accounts and notes receivable, and accounts and notes payable.

Nonmonetary assets or liabilities are those other than monetary assets or liabilities. Nonmonetary assets are generally restated for changes in current value. Examples of nonmonetary assets and liabilities are inventory, investments in common stock, property, plant and equipment, liability for advance rent collected, and common stock.

Because monetary assets are stated in fixed amounts of currency, they represent the amount of cash that is expected to be realized by them in the near future. Therefore, monetary assets are effectively stated at their net realizable value and do not usually have to be restated for current value financial statements.

Nonmonetary assets are not stated in fixed amounts of currency and thus do not reflect their net realizable value. Therefore, nonmonetary assets must be restated to their present current worth for current value financial statements.

Holding Gains

Regardless of the current value method used, holding gains will arise.

A holding gain is the difference between the current value of an asset and its historical cost. Realized holding gains result from the disposal of an asset, either by sale or use, during an accounting period. Unrealized holding gains result from increases in current values of assets during an accounting period in which such assets are retained by the entity.

Controversy exists as to whether holding gains should be reported in the current value income statement or in a separate statement of changes in holding gains.

Current Value Income

Under the current value concept, current operating income is the result of deducting from actual revenues the cost of goods sold and other expenses based on current values. Realized income is determined by adding realized holding gains to net operating income (current operating income less income taxes). Current value income is obtained by adding unrealized holding gains to realized income. The following illustration shows the steps required to determine current value income.

>Revenues (actual)
>Less: Current value of cost of goods sold and other expenses
>Current operating income
>Less: Income taxes
>Net operating income
>Plus: Realized holding gains
>Realized income
>Plus: Unrealized holding gains
>Current value income

The following example illustrates the computation of current value income.

Fair Value, Inc., paid $1,200,000 in December 1976 for certain of its inventory. In December 1977, one half of the inventory was sold for $1,000,000, when the replacement cost of the original inventory was $1,400,000. *Ignoring income taxes*, what amount should be shown as the total gain resulting from the above facts in a current fair value accounting income statement for 1977?

The computation of current value income is as follows:

Proceeds of sale	$1,000,000
Less: Current value of inventory sold (½ of $1,400,000)	700,000
Current operating income	$ 300,000
Plus: Realized holding gain—Inventory ($700,000 current value − $600,000 historical cost)	100,000
Realized income	$ 400,000
Plus: Unrealized holding gain—Inventory	100,000
Current value income	$ 500,000

Current Value Accounting

Comprehensive Illustration

This comprehensive illustration compares traditional historical cost accounting to the current value method of accounting.

Balance Sheet

Assets	Historical cost	Current value
Current assets:		
Cash	$ 1,700	$ 1,700
Accounts receivable	5,500	5,500
Investments	200	200
Inventory	2,500	3,000
Fixed assets:		
Plant	4,000	5,000
Accumulated depreciation	(400)	(500)
Total assets	$13,500	$14,900
Liabilities		
Current liabilities	$ 5,000	$ 5,000
Stockholders' equity:		
Common stock	4,000	4,000
Retained earnings	4,500	2,900
Revaluation reserve		3,000
Total liabilities and stockholders' equity	$13,500	$14,900

Comments:

Under the current value accounting method the monetary assets and liabilities are not restated, because they represent amounts fixed in terms of currency. However, the nonmonetary assets and liabilities (inventory, plant, and stockholders' equity) are restated to their net realizable values.

Statement of Income

	Historical cost		Current value	
Sales		$13,000		$13,000
Cost of goods sold		4,000		5,500
Gross margin		$ 9,000		$ 7,500
Less Expenses:				
Depreciation	$200		$ 250	
Others	600	800	600	850
Income before taxes		$ 8,200		
Current operating income				$ 6,650
Less: Provision for taxes		4,100		4,100
Net income		$ 4,100		
Net operating income				$ 2,550
Realized holding gains applicable to:				
Sale of inventory			$1,500	
Depreciation of plant			50	1,550
Realized income				$ 4,100
Unrealized holding gains applicable to:				
Replacement at cost of inventory at year end			$ 500	
Undepreciated value of plant			950	1,450
Current value income				$ 5,550

Comments:

Under the traditional historical cost method, net income is $4,100, whereas current value income is $5,550. Both methods use actual sales, but the current value method uses current values (replacement cost) in computing cost of goods sold and other expenses. In periods of inflation, gross margins will usually be less than under historical cost accounting, because current values are used.

Net income under historical cost accounting is always equal to realized income under current value accounting. In other words, historical cost accounting net income always includes realized holding gains. Holding gains are always separately identified in current value income statements. The only difference in dollar amounts between the two methods is unrealized holding gains. A current value income statement will reflect all unrealized holding gains,

Current Value Accounting

whereas these unrealized gains are never included in an historical cost income statement.

The provision for income taxes is the same for both historical cost and current value income statements. Depreciation expense is computed on the current value of an asset for current value accounting, whereas historical cost is used for historical cost purposes.

Statement of Changes in Revaluation Reserve
(Holding Gains)

Revaluation reserve (holding gains), beginning of the year:		—
Realized holding gains applicable to:		
Inventory sold	$1,500	
Depreciation on plant (5% of $1,000)	50	$1,550
Unrealized holding gains applicable to:		
Inventory at year end	$ 500	
Undepreciated value of plant	950	1,450
Total revaluation reserve (holding gains)		$3,000

Comments:
The revaluation reserve (which is shown on the balance sheet as $3,000) is a stockholders' equity account which reflects the difference between historical cost and current worth.

Statement of Retained Earnings

	Historical cost	Current value
Beginning balance	$ 400	$ 400
Add: Net income	4,100	
Current value income		5,550
Total	$4,500	$5,950
Less: Backlog depreciation		50
Revaluation reserve		3,000
Ending retained earnings	$4,500	$2,900

Comments:
Backlog depreciation (sometimes referred to as the "amortization gap") is the difference between accumulated depreciation under historical cost and accumulated depreciation based on current value.

DEFERRED COMPENSATION CONTRACTS

Background

The main source of promulgated GAAP for Deferred Compensation Contracts is APB-12, paragraphs 6–8. FASB-81 establishes the promulgated GAAP for the financial statement disclosure of postretirement health care and life insurance benefits that are provided by individual employers to their *retired* employees. Postretirement health care and life insurance benefits are generally considered a form of deferred compensation.

FASB-81 has been issued as an interim measure pending completion of a major project on employers' accounting for pensions and other postemployment benefits. The measurement and recognition of an employer's obligation for postretirement health care and life insurance benefits are not addressed by FASB-81. Death benefits, benefits provided by multiemployer-sponsored plans, and government-required employer contributions to a national health plan are also not addressed by FASB-81.

If individual deferred compensation contracts, as a group, are tantamount to a pension plan, they should be accounted for as a pension plan in accordance with existing GAAP.

Overview

Deferred compensation contracts should be accounted for on an individual basis for each employee. If a deferred compensation contract is based on current and future employment, only the amounts attributable to the current portion of employment should be accrued.

If a deferred compensation contract contains benefits payable for the life of a beneficiary, the total liability should be based on the beneficiary's life expectancy or on the estimated cost of an annuity contract that would provide sufficient funds to pay the required benefits.

The total liability for deferred compensation contracts is determined by the terms of each individual contract. The amount of the periodic accrual, computed from the first day of the employment contract, must total no less than the then present value of the benefits provided for in the contract. The periodic accruals should be made systematically over the active term of employment.

Deferred Compensation Contracts

A deferred compensation contract provides for the payment of $50,000 per year for five years, beginning one year after the end of the employee's 10-year contract. A 10% interest rate will be assumed.

We must find the present value for the five $50,000 payments at the end of 10 years, as follows:

Present value of $50,000 in five years	$ 31,045
Present value of $50,000 in four years	34,150
Present value of $50,000 in three years	37,565
Present value of $50,000 in two years	41,320
Present value of $50,000 in one year	45,455
Total present value of benefits at end of employment	$189,535

We now know that $189,535 must be accumulated over 10 years to have available the funds required to pay the benefits in accordance with the contract. We must find the amount of the annual accrual that earning 10% interest will total $189,535 at the end of 10 years. This may be found by using the formula for the value of an annuity due, as follows:

$$A = R\left[\Sigma\,(1+i)^n\right]$$
$$\$189,535 = \$10,811$$

The annual accrual is $10,811.

Postretirement Benefits

Postemployment benefits are those received by employees after termination of employment but before retirement, such as disability or termination benefits. In contrast to postemployment benefits, postretirement benefits include only those benefits that an employee receives after retirement. Health care benefits include all health-related benefits such as dental, hearing, and vision benefits.

Certain information concerning postretirement health care and life insurance benefits that are provided by an individual employer to its employees, their dependents, or survivors must be disclosed in the employer's financial statements. The following are the minimum financial statement disclosures required by FASB-81:

1. *Description of employee groups covered and benefits provided*
   An employer must disclose the types of postretirement health care and life insurance benefits that it provides for its employees, and disclose the groups of employees that are covered by these benefits. The financial statement disclosures that are required by FASB-81 may be presented for the total of all postretirement health care and life insurance benefits provided by the employer or for each type of benefit separately.

   Under FASB-81, health care benefits include dental, hearing, vision, and all other health-related benefits.

2. *Description of the accounting and funding policies used for the benefits*
   An employer must disclose the accounting and funding policies that are used to account for, and fund, its postretirement health care and life insurance benefits. The cost of postretirement health care and life insurance benefits that is included in net income of the period, under disclosure requirement 3, below, shall be based on these same accounting and funding policies.

3. *Cost of the benefits included in net income for the period*
   An employer must disclose the cost of postretirement health care and life insurance benefits that is included in its net income for the period. If the cost cannot be exactly determined, an employer is encouraged to use reasonable methods to approximate the cost of postretirement health care and life insurance benefits that is included in net income for the period. If the cost of postretirement health care and life insurance benefits that is included in net income of the period cannot be reasonably approximated or separated from other costs, the total cost of providing these benefits to both retired and active employees, and the number of retired and active employees, shall be disclosed by the employer. For purposes of this disclosure requirement, an employee and members of his or her family are counted as one employee.

   The cost of postretirement health care and life insurance benefits that is included in net income of the period shall be based on the same accounting and funding policies that are described for these benefits (see disclosure requirement 2, above).

4. *Effect of significant items that affect comparability of benefit costs for all periods presented*
   The cost of postretirement health care and life insurance benefits must be comparable for all periods presented. If an item affects the comparability of postretirement health care and life

insurance benefit costs in any of the periods presented, the effect of that item must be disclosed, if significant.

Additional disclosures encouraged FASB-81 encourages, but does not require, disclosure of other information such as the present value of estimated future health care and life insurance benefits for retirees, the amount of contributions to trusts established to pay retiree health care benefits, and the fair value of assets in trusts established to pay retiree health care benefits. In addition, paragraph 28 of FASB-81 suggests the following additional disclosures:

a. The average age and number of active employees potentially eligible for postretirement health care and life insurance benefits
b. The number of retirees covered by the employer's plan
c. Information concerning the significance of the potential future postretirement health care and life insurance benefits for both active and retired employees.
d. The average benefits per retiree for the most recent year for which that information is available. (According to FASB-81, the average benefits per retiree might be determined by dividing the total benefit payments for the year by the number of covered retirees.)

Effective date and transition The provisions of FASB-81 are effective for financial statements issued for periods ending after December 15, 1984. If the information concerning postretirement health care and life insurance benefits for an employer's foreign plans is unavailable, it need not be included in financial statements issued for periods ending on or before June 14, 1985. After June 14, 1985, disclosure of postretirement health care and life insurance benefits provided by an employer in both the United States and foreign countries is required in all financial statements presented for periods ending after December 15, 1984. Earlier disclosure is encouraged, but not required.

DEPRECIABLE ASSETS AND DEPRECIATION

Background

This chapter brings together the promulgated GAAP relating to depreciable assets and depreciation, in addition to nonpromulgated GAAP of importance.

The following is the promulgated GAAP discussed in this chapter:

> ARB-43 Chapter 9A—Depreciation and High Costs
> ARB-43 Chapter 9C—Emergency Facilities
> ARB-44 (Revised)—Declining-Balance Depreciation
> APB-1—New Depreciation Guidelines and Rules
> APB-6, paragraph 17—Depreciation on Appreciation
> APB-6, paragraph 20—Declining-Balance Depreciation
> APB-12, paragraphs 4 and 5—Disclosure of Depreciable Assets and Depreciation

Overview

The basic principle of matching revenue and expenses is applied to long-lived assets that are not held for sale in the ordinary course of business. The systematic and rational allocation used to achieve "matching" is usually accomplished by depreciation, amortization, or depletion, according to the type of long-lived asset involved.

Asset Cost

The basis of accounting for depreciable fixed assets is cost, and all normal expenditures of readying an asset for use should be capitalized. However, unnecessary expenditures that do not add to the utility of the asset should be charged to expense. An expenditure for repairing a piece of equipment that was damaged during shipment should be charged to expense.

Razing and removal costs (less salvage value) of structures located on land purchased as a building site are added to the cost of the land. Land itself is never depreciated.

> **OBSERVATION:** *Promulgated GAAP (ARB-43) requires that assets be recorded at cost, except in the case of quasi-reorganizations (corporate readjustments) in which it is permissible to write up or write down assets to market values (APB-6).*
>
> *When price-level accounting methods are used as supplemental statements, the distortion of assets and related depreciation resulting from inflation is somewhat ameliorated.*

Salvage Value

Salvage or residual value is an estimate of the amount that will be realized at the end of the useful life of a depreciable asset. Frequently, depreciable assets have little or no scrap value at the end of their estimated useful life and, if immaterial, the amount(s) may be ignored.

Estimated Useful Life

The estimated useful life of a depreciable asset may differ from company to company or industry to industry. A company's maintenance policy will affect the longevity of a depreciable asset.

> **OBSERVATION:** *Total utility of an asset, expressed in time, is called the* physical life. *The utility of an asset to a specific owner, expressed in time, is called the* service life.

Valuation of Assets

Under specific circumstances, assets may be valued in the following ways:

Historical costs   The actual amount paid at the date of acquisition, including all normal expenditures of readying an asset for use.

Replacement cost   The amount that it would cost to replace an asset. Frequently, replacement cost is the same as fair value.

Fair market value   The price at which a willing seller would sell to a willing buyer, neither under any compulsion to buy or to sell.

Present value   The value today of something due in the future.

General price-level restatement   The value of an asset restated in terms of current purchasing power.

Self-Constructed Fixed Assets

When a business constructs a long-lived asset for its own use, the following procedure should be observed:

1. All *direct costs* should be included in the total cost of the asset, which should be capitalized.
2. *Fixed overhead costs* should not be included unless they are increased by the construction of the asset.
3. *Interest costs* may or may not be capitalized as part of the construction cost of the fixed assets.

> **OBSERVATION:** Interest costs that are material must be capitalized on certain qualifying assets under the provisions of FASB-34. (See chapter entitled "Interest Costs Capitalized").

Write-Up of Assets to Appraisal Values

GAAP prohibit the write-up of fixed assets to market or appraisal values. However, although prohibiting such a procedure, GAAP state that if fixed assets are written up to market or appraisal values, depreciation should be based on the written-up amounts (ARB-43).

Improvement of Depreciable Assets

Expenditures that increase the capacity or operating efficiency of an asset, if they are substantial, should be capitalized. Minor expenditures are usually treated as period costs even though they may have the characteristics of capital expenditures. When the cost of improvements is substantial or when there is a change in the estimated useful life of an asset, depreciation charges for future periods should be revised on the basis of the new book value and the new estimated remaining useful life.

The revision of the estimated useful life of an asset is measured prospectively and accounted for in the current and future periods. No adjustment is made to prior depreciation.

A machine that originally cost $100,000 was being depreciated (no salvage value) over ten years, using the straight-line method. At the beginning of the fifth year $20,000 was expended, which considerably improved the operating efficiency of the machine and extended its useful life four years.

Original cost	$100,000
Less: Four years' depreciation	40,000
Balance (adjusted)	$ 60,000
New expenditure	20,000
New depreciable base	$ 80,000
Useful life (6 + 4) in years	10
Amount of annual depreciation	$ 8,000

Kinds of Depreciation

Physical depreciation is related to a depreciable asset's wear and deterioration over a period.

Functional depreciation arises from obsolescence or inadequacy of the asset to perform efficiently. Obsolescence may arise when there is no further demand for the product that the depreciable asset produces or from the availability of a new depreciable asset that can perform the same function for substantially less cost.

Depreciation Methods

The goal of a depreciation method should be to provide for a reasonable, consistent matching of revenue and expense, by systematically allocating the cost of the depreciable asset over its estimated useful life.

The actual accumulation of depreciation in the books is accomplished by using a *contra* account, called accumulated depreciation or allowance for depreciation.

The amount subject to depreciation is the difference between cost and residual or salvage value and is called the *depreciable base*.

Straight line *Straight-line depreciation* is determined by the formula:

$$\frac{\text{Cost less salvage value}}{\text{Estimated useful life}} = \text{annual depreciation}$$

Estimated useful life is usually stated in time periods, such as years or months.

Units of production The *units-of-production method* relates depreciation to the estimated production capability of an asset and is expressed in a rate per unit or hour.

The formula is:

$$\frac{\text{Cost less salvage value}}{\text{Estimated units or hours}} = \text{rate per unit}$$

A machine is purchased at a cost of $85,000 and has a salvage value of $10,000. It is estimated that the machine has a useful life of 750,000 hours.

$$\frac{\$85,000 - \$10,000}{750,000} = \$.10 \text{ per hour depreciation}$$

The units-of-production method is used in situations where the usage of the depreciable asset varies considerably from period to period, and in those circumstances in which the service life is more a function of use than passage of time.

Sum of the years' digits The *sum-of-the-years'-digits method* is one of the accelerated methods of depreciation that provides higher depreciation expense in the early years and lower charges in later years.

To find the sum of the years' digits, the digit of each year is progressively numbered and then added up. The sum of the years' digits for a five-year life would be:

$$5 + 4 + 3 + 2 + 1 = 15$$

For four years:

$$4 + 3 + 2 + 1 = 10$$

For three years:

$$3 + 2 + 1 = 6$$

Depreciable Assets and Depreciation

When dealing with an asset with a long life, it is necessary to use the general formula for finding the sum of the years' digits:

$$S = N\left(\frac{N + 1}{2}\right)$$

To find the sum of the years' digits for an asset with a 50-year life:

$$S = 50\left(\frac{50 + 1}{2}\right)$$
$$S = 50(25\frac{1}{2})$$
$$S = 1{,}275 \text{ sum of the years' digits for 50 years}$$

The sum of the years' digits becomes the denominator, and the digit of the highest year becomes the first numerator. For example, the first year's depreciation for a five-year life would be 5/15 of the depreciable base of the asset.

Assume that an asset cost $11,000, has a salvage value of $1,000, and has an estimated useful life of four years.

The first step is to determine the depreciable base:

Cost of asset	$11,000
Less: Salvage value	1,000
Depreciable base	$10,000

The sum of the years' digits for four years is:

$$4 + 3 + 2 + 1 = 10$$

The first year's depreciation is 4/10, the second year's 3/10, the third year's 2/10, and the fourth year's 1/10, as follows:

4/10 of $10,000	=	$ 4,000
3/10 of $10,000	=	3,000
2/10 of $10,000	=	2,000
1/10 of $10,000	=	1,000
Total depreciation		$10,000

When an asset is placed in service during the year, the depreciation expense is taken only for the portion of the year that the asset is used. For example, if an asset (of a company on a calendar-year basis) is placed in service on July 1, only six months' depreciation is taken. In our preceding illustration the six months' depreciation expense would be ½ of 4/10, or $2,000. If this occurs, then the second year's depreciation expense is calculated as follows:

½ of 4/10 of $10,000	=	$2,000
½ of 3/10 of $10,000	=	1,500
Depreciation expense second year	=	$3,500

Declining balance The most common of these accelerated methods is the *double-declining-balance method,* although other alternative (lower than double) methods are acceptable. Under double-declining balance, the first year's depreciation is double the straight-line rate. In succeeding years, the same percentage is applied to the remaining book value. No allowance is made for salvage, because the method always leaves a remaining balance, which is treated as salvage value. However, the asset should not be depreciated below the estimated salvage value.

An asset costing $10,000 has an estimated useful life of 10 years. Using the double-declining-balance method, the expense is computed as follows.

First, the regular straight line method percentage is determined, which in this case is 10% (10-year life). This amount is doubled to 20% and applied each year to the remaining book value, as follows:

Year	Percentage	Remaining book value	Depreciation expense
1	20	$10,000	$2,000
2	20	8,000	1,600
3	20	6,400	1,280
4	20	5,120	1,024
5	20	4,096	819
6	20	3,277	655
7	20	2,622	524
8	20	2,098	420
9	20	1,678	336
10	20	1,342	268
Salvage value		1,074	

Had the preceding illustration been 1½ times declining balance (150%), the rate would have been 15% of the remaining book value.

In the illustration above, if the asset (of a company on a calendar-year basis) had been placed in service on July 1, the first year's depreciation would have been $1,000 (½ of $2,000), and the second year's depreciation would have been 20% of $9,000 (remaining value after the first year), or $1,800.

The declining-balance method is sometimes referred to as the "fixed-percentage-on-book-value method."

Cost-Recovery Method

The cost-recovery method, also known as the sunk-cost theory, is used in situations where recovery of cost is undeterminable or very questionable. The procedure is simply that all cost is recovered before any gain is recognized. The cost-recovery method is also used for questionable receivables.

Other Types of Depreciation

Replacement depreciation   The original cost is carried on the books, and the replacement cost is charged to expense in the period the replacement occurs.

Retirement depreciation   The cost of the asset is charged to expense in the period it is retired.

Present-value depreciation   Depreciation is computed so that the return on the investment of the asset remains constant over the period involved.

Promulgated GAAP dictates that depreciation should systematically and rationally allocate the cost of an asset over its estimated useful life. Straight-line, sum-of-the-years'-digits, and declining-depreciation methods are considered acceptable, providing they are systematic and rational (ARB-44). For financial accounting purposes, companies should not use depreciation guidelines or other tax regulations issued by the IRS, but should estimate useful lives and calculate depreciation expense according to generally accepted procedures. When depreciation for tax purposes differs from depreciation for financial accounting purposes, income tax allocation (APB-11) should be used.

Depreciable Assets and Depreciation

In periods of inflation, depreciation charges based on historical cost of the original fixed asset may not reflect current price levels, and hence may not be an appropriate matching of revenues and expenses for the current period. In 1953, promulgated GAAP (ARB-43) took the position that it was acceptable to provide an appropriation of retained earnings for replacement of fixed assets, but not acceptable to depart from the traditional cost method in the treatment of depreciation, because a radical departure from the generally accepted procedures would create too much confusion in the minds of the readers of financial statements. Although inflation has become quite serious in recent years, depreciation based on historical cost remains the official, promulgated accounting principle.

Depletion

Cost depletion is the basic method of computing a deduction for depletion. An estimate is made of the amount of natural resources to be extracted, in units or tons, barrels, or any other measurement. The estimate of total recoverable units is then divided into the total cost of the depletable asset, to arrive at a depletion rate per unit. The annual depletion expense is the rate per unit times the number of units extracted during the fiscal year. If at any time there is a revision of the estimated number of units that are expected to be extracted, a new unit rate is computed. The cost of the natural resource property is reduced each year by the amount of the depletion expense for the year.

Disclosure

Allowances for depreciation and depletion should be deducted from the assets to which they relate (APB-12).

The following disclosures of depreciable assets and depreciation should be made in the financial statements or notes thereto:

1. Depreciation expense for the period
2. Balances of major classes of depreciable assets by nature or function
3. Accumulated depreciation allowances by classes or in total
4. The methods used, by major classes, in computing depreciation

> **OBSERVATION:** *Promulgated GAAP (APB-12) requires that the above disclosures be made in the financial statements or in footnotes. In addition, the effect of a change from one depreciation method to another must be disclosed (APB-20).*

GAAP GUIDE / **11.09**

DEVELOPMENT STAGE ENTERPRISES

Background

FASB-7 establishes the current promulgated GAAP for Accounting and Reporting by Development Stage Enterprises in all industries. It supersedes FASB Interpretation-5 in the area of research and development for development stage enterprises, and does not alter or amend any other promulgated or nonpromulgated GAAP. Promulgated GAAP in this area specifically states that FASB-7 does not alter nonpromulgated GAAP with respect to:

a. An established business in expansion phases
b. Extractive industries in exploration or development stages
c. Real estate firms developing properties

Applying FASB-7 to financial statements of established operating companies is covered by FASB Interpretation-7, which is covered later in this chapter.

Overview

A development stage company is one in which principal operations have not commenced or principal operations have generated an insignificant amount of revenue. During the development stage, a company devotes most of its activities toward establishing a new business. (For example, building production facilities or acquiring operational assets, training personnel, developing markets, etc.)

Accounting and Reporting

A development stage company must issue the same basic financial statements as any other enterprise, and such statements should be prepared in conformity with GAAP. A development stage company should follow GAAP in determining whether operating costs should be expensed, capitalized, or deferred. In the case of a subsidiary or a similar type of enterprise, this determination is made within the context of the entity presenting the financial statements. Thus, it would be possible to expense an item on the financial statements of a subsidiary and capitalize the same expense on the financial statements of the parent company (FASB Interpretation-7). For example, if a subsidiary purchases a machine that will be used only for research and development, it would expense the cost of the item in the year of acquisition. However, the parent company could capitalize the same machine, if in its normal course of business such a machine has an alternative future use.

Disclosure

The bulk of FASB-7 concentrates on establishing the disclosure requirements for a development stage company. The financial statements must disclose the following:

1. Accumulated losses should be described as "deficit accumulated during the development stage."
2. The income statement should show revenues and expenses for each period being presented and should also present a running cumulative total of both amounts from the company's inception. This provision also applies to dormant companies that have been reactivated at the development stage. In such cases, the totals begin from the time that development stage activities are initiated.
3. The statement of changes in financial position should reflect a cumulative total of the sources and uses of funds from the company's inception and amounts for the current period.
    The statement of changes in financial position need be presented only when required by promulgated GAAP. That is, it can be omitted if the financial statements are for internal use only or if they are prepared for a special purpose.
4. A separate statement of stockholders' equity shall be issued and shall contain the following information:
    a. The date and number of shares of stock (or other securities) issued for cash or other consideration and the dollar amount assigned.
    b. For each issuance of capital stock involving noncash consideration, a description of the nature of the consideration and the basis for its valuation.

A company can combine separate transactions of equity securities, provided that the same type of securities, consideration per equity unit, and type of consideration are involved and the transactions are made in the same fiscal period.

Modification of the statement of stockholders' equity may be required for a combined group of companies that form a development stage company or for an unincorporated development stage entity.

> **OBSERVATION:** *Promulgated GAAP does not indicate the types of modifications that might be necessary.*

5. The financial statements shall be identified as those of a development stage company and contain a description of the proposed business activities.
6. The first year that the company is no longer in the development stage, the financial statements shall indicate that in the prior year it was in the development stage. If the company includes prior-year figures for comparative purposes, the cumulative amounts required in 2 and 3 above should not appear.

When a development stage company which is a subsidiary adopts a new accounting principle, the parent should also reflect this accounting change by making the necessary adjustments on its financial statements in compliance with APB-20 (FASB Interpretation-7). Any such adjustments and related income tax effects should be recorded and disclosed.

EARNINGS PER SHARE

Background

The main source of promulgated GAAP for Earnings per Share is APB-15, which has been amended by FASB-55 (Determining Whether a Convertible Security is a Common Stock Equivalent) and by FASB-85 (Yield Test for Determining whether a Convertible Security Is a Common Stock Equivalent).

The promulgated GAAP apply to financial statements of corporations prepared in conformity with GAAP whose capital structure comprises common stock, including common stock equivalents, and/or senior securities. In this respect, the promulgated GAAP excludes mutual companies that do not have common stock, such as mutual savings banks, credit unions, cooperatives, and other similar entities. Also specifically excluded from the promulgated GAAP are registered investment companies, government-owned corporations and nonprofit entities.

In addition, statements prepared for special purposes, wholly owned subsidiaries and parent companies that accompany consolidated financial statements are not covered by the promulgated GAAP for obvious reasons.

Nonpublic Enterprise (FASB-21)

A nonpublic enterprise is an enterprise other than one:

1. Whose debt or equity securities are traded in a public market
2. That is required to file financial statements with the SEC

An enterprise loses its status as nonpublic when it issues financial statements in preparation for the sale of any class of securities in a public market.

A public market is a foreign or domestic stock exchange or an over-the-counter market.

A nonpublic enterprise is not required to disclose earnings per share (APB-15), or segment information (FASB-14), in a complete set of separately issued financial statements. The nonpublic enterprise may be a subsidiary, a joint venture, or any other investee.

If the nonpublic enterprise elects to disclose earnings per share or segment information, it must comply with the disclosure requirements of GAAP. It may not disclose this information on an arbitrary basis.

Overview

Earnings per share (EPS) or loss per share (LPS) is an important measure of performance for all users of financial statements, and should appear prominently on the face of the income statement for all periods presented. Earnings-per-share data should be consistent with the captions shown on the income statement, but EPS for continuing operations and EPS for net income are mandatory.

> **OBSERVATION:** *Although EPS for extraordinary items is not required, it is strongly recommended by APB-15 and APB-30. EPS for discontinued operations and the resulting gain or loss on the disposal of a segment may or may not be presented (APB-30).*
> *EPS for the cumulative effects of an accounting change is required by APB-20 and APB-30.*

If prior-period dollar amounts on an income statement have been restated as a result of a prior-period adjustment, the EPS data must also be restated, and the *effects* of such a restatement in per share amounts should be disclosed in the financial statements in the year of restatement.

When common stock equivalents or other dilutive securities cause a dilution in one of the EPS data presented on the face of the income statement, and at the same time cause an antidilutive effect in another EPS data presented on the same income statement, all the EPS data presented should be computed using the common stock equivalents or other dilutive securities, regardless of the dilution (APB-30).

In reporting the cumulative effects of an accounting change, two presentations of EPS data for each caption presented are required. The regular presentation includes the primary and fully diluted EPS (1) for the current year reflecting the new accounting principle and its cumulative effect on prior years and (2) for any prior years as previously presented. The *pro forma* presentation includes the primary and fully diluted EPS (1) for the current year reflecting the new accounting principle and (2) for any prior years presented, restated to include the effect of the new accounting principle (APB-20). (See Accounting Changes chapter for illustration of presentation.)

A "dual presentation" is the presentation of EPS data for both primary and fully diluted earnings per share. This information indicates the minimum and maximum levels of dilution for current earnings. GAAP requires that primary and fully diluted EPS be given equal prominence on the income statement.

If a conversion takes place during or after a current period (up to the issuance date of the financial report) that would have materially affected primary EPS if such conversions were included in primary EPS from the beginning of the period or from the date of issuance, if later, supplemental information reflecting the retroactive effect should be furnished in a footnote. Under no circumstances should such retroactive effect be included in EPS data on the face of the income statement.

Common Stock Equivalents

The concept of common stock equivalents (CSE) is essential to an understanding of reporting EPS in accordance with GAAP. The concept is based on the principle of *substance over form,* in that, although certain securities are not actually common stock, the terms and/or conditions under which they were issued usually contain provisions that enable the holder to become a common stockholder. For example, the holder of participating preferred stock is usually entitled to share in the earnings of a corporation when the earnings exceed a specified level. If the corporation has excellent earnings, the value of the participating preferred stock will undoubtedly increase, and its owner has a share in the earnings potential of the business. At the same time, the earnings potential of the common stockholder is decreased, usually as to dividends and possible price appreciation on his shares. This is the concept of *dilution.*

Consequently, the auditor wishes to identify and disclose the substance of these dilutive securities by disclosing their effect on the earnings of the common shareholder. Neither the conversion to common stock nor the imminence of conversion is a prerequisite to a security being considered a CSE.

The determination that a security is (or is not) a CSE is made at the time the security is issued and is based on conditions that existed at the time of issuance. Once a security has been classified as a CSE, it should not be changed thereafter as long as the security is outstanding. If a security is deemed to be a CSE and identical securities are subsequently issued, the identical securities must be classified as CSE.

> **OBSERVATION:** *In determining the "time of issuance" of a security for the purposes of CSE, all pertinent facts must be considered. The time of issuance is generally the date on which the terms of the offering were reached and announced even though they are subject to the approval of directors, stockholders, or others.*

Earnings Per Share

If a security is not classified as a CSE at the time of issuance but is subsequently reclassified as a CSE, it is excluded from primary EPS but included in computing fully diluted EPS (primary EPS and fully diluted EPS are discussed below).

Common stock equivalents are used only in respect to EPS, and the designation does not effect any other accounting treatment or financial statement presentation.

The following are common types of CSE:

Stock options, warrants, and similar instruments   Stock options, warrants, and other similar instruments should be considered CSE *at all times*. These types of security arrangements usually have no cash yield and their right to obtain common stock usually dictates their value.

Convertible debt and convertible preferred stock   FASB-55 and FASB-85 amend APB-15 (Earnings Per Share) by establishing new criteria for computing the yield test for determining whether a convertible security is a common stock equivalent. FASB-55 replaces the "prime interest rate" with the "average Aa corporate bond yield" as the basis for computing the yield test, and FASB-85 changes the "cash yield test" to an "effective yield test." Thus, under APB-15 as amended by FASB-55 and FASB-85, a convertible security is considered a common stock equivalent if its *effective yield* at the date of its issuance is less than 66⅔% of the then *current average Aa corporate bond yield*. The effective yield to maturity and, if any, the effective yield to all "call" dates must be computed, and the lowest effective yield is used for determining whether the convertible security is a common stock equivalent.

The average Aa corporate bond yield that is used on the date of issuance is determined by reference to the average Aa corporate bond yield for a brief period (about one week) prior to the issuance date of the convertible security.

In computing the effective yield of a convertible security, FASB-85 establishes the following rules:

1. The stated amount of annual interest or dividend payments, and any "original" or "call" premium or discount must be included in computing the effective yield of a convertible security. In computing effective yield, interest shall be compounded on a semiannual basis for bonds issued in the United States. For bonds that are sold or issued in other countries, interest shall be compounded on the same basis as publicly traded bonds in that particular country. Put options or chang-

ing conversion rates shall not be included in computing the effective yield.

2. The effective yield to maturity and, if any, the effective yield to all "call" dates must be computed, and the lowest effective yield is used for determining whether the convertible security is a common stock equivalent.

3. If a convertible security does not have a maturity date, the effective yield shall be computed as the ratio of the stated annual interest or dividend payments to the market price of the convertible security at the date of its issuance.

4. The effective yield of a convertible security with adjustable interest or dividend payments shall be based on its scheduled formula adjustments and formula information at issuance date.

On January 1, 19X1, Ace Company received proceeds of $95,000 from the sale of $100,000 of 12% Convertible Bonds at an original discount of 5%. The term of the bonds is 10 years, and interest is payable semi-annually on June 30 and December 31 of each year. On January 1, 19X6 (5 years), the bonds are callable at 102. The average Aa corporate bond yield for the immediate prior week from the date of issuance of the convertible securities was 21%. The effective yield on the bonds to the call date and to maturity are computed as follows:

Interest compounded semiannually at 12% for one year on $100,000	$12,360
Amount of proceeds from bond sale	$95,000
Effective yield to maturity ($12,360/$95,000)	13.01%
Interest for 5 years (5 × $12,360)	$61,800
Amount of call premium (2%)	2,000
Total	$63,800
Divided by five years ($63,800/5 years)	12,760
Amount of proceeds from bond sale	$95,000
Effective interest rate to call date ($12,760/$95,000)	13.43%

Under FASB-85, the effective yield to maturity is used to determine whether the convertible security qualifies as a common stock equivalent because it is less than the effective yield to the call date. Thus, the convertible security is classified as a common stock equivalent, since the effective yield to maturity of 13.01% is less than 66⅔% of the average Aa corporate bond yield (21%), which is 14.00%.

***

Moody and *Standard & Poor* are the two major bond rating organizations in the United States. An Aa bond rating indicates bonds of high quality which are very likely to be repaid (principal and interest) by the issuer. Many financial institutions issue bond yield information regularly and enterprises should encounter no difficulty in obtaining the "average Aa corporate bond yield." However, there are many different types of bond ratings and related bond yields, and care should be exercised to make sure that the correct information is obtained.

If convertible securities are sold or issued outside the United States, the most comparable *long-term yield* in the foreign country should be used instead of the "average Aa corporate bond yield."

FASB-85 is effective for convertible securities issued on or after April 1, 1985. Convertible securities issued prior to April 1, 1985, may be, but are not required to be, accounted for in accordance with FASB-85 if financial statements for the year have not been issued. Retroactive application of the provisions of FASB-85 to previously issued annual financial statements is permitted. The restated financial statement of the year of change shall disclose the nature of the restatement and its effect on income before extraordinary items, net income, and related per share amounts for each year presented.

A convertible security issued prior to the promulgation of FASB-55 (February 1982) shall be considered a common stock equivalent if, at the time of its issuance, its effective yield is less than 66⅔% of the then current prime interest rate.

Participating securities If a participation feature includes a share in the earnings potential of the corporation on substantially the same basis as that of the common shares, such participating securities are generally classified as CSE.

Contingent shares Contingent issuable shares depend on some future event or on certain conditions being met.

Generally, contingently issuable shares should not be considered CSE unless the contingent event has been attained as of the reporting date for the EPS. The following general rules apply to contingent issuable shares.

Attainment or maintenance of a certain level of earnings (1) If the level is currently being attained, the contingent shares should be considered CSE for both primary and fully diluted earnings. (2) If the attainment or maintenance contingency is above the present level of earnings, the contingent shares should be considered CSE only for the purpose of fully diluted earnings, in which case earnings for the period are adjusted to the specified earning level before computing EPS. Prior-period EPS should not be restated to reflect the year-to-year effect of the above changes.

Contingent on future market price CSE for both primary and fully diluted earnings should be considered only for the number of contingent shares that would be issued based on the market price at the close of the period being reported on. Prior-period EPS is restated to reflect the market price changes from year to year.

Both future earnings and future market price Some contingent issuable shares are conditioned on both future earnings and a future market price. Under these conditions only the number of shares that would be issuable by meeting both conditions at the end of the period being reported on should be considered CSE for both primary and fully diluted earnings. Prior-period EPS is restated to reflect the change in the number of shares from year to year.

Some options, warrants, and other CSE are not convertible until some future date. Usually these securities receive no cash dividends, derive their worth solely from their conversion feature, and thus can be considered CSE depending on the time they become directly convertible. If they can be converted within five years after the period being presented, they are CSE for both primary and fully diluted EPS; if they can be converted before ten years but after five, they are used only in fully diluted EPS calculations; any conversion after ten years can be ignored on the basis of its questionable relevance to the current period (APB-15).

Shares placed in escrow accounts that are contingently returnable shall be accounted for in the same manner as contingently issuable shares, for the purposes of computing EPS.

Sometimes subsidiaries issue convertible securities, options, warrants, or common stock that are in the hands of the public, which should be considered CSE from the standpoint of consolidated and parent company financial statements for the purpose of computing EPS. In this event, the subsidiary should compute its EPS in accordance with the promulgated GAAP, and then the consolidated group or parent company would compute its proportionate share of the subsidiary's primary and/or fully diluted EPS based on the number of shares held. In other words, the consolidated group or parent company would include as income from the subsidiary only an amount equal to the number of shares held in the subsidiary multiplied by the subsidiary's primary and/or fully diluted EPS computed in accordance with GAAP.

Sometimes a subsidiary will issue a security that is convertible into parent company stock, or issue options or warrants to purchase parent company stock. In this case, the options and warrants should be considered CSE by the parent company in computing consolidated and parent company primary and fully diluted EPS. However, subsidiary securities convertible into parent company stock must be evaluated to determine whether they are CSE and enter into the computation of the parent company's primary EPS, or whether they are not CSE and enter only into the parent company's computation of fully diluted EPS. The test for CSE in this case is the same as that for any other convertible security: If at the time of issuance, a convertible security has terms or conditions that make it a CSE, and its effective yield at the date of issuance is less than 66⅔% of the average Aa corporate bond yield, the convertible security should be considered a CSE.

Although most dividends are reported as historical facts for the purposes of EPS, stock dividends, splits or reverse splits should be presented in terms of the current equivalent number of common shares outstanding at the date of declaration. When this procedure is used, the basis for reporting such dividends should be fully disclosed. In this connection, presenting data as to dividends per share following a pooling of interests creates a disclosure problem. Therefore, in such cases it is usually preferable to disclose the dividends per share by the principal constituent on a historical basis, and in addition, the amount per equivalent share, or the total amount, for the other constituents in the pooling for each period, along with adequate disclosure of all pertinent facts. In all cases, where dividends are reported on other than a historical basis, full disclosure of such basis should be made in the financial statements or footnotes thereto.

CSE Materiality

If the dilution in EPS from all CSE is less than 3%, the dilution may be ignored (APB-15). This is an application of the basic principle of materiality.

The rule is that "common stock equivalents that in the aggregate dilute EPS by less than 3% need not be taken into consideration." However, in order to determine the 3% rule, primary and fully diluted EPS must be computed without and with the CSE.

Antidilution

If the inclusion of a CSE has the effect of increasing EPS or of decreasing LPS (loss per share), such CSE should be excluded from the EPS computation. As a result, a CSE may enter into the determination of primary EPS in one year and not another, because once a security has been classified as a CSE it always retains that status.

The following example illustrates the effects of antidilution.

During January the XYZ Company issued 10,000 shares of 100 par value 5% preferred stock when the average Aa corporate bond yield was 7%. The preferred shares were sold for $110 per share and were convertible into five shares of common stock. XYZ Company also had 300,000 shares of common stock outstanding at the beginning of the year. Net income was $220,000. What was the EPS for XYZ Company for the year?

Computation of Weighted Average Shares

Common stock outstanding, beginning of year	300,000
CSE-Preferred stock (issued for less than ⅔ of the average Aa corporate bond yield)	50,000
Weighted average shares	350,000

Adjustments to Net Income

Net income	$220,000
Less: Preferred dividends	50,000
Adjusted	$170,000
EPS, assuming conversion ($220,000 ÷ 350,000)	$ 0.63
EPS, assuming no conversion ($170,000 ÷ 300,000)	$ 0.57

Note: EPS with conversion is antidilutive and is not used.

Computation of Preferred Stock Yield

The effective yield is determined by dividing the initial issuance price into the stated amount of interest. The preferred stock was sold at issuance for $110 per share and the stated interest was 5%:

$$\$5 \div \$110 = 0.0454 = 4.5\%$$

The result of this computation indicates that the effective yield at the date of issuance was 4.5%. The effective yield is compared to ⅔ of the average Aa corporate bond yield for the week prior to the date of issuance, which was 4.7%:

$$\text{⅔ of } 7\% = 0.0466 = 4.7\%$$

The effective yield of 4.5% was less than ⅔ of the 7% average Aa corporate bond yield (4.7%) for the week prior to the date of issuance, which makes the preferred stock a CSE. However, because of its antidilutive effect, the preferred stock is not used.

Simple Capital Structures

A corporation with a simple capital structure is one that consists of only capital stock, or which includes no potentially dilutive CSE that could dilute EPS by more than 3% in the aggregate.

For organizations with simple capital structures, the presentation of EPS in the income statement should appear as follows:

	19XX	19XX
Income before extraordinary items	$XX,XXX	$XX,XXX
Extraordinary items (describe)	XXX	–
Net income	$XX,XXX	$XX,XXX
Earnings per common share:		
Income before extraordinary items	$ X.XX	$ X.XX
Extraordinary item (Note 1)	.XX	–
Net income per share	$ X.XX	$ X.XX

EPS data are presented before and after extraordinary items. The per share amounts for extraordinary items are arrived at simply by subtraction.

Complex Capital Structures

For organizations with complex capital structures the procedure for determining EPS requires that the auditor gather information regarding various outstanding securities, use that information in computing two EPS figures (which is called a dual presentation), and then present the two EPS amounts with equal prominence on the face of the income statement. The captions for the two EPS figures are "Earnings per common share and common stock equivalents" and "Earnings per common share—assuming full dilution."

The first of these captions is referred to as *primary earnings* and the second as *fully diluted earnings*. The difference between primary EPS and fully diluted EPS is that primary EPS considers only securities that are common stock or CSE, whereas fully diluted EPS indicates the maximum dilution.

Under both methods, antidilutive securities are excluded. Antidilutive securities are those which have the effect of increasing EPS or reducing loss per share.

Three types of securities that might enter into the computation of fully diluted EPS are:

1. Senior stock or debt that is convertible but not a CSE
2. Options or warrants
3. Contingently issuable shares

The difference between primary and fully diluted EPS is whether the securities are CSE. Only CSE enter into primary EPS, whereas all potentially dilutive securities are part of fully diluted EPS.

Dual Presentation of Net Income

A dual presentation includes primary EPS and fully diluted EPS. Only CSE enter into the computation of primary EPS, whereas CSE plus any other dilutive securities enter into the computation of fully diluted EPS.

Any securities that increase EPS are excluded from all computations. These types of securities are called "antidilutive" and either increase EPS or decrease LPS (loss per share).

$$\text{Primary EPS} = \text{common stock} + \text{CSE}$$
$$\text{Fully diluted EPS} = \text{primary EPS} + \text{any additional dilutive securities}$$

Earnings Per Share

Weighted Average Shares

Computations of EPS are based on the weighted number of shares outstanding for each period presented. A separate computation of the weighted number of shares outstanding must be made for primary EPS and fully diluted EPS.

The following example for ABC Company demonstrates how the weighted average shares are determined.

Common stock outstanding, 1/1/77	200,000 shares
Preferred stock (convertible into 2 shares of common stock), outstanding 1/1/77	50,000 shares
Convertible debentures (convertible into 100 shares of common stock for each $1,000 bond)	$100,000

On March 31, ABC reacquired 5,000 shares of its own common stock.

On May 1, ABC converted 20,000 shares of preferred stock into common.

On July 1, ABC converted $50,000 of convertible debentures into common stock.

On September 30, ABC reacquired 5,000 shares of its common stock.

Computation of Weighted Average Shares

1. Common stock outstanding, 1/1/77	200,000
2. Common stock reacquired, 3/31/77	(3,750)
3. Conversion of preferred stock on 5/1/77	26,667
4. Conversion of convertible debentures on 7/1/77	2,500
5. Common stock reacquired on 9/30/77	(1,250)
Total weighted average shares, 1977	224,167

1. Common stock outstanding Since the 200,000 shares of common stock were outstanding for the entire year, all the shares are included in the weighted average shares.

2. Common stock reacquired 5,000 shares were reacquired on March 31, 1977, which means that $9/12$ of the year they were not outstanding. Since the 5,000 shares are already included in the 200,000 shares (1 above), we must deduct that portion which was not outstanding during the full year. Thus, $9/12$ of the 5,000 shares, or 3,750 shares, should be excluded from the computations, which means that only 196,250 of the 200,000 shares were outstanding for the full year.

3. **Conversion of preferred** On May 1, 1977, 20,000 shares of the preferred were converted into common stock. Since the conversion rate is 2 for 1, an additional 40,000 shares were outstanding from May 1 to the end of the year. Thus, 8/12 of the 40,000 shares, or 26,667 shares, should be included in the weighted average shares outstanding for the year.

4. **Conversion of convertible debentures** On July 1, 1977, $50,000 of the convertible debentures were converted into common stock. The conversion rate is 100 shares for each $1,000 bond, which means that the $50,000 converted consisted of fifty $1,000 bonds, or 5,000 shares of common stock. Since the conversion was on July 1, only 6/12 of the 5,000 shares (2,500) are included in the weighted average shares outstanding for the year.

5. **Common stock reacquired** 5,000 additional shares out of the 200,000 shares outstanding at the beginning of the year were reacquired on September 30, which means that for 3/12 of the year they were not outstanding. Thus, 3/12 of 5,000 shares, or 1,250 shares, must be excluded from the computation of weighted average shares outstanding for the year.

The weighted average number of shares must be used so as to reflect the period in which each security affected operations.

Any stock splits or stock dividends (or reverse splits or dividends) must be retroactively recognized in all periods presented in the financial statements. A stock split or stock dividend should be recognized if it occurs after the close of the period but before issuance of the financial statements. If this situation occurs, it must be fully disclosed in the statements. Also, as mentioned previously, the dividends per share must be reported in terms of the equivalent number of shares outstanding at the time the dividend is declared.

Before computing EPS a company must subtract from net income any earnings pledged to senior security holders. If such a security is cumulative preferred, all dividends, whether the company has earnings to cover them or not, must be deducted from net income. In the case of a net loss, the loss is increased by the amount of cumulative dividends in arrears. If the senior security stipulates that dividends are limited to earnings, then adjustments are obviously made to the extent of available earnings.

Earnings Per Share

A company adjusts noncumulative interest or dividends only to the extent they are accruable or declared.

All the above adjustments must be given adequate disclosure in the financial statements or footnotes thereto.

As mentioned earlier, it is possible for a security to be dilutive with respect to one of the EPS figures presented in the financial statements and at the same time be antidilutive to another. In such an instance the effects of such a security should be included in all EPS calculations.

Treasury Stock Method

When potential dilution from stock options and similar instruments is less than 20% of the number of common shares outstanding, the treasury stock method is used to compute the dilution.

When the market price of the underlying stock exceeds the exercise price for substantially all of three consecutive months, the treasury stock method is used to determine the amount of dilution.

The treasury stock method assumes that the stock options or similar instruments are exercised and the money received by the company is used to purchase as much common stock on the open market as possible. The average market price is used for primary EPS and the ending market price is used for fully diluted EPS, unless the average market price is higher. The amount of stock that cannot be purchased because of the lack of money is considered additional outstanding shares, which could have a dilutive effect on EPS. The computations are made by quarters in the year, unless the market price is relatively stable during the year, in which case one computation for the year can be used. The formula to compute CSE for stock options and similar instruments is:

$$\text{Number of shares} - \left[\frac{\text{number of shares} \times \text{exercise price}}{\substack{\text{average market price*} \\ or \\ \text{ending market price**}}} \right] = \text{additional shares outstanding}$$

*Average market price is used for primary EPS.
**Ending market price is used for fully diluted EPS, unless average market price is higher.

> **OBSERVATION:** *Frequently an option or similar instrument is excluded from the computation of primary EPS, but must be included in the determination of fully diluted EPS.*

Earnings Per Share

The following problem illustrates how the incremental shares by quarters are computed for stock options and similar instruments.

A company has 10,000 stock options outstanding, which are exercisable at $60 each. Given the market prices below, determine the incremental shares by quarters, and the number of shares that should be included for both primary and fully diluted EPS.

	Quarters			
	1	2	3	4
Average market price	56	64	70	68
Ending market price	60	68	72	64

The formula for determining the incremental shares by quarters for primary EPS using the *average market price* is as follows:

$$\text{1st quarter} \quad 10{,}000 - \frac{10{,}000 \times \$60}{\$56} = 0^*$$

$$\text{2nd quarter} \quad 10{,}000 - \frac{10{,}000 \times \$60}{\$64} = 625$$

$$\text{3rd quarter} \quad 10{,}000 - \frac{10{,}000 \times \$60}{\$70} = 1{,}429$$

$$\text{4th quarter} \quad 10{,}000 - \frac{10{,}000 \times \$60}{\$68} = 1{,}176$$

$$\text{Total incremental shares by quarters} = 3{,}230$$

$$\text{Divided by 4 quarters} = 808$$

*The exercise price of $60 is higher than the average market price.

The reason why we divide by four quarters is that four quarters entered into our computation. The 808 shares must be included in the computation of primary EPS.

The computation of fully diluted EPS uses the *ending market price* unless the average market price is higher.

Earnings Per Share

$$\text{1st quarter } 10{,}000 - \frac{10{,}000 \times \$60}{\$60} = 0^*$$

$$\text{2nd quarter } 10{,}000 - \frac{10{,}000 \times \$60}{\$68} = 1{,}176$$

$$\text{3rd quarter } 10{,}000 - \frac{10{,}000 \times \$60}{\$72} = 1{,}667$$

$$\text{4th quarter } 10{,}000 - \frac{10{,}000 \times \$60}{\$68 \text{ (Note 1)}} = 1{,}176$$

$$\text{Total incremental shares by quarters} = \underline{4{,}019}$$

$$\text{Divided by 4 quarters} = \underline{1{,}005}$$

*The exercise price of $60 is the same as the ending market price.

Note 1. Since the average market price is higher in the fourth quarter, it is used.

The computation of the incremental shares by quarters when divided by the number of quarters involved gives us the number of shares that could not be purchased with the proceeds from the hypothetical exercise of all the stock options. The computation could be determined by just dividing either the average or ending market price (whichever is applicable) into the hypothetical funds received by the exercise of the stock options, and whatever number of shares cannot be purchased are considered additional outstanding shares.

Under the treasury stock method, the funds that would have been received from the exercise of the options or similar instruments are calculated and:

1. The amount calculated as received is applied as if the funds were used to purchase common stock at the *average market price during the period*, except that for *fully diluted EPS* the market price at the end of the year is used, *if it is higher than the average market price.*
2. All options are considered to be exercised as at the beginning of the period (or time of issuance, if later).
3. Any remaining shares of common stock that theoretically could not be purchased because of the lack of funds are considered outstanding and are added to the total outstanding shares of common stock used to compute EPS.

The theory behind the treasury stock method is that any number of shares of common stock that could have been purchased on the open market with the exercised price funds from the options or similar instruments are not additional outstanding stock and have no dilutive effect on EPS.

The treasury stock method is not used for options and similar instruments that contain a provision which permits or requires the holder to pay part or all of the exercise price by tendering debt or other security of the issuer. The amount of dilution caused by these options and similar instruments is determined by the "if converted" method, which is discussed later in this chapter.

Modified Treasury Stock Method

When the number of shares of common stock that can be purchased with the hypothetical funds from the exercise of the options or similar instruments exceeds 20% of the number of common shares outstanding, the modified treasury stock method is used to determine the dilution, if any.

A maximum of 20% of the outstanding number of common shares may be purchased with the money received from the hypothetical exercise of all the stock options and similar instruments involved.

If any hypothetical money is still left after purchasing the 20% maximum, it is applied as follows (hypothetically):

1. Reduction of existing debt
2. Investment in short-term paper

Net income is adjusted for any interest expense (income) saved or created by 1 and 2, and the related tax effects are taken into consideration.

The following problem demonstrates how the modified treasury stock method is used in those situations where the stock options outstanding exceed 20% of the authorized and issued common stock.

Assume the following data:

Common stock	500,000 shares
Stock options (exercisable at $28)	120,000 shares
6% debt outstanding	$500,000
Net income	$400,000

Average and year-end market price of common stock	$30
Tax rate	50%

What is the primary EPS?

Since the number of stock options exceeds 20% of the total outstanding shares before exercise, the modified treasury stock method must be used.

The first step is to assume that all the outstanding stock options are exercised.

Proceeds of exercise of options (120,000 × $28) $3,360,000

The next step is to apply the proceeds as follows:

1. To purchase the maximum (20%) amount of common stock in the open market at either (a) the average market price in the case of primary EPS computation or (b) the ending market price or the average market price, whichever is higher, in the case of fully diluted EPS computations.
2. If any of the hypothetical funds remain after purchasing the maximum (20%) amount of common stock on the open market, they are applied:
    a. first, to reduce any long-term debt of the enterprise,
    b. secondly, to purchase short-term paper (hypothetically)

In this problem the application of the proceeds would be:

Application of Proceeds

Purchase of maximum 100,000 shares (20%)	$3,000,000
Reduction in 6% debt	360,000
Total application of proceeds	$3,360,000

After the excess funds are applied to the reduction of $360,000 of 6% long-term debt, we must compute what effect this has on net income, because interest expense is hypothetically reduced by the reduction of the long-term debt.

Adjustment to Income

Net income	$400,000
Add: Net reduction of interest on 6% debt, less 50% taxes (0.06 × $360,000 × 0.5)	10,800
Adjusted net income	$410,800

Since 120,000 stock options were outstanding and we were restricted to purchasing 100,000 (20% maximum), the remaining 20,000 shares must be considered outstanding for the computations of both primary and fully diluted EPS.

Adjustment to Common Stock

Common stock outstanding	500,000
Additional shares (120,000 − 100,000)	20,000
Adjusted common stock	520,000
Primary EPS ($410,800 ÷ 520,000)	$ 0.79

The last item we must check is whether the addition of the stock options to the computation of primary EPS has had an antidilutive effect. This is determined by computing primary EPS without the stock options, as follows:

Primary EPS before options ($400,000 ÷ 500,000) $0.80

Since primary EPS excluding the stock options is higher than it is including them, there is no antidilutive effect. However, in this case the dilutive effect is less than the 3% materiality rule and can be ignored.

The following is a summary of the steps in the modified treasury stock method:

1. The regular treasury stock method is followed except that a maximum of 20% of the outstanding number of common shares may be theoretically purchased.
2. The regular steps are followed for the treasury stock method.
3. Any remaining theoretical funds are applied in the following order:

a. Reduction of any borrowings
b. Investment in short-term government or commercial paper
c. Recognition of any tax effect of a and b
4. The total effect of all steps are aggregated; if the net effect is dilutive, it is recognized in EPS.

If-Converted Method

Convertible debt and convertible preferred stock are considered common stock equivalents (CSE) if their effective yield, at the date of issuance, is less than ⅔ of the then current average Aa corporate bond yield.

When convertible debt or convertible preferred stock is CSE and enter into primary EPS, or when these same types of securities are not CSE but enter into the computation of fully diluted earnings, the *if-converted* method is used to determine dilution.

The principal objective of the if-converted method is to adjust net income for the effects of including a security in primary or fully diluted EPS. These adjustments are usually preferred dividends or interest on convertible securities.

> **OBSERVATION:** *Nondiscretionery items that would have been made on the basis of net income, such as profit-sharing expense, royalties, and investment credits, must also be taken into consideration.*

The if-converted method assumes that convertible issues are converted at the beginning of the year or at issuance date, if later.

Some convertible debt and preferred stock require the holder to pay a stipulated amount of cash on conversion. The treasury stock method is used to account for any cash received when the if-converted method is used. However, theoretical stock purchases are assumed only if the market price exceeds the exercise price or if the exercise price is less than market because the convertible security is selling at a discount.

It stands to reason that if you are going to consider one of these types of securities a CSE, the applicable dividend and interest must be added back to net income, *if either was previously deducted.*

The following example illustrates the application of the if-converted method.

Earnings Per Share

X Company has outstanding 100,000 shares of common stock and $500,000 in 6% debentures convertible into 10 shares for each $1,000 bond. The convertible debentures are CSE, and net income for the year was $100,000. What is primary EPS, assuming a 50% tax rate?

Primary shares outstanding:	
Common stock	100,000
Convertible debentures (500 × 10)	5,000
Total primary shares—outstanding	105,000

Primary net income:	
Net income	$100,000
Add back interest on bonds, less tax effects (0.06 × $500,000 × 0.5)	15,000
Total primary net income	$115,000

Primary EPS (with conversion) ($115,000 ÷ 105,000 shares)	$ 1.10

Once again we must check to see whether the inclusion of the convertible debentures in the computation of primary EPS is antidilutive, by comparing primary EPS computed with the bonds to primary EPS computed without the bonds, as follows:

Primary EPS (without conversion) ($100,000 ÷ 100,000 shares)	$1.00

Primary EPS with conversion of the convertible bonds ($1.10) is more than primary EPS without the conversion ($1) and is therefore antidilutive.

In the above example, assume that instead of the convertible debenture, there were 10,000 shares of 3% preferred stock ($100 par) convertible into five shares for each share of preferred. What is the primary EPS?

Primary shares outstanding:	
Common stock	100,000
Convertible preferred (10,000 × 5)	50,000
Total primary shares	150,000

Primary net income (with conversion)	$100,000

No adjustment is made when considering preferred stock as CSE, because dividends are deducted from net income.

Primary net income (without conversion):
($100,000 − $30,000 for preferred dividends) $ 70,000

Primary EPS (with conversion):
($100,000 ÷ 150,000 shares) $ 0.67

Primary EPS (without conversion)
($70,000 ÷ 100,000 shares) $ 0.70

Primary EPS with conversion is *not antidilutive* and is therefore used.

The *if-converted method* recognizes that the holders of a convertible bond or other debt instrument may share in equity (through conversion to common stock) or in debt (from holding the bond), but not in both. Many convertible securities are such that in order to convert to common stock, the holder must surrender his security.

In summary, convertible issues of this type that are CSE are assumed to be converted as at the beginning of the period (or at the date of issuance, if later), and the following steps are taken:

1. Net income must be recomputed to reflect the conversion of these securities from the beginning of the period. Interest charges and other expenses attributable to the convertible issues, along with any preferred dividends, must be taken into consideration in recomputing net income.

2. EPS is computed on the basis of the amount of common stock that would have been outstanding if these types of convertible securities were converted as at the beginning of the period (or at the date of issuance, if later).

Some warrants and convertible securities require a cash payment on conversion. In these cases, if the market price of the underlying stock exceeds the exercise price or if the security being converted is selling for a discount that results in an exercise price lower than the market price of the underlying common stock, then (1) the theoretical proceeds should be applied in accordance with the treasury stock method *and* (2) the if-converted method should apply as to the retirement or conversion of such warrants or convertible securities.

Two-Class Method

Although the *two-class method* is considered inappropriate when other acceptable methods can be used, it may be necessary in the case of *participating securities and two classes of common stock.*

Under the *two-class method,* CSE are treated as common stock, but with a dividend rate different from that of the common stock, there is no conversion of any convertible securities, and:

1. No use of theoretical proceeds is considered.
2. All required distributions to senior securities, CSE, and common stock are assumed to be deducted from net income.
3. The remaining amount is divided by the CSE and common shares, after adding back distributions under 2 above to arrive at primary EPS.

Loss per Share

Loss per share is generally based on the number of outstanding common shares, and any assumption of conversion would be antidilutive because the loss is spread over more shares, thereby reducing the loss per share.

Business Combinations

Shares issued in a combination accounted for by the *purchase method* are accounted for in the EPS calculation from the date of the acquisition. When the *pooling method* is used, the calculation is based on the total weighted average number of shares of the constituent firms, adjusted to the equivalent shares of the surviving company.

The difference in treatment is based on the difference between the purchase method, in which results of operations appear in the parent's net income only from the date of acquisition, and the pooling method, in which results are "pooled" for all periods presented.

> **OBSERVATION:** As mentioned previously, data as to dividends per share following a pooling of interests may create a disclosure problem. In such cases, it is usually preferable to disclose on a historical basis the dividends per share paid by the principal constituent of the pooling and the amount of dividends per equivalent share, or the total amount of dividends, for the other constituents in the pooling. This type of presentation should be made for each

Earnings Per Share

period presented, along with adequate disclosure of all the pertinent facts.

In all cases, where dividends are reported on other than a historical basis, full disclosure of such basis is required in the financial statements or footnotes thereto.

Disclosure

Disclosure should be made of all pertinent rights and privileges of the various security holders, including dividend and liquidation preferences, participation rights, call prices and dates, and conversion and exercise prices.

The bases on which primary and fully diluted EPS have been calculated should be disclosed in a schedule or a footnote to the financial statements. This disclosure should include the identification of any CSE in determining primary and fully diluted EPS, describe all assumptions used, and reveal the number of shares issued on conversion, exercise, or otherwise during the most recent annual fiscal period and any subsequent periods presented.

It may be desirable to provide clear-cut computations or reconciliations of each security entering into the computation of primary and fully diluted EPS. However, this type of information which shows the historical amount of outstanding common shares should not be shown on the face of the income statement.

A company should also disclose, preferably in a footnote, the effect of any recapitalization. For instance, if common stock is sold and the proceeds are used to retire preferred stock or bonds, supplemental EPS information should be supplied, showing the effects of such a transaction if it had occurred at the beginning of the period.

The following specific disclosures mentioned in this chapter are repeated here for convenience:

1. EPS should appear prominently on the face of the income statement for all periods presented.
2. The effects of prior-period EPS restated in per share amounts should be disclosed in the financial statements in the year of restatement.
3. If CSE or conversions occur during or after a current period that would have materially affected primary EPS, supplemental information reflecting the retroactive effect should be furnished in a footnote, if such CSE had been included in the

computation of EPS for the current period. Under no circumstances should such retroactive effect be actually included in EPS data on the face of the income statement.

4. When stock dividends, splits, or reverse splits are presented in terms of the current equivalent number of common shares outstanding, as they should be, the basis for reporting such dividends should be fully disclosed.
5. A stock dividend, split, or reverse split that occurs after the close of a period but before issuance of the financial statements should be retroactively recognized in all periods presented in the financial statements. Full disclosure of the fact must be made in the financial statements or footnotes thereto.
6. All adjustments made to net income for the computation of EPS must be adequately disclosed.

Comprehensive Illustration

The following problem illustrates the application of all the components of determining EPS in accordance with the promulgated GAAP (APB-15).

Assume the following information for Black Corporation for 19X2 and 19X1. On the basis of this information compute the primary and fully diluted EPS for 19X2 and 19X1. Show your computation by supporting schedules in good form.

Common stock ($1 par) issued prior to 19X1	1,000,000 shs.
Common stock ($1 par) issued for cash, 7/1/X2	100,000 shs.
Stock options to acquire one share of $1 common for $50 issued 1/1/70 expire 1/1/80	100,000 shs.
3% preferred stock ($100 par) convertible into 1.5 shares of $1 common. Sold at par (3/1/X0) when the average Aa corporate bond yield was 7%	200,000 shs.
6% debentures issued at par 4/1/X2, convertible into 15 shares of $1 common for each $1,000 bond. The debentures are not CSE.	$500,000

Earnings Per Share

Market price of common stock ($1 par):

	Average	Ending
19X2	64	66
19X1	48	47

Income tax rate: 50%

	19X2	19X1
Income before extraordinary item	$3,200,000	$2,600,000
Extraordinary item	(400,000)	(600,000)
Cumulative effect of a change in accounting for depreciation	100,000	–
Net income	$2,900,000	$2,000,000

Computation of Weighted Average Shares

	19X2	19X1
Common stock ($1 par)	1,000,000	1,000,000
Common stock ($1 par) issued 7/1/X2 equivalent shares (100,000 × 6/12)	50,000	–
Stock option (CSE) (Schedule A)	21,875	–
3% Preferred stock (CSE) (Schedule B)	300,000	300,000
Primary weighted average shares	1,371,875	1,300,000
Stock options (Schedule A)	2,368	–
Convertible debentures (Schedule C)	5,625	–
Fully diluted weighted average shares	1,379,868	1,300,000

Schedule A—Computation of CSE, Stock Options

19X2—Primary EPS (use average market price = 64)

$$100,000 - \frac{100,000 \times \$50}{\$64} = 21,875$$

19X2—Fully diluted EPS (use ending market price = 66, unless average is higher = 64)

$$100,000 - \frac{100,000 \times \$50}{\$66} = 24,243$$

Less included in primary EPS (above)	21,875
Additional shares for fully diluted EPS	2,368

13.26 / GAAP GUIDE

19X1—The average and ending market prices are less than the $50 exercise price, which results in no CSE.

Schedule B—Computation of CSE, Preferred Stock

Because the effective yield (3%) is less than ⅔ of the average Aa corporate bond yield of 7% (⅔ of 7% = 4.67%) at the date of issue, the preferred stock is a CSE.

200,000 shares × 1.5 (conversion rate) = 300,000

Schedule C—Convertible Debenture Dilution

The 6% convertible debentures are not CSE, because they were issued to yield 6%, which is more than ⅔ of the average Aa corporate bond yield (⅔ of 7% = 4.67%). However, they do enter into the computation of fully diluted EPS because of their potential dilution (convertibility).

Issued 4/1/X2 and convertible into 15 shares per $1,000.

Fully converted (500 × 15)	7,500
Issued 4/1/X2 (7,500 × 9/12)	5,625

Antidilution test—3% preferred stock:

	19X2	19X1
Without preferred:		
Net income	$2,900,000	$2,000,000
Less: Preferred dividends ($3 × 200,000)	600,000	600,000
Adjusted	$2,300,000	$1,400,000
Weighted average shares (1,000,000 + 50,000 + 21,875)	1,071,875	1,000,000
Primary EPS without conversion	$ 2.15	$ 1.40
With preferred:		
Net income	$2,900,000	$2,000,000
Weighted average shares	1,371,875	1,300,000
Primary EPS, with conversion	$ 2.11	$ 1.54

Earnings Per Share

Antidilution test—6% convertible debentures:

	19X2
Without conversion:	
Net income	$2,900,000
Weighted average shares (1,000,000 + 50,000 + 21,875 + 300,000 + 2,368)	1,374,243
Fully diluted EPS without conversion	$2.11
With conversion:	
Net income	$2,900,000
Plus: Interest expense ($500,000 × 6% × 9/12 × 50% tax rate)	11,250
Adjusted net income	$2,911,250
Weighted average shares (1,374,243 + 5,625)	1,379,868
Fully diluted EPS with conversion	$2.11

Statement Presentation

	19X2	19X1
Income before extraordinary item	$3,200,000	$2,600,000
Extraordinary item (Note ____)	(400,000)	(600,000)
Cumulative effect of change in accounting principle (depreciation)	100,000	–
Net income	$2,900,000	$2,000,000

Earnings per share and common stock equivalents:

	19X2	19X1
Income before extraordinary item	$ 2.33	$ 2.00
Extraordinary item (Note ____)	(0.29)	(0.60)
Cumulative effect of change in accounting for depreciation	0.07	–
Net income	$ 2.11	$ 1.40
Shares outstanding	1,371,875	1,000,000

Earnings per share assuming full dilution:

Income before extraordinary item	$ 2.33	$ 2.00
Extraordinary item (Note _____)	(0.29)	(0.60)
Cumulative effect of change in accounting for depreciation	$ 0.07	–
Net income	$ 2.11	$ 1.40
Shares outstanding	1,379,868	1,000,000

Comments:

1. In 19X1 the preferred stock was excluded from primary and fully diluted EPS because it was antidilutive ($1.40 versus $1.54).
2. Any CSE that in the aggregate dilutes EPS (primary or fully diluted) by less than 3% can be ignored (materiality rule). In this comprehensive illustration the aggregate dilution of the CSE included in the computation of EPS was greater than 3% ($2.19 − $2.11 = $.08 or 3.65%).

NOTE: The pro forma presentation required for a change in an accounting principle has been excluded from the above illustration for the sake of brevity.

EQUITY METHOD

Background

The promulgated GAAP for the Equity Method of Accounting for Investments in Common Stock is APB-18 (as amended) and FASB Interpretation-35 (Criteria for Applying the Equity Method of Accounting for Investments in Common Stock). In addition, Statement of Position 78-9 (Accounting for Investments in Real Estate Ventures) covers the application of the equity method of accounting to unincorporated real estate ventures.

FASB-13, paragraph 31, requires that subsidiaries whose principal business is leasing property to its parent company should be consolidated and the equity method is unacceptable.

The promulgated GAAP extends the use of the equity method to investments in common stock of corporate joint ventures and to investments included in parent company financial statements which are prepared for stockholders. The promulgated GAAP does not cover investment companies registered under, or those which would be included in, the Investment Company Act of 1940, or nonbusiness entities, such as individuals, trusts, and estates.

> **OBSERVATION:** *An investor's qualifying assets, for the purposes of capitalizing interest costs under FASB-34, shall include equity funds, loans, and advances made to investees accounted for by the equity method, provided that the investee (a) is undergoing activities necessary to start its planned principal operations and (b) the activities include the use of funds to acquire qualifying assets for its operations (FASB-58). For further discussion, see chapter on "Interest Costs Capitalized."*

Overview

Domestic and foreign unconsolidated subsidiaries and corporate joint ventures should be presented in consolidated financial statements on the *equity basis* by an investor (usually the parent company), whose investment in the voting stock gives it the ability to *exercise significant influence over the operating and financial policies* of the unconsolidated subsidiary, although control may be less than majority.

Under the equity basis of accounting for investments in common stock, consolidated net income during a time period includes the parent company's proportionate share of the net income reported by the subsidiary or affiliate for the periods subsequent to acquisition. *The effect of this treatment is that net income for the period and stockholders' equity at the end of the period are the same as if the companies had been consolidated.* Any dividends received are treated as adjustments of the amount of the investment under the equity basis.

The equity method of accounting for investments in common stock is not a substitute for consolidated statements when circumstances indicate that consolidation is more meaningful and appropriate.

When appropriate, investors should use the equity method to account for investments in common stock, in all unconsolidated subsidiaries, in corporate joint ventures, and in other common stock investments (domestic and foreign).

Generally, a subsidiary whose principal business is leasing property to its parent must be consolidated and the equity method is unacceptable for a fair presentation (FASB-13, paragraph 31).

It is presumed, absent evidence to the contrary, that an investment (directly or indirectly) of less than 20% of the voting stock of an investee indicates lack of significant influence, and the use of the equity method or consolidated statements is not required.

It is assumed, absent evidence to the contrary, *that an investment (directly or indirectly) of 20% or more of the voting stock of an investee indicates the ability to exercise significant influence and control, and the equity method or consolidated statements, whichever is more meaningful, is required for a fair presentation.*

The 20% ownership is based on current outstanding securities that have voting privilege. Potential ownership and voting privileges should be disregarded.

Presumption of Significant Influence

In order to establish a uniform application of the Equity Method, the presumption in APB-18 is that, absent evidence to the contrary, an investment (direct or indirect) of 20% or more of the voting stock of an investee indicates that the investor has the ability to exercise significant influence over the operating and financial policies of the investee. Evidence that the investor has such significant influence over the investee includes the following:

1. Investor has representation on the board of directors of the investee.

2. Investor participates in the policy-making process of the investee.
3. Material intercompany transactions occur between the investor and the investee.
4. Interchange of managerial personnel between the investor and the investee.
5. Technological dependency of the investee on the investor.
6. Extent of ownership of the investor in relation to the concentration of other shareholders.

The determination of the investor's influence in an investment may be difficult to reach and the application of sound judgment may frequently be necessary. However, the presumption is that significant influence does exist in an investment of 20% or more, unless sufficient evidence to the contrary outweighs the presumption.

> **OBSERVATION:** *There is also a presumption in APB-18 that significant influence does not exist in an investment of less than 20%. However, APB-18 makes it perfectly clear that this presumption may be overcome by enough evidence to the contrary. Thus, significant influence over the operating and financial policies of an investment of less than 20% can occur.*

In an investment of 20% or more, enough evidence may exist to demonstrate that the investor cannot exercise significant influence over the operating and financial policies of the investee. Thus, the presumption of significant influence in investments of 20% or more may be overcome by sufficient evidence.

The following conditions may indicate that an investor is unable to exercise significant influence over the operating and financial policies of an investee:

1. The investee opposes the investment and files a lawsuit or complaint, indicating that the investor does not have significant influence.
2. An agreement is executed between the investee and the investor which indicates that significant influence does not exist.

> **OBSERVATION:** *These types of agreements are generally referred to as* **standstill agreements** *and are frequently used to settle disputes between an investor and an investee. They may contain information as to whether the investor can or cannot exercise significant influence over the investee. The following are some of the typical provisions of the standstill agreement:*

Equity Method

    a. The investee agrees to use its best efforts to obtain representation for the investor on its board of directors.
    b. The investor agrees not to seek representation on the investee's board of directors.
    c. The investee may agree to cooperate with the investor.
    d. The investor may agree to limit its ownership in the investee.
    e. The investor may agree not to exercise its significant influence over the investee.
    f. The investee may acknowledge or refute the investor's ability to exercise significant influence.

    If a standstill agreement contains provisions indicating that the investor has given up some significant rights as a shareholder, the agreement is regarded, under FASB Interpretation-35, as a factor in determining that the equity method should not be used.

3. Significant influence is exercised by a small group of shareholders representing majority ownership of the investee.
4. The investor attempts, but cannot obtain, the financial information that is necessary to apply the equity method.

    OBSERVATION: The Codification of Statements on Auditing Standards *(AU 332.09)* states that, "The refusal of an investee to furnish necessary financial data to the investor is evidence (but not necessarily conclusive evidence) that the investor does not have the ability to exercise significant influence over operating and financial policies of the investee such as to justify the application of the equity method of accounting for investments in 50% or less owned companies in accordance with the provisions of APB-18."

5. The investor attempts and fails to obtain representation on the investee's board of directors.

    OBSERVATION: FASB Interpretation-35 implies that the investor must actually try to obtain financial information or try to obtain representation on the investee's board. It seems logical that the same effect should result in the event that the investor had prior knowledge that he would fail in these attempts and, therefore, did not even attempt them.

Many other factors, not listed above, may affect an investor's ability to exercise significant influence over the operating and financial policies of an investee. An investor must evaluate all existing circumstances to determine whether factors exist that overcome the presumption of significant influence in an investment of 20% or more of an investee.

> **OBSERVATION:** On the other hand, an investor must also evaluate existing circumstances in an investment of less than 20% of an investee. The presumption that significant influence does not exist in an investment of less than 20% may be overcome by factors that indicate that significant influence does exist.
>
> If there is not enough evidence to reach a definitive conclusion at the time that the investment is made, it may be advisable to wait until more evidence becomes available.

FASB Interpretation-35 is effective for fiscal years ending on or after June 15, 1982, and earlier application is encouraged. Accounting changes caused by the application of FASB Interpretation-35 shall not be accounted for as accounting changes (APB-20). Instead, accounting changes required by FASB Interpretation-35 shall be accounted for in accordance with the provisions of paragraphs 19 (l) and (m) of APB-18 (Equity Method), as follows:

1. If an investment in voting stock falls below the 20% level, or other factors indicate that the investor can no longer exercise significant influence, the presumption is that the investor has lost the ability to exercise significant influence and control, in which case the equity method should be discontinued. The carrying amount at the date of discontinuance becomes the cost of the investment. Subsequent dividends are accounted for by the cost method from the date the equity method was discontinued.

2. An investor who, because of other factors, obtains significant influence or who acquires more than 20% ownership in an investee after having had less than 20% *must retroactively adjust its accounts to the equity method on the basis of a step-by-step acquisition of an investment.* In this event, at the date of each step in the acquisition, the carrying value of the investment must be compared with the underlying net assets of the investee to determine whether goodwill (positive or negative) is involved.

Cost Method

The cost method is generally used when ownership is less than 20%. The original investment under the cost method is recorded at cost, and income is recognized from dividends received out of accumulated earnings earned after the date of acquisition.

Dividends received out of accumulated earnings prior to the date of acquisition are recorded as a return on investment and reduce the cost of the investment.

Equity Method

Certain factors, such as continuing operating losses, may indicate that a substantial decline in the value of the investment has occurred. If such a decline is not temporary, it should be recognized in the accounts.

Special rules apply to the cost method when it is used to account for unconsolidated subsidiaries (see chapter on Consolidated Financial Statements).

Equity Method

Under the equity method the original investment is recorded at cost and is adjusted periodically to recognize the investor's share of earnings or losses after the date of acquisition. *Dividends received reduce the basis of the investment.* Continuing operating losses from the investment may indicate the necessity for an adjustment in the basis of the investment in excess of those recognized by the application of the equity method.

An investor's share of earnings or losses from its investment is usually shown as a *single amount* (called a *one-line consolidation*) in the income statement, after the following adjustments:

1. Intercompany profits and losses are eliminated, unless realized, in the same manner as if the investee were consolidated.
2. Any difference between the underlying equity in net assets of the investee and the cost of the investment should be accounted for on a consolidated basis. Therefore, goodwill should be amortized over a period of 40 years or less.
3. The investment should be shown in the investor's balance sheet as a single amount and earnings or losses should be shown as a single amount (one-line consolidation) in the income statement, *except for the investor's share of (a) extraordinary items and (b) prior-period adjustments, which should be shown in the income statement separately.*
4. Capital transactions of the investee that affect the investor's share of stockholders' equity should be accounted for on a consolidated basis.
5. Gain or loss is recognized when an investor sells the common stock investment, *equal to the difference between the selling price and the carrying amount of the investment at the time of sale.*
6. If the investee's financial reports are not timely enough for an investor to apply the equity method, the investor should use the most recent available financial statement, and the lag in time created should be consistent from period to period.

7. Other than temporary declines, a decrease in an investment should be recognized in the books of the investor.
8. Losses on an investment decrease the basis of the investment, which may not be reduced below zero, at which point the use of the equity method should be discontinued, unless the investor has guaranteed obligations of the investee or is committed to provide financial support. The investor should resume the equity method when the investee subsequently reports net income and the net income exceeds the investor's share of any net losses not recognized during the period of discontinuance.
9. Dividends for cumulative preferred stock of the investee must be deducted first before the investor's share of earnings or losses is computed, whether the dividend was declared or not.
10. An investor who acquires more than 20% ownership in an investee after having had less than 20% *must retroactively adjust its accounts to the equity method on the basis of a step-by-step acquisition of a subsidiary.* In this event, at the date of each step in the acquisition, the carrying value of the investment must be compared with the underlying net assets of the investee to determine whether goodwill (positive or negative) is involved.

> **OBSERVATION:** *When restating financial statements of prior periods, interest cost capitalized in accordance with FASB-58 shall not be changed. Thus, if an unconsolidated investee is subsequently consolidated in the investor's financial statements as a result of increased ownership or a voluntary change by the reporting entity, interest costs capitalized in accordance with FASB-58 shall not be changed if restatement of financial statements is necessary. For further discussion of the capitalization of interest costs on equity funds, loans, and advances made by an investor to an investee accounted for by the equity method, see chapter on "Interest Costs Capitalized."*

11. If an investment in voting stock falls below the 20% level, the presumption is that the investor has lost the ability to exercise significant influence and control, in which case the equity method should be discontinued. The carrying amount at the date of discontinuance becomes the cost of the investment. Subsequent dividends are accounted for by the cost method from the date the equity method was discontinued.
12. An investor's share of earnings or losses from an investment accounted for by the equity method is based on the outstand-

ing shares of the investee without regard to common stock equivalents (APB-15).
13. The equity method should not be used for investments of a temporary nature, for foreign investments subject to controls and restrictions, and for those investments that are dissimilar and for which separate, supplemental information would be more meaningful.

   OBSERVATION: This criterion is the same as that used for consolidated financial statements.

   OBSERVATION: It is interesting to note that the cost method and the equity method are both bookkeeping and reporting methods. For example, a company may account for an investment by the cost method and prepare financial statements on the equity method. On the other hand, consolidation would more likely be classified as a reporting method. The amount of detail reported in the financial statements is the main difference between the equity method and consolidation.

Disclosure

Full disclosure must be made for investments accounted for by the equity method and should include:

1. The name of the investment
2. The percentage of ownership
3. The accounting policies of the investor in accounting for the investment
4. The difference between the carrying value of the investment and the underlying equity in the net assets, and the accounting treatment of such difference
5. The quoted market price of the investment, except if it is a subsidiary
6. If material, a summary of the assets, liabilities, and results of operations presented as a footnote or as separate statements
7. The material effect on the investor of any convertible securities of the investee

If the equity method is not used for an investment of 20% or more, disclosure should be made of the name of the investment and reason(s) why the equity method was not used. Conversely, if the equity method is used for an investment of less than 20%, disclosure should be made of the name of the investment and reason(s) why the equity method was used.

In evaluating the extent of disclosure, the investor must weigh the significance of the investment in relation to its financial position and results of operations.

Unincorporated Real Estate Ventures

The thrust of Statement of Position 78-9 is to extend the provisions of APB-18 (Equity Method) to unincorporated real estate ventures. Thus, if an investor includes an investment in a real estate venture in its financial statements prepared in conformity with GAAP, the real estate venture should generally be accounted for in accordance with APB-18. Regulated investment companies and other enterprises that must account for their investments at quoted market value or fair value are not required to comply with SOP 78-9.

The promulgated GAAP on the equity method of accounting (APB-18) applies only to investments held in the form of common stock. APB-18 does not cover investments in unincorporated businesses such as general partnerships, limited partnerships and investments held as undivided interests. In November 1971, an AICPA staff interpretation of APB-18 concluded that many aspects of the equity method were, in fact, quite appropriate in accounting for investments in certain unincorporated entities.

The preferable accounting principles expressed in SOP 78-9 confirm that unincorporated investments in noncontrolled real estate ventures should, as a general rule, be accounted for and reported under the equity method. The exposure to joint and several liability and the special income tax considerations of nonincorporated joint ventures are the principal differences cited by SOP 78-9 between corporate joint ventures and nonincorporated joint ventures. Some of the special problems which may arise in applying the equity method to unincorporated real estate ventures which are not controlled are covered by SOP 78-9 and are discussed below.

Many unincorporated joint ventures are not taxable entities for income tax purposes and the tax liability is usually passed on to the individual partners or investors. In this event, the timing difference, if any, is the difference between income or loss recorded by a partner or investor using the equity method and the partner's or investor's share of distributable taxable income or loss reported by the unincorporated joint venture.

As mentioned previously the equity method is used in those situations where the partner or investor can exercise significant

Equity Method

influence over the operating and financial policies of the unincorporated investee, which is presumed to occur when the investment is 20% or more of the investee. However, in those situations where an investor, directly or indirectly, controls (usually 50% or more) an investee, a parent-subsidiary relationship exists and consolidated financial statements are usually required instead of the equity method. On the other hand, a limited partner's interest may be so insignificant that little, if any, influence can be exerted over the operating and financial policies of the limited partnership. When this, or a similar situation exists, it may be appropriate for the limited partner or investor to account for its investment by the cost method.

A general partner of a limited partnership should not use the equity method to account for its investment, if the limited partnership agreement provides for control of the partnership by the general partners. On the other hand, a limited partner may be in control, if it holds over 50% interest in the limited partnership.

The equity method should be used in accounting for undivided interests in real estate ventures provided that some level of joint control exists between the owners. Some level of joint control is usually present in most real estate ventures owned by undivided interests. Joint control exists where the approval of two or more owners is required to finance, develop, operate or sell the real property. An undivided interest in the assets, liabilities, revenue and expenses of a real estate venture may be present if joint control does not exist and each undivided interest is liable only for indebtedness it incurs, is entitled only to its pro-rata share of income, and is liable only for its pro-rata share of expenses.

Accounting for losses Losses in excess of amounts invested, including loans and advances, should be recorded by partners or investors in real estate ventures in which they are jointly and severally liable. Such excess losses should be reported as a liability on the balance sheet of the partner or investor.

Sometimes a partner or investor is unable to bear its share of losses in a real estate venture and the other partners or investors may become liable. Accounting for this type of loss by a partner or investor is governed by the promulgated GAAP on contingencies (FASB-5). Therefore, if it is probable that a partner or investor in a real estate venture will have to bear a proportionate share of another partner's or investor's losses, the loss should be recorded. However, the partner or investor who is unable to bear the loss should still continue to record the losses on its books until the liability for payment has been terminated by agreement or operation of law.

Purchased goodwill The excess of cost of a real estate investment over the fair value of the underlying net assets (tangible and intangible) should be recorded as goodwill. Purchased goodwill should be amortized by systematic charges to income over the period to be benefited, but not to exceed 40 years (APB-17).

Capital transactions with a real estate venture The amount of cash contributed by a partner or investor for the formation of a real estate venture should be recorded as an investment provided that all partners or investors contribute cash. A partner or investor who contributes real estate as a capital investment in a real estate venture should record as its investment the carrying cost of the real estate contributed. No profit should be recognized on a transaction that is, in economic substance, a capital contribution to a real estate venture.

Under all circumstances, a partner or investor who sells real estate to a real estate venture must comply with all of the applicable provisions of the industry accounting guide entitled "Accounting for Profit Recognition on Sales of Real Estate."

In the event a partner or investor contributes real estate to a real estate venture as a capital contribution and simultaneously receives a sum of cash from the venture which does not have to be reinvested back into the venture, the transaction is in substance an exchange to the extent of the amount of cash received. Thus, a partner or investor should recognize a profit on the amount of cash received.

The carrying amount of real estate contributed as capital by a partner or investor may exceed the proportionate amount of interest received in the venture compared to cash contributions by other partners or investors. In this event, the partner or investor contributing the real estate should recognize a loss on the transaction to the extent that a cash contribution for the same interest in the venture exceeds the carrying amount of the real estate.

Services or intangibles contributed to a real estate venture by a partner or investor should be accounted for in the same manner as that of a wholly-owned investment.

Interest income on partners' or investors' loans and advances to a real estate venture should be deferred if one of the following conditions exists:

1. The collectibility of the principal amount of the loans and advances or any remaining interest payments is in doubt.

Equity Method

2. The other partners or investors in the real estate venture are not reasonably expected to bear their share of present or future losses.

The entire amount of interest income accrued on loans and advances to a real estate venture should be recorded as earned if both of the above conditions do not exist but a third condition exists as follows:

3. The partner or investor has recorded its proportionate share of income or loss from the venture (equity method), which included interest expense on loans and advances.

If none of the above three conditions exist, a portion of the interest income on loans and advances should be deferred. The percentage of interest income which must be deferred is equal to the partner's or investor's percentage interest in the real estate venture.

If a real estate venture capitalizes costs of services performed by a partner or investor, the partner or investor may recognize profit on the services performed, but only to the extent of outside interests in the real estate venture and if:

1. The form and substance of the transaction are basically the same
2. No significant uncertainties exist pertaining to completion of performance by the partner or investor, and to the total costs involved, and other partners or investors are reasonably expected to be able to share their portion of any present or future losses

Similarly, if a partner or investor capitalizes costs of services performed by the real estate venture, the partner's or investor's share of the venture's profit on the services performed should be recorded as a reduction of the capitalized costs.

If a real estate venture sells real estate to a partner or investor, the partner's or investor's share of the venture's profit on the sale should be recorded as a reduction of the cost of the real estate purchased and not recognized as profit.

Conclusion

The basis of recording income from investments accounted for by the cost method is dividends arising from earnings after the date of acquisition. Dividends are frequently unrelated to the earnings or losses of an investment, because some companies pay dividends in excess of earnings and sometimes when there are no earnings at all. These types of shortcomings of the cost method make it difficult to relate earnings to the proper periods.

The market value method recognizes both dividends received and changes in the market price of the investment. Dividends received are included as income from the investment, as is the increase or decrease in the market value of the investment. The carrying amount of the investment in the balance sheet is the market value of the investment on that date. Thus the market value method more clearly reports the economic substance of holding the investment.

The promulgated GAAP requires that the equity method be used for domestic and foreign unconsolidated subsidiaries and noncontrolled investments in voting common stock. The equity method is used in those situations where the investor can exercise significant influence over the investee, which is presumed to occur when the investment is 20% or more of the investee. Under the equity method, dividends are credited to the investment account and are not considered income, and after all the necessary eliminating entries are made, the investor periodically records its share of the investee's net income as a debit to the investment account and a credit to income from the investment. The eliminating entries are the same as would be made for consolidated financial statements, including amortization of goodwill, if necessary. The equity method is usually called "one-line consolidation," because the investment is shown in the balance sheet as one amount and the income is likewise shown in the income statement, except for the extraordinary items and prior period adjustments. Gain or loss on investment accounted for by the equity method is the difference between the sales price and the carrying value of the investment on the date of sale. If a decline of the value of an investment accounted for under the equity method is other than temporary, it is recorded as a loss in the period it occurs.

The basic difference between consolidation and the equity method is the amount of detail reported in the financial statements.

Comprehensive Illustration

Cost method The original investment is recorded at cost in an investment account. Additions to, or returns of, the original investment are also recorded at cost in the investment account. Dividends received out of accumulated earnings prior to acquisition are recorded as a return of investment. *All other dividends are recorded as dividend income.*

Equity Method

The recording of dividends as dividend income is the major difference between the cost and the equity methods.

Equity method This method is exactly the same as the cost method except:

1. Dividends received are credited to the investment account and are not considered income.
2. The investor periodically records its share of the investee's net income by a debit to the investment account and a credit to income from subsidiary. Goodwill is amortized over a period of 40 years or less.

On December 31, 19X1, LKM Corporation acquired a 90% interest in Nerox Company for $700,000. Total stockholders' equity on the date of acquisition consisted of capital stock (common $1 par) of $500,000 and retained earnings of $250,000. During 19X2, Nerox Company had net income of $90,000 and paid a $40,000 dividend.

Cost method:

Investment in Nerox (90%)	$700,000	
Cash		$700,000
Cash	$ 36,000	
Dividend income		$ 36,000

On December 31, 19X2, the investment account on the balance sheet would show $700,000 and the income statement would show $36,000 dividend income.

Equity method:

Investment in Nerox (90%)	$700,000	
Cash		$700,000
Cash	$ 36,000	
Investment in Nerox (90%)		$ 36,000
Investment in Nerox (90%)	$ 81,000	$ 625
Net income from 90% subsidiary	625	81,000

The debit of $81,000 to the investment account represents 90% of the $90,000 of net income for Nerox Company for 19X2. The credit of $625 to the investment account represents amortization of goodwill of $25,000 which is assumed to be amortized over the maximum period of 40 years ($700,000 purchase price less 90% of $750,000 ($675,000) book value = $25,000 goodwill).

On December 31, 19X2, the investment account on the balance sheet would show $744,375 ($700,000 + $81,000 − $625 − $36,000), and the income statement would show $80,375 net income from 90% subsidiary.

The basic difference between the cost and equity methods of accounting for a stock investment is that the cost method records dividends as dividend income and the equity method does not record dividend income, but does record as income the proportionate share of the investee's net income.

Converting from Cost Method to Equity Method

Under the cost method the investment account is debited only with the cost of the stock acquired. Dividends received on the stock acquired are credited to dividend income and are reported in net income for the period. An exception occurs when dividends are received out of accumulated earnings prior to the date of the acquisition of the investment, which are recorded as a reduction of the investment and not as dividend income. Under the equity method the investment account changes to reflect the book value that the stock acquired actually represents. The difference between the two methods will always be the actual book value that the stock acquired represents less any dividends received that were reported as dividend income.

P acquires a 30% stock interest in S for $45,000. Stockholders' equity of S at the date of acquisition consisted of $100,000 of capital stock and retained earnings of $50,000 for a total of $150,000. During the year, S had net income of $30,000 and paid to P a dividend of $3,000 out of current earnings.

Cost method:

P will record in an investment account its investment in S of $45,000 and will report the $3,000 dividend as dividend income in determining its net income for the year. P's investment account at

Equity Method

the end of the year will still show a balance of $45,000, the original investment.

Equity method:

P will record as income 30% of the $30,000, or $9,000, as its share of the net income of S for the year, as follows:

Investment in S	$9,000	
Subsidiary income		$9,000

When the $3,000 dividend was received during the year, the entry was:

Cash	$3,000	
Investment in S		$3,000

P's investment in S at the end of the year was $51,000, as follows:

Original investment	$45,000
Add 30% of S's net income	9,000
Total	$54,000
Less: Dividend received	3,000
Investment at end of year	$51,000

The $51,000 investment at the end of the year should exactly agree with P's 30% interest in S at the end of the year, as follows:

Stockholders' equity, beginning of year	$150,000
Add net income for year	30,000
Total	$180,000
Less: Dividend paid (P received $3,000, which represents 30%; thus 100% = $10,000)	10,000
Stockholders' equity, end of year	$170,000
P's investment of 30% of $170,000	$ 51,000

EXTINGUISHMENT OF DEBT

Background

The following current promulgated GAAP that address the extinguishment of debt are discussed in this chapter:

>APB-26 – Early Extinguishment of Debt
>FASB-4 – Reporting Gains and Losses from the Extinguishment of Debt
>FASB-64 – Extinguishment of Debt Made to Satisfy Sinking Fund Requirements
>FASB-76 – Extinguishment of Debt
>Technical Bulletin 80-1 – Early Extinguishment of Debt Through Exchange for Common or Preferred Stock
>Technical Bulletin 84-4 – In-Substance Defeasance of Debt

APB-26 covers the extinguishment of all debt, whether early or not, except debt that is extinguished through a troubled debt restructuring (FASB-15), and convertible debt that is converted to equity securities of the debtor, which is covered by FASB-84 (see chapter entitled "Convertible Debt"). The classification of gain or loss on the extinguishment of debt is covered by FASB-4, which has been amended by FASB-64.

FASB-76 amends APB-26, to specify the criteria which shall be applied by a debtor in determining when an extinguishment of debt has occurred for the purposes of recognizing gain or loss on the extinguishment of debt. Under the provisions of FASB-76, certain in-substance defeasance transactions that were accounted for as extinguishments of debt under SOP 78-5 (Accounting for Advance Refundings of Tax-Exempt Debt) continue to be accounted for in the same manner.

FASB Technical Bulletin 80-1 deals with the issuance of equity securities in exchange for the extinguishment of debt.

FASB Technical Bulletin 84-4 provides guidance in the application of those provisions of FASB-76 (Extinguishment of Debt) that relate to (a) an instantaneous in-substance defeasance, (b) addressing remoteness of risk of trust assets, and (c) an in-substance defeasance of callable debt.

Overview

An extinguishment of debt is the reacquisition of debt prior to or at the maturity date of the debt. Gain or loss on the extinguishment of debt is the difference between the total reacquisition cost of the debt and the net carrying amount of the debt on the date of the extinguishment.

Most debt ageements issued in recent years contain a *call provision* and a *defeasance provision*. A call provision grants the issuer (debtor) the right to "call in" part or all of a debt before its scheduled maturity date, usually in exchange for a premium price. A defeasance provision allows the issuer to legally satisfy the debt and obtain a release of lien without necessarily retiring the debt. Thus, in a defeasance transaction the old debt is legally satisfied which results in the culmination of the earning process and recognition of gain or loss. In a nondefeasance transaction, there is no satisfaction of the old debt, no culmination of the earning process, and no gain or loss is recognized. However, under certain conditions a nondefeasance transaction may be accounted for as an in-substance defeasance, in which gain or loss is recognized, but the old debt is not legally satisfied. In an in-substance defeasance transaction, assets are deposited in a trust account for the sole purpose of paying the interest and principal on the outstanding debt as they become due, but the debt is not legally satisfied.

Accounting for Advance Refundings of Tax-Exempt Debt (SOP 78-5) was issued in 1978 by the AICPA to provide guidance in accounting for advance refundings of tax-exempt debt. When a defeasance transaction occurred in the advance refunding of tax-exempt debt, SOP 78-5 provided that the debtor had extinguished the debt and gain or loss on the extinguishment should be recognized. When a nondefeasance transaction occurred in the advance refunding of tax-exempt debt, SOP 78-5 provided that the debtor had not legally satisfied the debt and no gain or loss could be recognized. In addition, if certain conditions were met, a nondefeasance transaction could be accounted for as an in-substance defeasance transaction, in which gain or loss was recognized, even though the old debt was not legally satisfied.

When a refunding is desired because of lower interest rates or some other reason, the old debt issue may not be callable for several years. This is the usual circumstance for an advance refunding. In an advance refunding, a new debt issue is sold to replace the old debt issue that cannot be called. The proceeds from the sale of the new debt issue are used to purchase high grade investments which are placed in an escrow account. The earnings from the investments in the escrow account are used to pay the interest and/or principal payments on the existing debt, up to the date that the existing debt can be called. On the call date of the existing debt, whatever remains in the escrow account is used to pay the call premium, if any, and all remaining principal and interest due on the existing debt.

In a well-publicized transaction early in 1982, Exxon Corporation purchased enough U.S. government securities to generate a cash flow sufficient to pay, on a timely basis, the interest and principal on six outstanding Exxon debt issues. Exxon deposited the U.S. government securities in an irrevocable trust that was created for the sole purpose of paying the principal and interest on the six debt issues. Exxon removed the debt issues and the government securities from its balance sheet and reported an after-tax gain of $132 million from this "in-substance defeasance" of its debt. The gain on the extinguishment of debt was reported on Exxon's financial statements for calendar year 1982, accompanied by an unqualified report from Price Waterhouse dated February 28, 1983.

In its "Action Alert" dated August 11, 1982, the Financial Accounting Standards Board (FASB) temporarily prohibited the recognition of an extinguishment of debt, unless the debtor had no further legal obligation with respect to the debt. At the same time, the FASB announced its intention of looking into the possibility of relaxing this standard, so as to allow the extinguishment of debt in some special circumstances where the debtor remains liable on the debt. The FASB noted that SOP 78-5 (Advance Refundings of Tax-Exempt Debt) allowed the extinguishment of debt with regard to tax-exempt debt in some circumstances where the debtor remained liable.

In November 1983, the FASB issued Statement No. 76 (Extinguishment of Debt), resulting from the study which had been announced at the time of the 1982 "Action Alert." FASB-76 allowed the extinguishment of debt and the resulting recognition of gain or loss in some situations where the debtor remains liable, and this applied not only to the tax-exempt debt covered by SOP 78-5, but to all types of debt, whether taxable or tax-exempt. In order to qualify under FASB-76, the debtor must irrevocably place cash or other essentially risk-free monetary assets in a trust, solely for the purpose of satisfying the interest and principal payments on the debt. In addition, the possibility that the debtor will be required to make further payments must be remote. (A full discussion of FASB-76 follows.)

Questions arose in 1984, as to whether FASB-76 allows extinguishment of debt by an "instantaneous" type of in-substance defeasance, in which an enterprise borrows at one interest rate and at the same time invests in other securities that yield a higher interest rate. The "instantaneous" nature of this type of transaction distinguishes it from the Exxon type of defeasance, in which Exxon purchased new securities to be placed in trust for the payment of pre-existing Exxon debt. The proposed "instantaneous" in-substance defeasance transaction was for an enterprise to borrow by issuing zero coupon bonds in European bond markets, and at about the same time, to purchase U.S. Treasury bonds yielding a higher rate of interest. The U.S. Treasury bonds would be placed in an irrevocable trust created for the sole purpose of paying the zero coupon bonds. Finally, the U.S. Treasury bonds and the zero coupon bonds would be removed from the balance sheet and the gain on the extinguishment of debt would be reported in the enterprise's financial statements.

This type of "instantaneous" in-substance defeasance clearly conforms to the literal provisions of FASB-76. The FASB determined, however, that this "instantaneous" in-substance defeasance does not conform to the spirit of FASB-76. The result was FASB Technical Bulletin 84-4, issued on October 17, 1984, with earlier application encouraged for transactions in fiscal years for which annual financial statements have not previously been issued. In essence, Technical Bulletin 84-4 amends FASB-76, by prohibiting an in-substance defeasance if the assets that the debtor places in trust were acquired "at about the time" that the debt was incurred, or were acquired as part of a series of investment activities that were initiated "at about the time" that the debt was incurred.

Accounting for Extinguishments of Debt

Under APB-26 (Early Extinguishment of Debt), all extinguishments of debt prior to maturity are basically alike, and accounting for such transactions should be the same, regardless of the method used to achieve the extinguishment. Therefore, there should be no difference in accounting for an extinguishment of debt by (a) cash purchase, (b) exchange of stock for debt, (c) exchange of debt for debt, or (d) any other method.

Gain or loss on the extinguishment of debt is the difference between the reacquisition price and the net carrying amount of the debt on the date of the extinguishment.

Reacquisition price The amount paid for the extinguishment. Includes call premium and any other costs of reacquiring the portion of the debt which is being extinguished.

Net carrying amount The amount due at the maturity of the debt, adjusted for any unamortized premium or discount and any other costs of issuance (legal, accounting, underwriter's fees, etc.).

Note: When extinguishment is achieved through the exchange of securities, the reacquisition price is the total present value of the new securities being issued.

> **OBSERVATION:** *FASB Technical Bulletin 80-1 defines the term "stock" as any class of equity security, including redeemable and/ or fixed maturity preferred stock. In addition, the Technical Bulletin requires that the gain or loss be based on either the value of the stock issued in exchange or the value of the debt that is being extinguished, whichever is more clearly evident.*

When Debt Is Extinguished

Under the provisions of FASB-76, debt shall be considered extinguished for financial reporting purposes in the following circumstances:

1. On the date the debtor pays the debt to the creditor or on the date the debtor reacquires the debt in the public securities market.
2. On the date the debtor is *legally* released as the primary obligor under the debt and it is *probable* that the debtor will not be required to make future payments as guarantor of the debt. Under this provision of FASB-76, it makes no difference whether the creditor has been paid in full or not.

   Note: This provision of FASB-76 covers those situations where a debtor is legally released as the *primary obligor* on a debt and at the same time agrees to remain secondarily liable on the same debt.

   > **OBSERVATION:** *Direct and indirect guarantees of indebtedness of others, even if they have a remote possibility of materializing, must be disclosed in accordance with FASB-5 (Contingencies). Thus, any situation in which the debtor is released as the primary obligor under a debt, but remains contingently liable as a guarantor under the debt, must be appropriately disclosed in the financial statements of the debtor in accordance with FASB-5.*

3. On the date the debtor places cash or certain other assets (see below) in an irrevocable trust for the sole purpose of servicing

the interest and principal payments of debt with specified maturities and fixed schedule payments, and there is only a *remote* possibility that the debtor will be required to make any other future payments on the debt. In this circumstance, *remote* means that it is *unlikely* that the debtor will have to make any future payments on the debt.

This provision of FASB-76 covers "in-substance" defeasance transactions, which were previously covered by the AICPA Statement of Position 78-5. Under this provision of FASB-76, it makes no difference whether the debtor is or is not legally released as primary obligor on the debt.

Only debt with specified maturities and fixed payment schedules can be extinguished under this provision of FASB-76. Debt cannot be extinguished under this provision of FASB-76 unless the debt service requirements can be determined in advance. Thus, debt with variable terms, such as floating interest rates, does not qualify for this type of extinguishment.

Convertible debt cannot be extinguished under the in-substance defeasance provision of FASB-76 because the debt and the conversion option are inseparable, and because there will be no obligation to pay if the debentures are converted.

FASB Technical Bulletin 84-4 provides that callable debt may be extinguished under the in-substance defeasance provisions of FASB-76, provided that there is only a *remote* possibility that the debtor will exercise the call option. In the event the debtor does plan to exercise the call option at a specific future date, the debtor must irrevocably revise the maturity date of the debt to coincide with the intended call date of the debt. In this event, the cash flow from the assets in the irrevocable trust must be structured to approximately coincide, in timing and amount, with the revised scheduled interest and principal payments of the debt.

FASB Technical Bulletin 84-4 takes the position that most of the criteria for the extinguishment of debt are clearly specified in FASB-76, and any deviation from the specified criteria is not permitted. The Technical Bulletin suggests that a debtor use its judgment in those areas not specifically covered by FASB-76.

Based on the issuance of FASB-76, the SEC issued Financial Reporting Release No. 15, containing the following additional clarifications of certain provisions of FASB-76, which SEC reporting companies should observe:

a. an appropriate trustee is one that meets the eligibility requirements of the Trust Indenture Act of 1939 [Sections 310(a)(1) and 310(a)(2)]

b. an irrevocable trust is defined as a trust ". . . designed so that neither the corporation nor its creditors or others can rescind or revoke it, or obtain access to the assets"
c. an assessment is required to determine the likelihood of the debtor's being required to make future payments with respect to the debt, not only because of an inadequacy of trust assets, but also because of an acceleration of the debt's maturity as a result of a violation of a covenant of the debt issue or under cross-default provisions, or a violation of a covenant of another debt issue

Instantaneous in-substance defeasance is prohibited The use of an in-substance defeasance to extinguish debt in accordance with the provisions of FASB-76 is prohibited by FASB Technical Bulletin 84-4 under any of the following circumstances:

a. The assets that a debtor places in an irrevocable trust to consummate an in-substance defeasance of debt are acquired "at about the time that the debt is incurred."
b. The assets that a debtor places in an irrevocable trust to consummate an in-substance defeasance of debt are acquired as part of a series of investment activities that are initiated "at about the time that the debt is incurred." A series of investment activities includes the purchase of assets or entering into a purchase agreement or futures contract "at about the time that the debt is incurred."
c. The assets that a debtor places in an irrevocable trust to consummate an in-substance defeasance of debt are acquired "at about the time that the debt is incurred" pursuant to a forward contract.

> Note: FASB Technical Bulletin 84-4 refers to each of the above transactions as an "instantaneous in-substance defeasance."

According to FASB Technical Bulletin 84-4, an "instantaneous" type of defeasance of debt is considered a "borrow-and-invest activity," which, in effect, hedges the debtor against the risk of changes in interest rates. Furthermore, the gain or loss on a borrow-and-invest activity reflects principally the difference in interest rates that existed in different markets on the same date that the debt was issued, while the gain or loss on previously outstanding debt reflects the difference between the interest rate that existed on the date the debt was issued and the interest rate that existed on the date that the debt was extinguished.

> **OBSERVATION:** *The key term in FASB Technical Bulletin 84-4 is "at about the time the debt is incurred." However, the Technical Bulletin gives absolutely no indication as to what this term means.*

Allowable trust assets   Only monetary assets that are essentially risk free as to the collection of interest and principal may be placed in an irrevocable trust for the payment of the debt that is being extinguished. The monetary assets must be denominated in the same currency in which the debt is payable. Essentially risk-free monetary assets that are denominated in U.S. currency shall be limited to the following:

1. Direct obligations of the U.S. government.
2. Obligations that are guaranteed by the U.S. government.
3. Securities that are backed by U.S. government obligations under a collateral arrangement which provides that in the event of a default, interest and principal on the collateral flow immediately through to the holder of the security.

Timing and amount of trust assets   The maturity dates of the essentially risk-free monetary assets that are placed in the irrevocable trust must approximately coincide, in timing and amount, with the scheduled interest and principal payments on the debt that is being extinguished. In other words, the monetary assets held by the irrevocable trust must provide sufficient cash flow to approximately coincide with the timing and amount of the scheduled interest and principal payments on the debt that is being extinguished.

> **OBSERVATION:** *Under FASB-76, if a monetary asset can be paid before its scheduled maturity date, it is not essentially risk free as to the timing of the collection of its interest and principal and therefore cannot be owned by the irrevocable trust.*

Costs of administrating trust   Earnings from reinvesting trust assets and the expected costs of administrating the irrevocable trust, such as trustee fees and related costs, shall be considered in computing the total amount of essentially risk-free monetary assets which will be required by the trust to pay the expected administration costs and to satisfy, in a timely manner, all scheduled interest and principal payments of the debt being extinguished.

Any obligation for trustee fees, taxes on trust income, and other trust expenses that are incurred directly by the debtor shall be accrued in the period in which the debt is recognized as extinguished.

Partial in-substance defeasance transactions   Although in-substance defeasance transactions usually involve the entire debt issue, partial in-substance defeasance transactions are permitted by FASB-76. In this event, the amount of debt which is recognized as extinguished is either (a) a pro rata portion of all remaining interest and principal payments on the debt issue or (b) the principal and interest payments for a specific debt instrument with a specified scheduled maturity (paragraph 36 of FASB-76). Thus, a partial in-substance defeasance consisting only of interest payments or only of principal payments cannot be recognized by a debtor.

Disclosures for irrevocable trust   If a debtor places assets that are essentially risk free in an irrevocable trust to extinguish a specific debt in accordance with FASB-76, the debtor shall disclose the following information in its financial statements for as long as the specific debt remains outstanding:

1. A general description of the transaction.
2. The total amount outstanding at the end of the period.
3. The total amount that is considered extinguished at the end of the period.

FASB-76 is effective for extinguishments of debt that occur on or after January 1, 1984. The provisions of FASB-76 may be retroactively applied to previously *issued* annual financial statements, and earlier application of FASB-76 is encouraged in *unissued* annual financial statements.

Gain or Loss

The gain or loss on the extinguishment of debt is recognized immediately, in the year of extinguishment, and, if material, is reported as an extraordinary item, net of related tax effects (FASB-4). However, certain gains or losses on extinguishment of debt are not classified as extraordinary items. Under the provisions of FASB-64, gains or losses from the extinguishment of debt made within one year to meet sinking fund requirements shall not be classified as extraordinary items, but shall be included in income from continuing operations. This would also apply to any debt that has the same characteristics as sinking fund requirements, such as a required annual extinguishment of a specific percentage of outstanding debt prior to its maturity. However, gains or losses from the maturation of serialized debt are classified as extraordinary items, because under FASB-4 serial debt does not have the same characteristics as debt pursuant to sinking fund requirements.

> **OBSERVATION:** *FASB-64 is effective for all extinguishments of debt made on or after October 1, 1982. FASB-64 may be applied to previously unissued annual financial statements, but retroactive application of FASB-64 to previously issued annual financial statements is not permitted.*

Appropriate accounting recognition should be given to any stated or unstated rights or privileges arising from an extinguishment of debt.

Gains or losses on the extinguishment of debt should not be amortized over future periods.

In the early extinguishment of a debt, the recorded value of the new debt should not be affected in any way by the amount of the old debt.

Refunding of Tax Exempt Debt (FASB-22)

If a change in a lease occurs as a result of a refunding by the lessor of tax-exempt debt and (1) the lessee receives the economic advantages of the refunding, (2) the revised lease qualifies and is classified either as a capital lease by the lessee or as a direct financing lease by the lessor, the change in the lease shall be accounted for on the basis of whether or not an extinguishment of debt has occurred, as follows:

1. Accounted for as an extinguishment of debt
   a. The lessee adjusts the lease obligation to the present value of the future minimum lease payments under the revised agreement, using the effective interest rate of the new lease agreement. Any gain or loss shall be treated as a gain or loss on an early extinguishment of debt.
   b. The lessor adjusts the balance of the minimum lease payments receivable and the gross investment in the lease (if affected) for the difference between the present values of the old and new or revised agreement. Any gain or loss shall be recognized in the current period.
2. Not accounted for as an extinguishment of debt
   a. The lessee accrues any costs connected with the refunding that it is obligated to reimburse to the lessor. The interest method is used to amortize the costs over the period from the date of the refunding to the call date of the debt to be refunded.

b. The lessor recognizes as revenue any reimbursements to be received from the lessee for costs paid related to the debt to be refunded over the period from the date of the refunding to the call date of the debt to be refunded.

Disclosure

Gains or losses from the early extinguishment of debt which are classified as extraordinary items should be disclosed in the financial statements or in properly cross-referenced footnotes thereto, as follows:

1. A description of the transaction, including the sources, if identifiable, of any funds used to extinguish the debt
2. The income tax effect for the period of extinguishment
3. The gain or loss per share net of any related income taxes

Comprehensive Illustration

On December 31, 1985, a corporation decides to retire $500,000 of an original issue of $1,000,000 8% debentures, which were sold on December 31, 1980, at a price of 98 and are callable at 101. The legal and other costs for issuing the debentures was $30,000. Both the original discount and the issue costs are being amortized over the 10-year life of the issue. What gain or loss is recognized on this early extinguishment of debt?

Amount of original expenses of issue	$30,000
Amount of original discount (2% of $1,000,000)	$20,000
Amount of premium paid for redemption (debentures callable at 101, 1% of $500,000)	$ 5,000
Date of issue	12/31/80
Date of maturity	12/31/90
Date of redemption	12/31/85

Interest on debentures is irrelevant.

Computation discussion If the original legal and other expenses of $30,000 are being amortized over the 10-year life of the issue and five years have elapsed since that date, one-half of these expenses have already been amortized, leaving a balance of $15,000 at the date of redemption. However, only one-half of the outstanding debentures is being retired, which leaves $7,500 to account for in the computation of gain or loss.

The original discount of $20,000 (debentures sold at 98) is handled exactly the same as the legal and other expenses. Since one-half of the discount has already been amortized, leaving a $10,000 balance at the date of redemption, and since only one-half of the issue is being redeemed, this leaves $5,000 more that must go into the computation of gain or loss.

Obviously, any time that a security is redeemed at a premium, the amount of premium must also enter into the computation of gain or loss. In this case, the premium is $5,000.

Since there is no other relevant information in the problem relating to gain or loss, the following items enter into the final computation:

Original-issue expenses relating to retired debentures	$ 7,500
Original discount relating to the retired debentures	5,000
Premium paid for redemption	5,000
Loss on redemption of $500,000 of debentures	$17,500

FINANCIAL REPORTING AND CHANGING PRICES

Background

The primary source of promulgated GAAP concerning the effects of inflation on financial reporting is FASB-33 (Financial Reporting and Changing Prices). FASB-54 was subsequently issued to exempt certain investment companies from the provisions of FASB-33. FASB-82 was issued to eliminate the historical cost/constant purchasing power disclosures that were previously required by FASB-33. In addition, four FASB Statements entitled "Financial Reporting and Changing Prices: Specialized Assets" have been issued as supplements to FASB-33, as follows:

FASB-39 – Financial Reporting and Changing Prices:
    Specialized Assets–Mining and Oil and Gas
FASB-40 – Financial Reporting and Changing Prices:
    Specialized Assets–Timberlands and Growing Timber
FASB-41 – Financial Reporting and Changing Prices:
    Specialized Assets–Income-Producing Real Estate
FASB-46 – Financial Reporting and Changing Prices:
    Motion Picture Films

FASB-70 establishes the promulgated GAAP to implement the provisions of FASB-52 (Foreign Currency Translation) with the supplementary information on changing prices that is required by FASB-33 (Financial Reporting and Changing Prices). FASB-70 affects only those enterprises that report the supplementary information required by FASB-33 and have foreign operations whose functional currency is other than the U.S. dollar.

As originally promulgated, FASB-33 required certain minimum supplementary information to be disclosed both on a historical cost/constant dollar basis and on a current cost/constant purchasing power basis. However, in November 1984, FASB-82 was promulgated, which eliminated all of the historical cost/constant dollar disclosures required by FASB-33. FASB-82 did not change the acceptability of determining the current cost amounts of certain specialized assets by adjusting the historical cost amount of such an asset by a specific price index of general purchasing power.

The following FASB Technical Bulletins relating to financial reporting and changing prices have also been issued:

79-8 – Applicability of FASB Statements 21 and 33 to Certain Brokers and Dealers in Securities
79-13 – Applicability of FASB Statement 13 to Current Value Financial Statements
81-4 – Classification as Monetary or Nonmonetary Items

Scope and Applicability of FASB-33

Certain large *publicly held enterprises* that prepare their primary financial statements in accordance with U.S. generally accepted accounting principles are required by FASB-33 to disclose specific minimum information concerning the effects of changing prices. Investment companies that meet the definition of an "investment company" as provided for in the Investment Company Act of 1940 are exempt by FASB-54 from the provisions of FASB-33. The specific minimum information required by FASB-33 must be in supplementary form accompanying the basic financial statements of an enterprise. Publicly held companies that fall into either of the following two categories, as determined at the beginning of the year for which financial statements are being presented, must comply with FASB-33:

a. *Publicly held enterprises* that have inventories, property, plant, and equipment (exclusive of any depreciation), which amount to more than $125 million. (NOTE: Except as otherwise provided, land, natural resources, and capitalized leaseholds are considered "property.")
b. *Publicly held enterprises* that have total assets of more than $1 billion (net of depreciation).

A *publicly held enterprise* is a business enterprise (a) whose debt or equity securities are traded in a public market on a domestic stock exchange or in the domestic over-the-counter market (including securities quoted only locally or regionally) or (b) that is required to file financial statements with the Securities and Exchange Commission. An enterprise is considered to be a public enterprise as soon as its financial statements are issued in preparation for the sale of any class of securities in a domestic market.

The required supplementary information must be presented for consolidated financial statements, but does not have to be presented for the individual entities which make up the consolidated group. FASB-33 does not apply to an enterprise in the year of a business combination that is accounted for as a pooling if none of the combining companies is individually required to comply with FASB-33. It is encouraged that supplementary information required by FASB-33 be presented for segments of a business enterprise, but this is not required.

The provisions of FASB-33 (as amended) need not be applied to:

1. Interim financial statements
2. Foreign publicly held enterprises whose basic financial statements are not prepared in U.S. currency
3. Certain closely held brokers and dealers in securities (Technical Bulletin 79-8)

Closely held brokers and dealers in securities are considered nonpublic entities if their financial statements which are filed with the SEC are accompanied by a request that significant portions of the statements be held in confidence (FASB Technical Bulletin 79-8). Thus, these brokers and dealers in securities are exempt from FASB-33, and are also exempt from APB-15 (Earnings per Share) and FASB-14 (Segmental Information).

Monetary Assets and Liabilities

Assets and liabilities are called *monetary items* if their amounts are fixed by contract or otherwise in terms of number of dollars. Cash, accounts and notes receivable in cash, and accounts and notes payable in cash are examples of monetary items.

Monetary items automatically gain or lose general purchasing power during inflation or deflation as a result of changes in the general price-level index. For example, a holder of a $10,000 promissory note executed 10 years ago and due today will receive exactly $10,000 today, in spite of the fact that $10,000 in cash today is worth a lot less than $10,000 in cash was worth 10 years ago.

For the purposes of FASB-33, foreign currency on hand, claims to foreign currency, foreign currency obligations, and deferred income tax items are all treated as monetary items.

Nonmonetary Assets and Liabilities

Assets and liabilities that are not monetary items are called *nonmonetary items*. Inventories, investments in common stocks, property, plant, equipment, and deferred charges are examples of nonmonetary items. Holders of nonmonetary items may lose or gain with the rise or fall of the general price-level index if the nonmonetary items do not rise or fall in proportion to the change in the price-level index. In other words, a nonmonetary asset or liability is affected (1) by the rise or fall of the general price-level index and (2) by the increase or decrease of the fair value of the nonmonetary item. For example, the purchaser of 10,000 shares of General Motors common stock 10 years ago was subject (1) to the decrease in purchasing power and (2) to the rise in the fair value of his stock. If the decrease in purchasing power exactly offsets the increase in the price of the stock, the purchaser is, in effect, in the same position today as he was 10 years ago (that is, monetarily).

Net Monetary Position

The difference between monetary assets and monetary liabilities, at any specific date, is the net monetary position. The net monetary position may be either positive (monetary assets exceed monetary liabilities) or negative (monetary liabilities exceed monetary assets).

In periods in which the general price-level index is rising (inflation), it is advantageous for a business to maintain a net negative monetary position. The opposite is true during periods in which the general price-level index is falling (deflation). In periods of inflation, a business which has a net negative monetary position will experience general price-level gains, because it can pay its liabilities in a fixed number of dollars that are getting cheaper as time goes by. A net positive monetary position during periods of inflation results in a general price-level loss, because the value of the dollar is declining.

Some assets and liabilities have characteristics of both monetary and nonmonetary items. Convertible debt, for example, is monetary in terms of its fixed obligation, but nonmonetary in terms of its conversion feature.

The determination of whether an item is monetary or nonmonetary is made as at the balance sheet date. Therefore, if convertible debt has not been converted as of that date, it should be classified as a monetary item. Additionally, a bond receivable held for speculation would be classified as nonmonetary, because the amount that will be received when the bond is sold is no longer fixed in amount, as it would be if the same bond was held to maturity.

The following table reflects the monetary-nonmonetary classification of most assets and liabilities:

	Monetary	Nonmonetary
Cash (in most forms)	X	
Accounts and notes receivable	X	
Allowances for receivables	X	
Inventories		X
Inventories–under fixed contract price	X	
Employee loans	X	
Prepaid expenses	X	
Advances to subsidiaries	X	
Fixed assets		X
Accumulated depreciation		X
Cash surrender value of life insurance	X	
Intangible assets		X
Accounts and notes payable	X	
Accrued expenses	X	
Accrued losses on firm commitments	X	
Refundable deposits	X	
Taxes payable	X	
Most long-term liabilities	X	
Unamortized premium or discount on long-term liabilities	X	
Obligations under warranties		X
Deferred income tax credits	X	
Deferred investment tax credits		X
Capital stock (common)		X
Retained earnings		X
Minority interest		X

Current Cost Accounting

Current cost accounting is a method of measuring and reporting the use or sale of assets and expenses at their current cost or lower recoverable amount at the balance sheet date or at the date of their use or sale. Current cost/constant purchasing power accounting is a method of accounting based on measures of current cost or lower recoverable amounts in units of currency that each have the same general purchasing power. For business operations in which the U.S. dollar is the functional currency, the general purchasing power of the dollar is used. For business operations in which the functional currency is other than the U.S. dollar, the general purchasing power of either (a) the dollar or (b) the functional currency is used (see FASB-52, Foreign Currency Translation).

A publicly held enterprise that is subject to the provisions of FASB-33 must disclose, as supplementary information to its basic financial statements, certain selected financial data. An enterprise may elect to disclose the minimum supplementary information required by FASB-33, or alternatively may present comprehensive current cost/constant purchasing power financial statements. If an enterprise elects to disclose the minimum information required by FASB-33, the disclosures must be presented in average-for-the-year units of constant purchasing power. If an enterprise elects to disclose comprehensive current cost/constant purchasing power financial statements, the disclosures may be presented in either average-for-the-year or end-of-year units of constant purchasing power.

Determining Current Costs

Current cost is the current cost to purchase or reproduce a specific asset. Current reproduction cost must contain an allocation for current overhead costs (direct costing not permitted).

The current cost of inventory owned by an enterprise is the current cost to purchase or reproduce that specific inventory. The current cost of property, plant, and equipment owned by an enterprise is the current cost of acquiring an asset that will perform or produce in a manner similar to the owned asset.

An enterprise may obtain its current cost information internally or externally, including independent appraisals, and may apply the information to a single item or to groups of items. An enterprise is expected to select the types of current cost information that are most appropriate for its particular circumstances. FASB-33 lists the following types and sources of current cost information that an enterprise may utilize:

1. Current invoice prices
2. Vendor firms' price lists, quotations, or estimates
3. Standard manufacturing costs which reflect current costs
4. Unit pricing, which is a method of determining current cost for assets, such as buildings, by applying a unit price per square foot of space to the total square footage in the building
5. Revision of historical cost by the use of:
    (i) Externally generated price indexes for the services or goods being restated

(ii) Internally generated indexes for the services or goods being restated (NOTE: This method is sometimes referred to as indexation.)

Depreciation methods   Depreciation methods, useful lives, and salvage value should be the same for current cost purposes as those used for historical cost purposes. If historical cost computations already include an allowance for changing prices, then a different method may be used for current cost purposes. However, any material differences must be disclosed in the explanatory notes to the supplementary information.

Recoverable amounts   Recoverable amounts are reductions that represent additional write-downs during a current period, from the current cost amount to an amount that is considered recoverable. These reductions reflect a permanent decline in the value of the inventory or property, plant, and equipment. Recoverable amounts may be determined by reference to net realizable values or values in use.

Net realizable value   Net realizable value is the expected amount of net cash or other net equivalent to be received from the sale of an asset in the regular course of business. Net realizable value may be used only if the specific asset is about to be sold.

Value in use   Value in use is the total net present value of all future cash inflows which are expected to be received from the use of an asset. Value in use may be used only if there are no immediate intentions to sell or otherwise dispose of the asset. Value in use shall be estimated by taking into consideration an appropriate discount rate that includes an allowance for the risk involved in the circumstances.

Income tax expense   Income tax expense and the provision for deferred taxes, if any, are not restated in terms of current cost and are presented in the supplementary information at their historical cost. Disclosure must be made in the supplementary information to the effect that income tax expense for the current period is presented at its historical cost.

Minimum Supplementary Information

Under FASB-33, an enterprise must disclose certain minimum supplementary information for each of its five most recent years (Five-

Year Summary of Selected Financial Data). In addition, if income from continuing operations as shown in the primary financial statements differs significantly from income from continuing operations determined on a current cost/constant purchasing power basis, certain additional disclosures relating to the components of income from continuing operations for the current year must also be disclosed.

The minimum supplementary information required by FASB-33 must be disclosed in average-for-the-year units of constant purchasing power. The Consumer Price Index for All Urban Consumers (CPI-U) must be used to restate the current cost of an item into average-for-the-year units of constant purchasing power. An enterprise must disclose the following minimum supplementary information for the five most recent years:

- Net sales and other operating revenue
- Income from continuing operations on a current cost basis
- Purchasing power gain or loss on net monetary items
- Increase or decrease in the current cost or lower recoverable amount of inventory and property, plant, and equipment, net of inflation
- Aggregate foreign currency translation adjustment on a current cost basis, if applicable
- Net assets at the end of the year on a current cost basis
- Income per common share from continuing operations on a current cost basis
- Cash dividends declared per common share
- Market price per common share at year-end
- The average level of the Consumer Price Index for All Urban Consumers (CPI-U)

Each of the above disclosures that are included in the five-year summary of selected financial data is discussed below.

Net sales and other operating revenue Net sales and other operating revenue for each of the five most recent years is restated, by the use of the CPI-U, into average-for-the-year units of constant purchasing power.

Income from continuing operations on a current cost basis Income from continuing operations on a current cost basis for each of the five most recent years is computed in accordance with FASB-33 and then restated by the use of the CPI-U into average-for-the-year units of constant purchasing power. For purposes of the minimum supplementary information, only certain items that are included in income from continuing operations in the primary financial statements have to be adjusted to compute income from continuing operations on a current cost basis. Under FASB-33, the following items must be adjusted to compute income from continuing operations on a current cost basis:

   a. *Cost of goods sold* must be determined on a current cost basis or lower recoverable amount at the date of sale or at the date on which resources are used on or committed to a specific contract.
   b. *Depreciation, depletion, and amortization* must be determined on the basis of the average current cost of the assets' service potential or lower recoverable amount during the period of use.
   c. *Gain or loss on the sale, retirement, or write-down of inventory, property, plant, and equipment* is equal to the difference between the value of the consideration received or the written-down amount and the current cost or lower recoverable amount of the item prior to its sale, retirement, or write-down.

All other revenue, expenses, gains and losses that are included in the primary financial statements are not adjusted in computing income from continuing operations on a current cost basis. Thus, the amounts for these items included in income from continuing operations on a current cost basis are the same amounts that appear in the primary financial statements.

Income tax expense that is included in the primary financial statements is not adjusted in computing income from continuing operations on a current cost basis. Thus, income tax expense is included in income from continuing operations on a current cost basis at the same amount that it is included in the primary financial statements. Disclosure must be made in the minimum supplementary information to the effect that income tax expense for the current period is presented at its historical cost.

Purchasing power gain or loss on net monetary items Purchasing power gain or loss on net monetary items for each of the five most recent years is computed and then restated by the use of the CPI-U, into average-for-the-year units of constant purchasing power. The purchasing power gain or loss on net monetary items is determined by restating in units of constant purchasing power the opening and closing balances of, and transactions in, monetary assets and monetary liabilities.

Increase or decrease in inventory, property, plant, and equipment at current costs The increase or decrease in current costs for inventory and property, plant, and equipment for each of the five most recent years must be restated by the use of the CPI-U into average-for-the-year units of constant purchasing power. The increase or decrease in the current cost amounts of inventory and property, plant, and equipment represents the difference between the measures of the assets at their entry dates for the year and the measures of the assets at their exit dates for the year. The entry date is the beginning of the year or the date of acquisition, whichever is applicable. The exit date is the end of the year or the date of use, sale, or commitment to a specific contract, whichever is applicable.

The increase or decrease in the current cost amounts of inventory, property, plant, and equipment for the five-year summary is reported after the effects of each year's general inflation. The increase or decrease in the current cost amounts of inventory and property, plant, and equipment for the current year is reported both before and after the effects of general inflation.

Aggregate foreign currency translation adjustment (if applicable) Aggregate foreign currency translation adjustment (if applicable) for each of the five most recent years is computed on a current cost basis and then restated by use of the CPI-U into average-for-the-year units of constant purchasing power.

Current cost information for operations measured in a foreign functional currency is measured either (a) after translation and based on the CPI-U (the translate-restate method) or (b) before translation and based on a broad-based measure of the change in the general purchasing power of the functional currency (the restate-translate method). The same method must be used for all operations measured in foreign functional currencies, and the same method must be used for all periods presented.

Net assets at end of each fiscal year For purposes of the minimum supplementary information required by FASB-33, net assets at the end of each fiscal year are equal to all of the net assets appearing in the basic historical cost financial statements except inventories, property, plant, and equipment, which are included at their current costs or at a lower recoverable amount. (Total net assets at historical cost minus inventories, property, plant, and equipment at historical cost, plus inventories, property, plant, and equipment at current costs or lower recoverable amount, equals net assets as required by FASB-33). The amount computed for net assets at end of each fiscal year is then restated by use of the CPI-U into average-for-the-year units of constant purchasing power.

Where comprehensive restatement of financial statements is made in lieu of the minimum supplementary information, net assets for the five-year summary of selected financial data may be reported at the same amount shown in the comprehensive restated financial statements.

Income per common share from continuing operations on a current cost basis Income per common share from continuing operations on a current cost basis for each of the five most recent years is computed and then restated, by the use of the CPI-U, into average-for-the-year units of constant purchasing power. Income per common share from continuing operations on a current cost basis is found by dividing the outstanding number of shares of common stock into the total restated income from continuing operations on a current cost basis.

Cash dividends declared per common share Cash dividends declared per common share for each of the five most recent years are restated, by use of the CPI-U, into average-for-the-year units of constant purchasing power.

Market price per common share at year-end Market price per common share at year-end for each of the five most recent years is restated, by use of the CPI-U, into average-for-the-year units of constant purchasing power.

Average level of CPI-U The average level of CPI-U for each of the five most recent years shall be disclosed in a note to the minimum supplementary information. If an enterprise presents comprehensive current cost/constant purchasing power financial statements measured in year-end units of purchasing power, the year-end level of the CPI-U for each of the five most recent years shall be disclosed.

Explanatory disclosures An enterprise shall provide an explanation of the disclosures required by FASB-33 and a discussion of their significance in the circumstances of the enterprise. These explanatory statements should be sufficiently detailed so that a user who possesses reasonable business acumen will be able to understand the information presented.

Additional Disclosures for the Current Year

If income from continuing operations as shown in the primary financial statements differs significantly from income from continuing operations determined on a current cost/constant purchasing power basis, certain other disclosures for the current year are required by FASB-33 in addition to the minimum supplementary information. The additional disclosures for the current year are as follows:

- Income from continuing operations for the current year on a current cost basis
- Separate amounts for the current cost or lower recoverable amount at the end of the current year of (a) inventory and (b) property, plant, and equipment
- Increase or decrease in current cost or lower recoverable amount before and after adjusting for the effects of inflation of (a) inventory and (b) property, plant, and equipment
- The principal types and sources of information used to calculate current costs for the current year
- The differences, if any, in depreciation methods, useful lives, and salvage values used in the primary financial statements and the depreciation methods, useful lives, and salvage values used in the disclosure of current cost information for the current year

Each of the above additional disclosures is separately discussed below.

Income from continuing operations for the current year on a current cost basis Income from continuing operations for the current year on a current cost basis is computed in accordance with FASB-33, and then restated by the use of the CPI-U, into average-for-the-year units of constant purchasing power. The information for income from continuing operations for the current year on a current cost basis should be presented in either a "statement format" or in a "reconciliation format," which discloses all adjustments between the supplementary information and the basic historical cost financial statements. The same categories of revenue and expense as those appearing in the basic historical cost financial statements should be used for the presentation of income from continuing operations for the current year on a current cost basis. Account classifications may be combined if they are not individually significant for restatement purposes, or if the restated amounts are approximately the same as the historical cost amounts.

Income from continuing operations for the current year on a current cost basis does not include (a) the purchasing power gain or loss on net monetary items, (b) the increase or decrease in the current cost or lower recoverable amount of inventory and property, plant, and equipment, net of inflation, and (c) the translation adjustment (if applicable). However, an enterprise may include this information separately after the presentation of income from continuing operations for the current year on a current cost basis.

Only certain items that are included in income from continuing operations in the primary financial statements have to be adjusted to compute income from continuing operations for the current year on a current cost basis. Under FASB-33, the following items must be adjusted to compute income from continuing operations for the current year on a current cost basis:

a. *Cost of goods sold* must be determined on a current cost basis or lower recoverable amount at the date of sale or at the date on which resources are used or committed to a specific contract.
b. *Depreciation, depletion, and amortization* must be determined on the basis of the average current cost of the assets' service potential or lower recoverable amount during the period of use.
c. *Gain or loss on the sale, retirement, or write-down of inventory, property, plant, and equipment* is equal to the difference between the value of the consideration received or the written-down amount and the current cost or lower recoverable amount of the item prior to its sale, retirement, or write-down.

All other revenue, expenses, gains, and losses that are included in the primary financial statements are not adjusted and may be disclosed as one amount in computing income from continuing operations for the current year on a current cost basis. Thus, the amounts for these items included in income from continuing operations for the current year on a current cost basis are the same amounts that appear in the primary financial statements.

Income tax expense that is included in the primary financial statements is not adjusted in computing income from continuing operations for the current year on a current cost basis. Thus, the amount of income tax expense included in income from continuing operations for the current year on a current cost basis is the same amount that is included in the primary financial statements. Disclosure must be made in the minimum supplementary information to the effect that income tax expense for the current period is presented at its historical cost.

Separate amounts for the current cost or lower recoverable amount at the end of the current year of (a) inventory and (b) property, plant, and equipment The current cost or lower recoverable amount of inventory at the end of the current year must be disclosed as a separate item after the presentation of income from continuing operations for the current year on a current cost basis. The current cost or lower recoverable amount of property, plant, and equipment at the end of the current year must be disclosed as a separate item after the presentation of income from continuing operations for the current year on a current cost basis.

Increase or decrease in current cost or lower recoverable amount before and after adjusting for the effects of inflation of (a) inventory and (b) property, plant, and equipment The increase or decrease in the current cost or lower recoverable amount before and after the effects of inflation must be separately disclosed for inventory and for property, plant, and equipment.

The principal types and sources of information used to calculate current costs for the current year The principal types and sources of information used to calculate current costs for the year must be disclosed in an explanatory note to the current cost information. The explanatory note should be sufficiently detailed so that a user who possesses reasonable business acumen will be able to understand the information presented.

The differences, if any, in depreciation methods, useful lives, and salvage values used in (a) the primary financial statements and (b) the disclosure of current cost information for the current year Depreciation methods, useful lives, and salvage values should be the same for current cost purposes as for historical cost purposes. If historical cost computations already include an allowance for changing prices, then a different method may be used for current cost purposes. However, any material differences must be disclosed in the explanatory note to the supplementary information.

Specialized Assets

Mineral ore bodies and proved oil and gas reserves (FASB-39), timberlands and growing timber (FASB-40), income-producing real estate

(FASB-41), and motion picture films (FASB-46) are classified as specialized assets. Specialized assets are considered unique and the determination of their current costs is frequently difficult, if not impossible. For example, the current cost of an existing oil field may be difficult to determine because an oil field is one of a kind and cannot be duplicated. Yet, the definition of current cost is the current cost to purchase or reproduce the specific asset, and the current cost of property which is owned is the current cost of acquiring an asset that will perform or produce in a manner similar to the owned property.

Special rules are provided for determining the current costs of specialized assets. As a substitute for the current cost amounts and related expenses of timberlands and growing timber, income-producing real estate, and motion picture films, the historical cost amounts of such specialized assets may be adjusted for changes in specific prices by the use of a broad index of general purchasing power.

In the event an enterprise estimates the current cost of growing timber and timber harvested by adjusting historical costs for changes in specific prices, the historical costs may include either (a) only costs that are capitalized in the primary financial statements or (b) all direct costs of reforestation and forest management, even if such costs are not capitalized in the primary financial statements. Reforestation and forest management costs include planting, fertilization, fire protection, property taxes, and nursery stock.

Mineral resource assets The requirements for determining the current cost amounts for mineral resource assets are flexible because there is no generally accepted approach for measuring the current cost of finding mineral reserves. Specific price indexes applied to historical costs, market buying prices, and other statistical data may be used to determine the current replacement costs of mineral resource assets. An enterprise must disclose the types of data or information that are used to determine current cost amounts of mineral resource assets.

For enterprises that own significant mineral reserves, the following information on owned mineral reserves, excluding oil and gas, must be disclosed for each of the five most recent years.

1. The amount of estimated proved or proved and probable mineral reserves on hand at the end of the year. A date during the year is acceptable, but the date must be disclosed.
2. The estimated quantity of each significant mineral product that is commercially recoverable from the mineral reserves in 1.

above. The estimated quantity may be expressed in percentages or in physical units.
3. The quantities of each significant mineral produced during the year. In the case of ores, the quantity of each significant mineral product produced by milling or similar process must also be disclosed.
4. The quantity of mineral reserves (proved, or proved and probable) purchased or sold in place during the year.
5. The average market price of each significant mineral product. If transferred within the enterprise, the equivalent market price prior to further use should be disclosed.

In classifying and detailing the above information, current industry practices should prevail. The following illustrates a typical presentation for mining activities:

Mining Activities
Supplementary Operating Information
For The Five Years Ended 19X5

	19X1	19X2	19X3	19X4	19X5
Proved and probable mineral ore reserves (in tons):					
Beginning of year:					
Magnesium (20%)	XXX,XXX	XXX,XXX	XXX,XXX	XXX,XXX	XXX,XXX
Copper (40%)	XXX,XXX	XXX,XXX	XXX,XXX	XXX,XXX	XXX,XXX
Lead (40%)	XXX,XXX	XXX,XXX	XXX,XXX	XXX,XXX	XXX,XXX
Total	XXX,XXX	XXX,XXX	XXX,XXX	XXX,XXX	XXX,XXX
Produced during the year:					
Magnesium (15%)	XX,XXX	XXX,XXX	XXX,XXX	XXX,XXX	XXX,XXX
Copper (45%)	XXX,XXX	XXX,XXX	XXX,XXX	XXX,XXX	XXX,XXX
Lead (40%)	XXX,XXX	XXX,XXX	XXX,XXX	XXX,XXX	XXX,XXX
Total	XXX,XXX	XXX,XXX	XXX,XXX	XXX,XXX	XXX,XXX
Purchased during the year:					
Magnesium (80%)	XX,XXX	X,XXX	XXX	X,XXX	XX,XXX
Copper (20%)	X,XXX	X,XXX			
Lead (00%)		XXX	XXX	XXX	
Total	XX,XXX	X,XXX	XXX	X,XXX	XX,XXX
Sold during the year:					
Magnesium (25%)	XXX,XXX	XXX,XXX	XXX,XXX	XXX,XXX	XXX,XXX
Copper (35%)	XXX,XXX	XXX,XXX	XXX,XXX	XXX,XXX	XXX,XXX
Lead (40%)	XXX,XXX	XXX,XXX	XXX,XXX	XXX,XXX	XXX,XXX
Total	XXX,XXX	XXX,XXX	XXX,XXX	XXX,XXX	XXX,XXX
On hand at end of year:					
Magnesium (20%)	XXX,XXX	XXX,XXX	XXX,XXX	XXX,XXX	XXX,XXX
Copper (40%)	XXX,XXX	XXX,XXX	XXX,XXX	XXX,XXX	XXX,XXX
Lead (40%)	XXX,XXX	XXX,XXX	XXX,XXX	XXX,XXX	XXX,XXX
Total	XXX,XXX	XXX,XXX	XXX,XXX	XXX,XXX	XXX,XXX
Average market price (per lb.):					
Magnesium	$1.28	$1.14	$1.32	$1.42	$1.48
Copper	.71	.77	.83	.88	.93
Lead	.33	.38	.44	.49	.54

The following procedures shall be used in determining the quantities of mineral reserves that should be reported:

1. In consolidated financial statements, 100% of the quantities of mineral reserves attributable to both the parent company and all consolidated subsidiaries shall be reported regardless of whether a subsidiary is partially or wholly owned.
2. In a proportionately consolidated investment, an investor shall include only its proportionate share of the investee's mineral reserves.
3. Mineral reserve quantities attributable to an investment accounted for by the equity method shall not be included at all. However, if significant, the mineral reserve quantities should be reported separately by the investor.

FASB-33 contains the following definitions relating to mineral resource assets:

Mineral resource assets Mineral resource assets are assets that are directly associated with and derive value from all minerals extracted from the earth. Such minerals include oil and gas, ores containing ferrous and nonferrous metals, coal, shale, geothermal steam, sulphur, salt, stone, phosphate, sand, and gravel. Mineral resource assets include mineral interests in properties, completed and uncompleted wells and related equipment and facilities, and other facilities required for purposes of extraction (FASB Statement No. 19, Financial Accounting and Reporting by Oil and Gas Producing Companies, paragraph 11). The definition does not cover support equipment, because that equipment is included in the property, plant, and equipment for which current cost measurements are required by FASB-33.

Proved mineral reserves in extractive industries other than oil and gas Proved mineral reserves in extractive industries other than oil and gas are the estimated quantities of commercially recoverable reserves that, on the basis of geological, geophysical, and engineering data, can be demonstrated with a reasonably high degree of certainty to be recoverable in the future from known mineral deposits by either primary or improved recovery methods.

Probable mineral reserves in extractive industries other than oil and gas Probable mineral reserves in extractive industries other than oil and gas are the estimated quantities of commercially recoverable reserves that are less well defined than proved reserves and that may be estimated or indicated to exist on the basis of geological, geophysical, and engineering data.

FOREIGN OPERATIONS, AND EXCHANGE

Background

The major promulgated GAAP on Foreign Currency Translation is FASB-52, which supersedes the following prior GAAP:

- FASB-8, Accounting for the Translation of Foreign Currency Transactions and Foreign Currency Financial Statements
- FASB-20, Accounting for Forward Exchange Contracts
- FASB Interpretation-15, Translation of Unamortized Policy Acquisition Costs by a Stock Life Insurance Company
- FASB Interpretation-17, Applying the Lower of Cost or Market Rule in Translated Financial Statements

FASB Interpretation-37 (Accounting for Translation Adjustments upon Sale of Part of an Investment in a Foreign Entity) clarifies paragraph 14 of FASB-52 in that a sale of an investment in a foreign entity includes a partial, as well as a complete, sale or other disposition of an ownership interest in a foreign investment.

FASB-52 covers the translation of foreign currency financial statements for the purposes of consolidation, combination, or reporting by the equity method (APB-18), and the translation of foreign currency transactions, including forward exchange contracts.

FASB-52 also amends paragraph 13 of APB-22 (Disclosure of Accounting Policies) by deleting the words "translation of foreign currencies" as an example of disclosure "commonly required with respect to accounting policies." Thus, APB-22 no longer requires the disclosure of foreign currency translations. However, FASB-52 does require specific disclosures of foreign currency translations.

> **OBSERVATION:** FASB-52 was promulgated by a 4 to 3 vote of the seven members of the Financial Accounting Standards Board.

Overview

Business transactions and foreign operations that are recorded in a foreign currency must be restated in U.S. dollars in accordance with generally accepted accounting principles.

Transactions occur at various dates, and since the abandonment of the gold standard, exchange rates have tended to fluctuate considerably. Before an attempt is made to translate the records of a foreign operation, the records should be in conformity with GAAP. In addition, if the foreign statements have any accounts stated in a currency other than their own, they must be converted into the foreign statement's currency before translation into U.S. dollars or any other reporting currency.

The two major areas involved in foreign currency translations are:

I. The accounting and reporting of foreign currency transactions, including forward exchange contracts
II. The translation of foreign currency financial statements for the purposes of consolidation, combination, or reporting on the equity method (one-line consolidation)

A brief survey of FASB-52 follows:

1. Foreign currency financial statements must be in conformity with GAAP before they are translated.
2. Assets, liabilities, and operations of an entity must be expressed in the functional currency of the entity.
3. The functional currency of an entity is the currency of the primary economic environment in which the entity operates.
4. If a foreign entity's books of record are not kept in the functional currency, they must be remeasured into the functional currency prior to translation.
5. The current rate of exchange shall be used to translate the assets and liabilities of a foreign entity from its functional currency into the reporting currency.
6. The weighted-average exchange rate for the period shall be used to translate revenue, expenses, and gains and losses of a foreign entity from its functional currency to the reporting currency.
7. The current rate of exchange shall be used to translate changes in financial position other than those items found in the income statement, which are translated at the weighted-average exchange rate for the period.
8. Gain or loss on the translation of foreign currency financial statements is not recognized in current net income, but is reported as a separate component of stockholders' equity. However, if remeasurement from the recording currency to

the functional currency is necessary prior to translation, gain or loss on remeasurement is recognized in current net income.
9. The amounts accumulated in the separate component of stockholders' equity are realized on the sale or substantially complete liquidation of the investment in the foreign entity.
10. The financial statements of a foreign entity in a country that has had cumulative inflation of approximately 100% or more over a three-year period (highly inflationary) must be remeasured into the functional currency of the reporting entity.
11. A foreign currency transaction is one that requires settlement in a currency other than the functional currency of the reporting entity.
12. Gains or losses from foreign currency transactions are recognized in current net income, except for:
    a. gain or loss on a designated and effective economic hedge of a net investment in a foreign entity;
    b. gain or loss on certain long-term intercompany foreign currency transactions; or
    c. gain or loss on a designated and effective economic hedge of a firm identifiable foreign currency commitment which meets certain conditions
13. Taxable foreign exchange gains or losses that do not appear in the same period in taxable income and either (a) financial accounting income (books) or (b) a separate component of stockholders' equity (books) are timing differences for which deferred taxes must be provided in accordance with existing GAAP (APB-11).
14. Certain specific disclosures are required by FASB-52.

Translation Objectives

FASB-52 establishes accounting and reporting standards for (1) foreign currency transactions and (2) translation of foreign currency financial statements that are included by consolidation, combination, or the equity method in a parent company's financial statements. Foreign financial statements must conform to U.S. generally accepted accounting principles before they can be translated into dollars.

An important objective in translating foreign currency is to preserve the financial results and relationships that are expressed in the foreign currency. This is accomplished by using the *functional currency* of the foreign entity. The functional currency is then translated into the *reporting currency* of the reporting entity. FASB-52 assumes that the reporting currency for an enterprise is U.S. dollars. However, the reporting currency may be a currency other than U.S. dollars.

> **OBSERVATION:** Perhaps the ultimate objective of translating foreign transactions and financial statements would be to produce the same results that each individual underlying transaction would have produced on the date it occurred, if it had then been recorded in the reporting currency.

Functional Currency

FASB-52 requires that the assets, liabilities, and operations of an entity be measured in terms of the functional currency of that entity. The functional currency is the currency of the primary economic environment in which an entity generates and expends cash. The functional currency is generally the currency of the country in which the entity is located. However, the functional currency of a foreign operation may be the same as a related affiliated enterprise, if the foreign operation is a direct and integral component or extension of the related affiliated enterprise.

For the purposes of determining functional currency under FASB-52, foreign operations may be broken down into two models. The first model is the self-contained foreign operation, located in a particular country, whose daily operations are not dependent on the economic environment of the parent's functional currency. This type of foreign operation primarily generates and expends foreign currency; the net cash flows that it produces in foreign currency may be reinvested or converted and distributed to its parent company. The functional currency for this type of foreign operation is its foreign currency.

The second model of foreign operation is usually a direct and integral component or extension of the parent company's operation. Financing is usually in U.S. dollars and is frequently supplied by the parent. The purchase and sale of assets are usually made in U.S. dollars. In other words, the daily operations of this type of foreign operation are dependent on the economic environment of the parent's currency. In addition, the changes in the foreign operation's individual assets and liabilities directly affect the cash flow of the parent company. The functional currency for this type of foreign operation is the U.S. dollar.

In the event that the facts in a given situation do not clearly identify the functional currency, the determination rests on the judgment of management. The FASB has developed the following guidelines, based on certain indicators, that should be considered in determining the functional currency of a foreign operation:

Cash Flow Indicators

The foreign operation's cash flows are mostly in foreign currency which does not directly affect the parent company's cash flows. Under these circumstances, the functional currency is the foreign currency.

The foreign operation's cash flows directly affect the parent company's cash flows on a current basis, and are usually available for remittance through intercompany account settlement. Under these circumstances, the functional currency is the parent company's currency.

Sales Price Indicators

The foreign operation's sales prices for its products are primarily determined (on a short-term basis) by local competition, or local government regulation, and not by exchange rate changes. Under these circumstances, the functional currency is the foreign currency.

The foreign operation's sales prices for its products are mostly responsive (on a short-term basis) to exchange rate changes, such as worldwide competition and prices. Under these circumstances, the functional currency is the parent company's currency.

Sales Market Indicators

The foreign operation has an active local sales market for its products, although there also may be significant amounts of exports. Under these circumstances, the functional currency is the foreign currency.

The foreign operation's sales market is mostly in the parent's country, or sales contracts are mostly made in the parent company's currency. Under these circumstances, the functional currency is the parent company's currency.

Expense Indicators

The foreign operation's costs of production (labor, material, etc.) or service are mostly local costs, although there may also be imports from other countries. Under these circumstances, the functional currency is the foreign currency.

The foreign operation's costs of production or service, on a continuing basis, are primarily costs for components obtained from the parent's country. Under these circumstances, the functional currency is the parent company's currency.

Financing Indicators

Financing for the foreign operation is in foreign currency and funds generated by the foreign operation are sufficient to service debt obligations. Under these circumstances, the functional currency is the foreign currency.

Financing for the foreign operation is provided by the parent company or is obtained in U.S dollars. Funds generated by the foreign operation are insufficient to service its debt. Under these circumstances, the functional currency is the parent company's currency.

Intercompany Transactions

There is little interrelationship between the operations of the foreign entity and the parent company, except for competitive advantages, such as trademarks, patents, etc. Intercompany transactions are of a low volume. Under these circumstances, the functional currency is the foreign currency.

There is an extensive interrelationship between the operations of the foreign entity and the parent company. Intercompany transactions are numerous. Under these circumstances, the functional currency is the parent company's currency.

The functional currency of a foreign entity must be used consistently from one fiscal year to another, unless significant changes in economic facts and circumstances dictate a change.

> **OBSERVATION:** *A change in functional currency is accounted for as a change in an accounting estimate. Thus, the change is accounted for in the period of change and/or future periods (prospectively).*
>
> *If a change in functional currency occurs, the translation adjustments for prior periods are not removed from the separate component of stockholders' equity. Thus, the translated amounts of nonmonetary assets at the end of the period prior to the change in functional currency become the accounting basis for subsequent periods.*

After the functional currency of a foreign entity is determined, the financial statements must be remeasured in the functional currency before translation can be made under FASB-52. In other words, the functional currency is first determined. Then, the accounts and records and resulting financial statements of the foreign entity must be remeasured in the functional currency. Next, the financial statements are translated into the functional currency of the reporting entity. Usually, the functional currency of a foreign entity is either (1) the foreign currency of the country in which the foreign entity is located, (2) the foreign currency of a related affiliate, or (3) the U.S dollar.

If the foreign entity's financial statements are already stated in terms of its functional currency, translation can be made under the provisions of FASB-52. The translation provisions of FASB-52 are discussed later. However, if the foreign entity's financial statements are not stated in the functional currency, the financial statements must be remeasured into the functional currency before they can be translated. The remeasurement of the foreign entity's financial statements into the functional currency is required by FASB-52 prior to translation. Remeasurement of the financial statements shall be made in accordance with the provisions of FASB-52, and shall produce the same results as if the entity's accounts and records had always been maintained in the functional currency.

> **OBSERVATION:** *For example, if a foreign entity's books of record are kept in French francs and the functional currency is British pounds, the books of record must be remeasured into British pounds before the financial statements can be translated into the functional currency of the reporting entity. Any translation gain or loss from French francs to British pounds is included in the remeasured net income.*

The remeasurement process required by FASB-52 is the same as that which was required by FASB-8 (Temporal Method), except for deferred income taxes and deferred life insurance policy acquisition costs. Thus, *exchange adjustments resulting from the remeasurement process are included in the determination of remeasured net income.* Deferred income taxes and deferred life insurance policy acquisition costs are remeasured using the current rate of exchange, instead of the historical exchange rate, which was required by FASB-8. The following is a brief review, using FASB-52 terminology, of the translation provisions of FASB-8. They are relevant under FASB-52 only for the remeasurement process from the recording currency to the functional currency, prior to translation from the functional currency to the reporting currency.

There are two categories of exchange rates that may be used in remeasuring financial statements. Historical exchange rates are those which existed at the time of the transaction, and the current exchange rate is the rate that is current at the date of remeasurement.

Monetary assets and liabilities are those which are fixed in amount, such as cash, accounts receivable, and most liabilities. Under FASB-8, all monetary assets and liabilities are translated at the current rate of exchange. All other assets, liabilities, and stockholders' equity are remeasured by reference to money price exchanges based on the type of market and time. FASB-8 describes the four types of money price exchanges as follows:

1. *Past purchase exchange*—the historical or acquisition cost, because it is based on the actual past purchase price.
2. *Current purchase exchange*—the replacement cost, because it is measured by the current purchase price of a similar resource.
3. *Current sale exchange*—the market price, because it is based on the current selling price of the resource.
4. *Future exchange*—the present value of future net money receipts, discounted cash flow, or the discounted net realizable value, because it is based on a future resource.

All other assets, liabilities, and stockholders' equity are remeasured based on the four money price exchanges, as follows:

1. Accounts based on past purchase exchanges (historical or acquisition cost) are remeasured at historical exchange rates.
2. Accounts based on current purchase, current sale, and future exchanges are remeasured at the current exchange rate.

Revenue and expense transactions are remeasured at the average exchange rate for the period, except those expenses related to assets and liabilities, which are remeasured at historical exchange rates. For example, depreciation and amortization are remeasured at historical exchange rates, the rate that existed at the time the underlying related asset was acquired.

The following is a comprehensive list of assets, liabilities, and stockholders' equity items and their corresponding remeasurement rates under FASB-8:

Foreign Operations and Exchange

	Remeasurement Rates	
	Current	Historical
Cash (in almost all forms)	X	
Marketable securities—at cost		X
Marketable securities—at market	X	
Accounts and notes receivable	X	
Allowance for receivables	X	
Inventories—at cost		X
Inventories—at market, net realizable value, selling price	X	
Inventories—under fixed contract price	X	
Prepaid expenses		X
Refundable deposits	X	
Advances to subsidiaries	X	
Fixed assets		X
Accumulated depreciation		X
Cash surrender value—life insurance	X	
Intangible assets (all)		X
Accounts and notes payable	X	
Accrued expenses	X	
Accrued losses on firm commitments	X	
Taxes payable	X	
All long-term liabilities	X	
Unamortized premium or discount on long-term liabilities	X	
Obligations under warranties	X	
Deferred income		X
Capital stock		X
Retained earnings		X
Minority interests		X

Note: FASB-52 requires the current rate of exchange to be used for remeasuring deferred income taxes and deferred life insurance policy acquisition costs. In other respects, remeasurement under FASB-52 follows the above tabulation of exchange rates, derived from FASB-8.

As previously mentioned, revenue and expenses not related to any balance sheet items are remeasured at the average currency exchange rate for the period. The average may be based on a daily, weekly, monthly, or quarterly basis or on the weighted-average rate for the period, which will probably result in a more meaningful conversion. Revenue and expense items that are related to a balance sheet account, such as deferred income, depreciation, and beginning and ending inventories, are remeasured at the same exchange rate as the related balance sheet item.

In remeasuring the lower-of-cost-or-market rule, the remeasured historical cost is compared to the remeasured market, and whichever is lower in functional currency is used. This may require a write-down in the functional currency from cost to market, which was not required in the foreign currency financial statements. On the other hand, if market was used on the foreign statements and in remeasuring to the functional currency market exceeds historical cost, the write-down to market on the foreign statements will have to be reversed before remeasuring, which would then be done at the historical rate. Once inventory has been written down to market in remeasured functional currency statements, the resulting carrying amount is used in future translations until the inventory is sold or a further write-down is necessary. This same procedure is used for assets, other than inventory, that may have to be written down from historical cost.

The reason for the above procedure in applying the lower-of-cost-or-market rule in remeasuring foreign financial statements is that exchange gains and losses are a consequence of remeasurement and not of applying the lower-of-cost-or-market rule (FASB Interpretation-17). This means that remeasured market is equal to replacement cost (market) in the foreign currency remeasured at the current exchange rate, except that:

1. Remeasured market cannot exceed net realizable value in foreign currency translated at the current exchange rate.
2. Remeasured market cannot be less than 1 above, reduced by an approximate normal profit translated at the current exchange rate.

For remeasurement purposes, the current exchange rate is the one in effect as of the balance sheet date of the foreign statements. Therefore, if the parent company's financial statements are at a date different from the date(s) of its foreign operation(s), the exchange rate in effect at the date of the foreign subsidiary's balance sheet is used for remeasurement and translation purposes.

Any translation adjustment arising from the remeasurement process is included in remeasured net income. In other words, any gain or loss resulting from the remeasurement process which is required by FASB-52 is included in net income in the remeasured financial statements.

After the foreign entity's financial statements are remeasured in the functional currency, they are ready for translation. If the functional currency of a foreign entity is the U.S. dollar and the reporting currency of the parent is also the U.S. dollar, there will be no translation adjustment.

Translation of Foreign Operations—Highly Inflationary Economies

FASB-52 defines a highly inflationary economy as one in which the cumulative inflation over a three-year consecutive period approximates one hundred percent (100%). In other words, the inflation rate in an economy must be rising at the rate of about 35% per year for three consecutive years to be classified as highly inflationary.

For the purposes of FASB-52, a foreign entity in a highly inflationary economy does not have a functional currency. The functional currency of the reporting entity is used as the functional currency of the foreign entity in a highly inflationary economy. Thus, the financial statements for a foreign entity in a highly inflationary economy must be remeasured into the functional currency of the reporting entity. The remeasurement process required by FASB-52 is the same as that which is required for a foreign entity's financial statements that are not expressed in the functional currency. This remeasurement process, which was discussed in the prior section entitled "Functional Currency," is the same as that which was required by FASB-8 (Temporal Method), except for deferred income taxes and deferred life insurance policy acquisition costs.

> **OBSERVATION:** Apparently, exchange adjustments resulting from the remeasurement process for foreign entities in highly inflationary economies must be included in the determination of remeasured net income, rather than reported as a separate component of stockholders' equity. Paragraph 11 of FASB-52 is not clear on this point, but does state that the remeasurement process must be done in accordance with paragraph 10.

The International Monetary Fund (IMF) of Washington, D.C., publishes monthly statistics on international inflation rates. After the financial statements of a foreign entity in a highly inflationary economy are expressed in the functional currency of the reporting entity, they are ready for translation. However, since the financial statements are now expressed in the reporting currency, there will be no translation adjustment.

Translation of Foreign Currency Statements

Foreign currency financial statements must be in conformity with GAAP before they are translated into the functional currency of the reporting entity. FASB-52 covers the translation of financial statements from one functional currency to another for the purposes of consolidation, combination, or the equity method of accounting. Translation of financial statements for any other purpose is beyond the scope of FASB-52.

> **OBSERVATION:** *If the functional currency of a foreign operation is the same as its parent, there will be no need for translation. A translation adjustment will only occur if the foreign operation's functional currency is a functional currency different from that of its parent.*

The translation of foreign currency financial statements to the functional currency of the reporting entity does not produce realized exchange gains or losses. Instead, the gains or losses are considered unrealized and are recorded and reported as a separate component of stockholders' equity. In the year that FASB-52 is first applied, the beginning balance of the separate component of stockholders' equity should be equal to the difference between the net assets translated under FASB-8 and the net assets translated at the current exchange rate.

> **OBSERVATION:** *Paragraph 12 of FASB-52 states that "All elements of financial statements shall be translated by using a current exchange rate." This statement is obviously not correct because common stock, paid-in capital, donated capital, retained earnings, and similar items are not translated at the current exchange rate. Translation of these elements of the financial statements is made exactly as they were translated under FASB-8, as follows:*
>
> Capital Accounts—*are translated at their historical exchange rates when the capital stock was issued, or at the historical exchange rate when the capital stock was acquired.*
> Retained Earnings—*are translated at the translated amount at the end of the prior period, plus the translated amount of net*

income for the current period, less the translated amount of any dividends declared during the current period.

Assets and liabilities should be translated from the foreign entity's functional currency to the reporting entity's functional currency using the current exchange rate at the balance sheet date of the foreign entity. If a current exchange rate is not available at the balance sheet date of the foreign entity being translated, the first exchange rate available after the balance sheet date shall be used.

Revenue, expenses, and gains and losses should be translated from the foreign entity's functional currency to produce the approximate results that would have occurred if each transaction had been translated using the exchange rate in effect on the date that the transaction was recognized. Since the separate translation of every single transaction is impractical, an appropriate weighted-average exchange rate for the period should be used.

> **OBSERVATION:** *Translated amounts appearing on the statement of changes in financial position will usually consist of some items translated at the current exchange rate and some items translated at the weighted-average exchange rate. (A net adjustment may be required, resulting from the use of various exchange rates for various items appearing on the statement.) The increase or decrease in funds for a period is equal to the difference between funds translated at the current exchange rate at the beginning of the period and funds translated at the current exchange rate at the end of the period. Funds may be defined as working capital, net quick assets, cash, or some other concept of funds in accordance with existing GAAP (APB-19).*
>
> *APB-19 (Reporting Changes in Financial Position) requires the disclosure of all important changes in financial position. Thus, important effects of changes in exchange rates on amounts appearing in the statement of changes in financial position should be appropriately disclosed.*

Gains or losses on the translation of foreign currency financial statements for the purposes of consolidation, combination, or reporting on the equity method are not included in current net income. All adjustments resulting from the translation of foreign currency financial statements must be recorded and reported as a separate component of stockholders' equity. Thus, these adjustments are treated as unrealized gains and losses, similar to unrealized gains and losses of noncurrent marketable securities (FASB-12).

The translation process embodied in FASB-52 includes the following steps:

1. Financial statements must be in conformity with U.S. GAAP prior to translation.
2. The functional currency of the foreign entity must be determined.
3. The financial statements must be expressed in the functional currency of the foreign entity. Remeasurement of the financial statements into the functional currency may be necessary. Gains or losses from remeasurement are included in remeasured current net income.
4. If the foreign entity operates in a country with a highly inflationary economy, its financial statements must be remeasured into the functional currency of the reporting entity.
5. The functional currency financial statements of the foreign entity are translated into the functional currency of the reporting entity using the current rate of exchange method. Gains or losses from translation are not included in current net income.

Realization of Separate Component of Stockholders' Equity

Upon part, complete, or substantially complete sale or upon complete liquidation of an investment in a foreign entity, a *pro rata* portion of the accumulated translation adjustments attributable to that foreign entity, which have been recorded as a separate component of stockholders' equity, shall be included in determining the gain or loss on the sale or other disposition of that foreign investment (FASB Interpretation-37). Thus, if an enterprise sells a 50% ownership interest in a foreign investment, 50% of the accumulated translation adjustments related to that foreign investment shall be included in determining the gain or loss on the sale of the 50% ownership interest.

FASB Interpretation-37 is effective for the sale of part of a foreign investment that is consummated on or after July 1, 1983, with earlier application encouraged in previously unissued financial statements. Retroactive restatement of previously issued financial statements is not required, but is permitted.

> **OBSERVATION:** *Any required provision for the permanent impairment of a foreign investment should be determined before*

translation and consolidation (see Appendix C, paragraph 118, of FASB-52). Apparently, this means that the amounts accumulated in the separate component of stockholders' equity for a specific foreign investment are not included in determining whether the investment has become permanently impaired.

The separate component of stockholders' equity account for a foreign investment may contain amounts from the following sources:

1. Translation adjustments.
2. Deferred income taxes related to items in the separate component of stockholders' equity.
3. Gain or loss on an economic hedge of a net investment in a foreign entity.
4. Gain or loss on intercompany foreign currency transactions of a capital or long-term nature.
5. Under certain conditions, amounts deferred under FASB-8 on a forward exchange contract that hedged an identifiable foreign currency commitment of a nonmonetary asset (see "Effective Date and Transition").

Foreign Currency Transactions

A foreign currency transaction is one that requires settlement in a currency other than the functional currency of the reporting entity. As a general rule, gains and losses on foreign currency transactions are recognized in current net income. However, the following foreign currency transactions, which are discussed later, may require different treatment than that afforded all other foreign currency transactions:

1. Gain or loss resulting from a foreign currency transaction that is designated as an economic hedge of a net investment in a foreign entity.
2. Gain or loss resulting from intercompany foreign currency transactions of a capital nature or long-term financing nature, between an investor and investee where the investee entity is consolidated, combined, or accounted for by the equity method by the investor.
3. Forward exchange contracts.

If the exchange rate changes between the time a purchase or sale is contracted for and the time actual payment is made, a foreign exchange gain or loss will result. For example, if goods were purchased for 100,000 pesos when the rate of exchange was 10 pesos to a dollar, the journal entry in dollars would be:

Purchases	$10,000	
Accounts payable		$10,000

Assuming that when the goods are paid for, the exchange rate is 12:1, the journal entry in dollars would be:

Accounts payable	$10,000	
Cash		$ 8,333
Foreign exchange gain		1,667

The $8,333, at a 12:1 exchange rate, can purchase 100,000 pesos. The difference between the $8,333 and the original recorded liability of $10,000 is a foreign exchange gain.

A foreign exchange gain or loss must be computed at each balance sheet date on all recorded foreign transactions that have not been settled. The difference between the exchange rate that could have been used to settle the transaction at the date it occurred, and the exchange rate that can be used to settle the transaction at a subsequent balance sheet date, is the gain or loss on the foreign currency transaction, which is recognized in current net income. Generally, the current exchange rate is the rate that is used to settle a transaction on the date it occurs, or on a subsequent balance sheet date.

> **OBSERVATION:** *FASB-52 retains most of the provisions of FASB-8 regarding foreign currency transactions. The major difference is in the definition of a hedge of an identifiable foreign currency commitment, which is discussed in a later section.*

Forward Exchange Contracts

A forward exchange contract is a foreign currency transaction. A forward exchange contract is an agreement to exchange, at a future specified date and rate, currencies of different countries. Generally, a forward exchange contract is entered into either as a hedge or for speculation. Gains or losses on all foreign exchange contracts and foreign currency transactions are usually recognized in net income of the period in which the exchange rate changes. Gains and losses that are exceptions to this general rule are deferred and are discussed in a later section.

FASB-52 specifies two methods of determining gain or loss on forward exchange contracts, depending upon whether the contract is (1) a hedge (whether or not deferred) or (2) speculative.

Hedge contracts   Gain or loss is the difference between the balance sheet date spot exchange rate and the spot exchange rate at the inception of the contract, multiplied by the principal amount of foreign currency.

Speculative contracts   Gain or loss is the difference between the contracted forward exchange rate and the forward exchange rate available for the remaining maturity of the contract, multiplied by the principal amount of foreign currency.

> **OBSERVATION:** *The spot or forward exchange rate last used to measure gain or loss on a forward exchange contract for an earlier period may be used for either hedge or speculative contracts, if necessary.*

The discount or premium involved in a forward exchange contract is the difference between the contract rate and the spot rate on the date of purchase, multiplied by the principal amount of foreign currency. Discounts and premiums are disposed of as follows:

Identifiable hedges   Either separately accounted for and amortized to net income over the life of the contract, or not separately accounted for and recognized as part of the total gain or loss on the identifiable transaction.

Hedge of net investment   Either separately accounted for and amortized to net income over the life of the contract, or not separately accounted for and recognized as part of the total gain or loss on the transaction.

All other contracts   Discounts and premiums are separately accounted for and amortized to net income over the life of the forward exchange contract.

Deferred Foreign Currency Transactions

Certain gains and losses on forward exchange contracts and certain types of foreign currency transactions are not included in current net income, but are either (1) reported in the separate component of stockholders' equity, along with translation adjustments or (2) included in the overall gain or loss of the related foreign currency transaction. These deferred gains and losses may be classified as follows:

1. Gain or loss on a designated and effective economic hedge of a net investment in a foreign entity.
2. Gain or loss on certain long-term intercompany foreign currency transactions.
3. Gain or loss on a designated and effective economic hedge of a firm identifiable foreign currency commitment.

Gain or loss on a forward exchange contract or foreign currency transaction that is intended and effective as an economic hedge of a net investment in a foreign entity is not recognized in current net income. Instead, the gain or loss is recorded and reported as a separate component of stockholders' equity. The foreign currency transaction must be designated and effective as an economic hedge of a net investment in a foreign entity. The accounting required by FASB-52 commences with the designation date of the transaction.

> **OBSERVATION:** *As an example of a foreign currency transaction intended to be an economic hedge of a net investment in a foreign entity, take the case of a U.S. parent company with a net investment in a Greek subsidiary that borrows Greek currency in the amount of its net investment in the Greek subsidiary. The U.S. company designates the loan as an economic hedge of its net investment in the Greek subsidiary. In other words, the U.S. parent computes its net investment in the foreign currency of its foreign subsidiary and then borrows the same amount of foreign currency as the amount of its net investment. In this event, if the net investment in the foreign subsidiary declines because of a change in exchange rates, the change is made up in the foreign currency loan. The U.S company can buy a larger amount of the subsidiary's foreign currency with fewer U.S. dollars. When the net investment in the foreign subsidiary and the loan in the foreign currency of the foreign subsidiary are both translated into U.S. dollars, the change in the net investment in the foreign subsidiary (an asset) should be approximately equal to the change in the foreign currency loan, except for taxes, if any. Thus, the foreign currency loan acts as a hedge against any increase or decrease in the net foreign investment that is attributable to a change in the exchange rate. FASB-52 requires that both translated amounts be recorded and reported in a separate component of stockholders' equity. However, if the translated amount of the foreign currency loan (after taxes, if any) exceeds the translated amount of the net investment in the*

foreign subsidiary that was hedged, the gain or loss that is allocable to the excess must be included in net income, and not recorded and reported as a separate component of stockholders' equity.

Gains or losses on intercompany foreign currency transactions of a capital or long-term nature are not included in current net income, but are reported in the separate component of stockholders' equity, along with translation adjustments. The entities involved in the intercompany foreign currency transactions reported in this manner must be consolidated, combined, or accounted for by the equity method. Gain or loss on intercompany foreign currency transactions that are not of a permanent nature are included in net income.

Gain or loss on a forward exchange contract or foreign currency transaction that is intended and effective as a hedge of a firm identifiable foreign currency commitment is deferred and included in the overall gain or loss from the firm identifiable foreign currency commitment. However, a loss shall not be deferred if it is estimated that the loss would be recognized in later periods. Thus, any loss that is expected to be recognized in later periods cannot be deferred. The foreign currency transaction must be firm, and must be designated and effective as a hedge of a foreign currency commitment. The accounting required by FASB-52 commences with the designation date of the transaction.

> **OBSERVATION:** For example, a U.S company purchases a large piece of equipment from a Mexican company for 100,000 pesos when the exchange rate is 10:1 (ten pesos to 1 dollar). Delivery of the equipment will be made in one year, at which time the purchase price must be paid in Mexican pesos. In order to hedge against the rise or fall in the exchange rate of the Mexican peso, the U.S. company purchases, for $1,000, a forward exchange contract to purchase 100,000 Mexican pesos in one year at the exchange rate of 10:1. At the end of six months, financial statements are prepared and the exchange rate of Mexican pesos is 12:1. Thus, at the end of six months the cost of the equipment in U.S. dollars is $8,333, or 100,000 Mexican pesos, while at the date of purchase the cost in U.S. dollars was $10,000, or 100,000 Mexican pesos. The company has protected itself against an exchange rate change and at the end of the year will receive 100,000 Mexican pesos from the forward exchange contract upon payment of $10,000. However, at the interim six-month date, there is a loss on the forward exchange contract of $2,667 ($1,667, plus the cost of the forward exchange contract of $1,000). This loss cannot be deferred if the total cost of the asset, including the deferred loss on the forward exchange contract, is expected to exceed the estimated net realizable value of the asset.

Foreign Operations and Exchange

For the purposes of FASB-52, the amount of the forward exchange contract or foreign currency transaction cannot exceed the amount of the firm identifiable foreign currency commitment. If the amount of the transaction exceeds the amount of firm commitment, the gain or loss pertaining to the excess amount over the commitment may be deferred only to the extent that the transaction provides a hedge on an after-tax basis. Where gain or loss pertaining to amounts in excess of the foreign currency commitment is deferred, it is included as an offset to the related tax effects in the period in which such tax effects are recognized. Gains or losses in excess of the amount of commitment on an after-tax basis cannot be deferred. In addition, any gains or losses on a forward exchange contract or foreign currency transaction that are attributable to a period after the transaction date of the related commitment cannot be deferred.

Deferred gain or loss on a hedge of a foreign currency commitment that is sold or terminated is not recognized until the related identifiable transaction is consummated, unless the identifiable transaction is reasonably expected to result in a loss.

The major differences between FASB-52 and FASB-8 concerning a hedge of an identifiable foreign currency commitment are depicted in the following chart:

FASB-8 and 20	FASB-52
Covered forward exchange contracts only.	Covers all "designated" and "effective" hedges.
Life of the forward contract must extend from foreign currency commitment date to anticipated transaction date or later.	Commences at the "designation date."
Foreign currency commitment must be firm and noncancelable.	Foreign currency commitment must be firm.
Forward contract must be for the same currency as the identifiable commitment.	No rule, but Appendix C (paragraph 130) of FASB-52 suggests a hedge in another currency under certain conditions.

Deferred Taxes

Timing differences are taxable transactions that do not appear in financial accounting income (books) and taxable income (tax return) in the same reporting period. Under existing GAAP (APB-11, APB-23, and APB-24), deferred taxes are provided for timing differences. Thus, a reporting entity must determine its provision for deferred taxes to include taxable foreign currency transactions and taxable translation adjustments that are included in financial accounting income (books) and taxable income (tax return) in different reporting periods.

FASB-52 requires that deferred taxes be provided on taxable foreign currency transactions and taxable translation adjustments of foreign currency financial statements, regardless of whether the exchange gain or loss is charged to current net income or recorded and reported as a separate component of stockholders' equity. Thus, all taxable foreign exchange gains or losses that do not appear in the same period in taxable income and either (1) financial accounting income or (2) the separate component of stockholders' equity are timing differences, for which deferred taxes must be provided. The amount of the deferred taxes should be determined in accordance with existing GAAP.

> **OBSERVATION:** *There is a presumption in GAAP that all undistributed earnings of a subsidiary (domestic or foreign) will eventually be transferred to the parent company. Unless this presumption is overcome, the undistributed earnings included in a parent's consolidated income will result in a timing difference, and a provision for deferred taxes may be necessary. This same presumption exists for corporate joint ventures and investments accounted for by the equity method. Thus, unless this presumption is overcome by sufficient evidence to the contrary, a parent or investor will have to provide for deferred taxes on taxable translation adjustments that are included in financial accounting income and taxable income in different periods.*

Intraperiod income tax allocation should be disclosed in the financial statements in accordance with ABP-11. Thus, the total income tax expense for a period should be properly allocated to (1) income before extraordinary items, (2) extraordinary items, (3) adjustments of prior periods, and (4) direct entries to other stockholders' equity accounts. Therefore, the portion of income tax expense for a period that is attributable to items in the separate component of stockholders' equity should be allocated to the separate component of stockholders' equity, and should not appear as an increase or decrease of income tax expense for the period. In other words, deferred taxes related to items in the separate component of stockholders' equity account are charged or credited to the separate component of stockholders' equity account.

> **OBSERVATION:** *All aspects of income tax allocation are complicated, and these provisions of FASB-52 will require careful application to the specific facts of each situation. In particular, intercompany transactions of a long-term nature and discontinuance of a foreign operation may present peculiar problems.*

Elimination of Intercompany Profits

The exchange rate to be used to eliminate intercompany profits shall be the rate that existed on the date of the intercompany transaction. FASB-52 permits the use of approximations and/or averages as long as they are reasonable.

> **OBSERVATION:** *Intercompany profits occur on the date of sale or transfer. Thus, the exchange rate on the date of sale or transfer should be used to determine the amount of intercompany profit to be eliminated.*

Exchange Rates

The balance sheet date of the foreign entity which is consolidated, combined, or accounted for by the equity method is used for translation purposes, if different from the balance sheet date of the reporting entity. Thus, the current exchange rate for the translation of foreign currency financial statements is the rate in effect on the balance sheet date of the foreign entity which is being translated. If a current exchange rate is not available at the balance sheet date of the foreign entity being translated, the first exchange rate available after the balance sheet date should be used. The exchange rate used for dividend remittances, if available, shall be used to translate foreign currency financial statements.

> **OBSERVATION:** *If a preference or penalty rate is used to translate intercompany transactions and the dividend remittance exchange rate is used for all other translation, a difference may arise in the intercompany receivables and payables. In this event, the difference shall be accounted for as a receivable or payable until the difference is eliminated by settlement of the transaction.*

Conditions may exist where it will be prudent to exclude a foreign entity from financial statements which are consolidated, combined, or accounted for by the equity method. Disruption of a foreign operation caused by internal strife or severe exchange restrictions may make it impossible to compute meaningful exchange rates. Under these circumstances, it is best to include earnings of a foreign operation only to the extent that cash has been received in unrestricted funds (ARB-43). Adequate disclosure should be made of any foreign subsidiary or investment that is excluded from the financial statements of the parent or investor. This may be accomplished by separate supplemental statements or a summary describing the important facts and information (ARB-43).

For foreign currency transactions, the exchange rate that existed on the date of the transaction should be used for translation purposes. A foreign currency transaction is one that requires settlement in a currency other than the functional currency of the reporting entity. A foreign exchange gain or loss must be computed at each balance sheet date on all recorded foreign currency transactions that have not been settled. The difference between the exchange rate that could have been used to settle the transaction at the date it occurred and the exchange rate that can be used to settle the transaction at a subsequent balance sheet date is the gain or loss on the foreign currency transaction.

> **OBSERVATION:** *More frequently than not, the current exchange rate is the rate that could have been used to settle the transaction at the date it occurred; the current exchange rate at a subsequent balance sheet date is usually the rate used to settle a transaction at a subsequent balance sheet date.*

Financial statements should not be adjusted for a change in rate subsequent to the date of the financial statements. However, disclosure of such a rate change, if significant, may be required under the disclosure provisions of FASB-52.

Use of Averages and/or Approximations

Since detailed compliance may require significant record keeping, the promulgated GAAP (FASB-52) permits the use of averages and/or reasonable approximations, providing the results do not differ materially from the prescribed standards.

Financial Statement Disclosure

The aggregate transaction gain or loss that is included in determining net income for the period, including gain or loss on forward exchange contracts, shall be disclosed in the financial statements or footnotes thereto.

> **OBSERVATION:** *Transaction gains or losses of dealers in foreign exchange may be accounted for as dealer gains or losses, instead of transaction gains or losses under FASB-52.*

An analysis of the changes in the separate component of stockholders' equity account for cumulative translation adjustments for the period shall be disclosed in either (1) a separate financial statement or (2) notes to the financial statements, or (3) be included as part of a stockholders' equity or a similar statement. The following is the minimum information that must be disclosed in the analysis:

1. Beginning and ending cumulative balances.
2. The aggregate increase or decrease for the period from translation adjustments and gains and losses from (a) hedges of a net investment in a foreign entity and (b) long-term intercompany transactions.
3. The amount of income taxes for the period allocated to translation adjustments.
4. The amount of translation adjustment transferred to net income during the period as a result of a sale or complete or substantially complete liquidation of a foreign investment.

Disclosure of exchange rate changes and related effects on foreign currency transactions that occur subsequent to the balance sheet date should be disclosed, if the effects are material. No adjustment should be made to the financial statements for exchange rate changes that occur subsequent to the balance sheet date.

Effective Date and Transition

FASB-52 shall be initially applied from the start of an enterprise's fiscal year, and is effective for fiscal years commencing on or after December 15, 1982, although earlier compliance is encouraged. Financial summaries for periods prior to the effective date may be restated to comply with FASB-52. In the year of first compliance, the nature of any restatement and its effect on (1) income before extraordinary items, (2) net income, and (3) related per share data for each period restated must be disclosed. However, if the prior period is not restated, the disclosure of income before extraordinary items and net income is permitted on a *pro forma* basis.

> **OBSERVATION:** *To the extent practicable, financial statements restated for prior periods should contain all of the disclosures required by FASB-52.*

Gain or loss on forward exchange contracts, which under FASB-8 hedged an identifiable foreign currency commitment, shall be included in the opening balance of the separate component of stockholders' equity if the following conditions are met:

1. The forward exchange contract is canceled at the time FASB-52 is first applied.
2. The foreign currency commitment must involve the right to receive proceeds from the use or sale of nonmonetary assets that were translated at historical exchange rates under FASB-8.
3. The amount that can be included in the opening balance of the separate component of stockholders' equity may not exceed the amount of the related offsetting adjustment to the nonmonetary assets.

> **OBSERVATION:** For example, an enterprise has an operating lease or take-or-pay contract that represents the right to receive proceeds from the use or sale of a nonmonetary asset. Assume that the transaction qualified as an identifiable foreign currency commitment and the enterprise purchased a forward exchange contract to hedge the commitment, in accordance with the provisions of FASB-8. If the foreign exchange contract is canceled at the time that FASB-52 is first applied, any amounts that would have been deferred under the provisions of FASB-8 (up to the amount attributable to the related nonmonetary asset) shall be included in the opening balance of the separate component of stockholders' equity.

In the year that FASB-52 is first applied, the beginning balance of the separate component of stockholders' equity is equal to the difference between the beginning net asset translated at the current exchange rate at the beginning of the period. In addition, as discussed above, gain or loss on forward exchange contracts, which under FASB-8 hedged an identifiable foreign currency commitment, shall also be included in the opening balance of the separate component of stockholders' equity, if they meet the necessary conditions.

The difference between the historical exchange rate and the current exchange rate for deferred income taxes and insurance policy acquisition costs that arise as a result of remeasuring a foreign entity's financial statements shall be reported as an adjustment of the opening balance of retained earnings.

> **OBSERVATION:** In the event that a foreign entity's financial statements did not have to be remeasured because they were already expressed in its functional currency, the difference between the historical exchange rate and the current exchange rate for deferred income taxes and insurance policy acquisition costs would be reflected in the opening balance of the separate component of stockholders' equity.

If an enterprise first applies FASB-52 for fiscal years ending on or before March 31, 1982, disclosure in the year of change shall be made in the financial statements of the effects of adopting FASB-52 on (a) income before extraordinary items, (b) net income, and (c) related per share data. Subsequent to March 31, 1982, these disclosures for the year of change are not required.

Companies that adopt FASB-52 and are also required to comply with FASB-33 (Financial Reporting and Changing Prices) may prepare the supplementary information required by FASB-33 in accordance with (1) FASB-8 and the existing provisions of FASB-33 or (2) FASB-52 and the proposed amendment to FASB-33, which is expected to be issued in the near future.

If an enterprise must comply with FASB-33 because of early adoption of FASB-52, compliance with FASB-33 may be postponed until fiscal years beginning on or after December 15, 1982 (the effective date of FASB-52).

Comprehensive Illustration

The following is an illustration of how an enterprise should determine the beginning balance of the separate component of stockholders' equity.

DETERMINING THE BEGINNING BALANCE OF THE SEPARATE COMPONENT OF STOCKHOLDERS' EQUITY ACCOUNT

	Beginning of the Year			Beginning of the Year		
	Functional currency	FASB-8 exchange rates	U.S. dollars	Functional currency	Current exchange rates	U.S. dollars
Current Assets						
Cash	F 1,000	C*1.25	$ 800	F 1,000	C 1.25	$ 800
Accounts receivable	4,000	C 1.25	3,200	4,000	C 1.25	3,200
Inventory	10,000	H†2.00	5,000	10,000	C 1.25	8,000
Total	F15,000		$ 9,000	F15,000		$12,000
Property, plant, & equipment	F75,000	H 1.50	$50,000	F75,000	C 1.25	$60,000
Total assets	F90,000		$59,000	F90,000		$72,000
Current Liabilities	F20,000	C 1.25	$16,000	F20,000	C 1.25	$16,000
Deferred income taxes	5,000	H 2.00	2,500	5,000	C 1.25	4,000
Long-term obligations	20,000	C 1.25	16,000	20,000	C 1.25	16,000
Total liabilities	F45,000		$34,500	F45,000		$36,000
Net assets (equals stockholders' equity)	F45,000		$24,500	F45,000		$36,000

COMPUTATION OF THE BEGINNING BALANCE OF THE SEPARATE COMPONENT OF STOCKHOLDERS' EQUITY ACCOUNT

Net assets at beginning of the year at current exchange rate	$36,000
Net assets at beginning of the year at FASB-8 rates	$24,500
Beginning balance of separate component of stockholders' equity	$11,500

*C = Current exchange rate. †H = Historical exchange rate

GENERAL PRICE-LEVEL CHANGES

Background

Most information about restating financial statements for general price-level changes is contained in APB-3, which was issued in June 1969. APB Statements are not considered promulgated GAAP.

> **OBSERVATION:** *FASB-33 requires the application of some Current Value and General Price-Level Accounting techniques (see Financial Reporting and Changing Prices).*

Overview

The degree of inflation or deflation in an economy may become so great that conventional statements lose much of their significance, and general price-level statements clearly become more meaningful.

The unit of measure is the basic difference between historical and general price-level financial statements. General price-level financial statements do not represent replacement cost or an appraisal value, but merely represent what historical-cost statements reflect in general purchasing power, as at a specific date. GAAP used in historical-cost financial statements are also used in general price-level financial statements. Changes in the general price level are measured in terms of index numbers; the base year is given the index number of 100, and changes are expressed as percentages of the base year.

General

It is important to remember that general price-level adjusted statements are based on historical cost. The process of restatement simply converts the historical dollars into dollars of current purchasing power. Statements are adjusted to reflect the price level at the *end* of the current period.

Historically, the rate of inflation in the United States has not been significant enough to cause serious erosion of the *unit of measure principle*. However, the double-digit inflation of recent years has caused some to question the usefulness of historical-cost financial statements.

The price-level adjustment process consists of restating historical-cost financial statements into common dollars.

Monetary Assets and Liabilities

For purposes of general price-level accounting assets and liabilities are called *monetary items* if their amounts are fixed by contract or otherwise in terms of numbers of dollars. Cash, accounts and notes receivable in cash, and accounts and notes payable in cash are examples of monetary items.

Monetary items automatically gain or lose general purchasing power during inflation or deflation as a result of changes in the general price-level index. For example, a holder of a $10,000 promissory note executed 10 years ago and due today will receive exactly $10,000 today, in spite of the fact that $10,000 in cash today is worth a lot less than $10,000 in cash was worth 10 years ago! Such losses or gains of this nature are called *general price-level gains or losses*. Although monetary assets and liabilities are *not restated* on a general price-level balance sheet, the general price-level gains and losses are calculated and are recognized in the general price-level income statement.

Nonmonetary Assets and Liabilities

Assets and liabilities that are not monetary items are called *nonmonetary items* for purposes of general price-level accounting. Inventories, investments in common stocks, property, plant, equipment, and deferred charges are examples of nonmonetary items. Holders of nonmonetary items may lose or gain with the rise or fall of the general price-level index if the nonmonetary item does not rise or fall in proportion to the change in the price-level index. In other words, a nonmonetary asset or liability is affected (1) by the rise or fall of the general price-level index and (2) by the increase or decrease of the fair value of the nonmonetary item. For example, the purchaser of 10,000 shares of General Motors common stock 10 years ago was subject (1) to the decrease in purchasing power and (2) to the rise in the fair value of his stock. If the decrease in purchasing power exactly offsets the increase in the price of the stock, the purchaser is, in effect, in the same position today as he was 10 years ago (that is, monetarily).

By means of the general price-level index nonmonetary items are *restated* to current purchasing power at the end of the reporting period. The difference produced by the restatement of nonmonetary items does not represent replacement cost or current values, but presents the historical cost in terms of current purchasing power.

Inventory purchased at the end of a period, although a nonmonetary item, may well be already stated at approximately the general purchasing power at the end of a period.

Net Monetary Position

The difference between monetary assets and monetary liabilities, at any specific date, is the net monetary position. The net monetary position may be either positive (monetary assets exceed monetary liabilities) or negative (monetary liabilities exceed monetary assets).

In periods in which the general price-level index is rising (inflation), it is advantageous for a business to maintain a net negative monetary position. The opposite is true during periods in which the general price-level index is falling (deflation). In periods of inflation, a business which has a net negative monetary position will experience general price-level gains, because it can pay its liabilities in a fixed number of dollars that are getting cheaper as time goes by. A net positive monetary position during periods of inflation results in a general price-level loss, because the value of the dollar is declining.

Some assets and liabilities have characteristics of both monetary and nonmonetary items. Convertible debt, for example, is monetary in terms of its fixed obligation, but nonmonetary in terms of its conversion feature.

The determination of whether an item is monetary or nonmonetary is made as at the balance sheet date. Therefore, if convertible debt has not been converted as of that date, it should be classified as a monetary item. Additionally, a bond receivable held for speculation would be classified as nonmonetary, because the amount that will be received when the bond is sold is no longer fixed in amount, as it would be if the same bond was held to maturity.

Price Indexes

Price-level changes are measured by price indexes. Price indexes are stated in percentages to a base year, which is assigned a value of 100.

By using a price index, dollars of general purchasing power in one period can be restated to dollars of general purchasing power of another period. The formula for restating dollars of one period to those of another is:

$$\frac{\text{New index (converting to)}}{\text{Old index (converting from)}}$$

For example, assume that the current ending price index is 120, and a parcel of land was purchased for $10,000 in a year when the price index was 80. The conversion would be:

$$\frac{120}{80} \times \$10,000 = \$15,000$$

This conversion should not be interpreted to mean that the land is worth $15,000. What it means is that, historically, the purchasing power needed to buy the land is equal to $15,000 in terms of the dollar represented by the new price index.

Restating can be made in either direction—to current purchasing power or to purchasing power of a prior year.

In the United States the best price index for restating financial statements is the Gross National Product Implicit Price Deflator, which is *not* a specific-goods price index, but a broad index of general price changes.

General Price-Level Gain or Loss

Monetary items automatically gain or lose general purchasing power as a result of changes in price indexes. Assume that a comparative balance sheet showed cash of $10,000 and notes payable of $20,000 at both balance sheet dates in a year when the price index went from 110 to 117. Obviously, the current year's $10,000 in cash cannot purchase what the prior year's $10,000 in cash could. Using our formula the conversion of the current year to general price levels would be:

$$\frac{117}{110} \times \$10,000 = \$10,636$$

The $636 is a loss in the general purchasing power of the cash as measured by the change in the price indexes.

On the other hand, the current year's $20,000 of notes payable will be paid with cheaper dollars than the prior year's $20,000 in notes payable:

$$\frac{117}{110} \times \$20{,}000 = \$21{,}272$$

The $1,272 ($21,272 − $20,000) is a gain in the general purchasing power, because the liability will be paid with dollars of less general purchasing power.

If our hypothetical company had no other monetary assets and liabilities besides the cash of $10,000 and notes payable of $20,000, it would have a net general price-level gain of $636 ($1,272 − $636 = $636) for the year.

A change in the price index from one period to another can be expressed as a percentage. When the index moves from 110 to 117, it has increased 7 points, or 6.36% (7/110 = 6.36). Applying this percentage increase to the $10,000 cash and $20,000 notes payable in the preceding example:

$10,000 × 6.36% =	($ 636)
$20,000 × 6.36% =	1,272
Net price-level gain for the period	$ 636

Note that price-level increases arising from assets cause a price-level *loss*, whereas price-level increases arising from liabilities cause a price-level *gain*.

Instead of computing a gain or loss on each individual monetary item, it is easier to calculate the net monetary position. In our last example, the net monetary position (negative) was $10,000 ($10,000 in cash less $20,000 notes payable). We can now restate the beginning net monetary position for the change in the price index and then subtract the actual net monetary position at the end of the period, as follows:

Net monetary position (negative)	
$10,000 × $\frac{117}{110}$	$10,636
Less: Ending net monetary position	10,000*
Net general price-level gain	$ 636

*$10,000 cash less the $20,000 notes payable on the current year's balance sheet.

Advantages of Restatement

Advantages of general price-level financial statements are:

1. The dollar is not stable, and changes in its monetary value should be reflected in financial statements in order to produce more realistic information.
2. General price-level financial statements provide more meaningful information in terms of current economic conditions.
3. Management's effectiveness in periods of inflation or deflation can be more readily determined.
4. General price-level balance sheets more clearly approximate current values.

Disadvantages of Restatement

Disadvantages of general price-level financial statements are:

1. Historical-dollar financial statements are based on verifiable information.
2. There is no general agreement as to which price-level index to use and how it should be applied.
3. Most assets and liabilities that have been recently acquired are already valued close to current price levels.
4. Historical costs have been employed traditionally over many years with satisfactory results.

Schedule of General Price-Level Gain or Loss

Our previous discussion has been oversimplified in order to demonstrate the nature of general price-level gains or losses.

In reality, a business will have many transactions that cause a change in net monetary assets or liabilities. Cash and credit sales increase the net monetary position; purchases, operating expenses, and cash dividends decrease the net monetary position. Depreciation and amortization have no effect on the net monetary position. The procedure for preparing a schedule of general price-level gain or loss is:

1. Determine the net monetary position (positive or negative) at the beginning of the period (usually the monetary assets less

the monetary liabilities at the end of the prior period) adjusted to the general price-level index at the end of the period.
2. Add all increases in net monetary items from all sources (sales, miscellaneous revenue, proceeds from the sale of fixed assets, proceeds from the issuance of debt or stock, etc.), adjusted to the general price-level at the end of the period.
3. Deduct all decreases in net monetary items from all sources (expenditures for purchases, operating expenses, acquisition of assets, miscellaneous expenses, and the retirement of debt or stock), adjusted to the general price-level index at the end of the period.
4. Arrive at the *estimated* net monetary position at the end of the period, which is the difference between steps 1, 2, and 3 above.
 (1 + 2 − 3) = estimated net monetary position at the end of the period
5. Compute the *actual* net monetary position at the end of the period (monetary assets less monetary liabilities), and subtract this from the estimated net monetary position calculated in step 4.
 Note: The difference between the estimated net monetary items at the end of the period and the actual net monetary items at the end of the period is the general price-level gain or loss for the period. If the estimated net monetary items exceed the actual, a loss results. If the estimated net monetary items are less than the actual, a gain results.

This price-level gain or loss is shown in the income statement as the item immediately preceding net income.

General Price-Level Financial Statements

The following are general rules for preparing price-level adjusted financial statements:

1. All financial statements presented, including those of prior years, are restated to the purchasing power of the dollar at the most recent balance sheet date. This is called "rolling over" the previously restated statements. The prior restated statements are simply restated again to the current price level. This serves two purposes. It converts last year's statements into current-year dollars (comparability), and it translates last year's

ending retained earnings into current-year dollars for use in the current-year statement of retained earnings.
2. Sales and expenses incurred evenly throughout the year are converted by using the average general price index for the year.
3. The inventory method (FIFO, LIFO, etc.) will dictate the price index to use for restating inventory.
4. Depreciation is restated by using the price index of the related asset.
5. Buildings, equipment, and other fixed assets are restated by using the price index existing at the time of their purchase.
6. Common stock is restated by using the price index existing at the time the stock was issued.

Comprehensive Illustration

The following comprehensive problem illustrates how financial statements are restated for general price-level changes.

ABC Corporation's financial statements for the year ended December 31, 19X2, are shown below:

ABC Corporation
Balance Sheet
As of December 31, 19X2

Cash	$100,000
Accounts receivable	200,000
Inventory (FIFO)	50,000
Fixed assets	250,000
Total assets	$600,000
Accounts payable	$ 70,000
Common stock	200,000
Retained earnings	330,000
Total liabilities and equity	$600,000

ABC Corporation
Income Statement
For the year ended December 31, 19X2

Sales		$900,000
Cost of goods sold:		
Beginning inventory	$ 50,000	
Add: Purchases	700,000	
Total	$750,000	
Less: Ending inventory	50,000	
Cost of goods sold		700,000
Gross profit		$200,000
Operating expenses:		
Depreciation		$ 20,000
Other		80,000
Total operating expenses		$100,000
Income before taxes		$100,000
Income tax expense		20,000
Net income		$ 80,000

Relevant price indexes

Beginning of year	104
End of year	108
Average	106
Fixed assets acquired	92
Formation of company	90

Additional data:
The company's net monetary position at December 31, 19X1, was $130,000. Inventories are priced on a FIFO basis.

The first step in this problem is to compute the amount of the general price-level gain or loss.

The essence of creating the schedule of general price-level gain or loss is to compare the monetary items at year end with the amount at which the items would have been stated if they were nonmonetary items.

The steps in preparing this schedule for ABC Corporation are explained below.

General Price-Level Changes

1. The net monetary position at the beginning of the year (December 31, 19X1) is given as $130,000. Restate this to current dollars as follows:

$$\$130,000 \times \frac{108}{104} = \$135,000$$

The beginning index of 104 is used because this is the net monetary position at the *beginning* of the period.

2. Assemble all increases in monetary items and convert them, using the appropriate index.

Increases:

Sales	$900,000
Total increases	$900,000
Factor	108/106
Adjusted sales	$916,981

The average index of 106 is used because sales are assumed to occur evenly through the year.

3. Assemble all decreases in monetary items and convert them, using the appropriate index.

Decreases:

Purchases	$700,000
Other expenses	80,000
Income tax expense	20,000
Total decreases	$800,000
Factor	108/106
Adjusted expenses	$815,094

The average index of 106 is used because purchases and expenses, including income tax expense, are assumed to be incurred evenly through the year.

General Price-Level Changes

4. The net estimated monetary position at year end is calculated as follows:

Net monetary position—beginning	$135,000
Plus: Increases	916,981
Less: Decreases	(815,094)
Net estimated monetary position—ending	$236,887

5. The actual net monetary position at the end of the period is calculated from actual amounts appearing on the balance sheet for the end of the period, as follows:

Monetary assets:
Cash	$100,000
Accounts receivable	200,000
Total actual monetary assets	$300,000

Monetary liabilities:
Accounts payable	$ 70,000
Total actual monetary liability	$ 70,000
Net monetary position (positive)	$230,000

The general price-level gain or loss can now be calculated as follows:

Actual net monetary items	$230,000
Estimated net monetary items	236,887
General price-level gain (loss)	($ 6,887)

Since the estimated net monetary position exceeds the actual net monetary position, there is a loss.

The work papers for the restatement of the financial statements of ABC Corporation follow:

General Price-Level Changes

ABC Corporation
Income Statement
For the year ended December 31, 19X2

	Historical	Conversion factor	Adjusted
Sales	$900,000	108/106	$916,981
Cost of goods sold:			
Beginning inventory	$ 50,000	108/104	$ 51,923
Add: Purchases	700,000	108/106	713,208
Total	$750,000		$765,131
Less: Ending inventory	50,000	108/108	50,000
Cost of goods sold	$700,000		$715,131
Gross profit	$200,000		$201,850
Operating expenses:			
Depreciation	$ 20,000	108/92	$ 23,478
Other	80,000	108/106	81,509
Total	$100,000		$104,987
Net income before taxes	$100,000		$ 96,863
Income tax expense	20,000	108/106	20,377
Net income	$ 80,000		$ 76,486
General price-level gain (loss)			($ 6,887)
Net income–adjusted for changes in general price levels			$ 69,599

Schedule of General Price-Level Gain (Loss)

Historical		Converted for Price-Level Changes
$130,000	Beginning net monetary position [index at beginning of year (104) index at end of year (108) = conversion factor 108/104]	$135,000
900,000	Increases in monetary items during the year: sales $900,000 [average index during the year (106), index at end of year (108) = conversion factor 108/106]	916,981
(800,000)	Decreases in monetary items during the year: purchases $700,000, other expenses $80,000, income tax expense $20,000 [average index during the year (106), index at end of year (108) = conversion factor 108/106]	(815,094)
$230,000	Ending net estimated monetary position	$236,887
230,000	Ending actual net monetary position*	230,000
—	General price-level gain or (loss)	($ 6,887)

*Monetary assets–end of period	$300,000
Less: Monetary liabilities–end of period	70,000
Actual net monetary position–end of period	$230,000

General Price-Level Changes

ABC Corporation
Balance Sheet
As of December 31, 19X2

	Historical	Conversion factor	Adjusted
Cash	$100,000	108/108	$100,000
Accounts receivable	200,000	108/108	200,000
Inventory	50,000	108/108	50,000
Fixed assets	250,000	108/92	293,478
Total assets	$600,000		$643,478
Accounts payable	$ 70,000	108/108	$ 70,000
Common stock	200,000	108/90	240,000
Retained earnings	330,000		333,478
Total liabilities and equity	$600,000		$643,478

Note: Only the nonmonetary assets and liabilities are restated on the general price-level balance sheet. The changes in the net monetary assets and liabilities have already been taken into account in the general price-level income statement as a general price-level gain or loss.

GOVERNMENT CONTRACTS

Background

The promulgated GAAP which addresses itself to Government Contracts is as follows:

   ARB-43, Chapter 11A—Cost-Plus-Fixed-Fee Contracts
   ARB-43, Chapter 11B—Renegotiation
   ARB-43, Chapter 11C—Terminated War and Defense Contracts

Overview

More frequently than not, government contracts are performed under a cost-plus-fixed-fee (CPFF) arrangement which provides for possible renegotiation, if the contracting officer for the government believes that excess profits were made by the contractor. These contracts usually also provide that the government may terminate the contract for its convenience at any time.

CPFF Contracts

Cost-plus-fixed-fee contracts generally provide that the government pay a fixed fee in addition to all costs involved in fulfilling the contract. The contract may include the manufacture of a product or only the performance of services, and the government may or may not withhold a specified percentage of the interim payments until completion of the entire contract. Furthermore, CPFF contracts are usually cancellable by the government, and when such contracts are terminated the contractor is entitled to reimbursement for all costs, plus an equitable portion of the fixed fee.

One of the main problems in accounting for CPFF contracts is when profits should be recognized. As a general rule, profits should not be recognized until the right to full payment becomes unconditional, which is usually when the product has been delivered and accepted or the services fully rendered (completed-contract method).

However, when CPFF contracts extend over several years, the completed-contract method may be utilized; the percentage-of-completion method is acceptable, provided that costs and profits can be reasonably estimated and realization of the contract is reasonably assured.

An advance payment by the government may not be offset as a payment on account, unless it is expected to be applied as such with reasonable certainty. A distinction should be made in the balance sheet between unbilled costs and fees and billed amounts. In the event that an advance is offset, it must be clearly disclosed.

Renegotiation

Renegotiation involves the adjustment of the original selling price or contract. Since the government makes renegotiation adjustments an integral part of a contract, a provision for such probable adjustments is necessary. This provision for renegotiation should be based on the contractor's past experience or on the general experience of the particular industry, and it is shown in the income statement as a reduction of the related sales or income. If a reasonable estimate cannot be made, disclosure of the inability to provide for renegotiation should be fully disclosed in the financial statements or footnotes thereto. The provision for renegotiation is reported as a current liability in the balance sheet.

In those unusual cases where collection is not reasonably assured, it may be preferable to employ the installment-sale or cost-recovery method in accounting for a government contract.

When a provision for renegotiation is made in a particular year and the subsequent final adjustment differs materially, the difference should be shown in the income statement of the year of final determination.

Disclosure

When a significant part of a company's business is derived from government contracts, such disclosure should be made in the financial statements or footnotes thereto, indicating the uncertainties involved and the possibility of renegotiation in excess of the amount provided. In addition, the basis of determining the provision for renegotiation should be disclosed (prior experience, industry experience, etc.).

Terminated War and Defense Contracts

This section of the promulgated GAAP deals with both fixed-price and cost-plus-fixed-fee contracts. It addresses the problems involved in the termination of a government contract by the government but does not cover terminations resulting from default of the contractor.

The determination of profit or loss on a terminated government contract is made as of the effective date of termination. This is the date that the contractor accrues the right to receive payment on that portion of the contract which has been terminated.

Although most government contracts provide for a minimum profit percentage formula in the event agreement cannot be reached, the amount of profit to be reported in the case of termination for the convenience of the government is the difference between all allowable costs incurred and the amount of the termination claim.

If it is impossible to determine a reasonable estimate of the termination claim for reporting purposes, full disclosure of this fact should be made by footnote to the financial statements, which should describe the uncertainties involved. In other words, those parts of the termination claim which can be reasonably ascertained should be reported, and those which cannot be reasonably ascertained should be described in a footnote to the financial statements.

Termination claims should be classified as current assets. Prior to termination notice, advances received should be deducted from termination claims receivable for reporting purposes. Loans received on the security of the contract or termination claim should be separately shown as current liabilities.

The cost of items included in the termination claim that are subsequently reacquired by the contractor should be recorded as a new purchase, and the amount should be applied as a reduction of the termination claim. These types of reductions from the termination claim are generally referred to as *disposal credits*.

Disclosure

Material amounts of termination claims should be classified separately from other receivables in the financial statements.

Termination claims should be stated at the amount estimated as collectible, and adequate provision or disclosure should be made for items of a controversial nature.

Claims against the government, if material, should be segregated from other receivables.

INCOME TAXES

Background

The present promulgated GAAP on income taxes, which is covered herein, consists of the following:

    APB-10, paragraph 6—Tax Allocation Accounts-Discounts
    APB-10, paragraph 7—Offsetting of Securities Against Taxes Payable
    APB-11—Accounting for Income Taxes
    APB-23—Accounting for Income Taxes—Special Areas
    APB-24—Accounting for Income Taxes—Investments in Common Stocks Accounted for by the Equity Method
    FASB-31—Accounting for Tax Benefits Related to U.K. Tax Legislation Concerning Stock Relief
    FASB-37—Balance Sheet Classification of Deferred Income Taxes
    FASB Interpretation-18—Accounting for Income Taxes in Interim Periods
    FASB Interpretation-22—Applicability of Indefinite Reversal Criteria to Timing Differences
    FASB Interpretation-29—Reporting Tax Benefits Realized on Disposition of Investments in Certain Subsidiaries and Other Investees
    Note: APB-11 is considered the main source for general income tax GAAP. Accounting for Income Taxes—Oil and Gas Producing Companies (FASB-19) and Accounting for the Investment Credit (APB-2) are discussed elsewhere in this publication.

Overview

One of the basic principles in accounting is that business entities are presumed to continue in existence unless liquidation is imminent (going-concern principle). Therefore, a business currently subject to income taxes will ordinarily continue to pay such taxes in the future. Income tax expense is an important determinant of net income, and must be identified to, and measured with, the appropriate accounting periods.

  Income for federal tax purposes and financial accounting income frequently differ. Obviously, income for federal tax purposes is computed in accordance with the prevailing tax laws, whereas financial accounting income is determined in accordance with GAAP. In such a case, a company will have two different income tax liabilities: one for income tax purposes and the other for financial accounting purposes. This disparity is caused by timing differences.

Timing Differences

Timing differences are merely transactions that do not appear in financial accounting income and taxable income in the same reporting period. For example, accelerated depreciation for tax purposes and straight-line depreciation for financial accounting purposes create a timing difference in that taxable income will be different from financial accounting income in the same period. There are two types of timing differences:

1. Those which always reverse themselves in one or more future periods
2. Those which never reverse themselves, or permanent differences

Comprehensive interperiod income tax allocation includes the effects of timing differences in computing income tax expense for a period. This process balances the tax liability and income tax expense for a period by the use of tax deferrals and accruals.

Transactions that cause timing differences There are four basic causes of timing differences:

1. Income that is included in taxable income, after it has already been included in financial accounting income
   (*Example:* Installment sales are reported for tax purposes as they are collected, but in financial accounting the total income is recognized in the period the sale is made, so collections on the installment sale are included in taxable income, after the entire sale was recognized by financial accounting in the year of sale.)
2. Income that is included in taxable income before it is included in financial accounting income
   (*Example:* Rents collected in advance must be included in taxable income, but in financial accounting such rents are recognized only in the periods in which they are earned.)
3. Expenses deducted for taxable income after they have already been deducted for financial accounting income

(*Example:* Provision for estimated product warranty is not deductible in computing taxable income, but such provision is made in financial accounting at the time a sale is made.)
4. Expenses deducted for taxable income before they are deducted for financial accounting purposes
(*Example:* Accelerated depreciation is allowed in computing taxable income, but in financial accounting the straight-line method is usually used to more properly match revenue with its expired costs.)

Some timing differences reduce income taxes that would otherwise have to be paid, whereas other timing differences may increase income taxes.

> **OBSERVATION:** *The Tax Equity and Fiscal Responsibility Act of 1982 (TEFRA) provides that a taxpayer may elect to either (a) claim the full investment tax credit (ITC) and reduce the basis of the property by one half of its related ITC, or (b) claim an ITC that is reduced by two percentage points and not reduce the basis of the related property.*
>
> *FASB Technical Bulletin 83-1 requires that the reduction in the basis of property by one half of its related ITC (as may be required by TEFRA) must be accounted for as a timing difference in accordance with APB-11. Thus, deferred income taxes must be accrued in connection with the reduction of the basis of property in the same manner as deferred taxes are accrued in connection with a timing difference. See the section in Chapter 25.01 entitled "Reduction in basis of property" for more information.*

Permanent differences   Permanent differences arise from special tax laws regarding exempt income, dividends received exclusions, and certain other special deductions that, after taken, are permanent. Since permanent differences do not affect subsequent periods, no interperiod tax allocation need be made to account for them.

Permanent differences are either (a) nontaxable, (b) nondeductible, or (c) special tax allowances. Examples are:

1. Tax-exempt interest (municipal, state)
2. Proceeds from life insurance on officers
3. Amortization of goodwill
4. Life insurance premiums when corporation is beneficiary
5. Certain fines, bribes, kickbacks, etc.
6. Dividends received deduction for corporations
7. Excess percentage depletion over cost depletion

Bad debt allowances of savings and loan associations, and policyholders' surplus of stock life insurance companies that create a difference between taxable income and pretax financial accounting income are usually considered permanent differences, because the company controls the events that create the tax consequence. However, if circumstances dictate that income taxes will be paid because of a reduction in the bad debt allowance or in policyholders' surplus, a tax expense should be accrued on such reductions in the period they occur. In effect, these reductions do create a timing difference when they occur and should not be accounted for as an extraordinary item.

Disclosure of bad debt allowances and policyholders' surplus should be made in the financial statements or in footnotes, as follows:

Bad debt allowance (reserves):

1. The purpose of the allowance account and the rules and regulations pertaining thereto
2. The fact that income taxes may become payable if the allowance account is used for other purposes
3. The total amount of the allowance account for which income taxes have not been accrued

Policyholders' surplus:

1. Treatment of the policyholders' surplus under the provisions of the IRC
2. The fact that income taxes may become payable if the company takes specific action, which should be appropriately described
3. The total amount of policyholders' surplus for which income taxes have not been accrued

These disclosure requirements also apply to the parent company of the savings and loan association or the stock life insurance company.

Operating Losses

Under present tax regulations an operating loss of a period may be carried back or forward and may be applied as a reduction of income in those periods permitted by the tax laws. In such a case, the taxable income and the financial accounting income will change for the periods that the loss is carried back or forward.

If an operating loss is carried forward, the tax effects are not recognized because there is no assurance that they will be realized. For example, a loss carryforward would decrease the amount of taxes due in a certain future period, but if the company continues to lose money, there will be no profits to offset the carryforward and it may never be utilized. However, when the tax benefits of a loss carryforward are recognized in full or in part in subsequent periods, it is reported as an extraordinary item.

If an operating loss is carried back, the tax effect will certainly be realized in the form of a claim for taxes previously paid.

There is only one exception to not recognizing the effects of a loss carryforward. The tax effects of a loss carryforward may be realized in the books of accounts *providing that the realization is assured beyond any reasonable doubt.* In this event, in determining the results of operations for those periods the potential tax benefit (deferred tax credit) is recognized in the period(s) that gave rise to the loss. Estimates of the tax benefit should be based on the tax rates that are expected to exist at the time of realization. Any difference between the estimated amount and that received is applied as an adjustment of the tax expense of the period in which the benefit is received. Realization of a loss carryforward is assured beyond any reasonable doubt if the following conditions exist:

1. The company has been reasonably profitable over a long period or has experienced occasional losses which were subsequently offset by taxable income.
2. The loss carryforward is the result of an isolated, nonrecurring, and identifiable source.
3. Realization of future taxable income is large enough to offset the loss carryforward and will occur within the period allowed under tax law.

If tax benefits of loss carryforwards have not been recognized by a purchased subsidiary prior to the date of acquisition, they are recorded as assets purchased if realization is assured beyond any reasonable doubt. If they have not been recognized prior to the acquisition date, they are recognized when actually realized and treated as a retroactive adjustment of the purchase transaction. In this event, operating results for periods subsequent to the purchase may have to be retroactively adjusted if the affected balance sheet items have been subject to amortization.

A similar situation arises for loss carryforwards arising prior to a quasi-reorganization where realization is assured beyond a reasonable doubt. Under these circumstances, a previously unrecognized loss carryforward is recorded as an asset at the date of reorganization. If realization is not assured, the tax benefits of a loss carryforward are recognized when actually realized, and added to contributed capital, on the basis that the benefits are attributable to loss periods prior to the quasi-reorganization.

All other unused tax deductions and/or credits that may be carried back and forward in determining taxable income except investment tax credits are handled in the same manner as operating losses. That is, if realization is assured beyond any reasonable doubt, the tax deduction or credit is recognized for financial accounting purposes (books). As a general rule, investment tax credits may not be recognized even though their realization is assured beyond any reasonable doubt. However, in using the "with and without" method of computing deferred taxes, investment tax credits are recognized for financial accounting purposes (books) prior to their realization for tax return purposes (see- Investment Tax Credits).

The tax effects of any realizable loss carryback should be recognized in the determination of the loss period net income. A claim of refund for past taxes will result and is shown on the balance sheet as a separate item (from other deferred taxes) and classified as either current or noncurrent. In the income statement, the claim of refund for past taxes is shown as a reduction of income tax expense for the current period.

When the tax effects of a carryback loss are not recognized (when prior years already are losses) and at the same time a net deferred tax credit exists, an adjustment may have to be made. In such a case, the deferred tax credits should be (1) eliminated to the extent of the tax effect of the resulting loss carryforward or (2) amortized over the period of the resulting loss carryforward. If in subsequent periods the loss carryforward is realized, in part or in whole, the prior adjustments to the deferred tax credits will have to be readjusted or reinstated at the then current tax rates. This procedure is similar to the offsetting of unused investment tax credits against existing net deferred tax credits required by FASB Interpretation-25 (see- Investment Tax Credits).

Timing Differences—Special Areas

There is a presumption that all undistributed earnings of a subsidiary (domestic and foreign) will eventually be transferred to the parent. Unless the presumption is overcome, the undistributed earnings included in a parent's consolidated income will result in a timing difference, which should be recognized in the accounts. In addition, corporate joint ventures and investments in common stocks

Income Taxes

accounted for by the equity method present the same problem as a subsidiary in regard to timing differences and should be accounted for in the same manner.

> **OBSERVATION:** *Undistributed earnings of a subsidiary include those of a domestic international sales corporation (DISC) that qualify for tax deferral.*

An investor's proportionate share of operating losses from a subsidiary which files separate income tax returns, a joint venture, or an investment in common stock accounted for by the equity method, is accounted for in the same manner as other operating losses (see 19.04). As a result, an operating loss of this type is included in the investor's income or loss for the period, but is not treated as a timing difference unless it is realizable beyond any reasonable doubt. The journal entry to record the investor's proportionate share of an investee's operating loss is a debit to a loss account which appears on the income statement and a credit to the investment account. As a result, a difference is created between the accounting and tax basis of the investment. In addition, no deferred taxes are provided for, unless the operating loss is realizable beyond a reasonable doubt. Should the operating loss become realizable beyond a reasonable doubt a tax benefit is realized at that time. Because of the difference between the accounting and tax basis, a tax benefit will also be realized upon the ultimate disposition of the investment. FASB Interpretation-29 requires that these tax benefits be included as part of the gain or loss on the disposition of the investment. The result is that the tax benefit is given the same classification as the gain or loss on the investment (continuing operations, extraordinary item, disposal of a segment, etc.). Any significant variation in the usual relationship between income tax expense and pretax accounting income must be disclosed in the financial statements (APB-11).

> **OBSERVATION:** *There is a mistake in paragraph 3 of FASB Interpretation-29. The reference to paragraph 63(c) of APB-11, should be paragraph 62(c). There is no paragraph 63(c).*

Indefinite reversal criteria The presumption that all undistributed earnings of a subsidiary or corporate joint venture will be eventually distributed to the parent may be overcome by sufficient evidence that the subsidiary or corporate joint venture has invested or will invest such earnings indefinitely, or that they will be remitted in a tax-free liquidation—all in accordance with a specific plan. In the event the plans change and earnings will be remitted in the foreseeable future, the parent company should accrue as an expense

GAAP GUIDE / 19.07

of the current period the appropriate income tax expense. If the reverse occurs, where income taxes were accrued and the undistributed earnings will not be distributed in the foreseeable future, the parent company should adjust income tax expense of the current period. In either case, the adjustment of income tax expense should not be accounted for as an extraordinary item.

> **OBSERVATION:** Under the provisions of the Tax Reform Act of 1984, qualified earnings of a Domestic International Sales Corporation (DISC) that are not distributed to a stockholder(s), on or before December 31, 1984, are to be treated as previously taxed income, and thus, will be exempt from federal income taxes. As a result, deferred income taxes on undistributed earnings of a DISC that have been recorded on the books of a stockholder will have to be adjusted if the earnings are not expected to be distributed in a taxable transaction before January 1, 1985. FASB Technical Bulletin 84-2 provides that the adjustment to deferred taxes should be recognized as a reduction of income tax expense, in one interim period of the current year. The effect of the adjustment on income tax expense should be disclosed and may be shown as a separate component of income tax expense.
>
> FASB Technical Bulletin 84-2 is effective for financial statements and interim financial information issued after September 30, 1984, for fiscal years ending after July 18, 1984 (the enactment date of the Tax Reform Act of 1984). Earlier application is permitted, but not required. Interim financial information issued after September 30, 1984, for fiscal years ending after July 18, 1984, should be retroactively restated, if necessary.

The indefinite reversal criteria for investments in common stock accounted for by the equity method depend upon those interests that control the investment. Only the controlling interest (50% or more) of an investment in common stocks accounted for by the equity method, can determine that undistributed earnings will be reinvested for an indefinite period. The fact that the equity method presumes that an investor has the ability to exercise significant influence over the investee if the investor owns 20% or more control, is irrelevant in considering the indefinite reversal criteria.

Corporate joint ventures may be permanent or have a limited life depending on the nature of the venture. GAAP (APB-18) requires that corporate joint ventures, of less than 50% control, be accounted for by the equity method.

Changes in investment An investment (usually 50% or more) in a subsidiary may change to the extent that a subsidiary relationship no longer exists, and the equity method (20% to 49% control) or the cost method (less than 20% control) must be applied. In the event that a subsidiary changes to an investment in common stock accounted for by the equity method, the investor should recognize income taxes on its share of the current earnings of the investee in accordance with the equity method. If, previous to the change in an investment from a subsidiary to one accounted for by the equity or cost method, the parent had not accrued income taxes because of the indefinite reversal criteria, it should then accrue income taxes on the undistributed earnings in the period that it becomes apparent that part or all of the undistributed earnings will be remitted. This accrual should not be accounted for as an extraordinary item.

Deferred income taxes resulting from undistributed earnings of a subsidiary, corporate joint venture, and an investment in common stock accounted for by the equity method should be considered in accounting for a sale or other disposition of the underlying investment.

An investment in common stock accounted for by the equity method may fall below the 20% ownership that is presumed to indicate significant control, or may rise to 50% or more, which indicates that it has become a subsidiary. If the investment becomes a subsidiary, the deferred income taxes, if any, previously accrued should be included in the income of the parent only as dividends are received that exceed the parent's share of earnings subsequent to the date of becoming a subsidiary. If the investment falls below 20% ownership, the deferred income taxes previously accrued should be included in income only as dividends are received that exceed the allocable share of earnings subsequent to the date the investment fell below 20%.

In the event of a sale or other disposition of an investment in common stock accounted for by the equity method, deferred taxes attributable to the investment should be taken into consideration.

Railroad gradings and tunnel bores Income tax benefits resulting from the amortization of railroad gradings and tunnel bores are timing differences for which comprehensive interperiod tax allocation must be made (FASB Interpretation-18).

U.S. steamship companies Present promulgated GAAP does not cover deposits in capital construction funds or statutory reserves of U.S. steamship companies complying with the Merchant Marine Act of 1970.

Measuring timing differences Difficulties in measuring timing differences in these special areas do not justify ignoring the accrual of income taxes. Estimates and assumptions should be used that include all available related tax planning, tax credits, and deductions. Parent companies' income tax expense should also include a provision, if any, for taxes that would have been withheld if the undistributed earnings had been remitted as dividends.

The determination of whether the undistributed earnings of an investment in common stock accounted for by the equity method will be realized in dividends, the sale or other disposition, or a combination of both, must be made on the basis of the facts and circumstances of each individual investment. If it is determined that the undistributed earnings will be realized in dividends, the accrued income taxes should be based on any available dividend-received deduction, foreign-tax credit, and other tax credits or deductions that may be applicable in the circumstances. On the other hand, if the ultimate disposition will be realized by the sale of the investment, the accrued income taxes should be based on capital gain rates, if applicable, recognizing all other available credits and deductions.

The operating losses of a subsidiary, a joint venture, and an investment in common stock accounted for by the equity method are accounted for in the same manner as other operating losses previously mentioned.

Deferred Tax Method

The deferred tax method of allocating income taxes should be used (APB-11) and is considered the most useful and practical approach to interperiod allocation. The promulgated GAAP (APB-11) has rejected the use of other methods.

Under the deferred tax method, income taxes payable are computed twice: once on the amount that excludes any transaction causing a timing difference and once on the amount that includes the transaction causing a timing difference. The difference between the two income taxes payable is the deferred income tax for the period for that particular timing difference.

The promulgated GAAP (APB-11) states that "The tax effect of a timing difference should be measured by the differential between income taxes computed with and without inclusion of the transaction creating the difference between taxable income and pretax accounting income." Taxable income is further defined as "the excess of revenues over deductions or the excess of deductions over revenue to be reported for income tax purposes for a period . . . except that deductions do not include loss carryforwards or loss carrybacks."

The following is an illustration of the "with and without" method of computing deferred income taxes as required by APB-11.

Income Taxes

Assume the following facts for the XYZ Corporation for its calendar year ended December 31, 19XX:

- $362,500 allowable investment tax credit for the current year
- $1,000,000 of pretax financial accounting income (books)
- $200,000 of net timing differences which reduce taxable income
- 40% tax rate for the current period
- The maximum investment tax credit may not exceed the taxpayer's first $25,000 of tax liability, plus 90% of the tax liability over $25,000.

Discussion

Income tax expense is computed on all taxable items included in pretax financial accounting income. In this example, all items included in financial accounting income are eventually taxable.

There are no permanent differences in this example. In any event, permanent differences do not affect subsequent periods because they do not reverse in future periods, and no interperiod tax allocation need be made to account for them. Therefore, if a permanent difference is taxable, it is included in computing income tax expense (books) for the period. If a permanent difference is nontaxable, it is excluded in computing income tax expense for financial accounting purposes.

The first computation in solving this example illustration is to determine income tax expense on pretax financial accounting income (books) and the current income tax liability on taxable income (tax return), as follows:

Income Tax Expense on Pretax Financial Accounting Income:

Pretax financial accounting income	$1,000,000
Rate of tax	40%
Income tax expense before allowable investment tax credit	$ 400,000
Allowable investment tax credit [$25,000 plus 90% of ($400,000 less $25,000)]	362,500
Income tax expense (books)	$ 37,500

Current Income Tax Liability on Taxable Income:

Pretax financial accounting income	$1,000,000
Less: Timing difference	200,000
Taxable income	$ 800,000
Rate of tax	40%

GAAP GUIDE / 19.11

Income Taxes

Income tax liability before allowable investment tax credit	$ 320,000
Allowable investment tax credit [$25,000 plus 90% of ($320,000 less $25,000)]	290,500
Current income tax liability	$ 29,500

The $8,000 difference between income tax expense of $37,500 (books) and the current income tax liability of $29,500 (tax return) is the deferred tax expense on the net timing difference of $200,000, computed as follows:

Net timing difference	$ 200,000
Rate of tax	40%
Income tax expense before allowable investment tax credit	$ 80,000
Allowable investment tax credit (90% of $80,000)	72,000
Deferred tax expense on timing difference	$ 8,000

The journal entry to record the income tax expense for the current period and the deferred taxes is:

Income tax expense—current	$29,500	
Income tax expense—deferred	8,000	
Current tax liability		$29,500
Deferred taxes		8,000

The provision for income taxes in the income statement for the current period would appear as follows:

Provision for income taxes:	
Current	$29,500
Deferred	8,000
Total provision for income taxes	$37,500

Analysis of Solution:
From a practical standpoint, interperiod tax allocation is basically an accrual or prepayment process. In the above example, XYZ Corporation had $200,000 more pretax financial accounting income (books) than it showed on its tax return. Perhaps the reason for the difference was that for book income the straight-line method of depreciation was being used and for tax return purposes they used an accelerated method. The fact is that they showed $200,000 more

income per books than on their tax return and for that reason taxes computed on book income was $8,000 more than that reflected on the tax return. The credit of $8,000 to deferred taxes is actually an accrual of income taxes which will have to be paid in the future when the timing difference reverses itself.

It must be realized that a timing difference can either increase or decrease taxable income. In the illustration of the XYZ Corporation, suppose that the $200,000 timing difference arose because of rental income collected in advance. Advance rental income is taxable when received for tax purposes, but would be excluded from financial accounting income (books) because it would not be income for the current period. In that case, pretax financial accounting income would only be $800,000 and taxable income $1,000,000. Instead of accruing the tax on the $200,000 timing difference, XYZ would in fact have to prepay it. The computations using the "with and without" method follow:

Income Tax Expense on Pretax Financial Accounting Income:
Pretax financial accounting income	$ 800,000
Rate of tax	40%
Income tax expense before allowable investment tax credit	$ 320,000
Allowable investment tax credit [$25,000 plus 90% of ($320,000 less $25,000)]	290,500
Income tax expense	$ 29,500

Current Income Tax Liability on Taxable Income:
Pretax financial accounting income	$ 800,000
Add: Timing difference	200,000
Taxable income	$1,000,000
Rate of tax	40%
Income tax liability before allowable investment tax credit	$ 400,000
Allowable investment tax credit [$25,000 plus 90% of ($400,000 less $25,000)]	362,500
Current income tax liability	$ 37,500

The $8,000 difference between income tax expense of $29,500 (books) and the current income tax liability of $37,500 (tax return) is the deferred tax expense on the net timing difference of $200,000. However, this time the journal entry will reflect that the $8,000 of deferred taxes is actually a prepayment of future taxes, as follows:

Income tax expense—current	$37,500	
Deferred taxes	8,000	
Income tax expense—deferred		$ 8,000
Current tax liability		37,500

The provision for income taxes in the income statement for the current period would appear, as follows:

Provision for income taxes:	
Current	$37,500
Deferred	(8,000)
Total provision for income taxes	$29,500

The "short cut" approach which determines the deferred tax by applying the current tax rate to the transaction causing the timing difference works most of the time. However, in some instances involving the effect of the investment credit, foreign tax credit, and operating losses, the "short cut" approach does not theoretically work.

Timing differences may be considered individually, or in groups of similar timing differences which may be further determined by the gross change or net change method. However, the tax effect in all cases is based on a differential calculation of taxes involved.

> **OBSERVATION:** *Where a company is subject to more than one tax rate, the U.S. tax rate is usually increased by a percent equivalent, to take into consideration taxes imposed by other jurisdictions.*

Individual method The tax effect of a timing difference is computed separately on each timing difference.

Gross change method For each group of similar timing differences a computation is made for the tax effects of originating differences based on the current tax rate, and for the tax effects of reversing differences at the tax rate reflected in the account.

Net change method A single computation is made at current tax rates for the net cumulative tax effect of both originating and reversing differences occurring during a period for a particular similar group.

Groups of similar timing differences are determined on the basis of those arising from the same kind of transaction, such as depreciation, installment sales, and warranties.

Once a method for determining the tax effects of timing differences is selected, it must be consistently applied, because a change would probably require a consistency exception in the auditor's report.

Deferred taxes are amortized as the timing differences reverse in periods subsequent to their origination.

The total of all deferred federal income tax charges and all deferred federal income tax credits should be offset and the resulting net figure used for balance sheet purposes. (This does not include a claim of refund or offsets to future taxes arising from net operating loss carrybacks and carryforwards, which should be shown in separate accounts and classified as either current or noncurrent.)

Matching Concept

The principle of matching income tax expense with the related financial accounting income is the objective of comprehensive interperiod tax allocation.

ABC Construction Co. uses the completed-contract method for tax purposes and the percentage-of-completion method for financial accounting purposes. The realized gross profit recognized on one four-year contract was $5,000, $6,000, $7,000, and $12,000. Assuming a 50% tax rate in effect for the four years, tax allocation would be:

	1	2	3	4
Income	$5,000	$6,000	$7,000	$12,000
50% taxes	2,500	3,000	3,500	6,000
Net income	$2,500	$3,000	$3,500	$ 6,000

The journal entry the first three years was:

Income tax expense	$XXX	
Deferred taxes		$XXX

In the fourth year, when the contract was completed and appeared on the tax return, the journal entry was:

Income tax expense	$6,000	
Deferred taxes	9,000	
Income tax liability		$15,000

The matching concept includes accruing deferred taxes on undistributed earnings of subsidiaries, corporate joint ventures, and investment in common stock accounted for by the equity method. There is a presumption that these types of undistributed earnings will be paid, and deferred taxes should be accrued in the period such earnings are earned.

Control over the subsidiary, joint venture, or investment can determine that distributions of earnings will not be made or postponed indefinitely. Under these circumstances, deferred taxes need not be accrued.

Intraperiod Tax Allocation

Existing promulgated GAAP (APB-11) requires intraperiod tax allocation to contain the relationship between income tax expense and

1. Income before extraordinary items
2. Extraordinary items
3. Prior-period adjustments
4. Direct entries to other stockholders' accounts

Intraperiod tax allocation merely involves associating the income tax expense involved with each of the above categories, which are usually shown "net of tax" in the income statement.

When an operating loss occurs, the tax effects shoud be associated with it in the period of occurrence.

Discounting Tax Allocation Accounts

Under present promulgated GAAP (APB-10), deferred taxes should not be accounted for on a discounted basis.

Offsetting—Taxes Payable

As a general rule the offsetting of assets and liabilities in the balance sheet is unacceptable unless a right of offset exists.

When securities that are specifically acceptable as payment for taxes are purchased, a right of offset exists, and such securities may be deducted from the related taxes payable on the balance sheet.

Income Taxes—Interim Periods

The promulgated GAAP for Interim Financial Reporting (APB-28) requires that taxes for interim periods be determined in accordance with the existing promulgated GAAP for accounting for income taxes (APB-11). In addition, it requires that an estimated annual effective tax rate be established and used, which includes anticipated investment tax credits, foreign tax credits, percentage depletion, capital gain rates, and all other available tax planning alternatives used in determining ordinary income or loss. At the end of each interim period during the year, this effective tax rate is revised, if necessary, to the best current estimates of the annual effective tax rate.

The interim-period tax is determined by applying the established estimated annual effective tax rate to the year-to-date ordinary income or loss, and subtracting the previous interim year-to-date tax on the ordinary income or loss. Ordinary income or loss is defined as income or loss from continuing operations before a provision for income taxes, excluding significant unusual or nonrecurring items. This excludes extraordinary items, discontinued operations, and cumulative effects of changes in an accounting principle. Income tax is defined to include both current and deferred taxes.

The estimated annual effective tax rate shall include only the tax benefit of a loss that has already been realized, or future realization is assured beyond any reasonable doubt. Therefore the year-to-date tax benefit of a loss shall not exceed benefits that have already been realized or those for which future realization is assured beyond any reasonable doubt.

The estimated annual effective tax rate should include an adjustment for existing net deferred credits, if an estimated ordinary loss is projected for a fiscal year or the year-to-date ordinary loss exceeds the entire projected loss for the year, and if all or part of the tax benefit of the loss will not be realized or realization is not assured beyond a reasonable doubt. The adjustment to the existing net deferred credits is the lesser of:

1. The unrecognized tax benefits of the loss
2. The net deferred tax credits that would otherwise be amortized during the carryforward period of the loss

Adjustments to net deferred credits should be included in computing the maximum tax benefit for year-to-date amounts.

The adjustment to the net deferred credits should be cumulatively reinstated in subsequent periods at the then-current tax rates when the loss carryforward is realized in whole or in part.

The following illustration reflects the computation of the estimated annual effective tax rate and its application.

Income Taxes

A business estimates $1,000,000 of ordinary income for the year and anticipated realizable tax credits of $100,000. The income tax rate is 50%. Seasonable patterns in the fourth quarter assure the realization of the tax benefits beyond any reasonable doubt.

Tax on ordinary income (50%)	$500,000
Less: Anticipated credits	100,000
Net tax to be provided	$400,000
Estimated annual effective tax rate ($400,000 required tax divided by $1,000,000 income)	40%

Based on the estimated annual effective tax rate, the quarterly computations of taxes might appear as:

	Estimated Results		Estimated	Provision for taxes	
Period	Quarter	Cumulative	Tax rate	Quarter	Cumulative
1	($ 200,000)	($ 200,000)	40%	($ 80,000)	($ 80,000)
2	100,000	(100,000)	40%	40,000	(40,000)
3	150,000	50,000	40%	60,000	20,000
4	950,000	1,000,000	40%	380,000	400,000
	$1,000,000			$400,000	

If a reliable estimate cannot be made for the annual effective tax rate, the actual year-to-date annual effective tax rate should be used. If a reliable estimate of part of the ordinary income or loss, or of the related tax (or benefit), cannot be made, it should be reported in the interim period in which it actually occurs.

Significant, unusual, or extraordinary items that are reported separately net of their related tax effects are recognized in the interim period in which they occur. The related tax on these items is the difference between the tax on year-to-date ordinary income including the item, and the tax on year-to-date ordinary income excluding the item.

Assume the same facts as those in the preceding illustration; assume also that the business incurs a tax-deductible significant unusual extraordinary loss in the third quarter of $200,000 the benefit (50%) for which is assured beyond any reasonable doubt, because the loss can be carried back.

Since the estimated annual effective tax rate is unaffected under these circumstances, the tax on ordinary income or loss is the same, and the computation of the estimated annual effective tax rate is not reproduced.

	Income		Provision for Taxes	
Period	Ordinary	Extraordinary	Ordinary	Extraordinary
1	($ 200,000)		($ 80,000)	
2	100,000		40,000	
3	150,000	($200,000)	60,000	($100,000)
4	950,000		380,000	
	$1,000,000	($200,000)	$400,000	($100,000)

If the $200,000 tax-deductible unusual extraordinary loss in the third quarter was not realizable beyond any reasonable doubt, it would appear only in the third and succeeding periods to the extent that it could offset ordinary income for the year to date.

The tax benefit of a loss from significant, unusual, and extraordinary items or discontinued operations shall not be recognized until it is realized or realization is assured beyond a reasonable doubt. Realization is assured beyond a reasonable doubt by:

1. Offsetting year-to-date ordinary income
2. Offsetting taxable income from unusual, extraordinary, discontinued operations, or items credited directly to stockholders' equity accounts
3. Carrying back the loss to prior years
4. Future taxable income that is almost certain to occur shortly, especially from seasonal patterns of revenue

If all or part of such losses are not realized, and previously reported net deferred tax credits exist that would have been amortized during the carryforward period, the net deferred tax credits should be amortized in the same manner as previously stated.

The provision for taxes on income or loss from operations of a discontinued segment prior to measurement date, and the gain or loss on disposal of the discontinued operations, is determined (as stated earlier) by the difference between the tax on year-to-date ordinary income or loss including such items and the tax on year-to-date ordinary income or loss excluding the items. Thereafter the provision for taxes shall not be recomputed, but should be divided into two components: (1) for the remaining ordinary income or loss and (2) for the income or loss from operations of the discontinued

Income Taxes

segment. A revised estimated annual effective tax rate and resulting tax benefits is then recomputed for the remaining ordinary income or loss.

The following illustration depicts how a discontinued segment is accounted for:

A business estimates ordinary income of $1,000,000 for the year and tax credits of $100,000 that are realizable beyond any reasonable doubt. Income tax rates are 50%. The estimated annual effective tax rate is as follows:

Tax on pretax ordinary income (50%)	$500,000
Less: Anticipated credits	(100,000)
Net tax to be provided	$400,000
Estimated annual effective tax rate ($400,000 ÷ $1,000,000)	40%

The first two quarters appear as:

	Estimated Results			Provision for Taxes	
Period	Quarter	Cumulative	Rate	Quarter	Cumulative
1	$200,000	$200,000	40%	$ 80,000	$ 80,000
2	250,000	450,000	40%	100,000	180,000

During the third quarter the decision to discontinue a division of the company was made. The results of operations for the continuing divisions of the company and for the discontinued division are as follows:

	Revised	Discontinued Division	
Quarter	Ordinary Income	Operations	Loss on Disposal
1	$ 250,000	($ 50,000)	
2	350,000	(100,000)	
3	500,000	(100,000)	($550,000)
4 (Estimated)	500,000		
Total for Year	$1,600,000	($250,000)	($550,000)

The only assumptions that have changed for the estimated annual effective tax rate is that $20,000 of the $100,000 in tax credits was related to the discontinued operations. The recomputation of the estimated annual effective tax rate is:

Tax on ordinary income (50% of $1,600,000)	$800,000
Less: Anticipated tax credits	80,000
Net tax to be provided	$720,000
Estimated annual effective tax rate ($720,000 ÷ $1,600,000)	45%

The quarterly amounts, based on the revised ordinary income and estimated annual effective tax rate, are:

	Estimated results			Provision for taxes	
Period	Quarter	Cumulative	Rate	Quarter	Cumulative
1	$ 250,000	$ 250,000	45%	$112,500	$112,500
2	350,000	600,000	45%	157,500	270,000
3	500,000	1,100,000	45%	225,000	495,000
4	500,000	1,600,000	45%	225,000	720,000
	$1,600,000			$720,000	

The computation of the tax benefit attributable to the discontinued division for the first two quarters is the difference between the tax on year-to-date ordinary income or loss including the discontinued division, and the tax on the year-to-date ordinary income or loss, excluding the discontinued division, as follows:

	Tax on ordinary income		
Quarter	Previously Computed	Recomputed	Tax Benefit, Discontinued Div.
1	$ 80,000	$112,500	($32,500)
2	100,000	157,500	(57,500)
Totals	$180,000	$270,000	($90,000)

The third-quarter tax benefits for (1) the loss from operations and (2) the provision for the disposal of the discontinued division are computed on the revised estimated annual income with and without the effects of the discontinued division, as follows:

Income Taxes

	Discontinued Division	
	Loss on operations	Loss on disposal
Estimated revised ordinary income	$1,600,000	$1,600,000
Discontinued division loss on operations	250,000	
Discontinued division loss on disposal		550,000
Total	$1,350,000	$1,050,000
Tax at regular tax rate (50%)	$ 675,000	$ 525,000
Anticipated credits—continuing operations	(80,000)	(80,000)
Taxes—after effect of discontinued division	$ 595,000	$ 445,000
Previously computed taxes for year	720,000	720,000
Tax benefit—discontinued division	($ 125,000)	($ 275,000)
Less: Tax benefits recognized in first two quarters	(90,000)	—
Tax benefit for third quarter	($ 35,000)	($ 275,000)

The $20,000 in tax credits related to the discontinued division have not been recognized on the assumption that they will not be realized.

The tax benefit of a prior year's operating loss carryforward is recognized as an extraordinary item (APB-11) to the extent that offsetting income is available in each interim period.

The cumulative effect of a change in an accounting principle on the beginning-of-the-year retained earnings is reported in the first interim period of the fiscal year (FASB-3). The related income tax effects are computed as though the new accounting principle had been applied retroactively to all affected prior periods (APB-20). When the change is made in other than the first interim period, the prechange interim periods are restated, by applying the newly adopted accounting principle to those prechange interim periods. The tax or tax benefits for the prechange interim periods is then recomputed on the year-to-date and annual estimated amounts, modified only for the effect of the change in accounting principle.

Businesses subject to tax in more than one taxing jurisdiction shall compute one overall estimated annual effective tax rate, except that:

1. Ordinary income (loss) and related tax (benefit) shall be excluded in computing the estimated annual effective tax rate and interim-period tax (benefit), in any jurisdiction that anticipates an ordinary loss for the year, or has an ordinary loss for the year-to-date, for which a tax benefit cannot be recognized.
2. Ordinary income (loss) and related tax (benefit) shall be excluded in computing the estimated annual effective tax rate and interim-period tax (benefit) in any foreign jurisdiction where reliable estimates cannot be made. In this event, the tax (benefit) on ordinary income (loss) shall be recognized in the interim period in which it is reported.

Changes resulting from new tax laws should be reflected in a revised estimated annual effective tax rate for the first interim period affected.

Full disclosure should be made of any significant difference in the usual relationship between income tax expense and pretax accounting income, arising from the application of the promulgated GAAP for accounting for income taxes in interim periods.

> **OBSERVATION:** *FASB Technical Bulletin 79-9 reaffirms the fact that the effect of a change in tax rates during an interim period be reflected in a revised estimated annual effective tax rate. The revised annual effective tax rate is applied to pretax income for the year to date at the end of the interim period in which the change in tax rate took effect. If the effects are material, previous interim periods of the current fiscal year should be restated and any adjustment accounted for as a prior-period adjustment in accordance with FASB-16.*

Disclosure

Balance sheet accounts relating to tax allocations are of two types:

1. Deferred charges and deferred credits arising from timing differences
2. Claim of refunds for past taxes or offsets to future taxes arising from the tax effects of carrybacks and carryforwards

Deferred income tax charges and credits must be disclosed in classified balance sheets as either current or noncurrent. APB-11 requires that all current amounts (debits and credits) be presented in the balance sheet as one net current amount and that all non-current amounts (debits and credits) be presented in one net non-current amount. The problem that arises is determining when a

Income Taxes

deferred tax charge or credit is current and when it is noncurrent. FASB-37 (Balance Sheet Classification of Deferred Income Taxes) contains the criteria that must be used in determining whether a deferred tax charge or credit is current or noncurrent. The general rule depends on whether or not a deferred tax charge or credit is related to an asset or liability. If a relationship exists between a deferred tax charge or credit and an asset or a liability, then the current or noncurrent classification is exactly the same as the related asset or liability. If no relationship exists between the deferred tax charge or credit and an asset or liability, then the current or noncurrent classification is determined by reference to the normal operating cycle of the business. The timing differences that do reverse within the normal operating cycle of a business are classified as current and those timing differences that reverse after the normal operating cycle period are classified as noncurrent (FASB-37).

A deferred tax charge or credit is related to an asset or liability if reduction of the asset or liability would cause the underlying timing difference to reverse. In other words, the timing difference automatically reverses as a result of the reduction in the related asset or liability. A reduction of the related asset can arise as a result of amortization, sale, or other realization of the asset. A reduction of the related liability can arise as a result of amortization, or other satisfaction of the liability. The following examples demonstrate how deferred tax charges and credits are classified for balance sheet presentation:

1. For tax purposes, a company uses an accelerated method of depreciation for a fixed asset, but for financial statement purposes the straight-line method is used.

   The sale of the fixed asset will cause a reduction in the fixed asset which will automatically reverse the underlying timing differences. In other words, the related timing differences will reverse as a result of the reduction in the fixed asset. Thus, the deferred income taxes that resulted from the two depreciation methods are related to the fixed asset. In this event, the deferred income taxes are classified exactly the same as the related fixed asset. If the fixed asset is classified noncurrent then the income taxes must also be classified as noncurrent. If the fixed asset was classified as 20% current and 80% noncurrent, then the deferred income taxes must be classified as 20% current and 80% noncurrent.

2. For tax purposes a company uses the installment sales method, but for financial statement purposes, sales are reported when the goods are delivered.

Income Taxes

The collection of the installment receivables is a reduction of the asset which causes the underlying timing differences to reverse. Thus, the deferred income taxes are related to the installment receivables (an asset) and they both must be classified exactly the same. If 30% of the installment receivables are current because of the normal operating cycle of the business then 30% of the related deferred taxes are also classified as current.

3. For tax purposes, a company uses the completed-contract method for reporting profits on construction contracts, but for financial statement purposes the percentage-of-completion method is used.

The timing differences arising between the two methods of reporting profits will only reverse when the contracts are completed. Billing, collection, or retention of funds do not cause the timing differences to reverse. Thus, the deferred income taxes are not related to an asset or liability. Under these circumstances the deferred taxes are classified as current or noncurrent based on when they reverse. Those timing differences which reverse within the normal operating cycle of the business are classified as current and the balance are classified as noncurrent.

Claims for refunds and offsets to future taxes from the tax effects of carrybacks and carryforwards are classified as current or noncurrent on the basis of their expected realization during the current operating cycle.

The amounts and expiration dates of all operating-loss carryforwards not previously recognized should be disclosed, including those amounts which will be credited to deferred tax accounts.

All other significant unused deductions or credits including expiration dates should be fully disclosed.

The components of income tax expense for the period should be disclosed in the results of operations as:

1. Taxes estimated to be payable
2. Tax effects arising from timing differences
3. Tax effects of operating losses

In addition, as stated earlier, the income tax expense should be allocated to (1) income before extraordinary items, (2) extraordinary items, and (3) tax effects of any prior-period adjustments (see Intraperiod Tax Allocation section).

The tax benefit of an operating-loss carryforward that has not been recognized previously should be reported as an extraordinary item in the period in which it is realized.

The amount of tax effects of prior-period adjustments and direct entries to stockholders' equity should be disclosed.

Deferred taxes should not be included in the stockholders' equity section of a balance sheet or in the valuation of assets or liabilities.

Significant differences between taxable income and pretax accounting income and material variations between income tax expense and pretax accounting income should be fully disclosed unless apparent in the financial statements or from the nature of the entity's business activities.

Where income taxes have not been accrued on undistributed earnings because of the indefinite reversal criteria, the financial statements should contain a declaration of intention to reinvest the undistributed earnings or a statement that they will be remitted in the form of a tax-free liquidation, whichever is applicable. In addition, the cumulative amount of undistributed earnings for which income taxes have not been recognized should be disclosed.

United Kingdom Tax Benefits (FASB-31)

Recent changes in the tax law of the United Kingdom has created a potential six year recapture period for the "stock relief" deduction. For companies affected by this new legislation, any tax benefits arising from the "stock relief" deduction shall be deferred, unless it is "probable" that recapture of the tax benefits will not occur during the six year recapture period (FASB-31). If, in a subsequent period, it is determined that a previously recorded deferred tax benefit will not be recaptured because of a change in circumstances, then the tax benefit should be recognized in that period as a reduction of income tax expense. The reverse is also true. If, in a subsequent period, it is determined that a previously recognized tax benefit will be recaptured because of a change in circumstances, it should be deferred in that period by increasing income tax expense (FASB-31).

When the above requirements are initially included in interim financial statements, the recognition of previously deferred tax benefits shall be reported as an item of income tax expense for that interim period only, and shall not be classified as an extraordinary item. For subsequent interim reporting periods, adjustments due to changed circumstances shall be included as an adjustment of the estimated annual effective tax rate for the interim period in which circumstances change.

Tax benefits that are deferred under the provisions of FASB-31 are not timing differences and should be classified on the balance sheet based on the estimated recapture period (FASB-37, Balance Sheet Classification of Deferred Income Taxes).

Full disclosure must be made in the financial statements or footnotes thereto if a significant variation in the customary relationship between income tax expense and pretax accounting income occurs as a result of compliance with FASB-31.

GLOSSARY

Deferred taxes Tax effects to be charged to expense in subsequent periods.

Income tax expense That amount of income tax chargeable to the current period, whether or not currently payable (or refundable).

Income tax liability The amount of income tax due as calculated under the provision of the U.S. Internal Revenue Code.

Income taxes Taxes based on income as determined by the provisions of the U.S. Internal Revenue Code, as well as other foreign, franchising, state, and local taxes based on income.

Indefinite reversal criteria Sufficient evidence that a subsidiary has invested or will invest its undistributed earnings indefinitely, or such earnings will be remitted in a tax-free liquidation. In this event, income taxes need not be accrued on the undistributed earnings.

Interperiod tax allocation The process of using tax deferrals and accruals to balance the tax liability and expense among periods.

Intraperiod tax allocation The process of apportioning the tax expense within a period to the proper accounts, namely, income before extraordinary items, extraordinary items, prior-period adjustments, and direct entries to equity accounts.

"Net of tax" presentation Tax effects recognized under interperiod tax allocation are considered to be adjustments of the valuation of the related asset or liability.

Permanent differences Differences between the taxable income and the pretax accounting income that are caused by different rules of recognition of items affecting net income. Permanent differences do not reverse themselves in subsequent periods.

Pretax accounting income Profit or loss for a period, exclusive of income tax expense, as determined under the guidelines of GAAP.

Tax carrybacks or carryforwards Losses in years other than the current year that can be applied to prior years (carrybacks) or future years (carryforwards) to reduce net taxable income.

Tax effects Differences between the tax liability and the tax expense that are caused by timing differences. Included in tax effects are tax carrybacks and carryforwards and taxable adjustments to equity accounts.

Taxable income Net excess (or deficiency) of revenues over deductions (not including tax carrybacks or carryforwards) as specified in the Code.

Timing differences Differences between the taxable income and the pretax accounting income that are caused by different periods of recognition of items affecting net income. Timing differences reverse themselves in subsequent periods, so that the net long-term timing difference is zero.

INSTALLMENT METHOD OF ACCOUNTING

Background

APB-10, paragraph 12, and ARB-43, Chapter 1A, paragraph 1, constitute the promulgated GAAP for the installment method of accounting and unrealized profit.

Overview

Promulgated GAAP prohibits accounting for sales by any form of installment accounting except under exceptional circumstances where collectibility cannot be reasonably estimated or assured. The doubtfulness of collectibility can be caused by the length of an extended collection period or because no basis of estimation can be established. In such cases a company can use either the cost recovery method or the installment sales method of accounting (APB-10).

Cost Recovery Method

The cost recovery method, also known as the sunk-cost theory, is used in situations where recovery of cost is undeterminable or extremely questionable. The procedure is simply that all cost is recovered before any gain is recognized. Once all cost has been recovered, any other collections are recognized as revenue. The only expenses remaining to be charged against such revenue are those relating to the collection process.

For example, if a company sells for $100 an item that cost $40, and receives no down payment, the first $20 collected, regardless of the year collected, would be considered recovery of one-half the cost. The next $20 collected would be recovery of the balance of the cost, regardless of the year collected. The remaining $60 (all gross profit) would be recognized as income when received. The only additional expenses that could be charged against the remaining $60 would be those directly related to the collection process.

Recording Installment Sales

Under the installment sales method of accounting, each payment collected consists of part recovery of cost and part recovery of gross

Installment Method of Accounting

profit, in the same ratio that these two elements existed in the original sale. For example, assume that a furniture dealer sells for $100 a chair that cost him $70. The gross profit percentage for this sale is 30%. The dealer would recognize 70% of any payment as a recovery of cost and 30% as realized gross profit.

The entries to record the initial sale, assuming the use of a periodic inventory system and no down payment, are:

Accounts receivable—installment sales	$100	
Installment sales		$100
Cost of installment sales	$ 70	
Inventory		$ 70

At the end of the period, the company closes out the installment sales account and the cost of installment sales to unrealized gross profit on installment sales account, which in this example is $30. The entry is:

Installment sales	$100	
Cost of installment sales		$ 70
Unrealized gross profit on installment sales		30

In the period that the company collects $40, the entries are:

Cash	$ 40	
Accounts receivable—installment sales		$ 40
Unrealized gross profit on installment sales	$ 12	
Realized gross profit on installment sales		$ 12

The $40 collected includes $28 recovery of cost and $12 of realized gross profit on installment sales (70%/30% relationship).

Since gross profit ratios are different for most products and departments and fluctuate between years, it is necessary to keep a separate record of sales by year, product lines, and department. Separate accounts and records must be kept for receivables, realized gross profit, unrealized gross profit, and repossessions for each category of product. Under the installment sales method, selling and administrative costs are charged to expense in the period incurred.

Generally, the seller will protect its interest in an installment sale by retaining title to the goods through a conditional sales contract, lease, mortgage, or trustee. In the event of a default on an installment sales contract, the related account receivable and unrealized gross profit are written off. In many cases of default, the goods are repossessed by the seller. The loss (or gain) on a default of an installment sales contract is determined as follows:

$$\text{Loss (or Gain)} = \begin{bmatrix} \text{balance of} \\ \text{account} \\ \text{receivable} \end{bmatrix} \text{less} \begin{bmatrix} \text{unrealized} \\ \text{gross} \\ \text{profit} \end{bmatrix} \text{less} \begin{bmatrix} \text{inventory value of} \\ \text{repossessed} \\ \text{merchandise} \\ \text{(if any)} \end{bmatrix}$$

For example, continuing the preceding illustration, if the first payment of $40 was the only payment the company received and the goods were not repossessed, the journal entry to record the default and loss would be:

Unrealized gross profit	$18	
Loss on installment sales	42	
Accounts receivable—installment sales		$60

If the goods were repossessed and had an inventory value of $25, the journal entry would be:

Unrealized gross profit	$18	
Loss on installment sales	17	
Inventory	25	
Accounts receivable—installment sales		$60

When goods are repossessed, one of the major problems is determining the value of these inventory goods. Some of the methods of determining the value include:

1. Fair market value
2. Unrecovered cost (results in no gain or no loss)
3. Resale value less reconditioning costs plus a normal profit (net realizable value)
4. No value—a good method when no other method is appropriate, particularly when the actual value is minor

Deferred Income Taxes

The installment sales method is acceptable for tax purposes, because the government attempts to collect taxes when the taxpayer has the cash on hand rather than basing collection on a theoretical analysis of accounting principles. The use of installment accounting for tax purposes and normal accrual accounting for financial reporting purposes results in a timing difference and creates a deferred tax liability.

Disclosure

Accounts receivable on installment sales are shown separately in the balance sheet. They are classified as current assets in accordance with the normal operating cycle of the entity, which frequently extends for more than one year. Resources that are reasonably expected to be realized in cash, sold, or consumed (prepaid items) during the normal operating cycle of a business are classified as current assets. The amounts maturing each period for each class of installment receivable should also be disclosed.

Unrealized gross profit is presented in the balance sheet as a separate caption, immediately above stockholders' equity or as a contra account to the related installment receivable.

Since realized gross profit is recognized as a portion of each cash collection, a percentage relationship will always exist between the installment accounts receivable balance for a particular sales category and the related unrealized gross profit for that category. The percentage relationship will be the same as the gross profit ratio on the initial sale.

INTANGIBLE ASSETS

Background

The promulgated GAAP for Accounting for Intangible Assets is APB-17. Accounting for Intangible Assets of Motor Carriers is covered by FASB-44. A good source of nonpromulgated GAAP is Accounting Research Study No. 10, Accounting for Goodwill (AICPA).

The promulgated GAAP (APB-17) covers both internally developed intangibles and those acquired in a business combination. However, the promulgated GAAP (APB-17) does not cover research and development costs included in FASB-2.

> **OBSERVATION:** *APB-17 is effective for intangible assets acquired after October 31, 1970, and provides that intangible assets acquired prior to November 1, 1970, could continue to be accounted for in accordance with the preceding GAAP (ARB-43, Chapter 5). Under Chapter 5 of ARB-43, an intangible asset with an indeterminate life (type b) could be capitalized and subsequent amortization was not required, unless it became reasonably evident that the life of the intangible asset had become limited. Thus, under Chapter 5 of ARB-43, it was possible to "permanently capitalize" a type b intangible asset. To this day, the balance sheet of some enterprises reflects the cost of type b intangible assets which have never been amortized.*
>
> *APB-17, the present promulgated GAAP, requires that all intangible assets be amortized over their estimated useful lives, which cannot exceed 40 years.*

FASB-72 (Accounting for Certain Acquisitions of Banking or Thrift Institutions) is applicable to that portion of goodwill that arises from the excess of the fair value of assumed liabilities over the fair value of acquired identifiable assets which may result from the acquisition of a troubled banking or thrift institution. FASB-72 provides for a different method of amortization over a shorter period than that required by APB-17 (Intangible Assets). In addition, FASB Interpretation-9 provides guidance for recording the acquisition of a banking or thrift institution by the use of the net-spread method and the separate-valuation method. For a complete discussion of FASB-72 and FASB Interpretation-9, refer to Chapter 45.01 (Banking and Thrift Institutions), in the specialized industry accounting principles section of this Guide.

Overview

The term *intangible asset* refers to certain long-lived legal rights and competitive advantages developed or acquired by a business enterprise.

Intangible assets differ considerably in their characteristics, useful lives, and relationship to operations of an enterprise and may be classified as follows.

Identifiability   Patents, copyrights, franchises, trademarks, and other similar intangible assets that can be specifically identified with reasonably descriptive names. Other types of intangible assets lack specific identification, the most common being goodwill.

Manner of acquisition   Intangible assets may be purchased or developed internally and may be acquired singly, in groups, or in business combinations.

Determinate or indeterminate life   Patents are issued to inventors for a period of 17 years. Copyrights and most franchises also expire within a definite period. Other intangible assets such as organizational costs, secret processes, and goodwill have no determinable term of existence, or the expected period of benefit cannot be ascertained at the time of acquisition.

Transferability   The rights to a patent, copyright, or franchise can be separately identified and bought or sold. Organizational costs are an inseparable part of a business, and it is unlikely that a purchaser would purchase the organizational costs without the business. Similarly, goodwill is inseparable from a business and is transferable only as an inseparable intangible asset of an enterprise.

Cost of Intangibles

A company should record as assets the cost of intangible assets acquired from other enterprises or individuals. Costs of developing, maintaining, or restoring intangible assets that are not specifically identifiable, have indeterminate lives, or are inherent in a continuing business and related to an enterprise as a whole, such as goodwill, should be deducted from income when incurred.

> **OBSERVATION:** *For a discussion of the net-spread method and the separate-valuation method used to record the acquisition of a banking or thrift institution, refer to Chapter 45.01, Banking and Thrift Institutions.*

Cost is measured by (1) the amount of cash disbursed or the fair value of other assets distributed, (2) the present value of amounts to be paid for liabilities incurred, and (3) the fair value of consideration received for stock issued (cost may be determined either by the fair value of the consideration given or by the fair value of the property acquired, whichever is more clearly evident).

The cost of unidentifiable intangible assets is measured by the difference between the cost of the group of assets or of the enterprise acquired and the sum of the assigned costs to identifiable assets acquired, less liabilities assumed. Cost of identifiable assets should not include goodwill.

The cost of an intangible asset, including goodwill acquired in a business combination, may not be written off as a lump sum to capital surplus or to retained earnings, or be reduced to a nominal amount at or immediately after acquisition.

Amortization

The cost of each type of intangible asset should be amortized by systematic charges to income over the period estimated to be benefited, but not to exceed 40 years.

Usually, all methods of amortizing goodwill are criticized as arbitrary, because the life of goodwill is indefinite and an estimated period of existence is not measurable.

Amortizing the cost of intangible assets, on arbitrary bases, in the absence of evidence of limited lives or decreased values may recognize expenses and decreases of assets prematurely, but delaying amortization of the cost until a loss is evident may recognize the decreases after the fact.

Even if the estimated useful life of an intangible asset is more than 40 years, it must be amortized over 40 years or less.

A business enterprise should evaluate the periods of amortization continually to determine if later circumstances warrant revision of estimated useful lives. If estimates are changed, the unamortized cost should be allocated to the number of years in the revised useful life, but not to exceed 40 years after date of acquisition.

> **OBSERVATION:** FASB-72 concludes that goodwill arising in the acquisition of a troubled banking or thrift institution should be amortized over a relatively short period because of the uncertainty about the nature and extent of the estimated future benefits related to the goodwill (see Chapter 45.01).

Method   The straight-line method of amortization should be applied unless a company demonstrates that another systematic method is more appropriate. The method and estimated useful lives of intangible assets should be adequately disclosed in the financial statements.

Income tax effect   Amortization of acquired intangible assets not deductible in computing income taxes payable does not create a timing difference, and allocation of income taxes is inappropriate. Only goodwill acquired after November 1, 1970, should be amortized, and retroactive amortization of previously unamortized goodwill acquired prior to November 1, 1970, is prohibited (APB-17).

Negative Goodwill

The measurement or valuation of cost in financial accounting usually means the historical or acquisition cost. The sum of the market or appraised values of identifiable assets less liabilities assumed may sometimes exceed the cost of the assets or business enterprise being acquired. Under these circumstances, the values assigned to the noncurrent assets being acquired should be reduced proportionately (except long-term investments in marketable securities) to absorb the excess value. A deferred credit for an excess of assigned values of identifiable assets over cost (*negative goodwill*) should not be recorded unless the noncurrent assets have been reduced to zero. If, after reducing the noncurrent assets (except long-term investments in marketable securities) to zero, a deferred credit still remains, it should be classified as a deferred credit—excess of acquired net assets over cost, and amortized systematically to income over the period expected to benefit, but not in excess of 40 years. The method and period of amortization should be adequately disclosed in the financial statements. No part of the excess of acquired net assets over cost (negative goodwill) should be credited directly to stockholders' equity at the date of acquisition.

Disposal of Goodwill

Goodwill is unidentifiable apart from a business and cannot be disposed of separately from the enterprise as a whole. However, a large segment or a separable group of assets of an acquired company may be sold or otherwise liquidated, and all or a portion of the unamortized cost of goodwill recognized in the acquisition should be included in the cost of the assets sold.

Step-by-Step Acquisitions

If an enterprise purchases, on a step-by-step basis, a subsidiary that is consolidated or an investment that is accounted for under the equity method, the fair value of the underlying assets acquired and the goodwill for each step purchased must be separately identified.

Assume that Company P acquired an interest in Company S in two steps: (1) It acquired 20% of the outstanding common stock for $200,000. (2) The following year it acquired an additional 60% for $500,000. At the dates of acquisition, the equity book value for Company S was $900,000 and $1,100,000, respectively.

Computation of Excess of Cost over Book Value

First Acquisition
Cost of 20% acquired	$200,000
20% of equity book value of $900,000	180,000
Excess of cost over book value (goodwill)	$ 20,000

Second Acquisition
Cost of 60% acquired	$500,000
60% of equity book value of $1,100,000	660,000
Excess of book value over cost (negative goodwill)	($160,000)

Actually, as of the date of the second acquisition Company P had an investment of $700,000 for 80% of Company S. Company S at the second acquisition date had an equity book value of $1,100,000, and Company P's 80% is $880,000, for which it paid $700,000. Had Company P been recording its first acquisition of 20% on the equity method, it would have recorded its 20% of the $200,000 increase in Company S's book value (assuming that no dividends or other distributions were made to Company P by Company S), so that the adjusted equity in Company S on the books of Company P would include the original $200,000 purchase price plus 20% of the $200,000 increase in book value (from $900,000 to $1,100,000), or a total of

Intangible Assets

$220,000 ($180,000 + $40,000). The cost of the second acquisition of 60% for $500,000 and the adjusted basis for the 20% at $220,000 equals $720,000, which represents 80% of $1,100,000, or $880,000. The difference of $160,000 is the excess of book value over cost (negative goodwill), indicated by the computation for the second acquisition of 60%.

Disclosure

A description of intangible assets, method of amortization, and estimated useful lives should be appropriately disclosed in the financial statements or in footnotes.

In the event that a large part or all of the unamortized cost of an intangible asset is included as an extraordinary charge in the determination of net income, the reasons for the extraordinary deduction should be fully disclosed.

Intangible Assets of Motor Carriers

The cost of intangible assets of motor carriers may include (1) expected benefits from established routes, (2) marketing or operating efficiencies, (3) knowledge of business, (4) customer lists, (5) favorable leases, (6) operating rights, and (7) goodwill. Operating rights are franchises or permits issued by the ICC or a state agency that permit a motor carrier to transport specified commodities over a specified route. Operating rights usually result in limiting competition over a particular route. When issued by a Federal agency, they are referred to as "interstate operating rights," and when issued by a state agency, they are referred to as "intrastate operating rights." FASB-44 covers only interstate operating rights and those intrastate operating rights in states which have enacted legislation similar to the Motor Carrier Act of 1980.

> **OBSERVATION:** *As a result of the Motor Carrier Act of 1980, the FASB has found that the value of an interstate operating right of a motor carrier has become permanently and substantially impaired, as evidenced by a significant decline in the value of these rights for sale or use as collateral. The FASB has concluded that the unamortized cost of impaired operating rights should be com-*

pletely written off by a charge to income in the year in which their value was impaired. FASB-44 applies to intrastate operating rights in those states that enact legislation similar to the Motor Carrier Act.

The cost of previously acquired intangible assets of motor carriers must be separately identified and classified as (1) impaired operating rights, (2) other identifiable intangible assets, including unimpaired operating rights, and (3) goodwill. Cost is defined as the net carrying amount of the intangible asset on the date this Statement is first applied. However, net carrying amount shall include only the original or unamortized original cost of the intangible asset.

Costs of developing, maintaining, or restoring intangible assets after they were acquired must not be included in the cost of the intangible assets. In addition, those costs that are identified and assigned to previously acquired intangible assets shall not be merged with, or replaced by, any amounts relating to other identifiable intangibles or goodwill.

GAAP that existed on the date that the intangible assets were previously acquired should be used as the basis for identifying and assigning costs to (1) impaired operating rights, (2) other identifiable intangible assets, including unimpaired operating rights, and (3) goodwill.

If, for any reason, a motor carrier cannot separately identify and assign costs to its previously acquired intangible assets in accordance with this Statement, it shall be presumed that all such costs relate to impaired operating rights.

Previously acquired intangible assets which are classified as impaired operating rights in accordance with this Statement shall be charged to income in the period in which this Statement is first applied, and if material, such amounts shall be reported as an extraordinary item in accordance with existing GAAP (APB-30).

After this Statement is first applied, any intangible assets that must subsequently be charged to income in accordance with this Statement shall not be reported as an extraordinary item, even if such amounts are material.

Tax effects that arise from the application of this Statement should be accounted for in accordance with existing GAAP (APB-11).

Motor carriers shall account for operating rights which do not have to be charged to income in accordance with FASB-44, and other identifiable intangible assets, including goodwill, in accordance with APB-17 (Intangible Assets), or ARB-43, Chapter 5 (Intangible Assets). In other words, after charging all impaired operating rights to income

Intangible Assets

in accordance with this Statement, the remaining unimpaired operating rights and other identifiable assets, including goodwill, shall be reported in accordance with the GAAP that existed at the time the asset was acquired. If the intangible asset was acquired at the time ARB-43 (Chapter 5) was in effect, the intangible asset should be reported on the balance sheet at its original unamortized cost. If the intangible asset was acquired after APB-17 went into effect (November 1, 1970), it should be reported on the balance sheet at its original cost, less amortization over a period of 40 years or less.

FASB-44 is effective for financial statements covering fiscal periods that end after December 15, 1980. Earlier application of FASB-44 is encouraged for fiscal periods prior to its effective date, providing that the financial statements had not been issued before December 19, 1980.

FASB-44 should not be applied retroactively to previously issued financial statements.

Comprehensive Illustrations

The following examples depict the computation of goodwill using different facts.

---

1. Company P acquires for $725,000 an 80% interest in the outstanding common stock of Company S. At the date of acquisition Company S has capital stock of $600,000 and retained earnings of $150,000.

As at the Date of Acquisition

Cost of investment in Company S		$725,000
Company S stockholders' equity:		
Capital stock	$600,000	
Retained earnings	150,000	
Total	$750,000	
Acquired by Company P	80%	
Equity acquired by Company P		600,000
Excess of cost over book value (goodwill)		$125,000

2. Company P acquires for $500,000 cash all the assets and liabilities of Company S. An appraisal at the date of acquisition reflects the following values.

Accounts receivable (net)	$ 75,000
Inventories	125,000
Fixed assets	400,000
Long-term marketable securities	100,000
Total	$700,000
Liabilities assumed (present values)	250,000
Value of underlying assets	$450,000
Cost of assets acquired	500,000
Excess of cost over assets acquired (goodwill)	$ 50,000

In example 2. above, if the cost of the assets acquired was $400,000, creating negative goodwill of $50,000, only noncurrent assets, *except long-term marketable securities,* should be adjusted downward, but not below zero. The result in this case is that fixed assets are reduced to $350,000, and *no negative goodwill is recorded.* However, negative goodwill would have been recorded on the books if all the noncurrent assets (except long-term marketable securities) had been reduced to zero and a balance of the excess of book value over cost still remained.

3. When preferred stock is involved in an acquisition of a subsidiary, caution must be taken when (a) dividends are in arrears or (b) there is any preference in liquidation.
   Company P acquires for $900,000, 75,000 shares of Company S common stock. At the date of acquisition Company S has 100,000 shares of common stock outstanding with a stated value of $1,000,000, and 5,000 shares of 5% preferred stock $100 par outstanding with dividends in arrears of $50,000; the preferred stock is entitled to $105 per share in the event of liquidation.

Intangible Assets

Computation of Excess of Cost over Book Value

	Preferred	Common
5,000 shares of preferred stock par $100	$500,000	
Stated value of common stock		$1,000,000
Dividends in arrears	50,000	(50,000)
Liquidation preference on preferred stock	25,000	(25,000)
Retained earnings		225,000
Paid-in capital		100,000
Totals	$575,000	$1,250,000
75% of common equity acquired by P		$ 937,500
Cost of 75%		900,000
Excess of book value over cost (negative goodwill)		$ 37,500

INTEREST ON RECEIVABLES AND PAYABLES

Background

APB-21 is the main source of GAAP on imputing, if necessary, interest on receivables and payables. However, APB-21 excludes the following types of receivables and payables:

1. Arising in the ordinary course of business which are due in approximately one year or less
2. Whose terms of payments are in property or services and not in cash
3. Representing security or retainage deposits
4. Arising in the ordinary course of business of a lending institution
5. Arising from transactions between a parent and its subsidiaries, or between subsidiaries of a common parent
6. Whose interest rate is determined by a governmental agency

The present value techniques used in APB-21 should not be applied to estimates of contractual property or other obligations that are assumed in connection with a sale of property, goods, or services such as an estimated warranty for product performance.

> **OBSERVATION:** *Interest that is imputed on certain receivables and payables in accordance with APB-21, is eligible for capitalization under the provisions of FASB-34 (See chapter entitled "Interest Costs Capitalized").*

Overview

Those receivables and payables which are not specifically excluded from the provisions of APB-21 and which are contractual rights to receive or pay money at a fixed or determinable date must be recorded at their present value, if (1) the interest rate is not stated or (2) the stated interest rate is unreasonable. This is an application of the basic principle of substance over form.

A note issued or received solely for cash equal to its face amount is presumed to earn the interest stated. However, if rights or privileges are attached to the note, they must be evaluated separately. For example, a beer distributor lends a customer who wishes to purchase bar equipment $5,000 for two years at no interest. There is, of course, a tacit agreement that the customer will buy the distributor's products. In this event, a present value must be established for the note receivable, and the difference between the face of the note ($5,000) and its present value must be considered an additional cost of doing business for the beer distributor.

There is a general presumption that the interest stated on a note, resulting from a business transaction entered into at arm's length, is fair and adequate. However, if no interest is stated or the interest stated appears unreasonable, the substance of the transaction must be recorded.

A note issued or received in a noncash transaction contains two elements to be valued: (1) the principal amount for the property, goods, or services exchanged and (2) an interest factor for the use of funds over the time period of the note. These types of notes must be recorded at their present value. Any difference between the face amount of the note and its present value is a discount or premium that must be amortized over the life of the note.

Determining Present Value

There is no predetermined formula for computing an appropriate interest rate. *However, the objective is to approximate what the rate would have been, using the same terms and conditions, if it had been negotiated by an independent lender.* The following guidelines are recommended:

1. Credit rating of the borrower
2. Restrictive covenants or collateral involved
3. Prevailing market rates
4. Rate at which the debtor could borrow funds

The appropriate interest rate will frequently depend upon a combination of the above factors.

Amortization of Discount or Premium

The difference between the present value and the face amount of the receivable or the payable represents the amount of premium or discount. A discount exists if the present value of the total eventual proceeds of the note (face amount plus stated interest), using the appropriate rate of interest, is less than the face amount of the note. A premium exists if the present value of the total eventual proceeds of the note (face amount plus stated interest), using the appropriate rate of interest, is more than the face amount of the note.

The premium or discount should be amortized over the life of the note, using a constant rate on any outstanding balance. This method is called the *interest method* and is reviewed in the comprehensive illustration at the end of this chapter.

Statement Presentation of Discount or Premium

The premium or discount that arises from the use of present values on cash and noncash transactions is inseparable from the related asset or liability. Therefore, such premiums or discounts are deducted from their related asset or liability on the balance sheet. Discounts or premiums resulting from imputing interest must not be classified as deferred charges or credits.

Disclosure

A full description of the receivable or payable, the effective interest rate, and the face amount of the note should be disclosed in the financial statements or footnotes thereto.

Issue costs should be reported separately in the balance sheet as deferred charges.

Comprehensive Illustrations

The following example indicates how interest is imputed on a non-interest-bearing note.

A manufacturer sells a machine for $10,000 and accepts a $10,000 note receivable bearing no interest for five years; 10% is an appropriate interest rate. The initial journal entry would be:

Note receivable	$10,000.00	
Sales (present value at 10%)		$6,209.00
Unamortized discount on note		3,791.00

Interest on Receivables and Payables

End of 1st year:		
Unamortized discount on note	$ 620.90	
Interest income		$ 620.90
(10% of $6,209)		
End of 2nd year:		
Unamortized discount on note	$ 682.99	
Interest income		$ 682.99
(10% of $6,829.90)		
End of 3rd year:		
Unamortized discount on note	$ 751.29	
Interest income		$ 751.29
(10% of $7,512.89)		
End of 4th year:		
Unamortized discount on note	$ 826.42	
Interest income		$ 826.42
(10% of $8,264.18)		
End of 5th year:		
Unamortized discount on note	$ 909.06	
Interest income		$ 909.06
(10% of $9,090.60)		

In the example above the manufacturer records the note at its face amount but records the sale at the present value of the note because that is all the note is worth today. The difference between the face amount of the note and its present value is recorded as "unamortized discount on note."

The *interest method* is used to produce a constant rate which is applied to any outstanding balance. In the above example the present value of $6,209 was recorded for the $10,000 sale using the appropriate interest rate of 10% for the five year term of the note. The difference between the $10,000 sale and its present value of $6,209 is $3,791, which was recorded as unamortized discount on note. Since the present value was determined by using the 10% rate for five years, it stands to reason that the same 10% rate, when applied to each annual outstanding balance for the same five years, will result in full amortization of the discount on the note, as follows:

		Amortization of Discount on the Note
Original balance	$6,209.00	$3,791.00
Year 1, 10%	620.90	620.90
Remaining balance	$6,829.90	$3,170.10
Year 2, 10%	682.99	682.99
Remaining balance	$7,512.89	$2,487.11
Year 3, 10%	751.29	751.29
Remaining balance	$8,264.18	$1,735.82
Year 4, 10%	826.42	826.42
Remaining balance	$9,090.60	$ 909.40
Year 5, 10%	909.05	909.05
*Remaining balance	$9,999.65	$ 0.35

*Difference of $0.35 due to rounding.

The next example illustrates how a note with an unreasonable rate of interest should be recorded.

A company purchases a $10,000 machine and issues for payment a $10,000 four-year note bearing 2% compound interest per year; 10% is considered an appropriate rate of interest. The initial journal entry is:

Machine (present value of $10,824 @ 10%)	$7,393	
Unamortized discount on note	3,431	
Note payable		$10,000
Deferred interest payable		824
1st year:		
Interest expense	$739	
Unamortized discount on note		$739
2nd year:		
Interest expense	$813	
Unamortized discount on note		$813

3rd year:
    Interest expense $895
        Unamortized discount on note $895

4th year:
    Interest expense $984
        Unamortized discount on note $984

In the fourth year, when the note and the 2% interest are paid, the following journal entry is made:

Note payable $10,000
Deferred interest payable   824
    Cash $10,824

In the above example the company records a note payable ($10,000) and the deferred interest ($824) at their face amount. The total due in four years is $10,824, and the machine is valued at the present value of this amount ($7,393). This is because today the $10,824 is worth only $7,393, which is all that the sale should be recorded at. The difference between the total amount due in four years ($10,824) and its present value ($7,393) must be considered deferred interest ($3,431) for the use of the seller's funds.

INTEREST COSTS CAPITALIZED

Overview

FASB-34 (Capitalization of Interest Cost) covers the promulgated GAAP on the capitalization of interest costs on certain qualifying assets that are undergoing activities to get them ready for their intended use. FASB-42 (Determining Materiality for Capitalization of Interest Cost) is an amendment to FASB-34, which requires that the same materiality tests applied to regular GAAP be applied to the materiality of capitalizing interest cost.

FASB-58 (Capitalization of Interest Cost in Financial Statements That Include Investments Accounted For by the Equity Method) amends FASB-34 to provide for capitalization of interest cost on equity funds, loans, and advances which are made by investors to certain investees that are accounted for by the equity method (APB-18).

FASB-62 (Capitalization of Interest Cost in Situations Involving Certain Tax-Exempt Borrowings and Certain Gifts and Grants) amends FASB-34 to provide special treatment in capitalizing interest costs on qualifying assets that are acquired with (a) the proceeds of tax-exempt borrowings and (b) a gift or grant which is restricted for the sole purpose of acquiring a specific asset. In addition, FASB-62 supersedes FASB Technical Bulletin 81-5 (Offsetting Interest Cost to Be Capitalized with Interest Income).

FASB-34 (Capitalization of Interest Cost) supersedes the provisions for capitalizing interest costs that appear in the AICPA industry accounting guide entitled "Retail Land Sales." Thus, enterprises involved in retail land sales must apply the provisions of FASB-34 to determine the amount of interest cost that must be capitalized.

FASB-34 includes the capitalization of interest imputed on receivables and payables in accordance with APB-21 (Interest on Receivables and Payables). In other words, interest costs that are imputed in accordance with existing GAAP may qualify for capitalization in accordance with FASB-34. In addition, FASB-34 permits the capitalization of interest costs that are related to a lease which is capitalized in accordance with FASB-13 (Accounting for Leases). Thus, interest costs that would otherwise ultimately be expensed under APB-21 and FASB-13, are eligible for capitalization in accordance with FASB-34.

> **OBSERVATION:** *The seven member Financial Accounting Standards Board adopted FASB-34 by a vote of four to three.*

Background

The basis of accounting for depreciable fixed assets is cost, and all normal expenditures of readying an asset for use should be capitalized. However, unnecessary expenditures that do not add to the utility of the asset should be charged to expense. An expenditure for repairing a piece of equipment that was damaged during shipment should be charged to expense.

Razing and removal costs (less salvage value) of structures located on land purchased as a building site are added to the cost of the land. Land itself is never depreciated.

> **OBSERVATION:** *Promulgated GAAP (ARB-43) require that assets be recorded at cost, except in the case of quasi-reorganizations (corporate readjustments) in which it is permissible to write up or write down assets to market values (APB-6).*

Expenditures that increase the capacity or operating efficiency of an asset, if they are substantial, should be capitalized. Minor expenditures are usually treated as period costs even though they may have the characteristics of capital expenditures. When the cost of improvements is substantial or when there is a change in the estimated useful life of an asset, depreciation charges for future periods should be revised on the basis of the new book value and the new estimated remaining useful life.

The revision of the estimated useful life of an asset is measured prospectively and accounted for in the current and future periods. No adjustment is made to prior depreciation.

Capitalization of Interest—General

The FASB has concluded that, under certain conditions, interest costs should be capitalized as part of the total acquisition cost of an asset. The interest costs are incurred only during the period of time that is required to complete and get the asset ready for its intended use. Intended use means "sale" or "use within the business." Thus, there is usually a relationship between the length of the period necessary to acquire the asset and the amount of interest that will be capitalized.

The FASB has also concluded that a better measure of acquisition cost is achieved when certain interest costs are capitalized. This apparently results in a better matching of revenue and costs in future periods.

> **OBSERVATION:** *The basis of capitalizing certain interest costs is that the cost of an asset should include all costs necessary to bring the asset to the condition and location for its intended use. However, FASB-34 fails to mention that GAAP also provide that unnecessary expenditures that do not add to the utility of an asset should not be capitalized. Companies that are required to borrow funds to acquire an asset are placed on an equal basis as far as interest expense is concerned, as that of companies which do not have to borrow. The only difference is that the total cost of the asset to the company that borrows is increased by the amount of capitalized interest. For example, Company A and Company B both acquire an identical asset for $10 million that requires three years to complete for its intended use. Company A pays cash and at the end of three years the total cost of the asset is $10 million. In addition, let's assume that Company A also had net income of $2 million a year for each of the three years, and had no interest expense at all. Assume also that Company B, had $1.5 million net income for each of the three years, after deducting $500,000 of interest expense per year. Assuming that Company B qualifies for capitalized interest costs under FASB-34, it would reflect $2 million per year net income and not show any interest expense. However, on the balance sheet of Company B at the end of three years, the same identical asset would appear at a cost of $11.5 million! Thus, Company A has a cost of $10 million for the asset, while Company B will reflect a total cost of $11.5 million for the identical asset. Although the interest cost may be necessary to Company B, it obviously does not add to the utility of the asset.*

Qualifying Assets—Acquisition Period

Interest cost must be capitalized for all assets that require an "acquisition period" to get them ready for their intended use. "Acquisition period" is defined as the period commencing with the first expenditure for a qualifying asset and ending when the asset is substantially complete and ready for its intended use. Thus, before interest costs can be capitalized, expenditures must have been made for the qualifying asset and activities that are required to get the asset ready for its intended use must actually be in progress.

FASB-42 (Determining Materiality for Capitalization of Interest Cost) was issued to reaffirm that the usual rules of materiality embodied in GAAP must be followed in determining the materiality for the capitalization of interest costs. One of the purposes of FASB-42 was to eliminate language in FASB-34 which implies capitalization of interest costs could be avoided in certain circumstances. Thus, in applying the provisions of FASB-34, all the usual materiality tests used in applying other promulgated GAAP should also be used in determining the materiality for capitalization of interest costs.

Qualifying Assets—Intended Use

Certain interest costs, if material, must be capitalized and added to the acquisition cost of assets which require a period of time (acquisition period) to get them ready for their intended use. The cost of assets to which capitalized interest must be allocated include the cost of both those assets acquired for a company's own use and those acquired for sale in the ordinary course of business. Thus, inventory items which require a long time to produce, such as a real estate development, qualify for capitalization of interest costs. However, interest costs should not be capitalized for inventories which require a period of time to get them ready for their intended use, if such inventories are routinely produced in large quantities on a repetitive basis.

> *OBSERVATION:* The FASB concluded that the benefit of capitalizing interest costs on inventories that are routinely produced in large quantities does not justify the cost. Thus, interest costs should not be capitalized for inventories that are routinely produced in large quantities.

FASB-34 does not allow the capitalization of interest cost (1) for assets that are ready for their intended use or that are actually being used in the earning activities of a business, and (2) for assets that are not being used in the earning activities of a business that are not undergoing the activities required to get them ready for use. In other words, interest costs cannot be capitalized (1) for completed assets and (2) for incompleted assets that are not undergoing activities to be completed. Also, FASB-34 specifically prohibits imputing interest costs on any equity funds.

Amount of Interest Cost to Be Capitalized

The maximum amount of interest cost that may be capitalized for any accounting period may not exceed the actual interest cost (from any source) that is incurred by an enterprise during that same accounting period. In other words, capitalizing interest cost may not create a credit balance in the interest expense account. In consolidated financial statements, this limitation on the maximum amount of interest cost that may be capitalized in a period should be applied on a consolidated basis.

In order to compute the amount of interest cost to be capitalized for a particular accounting period, the average accumulated expenditures for the qualifying asset during the particular accounting period must be determined. To determine the average accumulated expenditures, each expenditure must be "weighted" for the time it was outstanding during the particular accounting period.

In the acquisition of a qualifying asset, a calendar year company expends $225,000 on January 1, 19X1, $360,000 on March 1, 19X1, and $180,000 on November 1, 19X1. The average accumulated expenditures for 19X1 are computed as follows:

Amount of Expenditure	Period From Expenditure to End of Year	Average Expenditure
$225,000	12 months	$225,000
360,000	10 months	300,000
180,000	2 months	30,000
$765,000		$555,000

If no specific borrowing is made to acquire the qualifying asset, the weighted-average interest rate incurred on other borrowings outstanding during the period shall be used to determine the amount of interest cost to be capitalized. Thus, the weighted-average interest rate is applied to the average accumulated expenditures for the period to calculate the amount of capitalized interest cost on the qualifying asset.

If a specific new borrowing is made to acquire the qualifying asset, the interest rate incurred on the new borrowing shall be used to determine the amount of interest costs to be capitalized. Thus, the interest rate on the specific new borrowing is applied to the average accumulated expenditures for the period to calculate the amount of capitalized interest cost on the qualifying asset. However, capitalized interest cost on average accumulated expenditures in excess of the amount of the specific new borrowing shall be calculated by the use of the weighted-average interest rate incurred on other borrowings outstanding during the period. In other words, the interest rate incurred on the specific new borrowing is used only on the average accumulated expenditures that are equal to, or less than, the amount of the new specific borrowing. The weighted-average interest rate is used on the average expenditures that exceed the amount of the new specific borrowing.

Progress payments received from the buyer of a qualifying asset must be deducted in the computation of the average amount of accumulated expenditures during a period. Nonetheless, the determination of the average amount of accumulated expenditures for a period may be reasonably estimated.

Judgment will be required to identify and select the appropriate specific borrowings which should be used in determining the weighted-average interest rate. The objective should be to obtain a reasonable cost of financing for the qualifying asset that could have been avoided if the asset was not acquired.

Capitalization Period

The interest capitalization period commences with the first expenditure for the asset and continues through the acquisition period. Interest is not capitalized during delays or interruptions, except for brief interruptions, which occur during the acquisition or development stage of the qualifying asset. When the qualifying asset is substantially complete and ready for its intended use, the capitalization of interest ceases. The qualifying asset may be completed in independent parts or in dependent parts. Interest capitalization ceases for an independent part when it is substantially complete and ready for its intended use. However, for dependent parts of a qualifying asset, interest capitalization does not stop until all dependent parts are substantially complete and ready for their intended use.

Before interest costs can be capitalized, expenditures must have been made for the qualifying asset and activities that are required to get the asset ready for its intended use must actually be in progress.

Investor's Qualifying Assets

Under the provisions of FASB-58, which amends FASB-34, an investor's qualifying assets, for the purposes of capitalizing interest costs under FASB-34, shall include equity funds, loans, and advances made to investees accounted for by the equity method, provided that the investee (a) is undergoing activities necessary to start its planned principal operations and (b) the activities include the use of funds to acquire qualifying assets for its operations. Thus, from the date of inception to the date that planned principal operations begin, an investor must capitalize interest costs on equity funds, loans, and advances made to an investee accounted for by the equity method, if during that period, the investee is undergoing activities necessary to start its planned principal operations and such activities include the use of funds to acquire qualifying assets for its operations. The investor cannot capitalize any interest costs on or after the date that the investee actually begins its planned principal operations. The term *planned principal operations,* under FASB-58, has the same meaning as used in FASB-7 (Accounting and Reporting for Development Stage Enterprises). Under the provisions of FASB-7, a development stage company is one which is devoting substantially all of its efforts to establishing a new business and (a) planned principal operations have not commenced or (b) planned principal operations have commenced, but there has been no significant revenue therefrom.

For the purposes of FASB-58, the term *investor* means both the parent company and all consolidated subsidiaries. Thus, all qualifying assets of a parent company and its consolidated subsidiaries which appear in the consolidated balance sheet are subject to the interest capitalization provisions of FASB-34 (as amended).

FASB-58 expressly states that it does not affect the accounting or reporting of capitalized interest cost in an investee's separate financial statements.

Capitalized interest costs on an investment accounted for by the equity method are included in the carrying amount of the investment. Up to the date on which the planned principal operations of the investee commence, the investor's carrying amount of the investment, which includes capitalized interest costs (if any), may exceed the underlying equity in the investment. If the investor cannot relate the excess carrying amount of the investment to specific identifiable assets of the investee, the difference is considered goodwill [paragraph 19(n) of APB-18]. Goodwill must be amortized to income over its estimated useful life, which may not exceed forty years (APB-17, Intangible Assets). The straight-line method of amortization must be used for goodwill unless another systematic and rational method can be justified.

Any interest cost capitalized under the provisions of FASB-58 shall not be changed in restating financial statements of prior periods. Thus, if an unconsolidated investee is subsequently consolidated in the investor's financial statements, as a result of increased ownership or a voluntary change by the reporting entity, interest costs capitalized in accordance with FASB-58 shall not be changed if restatement of financial statements is necessary.

FASB-58 is effective for investments (equity funds, loans, or advances) made by an investor to an investee accounted for by the equity method, on or after July 1, 1982. Earlier application of the provisions of FASB-58 are encouraged, but are not required.

Contractual obligations existing on July 1, 1982, for investments not made may be accounted for in the same manner as they were prior to July 1, 1982, or the provisions of FASB-58 may be applied.

FASB-58 may be applied to unissued annual financial statements, but shall not be retroactively applied to previously issued financial statements.

Tax-Exempt Borrowings and Gifts and Grants

Under the provisions of FASB-34, capitalized interest cost for a qualifying asset is determined by applying either a specific interest rate or a weighted-average interest rate to the average accumulated expenditures during a particular period for the qualifying asset. The actual interest cost incurred on the qualifying asset is not used under the provisions of FASB-34 and it is not necessary to identify a specific borrowing or loan to a specific qualifying asset in order to capitalize interest costs. Thus, an underlying premise in FASB-34 is that borrowings usually cannot be identified with specific qualifying assets. The financing policies of most enterprises are planned to meet general funding objectives, and the identification of specific borrowings with specific assets is considered highly subjective.

FASB-62 concludes that different circumstances are involved in the acquisition of a qualifying asset with tax-exempt borrowings, such as industrial revenue bonds and pollution control bonds. The tax-exempt borrowings, temporary interest income on unused funds, and construction expenditures for the qualifying asset are so integrated that they must be accounted for as a single transaction. Thus, FASB-62 amends FASB-34 to provide for the capitalization of interest cost for any portion of a qualifying asset that is acquired with tax-exempt borrowings, as follows:

Capitalization Period

Interest cost shall be capitalized from the date of the tax-exempt borrowings to the date that the qualifying asset is ready for its intended use.

Amount of Capitalized Interest Cost

The amount of capitalized interest cost allowable under FASB-62 is equal to the total actual interest cost on the tax-exempt borrowing, less any interest income earned on temporary investments of the tax-exempt funds. In other words, the actual net cost of interest on the tax-exempt borrowing is capitalized and added to the acquisition cost of the related qualifying asset.

External Restriction Requirement

FASB-62 applies only where the qualifying asset is financed by tax-exempt borrowing, in which the use of the borrowed funds is restricted to acquiring the assets or servicing the related debt. The restriction must be "external," that is, imposed by law, contract, or other authority outside the enterprise that borrows the funds.

After the qualifying asset is ready for its intended use and interest capitalization ceases, interest cost incurred on the related tax-exempt borrowing is eligible for capitalization on other qualifying assets of the enterprise.

As mentioned previously, FASB-62 supersedes FASB Technical Bulletin 81-5 (Offsetting Interest Cost to Be Capitalized with Interest Income). However, FASB-62 reaffirms that interest income earned on temporary funds that are earmarked for the construction of a qualifying asset cannot be used to offset the amount of interest cost that must be capitalized. As discussed above, the only exception to this rule is for qualifying assets that are acquired with tax-exempt borrowings.

Restricted gifts and grants   FASB-62 does not permit the capitalization of interest cost on any portion of a qualifying asset which is acquired with a gift or grant that is restricted to the acquisition of the specified qualifying asset. Restricted interest income on temporary investment of funds is considered an addition to the restricted gift or grant.

> **OBSERVATION:** *FASB-62 concludes that no interest cost should be capitalized on qualifying assets acquired by restricted gifts or grants, because there is no economic cost of financing involved in acquiring an asset with a gift or grant. In addition, any interest earned on temporary investment of funds from a gift or grant is, in substance, part of the gift or grant.*

FASB-62 is effective for tax-exempt borrowing transactions entered into on or after September 1, 1982, and for gifts and grants that are received on or after September 1, 1982. Earlier application of the provisions of FASB-62 is permitted in financial statements that have not been previously issued. FASB-62 expressly permits the retroactive application of its provisions to previously issued financial statements for fiscal years beginning on or after December 6, 1979. Any restated financial statements must include, in the year when FASB-62 is first applied, disclosure of the nature of the effects of the restatement on income before extraordinary items, net income, and related per share amounts for each restated year.

Disposition of Capitalized Interest

If capitalized interest costs are added to the overall cost of an asset, the total cost of the asset, including capitalized interest, may exceed the net realizable or other lower value of the asset that is required by GAAP. In this event, FASB-34 requires that the provision to reduce the asset cost to the lower value required by GAAP, be increased. Thus, the total asset cost, including capitalized interest, less the provision, should equal the lower value for the asset that is required by GAAP.

> **OBSERVATION:** *Paragraph 19 of FASB-34 is apparently directed to those situations in which GAAP provide for a contra or provision account that, in effect, reduces an asset to a lower value. However, in the event an asset is permanently impaired, GAAP require that the carrying amount of the asset be reduced to its net realizable value. In this case, no contra or provision account is generally utilized. Evidently, paragraph 19 of FASB-34 does not contemplate these situations.*
>
> *Capitalized interest costs will increase the total cost of an asset acquired for a company's own use. As a result of the capitalized interest, the net carrying amount of the asset in a subsequent year may exceed its net realizable value. If the decline in value of the asset is other than temporary, the net carrying amount of the asset has become impaired. Under existing promulgated GAAP, the impaired amount must be removed from the net carrying amount, by a charge to net income in the period in which the impairment occurs. Thus, it is likely that excessive amounts of capitalized interest may be a direct cause of an impairment of the carrying amount of an asset in years subsequent to interest capitalization.*

Capitalized interest costs become an integral part of the acquisition costs of an asset and should be accounted for as such in the event of disposal of the asset.

Full Cost Method in Extractive Industries

FASB Interpretation-33 covers the application of FASB-34 (Capitalization of Interest Costs) to oil and gas producing activities that are being accounted for by the full cost method.

Unproved properties and major developments that represent unusually significant investments are assets which qualify for capitalization of interest costs, if the following conditions are met:

a. Exploration or development activities are in progress
b. The assets are not currently being depreciated, depleted, or amortized

Other assets that qualify for capitalization of interest costs, in accordance with FASB-34, are significant properties or projects within a nonproducing cost center on which exploration or development activities are in progress.

All assets that are currently being depreciated, depleted, or amortized are considered in use in the earning activities of the business and in accordance with FASB-34, do not qualify for capitalization of interest costs.

FASB Interpretation-33 is effective for fiscal years beginning after December 15, 1979. Current and prior interim financial statements that are presented after the effective date, must be restated to reflect the provisions of FASB Interpretation-33. In addition, the following disclosures shall be made in current and prior financial statements that are presented after the effective date:

a. The nature of the change in method of applying FASB-34
b. The effect of the change on income from continuing operations, net income, and related per share amounts for each current and prior period presented after the effective date.

Disclosure, Effective Date, and Transition

The total amount of interest costs incurred and charged to expense during the period and the amount of interest costs, if any, which have been capitalized during the period, should be disclosed in the financial statements or footnotes thereto.

FASB-34 is effective for fiscal years beginning on and after December 15, 1979, although earlier application is permitted, but not required, for prior financial statements that have not been previ-

Interest Costs Capitalized

ously issued. Interest capitalization shall begin on December 16, 1979, for qualifying assets in existence at that time for which interest costs have not been previously capitalized. No adjustment need be made to qualifying assets for which interest costs have been capitalized prior to December 14, 1979. However, additional capitalized interest costs must be determined in accordance with FASB-34.

The provisions of FASB-34 shall not be applied retroactively for previously issued annual financial statements.

Comprehensive Illustration

The following is a comprehensive illustration of the application of FASB-34 (Capitalization of Interest Cost):

On January 1, Year One, Poll Powerhouse borrowed $300,000 from its bank at an annual rate of 18%. The principal amount plus interest is due on January 1, Year Three. The funds from this loan are specifically earmarked for the construction of a new plant facility. On February 1, Year One, Poll paid $15,000 for architects' fees and for fees for filing a project application with the state government.

On March 1, Year One, Poll received approval for the project from the state and construction of the plant was started. The following summarizes the costs incurred on this project.

Year One
February 1 (architects' and filing fees)	$ 15,000
April 1	150,000
September 1	60,000

Year Two
January 1	1,000
March 1	360,000
November 1	180,000
Total Project Cost	$766,000

The $1,000 is a miscellaneous cost and was expensed in Year Two, since it was determined by Poll to be immaterial.

The following schedule summarizes the borrowings of Poll as of December 31, Year Two.

Interest Costs Capitalized

Borrowing Date	Amount	Maturity Date	Annual Interest Rate
March 1, Year One	$1,000,000	Feb. 28, Year Three	17%
October 1, Year Two	500,000	Sept. 30, Year Four	14%

From February 1, Year Two, to March 31, Year Two, a major strike of construction workers was in effect. Therefore, all construction activity was halted during this period.

In August, Year Two, construction was voluntarily halted for the entire month by Poll. The chief executive officer did not want construction to continue without his supervision. Therefore, during his scheduled vacation construction was completely halted.

Solution to Problem

Poll's new plant facility is a qualifying asset under the provisions of FASB-34, and is subject to interest capitalization. The interest capitalization period begins on the first date that an expenditure is made by Poll, which was for architects' fees, February 1, Year One.

In order to compute the interest capitalization for Year One, the average accumulated expenditures for Year One must be calculated as follows:

Amount	Period From Expenditure to End of Year	Average Expenditure
$ 15,000	11 months	$ 13,750
150,000	9 months	112,500
60,000	4 months	20,000
$225,000		$146,250

The expenditures must be weighted by the period of time from the date they were made to the end of the year in order to determine the average expenditures for the entire year.

Next, the average expenditures must be multiplied by the interest rate on the borrowing (18%). This rate is used because Poll has specifically associated the borrowing with the construction of the new plant facility, and the average accumulated expenditures ($146,250) do not exceed the amount of the borrowing ($300,000). Therefore, the interest capitalized for Year One is computed, as follows:

Interest Costs Capitalized

Average accumulated expenditures	$146,250
Interest rate	18%
Capitalizable interest cost—Year One	$ 26,325

The final step is to determine that Poll actually incurred at least $26,325 of interest costs in Year One. Since in Year One Poll incurred $195,667 of interest costs ($300,000 × 18% + $1,000,000 × 17% × 10/12), the full $26,325 must be capitalized.

The next step is to compute the average accumulated expenditures for Year Two, which are calculated, as follows:

Amount	Period From Expenditure to End of Year	Average Expenditure
$225,000	12 months	$225,000
360,000	10 months	300,000
180,000	2 months	30,000
$765,000		$555,000

The $1,000 miscellaneous cost is not included, since Poll decided that this amount was immaterial and expensed it.

It is important to note that the expenditures for Year One are included as part of the base to compute Year Two capitalizable interest cost. FASB-34 requires that the average accumulated expenditures be calculated, and this would include those of prior accounting periods. Thus, the expenditures of $225,000 made by Poll in Year One are properly included in calculating the average accumulated expenditures for Year Two.

There is one further adjustment necessary to the above calculation of the average accumulated expenditures for Year Two. The plant facility was completed on December 31, Year Two, but there were two interruptions in construction in Year Two. Interest is not capitalized during delays or interruptions which are caused internally by an enterprise, unless they are brief. However, interest is capitalized during brief delays or interruptions which are externally imposed, or delays inherent in acquiring the qualifying asset. Thus, in this problem, the strike was an externally imposed interruption and interest capitalization continues during this period. However, the voluntary interruption in construction due to the supervisor's vacation is a period in which interest capitalization ceases. Therefore, interest is not capitalized during August, Year Two.

In order to give effect to the cessation of interest capitalization for the month of August, Year Two, it is necessary to adjust the calculation of the average accumulated expenditures for Year Two, as follows:

Amount	Period From Expenditure to End of Year, Less One Month of Interruption	Average Expenditure
$225,000	11 months	$206,250
360,000	9 months	270,000
180,000	2 months	30,000
$765,000		$506,250

Note: The $180,000 was expended on November 1, Year Two, after the interruption, so no adjustment need be made to the average expenditure of $30,000.

If the average accumulated expenditures for the qualifying asset exceed the amount of the specific borrowing made to construct the asset, the capitalization rate applicable to the excess is the weighted average interest rate incurred on other borrowings. In this problem, the computation of the excess expenditures over the original loan amount is as follows:

Average expenditures through December 31, Year Two	$506,250
Less: Amount of original loan	300,000
Excess expenditures	$206,250

Thus, in Year Two, $206,250 of the $506,250 average expenditures must be capitalized using the weighted-average borrowing rate, and the balance of $300,000 is capitalized using the interest rate on the original loan made to specifically acquire the qualifying asset. The weighted-average rate on the other borrowings is computed as follows:

Amount	Weighted Amount	Rate	Annual Interest
$1,000,000	$1,000,000	17%	$170,000
500,000	125,000	14% (3. mos.)	17,500
$1,500,000	$1,125,000		$187,500

$$\frac{\$187,500}{\$1,125,000} = 16.67\% \text{ weighted-average interest rate}$$

Interest Costs Capitalized

The interest cost to be capitalized for Year Two can now be computed, as follows:

$$\begin{aligned}\$300{,}000 \times 18.00\% &= \$54{,}000 \\ 206{,}250 \times 16.67\% &= \underline{34{,}382} \\ &\ \$88{,}382\end{aligned}$$

The final step is to determine whether Poll incurred at least $88,382 of interest expense in Year Two. Since in Year Two Poll incurred $241,500 ($300,000 × 18% + $1,000,000 × 17% + $500,000 × 14% × 3/12) of interest, the full $88,382 is capitalizable as part of the acquisition cost of the asset in Year Two.

The total amount of interest which Poll must capitalize on the new plant facility is $114,707 ($26,325 for Year One, and $88,382 for Year Two).

INTERIM FINANCIAL REPORTING

Background

APB-28 covers the general promulgated GAAP for accounting and reporting on interim periods. This opinion provides the accounting and disclosure requirements necessary for interim reporting and establishes the minimum disclosures for interim reports of publicly traded companies.

Income taxes for interim reporting are discussed in the chapter on Income Taxes; accounting changes for interim reporting are discussed in the chapter on Accounting Changes. Financial reporting for segments of a business enterprise is not required in interim financial statements (FASB-18).

Overview

Interim financial reports may be issued quarterly, monthly, or at other intervals, and may include complete financial statements or summarized data. In addition, they usually include the current interim period and a cumulative year-to-date period with comparative reports on the corresponding periods of the immediately preceding fiscal year.

The procedures and disclosures expressed in the promulgated GAAP (APB-28) are applicable whenever an entity issues interim financial reports.

Accounting and Reporting

Each interim period must be viewed as an integral part of the annual period, and accounting principles and reporting practices should be based on those of the latest annual reports of the entity, unless there has been a change in an accounting principle. A change in an accounting principle during an interim period is discussed in the chapter on Accounting Changes.

The accounting and reporting on the results of operation for interim financial statements is discussed in the following paragraphs.

Revenues are recognized as earned on the same basis as that for fiscal periods.

As closely as possible product costs are determined as those for the fiscal period with some exceptions for inventory valuation, as follows:

1. Companies using the gross profit method to determine interim inventory costs, or other methods different from those used for annual inventory valuation, should disclose the method used at the interim date and any material difference from the reconciliation with the annual physical inventory.
2. A liquidation of a base-period LIFO inventory at an interim date that apparently will be corrected by the end of the annual period should be valued at the expected cost of replacement. Cost of sales for the interim period should include the expected cost of replacement and not the cost of the base-period LIFO inventory.
3. Inventory losses from market declines should be included in the interim period in which they occur, and gains in subsequent interim periods should be recognized in such interim period but should not exceed the losses included in prior interim periods.

    Temporary market declines that are expected to be made up by the end of the annual period need not be recognized in interim periods.
4. Inventory and product costs computed by the use of a standard cost accounting system should be determined by the same procedures used at the end of a fiscal year. Variances from standard costs that are expected to be made up by the end of the fiscal year need not be included in interim-period statements.

Other costs and expenses should be charged or allocated to produce a fair presentation of the results of operation, changes in financial position, and financial position for all interim periods. The following should apply in accounting for other costs and expenses:

1. The general rule in preparing interim-period financial statements is that costs and expenses that clearly benefit more than one period should be properly allocated to the periods affected. This procedure should be consistently applied.
2. Companies that have material seasonal revenue variations must avoid the possibility that interim-period financial statements become misleading. Disclosure of material seasonal revenue variations should be made in the interim-period financial statements. In addition, it is desirable to disclose results for a full year, ending at the interim date.

3. Unusual and infrequent transactions that are material and not designated as extraordinary items, such as the effects of a disposal of a segment of business, should be reported separately in the interim periods in which they occur.
4. All other pertinent information, such as accounting changes, contingencies, seasonal results, and purchase or pooling transactions, should be disclosed to provide the necessary information for the proper understanding of the interim financial statements.

Interim reports should not contain arbitrary amounts of costs or expenses. Estimates should be reasonable and should be based on all available information applied consistently from period to period. An effective tax rate is used for income tax provision in interim periods. Income taxes for interim-period reports are discussed in the chapter on Income Taxes.

Material contingencies and other uncertainties that exist at an interim date must be disclosed in interim reports in the same manner as that required for annual reports. However, these contingencies and uncertainties, at an interim date, should be evaluated in relation to the annual report. The disclosure for such items must be repeated in every interim and annual report until the contingency is resolved or becomes immaterial.

Summarized Interim Financial Statements

Publicly traded companies reporting summarized financial information at interim dates should include the following minimum information:

1. Gross revenues, provision for income taxes, extraordinary items, effects of accounting changes (principles or practice), and net income
2. Primary and fully diluted earnings-per-share data
3. Material seasonal variations of revenues, costs, or expenses
4. Contingent items and effects of the disposal of a segment of a business
5. Material changes in financial position

Summarized interim financial statements based on these minimum disclosures *do not* constitute a fair presentation of financial position and results of operations in conformity with GAAP.

In the event that fourth-quarter results are not issued separately, the annual report should include disclosures for the fourth quarter on the aggregate effect of material year-end adjustments and infrequently occurring items, extraordinary items, and disposal of business segments that occurred in the fourth quarter.

When summarized interim financial data are not presented, significant changes in liquid assets, working capital, long-term liabilities, and stockholders' equity should be disclosed and disseminated to the public.

INVENTORY PRICING AND METHODS

Background

The main source of promulgated GAAP for inventories is ARB-43, Chapter 4 (as amended). Other promulgated GAAP relating to the subject of inventory are FASB Interpretation-1, Accounting Changes Related to the Cost of Inventory, and FASB Interpretation-17, Applying the Lower of Cost or Market Rule in Translated Financial Statements.

In addition to the above and other areas of promulgated GAAP, this chapter includes most of the nonpromulgated GAAP on inventories.

Overview

Inventories of goods must be periodically compiled, measured, and recorded in the books of accounts of a business. Inventory includes the total amount of tangible personal property and is usually classified as (1) finished goods, (2) work in process, and (3) raw materials.

Inventories exclude long-term assets that are subject to depreciation or assets that will be classified as such.

Inventories are classified as current assets, except when there are excessive quantities which may not reasonably be expected to be used or sold within the normal operating cycle of a business. In this event, the excess inventory is classified as noncurrent.

The periodic preparation of financial statements requires that revenues and costs be matched (one of the basic [pervasive] principles of GAAP), and the valuation of inventories is a major objective in that matching principle.

Inventory Systems

Periodic system The inventory is determined by a physical count as of a specific date. As long as the count is made frequently enough for reporting purposes, it is not necessary to maintain extensive inventory records. The inventory shown on the balance sheet is determined by the physical count and is priced in accordance with the inventory method used. The net change between the beginning and ending inventories enters into the computation of the cost of goods sold.

Perpetual system With this system, inventory records are maintained and updated regularly. The system has the advantage of providing inventory information on a timely basis, but requires the maintenance of a full set of inventory records. Theoretically, physical counts are not necessary, but they are normally taken to verify the inventory records. GAAP require that a physical check of perpetual inventory records be made periodically. The maintenance of the inventory information consists of posting each individual transaction.

Title to Goods

Legal title to merchandise usually determines whether or not it is included in the inventory of an enterprise. According to the Uniform Commercial Code, title to goods passes from the seller to the buyer in any manner and on any conditions explicitly agreed on by the parties. If no conditions are explicitly agreed on, title to goods passes from the seller to the buyer at the time and place at which the seller completes his performance with reference to the physical delivery of the goods. Title passes to the buyer at the time and place of shipment if the seller is required only to send the goods. However, if the contract requires delivery at destination, title passes when the goods are tendered at the destination. The following is the most commonly used terminology in passing title from the seller to the buyer:

- *F.O.B.*—means "free on board" and requires the seller, at his expense, to deliver the goods to the destination indicated as F.O.B.
- *F.A.S.*—means "free alongside" and is usually used in conjunction with a dock or a seaport. The seller must at his expense deliver the goods to the vessel indicated on the F.A.S.
- *C.I.F.*—means that the price of the goods includes the cost of the goods and the insurance and freight to the named destination.
- *C &F*—means that the price of the goods includes the cost of the goods and the freight to the named destination.
- *C.O.D.*—means "collect on delivery" and requires the buyer to pay for the goods at the time and place of delivery.

Costs

The basis of accounting for inventories is cost (basic principle), which has been defined as the price paid or consideration given to acquire an asset. In inventory accounting, cost is the sum of the expenditures and charges, direct and indirect, in bringing goods to their existing condition or location.

The principles of measuring inventory costs can be easily stated, but the application of the principles, particularly to items in work in process and finished goods, is difficult because of the problem involved in allocating the various costs and charges. For example, idle factory expense, excessive spoilage, double freight, and rehandling costs can be so abnormal that they may have to be charged to the current period, rather than as a portion of the inventory costs. Selling expenses should not be considered as any part of inventory costs. *The exclusion of all overhead from inventory costs is an unacceptable accounting procedure* (direct or variable costing).

Departure from the Cost Basis

When the utility of the goods, in the ordinary course of business, is no longer as great as their cost, a departure from the cost basis principle of measuring the inventory is required. Whether the cause be from obsolescence, physical deterioration, changes in price levels, or any other, the difference should be recognized as a loss of the current period. This is usually accomplished by stating such goods at a lower level designated as market (lower of cost or market principle).

Lower of Cost or Market

In the phrase *lower of cost or market*, the term market means current replacement cost, whether by purchase or by reproduction, *but is limited to the following maximum and minimum amounts:*

1. *Maximum:* cannot exceed the estimated selling price less any costs of completion and disposal. The maximum cost is also the net realizable value.
2. *Minimum:* the maximum less an allowance for normal profit.

Inventory Pricing and Methods

Item	Cost	Replacement Cost	(1) Selling Price	(2) Cost of Completion	(1 − 2) Maximum*	(3) Normal Profit	[(1 − 2) − 3] Minimum
1	$20.50	$ 19.00	$ 25.00	$ 1.00	$ 24.00	$ 6.00	$ 18.00
2	26.00	20.00	30.00	2.00	28.00	7.00	21.00
3	10.00	12.00	15.00	1.00	14.00	3.00	11.00
4	40.00	55.00	60.00	6.00	54.00	4.00	50.00
	$96.50	$106.00	$130.00	$10.00	$120.00	$20.00	$100.00

*The maximum is equal to the net realizable value.

The lower of cost or market for the above four items is:

Item 1	$19.00	Item 3	$10.00
Item 2	$21.00	Item 4	$40.00

If the lower of cost or market is applied to each individual item in the above illustration, items 1 and 2 must be written down by $1.50 and $5.00, respectively, or a total of $6.50. However, if the lower of cost or market is applied to the entire inventory, there is no write-down, because total cost of $96.50 is lower than market of $106.00.

The correct procedure in applying the lower-of-cost-or-market principle is first to determine what market is and then to compare it to cost. Market can be either replacement cost or the maximum or minimum restriction on replacement cost.

When market is lower than cost, the purposes of the maximum and minimum limitation are:

1. The maximum prevents a loss in future periods by at least valuing the inventory at its estimated selling price less costs of completion and disposal.
2. The minimum prevents any future periods from realizing any more than a normal profit.

The write-down of inventory to market is usually reflected in cost of goods sold, unless the amount is unusually material, in which case the loss should be identified separately in the income statement.

The journal entry to record the write-down to a separate account is:

Inventory loss due to decline in market $XXX
    Inventory $XXX

The lower-of-cost-or-market principle may be applied to a single item, a category, or the total inventory, provided that the method most clearly reflects periodic income.

The purpose of reducing inventory to the lower of cost or market is to reflect fairly the income of the period (matching-of-revenue-and-cost principle).

The basic principle of consistency must be applied in the valuation of inventory, and the method should be disclosed in the financial statements.

In the event that a significant change occurs in the measurement of inventory, adequate disclosure of the nature of the change and, if material (materiality principle), the effect on income should be disclosed in the financial statements.

Exceptions Exceptional cases, such as precious metals having a fixed determinable monetary value with no substantial cost of marketing, may be stated at such monetary value. When inventory is stated at a value in excess of cost, this fact should be fully disclosed in the financial statements.

The prerequisites of this exception are (1) immediate marketability at quoted prices and (2) cost difficult to obtain.

Cost Methods

For inventory purposes, cost may be determined by specific identification or by the association of the flow of cost factors—first-in, first-out (FIFO), last-in, last-out (LIFO), and average.

In selecting an inventory cost method the primary objective is the selection of the method that under the circumstances most clearly reflects periodic income. When similar goods are purchased at different times, it may not be possible to identify and match the specific costs of the item sold. Frequently, the identity of goods and their specific related costs are lost between the time of acquisition and the time of sale. This has resulted in the development and general acceptance of several assumptions with respect to the flow of cost factors (FIFO, LIFO, and average cost) to provide practical bases for the measurement of periodic income.

Inventory identification In some lines of business, specific items or lots of inventory are clearly identifiable from the time of purchase through the time of sale and are costed on this basis. Usually, the identity of goods is lost between the time of acquisition and the time of sale, and inventories are identified on the flow-of-cost factors. When a flow-of-cost method is used, the actual physical movement of the inventory is irrelevant.

Standard Costs

The use of standard costs is a management tool that identifies favorable or unfavorable variances from predetermined estimates established by past performance or time and motion studies. Inventory valuation by the use of standard costs is acceptable, if adjusted at reasonable intervals to reflect the approximate costs computed under one of the recognized methods, and adequate disclosure is made in the financial statements.

At the end of the reporting period the physical inventory is costed at LIFO, FIFO, or some other generally accepted method. Any variation between this result and the carrying value of the inventory at standard cost must be closed out to cost of goods sold and ending inventory such that the reported figure represents that which the generally accepted method would yield.

First-in, First-out Method (FIFO)

The *FIFO method* of identifying inventory is based on the assumption that costs should be charged against revenue in the order in which they occurred. The inventory remaining on hand is presumed to consist of the most recent costs. In other words, the first goods acquired are the first goods out, and the last goods acquired are in the ending inventory (assuming that there is an ending inventory).

Theoretically, FIFO approximates the results that would be obtained by the specific identification method.

Last-in, First-out Method (LIFO)

The last-in, first-out method of determining inventory (LIFO) requires that records be maintained as to the base year layer and additional layers that may be created or used up. An additional LIFO layer is created in any year in which the ending inventory is more than the beginning inventory. An additional LIFO layer is priced at the earliest or average costs of the year in which it was created, because the LIFO method matches the last costs incurred with current revenue, leaving the first cost incurred to be included in any inventory increase.

After an original LIFO layer is created (base year), it may decrease or additional layers may be created each year according to the quantity of ending inventory.

When the ending inventory is less than the beginning inventory, one or more LIFO layers may be used up. It is important to remember that once a LIFO layer is used up, any future new LIFO layer is priced at the cost of the year in which it is created, and not by reference to a prior LIFO layer cost.

In addition to the disclosure of significant accounting policies (APB-22) and of composition of inventories (ARB-43, Chapter 4), a business using the LIFO method of reporting inventory must disclose the following data, if it reports to the SEC:

1. Current replacement value of the LIFO inventories at each balance sheet date presented
2. The effect on the results of operations for any reduction of a LIFO layer

> **OBSERVATION:** *Certain restrictions on LIFO inventory disclosure are imposed by the IRS. An election (FORM 970) must be made to use the LIFO method for tax purposes. If the LIFO method is used for tax purposes, the IRS requires that it also be used for financial reporting purposes.*

Dollar-Value LIFO

A variation of the conventional LIFO method is the dollar-value LIFO method. Under the regular LIFO method, units of inventory are priced at unit prices. Under the dollar-value LIFO method, the base-year inventory is priced in dollars; for inventories of all subsequent years, price indices are used, with the base year as 100.

Year	Inventory at base-year prices	Price index	$ LIFO inventory amount
1	$100,000	100	$100,000
2	20,000	105	21,000
3	10,000	110	11,000
4	20,000	120	24,000
5	20,000	125	25,000
Totals	$170,000		$181,000

Weighted-Average Method

The weighted-average method of inventory valuation assumes that costs are charged against revenue on the basis of an average of the number of units acquired at each price level. The resulting average price is applied to the ending inventory to find the total ending inventory value. The weighted average is determined by dividing the total costs of the inventory available, including any beginning inventory, by the total number of units, as follows:

	Units	Cost per unit	Total cost
Beginning inventory	10,000	$4.00	$ 40,000
Purchase, July 25	8,000	4.20	33,600
Purchase, August 15	5,000	4.13	20,650
Purchase, September 5	7,000	4.30	30,100
Purchase, September 25	12,000	4.25	51,000
Totals	42,000		$175,350

Total cost $175,350 ÷ total units 42,000 = $4.175 weighted-average cost per unit.

Assume that the ending inventory consisted of 14,000 units. Value of ending inventory = 14,000 units × $4.175 per unit, or $58,450.

Moving-Average Method

The moving-average method can be used only with a perpetual inventory. The cost per unit is recomputed after every addition to the inventory.

	Total units	Total cost	Unit cost
Beginning inventory	1,000	$ 5,000	$5.00
Sale of 200 units	800	4,000	5.00
Purchase of 1,200 @ $6	2,000	11,200	5.60
Sales of 1,000 units	1,000	5,600	5.60
Purchase of 1,000 @ $5	2,000	10,600	5.30

Note: Only purchases change the unit price as sales are taken out at the prior moving-average unit cost.

Under the moving-average method, the ending inventory is costed at the last moving-average unit cost for the period.

Retail Inventory Method

Because of the great variety and quantity of inventory in some types of businesses, the reversed markup procedure of inventory pricing, such as the retail inventory method, may be both practical and appropriate.

It is necessary to maintain records of purchases at both cost and selling price and of sales at selling price in order to use the retail inventory method. With the information available, a ratio of cost to retail can be calculated and applied to the ending inventory at retail to compute the approximate cost.

	Cost	Retail
Inventory, at beginning of period	$ 100,000	$ 150,000
Purchases during the period	1,100,000	1,850,000
Totals	$1,200,000	$2,000,000
Sales during the period		1,800,000
Estimated ending inventory at retail		$ 200,000
Estimated ending inventory at cost (60% of retail)		$ 120,000

<u>Computation of Ratio of Cost to Retail</u>

$$\frac{\$1,200,000}{\$2,000,000} = 60\% \text{ of } \$200,000 = \$120,000$$

Physical inventories measured by the retail method should be taken periodically as a check on the accuracy of the estimated inventories.

The above illustration ignores the problem of changes made in selling prices after the original pricing of goods.

Original selling prices are revised or modified, thus necessitating an understanding of the following terminology:

> *original retail:* the first selling price at which goods are offered for sale
> *markup:* the selling price raised above the original selling price
> *markdown:* the selling price lowered below the original selling price
> *markup cancellation:* markup selling price decreased, but not below the original selling price

markdown cancellation: markdown selling price increased, but not above the original selling price
net markup: markup minus markup cancellation
net markdown: markdown minus markdown cancellation
markon: difference between the cost and the original selling price, plus any net markups

Original cost	$100
Original selling price ($50 markon)	$150
Markup	50
Original selling price plus markup	$200
Markup cancellation	25
Original selling price plus net markup	$175
Markdown (consists of $25 markup cancellation and a $25 markdown)	50
Original selling price minus markdown	$125
Markdown	25
Original selling price minus markdown	$100
Markdown cancellation	25
Original selling price minus net markdown	$125
Markup (consists of a $25 markdown cancellation and a $25 markup)	50
Original selling price plus net markup	$175

Theoretically speaking, the last selling price consisted of:

$50	markup
25	markup cancellation
25	markup cancellation
25	markdown
25	markdown
25	markdown cancellation
25	markdown cancellation
25	markup
$25	net plus change

and now the goods are priced at the original selling price plus a net markup of $25, or a total of $175.

The purpose of the conventional retail inventory method is to produce an inventory valuation (measurement) closely approximating what would be obtained by taking a physical inventory and pricing the goods at the lower of cost or market.

In order to approximate the lower of cost or market in the computations, *markdowns and markdown cancellations are excluded in calculating the ratio of cost to retail and are added to the retail inventory after the ratio is determined.*

In calculating the cost-to-retail ratio, any adjustment to the retail value will necessarily affect the ratio and hence the resultant cost figure. Adjustments that decrease the denominator of the ratio increase the ratio and the value for ending inventory at cost, thus increasing gross profit. In the interests of conservatism, as well as for other reasons, adjustments that decrease the retail figure should be avoided. Markups, which increase the denominator, however, are included *net* of cancellations.

Net markdowns (markdowns less markdown cancellations) are an example of adjustments that decrease the denominator. Including them in the retail figure violates the lower-of-cost-or-market rule. As shown below, net markdowns are not included in the calculation of the ratio, but *are* included in the determination of ending inventory after computing the ratio. The rationale for this is that the cost-to-retail ratio is presumed to be based on normal conditions, and a markdown is not a normal condition. When *applying* the ratio, however, to conform to the lower-of-cost-or-market rule, the retail value must be reduced by the amount of the markdowns.

Employee discounts obviously apply only to goods sold, not those remaining on hand. A sale at less than normal retail price to an employee does not represent a valid reduction to lower of cost or market, nor does it represent a valid adjustment of the cost-to-retail ratio or the value of the ending inventory. Hence, employee discounts should not enter into any of the calculations, but are deducted from retail, in the same way as markdowns, after the computation of the cost-to-retail ratio.

Inventory spoilage and shrinkage do affect the ending inventory figure, but should not enter into the cost-to-retail ratio calculation. It is an obvious distortion to make cost a higher percentage of retail merely because some items are missing from the retail inventory. When arriving at the final figure for inventory at cost, the amount of shrinkage is deducted either at cost or at retail depending upon whether shrinkage is stated at cost or at retail.

Assume the following information:

	Cost	Retail
Inventory, beginning of the period	$200,000	$ 300,000
Purchases	550,000	800,000
Transportation-in	50,000	
Markups		100,000
Markup cancellations		20,000
Markdowns		70,000
Markdown cancellations		10,000

The calculations would be:

	Cost	Retail
Inventory, at beginning of period	$200,000	$ 300,000
Purchases	550,000	800,000
Transportation-in	50,000	
Markups		100,000
Markup cancellations		(20,000)
Totals (ratio of cost to retail 67.8%)	$800,000	$1,180,000
Markdowns		(70,000)
Markdown cancellations		10,000
Total goods at retail		$1,120,000
Less: Sales during the period		860,000
Inventory, ending (at retail)		$ 260,000
Inventory, ending (67.8% of $260,000)*		$ 176,280

*At estimated lower of cost or market

LIFO application   The LIFO method of evaluating inventory can be applied to the retail inventory method by using procedures somewhat different from the conventional retail method. Basically two differences have to be taken into consideration:

1. Since the LIFO method produces a valuation approximating cost, and the conventional retail method produces a valuation approximating the lower of cost or market, to apply the LIFO concept to the conventional retail method it is necessary to include all markdowns as well as markups in determining the ratio of cost to retail.

2. With the LIFO method, the quantity of inventory on hand is from the earliest purchases during the year or from prior years' LIFO layers. The cost-to-retail ratio considers the current rela-

tionship between cost and selling price. Therefore, the beginning inventory is omitted from the cost-to-retail ratio, because it may cause a distortion. In short, to apply the LIFO concept to the retail inventory method:

    a. All markdowns as well as markups are included in the cost-to-retail ratio.

    b. The beginning inventory data are not used to compute the cost-to-retail ratio.

	Cost	Retail
Inventory, beginning of period	omitted	omitted
Purchases	$550,000	$ 800,000
Transportation-in	50,000	
Markups		100,000
Markup cancellations		(20,000)
Markdowns		(70,000)
Markdown cancellations		10,000
Totals (ratio of cost to retail 73.2%)	$600,000	$ 820,000
Add: Inventory, beginning of period		300,000
Total goods at retail		$1,120,000
Less: Sales during period		860,000
Inventory, ending of period (at retail)		$ 260,000

Since the $260,000 ending LIFO inventory (at retail) is less than the $300,000 beginning LIFO inventory (at retail), it is obvious that a prior LIFO layer was partially depleted:

	Retail
Beginning inventory	$300,000
Ending inventory	260,000
LIFO layer depleted	$ 40,000

The $40,000 difference is multiplied by the beginning inventory cost-to-retail ratio (66.67%) and then subtracted from the beginning inventory at cost, as follows:

	Cost
Beginning inventory	$200,000
$40,000 × 66.67%	(26,668)
Ending inventory (at cost)	$173,332

GAAP GUIDE / **24.13**

If the ending LIFO inventory (at retail) had been greater than the beginning LIFO inventory (at retail), a new LIFO layer would have been created which would have been costed at the new cost-to-retail ratio (73.2%).

The basic assumption of the retail inventory method is that there exists an equal distribution of goods (high-cost ratio and low-cost ratio) between sales, beginning inventory, and ending inventory. In instances where this basic premise does not prevail, cost ratios should be determined by departments or smaller units. This would require keeping (by departments) separate sales, purchases, markups, markdowns, and beginning and ending inventories.

Base Stock Method

The base stock method is similar to the LIFO method. It assumes a continuous permanent stock of inventory that is, in effect, a fixed asset. Excesses over this base stock are considered temporary inventory, and are priced at *current replacement cost*. Amounts below the base stock are similarly considered temporary, and are charged against revenue at replacement cost. The essential difference between the base stock method and LIFO is that the former uses replacement cost whereas LIFO relies on actual costs exclusively. Since the base stock method is not allowed for tax purposes, it is seldom encountered in practice.

Relative Sales Value Costing

This method is used when costs cannot be determined individually. Joint products, lump-sum purchase of assets (basket purchase), and large assets that are subdivided (real estate tracts) are examples of items that would be costed by their relative sales value.

ABC Company purchases four large pieces of machinery for $100,000. At the time of purchase an appraisal discloses the following fair values:

Machine #1	$ 12,000
Machine #2	28,000
Machine #3	40,000
Machine #4	30,000
Total	$110,000

The machines are priced at their relative fair values, as follows:

Machine #1	12/110 × $100,000 =	$ 10,909
Machine #2	28/110 × $100,000 =	25,455
Machine #3	40/110 × $100,000 =	36,364
Machine #4	30/110 × $100,000 =	27,272
Total cost allocated		$100,000

Firm Purchase Commitments

Losses on firm purchase commitments for inventory goods should be measured in the same manner as inventory losses and, if material, should be recognized in the accounts and disclosed separately in the income statement.

The recognition of losses, which are expected to arise from firm, noncancelable commitments and which arise from the decline in the utility of a cost expenditure, should be disclosed in the current period income statement.

In addition, all significant firm purchase commitments must be disclosed in the financial statements or in footnotes, whether or not any losses are recognized.

Disclosure

The general disclosure requirements for inventories are:

1. A description of accounting principles used and the methods of applying those principles (APB-22)
2. Any accounting principles or methods that are peculiar to a particular industry (APB-22)
3. Classification of inventories (ARB-43)
4. Basis of pricing inventories (ARB-43)
5. Method of determining inventories (LIFO, FIFO, average, etc.) (ARB-43)

All the above disclosures must be consistent from year to year, and if a significant change occurs, the following additional disclosures are necessary:

1. The nature of the change
2. If the change is significant, the effect on net income

Businesses dependent upon a limited number of sources for raw material or inventory or upon precarious sources (labor problems, foreign governments, etc.) should disclose the pertinent facts in their financial statements or footnotes thereto.

Inventory of Discontinued Segments

Inventories used in discontinued segments of a business should be written down to their net realizable value and the amount of write-down included as part of the gain or loss recognized on the disposal of the discontinued segment. However, such a write-down should not be attributable to any inventory adjustment that should have been recognized prior to the measurement date of the loss on disposal. In this event, the loss on the write-down should be included in the operating results of the discontinued segment (APB-30).

Inventory for Interim Financial Reporting

Generally, the same principles and methods are used to value inventories for interim financial statements as are used for annual reports. However, for practical purposes or otherwise there are some exceptions.

The use of estimated gross profit is frequently utilized to determine the cost of goods sold during an interim period. This procedure is acceptable for GAAP, as long as periodic physical inventories are taken to adjust the gross profit percentage used. Companies using the gross profit method for interim financial statements should disclose that fact and any significant adjustments that may occur in amounts determined by a physical count (APB-28).

When the LIFO method is used for interim financial statements and a LIFO layer is depleted, in part or in whole, that is expected to be replaced before the end of the fiscal period, it is acceptable to use the expected cost of replacement for the depleted LIFO inventory in determining cost of goods sold for the interim period (APB-28).

Inventory losses from market declines, other than those which are expected to be recouped before the end of the fiscal year, should be included in the results of operations of the interim period in which the loss occurs. Subsequent gains from market price recovery in later interim periods should be included in the results of operation in which the gain occurs, but only to the extent of the previously recognized losses (APB-28).

Standard costs are acceptable in determining inventory valuations for interim financial reporting. Unplanned or unanticipated purchase price, volume, or capacity variances should be included in the results of operations of the interim period in which they occur. Anticipated and planned purchase price, volume, or capacity variances that are expected to be recouped by the end of the fiscal year should be deferred at interim dates. In general, the same procedures for standard costs used at the end of the fiscal year should be used for interim financial reporting (APB-28).

Inventories in Business Combinations

Inventory acquired in a business combination accounted for by the purchase method is valued as follows:

> *Raw materials*—current replacement cost
> *Finished goods*—net realizable value less a reasonable profit
> *Work in process*—net realizable value less a reasonable profit

Inventories acquired in a business combination accounted for as a pooling of interests are valued at the same cost as that to the acquired entity.

Inventory for Terminated Contracts

When inventory is acquired for a specific customer contract that is subsequently terminated for any purpose, the carrying value of such inventory should be adjusted to reflect any loss in value.

Inventories—Research and Development

Inventories of supplies used in research and development activities should be charged to expense unless they clearly have an alternative use or can be used in future research and development projects.

When research and development activities consume goods, supplies, or materials from other sources within an organization, the carrying value of such inventory should be charged to research and development expense. Goods produced by research and development activities that may be used in the regular inventory of the organization may be transferred physically to regular inventory, at which time a credit in the amount of the costs assigned to the goods should be made to the research and development department (FASB-2).

Inventories—General Price-Level Changes

When preparing general price-level financial statements, the inventory method (FIFO, LIFO, average, etc.) will dictate the price index that must be used to restate inventory amounts (see General Price-Level Changes chapter).

Inventories—Intercompany Profits

Regardless of any minority interest, all (100%) of any intercompany profits in inventory must be eliminated for consolidated financial statements and investments in common stocks accounted for by the equity method (see Consolidated Financial Statements).

Inventories—Long-Term Construction-Type Contracts

The construction in progress account used in both the completed-contract and percentage-of-completion methods of accounting for long-term construction-type contracts is in fact an inventory account.

Inventories—Tax Allocation

Inventories accounted differently for financial accounting and tax purposes may create timing differences for which interperiod tax allocation may be necessary (APB-11).

Inventories—Accounting Change

An accounting change involving inventories in interim or annual reports necessitates accounting for the cumulative effect of the change and/or restatement of prior-period reports, including certain required *pro forma* information (APB-20).

Inventories—Nonmonetary Exchanges

A nonmonetary exchange of inventory held for sale in the ordinary course of business for similar property to be held for the same purpose does not complete the earning process and no gain or loss is recognized. The inventory received in the nonmonetary exchange should be recorded at the book value of the inventory surrendered, unless cash is also involved in the transaction (APB-29).

Inventory Profits

Profits from the sale of inventory, whose cost and selling price have increased significantly since acquisition, will probably include "ghost profits" or "inventory profits." These profits are considered fictitious, because the cost to replace the inventory has increased significantly and the normal gross profit on the inventory is considerably less than the gross profit containing the ghost or inventory profits.

During periods of rapid inflation, a significant portion of reported net income of a business may actually be ghost or inventory profits. The use of the LIFO method for pricing inventories may offset part or all of any ghost or inventory profits, because current purchases or production costs are matched against current revenue, leaving the earliest inventory on hand.

Certain publicly held companies are required by the SEC to disclose in a supplemental statement the current replacement cost for cost of goods sold, inventories, and resulting ghost or inventory profits.

Conclusion

Inventory is tangible personal property held for sale in the ordinary course of business. Inventory may be raw materials, in various stages of being produced (work in process), or finished goods.

Matching of revenue and costs is an important objective in accounting for inventory to ensure the proper determination of income in accordance with GAAP.

Accounting for inventories is cost (basic principle), which has been defined as the price paid or consideration given to acquire an asset. In inventory accounting, cost is the sum of the expenditures and charges, directly or indirectly, in bringing goods to their existing condition or location. For inventory purposes, cost may be determined by specific identification or by the association of the flow of cost factors such as LIFO, FIFO, or average. In selecting an inventory cost method the primary objective is the selection of the method that under the circumstances most clearly reflects periodic income.

When the utility of the inventory, in the ordinary course of business, is no longer as great as its cost, a departure from the cost basis is required. This is accomplished by pricing the inventory at the lower of cost or market on an item-by-item basis or on the entire inventory.

Market is defined as current replacement cost, either by purchase or reproduction, except that a maximum and minimum limitation is imposed. The valuation of inventories at the lower of cost or market results in recording losses but not profits prior to the sale of the inventory. The reason that beginning and ending inventories are included in the computation of net income is to arrive at the cost of goods sold during the period of time covered by the statement.

FIFO and LIFO are inventory costing methods employed to measure the "flow of costs." FIFO matches the first cost incurred with the first revenue produced, whereas LIFO matches the last cost incurred with the first revenue produced. In periods of changing prices, different costs are matched with revenue for the same quantity sold, depending on whether LIFO or FIFO is used.

The LIFO method matches current costs and current revenue. When prices are rising, higher costs are matched to current revenue; when prices are falling, lower costs are matched to current revenue. This minimizes recognition of inventory profits or losses that arise from fluctuations in the value of the inventory.

If the base of a LIFO inventory is substantially depleted after a long period of price increases, the cumulative effect of the old costs being matched against current revenue may distort net income for the period.

Comprehensive Illustration

To illustrate the application of FIFO, LIFO, and the weighted-average methods of inventory valuation, assume the following facts:

Units Purchased During the Year

Date	Units	Cost per Unit	Total Cost
January 15	10,000	$5.10	$ 51,000
March 20	20,000	5.20	104,000
May 10	50,000	5.00	250,000
June 8	30,000	5.40	162,000
October 12	5,000	5.30	26,500
December 21	5,000	5.50	27,500
Totals	120,000		$621,000

Beginning inventory consisted of 10,000 units at $5.
Ending inventory consisted of 14,000 units.

Under *FIFO*, the first units in stock are the first units out, which means that the ending inventory is of the units purchased last. Since the ending inventory is 14,000 units and the December purchases were only 5,000 units, we must go back to October's purchases for another 5,000 units; and in order to make up the 14,000 units in the ending inventory, we need to take 4,000 units from the June purchases, as follows:

December purchases	5,000 units @ $5.50	=	$27,500
October purchases	5,000 units @ 5.30	=	26,500
June purchases	4,000 units @ 5.40	=	21,600
Ending inventory using FIFO	14,000 units		$75,600

Inventory Pricing and Methods

Under *LIFO*, the last units in stock are the first units out, which means that the ending inventory is composed of the units purchased first. Using LIFO, we must go back to the earliest inventory to start our calculations. The earliest inventory available is the *beginning inventory* of 10,000 units at $5, but the ending inventory is 14,000 units. Thus, we must go to the next earliest purchase, which is January, and use 4,000 units at the January price to complete the ending inventory valuation, as follows:

Beginning inventory	10,000 units @ $5.00 =	$50,000
From January's purchase	4,000 units @ 5.10 =	20,400
Ending inventory using LIFO	14,000 units	$70,400

Under the *weighted-average* method we must find out what the weighted-average cost per unit is and then multiply it by the 14,000 units in the ending inventory, thus:

	Units	Cost per Unit	Total Cost
Beginning inventory	10,000	$5.00	$ 50,000
Purchases:			
January 15	10,000	5.10	51,000
March 20	20,000	5.20	104,000
May 10	50,000	5.00	250,000
June 8	30,000	5.40	162,000
October 12	5,000	5.30	26,500
December 21	5,000	5.50	27,500
Totals	130,000		$671,000

Weighted average = total costs divided by total units

= $671,000 divided by 130,000

= $5.1615 per unit

Ending inventory = 14,000 × $5.1615 per unit = $72,261

Comparison of Three Methods

Ending inventory, FIFO	$75,600
Ending inventory, LIFO	70,400
Ending inventory, weighted average	72,261

In periods of inflation, the FIFO method will always produce the highest ending inventory, resulting in the lowest cost of goods sold and the most gross profit. LIFO will produce the lowest ending inventory, resulting in the highest cost of goods sold and the least gross profit. The weighted-average method will yield results that will fall between those of LIFO and FIFO.

INVESTMENT TAX CREDIT

Background

The present promulgated GAAP on Accounting for the Investment Credit is APB-2, which has been amended by APB-4 and FASB Interpretation-25, Accounting for an Unused Investment Tax Credit. FASB Interpretation-32 (Application of Percentage Limitations in Recognizing Investment Tax Credit) represents an interpretation of APB-2, APB-4, and FASB Interpretation-25.

Overview

The investment credit may be a significant factor in influencing the determination of net income. The problem remains as to *when* the investment credit should be reflected in an operating statement.

The three suggested methods are (1) a direct contribution to capital, (2) a deduction of taxes for the period in which the credit arises, and (3) amortization over the life of the property.

The preferred method is to amortize the investment credit to net income over the productive life of the acquired property (deferral method).

An alternative method, but probably not as acceptable, is to treat the credit as a reduction of taxes of the year in which the credit arises (flow-through method). In practice today, the flow-through method is used by most companies.

The argument to amortize the investment credit to net income (deferral method) is based on the basic principle of matching costs with revenue. The theoretical support for deducting the investment credit from the tax liability in the year the credit arises is based on the literal translation of the IRC in that the investment credit is a credit against taxes due.

Using an investment credit as a direct contribution to capital is irrational and unacceptable, because it bypasses the income statement entirely.

The SEC has issued a statement (ASR 96) to the effect that the only two acceptable methods are (1) amortization of the credit over the life of the acquired property and (2) a direct reduction of taxes in the year in which the credit arose.

Investment Tax Credit

Internal Revenue Code Provisions

The investment tax credit is available to all taxpayers who place into service any "qualified Section 38" property having a useful life of three years or more. Section 38 property is new or used "recovery property" or other depreciable or amortizable tangible personal property, which is usually Section 1245 property. Generally, real property is not Section 38 property, but there are some exceptions.

There is no dollar limit on new Section 38 property for which the investment tax credit can be claimed. However, the maximum amount of used Section 38 property for which the investment tax credit can be claimed is $125,000 ($150,000 for years beginning after 1987).

The maximum investment tax credit may not exceed the taxpayer's first $25,000 of tax liability, plus 85% of the tax liability over $25,000. Generally, unused investment tax credits may be carried back three years or carried forward fifteen years. The investment tax credit allowable is deducted in full against the tax liability in the taxable year in which the qualified Section 38 property is placed into service by the taxpayer.

"Recovery property" which is eligible under the Accelerated Cost Recovery System (ACRS) includes most depreciable property (Section 1245 and Section 1250 assets) placed into service after December 31, 1980. However, ACRS does not generally apply to (a) property not depreciated in terms of years, such as the "units of production method," and (b) property that is amortized, such as leasehold improvements. In addition, pre-1981 property that is "churned" or acquired for the primary purposes of bringing the property under the ACRS is prohibited.

The investment tax credit is computed differently for "recovery property" than for other depreciable or amortizable personal property which is not "recovery property."

Recovery property The investment tax credit is 6% for three year recovery property and 10% for five, ten, or fifteen year recovery property. Investment tax credits are subject to recapture rules if the related Section 38 property is disposed of within a certain period. The amount of investment tax credit recaptured on the early disposition of Section 38 property is a percentage of the original investment tax credit, which was deducted against the taxpayer's tax liability, or is being carried forward to future taxable years. The recapture percentages for "recovery property" are as follows:

Year of Disposition	Three-Year Recovery Property	All Other Recovery Property
1	100%	100%
2	66⅔%	80%
3	33⅓%	60%
4		40%
5		20%

Other than "recovery property" The investment tax credit is 10% of the qualified Section 38 property placed into service during the taxable year. However, the qualified Section 38 property must have an estimated useful life of at least seven years to be included 100% in determining the tax credit. If the useful life is at least 5 years, then ⅔ of the cost of the qualified Section 38 property is included in determining the investment tax credit, and if the useful life is at least three years, then only ⅓ of the cost is included in determining the 10% credit.

If an investment tax credit was taken on Section 38 property that is not "recovery property" and the property is disposed of before the end of its estimated useful life, certain recapture rules apply. In this event, the investment tax credit must be recomputed based on the early disposition of the Section 38 property, and any difference between the original investment tax credit and the recomputed investment tax credit must be added to the tax liability in the year of disposition.

A Section 38 asset, costing $10,000, with an estimated useful life of 10 years, is disposed of at the end of five years.

Original investment tax credit taken	$1,000
Recomputed investment tax credit based on five years (2/3 of $10,000 × 10%)	667
Additional tax liability in the year of disposition	$ 333

Reduction in basis of property The Tax Equity and Fiscal Responsibility Act of 1982 (TEFRA) provides that a taxpayer may elect to reduce the basis of property by one half of the investment tax credit (ITC) that is claimed for the property. The basis of the property is reduced by one half of the amount of the related ITC for the purposes of ACRS deductions, depreciation, and determining the gain or loss on the sale or other disposition of the property. In lieu of reducing the basis of the property, a taxpayer may elect to claim a reduced ITC. In this event, for three-year recovery property, the reduced ITC is 4% instead of 6%; for all other recovery property, the reduced ITC is 8% instead of 10%. In other words, a taxpayer may elect to reduce the basis of the property by one half of its related ITC, or to claim an ITC that is reduced by two percentage points.

If a taxpayer elects to reduce the basis of the property by one half of the ITC, ACRS deductions and depreciation are computed for tax purposes on the reduced basis. In addition, gain or loss on the sale or other disposition of the property is determined by reference to the reduced basis. If a taxpayer elects to claim the reduced ITC instead of reducing the basis of the property, ACRS deductions, depreciation, and gain or loss on the disposition of the property are calculated without any reduction to the basis of the property on account of the ITC.

FASB Technical Bulletin 83-1 requires that the reduction in the basis of property by one half of its related ITC (as required by TEFRA) must be accounted for as a timing difference in accordance with the APB-11 (Income Taxes). Thus, deferred taxes must be accrued in connection with the reduction of the basis of property in the same manner as deferred taxes are accrued in connection with a timing difference.

Accounting for Investment Tax Credits

The total amount of tax benefits which become available in a current period must be included in computing income tax expense (books) for that current period (FASB Interpretation-25). The deferral method of tax allocation must be used. Investment tax credits are recognized for financial accounting purposes even though the same investment tax credits have not yet been realized for tax purposes. The theory that apparently justifies this treatment is that investment tax credits recognized in this manner will subsequently be realized as a reduction of an income tax liability of a future period.

> *OBSERVATION:* This promulgated GAAP (FASB Interpretation-25) requires that an investment tax credit be realized for financial accounting purposes before the same investment tax credit is

realized for tax purposes. This is a violation of another existing promulgated GAAP (APB-2) which specifically prohibits the recognition of an investment tax credit before it is actually used as an offset against income tax liability.

This conflict in GAAP can be apparently traced to the use of the "with and without" method used to compute deferred taxes. Under the "with and without" method, investment tax credits are recognized in computing deferred taxes. Thus, investment tax credits are recognized on timing differences for financial accounting purposes.

FASB Interpretation-25 further requires that any excess available investment tax credits not used in determining income tax expense for the current period must be used to reduce any existing net deferred tax credits which will reverse during the allowable carryforward periods of the related investment tax credits. Those investment tax credits which are used to offset existing net deferred tax credits will eventually be realized, as a reduction of income taxes payable, during the allowable carryforward period(s). When this occurs, a corresponding amount of net deferred tax credits must be reinstated and amortized over the period of its related timing difference.

FASB Interpretation-25 requires that all available investment tax credits be first applied to the current year using the statutory percentage limitation in effect for the current year. However, if excess investment tax credits still remain, they should be used to offset any existing net deferred tax credits which will reverse during the allowable carryforward periods. The statutory percentage limitations that must be used under these circumstances are the limitations applicable to the years in which previously recorded deferred tax credits are expected to reverse (FASB Interpretation-32). In other words, the reversal of the deferred tax credits must be scheduled by years to determine the total amount that is expected to reverse in each year. The statutory percentage limitation for each year is then multiplied by the amount that is expected to reverse in each year.

As mentioned previously, unused investment tax credits can be carried back three years and carried forward fifteen years on a first-in, first-out basis. When investment tax credits are carried forward they are included in computing income tax expense (books) for the current period (FASB Interpretation-25). Any excess investment tax credits not used in computing income tax expense for the current period are used to offset existing net deferred tax credits (FASB Interpretation-25).

Any investment tax credits not used in computing income tax expense for the current period, or used to offset existing net deferred tax credits, should be disclosed, if material, in the financial statements by footnote (APB-4).

When investment tax credits are carried back to prior years, income tax expense (per books) is reduced in the current period by the amount of refund of federal income taxes previously paid. In addition, the amount of investment tax credits which is carried back must be added to the total amount of investment tax credits recognized (per books) for the current period. The two preferable methods of accounting for the investment tax credit in the income statement when a carryback is involved are (APB-4):

1. The tax credit attributable to the carryback or carryforward is included in the total tax expense and is disclosed parenthetically or in a footnote.
2. The tax credit attributable to the carryback or carryforward is deducted as a separate item from the total tax expense.

Companies that defer and amortize investment tax credits over the productive life of the related asset (deferral method) should only include as a tax benefit for a current period the amount of amortization for the current year.

The following example will illustrate the major requirements of FASB Interpretation-25.

Assume the following facts for XYZ Corporation for its calendar year ended December 31, 1981.

- $900,000 of available unused investment tax credits for the current period.
- $1,000,000 of pretax financial accounting income (per books).
- $200,000 of net timing differences which reduce taxable income.
- $800,000 of taxable income.
- 40% tax rate for current period.
- $900,000 of existing net deferred tax credits of which $600,000 will reverse (amortize) in the carryforward period of the unused investment tax credits.
  The $600,000 will reverse as follows: $200,000 in 1982, $200,000 in 1983, and $200,000 in 1984.
- For the purposes of this illustration, assume that the investment tax credit for 1981 is limited to the first $25,000 of tax liability, plus 80% of any tax liability in excess of $25,000. Also

assume that the investment tax credit for tax years ending in 1982 and thereafter is limited to the first $25,000 of tax liability, plus 90% of any tax liability in excess of $25,000.

Discussion

Income tax expense is computed on all taxable items included in pretax financial accounting income. In this example, all items included in financial accounting income are eventually taxable.

There are no permanent differences in this example. However, in any event, permanent differences do not affect subsequent periods (they do not reverse) and no interperiod tax allocation (deferred taxes) need be made to account for them. Therefore, if a permanent difference is taxable it is included in computing income tax expense (books) for the period. If a permanent difference is nontaxable it is excluded in computing income tax expense for financial accounting purposes.

The first computation in solving this example is to determine income tax expense on pretax financial accounting income (per books) and the current income tax liability on taxable income (tax return), as follows:

Income Tax Expense on Pretax Financial Accounting Income:

Pretax financial accounting income	$1,000,000
Rate of tax	40%
Income tax expense before allowable investment tax credit	$ 400,000
Allowable investment tax credit [$25,000 plus 80% of ($400,000 − $25,000)]	325,000
Income tax expense (per books)	$ 75,000

Current Income Tax Liability on Taxable Income:

Pretax financial accounting income	$1,000,000
Less: Timing difference	200,000
Taxable income	$ 800,000
Rate of tax	40%
Income tax liability before allowable investment tax credit	$320,000
Allowable investment tax credit [$25,000 plus 80% of ($320,000 − $25,000)]	261,000
Current income tax liability	$ 59,000

The $16,000 difference between income tax expense of $75,000 (books) and the current income tax liability of $59,000 (tax return) is the deferred tax expense on the net timing differences of $200,000, computed as follows:

Net timing differences	$200,000
Rate of tax	40%
Income tax expense before allowable investment tax credit	$ 80,000
Allowable investment tax credit (80% of $80,000)	64,000
Deferred tax expense on timing difference	$ 16,000

The allowable investment tax credit for financial accounting income purposes is $325,000. The promulgated GAAP (FASB Interpretation-25) requires that any excess available investment tax credits not used in the current period in determining income tax expense (books) must be used to reduce any net deferred tax credits which will reverse within the carryforward period of the available investment tax credit. From the information given, there are $900,000 of existing net deferred tax credits of which $600,000 will reverse (amortize) within the carryforward period. For financial accounting purposes, the maximum amount of existing net deferred tax credits which can be used to offset the excess available investment tax credit not used in the current period is $540,000. The $540,000 is arrived at by applying the statutory percentage limitation which is in effect in the year of reversal, to the net deferred tax credits that reverse (FASB Interpretation-32). Thus, the $200,000 that reverses in 1982 is multiplied by the statutory percentage limitation in effect for 1982 ($200,000 × 90% = $180,000). The $200,000 that reverses in 1983 is multiplied by the statutory percentage limitation in effect for 1983 ($200,000 × 90% = $180,000). And the $200,000 that reverses in 1984 is multiplied by the statutory percentage limitation in effect for 1984 ($200,000 × 90% = $180,000). The total of the three computations is $540,000 ($180,000 + $180,000 + $180,000). Therefore, the maximum investment tax credit which can be recognized in this current period for financial accounting purposes in accordance with FASB Interpretation-25 and FASB Interpretation-32, is as follows:

Allowable investment tax credit on pretaxed financial accounting income (see first computation)	$325,000
Allowable investment tax credit on existing net deferred tax which will reverse within the carryforward period (1982 = $180,000, 1983 = $180,000 and 1984 = $180,000)	540,000

Maximum investment tax credit which can be recognized for financial accounting purposes	$865,000
Available investment tax credits	$900,000

The journal entry to record the current income tax expense, deferred taxes for the current period and the offset of the excess available investment tax credits against the maximum amount of deferred tax credits is:

Income tax expense—deferred	$ 16,000	
Income tax expense—current	59,000	
Deferred tax credits	540,000	
Current tax liability		$ 59,000
Provision for deferred taxes		540,000
Deferred taxes		16,000

The credit to deferred taxes of $16,000 represents the deferred tax on the net timing difference which arose in the current period. The credit to the provision for deferred taxes is an income statement account and appears in the total provision for income taxes for the current period, as follows:

Provision for income taxes:	
Current	$ 59,000
Deferred	16,000
Provision for deferred taxes	(540,000)
Total provision for income taxes	$(465,000)

The balance in the net deferred tax credit account which will appear on the balance sheet is computed as follows:

Balance, beginning of period	$ 900,000
Add: Deferred tax on net timing difference for current period	16,000
Less: Net deferred tax credit offset against excess available investment tax credit	(540,000)
Balance, end of period	$ 376,000

The computation of the ending balance and changes in investment tax credits for financial accounting and tax purposes is as follows:

Investment Tax Credit

	Financial	Tax
Beginning balance	$ 900,000	$ 900,000
Used in determining current income taxes	(325,000)	(261,000)
Used to offset existing net deferred tax credits	(540,000)	
Ending balance	$ 35,000	$ 639,000

In accordance with FASB Interpretation-25, the $35,000 of unused investment tax credits for financial accounting purposes may not be recorded on the books as an asset. However, if unused investment tax credits are material they should be disclosed by footnote in the financial statements (APB-4).

FASB Interpretation-25 also requires that deferred tax credits, which have been offset by investment tax credits, be reinstated in the subsequent period in which the investment tax credits are realized. In continuing the example of XYZ Corporation for its next succeeding calendar year, we will assume the following additional data to demonstrate the reinstatement of deferred taxes previously offset by investment tax credits:

- $35,000 of available unused investment tax credits for financial accounting purposes (balance from previous year)
- $639,000 of available unused investment tax credits for tax purposes (balance from previous year)
- $100,000 of available unused investment tax credits arising in current year
- $376,000 of existing net deferred tax credits (balance from previous year)
- $1,000,000 pretax financial accounting income
- $200,000 of net timing differences which reduce taxable income
- $800,000 of taxable income
- 40% tax rate
- For the purposes of this illustration, assume that the investment tax credit for 1982 is limited to the first $25,000 of tax liability, plus 90% of any tax liability in excess of $25,000.

Income Tax Expense on Pretax Financial Accounting Income:
Pretax financial accounting income	$1,000,000
Rate of tax	40%

Investment Tax Credit

Income tax expense before allowable investment tax credit	$ 400,000
Allowable investment tax credit [$25,000 plus 90% of ($400,000 − $25,000) = $362,500. However, for book purposes there is only $135,000 available ($35,000 + $100,000)].	135,000
Income tax expense (per books)	$ 265,000

Current Income Tax Liability on Taxable Income:

Pretax financial accounting income	$1,000,000
Less: Timing difference	200,000
Taxable income	$ 800,000
Rate of tax	40%
Income tax liability before allowable investment tax credit	$ 320,000
Allowable investment tax credit [$25,000 plus 90% of ($320,000 − $25,000)]	290,500
Current income tax liability	$ 29,500

The $235,500 difference between income tax expense of $265,000 (books) and the current income tax liability of $29,500 (tax return) consists of $8,000 deferred tax expense on the current year's net timing difference of $200,000, and the balance of $227,500 represents net deferred tax credits that must be reinstated. The journal entry to record the current income tax expense, deferred taxes for the current period and to reinstate the deferred tax credits, is as follows:

Income tax expense—current	$ 29,500	
Provision for deferred taxes	227,500	
Income tax expense—deferred	8,000	
Current tax liability		$ 29,500
Deferred tax credits		235,500

The credit to deferred tax credits consists of $8,000 arising in the current period and $227,500 of deferred tax credits being reinstated. The debit to the provision for deferred taxes is an income statement account and appears in the total provision for income taxes, as follows:

Provision for income taxes:

Current	$ 29,500
Deferred	8,000
Provision for deferred taxes	227,500
Total provision for income taxes	$265,000

The balance in the net deferred tax credit account which will appear on the balance sheet is computed as follows:

Balance, beginning of period	$376,000
Add: Deferred tax on net timing difference for current period	8,000
Deferred taxes reinstated for investment tax credits realized	227,500
Balance, end of period	$611,500

The computation of the ending balance and changes in investment tax credits for financial accounting and tax purposes is as follows:

	Financial	*Tax*
Beginning balance	$ 35,000	$ 639,000
New investment tax credits for current year	100,000	100,000
Used for determining current income taxes	(135,000)	(290,500)
Ending balance	$ NONE	$ 448,500

The tax benefit of a net operating loss carryforward may be recognized when future realization is assured beyond any reasonable doubt (APB-11). This same treatment is not allowed for an investment tax credit carryforward which may not be recognized even though future realization is assured beyond any reasonable doubt (FASB Interpretation-25).

Business combinations When an unused investment tax credit is acquired in a business combination accounted for as a purchase transaction, no value is assigned to it (FASB Interpretation-25). This is because existing promulgated GAAP (APB-2) prohibits the recording of an unused investment tax credit as an asset under any circumstances. The treatment of unused investment tax credits acquired in a purchase transaction as promulgated by FASB Interpretation-25 is as follows:

1. At the date of the purchase transaction no value is assigned to any unused investment tax credits acquired in the transaction.
2. At the date that a tax benefit is realized from the acquired unused investment tax credit, any unamortized goodwill (positive or negative) which arose from the same purchase transaction is reduced or increased by the amount of the tax benefit realized. The adjustment to goodwill is not made retroactively but is made prospectively. That is, there is no restatement of previously issued financial statements. The adjustment to goodwill is made in the period in which the tax benefit is realized and future periods. This means that the remaining amount of unamortized goodwill at the beginning of the period in which the tax benefit is realized is adjusted and the new balance is amortized over the current and remaining periods of amortization.
3. In the event that there is no unamortized goodwill at the beginning of the period in which the tax benefit is realized, then the noncurrent assets, if any, acquired in the same purchase transaction are reduced proportionately by the amount of the realized tax benefit. The adjustment is made prospectively in the same manner as goodwill (see 2 above).
4. If there is no unamortized goodwill or balances of noncurrent assets acquired in the same purchase transaction as the unused investment tax credit, or if the noncurrent assets are reduced to zero and realized tax benefits still exist, then any remaining realized tax benefits should be recorded as deferred credits and amortized to income over a period not to exceed forty years.

Other Considerations

Once a method of reporting the investment tax credit is selected, it should not be changed. A change may result in a consistency exception in the auditor's report (APB-4).

Only one method should be established for consolidated statements even though the members of the consolidating group may employ several different methods (APB-4).

In accounting for leverage leases the lessor must use the deferral method of accounting for the investment credit, or else the lease must be accounted for as a direct financing lease (FASB-13).

Disclosure

The two most acceptable forms of balance sheet presentation for the investment tax credit are (1) as a deduction from the corresponding asset and (2) as a deferred credit.

In the first case, the income statement will show a lower depreciation expense for the year, because the depreciable base of the asset has been reduced by the credit and so the credit will not appear on the income statement. If, however, this year's amount of the credit is shown directly on the income statement, then the depreciation expense for the year should be higher by the same amount.

Whatever method is used to account for the investment tax credit, full disclosure of the method and amounts involved should be made, as should material amounts of unused investment credits.

Conflict in GAAP

APB-2 and APB-4 require that investment tax credits be disclosed parenthetically or by footnote unless they can actually be used as an offset against the current income tax liability, or carried back to prior years for a claim of refund. In other words, investment tax credits are not to be recorded on the books of an enterprise, or be used as an offset against the income tax liability unless they can be actually realized for tax purposes and represent an available tax benefit. The justification for this treatment is apparently based on the limited life of the investment tax credit as provided by federal tax regulations. Under current tax regulations, an investment tax credit can be carried back three years and carried forward fifteen years, which are the same periods allowed for net operating losses.

The deferred tax method of interperiod tax allocation is required by APB-11 (Accounting for Income Taxes). APB-11 states that, "The tax effect of a timing difference should be measured by the differential between taxes computed with and without inclusion of the transaction creating the difference between taxable income and pretax accounting income." Thus, the "with and without" method of computing deferred taxes was established and investment tax credits are included in determining income tax expense (books) before the same investment tax credits are actually realized for tax purposes (see Deferred Tax Method in chapter on Income Taxes).

FASB Interpretation-25 condones the practice of recognizing investment tax credits for financial accounting purposes prior to their realization for tax purposes.

APB-11 permits the recognition, for financial accounting purposes, of a tax benefit resulting from an operating loss carryforward, providing that the realization of the tax benefit is assured beyond any reasonable doubt. Thus, income tax expense (books) can be reduced by the recognition of such an operating loss carryforward before the tax benefit is actually realized for tax purposes. However, FASB Interpretation-25 prohibits the recognition of a tax benefit resulting from an investment tax credit, even if the realization of the tax benefit is assured beyond any reasonable doubt. Thus, the tax benefit of an operating loss carryforward can be recognized for financial accounting purposes before the same loss is realized for tax purposes, but the tax benefit of an investment tax credit cannot be recognized under any circumstances prior to its realization for tax purposes.

To add further confusion, FASB Interpretation-25 requires that any excess available investment tax credits, not used to determine the current income tax expense (books), must be used to reduce any existing net deferred tax credits which will reverse in the available carryforward period. The journal entry to record the use of the excess available investment tax credits to reduce existing net deferred tax credits is, as follows:

Deferred tax credits	$XX,XXX	
Provision for deferred taxes		$XX,XXX

The "provision for deferred taxes" appears in the income statement as part of the total current provision for income taxes. Thus, once again, current income tax expense is being reduced by the tax benefits of investment tax credits which have not yet been realized for tax purposes.

LEASES

Background

The main source of promulgated GAAP on Accounting for Leases is FASB-13, which has subsequently been amended or interpreted by the following:

    FASB-17—Accounting for Leases—Initial Direct Costs
    FASB-22—Changes in the Provisions of Lease Agreements Resulting from Refunding of Tax Exempt Debt
    FASB-23—Inception of the Lease
    FASB-26—Profit Recognition on Sales-Type Leases of Real Estate
    FASB-27—Classification of Renewals or Extensions of Existing Sales-Type or Direct Financing Leases
    FASB-28—Accounting for Sales with Leasebacks
    FASB-29—Determining Contingent Rentals
    FASB Interpretation-19—Lessee Guarantee of the Residual Value of Leased Property
    FASB Interpretation-23—Leases of Certain Property Owned by a Governmental Unit or Authority
    FASB Interpretation-24—Leases Involving Only Part of a Building
    FASB Interpretation-26—Accounting for Purchase of a Leased Asset by the Lessee during the Term of the Lease
    FASB Interpretation-27—Accounting for a Loss on Sublease

In addition, the staff of the Financial Accounting Standards Board has issued the following Technical Bulletins (nonpromulgated GAAP) concerning leases:

    79-10 Fiscal Funding Clauses in Leases
    79-11 Effect of a Penalty on the Term of a Lease
    79-12 Interest Rate Used in Calculating the Present Value of Minimum Lease Payments
    79-14 Upward Adjustment of Guaranteed Residual Values
    79-15 Accounting for a Loss on a Sublease Not Involving the Disposal of a Segment
    79-16 Effect of a Change in Income Tax Rate
    79-17 Reporting Cumulative Effect Adjustment from Retroactive Application of FASB Statement 13
    79-18 Transition Requirement of Certain FASB Amendments and Interpretations of FASB Statement 13
    85-3   Accounting for Operating Leases with Scheduled Rent Increases

FASB Technical Bulletins are issued by the Staff of the FASB to provide timely guidance on specific accounting questions. Technical Bulletins are not approved by the FASB and are not considered promulgated GAAP.

The promulgated GAAP (FASB-13) defines a lease as an agreement that conveys the right to use assets (tangible or intangible) for a stated period. This broad definition includes certain transactions not generally considered leases and excludes leases of natural resources (oil, gas, minerals, and timber) and licensing agreements for manuscripts, patents, motion pictures, and copyrights.

Substance over Form

Some lease agreements are such that an asset and a related liability should be reported on the balance sheet of an enterprise. The distinction is one of *substance over form* (basic principle) when the transaction actually *transfers substantially all the benefits and risks inherent in the ownership of the property*.

Established in GAAP are criteria to determine whether a lease transaction is in substance a transfer of the incidents of ownership. If at its inception a lease meets one or more of the following four criteria, the lease should be classified as a transfer of ownership:

1. By the end of the lease term, ownership of the leased property is transferred to the lessee.
2. The lease contains a bargain purchase option.
3. The lease term is substantially (75% or more) equal to the estimated useful life of the leased property.
4. At the inception of the lease the present value of the minimum lease payments, with certain adjustments, is 90% or more of the fair value of the leased property.

We shall examine the four criteria in more detail later.

A lease that transfers substantially all the benefits and risks inherent in the ownership of property is called a *capital lease*. Such a lease should be accounted for by the lessee as the acquisition of an asset and the incurrence of a liability. The lessor should account for such a lease as a sale or financing. These leases are referred to as *sales-type* or *direct financing leases*. All other leases, called *operating leases*, are accounted for as true leases.

Terminology

It is essential that the various terms used in accounting for leases be thoroughly understood.

Capital lease   a lease that transfers substantially all the benefits and risks inherent in the ownership of the property to the lessee, who accounts for the lease as an acquisition of an asset and the incurrence of a liability.

Sales-type lease   a lease that usually results in a manufacturer's or dealer's profit or loss to the lessor, transfers substantially all the benefits and risks inherent in the ownership of the leased property to the lessee; in addition, (1) the minimum lease payments are reasonably predictable of collection and (2) no important uncertainties exist regarding cost to be incurred by the lessor under the terms of the lease.

Direct financing lease   a lease that does not result in a manufacturer's or dealer's profit or loss to the lessor, but does transfer substantially all the benefits and risks inherent in the ownership of the leased property to the lessee; in addition, (1) the minimum lease payments are reasonably predictable of collection and (2) no important uncertainties exist regarding costs to be incurred by the lessor under the terms of the lease.

Comparison of Sales-Type and Direct Financing Leases

Both sales-type and direct financing leases transfer substantially all the benefits and risks inherent in the ownership of the leased property to the lessee, who records the transaction as a *capital lease*.

A sales-type lease usually gives rise to a manufacturer's or dealer's profit or loss, whereas a direct financing lease does not give rise to a manufacturer's or dealer's profit or loss.

In a sales-type lease, the *fair value* of the leased property at the inception of the lease differs from the cost or carrying amount; in a direct financing lease, the fair value of the leased property at the inception of the lease is the same as the cost or carrying amount. This is because a manufacturer's or dealer's profit or loss usually exists in a sales-type lease and fair value is usually the *normal selling price* of the property. In a direct financing lease fair value is usually cost.

It must be remembered that a lessor need not be a dealer or manufacturer to realize a profit or loss, if at the inception of the lease the fair value differs from the cost or carrying amount.

Fair value   the price the leased property could be sold for between unrelated parties in an arm's-length transaction.

For the manufacturer or dealer, the fair value is usually the normal selling price less trade or volume discounts. However, fair value may be less than the normal selling price, and sometimes less than the cost of the property.

For others the fair value is usually cost less trade or volume discounts. However, fair value may be less than cost, especially in circumstances where a long period elapses between the acquisition of the property by the lessor and the inception of a lease.

Fair rental   the rental rate for similar property under similar lease terms and conditions.

Related parties   one or more entities subject to the significant influence over the operating and financial policies of another entity.

Executory costs   usually insurance, maintenance, and taxes paid in connection with the leased property.

Bargain purchase option   a lessee's option to purchase the leased property at a bargain price that makes the exercise of the option almost certain.

Bargain renewal option   a lessee's option to renew the lease at a bargain rental price that makes the exercise of the option almost certain.

Estimated economic life   the estimated remaining useful life of the property for the purpose for which it was intended, regardless of the term of the lease.

Estimated residual value   the estimated fair value of the leased property at the end of the lease term. The estimated residual value shall not exceed the amount estimated at the inception of the lease except for the effect of any increases that result during the construction or preacquisition period due to escalation provisions in the lease (see Leases with Escalation Clauses).

Unguaranteed residual value the estimated fair value of the leased property at the end of the lease term that is not guaranteed by the lessee or a third party unrelated to the lessor. A guarantee by a third party related to the lessee shall be considered a lessee guarantee.

Lessee's incremental borrowing rate the rate of interest that the lessee would have had to pay at the inception of the lease to borrow the funds, on similar terms, to purchase the leased property.

> *OBSERVATION:* FASB Technical Bulletin 79-12 precludes the use of the lessee's secured borrowing rate as a substitute for its incremental borrowing rate, as long as the incremental borrowing rate is determinable, reasonable, and consistent with the alternative financing the lessee could obtain.

Inception of lease The date of the lease agreement or the date of a written commitment signed by the parties involved which sets forth the principal provisions of the lease transaction.

A written commitment which does not contain all of the principal provisions of the lease transaction does not qualify under the promulgated GAAP (FASB-23).

> *OBSERVATION:* The first sentence of the definition of "inception of lease" in FASB-23 reads "The date of the lease agreement or commitment, if earlier." The last two words of the sentence ("if earlier") may be somewhat confusing to the reader. The commitment referred to is ostensibly an agreement to agree to enter into a lease. It is unlikely that such an agreement will ever be entered into after the lease agreement has been signed.

Interest rate implicit in the lease the discount rate that, when applied to certain items (enumerated below), results in an aggregate present value equal to the fair value of the leased property at the beginning of the lease term, less any investment credit expected to be realized and retained by the lessor. The items that the discount rate is applied to are (1) the minimum lease payments, excluding executory costs such as insurance, maintenance, and taxes (including any profit thereon) that are paid by the lessor; and (2) the estimated fair value of the property at the end of the lease term, exclusive of any portion guaranteed by the lessee or third party unrelated to the lessor (unguaranteed residual value).

Initial direct costs (FASB-17)   Initial direct costs are those directly incurred by the lessor to negotiate and consummate a lease transaction. Initial direct costs include any portion of compensation paid to salespersons or others that is applicable to time spent in negotiating and succesfully consummating a lease transaction. If the lease transaction is not successfully consummated, compensation paid to salespersons or others is not included in initial direct costs.

Other initial direct costs are:

1. Legal fees
2. Commissions
3. Credit investigations
4. Preparing and processing documents

Contingent rentals   are those which cannot be determined at the inception of the lease because they depend on future factors or events. Rental payments based on future sales volume, future machine hours, future interest rates and future price indexes are examples of contingent rentals. Contingent rentals can either increase or decrease lease payments (FASB-29).

Increases in minimum lease payments that occur during the preacquisition or construction period as a result of an escalation clause in the lease are not considered contingent rentals (see Leases with escalation clauses).

Lease Term

The term of a lease shall include the following time periods:

1. Any fixed noncancelable term
2. Any period(s) covered by a bargain renewal option
3. Any period(s) in which penalties are imposed in an amount that reasonably assures the renewal of the lease by the lessee
4. Any period(s) in which a guarantee by the lessee of the lessor's debt (related to the leased property) is expected to be in effect
5. Any period(s) up to the exercisable date of a bargain purchase option
6. Any period(s) in which the lessor has the option to renew or extend the lease term

Under no circumstances shall a lease term extend beyond the date a bargain purchase option becomes exercisable.

FASB Technical Bulletin 79-11 states that a penalty which provides reasonable assurance that a lease will be renewed, need not be expressly made in the lease. The penalty may result from outside factors. Thus as long as the penalty is known to exist at the inception of the lease and the amount of penalty is sufficient to reasonably assure the renewal of the lease, the lease term should include the renewal period covered by the penalty.

Noncancelable lease term a lease that is cancelable only (1) on some remote contingency, (2) with permission of the lessor, or (3) if the lessee enters into a new lease with the same lessor.

FASB Technical Bulletin 79-10 deals with fiscal funding clauses that are frequently found in governmental unit leases. The fiscal funding clause permits cancellation of a lease by a governmental unit if the necessary governmental appropriations are not made to pay for the lease. FASB Technical Bulletin 79-10 reaffirms the definition in FASB-13 of a noncancelable lease term. Thus, if there is a remote possibility that a fiscal funding clause will be exercised by a governmental unit, the lease should be classified as noncancelable. On the other hand, if the possibility is more than remote, the lease should be classified as cancelable in accordance with the provisions of FASB-13.

Lessee's Minimum Lease Payments

Normal minimum lease payments include:

1. The minimum rent called for during the lease term
2. Any payment(s) or guarantee(s) that the lessee must make or is required to make concerning the leased property at the end of the lease term (residual value), including:
   a. any amount stated to purchase the leased property
   b. any amount stated to make up any deficiency from a specified minimum
   c. any amount payable for failure to renew or extend the lease at the expiration of the lease term

When a lease contains a *bargain purchase option*, the minimum lease payments include only (1) the *minimum rental payments over the lease term* and (2) *the payment required to exercise the bargain purchase option.*

Under any circumstances, the following should be excluded from any minimum lease payments:

1. A guarantee by the lessee to pay the lessor's debt on the leased property
2. The lessee's obligation (separate from the rental payments) to pay executory costs (insurance, taxes, etc.) in connection with the leased property
3. Contingent rentals are never included in determining the minimum lease payments

> **OBSERVATION:** *FASB Interpretation-19 clarifies certain guarantees of the residual value of leased property made by a lessee, as follows:*
>
> 1. *A guarantee by a lessee to make up a residual value deficiency caused by damage, extraordinary wear and tear, or excessive usage is similar to a contingent rental, since the amount is not determinable at the inception of the lease. Therefore, this type of lessee guarantee does not constitute a lessee guarantee of residual value for purposes of computing the lessee's minimum lease payments.*
> 2. *A lessee's guarantee to make up a residual value deficiency at the end of a lease term is limited to the specified maximum deficiency called for by the lease.*
> 3. *Unless the lessor explicitly releases the lessee, a guarantee of residual value by an unrelated third party for the benefit of the lessor does not release the obligation of the lessee. Therefore, such a guarantee by an unrelated third party shall not be used to reduce the lessee's minimum lease payments. Costs incurred in connection with a guarantee by an unrelated third party are considered executory costs and are not included in computing the lessee's minimum lease payments.*

Lessor's Minimum Lease Payments

The minimum lease payments to a lessor are the sum of:

1. The minimum lease payments made by the lessee
2. Any guarantee by a third party, unrelated to the lessee and lessor, of the residual value or rental payments beyond the lease term, providing such guarantor is financially capable of discharging the potential obligation

Classification of Leases by Lessees

If one or more of the following four criteria are present at the inception of a lease, it should be classified as a capital lease by the lessee.

   I. Ownership of the property is transferred to the lessee by the end of the lease term.
  II. The lease contains a bargain purchase option.
 III. The lease term, at inception, is substantially (75% or more) equal to the estimated economic life of the leased property, including earlier years of use. (*Exception:* This particular criterion cannot be used for a lease that begins within the last 25% of the original estimated economic life of the leased property. For example: A jet aircraft that has an estimated economic life of 25 years is leased for five successive five-year leases. If the first four five-year leases were classified as operating leases, the last five-year lease could not be classified as a capital lease because the lease would commence within the last 25% of the estimated economic life of the property and would fall under this exception.)
  IV. The present value of the minimum lease payments at the beginning of the lease term, excluding executory costs and profits thereon to be paid by the lessor, is 90% or more of the fair value of the property at the inception of the lease, less any investment tax credit retained by the lessor and expected to be realized by him. (*Exception:* This particular criterion cannot be used for a lease that begins within the last 25% of the original estimated economic life of the leased property.)

Lessee's discount rate A lessee shall use the present value of the minimum lease payments, using his incremental borrowing rate unless he has knowledge of the implicit rate used by the lessor that is *lower* than his incremental borrowing rate.

Lessor's discount rate A lessor shall compute the present value of the minimum lease payments, using the interest rate *implicit in the lease*.

Classification of Leases by Lessors

If at inception, a lease meets any one of the four criteria indicating that substantially all the benefits and risks of ownership have been transferred to the lessee, *and meets both the following conditions*, it shall be classified by the lessor as a sales-type or direct financing lease, whichever is appropriate.

1. *Collection of the minimum lease payments is reasonably predictable.* A receivable resulting from a lease subject to an estimate of uncollectibility based on experience shall not be precluded from being classified as either a sales-type or a direct financing lease.
2. *No important uncertainties exist for unreimbursable costs yet to be incurred by the lessor under the lease.* Important uncertainties include extensive warranties and material commitments beyond normal practice. The necessity of estimating *executory costs,* such as insurance maintenance and taxes, shall not be considered important uncertainties.

NOTE: In the event the leased property is not acquired or constructed before the inception of the lease, this condition is not applied until such time as the leased property is acquired or constructed by the lessor (FASB-23) (see Leases with Escalation Clauses).

Changing a Provision of a Lease

If a change in a provision of a lease would have resulted in a different lease classification at the inception of the lease because of different criteria, a new lease agreement is created that must be reclassified according to its new criteria. Renewal, extension, or a new lease under which the lessee continues to use the same property is not considered a change in a lease provision.

Any action that extends the lease term, except to void a residual guarantee, or a penalty for failure to renew the lease at the end of the lease term, shall be considered a new lease agreement that must be classified according to this criteria.

Mere changes in estimates or circumstances do not cause a reclassification.

Refunding of tax-exempt debt If a change in a lease occurs as a result of a refunding by the lessor of tax-exempt debt and (1) the lessee receives the economic advantages of the refunding, (2) the revised lease qualifies and is classified either as a capital lease by the lessee or as a direct financing lease by the lessor, the change in the lease shall be accounted for on the basis of whether or not an extinguishment of debt has occurred, as follows:

1. Accounted for as an extinguishment of debt
   a. The lessee adjusts the lease obligation to the present value of the future minimum lease payments under the revised agreement, using the effective interest rate of the new lease agreement. Any gain or loss shall be treated as a gain or loss on an early extinguishment of debt.
   b. The lessor adjusts the balance of the minimum lease payments receivable and the gross investment in the lease (if affected) for the difference between the present values of the old and new or revised agreement. Any gain or loss shall be recognized in the current period.
2. Not accounted for as an extinguishment of debt
   a. The lessee accrues any costs connected with the refunding that it is obligated to reimburse to the lessor. The interest method is used to amortize the costs over the period from the date of the refunding to the call date of the debt to be refunded.
   b. The lessor recognizes as revenue any reimbursements to be received from the lessee for costs paid related to the debt to be refunded over the period from the date of the refunding to the call date of the debt to be refunded.

Accounting and Reporting by Lessees

Initial recording The lessee records a capital lease as an asset along with a corresponding liability. The initial recording value of a lease is the *lesser* of the fair value of the leased property or the present value of the minimum lease payments, excluding any portion representing executory costs and profit thereon to be paid by the lessor. Fair value is determined as at the inception of the lease and the present value of the minimum lease payments is computed as at the beginning of the lease term. The inception of the lease and the beginning of the lease term are not necessarily the same dates.

Since the definition of minimum lease payments (lessee's) *excludes* a lessee's obligation to pay executory costs (apart from the rental payments), any executory costs included in the minimum lease payments must be part of the rental payments, identified separately or not. Thus, there may be no executory costs at all to exclude from the minimum lease payments; or if such costs are included in the rental payments and are not separately identified (which is probably the most likely case), an estimate of the amount will be necessary.

The discount rate that the *lessee* uses to arrive at the present value of the minimum lease payments is his *incremental borrowing rate*, unless he has knowledge of the *interest rate implicit in the lease* used by the lessor, and it is lower. A *lessor* shall compute the present value of the minimum lease payments using the interest rate implicit in the lease that results in a present value equal to the fair value.

Leases with escalation clauses In lease agreements or written commitments in which the leased property is to be acquired or constructed by the lessor, there may be a provision for the escalation of the minimum lease payments during the construction or preacquisition period. Usually, the escalation is based on increased costs of acquisition or construction of the leased property. A provision to escalate the minimum lease payments during the construction or preacquisition period can also be based on other measures of cost or value, including general price-level changes, or changes in the consumer price index.

The relationship between the total amount of minimum lease payments and the fair value of a lease is such that when one increases so does the other. For example, assume that the total minimum lease payments of a particular lease are $100,000 payable in five equal annual installments, and the fair value of the same lease is $350,000. If the minimum lease payments are increased 20% to $120,000, it is quite likely that the fair value of the lease will increase correspondingly because the lease is just worth more money to an investor.

Promulgated GAAP (FASB-23) requires that increases in the minimum lease payments that occur during the preacquisition or construction period as a result of an escalation clause are to be considered in determining the fair value of the leased property at the inception of the lease for the purposes of the initial recording of the lease transaction by the lessee, or where fair value is used as a basis of allocation (see Leases involving land and buildings).

The initial recording value of a lease transaction by the lessee, which is required by FASB-13, is the lesser of the fair value of the leased property or the present value of the minimum lease payments. FASB-23 changes the lessee's determination of fair value for leases which contain escalation clauses from the fair value on the inception date to a fair value amount that includes the effect of any increases which have occurred as a result of the escalation clause. The changes embodied in FASB-23 are intended to create lease classifications that more closely reflect the substance of a lease transaction.

OBSERVATION: *The question arises as to when leases of this type should be recorded on the books of the lessee. The promulgated GAAP appears to indicate that the initial recording should be made only after the effects of the escalation clause on the fair value of the leased property is determined. Otherwise, FASB-23 is silent in all respects as to when the lease transaction should be recorded. In the case of significant amounts of leases, it would appear to be illogical to wait several years to record the transaction. However, if this is the only viable alternative, full disclosure of all pertinent facts pertaining to the lease agreement or commitment should be made in a prominent footnote.*

The other alternative is to record these types of lease transactions immediately at the inception of the lease, utilizing whatever information is available and subsequently adjusting the recorded amounts when the effects of the escalation clauses are known. This alternative does not appear to be viable because of the difficulties mentioned in the following paragraphs.

The last-enumerated criterion in FASB-13 for capitalizing a lease is when the present value of the minimum lease payments is 90% or more of the fair value of the leased property at the inception of the lease. When we consider this criterion for capitalizing a lease in conjunction with the alternative of recording lease transactions covered by FASB-23 at the inception of the lease and then subsequently adjusting the recorded amounts when the effects of the escalation clauses become known, the following problems arise, which are not addressed by either FASB-13 or FASB-23:

1. *If we assume that FASB-23 requires that the fair value of leases with escalation clauses be determined at a future date, what fair value should be used to determine whether the lease is or is not a capital lease in accordance with the criterion of whether the present value of the minimum lease payments is 90% or more of the fair value of the leased property at the inception of the lease?*

2. *What if a lease of this type is capitalized in accordance with the criterion that the present value of the minimum lease payments is 90% or more of the fair value at inception of the lease, and subsequently as a result of the escalation clause the present value becomes less than 90% of the fair value, so that the lease should not have been capitalized?*

3. *Suppose a lease with an escalation clause is properly classified as an operating lease at inception of the lease and subsequently, as a result of the escalation clause, the lease qualifies as a capital lease?*

The above are just a few of the complications that could arise in applying the provisions of FASB-23 to lease transactions. Some clarification must be forthcoming before this promulgated GAAP can be pragmatically applied.

FASB-23 also permits increases in the estimated residual value (see definition) that occur as a result of escalation provisions in leases in which the leased property is to be acquired or constructed by the lessor. For example, if the estimated residual value is 10% of the fair value at the inception of a lease and during the construction or preacquisition period of the leased property the effects of the escalation clause increase the fair value, then the estimated residual value is also allowed to increase above the amount which was estimated at the date of the inception of the lease.

Amortization The asset(s) recorded under a capital lease shall be amortized in a manner consistent with the lessee's normal depreciation policy for other owned assets. The period for amortization is either (1) the estimated economic life or (2) the lease term, depending on which criterion was used to classify the lease. If the criterion used to classify the lease as a capital lease was either I (ownership of the property is transferred to the lessee by the end of the lease term) or II (lease contains a bargain purchase option), the asset is amortized over its estimated economic life. In all other cases, the asset is amortized over the lease term. Any *estimated residual value* is deducted from the asset to determine the amortizable base.

Interest expense: Interest method The interest method is used to produce a constant rate of interest on the remaining lease liability. A portion of each minimum lease payment is allocated to interest expense and/or amortization, and the balance is applied to reduce the lease liability. Any *residual guarantee(s)* by the lessee or penalty payments are automatically taken into consideration by using the interest method and will result in a balance at the end of the lease term equal the amount of the guarantee or penalty payments at that date.

Jones Company leases a tractor-trailer for $8,000 per year on a noncancelable five-year lease. Jones guarantees to the lessor that the tractor-trailer will have a residual value of at least $5,000 at the end of the lease term.

Assume that all other assumptions have been eliminated and that a 12% interest rate is used.

Present value of $8,000 payments × 5 years	12%	= $28,838
Present value of $5,000 one payment	12%	= 2,837
Total asset and lease obligation		$31,675

Note: The present value of the $8,000 series of annual rental payments is found in the present value of annuity tables, and the present value of the $5,000 residual guarantee (one payment) is found in the present value tables.

A schedule of interest expense, amortization, and reduction of the lease obligation of $31,675 to the $5,000 residual guarantee using the interest method, follows:

Book Value Lease Obligation Beginning of Year	Rental Payments	12% Interest on Beginning Book Value	Amortization	Book Value Lease Obligations End of Year
$31,675	$ 8,000	$ 3,801	$ 4,199	$27,476
27,476	8,000	3,297	4,703	22,773
22,773	8,000	2,733	5,267	17,506
17,506	8,000	2,101	5,899	11,607
11,607	8,000	1,393	6,607	5,000
	$40,000	$13,325	$26,675	

Accounting for Lease Changes—Lessee

If a guarantee or penalty is rendered inoperative because of a renewal or other extension of the *lease term*, or if a new lease is consummated where the lessee continues to lease the same property, an adjustment must be made to the asset and lease obligation for the difference between the present values of the old and the revised agreements. In these cases, the present value of the future minimum lease payments under the new or revised agreement should be computed by using the original rate of interest on the initial lease.

Other lease changes should be accounted for as follows:

1. If a lease change results in revised minimum lease payments, but is also classified as a capital lease, an adjustment is made to the asset and lease obligation for the difference between the present values of the old and the new or revised agreement. The present value of the future minimum lease payments under the new or revised agreement should be computed by using the original rate of interest used on the initial lease.
2. If a new or revised agreement results from a lease change and is classified as an operating lease, gain or loss is recognized

and the asset and lease obligation is eliminated from the books of account.
3. A renewal, extension, or new lease under which the lessee continues to use the same property, except when a guarantee or penalty is rendered inoperative (see above), is accounted for as follows:
   a. *Renewal or extension classified as a capital lease:* an adjustment is made for the difference between the original and revised present values, using the original discount rate
   b. *Renewal or extension classified as an operating lease:* the existing lease continues to be accounted for as a capital lease to the end of its lease term, and the renewal or extension is accounted for as an operating lease

When leased property under a capital lease is purchased by the lessee, it is accounted for as a renewal or extension of a capital lease (FASB Interpretation-26). Thus, any difference between the carrying amount and the purchase price on the date of purchase is treated as an adjustment of the carrying amount of the property.

Termination of a Capital Lease—Lessee

Gain or loss, if any, is recognized on the termination of a capital lease, and the asset and lease liability must be removed from the books of account.

Lessee's Operating Leases

Leases that do not qualify as capital leases in accordance with the provisions of FASB-13 are classified as operating leases. FASB-13 requires that rental expense payments on an operating lease be amortized over the time periods in which the lessee derives benefit from the physical usage of the leased property. Thus, rental expense must be amortized over the lease term on a straight-line basis, unless some other systematic and rational basis is more representative of the time pattern in which the benefits of the leased property are derived by the lessee.

Contingent rental expense   Some operating lease agreements provide for rental increases or decreases based on one or more future conditions, such as future sales volume, future machine hours, future interest rates, or future price indexes. Under FASB-13, these types of rental increases or decreases are classified as *contingent rentals*. Contingent rentals are defined as those which cannot be determined at the inception of the lease because they depend on future conditions or events. A lessee's contingent rental payments are deducted as an expense in the period in which they arise.

Scheduled rent increases or decreases   To accommodate the lessee, a lessor may structure an operating lease agreement to provide for smaller rental payments in the early years of the lease, and higher rental payments toward the end of the lease. For example, a six-year operating lease agreement may provide for rental payments of $1,000 per month for the first two years; $1,500 per month for the next two years; and $2,000 per month for the last two years; for a total rental payment of $108,000 for the six years. Under this circumstance, FASB-13 requires that the $108,000 total rental payments be amortized over the six-year lease term on a straight-line basis. The monthly amortization for the first two years of the lease term is $1,500, even though only $1,000 per month is paid by the lessee under the terms of the lease.

It can be argued that in the early years of the above type of lease agreement, the lessee receives not only the use of the leased property, but also the temporary use of cash, equal to the excess of the fair rental value of the leased property over the actual rental payments. To recognize the economic substance of this lease transaction, it would appear that both the lessee and the lessor should record imputed interest on the difference between the actual amount of rental payments and the computed amount of level rental payments. However, FASB Technical Bulletin 85-3 reconfirms that under the provisions of FASB-13 it is unacceptable to use the time value of money as a factor in recognizing rentals under operating leases.

Lessee's Financial Statement Disclosure

Assets, accumulated amortization, and liabilities from capital leases should be reported separately in the balance sheet and classified as current or noncurrent in the same manner as other assets and liabilities.

Current amortization charges to income must be clearly disclosed, along with the additional information:

1. *Gross assets:* as of each balance sheet date presented, in aggregate and by major property categories (this information may be combined with comparable owned assets)

2. *Minimum future lease payments:* in total and for each of the next five years, showing deductions for executory costs, including any profit thereon, and the amount of imputed interest to reduce the net minimum lease payments to present values
3. *Minimum sublease income:* due in future periods under noncancelable subleases

Operating leases The following financial statement disclosure is required for all operating leases of lessees having noncancelable lease terms *in excess of one year.*

1. *Minimum future rental payments:* in total and for each of the next five years
2. *Minimum sublease income:* due in future periods under noncancelable subleases
3. *Schedule of total rental expense:* showing the composition by minimum rentals, contingent rentals, and sublease income (excluding leases with terms of a month or less that were not renewed)

General disclosure A general description of the lessee's leasing arrangements, including (1) basis of contingent rental payments; (2) terms of renewals, purchase options, and escalation clauses; and (3) restrictions imposed by lease agreements, such as additional debt, dividends, and leasing limitations. Following is an illustration of a lessee's financial statement disclosure.

Lessee's Financial Statement Disclosure

Lessee's Balance Sheet

	December 31	
Assets	1978	1977
Leased property:		
Capital leases, less accumulated amortization (Note ___)	$XXX,XXX	$XXX,XXX
Liabilities		
Current:		
Obligations under capital leases (Note ___)	$XXX,XXX	$XXX,XXX
Noncurrent:		
Obligations under capital leases (Note ___)	$ XX,XXX	$ XX,XXX

Capital Leases
Gross Assets and Accumulated Amortization

	December 31	
Type of Property	1978	1977
Manufacturing plants	$ XX,XXX	$XX,XXX
Retail stores	X,XXX	X,XXX
Other	XXX	XXX
Total	$XXX,XXX	$XX,XXX
Less: Accumulated amortization	XX,XXX	X,XXX
Capital leases, net	$XXX,XXX	$XX,XXX

Capital Leases
Minimum Future Lease Payments and Present Values of the Net Minimum Lease Payments

Year Ended December 31	
1979	$ XX,XXX
1980	X,XXX
1981	X,XXX
1982	X,XXX
1983	X,XXX
After 1983	XXX
Total minimum lease payments	$XXX,XXX
Less: Executory costs (estimated)	X,XXX
Net minimum lease payments	$XXX,XXX
Less: Imputed interest	XX,XXX
Present value of net minimum lease payments	$ XX,XXX

In addition to the foregoing statements and schedules, footnotes describing minimum sublease income and contingent rentals should be included, if required.

Operating Leases
Schedule of Minimum Future Rental Payments

Year Ended December 31	
1979	$ XX,XXX
1980	XXX,XXX
1981	XX,XXX

1982	XX,XXX
1983	XX,XXX
After 1983	XXX,XXX
Total minimum future rental payments	$XXX,XXX

In addition to the above information on operating leases, a footnote should be included describing minimum sublease income due in the future under noncancelable subleases.

Operating Leases
Composition of Total Rental Expense

	December 31	
	1978	1977
Minimum rentals	$XXX,XXX	$XXX,XXX
Contingent rentals	XX,XXX	XX,XXX
Less: Sublease rental income	(X,XXX)	(X,XXX)
Total rental expense, net	$XXX,XXX	$XXX,XXX

Note: The above schedule of total rental expense excludes leases with terms of one month or less that were not renewed.

In addition to the foregoing information on capital and operating leases, a footnote describing the general disclosure policy for the lessee's leases should be included containing (1) general leasing arrangements; (2) basis of contingent rental payments; (3) terms of renewals, purchase options, and escalation clauses; and (4) restrictions imposed by lease agreements, such as additional debt, dividends, and leasing limitations.

Accounting and Reporting by Lessors

Leases are classified for the lessor as either (1) sales-type, (2) direct financing, or (3) operating.

Sales-type leases are usually used by sellers of property to increase the marketability of expensive assets. The occurrence of a manufacturer's or dealer's profit or loss is generally present in a sales-type lease.

Direct financing leases do not give rise to a manufacturer's or dealer's profit or loss, and the fair value is usually the cost or the carrying amount of the property.

Recording Leases by Lessors

There are two steps in recording both sales-type and direct financing leases. Step 1 is to compute the gross investment in the lease, which is identical in each case. Step 2 will be explained for each kind of lease.

Step 1. Sales-type and direct financing leases The lessor's gross investment in a lease is the sum of the following:

1. The lessor's minimum lease payments
2. Any unguaranteed residual value accruing to the benefit of the lessor (this is the estimated fair value of the lease property at the end of the lease term, which is not guaranteed) less any executory costs and profit thereon to be paid by the lessor. [*Note:* If the residual value is guaranteed, it would be included in the minimum lease payments.]

Step 2. Sales-type leases Using the interest rate implicit in the lease, the gross investment arrived at in step 1 is discounted to its present value, which becomes the sales price included in income for the period. [*Note:* When using the interest rate implicit in the lease, the present value will always be equal to fair value.]

The cost or carrying amount of the property sold, plus any *initial direct costs* (costs incurred by the lessor in negotiating and consummating the lease, such as legal fees and commissions) less the present value of the *unguaranteed residual value* accruing to the benefit of the lessor, is charged against income in the period of the sale.

The difference between the gross investment computed in step 1 and the sales price computed above is recorded as unearned income, which is amortized to income over the lease term in proportion to the remaining balance (interest method). The unearned income is included in the balance sheet as a deduction from the related gross investment, which results in the net investment in the lease.

Step 2. Direct financing leases The difference between the gross investment computed in step 1 and the (a) cost or carrying amount of the property plus (b) any initial direct costs (legal fees, commissions, etc.) is recorded as unearned income, which is amortized to income over the lease term in proportion to the remaining balance (interest method). The unearned income is included in the balance sheet as a deduction from the related gross investment, which results in the net investment in the lease.

Other methods Other methods of recognizing income may be used for both sales-type and direct financing leases, provided the results are not materially different from those produced by the method prescribed.

Sales-type leases involving real estate FASB-26 covers a gain on a sales-type lease involving real estate. Losses on sales-type leases involving real estate are recognized and are not covered by FASB-26. A real estate lease that would otherwise be classified as a sales-type lease at the inception date shall be classified as an operating lease unless at the beginning of the lease term such a lease meets the criteria for full and immediate profit recognition as defined in FASB-66 (Accounting for Sales of Real Estate). The criteria are as follows:

1. The buyer's initial investment in the real estate is large enough that there is a reasonable likelihood that the seller will collect the receivable from the buyer. The minimum down payment required, which depends on the type of property, ranges from 5% to 25% and is illustrated on the following schedule appearing in FASB-66.

	Minimum down payment (% of Sales Value)
Land:	
Held for commercial, industrial, or residential development to commence within two years after sale	20%
Held for commercial, industrial, or residential development after two years	25%
Commercial and Industrial Property:	
Office and industrial buildings, shopping centers, etc.:	
Properties subject to lease on a long-term lease basis to parties having satisfactory credit rating; cash flow currently sufficient to service all indebtedness	10%
Single tenancy properties sold to a user having a satisfactory credit rating	15%
All other	20%
Other Income-Producing Properties (hotels, motels, marinas, mobile home parks, etc.):	
Cash flow currently sufficient to service all indebtedness	15%
Start-up situations or current deficiencies in cash flow	25%

Multi-Family Residential Property:
    Primary residence:
        Cash flow currently sufficient to service all indebtedness   10%
        Start-up situations or current deficiencies in cash flow   15%
    Secondary or recreational residence:
        Cash flow currently sufficient to service all indebtedness   15%
        Start-up situations or current deficiencies in cash flow   25%
Single Family Residential Property (including condominium or cooperative housing):
    Primary residence of the buyer   5%[1]
    Secondary or recreational residence   10%[1]

---

[1] *If collectibility of the remaining portion of the sales price cannot be supported by reliable evidence of collection experience, a higher down payment is indicated and should not be less than 60% of the difference between the sales value and the financing available from loans guaranteed by regulatory bodies, such as FHA or VA, or from independent financial institutions.*

2. The terms of the contract must require the buyer to increase his investment in the property each year after the appropriate down payment is made. The payments must be at least equal to an amount which will pay the total debt owed on the property, including any interest, over a maximum period, not to exceed twenty years.

3. If the seller continues to be involved with the property sold, his potential loss of profit as a result of continued involvement must be definitely limited by the contract in order to recognize profit at the time of sale. A seller's continued involvement after the sale may include arranging financing for the buyer, managing or constructing the property, or providing other services to the buyer in relation to the property after it is sold.

If the three conditions mentioned above are not met at the beginning of the lease term, then the lease must be classified as an operating lease by the lessor (FASB-26).

> **OBSERVATION:** *It is important to distinguish between the inception of the lease and the beginning of the lease term. The inception of the lease is the date on which the lease agreement or commitment is executed (FASB-23). The beginning of the lease term is the date that the actual lease term commences (FASB-19). For example, ABC Company executes a lease agreement on September 1, 1979. The lease term is to begin on January 1, 1980, and run for five years to December 31, 1984. The inception of the lease is September 1, 1979, and the beginning of the lease term is January 1, 1980.*

Balance Sheet Classification—Lessor

The resulting net investment in both sales-type and direct financing leases is subject to the same treatment as other assets in classifying as current or noncurrent.

Annual Review of Residual Values—Lessor

The unguaranteed residual values of both sales-type and direct financing leases should be reviewed at least annually to determine whether a decline, other than temporary, has occurred in their estimated values. If a decline is not temporary, the accounting for the transaction should be revised using the new estimate, and the resulting loss should be recognized in the period that the change is made. *Upward adjustments are not allowed.*

FASB Technical Bulletin 79-14 states that the prohibition of upward adjustments in residual values also applies to guaranteed residual values, even if the guaranteed residual value results from renegotiation of the value between the lessee and the lessor.

Accounting for Lease Changes—Lessor

The definition of lease term includes any periods in which penalties are imposed in an amount that reasonably assures the renewal of the lease by the lessee. The definition of minimum lease payments includes any payments or guarantees that the lessee is required to make concerning the leased property including any amount (1) to purchase the leased property, (2) to make up any deficiency from a specified minimum, and (3) for failure to renew or extend the lease at the expiration of the lease term. Guarantees and penalties, such as these, are usually canceled and become inoperative in the event the lease is renewed, is extended, or a new lease for the same property is consummated.

If a sales-type or direct financing lease contains a residual guarantee or a penalty for failure to renew and is rendered inoperative as a result of a lease renewal or other extension of the lease term, or if a new lease is consummated where the lessee continues to lease the same property, an adjustment must be made to the unearned income account for the difference between the present values of the old and the revised agreements. The present value of the future minimum lease payments under the new agreement should be computed by using the original rate of interest used for the initial lease. [*Note:* Care must be exercised in these circumstances to avoid an upward adjustment of any previously recorded residual values.]

In sales-type and direct financing leases which do not contain residual guarantees or penalties for failure to renew, an adjustment must be made to account for lease changes, renewals, or other extensions, including a new lease in which the lessee continues to lease the same property. If the classification of the lease remains unchanged or is classified as a direct financing lease and the amount of the remaining minimum lease payments is changed, an adjustment must be made to unearned income to account for the difference between the present values of the old and the new agreements. If a new classification results in a sales-type lease, it shall be classified and treated as a direct financing lease unless the transaction occurs within the last few months of the original lease, in which case it shall be classified as a sales-type lease (FASB-27).

If the classification of a lease is changed to an operating lease, the accounting treatment depends upon whether the operating lease starts immediately or at the end of the existing lease, as follows:

Starts immediately The remaining net investment is eliminated from the accounts and the leased property is recorded as an asset using the lower of (1) original cost, (2) present fair value, or (3) present carrying amount. The difference between the remaining net investment and the new recorded value of the asset is charged to income in the period of change.

Starts subsequently The existing lease continues to be accounted for as a sales-type or direct financing lease until the new operating lease commences, at which time the accounting treatment is the same as if the operating lease started immediately. Renewals and extensions usually commence at the end of the original sales-type or direct financing lease. Under these circumstances there should not be any remaining investment to eliminate from the books and the leased property is not recorded as an asset.

Termination of a Lease—Lessor

A termination of a lease is recognized in the income of the period by the following entries:

1. The remaining net investment is eliminated from the accounts.
2. The leased property is recorded as an asset using the lower of the (a) original cost, (b) present fair value, or (c) present carrying amount.

The resulting net adjustment from 1 and 2 is charged to income in the period of change.

Lessor's Operating Leases

Leases that do not qualify as capital leases in accordance with the provisions of FASB-13 are classified as operating leases. The cost of the property leased to the lessee is included in the lessor's balance sheet as property, plant, and equipment. The lessor's income statement will normally include the expenses of the leased property (unless it is a net lease), such as depreciation, maintenance, taxes, insurance, and other related items. However, if material, initial direct costs (those directly related to the negotiation and consummation of the lease) should be deferred and allocated to income over the lease term.

FASB-13 requires that rental income from an operating lease be amortized over the time periods in which the lessor's benefits in the leased property are depleted. Thus, rental income must be amortized over the lease term on a straight-line basis, unless some other systematic and rational basis is more representative of the time pattern in which the benefits of the leased property are depleted.

Contingent rental income Some operating lease agreements provide for rental increases or decreases based on one or more future conditions, such as future sales volume, future machine hours, future interest rates, or future price indexes. Under FASB-13, these types of rental increases or decreases are classified as *contingent rentals*. Contingent rentals are defined as those which cannot be determined at the inception of the lease because they depend on future conditions or events. A lessor's contingent rental income is accrued in the period in which it arises.

Scheduled rent increases or decreases To accommodate the lessee, a lessor may structure an operating lease agreement to provide for smaller rental payments in the early years of the lease, and higher rental payments toward the end of the lease. For example, a six-year operating lease agreement may provide for rental payments of $1,000 per month for the first two years; $1,500 per month for the next two years; and $2,000 per month for the last two years; for a total rental payment of $108,000 for the six years. In this event, FASB-13 requires that the $108,000 total rental income be amortized by the lessor over the six-year lease term on a straight-line basis. The monthly amortization for the first two years of the lease term is $1,500, even though only $1,000 per month is received by the lessor under the terms of the lease.

It can be argued that in the early years of the above type of lease agreement, the lessee receives not only the use of the leased property, but also the temporary use of cash, equal to the excess of the fair rental value of the leased property over the actual rental payments. To recognize the economic substance of this lease transaction, it would appear that both the lessee and the lessor should record imputed interest on the difference between the actual amount of rental payments and the computed amount of rental payments (straight-line or other systematic basis). However, under the provisions of FASB-13 it is unacceptable to use the time value of money as a factor in recognizing rentals under operating leases (FASB Technical Bulletin 85-3).

Lease Sale or Assignment to Third Parties

Sales or assignment of a sales-type or a direct financing lease does not negate the original accounting treatment. Profit or loss is recognized at the time of a sale or assignment, unless the seller assumes *substantial risks*.

Frequently, a sale of property *subject to an operating lease* is complicated by some type of indemnification agreement by the seller. The seller may guarantee that the property will remain leased or may agree to reacquire the property if the tenant does not pay the specified rent. These types of transactions cannot be accounted for as a sale because of the substantial risk assumed by the seller. The principle of *substance over form* must be applied to such situations and treated accordingly. Examples of *substantial risk* on the part of the seller are:

1. Agreements to reacquire the property or lease
2. Agreements to substitute another existing lease
3. Agreements to use "best efforts" to secure a replacement buyer or lessee

Examples of *nonsubstantial risk* situations on the part of the seller are:

1. Execution of a remarketing agreement that includes a fee for the seller
2. When the seller does not give priority to the releasing or other disposition of the property owned by a third party

If a sale to a third party purchaser is not recorded as a sale because of the substantial risk factor assumed by the seller, it should be accounted for as a *borrowing*. The proceeds from the "sale" are recorded as an obligation on the books of the seller. Rental payments made by the lessee under the operating lease are recorded as revenue to the seller, even if the rentals are paid to the third party. Each rental payment shall consist of imputed interest, and the balance as a reduction of the obligation. Any sale or assignment of lease payments under an operating lease, by the lessor, shall be accounted for as borrowings.

Lessor's Financial Statement Disclosure

The following financial statement disclosure is required by lessors whose *significant business activity is leasing* (not including "leveraged" leasing):

For sales-type and direct financing leases:

1. A schedule of the components of the *net investment* in leases, as of each balance sheet date, which shall include:
   a. future minimum lease payments
   b. executory costs
   c. allowance for uncollectibles
   d. unguaranteed residual values accruing to the benefit of the lessor
   e. unearned income
   f. contingent rentals
   g. amount of unearned income used to offset initial direct costs for direct financing leases
2. A schedule of the minimum lease payments, in total for the next five years

For operating leases:

1. A schedule of the investment in property on operating leases, and property held for lease, by major categories, less accumulated depreciation, as at each balance sheet presented
2. A schedule of future minimum rentals on noncancelable operating leases, in total and for the next five years
3. The amount of contingent rentals included in each income statement presented.

General disclosure for leases of lessors: a general description of the lessor's leasing arrangements.

Lessor's Financial Statement Disclosure

Lessor's Balance Sheet

	December 31	
Assets	1978	1977
Current assets:		
Net investment in sales-type and direct financing leases (Note ___)	$ XXX,XXX	$ XXX,XXX
Noncurrent assets:		
Net investment in sales-type and direct financing leases (Note ___)	$ XX,XXX	$ XX,XXX
Property on operating leases and property held for leases (net of accumulated depreciation of $X,XXX and $XX,XXX for 1978 and 1977, respectively) (Note ___)	$ XX,XXX	$ XX,XXX

*Schedule of Components—Net Investment in Leases
Sales-Type and Direct Financing Leases*

	1978	1977
Total minimum lease payments receivable	$X,XXX,XXX	$X,XXX,XXX
Less: Estimated executory costs, including profit thereon	XX,XXX	XX,XXX
Minimum lease payments	$X,XXX,XXX	$X,XXX,XXX
Less: Allowance for uncollectibles	XXX,XXX	XXX,XXX
Net minimum lease payments receivable	$X,XXX,XXX	$X,XXX,XXX
Add: Estimated unguaranteed residual values of leased properties	XXX,XXX	XXX,XXX
	$X,XXX,XXX	$X,XXX,XXX
Less: Unearned income	XXX,XXX	XXX,XXX
Net investment in sales-type and direct financing leases	$X,XXX,XXX	$X,XXX,XXX

A footnote should be included for contingent rentals.

Lessor's Schedule of Minimum Lease Payments

Year Ended December 31	
1979	$ XXX,XXX
1980	XXX,XXX
1981	XXX,XXX
1982	X,XXX,XXX
1983	XXX,XXX
After 1983	X,XXX,XXX
Total minimum lease payments receivable	$X,XXX,XXX

Lessor's Schedule of Investment in Property on Operating Leases and Property Held for Lease (by Major Class Categories)

Data-processing equipment	$X,XXX,XXX
Transportation equipment	XXX,XXX
Construction equipment	XXX,XXX
Other	XX,XXX
Total	$X,XXX,XXX
Less: Accumulated depreciation	XXX,XXX
Net investment	$X,XXX,XXX

Lessor's Schedule of Future Minimum Rentals on Noncancelable Operating Leases

Year Ended December 31	
1979	$ XXX,XXX
1980	XXX,XXX
1981	XXX,XXX
1982	XXX,XXX
1983	XX,XXX
After 1983	XXX,XXX
Total future minimum rentals	$X,XXX,XXX

A footnote should be included for contingent rentals.

Leases Involving Real Estate

Leases involving real estate are divided into leases involving:

1. Land only
2. Land and building(s)
3. Land, building(s), and equipment
4. Only part of a building(s)

Review of classification of leases by lessees   A review of the classifications of leases by lessees is necessary because accounting for leases involving real estate depends primarily on the criteria for classifying leases.

If one or more of the following four criteria are present at the inception of a lease, it should be classified as a capital lease by the lessee:

  I. Ownership of the property is transferred to the lessee by the end of the lease term.
 II. The lease contains a bargain purchase option.
III. The lease term, at inception, is substantially (75% or more) equal to the estimated economic life of the leased property, including earlier years of use. [*Exception:* This particular criterion cannot be used for a lease that begins within the last 25% of the original estimated economic life of the leased property.]
IV. The present value of the minimum lease payments at the beginning of the lease term, excluding executory costs and profits thereon to be paid by the lessor, is 90% or more of the fair value of the property at the inception of the lease, less any investment tax credit retained by the lessor and expected to be realized by him. [*Exception:* This particular criterion cannot be used for a lease that begins within the last 25% of the original estimated economic life of the leased property.]

Leases involving land only   A lessee shall account for a lease involving land only as a capital lease if either criterion I (ownership of property is transferred) or II (lease contains a bargain purchase option) is met. All other leases involving land only shall be classified as operating leases by the lessee.

A lessor shall account for a lease involving land only as a sales-type or a direct financing lease, whichever is appropriate, if either criterion I (ownership of property is transferred), or II (lease contains a bargain purchase option) is met; and (a) the collection of the minimum lease payments are reasonably predictable and (b) no important uncertainties exist regarding costs yet to be incurred by the lessor under the lease. All other leases involving land only shall be classified as operating leases by the lessor.

Leases involving land and building(s)   Leases involving land and building(s) may be broken down into three categories, as follows:

1. Leases that meet criterion I or II
2. Leases in which the fair value of the land is less than 25% of the total fair value
3. Leases in which the fair value of the land is 25% or more of the total fair value

1. Leases that meet either criterion I (ownership of the property is transferred) or II (lease contains a bargain purchase option) are accounted for as follows:

Lessee   The present value of the minimum lease payments, less executory costs and profits thereon (to be paid by the lessor), is allocated between the land and building(s) in proportion to their fair value at the inception of the lease. The present value assigned to the building(s) is amortized in accordance with the lessee's normal depreciation policy.

Lessor   A lessor must additionally meet the criteria that (a) the collection of the minimum lease payments is reasonably predictable and (b) no important uncertainties exist regarding costs yet to be incurred by the lessor under the lease. If the additional criteria are met, a lessor shall account for a lease involving land and building(s) as a sales-type or a direct financing lease, whichever is appropriate. If the additional criteria are not met, the lessor shall account for the lease as an operating lease.

2. Fair value of the land is less than 25% of the total fair value at the inception of the lease.

(When applying criterion III (lease term substantially—75% or more—equal to the economic life) and IV (present value of the minimum lease payments—excluding executory costs—is 90% or more of the fair value at inception), both the lessee and lessor shall consider the land and building(s) as a single unit, and the estimated economic life of the building(s) shall be the estimated economic life of the single unit.

Lessee The land and building(s) are accounted for as a single capitalized asset and amortized in accordance with the lessee's normal depreciation policy over the lease term if either criterion III (lease term is substantially—75% or more—equal to the economic life) or IV (present value of the minimum lease payments—excluding executory costs—is 90% or more of the fair value at inception) is met.

Lessor A lessor must additionally meet the criteria that (a) the collection of the minimum lease payments is reasonably predictable and (b) no important uncertainties exist regarding costs yet to be incurred by the lessor under the lease. If the additional criteria are met, the lessor accounts for the land and building(s) as a single capitalized asset, either as a sales-type or a direct financing lease, whichever is appropriate.

3. Fair value of the land is more than 25% of the total fair value at the inception of the lease.

When applying criteria III (*lease term* substantially—75% or more—equal to the economic life) and IV (present value of the minimum lease payments—excluding executory costs—is 90% or more of the fair value at inception), both the lessee and lessor shall consider the land and building(s) separately. To determine the separate values for the land and building(s), the lessee's incremental borrowing rate is applied to the fair value of the land to determine the annual minimum lease payments applicable to the land. The balance of the minimum lease payments remaining shall be attributed to the building(s).

Lessee The building(s) portion is accounted for as a capital lease and amortized in accordance with the lessee's normal depreciation policy over the lease term if the building(s) portion meets either criterion III (lease term substantially—75% or more—equal to the economic life) or IV (present value of the minimum lease payments—excluding executory costs—is 90% or more of the fair value at inception) is met.

The land portion shall be accounted for separately as an operating lease.

Lessor A lessor must additionally meet the criteria that (a) the collection of the *minimum lease payments* is reasonably predictable and (b) no important uncertainties exist regarding costs yet to be incurred by the lessor under the lease. If the additional criteria are met, the lessor accounts for the building(s) portion as a sales-type or a direct financing lease, whichever is appropriate.

The land portion shall be accounted for separately as an operating lease.

All other leases involving land and building(s) shall be accounted for as operating leases.

Leases involving land, building(s), and equipment   Equipment values, if material, should not be commingled with real estate values in leases. The minimum lease payments attributed to the equipment shall, if necessary, be appropriately estimated and separately stated. The criteria for the classification of leases should be separately applied to the equipment to determine proper accountability.

Leases involving only part of a building(s)   If the cost and fair value of a lease involving only part of a building(s) can be objectively determined, the lease classification and accountability shall be the same for any other land and building(s) lease. An independent appraisal of the leased property or replacement cost can be made as a basis for the objective determination of fair value (FASB Interpretation-24). In the event that cost and fair value cannot be objectively determined, leases involving only part of a building(s) should be classified and accounted for, as follows:

Lessee   The lessee shall classify the lease only in accordance with criterion III, as follows: "The lease term, at inception, is substantially (75% or more) equal to the estimated economic life of the leased property, including earlier years of use." [*Exception:* This particular criterion cannot be used for a lease that begins within the last 25% of the original estimated economic life of the leased property.]

In applying the above criterion, the estimated economic life of the building(s) in which the leased premises are located shall be used.

In the event the above criterion is met, the leased property is capitalized as a single unit and amortized in accordance with the lessee's normal depreciation policy over the lease term. In all other cases, the lease shall be classified as an operating lease.

Lessor   In all cases where the cost and fair value are indeterminable, the lessor shall account for the lease as an operating lease.

Leases Involving Government Units

Leases with government units usually lack fair values, have indeterminable economic lives, and cannot provide for transfer of ownership. These special provisions usually prevent their classification as any other than operating leases.

However, leases involving government units are subject to the same criteria as any other lease unless all of the following conditions exist and in that event they are classified as operating leases.

1. A government unit or authority owns the leased property.
2. The leased property is operated by or on behalf of a government unit or authority and is part of a larger facility such as an airport.
3. The leased property cannot be moved to another location because it is a permanent structure or part of a permanent structure.
4. Any government unit or authority can terminate the lease agreement at any time under the terms of the lease agreement, existing statutes, or regulations.
5. Ownership is not transferred to the lessee and the lessee cannot purchase the leased property.
6. Equivalent property in the same area as the leased property cannot be purchased or leased from anyone else.

Related Party Leases

Except in cases where the substance of a lease transaction clearly indicates that the terms and conditions have been significantly influenced by the related parties, these types of leases are classified and accounted for as if the parties were unrelated.

It is important to note that generally a subsidiary whose principal business activity is leasing property to its parent must be consolidated with the parent's financial statements.

> **OBSERVATION:** *Specific financial statement disclosures pertaining to related parties are required by FASB-57 (Related Party Disclosures).*

Sale-Leaseback Transactions

With the promulgation of FASB-28, Accounting for Sales with Leasebacks, these types of transactions have become quite difficult to classify and record. The following terminology must be understood in order to comprehend the promulgated GAAP:

Sale-leaseback   an owner sells property and then leases back part or all of the same property. Such an owner is referred to as the seller-lessee.

Purchaser-lessor   the party who purchases the property and leases back the same property to the seller-lessee.

Profit or loss on the sale   is the amount which would have been recognized on the sale by the seller-lessee assuming there was no leaseback.

"Substantially all" or "minor"   Under the terms of the lease, the seller-lessee may have a "minor" portion or "substantially all" of the rights to the remaining use of the property. This is determined by the present value of a total "reasonable rental" for the rights to the remaining use of the property retained by the seller-lessee. The seller-lessee has transferred "substantially all" of the rights to the remaining use of the property to the purchaser-lessor if the present value of the total "reasonable rental" under the terms of the lease is 10% or less than the fair value of the property sold at the inception of the lease. The seller-lessee has transferred a "minor" portion of the remaining rights to the purchaser-lessor if the terms of the leaseback include the entire property sold and qualifies as a capital lease under FASB-13.

> **OBSERVATION:** *The promulgated GAAP (FASB-28) does not define "reasonable rental" or "fair value." However, FASB-13 defines "fair value" as the price the leased property could be sold for between unrelated parties in an arm's-length transaction. FASB-13 defines "fair rental" as the rental rate for similar property under similar lease terms and conditions.*

Accounting for Sale-Leasebacks

When an owner sells property and then leases the same property back again, the transaction is called a sale-leaseback. If the lease meets the criteria for capitalization, the purchaser-lessor records the acquisition of the property as a purchase and the lease as a direct financing lease. If the lease does not meet the criteria for capitalization, the acquisition of the property is recorded as a purchase and the lease as an operating lease.

Accounting for the sale-leaseback by the seller-lessee is determined by the degree of rights in the remaining use of the property the seller-lessee retains, as follows:

a. Substantially all
b. Minor
c. More than minor but less than substantially all

Substantially all   If the entire property sold is leased back and the seller-lessee retains the rights to "substantially all" of the remaining use in the property, the seller-lessee records the lease as a capital lease provided it meets the criteria for capitalization under FASB-13. If the lease does not meet the criteria for capitalization, the seller-lessee records it as an operating lease. Whether the lease is recorded as a capital lease or an operating lease, any profit or loss (see definition) on the sale by the seller-lessee must be deferred and amortized as follows:

Capital lease   The deferred profit or loss on the sale is amortized in proportion to the amortization of the leased property.

Operating lease   The deferred profit or loss on the sale is amortized in proportion to the gross rental charged to expense over the lease term.

Whether a capital lease or an operating lease, if the leased asset is land only, the amortization of the deferred profit or loss on the sale must be on a straight-line basis over the lease term.

Minor   If the seller-lessee retains the rights to a "minor" portion of the remaining use in the property, the seller-lessee shall account for the sale and leaseback as two independent transactions based on their separate terms. However, the lease must provide for a reasonable amount of rent, considering prevailing market conditions at the inception of the lease. The seller-lessee must increase or decrease the profit or loss on the sale by an amount, if any, which brings the total rental for the leased property to a reasonable amount. Any amount created by this adjustment shall be amortized, as follows:

Capital lease   the deferred or accrued amount is amortized in proportion to the amortization of the leased property.

Operating lease   the deferred or accrued amount is amortized in proportion to the gross rental charged to expense over the lease term.

Whether a capital lease or an operating lease, if the lease asset is land only, the amortization of the deferred or accrued amount must be on a straight-line basis over the lease term.

> **OBSERVATION:** *If the total rental on the lease is less than a reasonable amount compared to prevailing market conditions at the inception of the lease, a profit on the sale would have to be increased and a loss on the sale would have to be decreased.*
>
> *In the case of an operating lease, the journal entry would be a debit to prepaid rent and a credit to profit or loss. The prepaid rent is amortized in an amount which increases the periodic rental expense over the lease term to a reasonable amount. Conversely, if the total rental on the lease is more than a reasonable amount compared to prevailing market conditions at the inception of the lease, a profit on the sale would have to be decreased and a loss on the sale would have to be increased. The journal entry would be a debit to profit or loss and a credit to deferred rent. The deferred rent is amortized in an amount which decreases the periodic rental expense over the lease term to a reasonable amount.*
>
> *In the case of a capital lease, the debit to prepaid rent or the credit to deferred rent is not made. Instead, the debit or credit increases or decreases the amount which is recorded for the leased property. The leased property is then amortized in the usual manner.*

More than minor but less than substantially all If the seller-lessee retains the rights to more than a minor but less than substantially all of the remaining use in the property, the seller-lessee shall recognize any excess profit (not losses) determined at the date of sale, as follows:

Capital lease The excess profit (if any) on a sale-leaseback transaction is equal to the amount of profit that exceeds the seller-lessee's recorded amount of the property as determined under the provisions of FASB-13 (the lesser of the fair value of the leased property or the present value of the minimum lease payments). For example, if the seller-lessee's recorded amount of the sale-leaseback property is $100,000 as determined under the provisions of FASB-13, and the amount of profit on the sale-leaseback transaction is $120,000, the excess profit that is recognized by the seller-lessee is $20,000. The balance of the profit ($100,000) is deferred and amortized in proportion to the amortization of the leased property.

Operating lease The excess profit (if any) on a sale-leaseback transaction is equal to the amount of profit that exceeds the present value of the minimum lease payments over the term of the lease. The amount of profit on the sale-leaseback transaction that is not recognized at the date of the sale is deferred and amortized over the lease term in proportion to the gross rentals charged to expense.

Whether a capital lease or an operating lease, if the lease property is land only, the amortization of the deferred profit (if any) must be on a straight-line basis over the lease term.

Accounting for Certain Losses on Sale-Leasebacks

Under any circumstances, if the fair value of the property at the time of the sale-leaseback is less than its undepreciated cost, the seller-lessee shall recognize immediately a loss in an amount not to exceed the difference between the fair value and the undepreciated cost of the property sold.

Subleases and Similar Transactions

Unless the original lease agreement is replaced by a new agreement, the original lessor shall continue to account for the lease as before.

A termination of a lease is recognized by a lessor in the income of the period in which termination occurs, by the following entries:

1. The remaining net investment is eliminated from the accounts.
2. The leased property is recorded as an asset using the lower of the (a) original cost, (b) present value at termination, or (c) present carrying amount at termination.

If an original lessee is relieved of the primary obligation under an original lease, the transaction should be accounted for by the lessee, as follows:

Capital leases Termination of the lease occurs and gain or loss is recognized in income of the period. A loss contingency should also be provided for if the original lessee remains secondarily liable on the lease.

Operating leases A loss contingency should be provided for if the original lessee remains secondarily liable on the lease.

When a lessee subleases leased property, the original lease continues and a simultaneous new lease is created in which the lessee becomes a sublessor. The results are that the original lessee is both a lessee in the original lease and at the same time, a sublessor in the new lease. In situations like this the original lease continues to be accounted for as if nothing happened, but the new lease must be classified and accounted for separately.

If an original lessee is not relieved of the primary obligation under an original lease, the transaction should be accounted for by the original lessee-sublessor, as follows:

1. If the criterion for the original lease was I (ownership of the property is transferred before the end of the lease term) or II (lease contains a bargain purchase option), the new lease shall be classified based on its own new criteria. If the new lease qualifies for capitalization, it shall be accounted for as a sales-type or a direct financing lease, whichever is appropriate, and the unamortized balance of the asset under the original lease shall be treated as the cost of the leased property to the sublessor (original lessee).

    In the event that the new lease does not qualify for capitalization, it shall be treated as an operating lease. [*Note:* As stated earlier, the original lease continues to be accounted for in the usual manner.]

2. If the criterion for the original lease was III (lease term is substantially—75% or more—equal to the estimated economic life of the leased property at the inception of the lease) or IV (present value of the minimum lease payments—excluding executory costs—is 90% or more of the fair value at inception), the new lease shall be capitalized only if it meets criterion III and (a) the collection of the minimum lease payments is reasonably predictable and (b) no important uncertainties exist regarding costs yet to be incurred by the lessor under the lease. If the new lease meets the criteria above, it is accounted for as a direct financing lease, with the unamortized balance of the asset under the original lease as the cost of the leased property.

    If the new lease does not meet the specific conditions above, it is accounted for as an operating lease. [*Note:* As stated earlier, the original lease continues to be accounted for in the usual manner.]

In any event, if the original lease is an operating lease, the sublease is accounted for as an operating lease also.

Even though the sublessor (original lessee) remains primarily obligated under an original lease, a loss may be recognized on a sublease (FASB Interpretation-27). The loss is measured as the difference between the unamortized cost of the leased property (net carrying amount) and the present value of the minimum lease payments which will be received under the terms of the sublease.

> **OBSERVATION:** FASB Interpretation-27 is silent as to recognition of any gain on subleases in which the sublessor (original lessee) remains primarily obligated under the original lease. However, FASB-13, paragraph 39, implies that both gain or loss may be recognized on sales-type and direct financing leases.

FASB Interpretation-27 also reaffirms that estimated costs and expenses directly associated with a decision to dispose of a business segment should include future rental payments on long-term leases less any future rentals to be received from subleases of the same properties (APB-30). The gain or loss is measured as the difference between the unamortized cost of the leased property (net carrying amount) and the present value of the minimum lease payments which will be received under the terms of the sublease. The gain or loss is included in the overall gain or loss on the disposal of the business segment.

> **OBSERVATION:** FASB Interpretation-27 is not clear on its coverage of subleases which are classified as operating leases. There is a strong argument that gain or loss on an operating sublease be included as part of the overall gain or loss on disposal of a business segment. APB-30 specifically states that all costs and expenses which are directly associated with the decision to dispose of a business segment be included in the overall gain or loss on the disposal. If a business segment has a long-term operating lease which is subleased and classified as an operating lease as part of the overall disposal of the segment, then any gain or loss would obviously be directly associated with management's decision to dispose of the segment. The gain or loss would be measured as the difference between the present value of the future rental payments which must be paid on the original lease and the present value of the future rental receipts which will be collected on the operating sublease. The journal entry to record a loss would be a debit to the gain or loss account for disposal of the business segment and a credit to a deferred account. The deferred credit account would be amortized each year in an amount which would make up the difference between the payment made on the original lease and the rental collected on the operating sublease.

FASB Technical Bulletin 79-15 reaffirms that a loss on a sublease not connected with the disposal of a business segment should be accounted for as any other loss on a sublease in accordance with FASB-13.

Accounting and Reporting for Leverage Leases

A lessee shall classify and account for "leveraged" leases in the same manner as "nonleveraged" leases. *Only a lessor* must classify and account for leveraged leases in the specific manner prescribed herein.

GAAP define a leveraged lease as a lease having all the following characteristics:

1. A leveraged lease meets the definition of a direct financing lease, as follows:
   A direct financing lease is a lease that does not result in a manufacturer's or dealer's profit or loss (this is because the fair value of the leased property at the inception of the lease is the same as the cost or carrying amount), but does transfer substantially all the benefits and risks inherent in the ownership of the lease property to the lessee; in addition:
   a. The minimum lease payments are reasonably predictable of collection.
   b. No important uncertainties exist regarding costs to be incurred by the lessor under the terms of the lease.
2. It involves at least three parties: (a) a lessee, (b) a lessor, and (c) a long-term creditor. [*Note:* The lessor is sometimes referred to as the "equity participant."]
3. The financing is sufficient to provide the lessor with substantial leverage in the transaction and is nonrecourse as to the general credit of the lessor.
4. Once the lessor's net investment is completed, it declines in the early years and rises in later years before being liquidated. These fluctuations in the lessor's net investment can occur more than once in the lease term.

If the investment tax credit is accounted for as provided herein and a lease meets the preceding definition, it shall be classified and accounted for as a leveraged lease.

The initial and continuing investment of the lessor in a leveraged lease shall be recorded "net" of the nonrecourse debt, as follows:

1. Rentals receivable, net of that portion applicable to principal and interest on the nonrecourse debt
2. A receivable for the amount of the investment tax credit to be realized on the transaction
3. The estimated residual value of the leased property

4. Unearned and deferred income consisting of (a) the estimated pretax lease income or loss, after deducting initial direct costs of negotiating and consummating the lease transaction, that remains to be allocated to income over the lease term, and (b) the investment tax credit that remains to be allocated to income over the lease term

FASB Technical Bulletin 79-16 requires that the effect of an income tax rate change be recognized in net income of the period in which the rate change occurs. If the effect of the income tax rate change creates a significant variation between the usual relationship of taxable income and pretax accounting income, disclosure should be made in accordance with APB-11 (Accounting for Income Taxes).

The investment in a leveraged lease, less applicable deferred taxes, shall represent the lessor's net investment for purposes of computing periodic net income from the leveraged lease. The following method is used to compute periodic net income:

1. A projected cash flow analysis is prepared for the lease term.
2. The rate of return on net investment in the years it is positive is computed (usually by trial and error).
3. Every year the net investment is increased or decreased by the difference between the net cash flow and the amount of income recognized, if any.

The amount of net income that is recognized each year consists of:

1. Pretax lease income or loss (allocated from the unearned income portion of the net investment)
2. Investment tax credit (allocated from the deferred income portion of the net investment)
3. The tax effect of the pretax lease income or loss recognized (which is reflected in tax expense for the year)

Any tax effect on the difference between pretax accounting income or loss and taxable income or loss is charged or credited to deferred taxes.

All the important assumptions affecting the estimated net income from the leveraged lease, including any estimated residual values, should be reviewed at least annually.

If at the inception or at any time during the lease, the projected net cash receipts over the initial or remaining lease term are less than the lessor's initial or current investment, the resulting loss shall be immediately recognized.

Upward adjustments of the estimated residual value are not permitted.

The lessor's financial statement disclosure for leveraged leases shall include the amount of deferred taxes separately stated.

When leveraged leasing is a significant part of the lessor's business activity, a schedule of the components of the net investment in leveraged leases shall be fully disclosed in the footnotes to the financial statements.

Business Combinations

A business combination, in itself, does not affect the classification of a lease. However, if as a result of a business combination, a lease is revised or modified to the extent that under the promulgated GAAP (FASB-13) it is considered a new agreement, it should be reclassified on the basis of its revision or modification.

Ordinarily, under the purchase method or pooling-of-interests method of effecting a business combination, a lease retains its previous classification under FASB-13 and is accounted for in the same manner as it was prior to the combination.

The acquiring company in a business combination accounted for by the purchase method shall account for a leverage lease by assigning a fair value (present value, net of tax) to the net investment in a leveraged lease based on the remaining future cash flows with appropriate recognition for any future estimated tax effects. After the fair value (present value, net of tax) of the net investment is determined, it should be allocated to net rentals receivable, estimated residual value, and unearned income. Thereafter, a company should account for the leveraged lease by allocating the periodic cash flow between the net investment and the lease income.

In a business combination where an acquired lease has not been conformed to FASB-13, the acquiring company should classify such a lease to conform retroactively to FASB-13.

Effective Date and Transition

FASB-13 is effective for leasing transactions entered into on or after January 1, 1977, and earlier application is encouraged. Leasing transactions entered into prior to January 1, 1977, and concluded after that date are excluded from FASB-13 if they are supported by a written commitment signed by the parties.

Financial statements presented for fiscal years beginning after December 31, 1980, shall be retroactively restated to the provisions of FASB-13.

> **OBSERVATION:** *The preceding discussion of the transitional procedures of FASB-13 is brief and incomplete. The reader is advised to refer to the actual transitional procedures enumerated in FASB-13. In addition, FASB Technical Bulletins 79-17 and 79-18 contain information relating to the transitional period in FASB-13.*

Comprehensive Illustration—Capital Lease

Paine Corporation leases a computer under a noncancelable five-year lease for annual rental payments of $10,000. The fair value of the computer at the inception of the lease is $36,048, and the incremental borrowing rate of Paine is 10%. There are no executory costs and no investment tax credit available. The annual rent of $10,000 is considered a fair rental as opposed to a bargain rental. The estimated economic life of the computer is 10 years.

Classification of Lease by Paine as Lessee

A review is made of the criteria involved in the provisions of the lease to determine its classification.

1. Criterion I is not met, because there is no transfer of the ownership of the lease property before the end of the lease term.
2. Criterion II is not met, because the lease does not contain a bargain purchase option.
3. Criterion III is not met, because the lease term (five years) is not equal to 75% or more of the estimated economic life (10 years) of the leased property. [*Note:* There are no other provisions affecting the lease term other than the five-year noncancelable term.]
4. Criterion IV is met, because the present value ($37,908) of the minimum lease payments, excluding executory costs and profits thereon paid by the lessor, is 90% or more of the fair value ($36,048) of the leased property. [*Note:* The present value computations are given below.]

Paine Corporation should record the transaction as a capital lease.

Accounting for the Lease by Paine

The initial recording value of the leased property, at the inception of the lease, is the lesser of the fair value of the leased property or the present value of the minimum lease payments, excluding any portion that represents executory costs and profit thereon to be paid by the lessor.

The discount rate used by the lessee to find the present value of the minimum lease payments is his incremental borrowing rate of 10%, unless the lessee has knowledge of the interest rate implicit in the lease, used by the lessor, which is lower.

The interest rate implicit in the lease is 12%, which is the discount rate that, when applied to the minimum lease payments of $10,000 per year for five years, results in a present value equal to the fair value of the leased property at the inception of the lease.

This means that Paine must use its incremental borrowing rate of 10% to discount the minimum lease payments to their present value, which is $37,908.

The initial recording value of the leased property is the lesser of the fair value of the leased property at inception or the present value of the minimum lease payments using the lower interest rate. Therefore, the $36,048 fair value is less than the minimum lease payments of $37,908 (computed by using the lower incremental borrowing rate) and is used to initially record the lease, as follows:

Lease property, capital leases	$36,048	
Obligations, capital leases		$36,048

[*Note:* The present value of the minimum lease payments using the interest rate implicit in the lease will always be the same as the fair value of the property at the inception of the lease.]

Amortization by Lessee

The asset(s) recorded under a capital lease shall be amortized in a manner consistent with lessee's normal depreciation policy for other owned assets. The period for amortization is either (1) the estimated economic life or (2) the lease term, depending on which criterion was used to classify the lease. If the criterion used to classify the lease as a capital lease was either criterion I (ownership of the property is transferred to the lessee by the end of the lease term) or criterion II (lease contains a bargain purchase option), the asset is amortized over its economic life. In all other cases, the asset is amortized over the lease term. Any residual value is deducted from the asset to determine the amortizable base.

Since the Paine Corporation's lease qualified under criterion IV (present value of the minimum lease payments, excluding executory costs and profit thereon paid by the lessor, is 90% or more of the fair value of the leased property), the amortization period must be over the lease term.

A schedule of amortization, interest expense, and lease obligation payments for Paine Corporation's computer lease, using the interest method, follows:

Book Value Lease Obligations Beginning of Year	Rental Payments	12% Interest on Beginning Book Value	Amortization	Book Value Lease Obligations End of Year
$36,048	$10,000	$ 4,326	$ 5,674	$30,374
30,374	10,000	3,645	6,355	24,019
24,019	10,000	2,882	7,118	16,901
16,901	10,000	2,028	7,972	8,929
8,929	10,000	1,071	8,929	—
	$50,000	$13,952	$36,048	

Note: The interest rate used is 12%, which is the interest rate implicit in the lease.

LONG-TERM CONSTRUCTION CONTRACTS

Background

ARB-45 is the main source of promulgated GAAP on Long-Term Construction-Type Contracts. Governmental contracts are specifically excluded from the promulgated GAAP and are discussed elsewhere in the chapter on Government Contracts.

> **OBSERVATION:** *The specialized accounting and auditing practices for construction contractors appear in the AICPA industry audit and accounting guide titled "Construction Contractors." Specialized accounting practices also appear in the AICPA Statement of Position 81-1 (Accounting for Performance of Construction-Type and Certain Production-Type Contracts).*
>
> *The Construction Contractors Guide and SOP 81-1 were issued concurrently in 1981 and supersede the previous audit guide (Audits of Construction Contractors) issued in 1965. The Construction Contractors Guide primarily focuses on the construction industry, whereas SOP 81-1 makes recommendations on accounting issues that apply to a broad range of contracting activities.*
>
> *In the case of construction-type contracts, revenue may be recognized either by the completed-contract method or by the percentage-of-completion method. The percentage-of-completion method is preferable when the estimated cost to complete the contract and the extent of progress made on the contract are reasonably determinable. When estimates are unreliable, the completed-contract method should be used.*

Overview

Because of the length of time involved in long-term construction contracts, the problem exists as to when income should be recognized. Two methods are generally followed to account for these long-term contracts: the completed-contract method and the percentage-of-completion method.

Completed-Contract Method

The completed-contract method recognizes incomes only on completion or substantial completion of the contract.

A contract is regarded as substantially complete if the remaining costs are insignificant.

Excess of accumulated costs over related billings should be reflected in the balance sheet as a current asset, and excess of accumulated billings over related costs should usually be reflected as a current liability. In the case of more than one contract, the accumulated costs or liabilities should be separately stated on the balance sheet. The preferred terminology for the balance sheet presentation should be "(Costs) (Billings) of uncompleted contracts in excess of related (billings) (costs)."

In some cases, it is preferable to allocate general and administrative expenses to contract costs as opposed to period income. In years when no contracts are completed, a better matching of costs and revenues is achieved by carrying general expense as a charge to the contract. If a contractor has many jobs, however, it is more appropriate to charge these expenses to current periods.

In all cases, although income is not recognized until completion of the contract, a provision for an expected loss should be recognized when it becomes evident that a loss on the contract is apparent.

The primary advantage of the completed-contract method is that it is based on final results rather than on estimates. The primary disadvantage of the completed-contract method is that it does not reflect current performances when the period of the contract extends over more than one accounting period.

Accounting for the Completed-Contract Method

The following are important points to remember in accounting for contracts under the completed-contract method:

1. Charge applicable overhead and direct costs to a construction in progress account (an asset).
2. Credit billing and/or cash received to advances on construction in progress account (a liability).
3. At completion of the contract, gross profit or loss is recognized as follows:

    Contract price − total costs = gross profit or loss
4. At interim balance sheet dates, the excess of either the construction in progress account or the advances account over the other is classified as a current asset or a current liability. It is a *current* asset or a *current* liability because of the *normal operating cycle concept*.
5. An expected loss on the total contract is discovered by:

a. adding estimated costs to complete to the recorded costs to date to arrive at total contract costs
b. adding to advances any additional revenue expected to arrive at total contract revenue
c. subtracting b from a to arrive at total estimated loss on contract

Losses should be recognized in full in the year they are discovered.

Percentage-of-Completion Method

Revenues are generally recognized when (1) the earning process is complete or virtually complete and (2) an exchange has taken place.

Accounting for long-term construction contracts on the percentage-of-completion method is an exception to the basic realization principle. This exception is based on the evidence that the ultimate proceeds are available and the consensus that a better measure of periodic income results (matching-of-revenue-and-cost principle).

The principal advantages of the percentage-of-completion method are the reflection of the status of the uncompleted contracts and the periodic recognition of income currently rather than irregularly as contracts are completed.

The principal disadvantage of the percentage-of-completion method is the necessity of relying on estimates of the ultimate costs.

The percentage-of-completion method recognizes income as work progresses on the contract.

The recommended method for recognizing income is to determine the percentage of estimated total income either (1) that incurred costs to date bear to total estimated costs based on the most recent costs information or (2) that may be indicated by such other measure of progress toward completion appropriate to the work performed.

During the early stages of a contract, all or a portion of items such as material and subcontract costs may be excluded if it appears that the results would produce a more meaningful allocation of periodic income.

When current estimates of the total contract costs indicate a loss, a provision for the loss on the entire contract should be made. However, when a loss is indicated on a total contract that is part of a related group of contracts, the group may be treated as a unit in determining the necessity of providing for losses.

Income to be recognized under the percentage-of-completion method at various stages should not ordinarily be measured by interim billings.

Accounting for the Percentage-of-Completion Method

The following are important points to remember in accounting for contracts under the percentage-of-completion method:

1. Journal entries and interim balance sheet treatment are the same as the completed-contract method *except* that the amount of estimated gross profit earned in each period is recorded by charging the construction in progress account and crediting realized gross profit.
2. Gross profit or loss is recognized in each period by the following formula:

$$\frac{\text{Total cost to date}}{\text{estimated total cost}} \times \text{total estimated gross profit or loss} - \text{gross profit recognized to date} = \text{realized gross profit}$$

3. An estimated loss on the total contract is recognized immediately in the year it is discovered. However, any previous gross profit or loss reported in prior years must be deducted from the total estimated loss.

Choice of Method

The percentage-of-completion method is preferred when the estimated cost to complete and the extent of construction progress are reasonably determinable. When estimates are unreliable, the completed-contract method should be used.

Disclosure

Generally, long-term construction-type contracts require no special disclosure, since they are, in fact, the nature of the contractor's business. However, unusual extraordinary commitments should be fully disclosed in the financial statements or footnotes thereto.

Comprehensive Illustration

The following example demonstrates the accounting involved in both the completed-contract and percentage-of-completion methods:

The following data pertain to a $2,000,000 long-term construction contract:

	19X5	19X6	19X7
Costs incurred during the year	$ 500,000	$700,000	$ 300,000
Year-end estimated costs to complete	$1,000,000	$300,000	–
Billing during the year	$ 400,000	$700,000	$ 900,000
Collections during the year	$ 200,000	$500,000	$1,200,000

The journal entries for both the completed-contract method and the percentage-of-completion method for the three years are as follows:

19X5	Completed Contract		% of Completion	
Construction in progress	$ 500,000		$ 500,000	
Cash or liability		$ 500,000		$ 500,000
Accounts receivable	$ 400,000		$ 400,000	
Advance billings		$ 400,000		$ 400,000
Cash	$ 200,000		$ 200,000	
Accounts receivable		$ 200,000		$ 200,000
Construction in progress	no entry		$ 166,667	
Realized gross profit (P&L)				$ 166,667
19X6				
Construction in progress	$ 700,000		$ 700,000	
Cash or liability		$ 700,000		$ 700,000
Accounts receivable	$ 700,000		$ 700,000	
Advance billings		$ 700,000		$ 700,000
Cash	$ 500,000		$ 500,000	
Accounts receivable		$ 500,000		$ 500,000
Construction in progress	no entry		$ 233,333	
Realized gross profit (P&L)				$ 233,333
19X7				
Construction in progress	$ 300,000		$ 300,000	
Cash or liability		$ 300,000		$ 300,000
Accounts receivable	$ 900,000		$ 900,000	
Advance billings		$ 900,000		$ 900,000
Cash	$1,200,000		$1,200,000	
Accounts receivable		$1,200,000		$1,200,000
Construction in progress	no entry		$ 100,000	
Realized gross profit (P&L)				$ 100,000
Advance billings	$2,000,000		$2,000,000	
Cost of construction		$1,500,000		$2,000,000
Realized gross profit (P&L)		500,000		–

Long-Term Construction Contracts

<u>Computation of Realized Gross Profit</u>
19X5

$$\frac{\$\ 500{,}000}{\$1{,}500{,}000} \times \$500{,}000 - 0 = \$166{,}667$$

19X6

$$\frac{\$1{,}200{,}000}{\$1{,}500{,}000} \times \$500{,}000 - \$166{,}667 = \$233{,}333$$

19X7

$$\frac{\$1{,}500{,}000}{\$1{,}500{,}000} \times \$500{,}000 - \$400{,}000 = \$100{,}000$$

Total gross profit $\underline{\$500{,}000}$

LONG-TERM OBLIGATIONS

Overview

FASB-47 contains disclosure requirements for certain unconditional purchase obligations associated with financing arrangements that have not been recorded on the books, and separate disclosure requirements for (1) unconditional purchase obligations that have been recorded on the books, (2) maturities and sinking funds for long-term borrowing, and (3) redemptions of capital stock. The disclosure requirements in FASB-47 pertain to long-term obligations that have a remaining term in excess of one year. An unconditional purchase obligation is considered unconditional even if the agreement provides for cancellation in the event of some remote occurrence. FASB-47 encourages, but does not require, the disclosure of certain unconditional purchase obligations at their present values.

Background

Under existing accounting principles, exchanges between enterprises or individuals are usually recorded when the actual transfer of resources, services, and/or obligations occurs (APB Statement-4). However, unfulfilled purchase commitments for the future exchange of resources, services, and/or obligations, are not recorded until the commitment is at least partially fulfilled by one of the contracting parties (APB Statement-4). Exceptions to the general rule for unfulfilled purchase commitments are certain leases and losses on firm noncancelable purchase commitments which are recorded under existing accounting principles. Commitments for leases that qualify for capitalization in accordance with FASB-13 are recorded for financial accounting purposes. In addition, losses on firm noncancelable purchase commitments are recognized in the accounts and, if material, disclosed separately in the income statement.

Enterprises and/or individuals frequently acquire assets or liabilities by written contract. A contract may contain unconditional rights and obligations, or conditional rights and obligations. A right or obligation is unconditional when nothing but the passage of time is necessary for the right or obligation to mature. On the other hand, a conditional right or obligation is one that matures only on the occurrence of one or more events that are specified in the contract.

If a significant period elapses between the execution and subsequent performance of a contract, a problem may arise as to when, if at all, the asset and/or liabilities created by the contract should be recognized by the contracting parties. Under existing accounting practices, assets and/or liabilities that are created by a contract may not be recognized at all, or may be either recognized in the accounts, or disclosed by footnote.

> **OBSERVATION:** *An FASB Research Report entitled "Recognition of Contractual Rights and Obligations," by Yuji Ijiri (December 1980), contains an excellent discussion on this topic.*

The disclosure of certain contractual rights or obligations is sometimes confused with the disclosure of a contingency. However, the disclosure of a contingency is only necessary when there is a contingent "gain" or "loss" in accordance with the provisions of FASB-5. If there is no contingent "gain" or "loss," disclosure is not required. On the other hand, the disclosure of information on certain contractual rights or obligations may be required by GAAP to avoid misleading financial statements.

A situation may arise in which the disclosure of a contractual obligation is required by GAAP and, at the same time, a "loss contingency" may exist involving the same contractual obligation. In this event, the disclosure of the information concerning the contractual obligation would have to be presented in accordance with GAAP, and the disclosure of the "loss contingency" would also have to be made in accordance with GAAP.

Unconditional Purchase Obligations

For the purposes of FASB-47, an unconditional purchase obligation is one in which one party is required to transfer funds to another party in return for future delivery of specified quantities of goods or services, at specified prices.

> **OBSERVATION:** *The definition of an unconditional purchase obligation, for the purposes of FASB-47, is one in which one party is required to make a transfer of funds to another party in return for specified quantities of goods or services at specified prices. Thus, an unconditional purchase obligation to transfer assets, other than funds, to another party in return for specified quantities of goods or services at specified prices, is not considered an unconditional obligation and, apparently, would not be covered by FASB-47.*

Under FASB-47, the unconditional purchase obligation must be associated with the financing arrangements (a) for the facilities that will provide the contracted goods or services or (b) relating to the costs of the contracted goods or services (such as carrying costs, etc.). Unconditional purchase obligations that have a remaining term of one year or less are excluded from the provisions of FASB-47. In addition, an unconditional purchase obligation qualifies for FASB-47, even though it is cancelable, because of:

1. A remote contingency
2. Permission of the other party
3. A replacement agreement between the same parties
4. A provision for a penalty payment in an amount which reasonably assures the continuation of the agreement.

The provisions in FASB-47 concerning unconditional purchase obligations cover the purchaser's disclosure requirements, and are primarily directed to take-or-pay contracts and throughput contracts.

> **OBSERVATION:** *In a take-or-pay contract a buyer agrees to pay certain periodic amounts for certain products or services. The buyer must make the specified periodic payments, even though it does not take delivery of the products or services.*
>
> *In a throughput contract, one party agrees to pay certain periodic amounts to another party for the transportation or processing of a product. The periodic payments must be made, even though the minimum quantities specified in the agreement in each period have not been sent to the other party for transporting or processing.*
>
> *In a take-or-pay contract and a throughput contract, the periodic payments are unconditional, and are not dependent on the occurrence of a specified event or the fulfillment of a condition.*

Minimum lease payments that are required to be disclosed in accordance with FASB-13 need not be disclosed in accordance with FASB-47. However, minimum lease payments that are not required to be disclosed in accordance with FASB-13 must be disclosed in accordance with FASB-47, if they meet the requirements for disclosure outlined in FASB-47.

> **OBSERVATION:** *Apparently, FASB-47 requires the disclosure of certain leases that were specifically excluded from FASB-13, if such leases are (1) substantially noncancelable, (2) part of the financing arrangements for the facilities that will provide specified goods or services, or related to the costs for the specified goods or services, and (3) for a remaining term in excess of one year. The following*

types of leases and similar agreements were expressly excluded from FASB-13, and may require disclosure under the provisions of FASB-47:

1. Natural resource leases, including oil, gas, minerals, and timber
2. Leases involving services only
3. Licensing agreements, including motion picture films, plays, manuscripts, patents, and copyrights

Furthermore, despite the similarity to take-or-pay contracts, "nuclear fuel heat supply contracts" are specifically included in FASB-13 as leases and are therefore not covered by FASB-47.

Disclosure of Unrecorded Unconditional Purchase Obligations

Unrecorded unconditional purchase obligations that are (1) substantially noncancelable, (2) associated with the financing arrangements (a) for the facilities that will provide the contracted goods or services or (b) relating to the costs of the contracted goods or services (such as carrying costs, etc.), and (3) for a remaining term in excess of one year, must be disclosed by footnote in the purchaser's financial statements. The disclosures must include:

1. A description of the nature and term of the obligation
2. The total determinable amount of unrecorded unconditional purchase obligations as of the latest balance sheet date, and the total determinable amount of unrecorded unconditional purchase obligations for each of the five years after the latest balance sheet date
3. A description of the nature of any variable component of the unrecorded unconditional purchase obligations
4. For each income statement presented, the amounts actually purchased under the unconditional purchase obligations

> **OBSERVATION:** An unconditional obligation may consist of a determinable portion and a variable portion. The determinable portion is quantified and disclosed in accordance with item #2 above. The variable portion need not be quantified, but the nature of such amounts must be disclosed in accordance with item #3 above.

Similar or related obligations may be combined and disclosures are not required if the aggregate commitment of all unrecorded unconditional purchase obligations is immaterial.

FASB-47 does not require, but does encourage, the disclosure of the present value of the total determinable amounts of unrecorded unconditional purchase obligations for each of the five years after the latest balance sheet date (item #2 above). In computing the present value of the obligations, the discount rate will usually be evident. In most cases, the discount rate is the effective interest rate at the inception of the borrowings that (1) financed the project, or (2) are associated with the unrecorded unconditional purchase obligations. If it is not practical to determine the discount rate, or if there are no borrowings associated with the obligations, the discount rate that should be used is the purchaser's incremental borrowing rate. The purchaser's incremental borrowing rate is the rate the purchaser would have incurred, at the inception of the obligation, to borrow funds, on similar terms, to discharge the unconditional purchase obligation.

The disclosure of the present value of the total determinable amount of unconditional purchase obligations, and the disclosure of the nature of any variable component of the unconditional purchase obligations, should be presented, as follows:

Year	Total Required Payments
19X1	$ 100,000
19X2	100,000
19X3	200,000
19X4	200,000
19X5	200,000
Subsequent years	700,000
Total	$1,500,000
Less: Imputed interest	350,000
Present value of required payments	$1,150,000

In addition to the determinable required payments presented above, the Company is required to periodically pay 12% of the variable operating expenses of the plant of the X Corporation. (Note: For each income statement presented, the amounts actually purchased under the unconditional purchase obligations would also have to be disclosed.)

Long-Term Obligations

Disclosure of Other Unconditional Obligations

FASB-47 does not change prior GAAP related to recording, as liabilities, certain unconditional purchase obligations, or the accounting treatment of future obligations that are substantially the same as certain obligations that are recorded as liabilities. In addition, FASB-47 reaffirms that the economic substance of a transaction should be recorded, rather than the legal form of the transaction.

The following specific disclosures must be made as of the date of the latest balance sheet presented:

1. For each of the five years immediately following the latest balance sheet date, the amount of payments for recorded unconditional purchase obligations that meet the disclosure provisions of FASB-47. In addition, all amounts due after the fifth year shall be disclosed in a caption labeled "subsequent years" (see illustration #1 below). The disclosure provisions of FASB-47 require that an unconditional purchase obligation be (1) substantially noncancelable, (2) associated with the financing arrangements (a) for the facilities that will provide the contracted goods or services or (b) relating to the costs of the contracted goods or services (such as carrying costs, etc.), and (3) for a remaining term in excess of one year.

   > **OBSERVATION:** The above disclosure requirements cover unconditional purchase obligations that meet the criteria of paragraph 6 of FASB-47, and which have been recorded on the purchaser's balance sheet. Thus, the asset and corresponding liability is recorded on the books and, in addition, the above disclosure requirements of FASB-47 must also be made.

2. For each of the five years immediately following the latest balance sheet date, the combined total of maturities and sinking fund requirements for all long-term borrowings (see illustration #2 below).

3. For each of the five years immediately following the latest balance sheet date, the total of required redemptions (separately or combined) for all classes of capital stock that are redeemable at determinable prices on determinable dates (see illustration #3 below).

Illustration #1—Take-or-Pay, Throughput, and Similar Contracts

X Company has entered into a long-term contract to purchase all of the widgets produced by a supplier. The contract expires in 1995, and X Company must make minimum annual payments to the supplier, whether or not it is able to take delivery of the widgets. The minimum total payments for each of the five years and later years succeeding December 31, 19X1, are as follows:

Year	Total Payments (in thousands)
19X2	$ 4,000
19X3	12,000
19X4	14,000
19X5	10,000
19X6	12,000
Subsequent years	28,000
Total	$ 80,000
Less: Imputed interest	30,000
Present value of payments	$ 50,000

(Note: FASB-47 requires the disclosure of the above information for periods subsequent to the fifth year, as reflected in the above illustration.)

Illustration #2—Maturities and Sinking Fund Requirements

Maturities of long-term debt and sinking fund requirements on long-term debt for each of the five years succeeding December 31, 19X1, are as follows:

Year	Long-Term Debt and Sinking Fund Requirements
19X2	$ 50,000
19X3	50,000
19X4	100,000
19X5	100,000
19X6	50,000

(Note: FASB-47 does not require the disclosure of the above information for periods subsequent to the fifth year.)

Long-Term Obligations

Illustration #3—Redemption of Capital Stock

Mandatory redemption requirements for all classes of capital stock for each of the five years succeeding December 31, 19X1, are as follows:

Year	4% Preferred	7% Preferred
19X2	$200,000	$400,000
19X3	200,000	400,000
19X4	200,000	400,000
19X5	none	400,000
19X6	none	400,000

(Note: FASB-47 does not require the disclosure of the above information for periods subsequent to the fifth year.)

> **OBSERVATION:** *If an unconditional obligation is not recorded on the books of an enterprise, the disclosures required by FASB-47 may be misleading to readers of financial statements because the benefits, if any, that are associated with the disclosed obligations are not required to be disclosed. When a lease is capitalized in accordance with FASB-13, both the asset (benefit) and a liability (obligation) are recognized on the books. However, if the unconditional obligation is not recorded, an enterprise may be unconditionally obligated to pay millions of dollars over a specified period, under a take-or-pay contract, for a continuous supply of natural gas. Under FASB-47, the unconditional obligation would have to be disclosed. However, the associated benefits, such as an assured supply of natural gas at a fixed price, are not required to be disclosed.*
>
> *Paragraph 7 (a) of FASB-47, which requires a statement about the nature and term of the obligation, may be the place for an enterprise to appropriately describe the associated benefits, if any. The last sentence of paragraph 19, Appendix A, of FASB-47 states that, "The lack of explicit requirements to disclose associated benefits does not preclude an enterprise from describing those benefits."*

Effective Date

FASB-47 is effective for fiscal years ending on or after June 16, 1981, and earlier application is encouraged. However, the amounts actually purchased under unconditional purchase obligations for each income statement presented, do not have to be disclosed for comparative purposes for periods that began prior to the effective date of FASB-47.

Product Financing Arrangements

FASB-47 contains specific disclosure requirements for recorded and unrecorded take-or-pay and throughput contracts. Both of these types of contracts are considered unconditional obligations under the provisions of FASB-47. However, a take-or-pay or throughput contract may, in substance, be a product financing arrangement. A product financing arrangement may also require unconditional periodic payments that are not dependent on the occurrence of a specified event or the fulfillment of a specified condition. The problem is that product financing arrangements that are unconditional obligations are accounted for much differently from take-or-pay and throughput contracts. Product financing arrangements are covered elsewhere in this publication in the chapter entitled "Product Financing Arrangements."

MARKETABLE SECURITIES

Background

Accounting for certain marketable securities is covered by FASB-12 and four subsequent FASB Interpretations, as follows:

> 11—Changes in Market Value After Balance Sheet Date
> 12—Accounting for Previously Established Allowance Accounts
> 13—Consolidations Involving Different Balance Sheet Dates
> 16—Clarification of Definitions and Accounting for Marketable Equity Securities That Become Nonmarketable

FASB-80 (Accounting for Futures Contracts) is discussed at the end of this section, after the discussion on marketable securities. FASB Technical Bulletin 85-2 (Accounting for Collateralized Mortgage Obligations (CMOs)) is discussed at the end of the chapter entitled "Mortgage Banking Industry."

FASB Technical Bulletin 79-19 was issued to provide guidance to an investor in accounting for its proportionate share of an investee's valuation allowance account for noncurrent marketable securities.

The procedures enumerated herein apply to all companies, including mutual savings banks, that do not have specialized accounting practices in accounting for marketable securities. In addition, some of the promulgated GAAP apply to those companies in industries that do have specialized accounting practices in accounting for marketable securities.

Nonprofit organizations, mutual life insurance companies, and employee benefit plans are specifically excluded from complying with the promulgated GAAP. Nonmarketable securities are not covered and are completely excluded.

Investments accounted for by the equity method are generally not covered by FASB-12.

Overview

The promulgated GAAP (FASB-12) differentiates between those industries having specialized accounting practices with respect to marketable equity securities and those which have no specialized practices.

Marketable Securities

An equity security is defined as any instrument that represents an ownership share or the right to acquire or sell an ownership share at a determinable price. This includes stock options, warrants, rights, puts, calls, and common, preferred, and other forms of capital stock. Preferred stock that is redeemable at the option of the owner or must be redeemed by the issuer is specifically excluded from the definition of an equity security for purposes of the promulgated GAAP, as are treasury stock and convertible bonds.

> *Realized gain or loss* is the difference between the net proceeds from the sale of a marketable security and its cost.
> *Unrealized gain or loss* is the difference between the market value and the cost of a marketable security.

Marketability

In order for a security to be classified as a marketable security, it must be marketable. Marketability is evidenced by whether a security can be readily bought or sold. A current *bid* and *ask* price is evidence of marketability for both over-the-counter stocks and stocks traded on a national exchange, except that over-the-counter quotations issued by the National Quotations Bureau, Inc., may not be used unless three quotations are available.

The determination of marketability is made as of the balance sheet date.

Marketability of equity securities traded on foreign markets is determined in the same way, provided the foreign market's trading volume and scope of activities are comparable to a U.S. counterpart.

Restricted or legend stock is not considered marketable unless it can qualify for sale within one year and is marketable as defined herein. Market prices for unrestricted shares of the same class of stock that is restricted can be used in determining marketability.

A temporary lack of market (no trades or quotations) at the balance sheet date does not render an equity security nonmarketable if a market closely precedes the balance sheet date. Moreover, if the balance sheet date falls on a day when markets are closed, the first trading day afterward should be used. Where the lack of quotations by NASDAQ or the lack of three quotations from the National Quotations Bureau, Inc., for the over-the-counter securities is temporary, a market price may be determined by:

1. The first quotation by NASDAQ preceding the balance sheet date

2. One quotation from the National Quotations Bureau, Inc., on the balance sheet date or on the first day preceding the balance sheet date that quotations are available

Industries Not Having Specialized Practices

Any company that does not account for marketable securities by a specialized industry practice should follow these procedures for accounting for them:

1. Marketable securities should be classified into two groups: current group and noncurrent group. *In the case of unclassified balance sheets, all marketable securities are to be classified as noncurrent.*
2. The total cost and the total market for each group should be determined.
3. The carrying amount of each group is the lower of cost or market for each group.
4. Unrealized losses on the group classified as current are deducted on the income statement in determining net income for the period. The credit side of the entry is to a valuation account, as follows:

    Loss on marketable securities $X,XXX
        Allowances for losses,
        marketable securities $X,XXX

5. Unrealized losses on the group classified as noncurrent are reported separately as a reduction of stockholders' equity. The credit side of the entry is to a valuation account, as follows:

    Stockholders' equity $X,XXX
        Allowances for losses,
        noncurrent marketable
        securities $X,XXX

6. Subsequent unrealized gains or losses are reported in the same manner (the current group through the income statement and the noncurrent group through the equity section of the balance sheet). *However, under no circumstances can either the current group or the noncurrent group be valued in excess of the original cost of the group.*

    Unrealized losses on the noncurrent group of marketable securities are reported as a reduction of stockholders' equity,

Marketable Securities

whereas unrealized losses on the current group are reported as a reduction of net income.

Allowance for losses accounts for both groups are *contra accounts* and are deducted from the related groups for balance sheet purposes.

Reclassification   Any change of a particular security from one group (current or noncurrent) to the other group (current or noncurrent) must be made at the lower of cost or market on the date of transfer. The lower of cost or market on the date of transfer becomes the new cost basis, and any gain (to the extent of prior realized or unrealized losses) or loss is accounted for as if realized, and is included in the determination of net income for the period.

Subsequent unrealized gains or losses   are recorded by adjusting the allowance for losses account, except that under no circumstances can either group be valued in excess of its original cost.

Sale of a security   A sale of a security from either the current or the noncurrent group results in a realized gain or loss and is reported in the income statement for the period. The cost of the security sold will usually be its original cost unless it was transferred from one group to another or a security in the noncurrent group was written down as a result of a decline in market value that was not temporary.

> *OBSERVATION: Since unrealized losses in both the current and noncurrent portfolios are based on the aggregate cost or market of the entire portfolio, the original cost of each security in each portfolio is not changed. Therefore, when a security is sold, its original cost is deducted from the portfolio and the aggregate cost, market, and related valuation account are recomputed. The only time an original cost of a security is changed is when it is transferred from one group to another or if a security in the noncurrent group is written down as a result of a decline in its market price that is other than temporary.*

An entity that is consolidated with a parent shall first determine its total cost and market for its current group and its noncurrent group before combining those aggregate totals with the parent's aggregate totals.

In the consolidation of a parent's statements with a subsidiary's statements of a different balance sheet date, the following applies (FASB Interpretation-13):

1. The parent and each subsidiary comply with the promulgated

GAAP as at the date of their own balance sheet, and then the aggregate totals are combined for consolidation purposes.
2. Intervening events occurring between the balance sheet date of the subsidiary and that of the parent which materially affect the financial position or the results of operations should be adequately recognized or disclosed in the consolidated financial statements (ARB-51).

The marketable securities of an investment accounted for by the equity method shall not be combined with those of the investor. Obviously, such an entity could, itself, be subject to the provisions of the promulgated GAAP (FASB-12).

> **OBSERVATION:** Changes in the stockholders' equity of an investment accounted for by the equity method (APB-18), which is the result of a decline in the market value of noncurrent marketable securities, is not covered by FASB-12. APB-18 requires that an investor record its proportionate share of the capital transactions of an investment accounted for by the equity method. FASB Technical Bulletin 79-19 requires that an investor reduce its investment accounted for by the equity method, by its proportionate share of the investee's valuation allowance account for noncurrent marketable securities. In addition, the investor should include in its stockholders' equity its proportionate share of the investee's valuation allowance account.

Disclosure The following disclosures for marketable securities shall be made in the financial statements or footnotes thereto by a company which does not follow specialized industry accounting practices for marketable equity securities.

1. As at the date of each balance sheet presented, the total cost and market value of marketable equity securities indicating which is the carrying value for:
   a. total marketable securities
   b. total current marketable securities
   c. total noncurrent marketable securities
2. As at the date of the most recent balance sheet presented, the total gross unrealized gains and the total gross unrealized losses for:
   a. total marketable securities
   b. total current marketable securities
   c. total noncurrent marketable securities

Marketable Securities

3. For each income statement presented:
    a. the net realized gain or loss included in net income
    b. the cost basis that was used in computing realized gain or loss
    c. the change in any valuation account that has been included in the equity section of the balance sheet, and the amount of any change that was included in the determination of net income

    In unclassified balance sheets, the above disclosures for the current portfolio are omitted.
4. In consolidated balance sheets that contain both specialized and nonspecialized practices for accounting for marketable securities, the disclosure requirements for both should be made.
5. Significant net realized and net unrealized gains and losses on marketable securities arising after the date of the balance sheet and prior to their issuance should be disclosed.

Financial statements should not be adjusted for realized gains and losses or for changes in market values of marketable securities that occur subsequent to the balance sheet date. A special procedure is discussed later for permanent declines in the noncurrent portfolio of marketable securities.

Industries Having Specialized Practices

Investment companies, brokers, and dealers in securities, stock life and casualty insurance companies, and other industries that follow specialized practices in accounting for marketable securities must comply with the promulgated GAAP (FASB-12) to a limited extent, as follows:

1. Marketable equity securities must be carried at the lower of cost or market, except market has a broader definition in those industries which do have specialized practices for marketable securities.
2. Market value may be whatever is permitted in a specific specialized industry, such as appraised value or fair value.

    OBSERVATION: *In industries in which either the cost basis or the market basis is accepted practice, an election to use the market basis does not require justification as an accounting change (APB-20) or compliance with the related disclosure requirements (FASB-12).*

Marketable Securities

3. Marketable securities should be classified into a current group and a noncurrent group. In unclassified balance sheets, all marketable securities are to be classified as noncurrent. This provision is exactly the same as that for industries which do not have specialized practices.
4. The aggregate carrying amount of a portfolio of marketable securities is the lower of cost or market (as defined herein) at the balance sheet date. A valuation account shall be used to record any excess of aggregate cost of a portfolio over aggregate market value. This provision is exactly the same as for industries which do not have specialized practices in accounting for marketable securities, except for the broader definition of market value.
5. Marketable securities portfolios of investments accounted for by the equity method should not be combined with portfolios of the investors.
6. Portfolios of entities that use the same specialized industry accounting practices for marketable securities should be combined into a single portfolio to determine the aggregate lower of cost or market value.
7. Specialized industry practices for reporting realized or unrealized gains or losses on marketable securities are not changed by the promulgated GAAP.
8. If a parent company recognizes realized gains or losses on marketable securities in determining net income, all subsidiaries and investments accounted for by the equity method must conform to this practice for the purposes of consolidation. Otherwise, accepted accounting practices for marketable securities followed by a subsidiary or an investment accounted for by the equity method shall be retained in consolidating, even if such practices differ from those of the parent.

> **OBSERVATION:** Since realized gains and losses are almost always recognized (GAAP), the only subsidiary or investment accounted for by the equity method that could logically be subject to conforming is one which follows a specialized industry practice that does not recognize realized gains or losses.

9. When two or more subsidiaries do not follow specialized industry practices and are consolidated with a parent which does follow specialized industry practices, the current and noncurrent portfolios of such subsidiaries are kept separate from those of the parent in consolidating, for the purpose of determining carrying amounts.

Marketable Securities

Disclosures The following disclosures for marketable securities shall be made in the financial statements or footnotes thereto by a company which follows specialized industry accounting practices for marketable equity securities.

1. For companies that include unrealized gains and losses on marketable securities in the equity section of the balance sheet and not in the determination of net income:
   a. as at the most recent balance sheet the gross unrealized gains and the gross unrealized losses
   b. for each income statement presented, the changes in net unrealized gains or losses
2. In consolidated balance sheets that contain both specialized and nonspecialized practices for accounting for marketable securities, the disclosure requirements for both should be made.
3. Significant net realized and net unrealized gains and losses on marketable securities arising after the balance sheet date and prior to their issuance should be disclosed.

Financial statements should not be adjusted for realized gains and losses or changes in market values of marketable securities that occur subsequent to the balance sheet date. A special procedure is discussed later for permanent declines in the noncurrent portfolio of marketable securities.

For the purposes of companies that follow specialized accounting practices, unrealized gains and losses are those which constitute the present accepted practice in a particular industry (FASB-12).

Other Than Temporary Declines—Noncurrent Group

The provisions in this section apply to all companies, whether or not they follow specialized industry practices in accounting for marketable equity securities.

As mentioned previously, a decline in one or more securities of the noncurrent group is handled as a reduction of the equity section of the balance sheet and does not enter into the determination of net income for the period. Under these circumstances, a permanent decline in a security of the noncurrent group would never be recognized in net income. However, FASB-12 provides an exception for declines in securities of the noncurrent group that are *other than temporary.* Under FASB-12, an other than temporary decline in a marketable security that exists on the balance sheet date must be recognized in the net income of the period in which the decline is discovered. The decline is usually equal to the difference between the recorded cost of the security and its current market price, or net realizable value, at the balance sheet date. *Thus, if a decline in one or more securities of the noncurrent group is other than temporary, the loss is recognized in the income statement for that period and not as a reduction of the equity section of the balance sheet.* The journal entry is:

Realized loss on marketable securities $XX,XXX
   Investment in marketable securities $XX,XXX

If a noncurrent marketable security is written down because of a loss that is other than temporary, and the security remains a part of the noncurrent group, any subsequent increase in value is not recognized in the income statement, but is used in the computation of the total unrealized gain or loss on the noncurrent group and is applied as a reduction or increase of the equity section of the balance sheet.

To determine whether a decline at the balance sheet date is permanent or temporary, reference to changes in market price or a realized gain or loss that occurs subsequent to the balance sheet date but prior to the issuance of the financial statements should be taken into consideration. However, the amount of permanent decline for an individual marketable security cannot exceed the amount that existed at the date of the balance sheet. Recoveries of a permanent decline in a marketable security after the balance sheet date and prior to the issuance of the financial statements should be taken into consideration, because such a recovery tends to indicate that all or part of the decline was, in fact, not permanent (FASB Interpretation-11).

FASB-12 does not discuss the difference between a decline in a current or noncurrent marketable security that is (a) permanent, (b) other than temporary, or (c) temporary. An Auditing Interpretation issued in January 1975 by the AICPA states that declines in marketable securities that reflect general market conditions may or may not be indicative of the ability of an enterprise to ultimately recover the carrying amount of an investment. However, the continued existence of a decline in a particular marketable security is indicative of an uncertainty, which may necessitate financial statement disclosure or a qualification of the auditor's opinion. If specific adverse conditions exist for a particular marketable security, a write-down in the carrying amount is necessary, unless persuasive evidence exists to the contrary.

The staff of the SEC takes the position that the phrase *other than temporary* in FASB-12 is not intended to mean *permanent impairment*, as that term is used elsewhere in professional accounting literature (SEC Staff Bulletin No. 59). The SEC staff believes that the following factors, individually or in combination, indicate that a decline is other than temporary and that a write-down of the carrying value of the noncurrent marketable security is required:

- The length of time and the extent to which the market value of the security has been less than its cost
- The financial condition and near-term prospects of the issuer, including any specific events which may influence the operations of the issuer such as changes in technology that may impair the earnings potential of the investment or the discontinuance of a segment of the business that may affect the future earnings potential
- The intent and ability of the holder to retain its investment in the issuer for a period of time sufficient to allow for any anticipated recovery in the market value of the security.

The SEC staff concludes that unless evidence exists to support a realizable value equal to or greater than the carrying value of the noncurrent marketable security, a write-down accounted for as a realized loss should be recorded.

Income Tax Effects

Tax effects of unrealized gains or losses entering into the determination of net income must be reflected in the computation of deferred income taxes. *However, the tax effects of unrealized capital losses should only be recognized when it is absolutely certain that the benefit will be realized by the offset of the capital losses against capital gains.*

Comprehensive Illustration

The following schedule of marketable securities was prepared for the LKM Corporation:

Schedule 1
MARKETABLE SECURITIES PORTFOLIO

	First Year			Second Year		
	Cost	Market	Unrealized Gain (Loss)	Cost	Market	Unrealized Gain (Loss)
Current Group:						
Security A	$1,000	$1,500	$ 500	$1,000	$1,500	$ 500
Security B	4,000	3,500	(500)	4,000	4,500	500
Security C	3,000	2,000	(1,000)	3,000	3,500	500
Totals	$8,000	$7,000	$(1,000)	$8,000	$9,500	$ 1,500
Noncurrent Group:						
Security X	$2,000	$2,500	$ 500	$2,000	$2,000	–
Security Y	1,500	1,000	(500)	1,500	2,000	500
Security Z	6,000	5,500	(500)	6,000	5,200	(800)
Totals	$9,500	$9,000	$ (500)	$9,500	$9,200	$ (300)

At the end of the first year, the carrying amount of the current group is the total market value of $7,000. Since the original cost was $8,000, the $1,000 unrealized loss must be recorded, as follows:

Loss on marketable securities	$1,000	
Allowance for losses,		
current marketable securities		$1,000

The carrying value of the noncurrent group at the end of the first year is the market value of $9,000. Since the original cost was $9,500, the unrealized loss of $500 must be recorded, as follows:

Stockholders' equity	$ 500	
Allowance for losses,		
noncurrent marketable securities		$ 500

The unrealized loss of $500 on the noncurrent marketable securities is deducted from the equity section of the balance sheet and does not enter into the determination of net income for the period.

At the end of the second year, the carrying value of the current group is $8,000 (the original cost), even though the market value is $9,500, because *the valuation may never exceed the original cost.* The journal entry to adjust the valuation account is:

Marketable Securities

Allowance for losses, current marketable securities	$1,000	
Gain on marketable securities		$1,000

The gain on marketable securities appears in the income statement for the period.

The carrying value of the noncurrent group at the end of the second year is the market value of $9,200, which is $300 less than the original cost of $9,500. However, the net book value is $9,000 ($9,500 original cost, less allowance for losses account of $500), so the allowance for losses account must be reduced from $500 to $300, as follows:

Allowance for losses, noncurrent marketable securities	$ 200	
Stockholders' equity		$ 200

The unrealized gain of $200 on the noncurrent group is not reported in the income statement, but reduces the allowance for losses account set up the previous year.

Reversals of previous year's writedowns are not considered as unrealized gains, but as a change in an accounting estimate of a prior realized loss. Actually, the original writedown represented a reduction in the net realizable value of the marketable securities, and any subsequent recovery reduces or eliminates the need for an allowance for losses account.

ACCOUNTING FOR FUTURES CONTRACTS

Overview

FASB-80 establishes the promulgated GAAP for reporting futures contracts that are traded on commodities and other exchanges. Neither foreign currency futures contracts nor forward placement or delayed delivery contracts are covered by FASB-80. Foreign currency futures contracts should be accounted for in accordance with FASB-52 (Foreign Currency Translation). Forward placement or delayed delivery contracts should be accounted for in accordance with prevailing accepted accounting principles and practices. FASB-80 applies to general purpose financial statements of all enterprises.

FASB-80 rescinds FASB Technical Bulletin 81-1 (Disclosure of Interest Rate Futures Contracts and Forward and Standby Contracts).

The thrust of FASB-80 is that changes in the market value of a futures contract must be recognized in the period of change, unless the futures contract qualifies as a hedge.

Background

Many types of commodities are traded on various commodity exchanges. Examples of some of the many types of commodities traded include grains such as wheat, barley, corn, oats, etc.; metals such as gold, silver, platinum, copper, lead, zinc, etc.; meats such as cattle, pork bellies, turkeys, etc.; financial instruments such as commercial paper, Treasury bills, bonds and notes, GNMA mortgages, etc.; and miscellaneous items such as cotton, plywood, eggs, soybeans, etc. Commodities, like securities, may be purchased long or sold short. Each commodity contract involves a specified quantity of the commodity.

A commodity may be traded in the form of a spot contract or a futures contract. A spot contract is for the current month and usually involves paying cash and taking physical delivery of the commodity. However, the great majority of commodity transactions involve futures contracts. This is because most investors do not want actual delivery of the commodity and therefore "cover" their positions before the spot month (the month in which the commodity contract expires). Some commodity contracts, such as stock index futures and Eurodollar time deposit futures, do not involve the delivery of a commodity and all outstanding contracts are settled for cash on their last day of trading. For every "buy" or "long" futures contract there must be a corresponding "sell" or "short" futures contract.

Futures contracts are traded on the basis that an investor agrees to buy or sell a certain quantity of a specific commodity in a specific future month and at a specific price. Thus, in June 19X1 an investor can agree to buy 100 ounces of gold in June 19X2, at a price that is agreed upon at the inception of the contract (June 19X1). If the price of gold rises six months later, the value of the June 19X2 gold futures contract will increase proportionately. In this event, the investor can make a profit by disposing of his "long" position. On the other hand, if the investor thought that the price of gold was going to decrease over the next year, a contract for 100 ounces of June 19X2 gold should be sold short. In this event, if the price of gold does decline, the investor can make a profit by disposing of his "short" position. The difference between the purchase price and selling price of a contract, less brokerage commission, is the investor's profit. If commodities are purchased or sold on margin, an investor's profit is decreased by the amount of interest paid on the margin account.

The commodity markets play an important role in the economy of the United States. The process of hedging is an integral part of many businesses and would not be possible without the existing commodity futures markets. Over the past few years, there has been a significant increase in the volume of futures transactions involving prime financial paper and future interest rates. Most of the increase in activity can be associated with hedging transactions. For example, savings and loan associations frequently hedge their actual position in GNMA mortgages by buying or selling futures contracts of GNMA mortgages which trade on the Chicago Board of Trade. Farmers, food processors, metal manufacturers, millers, and others who must store large quantities of commodities as inventory can minimize their exposure to price fluctuation by hedging their positions. For example, if a farmer believes that the price of his crop of corn is going to be substantially less at his expected harvest time, he can sell corn futures today and make actual delivery of the corn when his crop is ready for harvest. Alternatively, the farmer can close out his short position by purchasing spot contracts of corn in the month he is ready to sell his crop. The profit made on the commodity contracts will offset the decline in the market value of the farmer's corn.

Some commodities are regulated by the Commodities Exchange Act and some commodities are not regulated. Most regulated commodities are in the agricultural industries, such as grains, eggs, potatoes, cotton, and soybeans. The most important federal regulations (a) require that commodity exchange members submit daily reports of their commodity trading activity and (b) limit the number of futures contracts in any one commodity that any one person or enterprise can acquire for speculation purposes.

Transactions on commodity exchanges are cleared and settled by a clearing association appointed by the exchange. Thus, all buy and sell transactions in futures commodity contracts are handled by a clearing association. A settlement price for all open commodity contracts is established at the close of business each day by all commodity exchanges. This process is referred to as "marking-to-market." Each broker must settle his net difference on all open contracts in cash each day with the clearing association. On the broker's books the daily settlement is posted to a contract difference account which is subsequently posted to each customer's account to reflect any gain or loss.

Accounting for Speculative Futures Contracts

The minimum contract deposit that is paid to a commodity broker for the purchase of a futures contract is usually recorded by an enterprise as an asset (due from commodity broker). The recorded asset is then increased or decreased, during the period the futures contract is outstanding, to take into account the changes in the market value of the futures contract. The changes in the market value of a futures contract that does not meet the hedge criteria established by FASB-80 (see below) must be reported by an enterprise as a gain or loss in the period in which the change occurs. A change in the market value of a futures contract is calculated by multiplying the size of the contract by the change in the contract's quoted market price.

> *OBSERVATION:* Broker's commissions and related costs should be capitalized as part of the cost of acquiring the asset.

Hedge Criteria Established by FASB-80

Under FASB-80, a futures contract that hedges an existing or anticipated exposure to price or interest rate changes shall qualify as a hedge if all of the following conditions are met:

Must be designated as a hedge   A futures contract must be designated by an enterprise as a hedge of identifiable assets, liabilities, firm commitments, or anticipated transactions. A futures contract cannot be accounted for as a hedge until the date it is designated as a hedge by the enterprise. In order to be designated as a hedge, a futures contract must effectively reduce the enterprise's exposure to the risk of changes in price or interest rates.

> *OBSERVATION:* FASB-80 gives management the opportunity to choose how to report changes in the market value of futures contracts that relate to hedge situations. If management designates the contract as a hedge (and all the other criteria are satisfied), a change in the market value of the contract is not reflected in income until the related transaction is completed. On the other hand, if management does not designate the contract as a hedge, a change in the market value of the contract is recognized as gain or loss when it appears.

Exposure to the risk of changes in price or interest rates   The hedged item must be exposed to the risk of changes in market prices or interest rates. Thus, in order for the transaction to qualify as an economic hedge, the hedged item must contribute to the enterprise's risk associated with changes in prices or interest rates. The existence of risk associated with changes in prices or interest rates and whether a futures contract reduces that risk may be apparent or may require extensive analysis and judgment. However, FASB-80 does not permit a futures contract to be accounted for as a hedge of any item that is already effectively hedged by other assets, liabilities, commitments, or other transactions of an enterprise.

The assessment of price risk may be done on a decentralized basis if an enterprise cannot otherwise assess such risk on the basis of the enterprise as a whole and the risk management activities can be assessed on a decentralized basis.

Must reduce exposure to the risk of changes in price or interest rates The changes in the market value of a futures contract must be highly correlated, at the inception of the contract and throughout the hedge period, to the changes in the fair value of the hedged item(s). It must also be *probable* (likely) that changes in the market value of the futures contract will substantially offset the price changes or interest rate changes associated with the hedged item. Thus, the underlying commodity or financial instrument of a futures contract should be identical to the commodity or financial instrument which is hedged. However, the underlying commodity or financial instrument of a futures contract may differ from the underlying item being hedged, if (a) there is a clear economic relationship between the prices of the two commodities or financial instruments, and (b) a high degree of price correlation is probable (likely).

Hedged items reported at fair value For an item to qualify as an economic hedge under FASB-80, it must generally be accounted for at historical cost or the lower of cost or market, such as investments carried at cost, liabilities carried at historical proceeds, and inventories carried at the lower of cost or market. Thus, enterprises that hedge assets reported at fair value, in accordance with generally accepted accounting principles or specialized industry practices, are required to include the changes in value of both the hedged assets and the related futures contracts in income of the same accounting period.

Accounting for Hedges

Changes in the market value of a futures contract associated with a hedged item must not be recognized in income until the related change in the fair value of the hedged item is also recognized in income. To recognize a change in the market value of a futures contract in a different period from the related change in the fair value of the hedged item would negate the underlying economic effect of the hedging transaction. FASB-80 recognizes the underlying economic effect of a hedging transaction by providing for delayed income recognition of the changes in the market value of futures contracts that meet the hedge criteria. However, FASB-80 does not change current accounting principles or practices for assets, liabilities, or commitments.

Accounting for hedges of existing items In order to qualify as a hedge, a futures contract must meet the hedge criteria established by FASB-80 (see above). If a futures contract qualifies under FASB-80 as a hedge of an existing asset, liability, or firm commitment, changes in the market value of the futures contract are recognized in income at the same time as the effects of the price or interest rate changes of the hedged item. Adjustments of the carrying amount of a hedged item must be accounted for in the same manner as the carrying amount of the item, except for hedged interest-bearing financial instruments that are otherwise reported at amortized cost. Adjustments of the carrying amount of hedged interest-bearing financial instruments that are otherwise reported at amortized cost must begin on the date the hedge is closed out, and be amortized as either interest income or interest expense over the expected remaining life of the instrument. If a futures contract qualifies under FASB-80 as a hedge of a firm commitment to purchase or sell a commodity or financial instrument at a fixed price, changes in the market value must be included in the ultimate gain or loss on the transaction.

If it is *probable* that both the hedged item and the futures contract will be retained to the delivery date specified in the futures contract, an enterprise may recognize the premium or discount on a hedge contract in income over the life of the contract. The premium or discount is computed at the inception of the hedge by reference to the contracted futures price and the fair value of the hedged item.

> **OBSERVATION:** *A futures contract may qualify as a hedge of a fixed-rate financial instrument which an enterprise intends to hold to maturity, if the funding for the enterprise's assets has been made with instruments having earlier maturities or repricing dates.*

Commodity dealers and others who use futures contracts to hedge a net exposure consisting of inventory held for sale and firm commitments to purchase and sell similar assets may find it impractical to associate specific futures contracts with related hedges, because of the volume and frequency of transactions. In this event, it is permissible to make reasonable allocations of the results of futures contracts between the assets on hand or specific commitments on hand at the end of a reporting period and the assets sold during the period.

Assessment of correlation   FASB-80 requires that an ongoing assessment be made of the correlation between the changes in the market value of a futures contract and the changes in the fair value of the related hedged item to determine the effectiveness of the hedged transaction. If a high correlation has not been achieved, the enterprise must cease to account for the futures contract as a hedge, and must recognize, as a gain or loss in current income, the amount of change in the market value of the futures contract since inception that has not been offset by the change in the fair value of the hedged item.

Accounting for certain anticipated transactions   A futures contract may be used to hedge a purchase or sale transaction that an enterprise expects, but is not legally required, to enter into. This type of futures contract is referred to as an "anticipatory hedge." In an anticipatory hedge, the futures contract does not relate to an enterprise's existing assets, liabilities, or firm commitments.

In order to qualify as an anticipatory hedge, a futures contract must meet the hedge criteria established by FASB-80 (see above). If a futures contract qualifies under FASB-80 as an anticipatory hedge, changes in the market value of the futures contract shall be included in the ultimate gain or loss on the hedged transaction. If gain or loss in the fair value of an asset or liability will be recognized in income subsequent to its acquisition or issuance, gain or loss on the related futures contract must be recognized at the same time. However, if the futures contract is closed out before the date of the anticipated transaction, the accumulated change in the market value of the contract must be carried forward and included in the ultimate gain or loss on the transaction. When it becomes *probable* that the quantity of the anticipated transaction will be less than originally identified, a pro rata portion of the changes in the market value of the futures contract must be recognized as a gain or loss and a pro rata portion must be included in the ultimate gain or loss on the transaction.

Subject to the limitations described above, changes in the market value of a futures contract which hedges an anticipated transaction that an enterprise expects to occur, must be included in the ultimate gain or loss on the anticipated transaction if both of the following conditions are met:

Significant Terms Are Identified   An enterprise must identify the significant terms of the anticipated transaction, including (a) the commodity or type of financial instrument involved, (b) the quantity to be purchased or sold, and (c) the expected date of the transaction. As long as all other conditions are met for each possible transaction, an enterprise may identify more than one similar transaction, if identification of a single transaction is not possible.

Probable That the Anticipated Transaction Will Occur   It must be *probable* (likely) that the anticipated transaction will occur during the normal course of an enterprise's business. In other words, there must be a high level of assurance that the anticipated transaction will occur. The probability that the anticipated transaction will occur must be supported by observable facts and should not be based on management's intent (paragraph 56 of FASB-80). Under FASB-80, the likelihood that the anticipated transaction will occur is not sufficiently probable if the anticipated transaction can be abandoned by the enterprise with little cost or disruption of operations.

Disclosure and Effective Date

Enterprises that apply the accounting required by FASB-80 for hedges and anticipated transactions must disclose the following information in their financial statements:

- The nature of the items that are hedged or related to futures contracts
- The accounting method(s) used for the futures contracts
- A description of the events or transactions that will result in recognition in income of the changes in value of the futures contracts

Rescission of FASB Technical Bulletin 81-1   Upon the issuance of FASB-80, FASB Technical Bulletin 81-1 (Disclosure of Interest Rate Futures Contracts and Forward and Standby Contracts) was rescinded.

Effective date   The provisions of FASB-80 shall be applied to futures contracts entered into on or after January 1, 1985, and earlier application of FASB-80 is encouraged in annual financial statements that have not been previously issued. The disclosure requirements of FASB-80 must be complied with in financial statements for periods ending on or after December 16, 1984, for all open futures contracts that have been designated as hedges, whether or not other provisions of FASB-80 have been applied. Prospective application of the provisions of FASB-80 is permitted to all futures contracts owned by an enterprise on the date FASB-80 is first applied.

NONMONETARY TRANSACTIONS

Background

The promulgated GAAP on Nonmonetary Transactions is APB-29 and FASB Interpretation-30, Accounting for Involuntary Conversions of Nonmonetary Assets. The following types of transactions are specifically excluded from the promulgated GAAP:

1. Accounting for business combinations (purchase and pooling-of-interests methods)
2. A nonmonetary transfer of assets between companies or persons under common ownership control
3. Issuance of capital stock for the acquisition of nonmonetary assets or services
4. Stock dividends and stock splits, issued or received

FASB Technical Bulletin 85-1 (FASB:TB 85-1), issued on March 18, 1985, provides guidance, to members of the Federal Home Loan Banking System (primarily savings and loan institutions), on accounting for the receipt of the new Federal Home Loan Mortgage Corporation (FHLMC) Participating Preferred Stock.

Monetary Assets or Liabilities

Business transactions usually involve cash or monetary assets or liabilities that are exchanged for goods or services.

Monetary assets or liabilities are fixed in terms of currency and are usually contractual claims to fixed amounts of money. Examples of monetary assets and liabilities are cash, accounts and notes receivable, and accounts and notes payable.

Nonmonetary Assets or Liabilities

Some business transactions involve the exchange or transfer of nonmonetary assets or liabilities which are not fixed in terms of currency.

Nonmonetary assets or liabilities are those other than monetary assets or liabilities. Examples of nonmonetary assets and liabilities are inventory, investments in common stock, property, plant, and equipment, liability for advance rent collected, and common stock.

Under certain circumstances, a monetary asset or liability may become nonmonetary. For example, a marketable bond being held to maturity would qualify as a monetary asset because its face amount is fixed in terms of currency. However, if the same bond was being held for speculation, it would properly be classified as a nonmonetary asset because the amount that will be received when it is sold is not determinable and therefore not fixed in terms of currency.

Exchange (Reciprocal Transfer)

An exchange is a reciprocal transfer, in which each party to the transaction receives and/or gives up assets, liabilities, or services. Exchanges can be either monetary or nonmonetary, or a combination of both. Nonmonetary exchanges are usually for the mutual convenience of two businesses. Examples include an exchange of inventory for trucking services or a trade of a starting quarterback for three linemen and a future draft choice.

Nonreciprocal Transfer

A nonreciprocal transfer is a transaction in one direction, in which one party to the transaction usually acquires either an intangible asset or nothing. Examples of nonreciprocal transfers are:

1. Declaration and distribution of a dividend
2. Acquisition of treasury stock
3. Sale of capital stock
4. Conversion of convertible debt
5. Charitable contributions

Fair Value

Accounting for the transfer or distribution of a nonmonetary asset or liability should be based on the fair value of the asset or liability that is received or surrendered, whichever is more clearly evident (APB-29). The only exceptions to this rule are (a) when fair value is not determinable, (b) certain nonreciprocal transfers to owners, and (c) when the earning process is not completed (APB-29). Fair value of the assets in a nonmonetary transfer should be determined by reference to the estimated realizable value of similar assets that are sold for cash, quoted market prices, independent appraisals, and other available evidence. If cash could have been received in lieu of the nonmonetary asset, then the amount of cash may be the basis for the valuation of the nonmonetary asset.

Fair Value Not Determinable

Because of uncertainties, there may be situations where the fair value of the nonmonetary assets received and surrendered cannot be determined with reasonable accuracy. In these situations, the only valuation available may be the recorded book values of the nonmonetary assets (APB-29). Thus APB-29 suggests, but does not require, that the recorded amount of a nonmonetary asset be used in those situations in which fair value cannot be reasonably determined.

Nonreciprocal Transfers to Owners

If the fair value of the nonmonetary assets in a nonreciprocal transfer to owners can be objectively determined and realized in an outright sale at or near the date of transfer, the transfer shall be accounted for at fair value (APB-29). However, in a reorganization or liquidation (including spin-offs), or in a rescission of a business combination, the nonreciprocal transfer of nonmonetary assets shall be accounted for at their recorded amount, less any necessary reduction for impairment in values (APB-29). In other words, these types of nonmonetary transfers to owners must be accounted for either at the assets' recorded amount or at the assets' net realizable value, as follows:

1. If the recorded amount of the nonmonetary assets is less than fair value, the transfer is accounted for at the recorded amount because there is no reduction necessary for impairment.
2. If the recorded amount of the nonmonetary assets is more than fair value, the transfer is accounted for at net realizable value, which is equal to the recorded amount less a reduction for impairment.

A *pro rata* distribution to owners of the shares of a subsidiary or investee that is or will be consolidated or accounted for by the equity method is considered a spin-off for the purposes of APB-29.

FHLMC Participating Preferred Stock On December 6, 1984, the Federal Home Loan Mortgage Corporation declared a distribution consisting of a new class of participating preferred stock, payable to the 12 district FHL Banks in proportion to their respective holdings of FHLMC's non-voting common stock. Between December 8, 1984, and December 14, 1984, each FHL Bank declared a dividend of the new class of participating preferred stock to its stockholders of record (the "Members") as of the close of business on December 3, 1984. Shares of the new class of participating preferred stock were allocated to Members in the same manner and on the same basis as cash dividends would be allocated to Members as of such record date pursuant to 12 C.F.R. Sec. 522.6.

With certain exceptions, shares of the new class of participating preferred stock may be sold, transferred, pledged or otherwise disposed of *only* to and among Members and the FHLMC.

Each Member was treated as receiving a distribution in an amount equal to the fair market value of the shares of the new class of participating preferred stock received. The distribution was treated as a dividend to the extent of the earnings and profits of the FHL Bank from which the distribution was received. No amount treated as a dividend was eligible for the dividends received deduction. Any remainder of the distribution was treated as an adjustment of the Member's basis in its FHL Bank Stock to the extent of such basis, with any excess treated as a gain from the sale or exchange of FHL Bank Stock.

Under APB-29 (Nonmonetary Transactions), the distribution of the Federal Home Loan Mortgage Corporation's participating preferred stock, to the savings and loan associations who are members of the Federal Home Loan Banking System, represents a nonreciprocal transfer of a nonmonetary asset to owners. If the fair value of a nonmonetary asset, in a nonreciprocal transfer to owners, can be objectively determined and realized in an outright sale at or near the date of transfer, the transfer shall be accounted for at fair value (APB-29).

An independent appraisal of the price range at which the preferred stock was expected to trade on the New York Stock Exchange was obtained by the FHLMC before the stock began trading on January 23, 1985. Under FASB:TB 85-1, the preferred stock should be recognized by member institutions at its fair value on December 31, 1984, in accordance with APB-29.

Under FASB:TB 85-1, accounting for the preferred stock at fair value will result in income to a member institution, which should be reported as an extraordinary item (APB-30), because of the infrequency of occurrence, and unusual nature, of the distribution. The amount recorded by a member institution as fair value as at December 31, 1984, becomes the cost of the preferred stock. Under FASB:TB 85-1, the preferred stock should be reported in the financial statements of a member institution in accordance with FASB-12 (Marketable Securities).

> **OBSERVATION:** Paragraph 3 of FASB:TB 85-1 states that the FHLMC preferred stock is a marketable equity security and should be reported in accordance with FASB-12. However, under FASB-12, restricted or legend stock is not considered a marketable security. The Distribution Circular, dated December 21, 1984, for the FHLMC preferred stock states that the preferred stock may be sold, transferred, pledged, or otherwise disposed of only to and among Freddie Mac and its member institutions, and that each stock certificate will bear a conspicuous legend as to this restriction on transfer. Thus, reporting the FHLMC preferred stock as a marketable security under the provisions of FASB-12 may not be appropriate.

FASB:TB 85-1 is effective for fiscal years and interim period financial statements ending after December 1, 1984, that are issued on or after April 1, 1985. If financial statements have been issued that did not report the distribution of the FHLMC preferred stock as required by FASB:TB 85-1, such financial statements should be retroactively restated when reissued. Earlier application of the provisions of FASB:TB 85-1 is encouraged, but not required.

Earning Process Not Complete

A basic principle states that "When the earning process is complete and an exchange has taken place, only then is the realization of revenue recognized." There are two types of nonmonetary exchanges that do not result in completion of the earning process:

1. An exchange of property held for sale in the ordinary course of business for similar property to be held for the same purpose
2. An exchange of productive assets used in business but not held for sale for similar property to be held for the same purpose

In these two cases the nonmonetary exchange should be based on the recorded amount (book value) of the nonmonetary asset surrendered, unless the exchange includes an amount of monetary consideration. The amount of the monetary consideration included in the nonmonetary exchange should be accounted for, as follows:

Recipient of the monetary consideration The recipient of the monetary consideration should recognize realized gain on the exchange to the extent that the monetary amount exceeds a proportionate share of the recorded amount of the asset relinquished.

If the transaction results in a loss, the entire loss on the exchange should be recognized.

Nonmonetary Transactions

Payor of the monetary consideration The payor of the monetary consideration should not recognize any gain on the exchange and should record the cost of the nonmonetary asset received at the amount of the nonmonetary asset surrendered, plus the amount of the monetary consideration paid.

If the transaction results in a loss, the entire loss on the exchange should be recognized.

Formula for recognition of gains or losses The following formula may be used in determining the recognition of nonmonetary gains or losses:

1. The gain or loss on the transaction is the difference between the fair market value and the net book value of the asset surrendered.
2. Losses on any nonmonetary assets are always recognized in full.
3. Gains are recognized in full if the earning process has been completed.
4. If the earning process has not been completed, gains are recognized as follows:

   a. no boot involved = no gain recognized

   b. boot is given = no gain recognized

   c. boot is received = a portion of the gain is recognized, as follows:

$$\frac{\text{Cash received}}{\text{cash received + fair market value of asset received}} \times \text{gain} = \text{recognized amount of gain}$$

An asset with a $6,000 cost is exchanged for $4,000 in cash and an asset with a fair value of $8,000. Both assets were held for sale in the ordinary course of business, and except for the cash the earning process would not have been completed and no gain would be recognized. Using the formula for recognition of gain the computation is:

$$\frac{\$4,000}{\$4,000 + \$8,000} \times \$6,000 = \$2,000$$

Basis of acquired asset:

Original cost	$6,000
Less: Cash received	4,000
	$2,000
Add: Recognized gain	2,000
Basis of acquired asset	$4,000

Losses are recognized in full (conservatism).

Gain or Loss

Gain or loss, when applicable, should be recognized in nonmonetary transactions. A difference in the gain or loss for tax purposes and that recognized for accounting purposes may constitute a timing difference in income tax provision.

Involuntary Conversion of Nonmonetary Assets to Monetary Assets

When a nonmonetary asset is involuntarily converted to a monetary asset, a monetary transaction results, and gain or loss must be recognized in the period of conversion (FASB Interpretation-30). The gain or loss is the difference between the carrying amount of the nonmonetary asset and the proceeds from the conversion.

Gain or loss from an involuntary conversion of a nonmonetary asset to a monetary asset should be classified as from continuing operations, extraordinary items, disposal of a segment, etc., according to the particular circumstances (APB-30). In addition, a gain or loss recognized for tax purposes in a period different from that for financial accounting purposes (books) creates a timing difference, for which interperiod tax allocation may be necessary (APB-11).

If the amount of proceeds that will be received, from the involuntary conversion of the nonmonetary asset, cannot be determined, the gain or loss shall be recognized and classified as a contingency (see chapter on Contingencies).

The involuntary conversion of a LIFO inventory layer, at an interim reporting date, does not have to be recognized if the proceeds are reinvested in replacement inventory by the end of the fiscal year (FASB Interpretation-30).

> **OBSERVATION:** *This is the same treatment afforded a temporary liquidation of a LIFO inventory layer at interim dates which is expected to be corrected by the end of the annual period (see Interim Financial Reporting).*

In the event the proceeds from an involuntary conversion of a LIFO inventory layer are not reinvested in replacement inventory by the end of the fiscal year, gain for financial accounting purposes need not be recognized providing the taxpayer does not recognize such gains for income tax reporting purposes (FASB Interpretation-30).

Examples of involuntary conversion are the total or partial destruction of property through fire or other catastrophe, theft of property, or condemnation of property by a governmental authority (eminent domain proceedings).

Disclosure

Adequate disclosure of the nature of the nonmonetary transaction, the basis of accounting for assets transferred, and gains or losses recognized should be disclosed in the financial statements for the period.

Conclusion

All nonmonetary transactions except those for which fair value is undeterminable or for which the earning process is not complete are based on the fair value of the asset surrendered or received, whichever is more clearly evident. Gain or loss is recognized on nonmonetary transactions. In the event that fair value cannot be reasonably determined, the recorded book value may be used. In exchanges where the earning process is not complete, gain is recognized to the extent "boot" is received, and losses are recognized in full.

A gain or a loss recognized for tax purposes in a period different from that for financial accounting purposes creates a timing difference, for which interperiod income tax allocation may apply (APB-11).

PENSION PLANS - EMPLOYERS

Background

Financial accounting and reporting standards for employers' pension plans are established by FASB-87 (Employers' Accounting for Pensions). FASB-87 supersedes APB-8, as amended (Accounting for Costs of a Pension Plan); FASB-36 (Disclosure of Pension Information); and FASB Interpretation-3 (Accounting for the Cost of Pension Plans Subject to the Employee Retirement Income Security Act of 1974). In addition, FASB-87 amends APB-16 to provide that the purchase of the assets and liabilities of a pension plan shall no longer be accounted for in accordance with paragraph 88h of APB-16 (Business Combinations), but shall be accounted for in accordance with paragraph 74 of FASB-87, entitled "Business Combinations." FASB-87 also amends FASB-5 (Contingencies) to delete references to APB-8, and to provide for the recognition of a loss contingency when an employer withdraws as a member of a multiemployer pension plan, and it is *probable* or *reasonably possible* that, as a result of the withdrawal, the employer has incurred a liability for a portion of the plan's unfunded benefit obligation.

FASB-87 does not change or supersede any of the provisions of FASB-35 (Accounting and Reporting by Defined Benefit Plans).

> **OBSERVATION:** *FASB Technical Bulletin 81-3 (FASB:TB 81-3) provides guidance on the accounting implications of the Multiemployer Pension Plan Amendments Act of 1980 (MPPAA). FASB:TB 81-3 makes reference to APB-8, FASB-36, and FASB Interpretation-3, all of which have been superseded by FASB-87. Furthermore, FASB:TB 81-3 suggests that employers participating in multiemployer plans that are deemed to be defined benefit plans subject to the MPPAA should look to FASB Interpretation-3 for guidance.*
>
> *It appears that FASB:TB 81-3 should have also been superseded by FASB-87, but was not. Although FASB:TB 81-3 remains technically effective, it obviously should not be relied upon.*

FASB-87 was promulgated by a four to three vote of the seven board members of the Financial Accounting Standards Board.

Deferred compensation plan is a contractual agreement that specifies that a portion of the employee's compensation will be set aside and paid in future periods as retirement benefits. Only those deferred compensation plans that in substance are pension plans are covered by FASB-87.

Postemployment and postretirement benefits are generally considered a form of deferred compensation to an employee because these types of benefits are provided by an employer in exchange for an employee's services. Thus, these benefits must be properly measured and recognized in the financial statements and, if the amount is material, financial statement disclosure may be required.

> **OBSERVATION:** For a detailed discussion of postemployment and postretirement benefits and their disclosure requirements, see chapter entitled "Deferred Compensation Contracts."

Overview

Employment between an employee and an employer is usually based on an exchange agreement. The employee agrees to provide services for the employer in exchange for a current wage, a pension benefit, and frequently other benefits such as death, dental, disability, etc. Although pension benefits and some other benefits are not paid currently, they represent deferred compensation that must be accounted for as part of the employee's total compensation package.

Pension benefits are usually paid on a periodic basis to retired employees or their survivors, but may be paid in a single lump sum. Other benefits, such as death, dental, disability, etc., may also be provided through a pension plan.

A pension plan may be contributory or noncontributory; that is, the employees may be required to contribute to the plan, or the entire cost of the plan may be borne by the employer. A pension plan may be funded or unfunded; that is, the employees and/or the employer may make cash contributions to a pension plan trustee, or the employer may make only credit entries on its books reflecting the pension liability under the plan. Pension plans are accounted for on the accrual basis, and any difference between net periodic pension cost charged against income and the amount actually funded is recorded as an accrued or prepaid pension cost.

Although interest cost on the pension liability and the return (or loss) on a pension plan's assets will increase or decrease net periodic pension cost, they are considered financial costs rather than employee compensation costs. Financial costs can be controlled by the manner in which the employer provides financing for the pension plan. An employer can eliminate interest cost by completely funding the plan or by purchasing annuity contracts to settle all pension obligations. The return on plan assets can be increased by the contribution of more assets to the pension fund.

Pension plan accounting The assets of a pension plan are usually kept in a trust account, completely segregated from the assets of the employer. Contributions to the pension trust account are periodically made by the employer and, if the plan is contributory, by the employees. The plan assets are invested in stocks, bonds, real estate, and other types of investments. Plan assets are increased by earnings and gains on investments and are decreased by losses on investments and the payment of pension benefits. Plan assets placed in a trust account cannot usually be withdrawn by the employer. However, an exception arises when the plan assets exceed the pension obligation. In this event, most pension plan agreements permit the employer to withdraw the excess amount of plan assets, providing that all other existing pension plan obligations have been satisfied by the employer. Under GAAP, pension plan assets that are not effectively restricted for the payment of pension benefits or segregated in a trust are not considered pension plan assets.

Accounting and reporting for a pension plan (defined benefit plan) is covered by FASB-35.

Scope and Applicability of FASB-87

Most of the provisions of FASB-87 address *defined benefit pension plans* of single employers. A defined benefit pension plan is one that contains a "pension benefit formula," which generally describes the amount of pension benefit that each employee will receive for services performed during a specified period of employment. The amount of the employer's periodic contribution to a defined benefit pension plan is based on the total pension benefits earned by all eligible employees during a specified period of employment.

A *defined contribution pension plan* does not contain a pension benefit formula, but generally specifies the periodic amount that the employer shall contribute to the pension plan and how that amount shall be allocated to the eligible employees who perform services during that same period. Each periodic employer contribution is allocated among separate accounts maintained for each employee, and pension benefits are based solely on the amount available in each employee's account at the time of his or her retirement.

FASB-87 does not apply to a plan that provides only life and/or health insurance benefits to retirees. Although not required, FASB-87 may be applied to postemployment health care benefits provided through a pension plan. If FASB-87 is not applied to postemployment health care benefits that are provided through a pension plan, the obligations and assets associated with the postemployment health care benefits must not be included in the pension plan's obligations and plan assets. Specific financial statement disclosures for postemployment health care benefits to retirees are required by FASB-81 (Disclosure of Postretirement Health Care and Life Insurance Benefits). Postretirement health care and/or life insurance benefits that are provided to retirees are generally considered a form of deferred compensation.

Frequently, defined contribution pension plans provide for some method of determining defined benefits for employees, as may be the case with many "target benefit" plans. If, in substance, a plan does provide defined benefits for employees, it shall be accounted for as a defined benefit pension plan.

For the purposes of FASB-87, any plan that is not a defined contribution pension plan is considered a defined benefit pension plan (see definition of a defined benefit pension plan in Appendix D of FASB-87). FASB-87 does not supersede or change any of the requirements of FASB-35 (Accounting and Reporting by Defined Benefit Plans).

FASB-87 requires that its provisions be applied to any arrangement, express or implied, that is similar in substance to a pension plan, regardless of its form or method of financing. Thus, a pension plan arrangement does not have to be in writing if the existence of a pension plan is implied by company policy.

An employer's settlement of a defined benefit pension obligation, curtailment of a defined benefit pension plan, and/or the termination of pension benefits are covered by FASB-88 (Employers' Accounting for Settlements and Curtailments of Defined Benefit Pension Plans and for Termination Benefits).

The use of estimates, averages, and/or computational shortcuts is permitted by FASB-87 to reduce the cost of compliance, providing that the results are not significantly different from those that would be obtained by detailed application.

Actuarial Assumptions

Actuarial assumptions are factors that are used to calculate the estimated cost of pension plan benefits. Employee mortality, employee turnover, retirement age, administrative expenses of the pension plan, interest earned on plan assets, and the date on which a benefit becomes fully vested are some of the more important actuarial assumptions.

Under FASB-87, each significant actuarial assumption must reflect the best estimate for that particular assumption. In the absence of evidence to the contrary, all actuarial assumptions shall be made on the basis that the pension plan will continue in existence (going-concern concept).

Discount rates that are used in actuarial valuations shall reflect the rates at which the pension benefits could be effectively settled. In selecting appropriate interest rates, employers should refer to current information on rates used in annuity contracts that could be purchased to settle pension obligations, including annuity rates published by the Pension Benefit Guaranty Corporation, or the rates of return on high-quality fixed-income investments that are expected to be available through the maturity dates of the pension benefits.

An actuarial gain or loss is the difference between an actuarial assumption and actual experience. Under FASB-87, actuarial gains and losses are not included in net periodic pension cost in the year in which they arise, but may be subject to amortization in subsequent periods if certain criteria are met.

Pension Plan Assets

The resources of a pension plan may be converted into (a) plan assets that are invested to provide pension benefits for the participants of the plan, such as stocks, bonds, and other investments (paragraph 19 of FASB-87) or (b) plan assets that are used in the operation of the plan, such as real estate, furniture, fixtures, etc., (paragraph 51 of FASB-87). Plan assets must be segregated in a trust or otherwise effectively restricted so that they cannot be used by the employer for other purposes. Under FASB-87, plan assets do not include amounts accrued by an employer as net periodic pension cost, but not yet paid to the pension plan. Plan assets may include securities of the employer if they are freely transferable.

Pension plan assets that are held as investments to provide pension benefits shall be measured at fair value. Pension plan assets that are used in the operation of the plan shall be measured, for all purposes, at cost less accumulated depreciation or amortization (paragraph 51 of FASB-87). All plan assets shall be measured as of the date of the financial statements or, if used consistently from year to year, as of a date not more than three months prior to that date (paragraph 52 of FASB-87).

For the purposes of FASB-87, plan liabilities that are incurred, other than for pension benefits, may be considered reductions of plan assets (Appendix D of FASB-87, under definition of "Plan Assets").

Capsule Analysis of FASB-87

This capsule analysis offers an overall perspective of some of the major provisions of FASB-87. It is intended to simplify the material covered and to expedite the reader's understanding of FASB-87.

Under FASB-87, an enterprise must make at least two types of journal entries to record its pension cost, as follows:

(a) Net periodic pension cost $XXX
  Accrued pension cost payable $XXX
  To accrue pension cost for a specific period.

(b) Accrued pension cost payable $XXX
  Cash $XXX
  To record cash contribution to pension plan trustee.

Most of the provisions of FASB-87 pertain to the computation of the amount to be recorded in entry type (a) as net periodic pension cost. This computation requires numerous worksheet calculations which are illustrated throughout FASB-87.

In some but not all situations, an enterprise may also be required to make a third type of entry, as follows:

(c) Intangible asset $XXX
  Excess of additional pension liability over unrecognized prior service cost (an offset to net worth) XXX
  Accrued pension cost payable $XXX

As is discussed later in this chapter, this third type of entry is generally required if the employer's pension liability exceeds the fair value of the pension plan assets.

FASB-87 also requires a schedule reconciling the funded status of an employer's pension plan with certain amounts reported in the employer's statement of financial position. The reconciliation schedule must be as of the date of the financial statements or, if used consistently from year to year, as of a date not more than three months prior to the date of the financial statements. The following illustrates such a reconciliation as of the date of initial adoption of FASB-87.

**Reconciliation of Pension Plan Funded Status
with Amounts Reported on Statement of Financial Position
(as of the date of initial application of FASB-87)**

(a)	Projected benefit obligation	$(100,000)
(b)	Fair value of plan assets	65,000
(c)	Funded status of plan	$ (35,000)
(d)	Unrecognized prior service cost	0
(e)	Unrecognized net (gain) or loss	0
(f)	Unrecognized net obligation or (net asset) at date of initial application of FASB-87	35,000
(g)	(Accrued) or prepaid pension cost	$ 0

Only item (g) is actually recorded on the books of the employer. The other items are usually recorded by the employer on worksheets.

Each item appearing in the above reconciliation schedule is discussed briefly below. Further details are provided in subsequent text and illustrations.

(a) *Projected benefit obligation* is the actuarial present value, as of a specified date, of the total cost of all employees' vested and nonvested pension benefits that have been attributed by the pension benefit formula to services performed by employees to that date.

The projected benefit obligation includes the actuarial present value of all pension benefits (vested and nonvested) attributed by the pension benefit formula, whether the benefits are based on future employee compensation levels or not. Vested benefits are pension benefits that an employee has an irrevocable right to receive at a date specified in the pension agreement, even if the employee does not continue to work for the employer. In the event a pension plan is discontinued, a vested benefit obligation remains a liability of the employer.

Payments of pension benefits decrease both the projected benefit obligation and the fair value of plan assets, while contributions to a plan decrease accrued pension cost (or increase the prepaid pension cost), and increase the fair value of plan assets.

The projected benefit obligation appears on the books of the pension plan but not on the books of the employer. However, the employer should maintain a record of the projected benefit obligation on a worksheet.

The *accumulated benefit obligation* is calculated in the same way as the projected benefit obligation, except that current or past compensation levels are used to determine pension benefits instead of future compensation levels, even if the pension benefit formula requires the use of future compensation levels to determine pension benefits. Under FASB-87, an employer must recognize an additional minimum liability in its statement of financial position, if its accumulated benefit obligation exceeds the fair value of pension plan assets as of a specified date. The amount of the additional minimum liability must at least equal the employer's *unfunded accumulated benefit obligation*, which is the amount by which the accumulated benefit obligation exceeds the fair value of plan assets. In the event a pension plan is discontinued, the balance of any unfunded accumulated benefit obligation remains a liability of the employer.

(b) *Fair value of plan assets* is the amount that a pension plan could reasonably expect to receive from a current sale of plan assets, that are held to provide pension benefits, between a willing buyer under no compulsion to buy and a willing seller under no compulsion to sell. Plan assets that are used in the operation of the pension plan (building, equipment, furniture, fixtures, etc.) are valued at cost less accumulated depreciation or amortization.

Pension plan assets are recorded on the books of the pension plan. However, an employer should maintain worksheet records of the cost and fair value of all pension plan assets.

(c) *Funded status of plan* is the difference between the projected benefit obligation and the fair value of plan assets as of a given date. If the projected benefit obligation exceeds the fair value of the plan assets, a pension plan liability exists. If the fair value of plan assets exceeds the projected benefit obligation, a pension plan asset exists.

(d) *Unrecognized prior service cost* is the portion of prior service cost that has not been recognized by the employer in net periodic pension cost of any period. The amount of unrecognized prior service cost as of the date of initial application of FASB-87 is zero by definition.

Upon the initial adoption of a pension plan or through a plan amendment, certain employees may be granted pension benefits for services performed in prior periods. These retroactive pension benefits are referred to as "prior service costs," and are usually granted by the employer with the expectation that they will produce future economic benefits, such as reducing employee turnover, improving employee productivity, and minimizing the need to increase employee compensation. Under FASB-87, an employer is required to amortize any prior service cost in equal amounts over the future periods of each active employee who is expected to receive the benefits.

An employer does not record unrecognized prior service cost on its books but should maintain worksheet records of such amounts. The total amount of any prior service cost is recorded on the books of the pension plan, as an increase in the projected benefit obligation, in the period in which the retroactive benefits become effective.

(e) *Unrecognized net gain or loss* is the amount of actuarial gain or loss for a period that has not been recognized by the employer in net periodic pension cost of any period. The amount of unrecognized net gain or loss as of the date of initial application of FASB-87 is zero by definition.

Actuarial gains or losses arise from the difference between (a) the actual and expected amount of projected benefit obligation at the end of a period and/or (b) the actual and expected amount of the fair value of pension plan assets at the end of the period. Under FASB-87, actuarial gains or losses are not recognized by the employer in the period in which they arise, but may become subject to amortization in subsequent periods if certain criteria are met.

An unrecognized net gain or loss that, as of the beginning of the year, exceeds 10% of (a) the projected benefit obligation or (b) the market-related value of plan assets, whichever is greater, is subject to amortization. The amount of unrecognized net gain or loss in excess of 10% is amortized by the employer in equal amounts over the average remaining service period of active employees expected to receive benefits under the plan.

Actuarial gains and losses are recognized on the books of a pension plan as they occur. However, an employer does not record actuarial gains or losses on its books but should maintain worksheet records of such amounts.

(f) *Unrecognized net obligation or net asset at date of initial application of FASB-87* is the difference between the projected benefit obligation and the fair value of plan assets plus previously recognized unfunded accrued pension cost or less previously recognized prepaid pension cost. In other words, the unrecognized net obligation or net asset is the difference between the funded status of a plan (projected benefit obligation less the fair value of plan assets), and the total amount of accrued or prepaid pension cost existing on the books of the employer as of the date of the initial application of FASB-87. Thus, if all contributions of prior periods were equal to all of the net pension cost of prior periods, there should be no accrued or prepaid pension cost on the books of the employer at the date of the initial application of FASB-87. In this event, the unrecognized net obligation or net asset is exactly equal to the funded status of the plan as of the date of the initial application of FASB-87.

The unrecognized net obligation or net asset as of the date of initial application of FASB-87 shall be amortized on a straight-line basis over the average remaining service period of employees expected to receive benefits under the plan, except (a) if the amortization period is less than 15 years, the employer may elect to use 15 years, and (b) if the plan is composed of all or substantially all inactive participants, the employer shall use those participants' average remaining life expectancy as the amortization period.

The amount of the employer's unrecognized net obligation or net asset is included in the projected benefit obligation which is recorded on the books of the pension plan, as of the date of the employer's initial application of FASB-87. However, an employer does not record its unrecognized net obligation or net asset on its books as of the date of the initial application of FASB-87 but should maintain a worksheet record of such amount.

(g) *Accrued or prepaid pension cost* Accrued pension cost is the total amount of net periodic pension cost that has been recognized but not funded. Prepaid pension cost is the total amount that has been funded in excess of the total amount of the net periodic pension cost that has been recognized.

Accrued or prepaid pension cost is recorded on the books of the employer.

Net Periodic Pension Cost

The employer's *net periodic pension cost* represents the net amount of pension cost for a specified period that is charged against income.

Under FASB-87, the components of net periodic pension cost are (a) service cost, (b) interest cost on the projected benefit obligation, (c) actual return on plan assets, (d) amortization of unrecognized prior service cost (if any), (e) amortization of unrecognized net gain or loss (if required by FASB-87), and (f) amortization of the unrecognized net obligation or net asset existing at the date of initial application of FASB-87.

It is important to note that all of the components of net periodic pension cost are recognized on the books of the pension plan trustee in the period in which they arise, but the same components are not necessarily recognized on the books of the employer at the same time. For example, the total prior service cost that results from a plan amendment is recognized in full on the books of the pension plan in the period in which it arises as an increase in the projected benefit obligation. However, under the provisions of FASB-87, the employer recognizes the total prior service cost in equal amounts over the future service periods of each active employee who is expected to receive the benefits. The employer does not record any unrecognized prior service cost on its books but should maintain a worksheet record of such amounts.

The components of net periodic pension cost that are either partially recognized or not recognized at all on the employer's books in the period in which they arise are (a) unrecognized prior service cost, (b) unrecognized net asset gain or loss, and (c) unrecognized net obligation or net asset existing at the date of the initial application of FASB-87.

Net periodic pension cost is estimated in advance at the beginning of a period based on actuarial assumptions relating to (a) the discount rate on the projected benefit obligation, (b) the expected long-term rate of return on pension plan assets, and (c) the average remaining service periods of active employees covered by the pension plan. At the end of the period, adjustments are made to account for the differences (actuarial gains or losses), if any, between the estimated and actual amounts.

The same actuarial assumptions used to calculate the previous year's net periodic pension cost shall be used to calculate the net periodic pension cost in subsequent interim and annual financial statements, unless more current valuations of plan assets and obligations are available or a significant event has occurred, such as a plan amendment, which would usually require new valuations.

The following illustration shows how the different components of net periodic pension cost are estimated.

Computation of Net Periodic Pension Cost Accrual

Service cost component	$2,000
Interest cost component	3,000
Estimated return on plan assets	(2,500)
Amortization of unrecognized prior service cost	1,000
Amortization of unrecognized net (gain) or loss	1,000
Amortization of initial unrecognized net obligation (asset)	1,500
Total net periodic pension cost accrual	$6,000

For simplicity, it is assumed that there are no differences (actuarial gains or losses) between the estimated and actual amounts at the end of the period, and that the employer made no contributions to the pension fund during the period.

	Beginning of period	End of period
(a) Projected benefit obligation	$(115,000)	$(120,000)
(b) Fair value of plan assets	65,000	67,500
(c) Funded status of plan	$ (50,000)	$ (52,500)
(d) Unrecognized prior service cost	10,000	9,000
(e) Unrecognized net (gain) or loss	5,000	4,000
(f) Unrecognized net obligation or (net asset) at date of initial application of FASB-87	35,000	33,500
(g) (Accrued) or prepaid pension cost	$ 0	$ 0

The following journal entry was made by the employer to record the net periodic pension cost accrual:

Net periodic pension cost	$6,000	
Accrued pension cost		$6,000

The following is an explanation of the changes in the accounts that were affected by the net periodic pension cost accrual.

(a) *Projected benefit obligation*   The $5,000 increase in the projected benefit obligation, between the beginning and end of the period, consists of the service cost component ($2,000) and interest cost component ($3,000) of the net periodic pension cost accrual.

An increase in the projected benefit obligation of $5,000 will be recorded on the books of the pension plan, representing the service cost component of $2,000 and interest cost component of $3,000 for the period.

(b) *Fair value of plan assets*   The $2,500 increase in the fair value of plan assets, between the beginning and end of the period, represents the increase in the fair value of plan assets for the period.

An increase in the fair value of plan assets of $2,500 will be recorded on the books of the pension plan.

(c) *Funded status of plan*   The $2,500 increase in the funded status of the plan, between the beginning and end of the period, is the difference between the $5,000 increase in the projected benefit obligation for the period and the $2,500 increase in the fair value of plan assets for the period.

(d) *Unrecognized prior service cost*   The $1,000 decrease in the unrecognized prior service cost, between the beginning and end of the period, is the amount of amortization of prior service cost that has been recognized by the employer as a component of net periodic pension cost ($6,000).

As mentioned previously, unrecognized prior service cost is not recorded on the books of the employer, but worksheet records should be maintained for such amounts. Thus, the employer should reduce the worksheet balance of the unrecognized prior service cost by $1,000.

The $1,000 decrease in the unrecognized prior service cost is not recorded on the books of the pension plan because the total effects of the plan amendment were included, in full, in the projected benefit obligation in the year in which the plan amendment became effective.

(e) *Unrecognized net gain or loss*   The $1,000 decrease in the unrecognized net gain or loss (actuarial gain or loss), between the beginning and end of the period, is the amount of amortization that has been recognized by the employer as a component of net periodic pension cost ($6,000).

As mentioned previously, unrecognized net gain or loss (actuarial gain or loss) is not recorded on the books of the employer, but worksheet records should be maintained for such amounts. Thus, the employer should reduce the worksheet balance of the unrecognized net gain or loss by $1,000.

The $1,000 decrease in the unrecognized net gain or loss is not recorded on the books of the pension plan because the total net gain or loss was included in the pension plan's records in the year in which the actuarial gain or loss occurred.

(f) *Unrecognized net obligation or net asset at date of initial application of FASB-87* The $1,500 decrease in the unrecognized net obligation, between the beginning and the end of the period, is the amount of amortization which has been recognized by the employer as a component of net periodic pension cost ($6,000) for the period.

As mentioned previously, unrecognized net obligation or net asset is not recorded on the books of the employer, but worksheet records should be maintained for such amounts. Thus, the employer should reduce the worksheet balance of the unrecognized net obligation or net asset by $1,500.

The $1,500 decrease in the unrecognized net obligation or net asset is not recorded on the books of the pension plan because the total amount of the unrecognized net obligation or net asset was included in the funded status of the plan, as of the date of the initial application of FASB-87.

(g) *Accrued or prepaid pension cost* The $6,000 increase in the accrued or prepaid pension cost, between the beginning and the end of the period, is the amount of the net periodic pension cost for the period which has not been funded by employer contributions.

Accrued pension cost is the total amount of net periodic pension cost that has been recognized to date but not funded by contributions to the pension plan. Prepaid pension cost is the total amount that has been funded by contributions to date, in excess of the total amount of net periodic pension cost that has been recognized.

Service Cost Component

A defined benefit pension plan contains a pension benefit formula that defines the pension benefit that an employee will receive for services performed during a specified period. FASB-87 requires that the terms in the pension benefit formula be used to determine the amount of pension benefit earned by each employee for services performed during a specified period. Under FASB-87, attribution is the process of assigning pension benefits or cost to periods of employee service, in accordance with the pension benefit formula.

The service cost component of net periodic pension cost is defined by FASB-87 as the actuarial present value of pension benefits attributed by the pension benefit formula to employee service during a specified period. For example, a pension benefit formula may state that an employee shall receive, at the retirement age stated in the plan, a pension benefit of $20 per month for life, for each year of service. To compute the total future value of the pension benefit for the year, the monthly benefit is multiplied by the number of months in the employee's life expectancy at retirement age. The number of months in the employee's life expectancy at retirement age is determined by reference to mortality tables. The actuarial present value of all employees' future pension benefits that are earned during a period is computed and included as the service cost component of the net periodic pension cost for the same period.

If the terms of the pension benefit formula provide for benefits based on estimated future compensation levels of employees, those estimated future compensation levels shall be used to determine the service cost component of net periodic pension cost. For example, if the pension benefit formula states that an employee's benefit for a period is equal to 1% of his or her final pay, an estimate of the employee's final pay shall be used to calculate the benefit for the period. Assumed compensation levels should reflect the best estimate of the future compensation levels of the employee involved and be consistent with assumed discount rates to the extent that they both incorporate expectation of the same future economic conditions (paragraph 202 of FASB-87). Thus, future compensation levels in final-pay plans or career-average-pay plans are reflected in the service cost component of net periodic pension cost. Assumed compensation levels shall also reflect changes due to general price levels, productivity, seniority, promotion, and other factors.

Changes resulting from a plan amendment that has become effective and automatic benefit changes specified by the terms of the pension plan, such as cost-of-living increases, shall be included in the determination of service cost for a period.

An employer's substantive commitment to make future plan amendments in recognition of employees' prior services may indicate pension benefits far in excess of those reflected in the existing pension benefit formula. Such a commitment may be evidenced by a history of regular increases in non-pay-related benefits, benefits under a career-average-pay plan, or other evidence. In this event,

FASB-87 requires that the pension plan be accounted for on the basis of the employer's substantive commitment, and that appropriate disclosure be made in the employer's financial statements.

A plan's pension benefit formula may provide a nonvested benefit of $10 per month for life in the first 19 years of an employee's service and a vested benefit of $1,000 per month for life in the 20th year of an employee's service. If a pension plan benefit formula attributes all or a disproportionate portion of total pension benefits to later years, the employee's *total projected benefit* shall be calculated and used as the basis of assigning the total pension benefits under the plan. In this event, the employee's total projected benefit shall be assumed to accumulate in proportion to the ratio of the total completed years of service to date to the total completed years of service as of the date the benefit becomes fully vested. An employee's total projected benefit from a pension plan is the actuarial present value of the total cost of pension benefits that the employee is likely to receive under the plan. If the pension benefit formula is based on future compensation, the future compensation shall be used in calculating the employee's total projected benefit.

In the event a pension benefit formula does not indicate the manner in which a specific benefit relates to specific services performed by an employee, the benefit shall be assumed to be accumulated as follows:

If the Benefit Is Includable in Vested Benefits

The benefit shall be accumulated in proportion to the ratio of total completed years of service to date, to the total completed years of service as of the date the benefit becomes fully vested.

A vested benefit is a benefit that an employee has an irrevocable right to receive. For example, an employee is entitled to receive a vested benefit whether or not he or she continues to work for the employer.

If the Benefit Is Not Includable in Vested Benefits

The benefit shall be accumulated in proportion to the ratio of completed years of service to date to the total projected years of service. (An example of a benefit that is not includable in vested benefits is a death or disability benefit that is payable only if death or disability occurs during the employee's active service.)

Interest Cost Component

The two factors used to determine the actuarial present value of a future pension benefit are (a) the probability that the benefit will be paid to the employee (through the use of actuarial assumptions), and (b) the time value of money (through the use of discounts for interest cost). The probability that a pension benefit will be paid is based on actuarial assumptions such as employee mortality, employee turnover, and the date the benefits become vested. An employer's liability for a retirement fund of $56,520 that is due in ten years is not equal to a present liability of $56,520. At an 8% discount rate the $56,520 has a present value today of only $26,169. The $26,169 increases each year by the amount of the employer's interest cost of 8%, and in ten years grows to $56,520 if the 8% interest rate does not change.

FASB-87 requires an employer to recognize, as a component of net periodic pension cost, the interest cost on the projected benefit obligation. The interest cost is equal to the increase in the amount of the projected benefit obligation due to the passage of time.

> **OBSERVATION:** *FASB-87 specifies that the interest cost component of net periodic pension cost shall not be considered to be interest for the purposes of applying the provisions of FASB-34 (Capitalization of Interest Cost).*

Actual Return on Plan Assets Component

The actual return on plan assets is equal to the difference between the fair value of plan assets at the beginning and end of a period, adjusted for employer and employee contributions (if a contributory plan) and pension benefit payments made during the period. Fair value is the amount that a pension plan could reasonably expect to receive from a current sale of an investment between a willing buyer under no compulsion to buy and a willing seller under no compulsion to sell. Plan assets that are used in the operation of the pension plan (building, equipment, furniture, fixtures, etc.) are valued at cost less accumulated depreciation or amortization.

A return on plan assets decreases the employer's cost of providing pension benefits to its employees, while a loss increases pension cost. Net periodic pension income can result from a significantly high return on pension plan assets during a period.

FASB-87 requires an employer to recognize, as a component of net periodic pension cost, the actual return (or loss) on pension plan assets.

> **OBSERVATION:** *FASB-87 requires the employer to recognize the actual return on plan assets, which may include both realized and unrealized gains and losses. One of the paradoxes of GAAP is that FASB-87 requires an employer to recognize the unrealized gains and losses on the assets of the pension plan trustee (an entity separate from the employer), but traditional GAAP prohibits the employer from recognizing any unrealized gains and losses on the employer's own investments.*

Amortization of Unrecognized Prior Service Cost Component

Upon the initial adoption of a pension plan or through a plan amendment, employees are granted pension benefits for services performed in prior periods. These retroactive pension benefits are usually granted by the employer in the expectation that they will produce future economic benefits, such as reducing employee turnover, improving employee productivity, and minimizing the need for increasing employee compensation. The cost of pension benefits that are retroactively granted to employees for services performed in prior periods is referred to as *prior service cost.*

Under FASB-87, only a portion of the total amount of prior service cost arising in a period, including retroactive benefits that are granted to retirees, is included in net periodic pension cost. FASB-87 requires that the total prior service cost arising in a period from an adoption or amendment of a plan be amortized in equal amounts over the future service periods of each *active* employee who is expected to receive the retroactive benefits.

> **OBSERVATION:** *Since retirees are not expected to render future services, the cost of their retroactive benefits cannot be recognized over their remaining service periods (paragraph 170 of FASB-87). Although not clear, FASB-87 appears to require that the total prior service cost arising from a plan adoption or amendment, including the cost attributed to the benefits of retirees, shall be amortized in equal amounts over the future service periods of only the active employees who are expected to receive benefits. (See below for exceptions.)*

If substantially all of the participants of a pension plan are inactive, the prior service cost attributed to the benefits of the inactive participants shall be amortized over the remaining life expectancy of those participants.

> **OBSERVATION:** *The last sentence of paragraph 25 of FASB-87 addresses the method of amortizing that portion of the cost of ret-*

roactive plan amendments that affect benefits of inactive participants of a plan composed of substantially all inactive participants, but does not address the method of amortizing the portion of the cost of the same retroactive plan amendments that affect benefits of the active participants of the same plan. Two assumptions can be made. The first is that the cost of the active participants' benefits is not amortized at all, and thus is charged to net income of the period. The second assumption is that the cost of the active participants' benefits is amortized in the same manner as if the plan was not composed of substantially all inactive participants. In this event, the cost attributed to the retroactive benefits of the active participants of a plan composed of substantially all inactive participants is amortized in equal amounts over the future service periods of each active employee who is expected to receive the retroactive benefits.

FASB-87 permits the consistent use of an alternative amortization approach which more rapidly reduces the amount of unrecognized prior service cost. For example, straight-line amortization of unrecognized prior service cost over the average future service period of active employees who are expected to receive benefits under the plan is acceptable. If an alternative method is used to amortize unrecognized prior service cost, it must be disclosed in the financial statements.

The period in which an employer expects to realize the economic benefits from retroactive pension benefits that were previously granted may be shorter than the entire remaining future service period of all active employees. Under this circumstance, FASB-87 requires that a more rapid rate of amortization be applied to the remaining balance of the unrecognized prior service cost, to reflect the earlier realization of the employer's economic benefits and to properly allocate the cost to the periods benefited.

An amendment to a pension plan usually increases the cost of employees' pension benefits and increases the amount of the projected benefit obligation. However, a pension plan amendment may decrease the cost of employees' pension benefits, which results in a decrease in the amount of the projected benefit obligation. Any decrease resulting from a pension plan amendment shall be applied to reduce the balance of any existing unrecognized prior service cost and any excess shall be amortized on the same basis as increases in unrecognized prior service cost.

Gains and Losses Component

Gains and losses are changes in the amount of either the projected benefit obligation or pension plan assets, resulting from the differences between estimates or assumptions used and actual experience. Thus, a gain or loss can result from the difference between (a) the expected amount and actual amount of the projected benefit obligation at the end of a period, and/or (b) the expected amount and actual amount of the fair value of pension plan assets at the end of a period. Technically, both of these types of gains and losses are considered *actuarial gains and losses*. However, under FASB-87, a gain or loss resulting from a change in the projected benefit obligation is referred to as an "actuarial gain or loss," while a gain or loss resulting from a change in the fair value of pension plan assets is referred to as a "net asset gain or loss." For the purposes of FASB-87, the sources of these gains and losses are not separately distinguished, and they include amounts that have been realized as well as amounts that are unrealized.

Under FASB-87, the gains and losses component of net periodic pension cost consists of (a) the difference between the actual return on pension plan assets and the expected return on pension plan assets ("net asset gain or loss"), and (b) if required, amortization of any unrecognized gain or loss from previous periods.

> **OBSERVATION:** *The difference between the actual return on pension plan assets and the expected return on pension plan assets ("net asset gain or loss") is not recognized in the period in which it arises, but is included in the gains and losses component of net periodic pension cost only as an offset or supplement to the actual return on pension plan assets which is also a separate component of net periodic pension cost (paragraph 54, footnote 13, of FASB-87).*

As discussed in a previous section, the actual return on pension plan assets is equal to the difference between the fair value of pension plan assets at the beginning and end of a period, adjusted for any contributions and pension benefit payments made during that period. Fair value is the amount that a pension plan could reasonably expect to receive from a current sale of an investment between a willing buyer under no compulsion to buy and a willing seller under no compulsion to sell.

The expected return on pension plan assets during the period is computed by multiplying the *market-related value* of plan assets by the *expected long-term rate of return*. The expected long-term rate of return is an actuarial assumption of the expected long-term interest rate that will be earned on plan assets during the period. Under FASB-87, the current rate of return earned on plan assets and the rates of return expected to be available for plan investments should be considered in estimating the long-term rate of return on plan assets. The expected long-term rate of return on plan assets should reflect the average rate of earnings expected on plan investments.

To reduce the volatility of changes in the fair value of pension plan assets and the resulting effect on net periodic pension cost, FASB-87 requires the use of a market-related value for plan assets to compute the expected return on such assets during a period. Market-related value is used only to compute the expected return on pension plan assets for the period (expected return = market-related value multiplied by the expected long-term rate of return).

Under FASB-87, the market-related value of a plan asset can be either (a) the actual fair value of the pension plan asset or (b) a calculated value that recognizes, in a systematic and rational manner, the changes in the actual fair value of the pension plan asset over a period of not more than five years. Thus, in computing the market-related value of a pension plan asset, an enterprise may use actual fair value or a calculated value based on a five-year moving average of the changes in the actual fair value of the pension plan asset. In this event, the calculated market-related value would include only 20% of the total changes in the actual fair value of the pension plan asset that have occurred during the past five years. For example, if the actual fair value of a plan asset at the end of each of the last six years was $8,000, $10,000, $12,000, $14,000, $16,000, and $13,000, the net gain for the five years is $5,000 ($2,000 + $2,000 + $2,000 + $2,000 less $3,000 = $5,000). In this event, only 20% of the $5,000 gain ($1,000) is included in computing the calculated market-related value of the pension plan asset for the current year.

The only difference between the actual fair value of a pension plan asset and its calculated market-related value is the amount of net gain or loss from previous years that has not yet been recognized in the calculated market-related value.

Market-related value may be computed differently for each class of plan assets, but the method of computing market-related value must be consistently applied from year to year for each class of plan assets. For example, fair value may be used for bonds and other fixed income investments, and a calculated market-related value for stocks and other equities.

The following illustrates one method of computing market-related value.

For computing the market-related value of a particular class of plan assets as of the end of each period, an employer uses a calculated value that includes 20% of the gains and losses on the plan assets that have occurred over the last five years. The total market-related value of this particular class of plan assets at the beginning of calendar year 19X6 was $100,000. The total fair value of the plan assets was $120,000 at the beginning of 19X6 and $130,000 at the end of 19X6. Actual gains and losses for the past five years as of the beginning of 19X6 were: 19X1 $10,000; 19X2 $(8,000); 19X3 $12,000; 19X4 $10,000; 19X5 $(4,000); which resulted in a net gain of $20,000 for the five years. Employer's contributions to the plan for 19X6 are estimated at $2,000 and benefit payments expected to be paid from the plan in 19X6 are also $2,000. The expected long-term rate of return on plan assets for 19X6 is 10%. The computation of the estimated market-related value as of December 31, 19X6, for this particular class of plan assets is determined as follows:

Market-related value at the beginning of period	$100,000
Add:	
Expected return on assets for 19X6 (market-related value, multiplied by expected long-term rate of return ($100,000 × 10%))	10,000
20% of the net gain or loss for the last 5 years (20% × $20,000)	4,000
Employer's contribution	2,000
Benefit payments made from plan	(2,000)
Estimated market-related value, Dec. 31, 19X6 (Note)	$114,000

Note: The difference between the fair value ($130,000) and market-related value ($114,000) of plan assets at the end of 19X6 is $16,000. This difference represents the amount of net gain from previous years that has not yet been recognized in the market-related value of plan assets.

The expected return on plan assets is based on market-related values, which do not include all of the net asset gains and losses from previous years (unless market-related values are equal to fair values). Thus, net asset gains and losses may include both (a) gains and losses of previous years that have been included in market-related value and (b) gains and losses of previous years that have not yet been included in market-related value.

As mentioned above, FASB-87 does not require the recognition of any gains and losses as components of net periodic pension cost of the period in which they arise, except to the extent that the net asset gain or loss for the period offsets or supplements the actual return of pension plan assets for the period. However, in subsequent years, all gains and losses, except those which have not yet been recognized in the market-related values of pension plan assets are subject to certain minimum amortization provisions of FASB-87.

Under FASB-87, an unrecognized net gain or loss which, as of the *beginning* of the year, exceeds 10% of (a) the projected benefit obligation or (b) the market-related value of plan assets, whichever is greater, is subject to amortization. The amount of unrecognized net gain or loss in excess of 10% is amortized in equal amounts over the average remaining service period of active employees expected to receive benefits under the plan. However, if substantially all of a plan's participants are inactive, the amount of unrecognized net gain or loss in excess of 10% is amortized in equal amounts over the average remaining life expectancy of the inactive participants. Amortization must have the effect of reducing the beginning balance of an unrecognized net gain or loss.

In lieu of the minimum amortization of unrecognized gains and losses specified by FASB-87, an employer may use an alternative amortization method provided that the method (a) is systematic and applied consistently, (b) is applied to both gains and losses similarly, (c) reduces the unamortized balance by an amount greater than the amount that would result from the minimum amortization method provided by FASB-87, and (d) is disclosed in the financial statements.

The following is a comprehensive illustration of the gains and losses component of net periodic pension cost.

ABC Corporation elected to apply the provisions of FASB-87 as of January 1, 19X7, and also elected to compute all pension-related amounts as of the end of the period. The unrecognized net obligation existing at the date of the initial application of FASB-87 was $400, of which $40 was amortized in 19X7. The net asset (gain) or loss for 19X7, resulting from changes in actuarial assumptions, was a loss of $400, which was deferred as an unrecognized net loss for the year. The market-related value of pension plan assets at 1/1/X8 is $1,600 and the average remaining service life of active employees is 10 years.

The expected net periodic pension cost for 19X8 is $340, broken down as follows: service cost $200; interest cost $240 (10%); amortization of unrecognized net asset loss $20; amortization of unrec-

Pension Plans - Employers

ognized net obligation $40; less a 10% expected return on plan assets of $160 (expected return = market-related value of plan assets of $1,600 multiplied by the expected long-term rate of return of 10%). No contributions were made to the pension plan in 19X8.

	Actual 12/31/X7	Expected 12/31/X8	Actual 12/31/X8
(A) Projected benefit obligation	$(2,400)	$(2,840)	$(2,900)
(B) Fair value of plan assets	1,640	1,800	1,750
Funded status of plan	$ (760)	$(1,040)	$(1,150)
Unrecognized prior service cost	0	0	0
Unrecognized net (gain) or loss	400	380	490
Unrecognized net obligation existing at 1/1/X7	360	320	320
(Accrued)/prepaid pension cost	$ 0	$ 340	$ 340

(A) The difference between the actual projected benefit obligation for 19X7 and the expected projected benefit obligation for 19X8 is $440, which consists of the expected service cost of $200, and the expected interest cost of $240. However, the actual projected benefit for 19X8 increased $500 over the actual projected benefit for 19X7. The difference between the expected increase in the projected benefit obligation of $440 and the actual increase of $500 represents a $60 actuarial loss. The $60 loss occurred because the actuarial assumptions used were different from actual experience.

The $40 amortization of the unrecognized net obligation does not affect the projected benefit obligation because the full amount of the net obligation was recognized in the projected benefit obligation as of the date of the initial application of FASB-87.

(B) The difference between the actual fair value of plan assets for 19X7 and the expected fair value of plan assets for 19X8 is $160, which represents the 10% expected return on plan assets (market-related value of plan assets of $1,600 x 10%). However, the actual fair value of plan assets for 19X8 of $1,750 increased only $110 over the actual fair value of plan assets of $1,640 for 19X7. The difference between the expected increase in the fair value of plan assets of $160 and the actual increase of $110 represents a $50 net asset loss for the period. The loss occurred because the actual rate of return on pension plan assets was less than the expected rate of return.

Cost Components of Net Periodic Pension Cost for 19X8

FASB-87 requires the financial statement disclosure of the amount of net periodic pension cost for the period. The disclosure shall separately indicate the service cost component, the interest cost component, the actual return on plan assets for the period, and the net total of other components. The following illustrates this disclosure:

Service cost	$200
Interest cost	240
Actual return on plan assets	(110)
Net amortization and deferral (see below)	10
Net periodic pension cost for 19X8	$340

Net amortization and deferral computation:	
Amortization of unrecognized net obligation	$ 40
Amortization of unrecognized prior service cost	0
Amortization of unrecognized net (gain) or loss	20
Net asset gain or (loss) for 19X8–deferred (Note 1)	(50)
Net amortization and deferral	$ 10

Note 1: A net asset gain or loss is not recognized in the period in which it arises (paragraph 29 of FASB-87), but is included in the gains and losses component of net periodic pension cost (paragraph 34 of FASB-87), but only as an offset or supplement to the actual return on pension plan assets, which is a separate component of net periodic pension cost (paragraph 54, footnote 13, of FASB-87).

Computation of the Amortization of the Unrecognized Gain or Loss for 19X8

Unrecognized net (gain) or loss 1/1	$400
Add asset gain or subtract asset loss not yet recognized in market-related values at 1/1 (difference between fair value of plan assets ($1,640) and market-related value ($1,600))	40
Unrecognized net (gain) or loss subject to the minimum amortization provisions of FASB-87	$440
10% of the greater of the projected benefit obligation or market-related value at 1/1	240
Unrecognized net (gain) or loss subject to amortization	$200
Amortization for 19X8 (over the 10-year average remaining service life of active employees)	$ 20

Note: The unrecognized net (gain) or loss at 1/1 must be adjusted to exclude asset gains and losses not yet reflected in market-related values, because these gains and losses are not required to be amortized (paragraph 31 of FASB-87).

Note: The $60 loss that occurred in 19X8 as a result of the difference between the expected and actual projected benefit obligation for 19X8, and the $50 loss that occurred in 19X8 as a result of the difference between the expected and actual fair value of plan assets for 19X8, will become subject to the minimum amortization provisions of FASB-87 as of 1/1/X9. The computation of the amount of unrecognized net (gain) or loss as at January 1, 19X9, is as follows:

Unrecognized net asset (gain) or loss 1/1/X8		$400
Less: Amortization for 19X8		20
Unrecognized net asset (gain) or loss 12/31/X8		$380
Add: Actuarial net (gain) or loss for 19X8	$60	
Net asset (gain) or loss for 19X8	50	110
Unrecognized net (gain) or loss as of January 1, 19X9		$490

Amortization of the Unrecognized Net Obligation or Net Asset (as of the date of initial application of FASB-87)

The *funded status* of a pension plan is equal to the difference between the projected benefit obligation and the fair value of pension plan assets. The funded status indicates whether the employer has underfunded or overfunded the pension plan.

The unrecognized net obligation or net asset of a pension plan shall be determined by the employer as of the date of its financial statements of the beginning of the year in which FASB-87 is first applied, or, if used consistently from year to year, as of a date not more than three months prior to that date (see also section entitled "Transition and Effective Date"). The unrecognized net obligation or net asset is equal to the difference between the projected benefit obligation and fair value of pension plan assets, plus previously recognized unfunded accrued pension cost or less previously recognized prepaid pension cost. In the event there is no accrued or prepaid pension cost on the employer's statement of financial position as of the date of transition to FASB-87, the funded status of the pension plan and the unrecognized net obligation or net asset are exactly equal.

An unrecognized net obligation or net asset shall be amortized by the employer on a straight-line basis over the average remaining service period of employees expected to receive benefits under the plan, as of the date of initial application of FASB-87, except under the following circumstances:

(a) if the amortization period is less than 15 years, an employer may elect to use 15 years, or

(b) if the plan is composed of all or substantially all inactive participants, the employer shall use those participants' average remaining life expectancy as the amortization period

The above amortization method shall also be used to recognize, as of the date of the initial application of FASB-87, any unrecognized net obligation or (net asset) of a defined contribution pension plan.

Recognition of Liabilities and Assets

If an employer's total contribution to its pension plan for the period is not equal to the amount of net periodic pension cost required to be recognized under the provisions of FASB-87, the difference shall be recognized by the employer either as a liability or as an asset. A liability (unfunded accrued pension cost) shall be recognized if the amount of contribution is less than the amount of net periodic pension cost. If the amount of contribution is more than the amount of net periodic pension cost, an asset (prepaid pension cost) shall be recognized.

The *projected benefit obligation* is the actuarial present value of all employee benefits that are attributed by the pension benefit formula to employees' services performed prior to a specific date. The projected benefit obligation includes all pension benefits attributed by the pension benefit formula, whether the benefits are based on future employee compensation levels or not. The *accumulated benefit obligation* is the amount of the projected benefit obligation as of a specific date, reduced by the actuarial present value of any pension benefits attributed by the pension benefit formula that are based on future employee compensation levels, including the indirect effects of changes in future compensation levels, such as increases in the social security wage base. In lieu of estimates of future compensation levels, current and/or past compensation levels of employees should be used to calculate the accumulated benefit obligation.

An employer's *unfunded accumulated benefit obligation* is the amount of the accumulated benefit obligation that exceeds the amount of the fair value of plan assets as of a specific date. Under FASB-87, an additional minimum liability must be recognized in the employer's statement of financial position if an unfunded accumulated benefit obligation exists and (a) an asset has been recognized as prepaid pension cost, (b) a liability has been recognized as unfunded accrued pension cost in an amount that is less than the amount of the existing unfunded accumulated benefit obligation, or (c) no accrued or prepaid pension cost has been recognized. If an asset has been recognized as prepaid pension cost, the additional minimum liability is the amount of the existing unfunded accumulated benefit obligation plus the amount of the prepaid pension cost. If a liability has been recognized as unfunded accrued pension cost in an amount that is less than the amount of the existing unfunded accumulated benefit obligation, the additional minimum liability is the amount of the existing unfunded accumulated benefit obligation reduced by the amount of the unfunded accrued pension cost. If no accrued or prepaid pension cost has been recognized, the additional minimum liability is the amount of the existing unfunded accumulated benefit obligation.

If an additional minimum liability is required to be recognized, an intangible asset in the same amount as the additional minimum liability shall also be recognized, but the amount of the intangible asset shall not exceed the total amount of any existing unrecognized prior service cost and any unrecognized net obligation. In the event that the intangible asset exceeds the total existing unrecognized prior service cost and unrecognized net obligation, the excess shall be reported as a separate component of stockholders' equity (a reduction of equity), net of related tax benefits.

Unless more current amounts are available, the amount of additional minimum liability reported in interim financial statements shall be the same amount as reported by the employer in its previous year-end statement of financial position, adjusted for subsequent accruals and contributions.

The calculation of the additional minimum liability is reflected in the following illustration.

Calculation of the Additional Minimum Liability

	As of End of Period		
	Year 1	Year 2	Year 3
Accumulated benefit obligation	$(3,762)	$(4,884)	$(4,848)
Fair value of plan assets	3,495	4,515	4,866
(Unfunded) or overfunded accumulated benefit obligation	$ (267)	$ (369)	$ 18
Projected benefit obligation	$(5,637)	$(7,326)	$(7,272)
Fair value of plan assets	3,495	4,515	4,866
Funded status of plan	$(2,142)	$(2,811)	$(2,406)
Unrecognized prior service cost	2,145	3,942	3,516
Unrecognized net (gain) or loss	(753)	(1,671)	(1,380)
Unrecognized net obligation at date of initial application of FASB-87	840	780	720
(Accrued) or prepaid pension cost	$ 90	$ 240	$ 450

(Accrued) or prepaid pension cost at beginning of period	$ 0	$ 90	$ 240
Less: Net periodic pension cost	912	1,005	1,191
Add: Contributions paid	1,002	1,155	1,401
(Accrued) or prepaid pension cost at end of period	$ 90	$ 240	$ 450
(Unfunded) or overfunded accumulated benefit obligation (computed above)	$ (267)	$ (369)	$ 18
Required adjustment for additional minimum liability	(357)	(252)	609
Intangible asset	357	252	(609)
Cumulative balance of the additional minimum liability	(357)	(609)	0

Note: The adjustment necessary to record the additional minimum liability is equal to the unfunded accumulated benefit obligation, plus the amount of any prepaid pension cost or minus the amount of any accrued pension cost (at the end of the period), less the previous balance of the additional minimum liability from the preceding year. Thus the adjustment in year 1 is $357, which is equal to the unfunded accumulated benefit obligation of $267, plus the prepaid pension cost of $90 at the end of the period (there was no previous balance of the additional minimum liability from the preceding year). The adjustment for year 2 is $252, which is equal to the unfunded accumulated benefit obligation of $369, plus the amount of prepaid pension cost of $240 at the end of the period, less the preceding year's balance of the additional minimum liability of $357.

In the third year, the balance of the unfunded accumulated benefit obligation was an $18 debit, which results in no unfunded accumulated benefit obligation. Thus, the adjustment consisted of simply eliminating the preceding year's balance of $609.

Note: The additional minimum liability that was required in all three years did not exceed the unrecognized prior service cost plus the unrecognized net obligation. Thus, no portion of the required additional minimum liability had to be reported as a separate component of stockholders' equity.

Measurement of Plan Assets

All pension plan assets that are held as investments to provide pension benefits shall be measured at their fair values as of the date of the financial statements or, if used consistently from year to year, as of a date not more than three months prior to that date (paragraph 49 of FASB-87). Fair value is the amount that a pension plan could reasonably expect to receive for a current sale of an investment between a willing buyer under no compulsion to buy and a willing seller under no compulsion to sell. If an active market exists for a plan investment, fair value shall be determined by the market price. If an active market does not exist for a particular plan investment, selling prices for similar investments, if available, should be appropriately considered. If no active market exists, an estimate of the fair value of the plan investment may be based on its projected cash flow, provided that appropriate consideration is given to current discount rates and the investment risk involved.

Pension plan assets that are used in the actual operation of a plan should be valued at amortized cost (paragraph 51 of FASB-87). Thus, buildings, leasehold improvements, furniture, equipment and fixtures that are used in the everyday operation of a pension plan should be valued at historical cost less accumulated depreciation or amortization.

Measurement Dates

For the purposes of FASB-87, plan assets and obligations shall be determined either (a) as of the date of the financial statements or (b) if used consistently from year to year, as of a date not more than three months prior to the date of the financial statements.

Unless more current amounts are available, the amount of additional minimum liability reported in interim financial statements shall be the same amount as reported by the employer in its previous year-end statement of financial position, adjusted for subsequent accruals and contributions.

The same assumptions used to calculate the previous year-end net periodic pension cost shall be used to calculate the net periodic pension cost in subsequent interim and annual financial statements, unless more current valuations of plan assets and obligations are available or a significant event has occurred, such as a plan amendment which would usually require new valuations.

Financial Statement Disclosure

The following financial statement disclosures shall be made by an employer who sponsors a defined benefit pension plan:

- A full description of the pension plan, including the employee groups covered, type of benefit formula, funding policy, types of assets held and significant nonbenefit liabilities (if any), and the nature and effect of significant matters affecting comparability of information for all periods presented.
- The amount of net periodic pension cost for the period detailing the separate amounts for the (a) service cost component, (b) interest cost component, (c) actual return on plan assets for the period, and (d) net total of other components.
- A schedule reconciling the funded status of the plan with amounts reported in the employer's statement of financial position, showing separately:
    (a) The fair value of plan assets.
    (b) The projected benefit obligation, separately identifying the accumulated benefit obligation and vested benefit obligation.
    (c) The amount of unrecognized prior service cost.
    (d) The amount of unrecognized net gain or loss, including asset gains and losses not yet reflected in market-related values.
    (e) The amount of any remaining unrecognized net obligation or net asset existing at the date of the initial application of FASB-87.
    (f) The amount of additional minimum liability equal to either (i) the unfunded accumulated benefit obligation plus any

prepaid pension cost, (ii) the unfunded accumulated benefit obligation reduced by any unfunded accrued pension cost, or (iii) the amount of the unfunded accumulated benefit obligation.

(g) The amount of the net pension asset or liability that has been recognized in the employer's statement of financial position. This amount must be equal to the total of items (a) through (f). For an illustration of a reconciliation schedule, see the Capsule Analysis of FASB-87, above.

- The weighted-average assumed discount rate and, if applicable, the rate of compensation increase used in determining the projected benefit obligation, and the weighted-average expected long-term rate of return on pension plan assets.
- If applicable, the amounts and types of securities of the employer and/or related parties that are included in plan assets, and the approximate amount of annual benefits of employees and retirees covered by annuity contracts issued by the employer and related parties. Also, if applicable, the alternative amortization method used for unrecognized prior service cost and the alternative amortization method used to reflect the substantive commitment of an employer to pay more employee benefits than its existing pension benefit formula indicates.

Employers with Two or More Pension Plans

If an employer sponsors more than one defined benefit pension plan, the provisions of FASB-87 shall be applied separately to each plan. An employer shall not apply the assets of one plan to reduce or eliminate the unfunded accrued pension cost and/or minimum additional liability of another plan, unless the employer clearly has the right to do so. An excess of plan assets over the accumulated benefit obligation or prepaid pension cost of one plan cannot be applied to reduce or eliminate a liability of another plan which is required to be recognized by FASB-87.

All of the disclosures required by FASB-87 for defined benefit pension plans of a single employer may be combined, or combined in particular groups to provide the most useful information, except for plans with assets that have a net pension plan liability or a net pension plan asset, which must be separately disclosed. Unless plans are based on similar economic assumptions, the required disclosures for plans outside the U.S. shall not be combined with U.S. plans.

Annuity Contracts

All or part of an employer's obligation to provide pension plan benefits to individuals may be effectively transferred to an insurance company by the purchase of annuity contracts. An annuity contract is an irrevocable agreement in which an insurance company unconditionally agrees to provide specific periodic payments, or a lump-sum payment to another party, in return for a specified premium. Thus, by use of an annuity contract, an employer can effectively transfer to an insurance company its legal obligation to provide specific employee pension plan benefits. For the purposes of FASB-87, an annuity contract is not considered an annuity contract if the insurance company is a captive insurer or there is reasonable doubt that the insurance company will meet its obligation. A captive insurer is one that does business primarily with the employer and its related parties.

An annuity contract may be participating or nonparticipating. In a participating annuity contract, the insurance company's investing activities with the funds received for the annuity contract are generally shared, in the form of dividends, with the purchaser (the employer or the pension fund). An annuity contract is not considered an annuity contract, for the purposes of FASB-87, unless all the risks and rewards associated with the assets and obligations assumed by the insurance company are actually transferred to the insurance company by the employer.

The cost incurred for currently earned benefits under an annuity contract shall be the cost of those benefits, except for the cost of participating rights of participating annuity contracts, which must be accounted for separately (see below). Thus, the service cost component of net periodic pension cost for the current period is the cost incurred for nonparticipating annuity contracts that cover all currently earned benefits. Pension benefits not covered by annuity contracts shall be accounted for in accordance with the provisions of FASB-87 that address accounting for the cost of pension benefits not covered by annuity contracts.

The projected benefit obligation and the accumulated benefit obligation shall not include the cost of benefits covered by annuity contracts. Except for the cost of participation rights (see below), pension plan assets shall not include the cost of any annuity contracts.

The difference in cost between a nonparticipating annuity contract and a participating annuity contract is usually attributable to the cost of the participation right. The cost of a participation right, at the date of its purchase, is recognized as a pension plan asset. In subsequent periods, a participation right is included in plan assets at its fair value, if fair value is reasonably determinable. If fair value is not reasonably determinable, a participation right is included in plan assets at its amortized cost and systematically amortized over the expected dividend period stated in the contract. In this event, amortized cost may not exceed the net realizable value of the participation right.

Other contracts with insurance companies The purchase of insurance contracts that are, in substance, annuity contracts shall be accounted for in accordance with the provisions of FASB-87 (see previous section). The purchase of other types of insurance contracts shall be accounted for as pension plan assets and reported at fair value. The best evidence of fair value for some insurance contracts may be their contract values. Under FASB-87, the cash surrender value or conversion value of an insurance contract is presumed to be its fair value.

Defined Contribution Pension Plans

A defined contribution pension plan provides for employer contributions that are defined in the plan, but does not contain any provision for defined pension benefits for employees. Thus, a defined contribution pension plan does not contain a "defined benefit pension formula." However, based on the amount of the employer's defined contributions, pension benefits are provided in return for services performed by employees.

Under FASB-87, a defined contribution pension plan provides for individual accounts for each plan participant and contains the terms that specify how contributions are determined for each participant's individual account. Each periodic employer contribution is allocated to each participant's individual account in accordance with the terms of the plan, and pension benefits are based solely on the amount available in each participant's account at the time of his or her retirement. The amount available in each participant's account at the time of his or her retirement is the total of the amounts contributed by the employer, plus the returns earned on investments of those contributions, and forfeitures of other participants' benefits that have been allocated to the participant's account.

Under FASB-87, the net periodic pension cost of a defined contribution pension plan is the amount of contributions in a period which are made to the individual accounts of participants who performed services during that same period. Contributions for periods after an individual retires or terminates shall be estimated and accrued during periods in which the individual performs services.

The amount of the unrecognized net obligation or net asset of a defined contribution pension plan, at the date of initial application of FASB-87, shall be amortized on a straight-line basis over the average remaining service period of employees expected to receive benefits under the plan, except (a) if the amortization period is less than 15 years, the employer may elect to use 15 years, and (b) if the plan is composed of all or substantially all inactive participants, the employer shall use those participants' average remaining life expectancy as the amortization period.

> **OBSERVATION:** *The above amortization method is the same as that used to amortize the unrecognized net obligation or net asset of a defined benefit pension plan at the date of the initial application of FASB-87. Although not specified by FASB-87, this seems to imply that an employer who sponsors a defined contribution pension plan is also required to record an unrecognized net obligation or net asset at the date of the initial application of FASB-87.*

An employer who sponsors one or more defined contribution pension plans shall disclose the following information separately from its defined benefit pension plan disclosures:

- A description of the plan(s) including employee groups covered, the basis for determining contributions, and the nature and effect of significant matters affecting comparability of information for all periods presented
- The amount of pension cost recognized during the period

Frequently, defined contribution pension plans provide for some method of determining benefits for employees, as may be the case with many "target benefit" plans. If, in substance, a plan does provide defined benefits for employees, it shall be accounted for as a defined benefit pension plan in accordance with the appropriate provisions of FASB-87.

For the purposes of FASB-87, any plan that is not a defined contribution pension plan is considered a defined benefit pension plan (see definition of a defined benefit pension plan in the Glossary of Appendix D of FASB-87).

Multiemployer Plans

A multiemployer plan is a pension plan to which two or more unrelated employers make contributions, usually pursuant to one or more collective-bargaining agreements. In a multiemployer pension plan, assets contributed by one employer are not segregated in separate accounts or restricted to provide benefits only to employees of that employer. Thus, assets contributed by one employer in a multiemployer plan may be used to provide benefits to employees of other participating employers.

The net periodic pension cost of an employer participating in a multiemployer plan is the amount of the required contribution for the period. An employer participating in a multiemployer plan shall also recognize as a liability any of its contributions that are due and unpaid.

> **OBSERVATION:** *A withdrawal from a multiemployer pension plan may result in a loss contingency if the withdrawing employer has a potential liability to the plan for a portion of its unfunded benefit obligation. Under FASB-87, if it is* probable *or* reasonably possible *that the loss contingency will develop into an actual loss, the withdrawing employer shall account for the loss contingency in accordance with the provisions of FASB-5 (Contingencies).*

An employer participating in a multiemployer plan shall disclose the following information separately from disclosures for a single-employer plan:

- A description of the multiemployer plan(s) including employee groups covered, the types of benefits provided (defined benefit or defined contribution), and the nature and effect of significant matters affecting comparability of information for all periods presented
- The amount of pension cost recognized during the period

> **OBSERVATION:** *FASB Technical Bulletin 81-3 (FASB:TB 81-3) provides guidance on the accounting implications of the Multiemployer Pension Plan Amendments Act of 1980 (MPPAA). FASB:TB 81-3 makes reference to APB-8, FASB-36, and FASB Interpretation 3, all of which have been superseded by FASB-87. Furthermore, FASB:TB 81-3 suggests that employers participating in multiemployer plans that are deemed to be defined benefit plans subject to the MPPAA should look to FASB Interpretation-3 for guidance.*
> *It appears that FASB:TB 81-3 should have also been superseded by FASB-87, but was not. Although FASB:TB 81-3 remains technically effective, it obviously should not be relied upon.*

Multiple-employer plans Some pension plans to which two or more unrelated employers contribute are not multiemployer plans, but are groups of single-employer plans combined to allow participating employers to pool assets for investment purposes and to reduce the cost of plan administration. Under FASB-87, multiple-employer plans are considered single-employer plans and each employer's accounting shall be based on its respective interest in the plan.

Non-U.S. Pension Plans

FASB-87 does not make any special provision for non-U.S. pension plans, except for a different effective date. FASB-87 is effective for employers who have non-U.S. pension plans for fiscal years beginning on or after December 16, 1988.

In some foreign countries it is customary or required for an employer to provide benefits for employees in the event of a voluntary or involuntary severance of employment. In this event, if the substance of the arrangement is a pension plan, it is subject to the provisions of FASB-87 (for example, benefits are paid for substantially all terminations).

Business Combinations

The total cost of a business combination accounted for by the purchase method must be allocated to the individual assets acquired and liabilities assumed (APB-16). Each identifiable asset is assigned a cost equal to its fair value. Liabilities are accounted for at the present value of the amount that will eventually be paid and, if certain criteria are met, appropriate consideration should be given to contingent assets and liabilities (FASB-38).

When a single-employer defined benefit pension plan is acquired as part of a business combination accounted for by the purchase method, an excess of the projected benefit obligation over the plan assets shall be recognized as a liability and an excess of plan assets over the projected benefit obligation shall be recognized as an asset. The recognition of a new liability or new asset by the purchaser, at the date of a business combination accounted for by the purchase method, results in the elimination of any (a) previously existing unrecognized net gain or loss, (b) unrecognized prior service cost, and (c) unrecognized net obligation or net asset that existed at the date of initial application of FASB-87.

In subsequent periods, the differences between the purchaser's net pension cost and contributions will reduce the new liability or new asset recognized at the date of combination to the extent that the previously unrecognized net gain or loss, unrecognized prior service cost, or unrecognized net obligation are considered in determining the amounts of contributions to the plan. In addition, the effects of an expected plan termination or curtailment shall be considered by the purchaser in calculating the amount of the projected benefit obligation at the date of a business combination accounted for by the purchase method.

> **OBSERVATION:** FASB-87 amends APB-16, to provide that the assets and liabilities of a pension plan acquired by the purchase method of accounting shall no longer be accounted for in accordance with paragraph 88h of APB-16 (Business Combinations), but shall be accounted for in accordance with paragraph 74 of FASB-87, which is discussed above.

Transition and Effective Date

For defined benefit pension plans consisting of 100 or fewer participants that are sponsored by employers that are *nonpublic enterprises* (see definition below), and for pension plans located outside the United States, FASB-87 is effective for fiscal years beginning on or after December 16, 1988. For all other pension plans, FASB-87 is effective for fiscal years beginning on or after December 16, 1986, except for paragraphs 36, 37, and 38, which are effective for fiscal years beginning on or after December 16, 1988. Paragraphs 36, 37, and 38 require the recognition of an additional minimum liability in the employer's statement of financial position, if the unfunded accumulated benefit obligation exceeds the fair value of plan assets.

Retroactive application of the provisions of FASB-87 to previously issued annual financial statements is not permitted. However, if FASB-87 is initially applied in other than the first interim period of a fiscal year, previously issued interim financial statements of the same fiscal year shall be restated.

Definition of nonpublic enterprise FASB-87 defines a nonpublic enterprise as, "An enterprise other than one (a) whose debt or equity securities are traded in a public market, either on a stock exchange or in the over-the-counter market (including securities quoted only locally or regionally), or (b) whose financial statements are filed with a regulatory agency in preparation for the sale of any class of securities."

Recognition of unrecognized net obligation or net asset The unrecognized net obligation or net asset of a pension plan shall be determined by the employer as of the date of its financial statements of the beginning of the year in which FASB-87 is first applied, or, if used consistently from year to year, as of a date not more than three months prior to that date. The unrecognized net obligation or net asset is equal to the difference between the projected benefit obligation and fair value of pension plan assets, plus previously recognized unfunded accrued pension cost or less previously recognized prepaid pension cost.

An unrecognized net obligation or net asset shall be amortized by the employer on a straight-line basis over the average remaining service period of employees expected to receive benefits under the plan, as of the date of initial application of FASB-87, except under the following circumstances:

(a) if the amortization period is less than 15 years, an employer may elect to use 15 years, or
(b) if the plan is composed of all or substantially all inactive participants, the employer shall use those participants' average remaining life expectancy as the amortization period

> **OBSERVATION:** *Recognition and amortization of the unrecognized net obligation or net asset is also discussed in the section entitled "Amortization of Unrecognized Net Obligation or Net Asset (as of the date of the initial application of FASB-87)."*

Change In Accounting Principle

After FASB-87 (Employers' Accounting for Pensions) was issued, the following article appeared in *The CPA Letter,* which is published by the AICPA:

> "Many companies will have a change in accounting principle as a result of implementing FASB Statement no. 87, *Employers' Accounting for Pensions.* SAS no. 1, *Consistency of Application of Generally Accepted Accounting Principles,* section 420, requires the auditor's opinion to be modified for consistency when there is a change in an accounting principle having a material effect on the financial statements.
> According to the AICPA's auditing standards division, if the change is made on a piecemeal basis as permitted by FASB Statement no. 87 and each change is material, the auditor should modify his report as to consistency for each change. If the change does not have a material effect in the

year it is made but may be expected to have such an effect in the future, no consistency modification is required in the auditor's report, but disclosure of the change, nevertheless should be made in the notes to the financial statements."

The above information should be verified before an enterprise reports a material change in accounting principle as a result of implementing FASB-87 on a piecemeal basis.

PENSION PLANS - SETTLEMENTS AND CURTAILMENTS

Background

FASB-88 establishes accounting and reporting standards for settlements and curtailments of defined benefit pension plans and for termination benefits that are offered to employees. FASB-88 supersedes FASB-74 (Accounting for Special Termination Benefits Paid to Employees).

> **OBSERVATION:** FASB-88 is effective for events occurring during and after the fiscal year in which FASB-87 (Employers' Accounting for Pensions) is first applied. FASB-87 is generally effective for fiscal years beginning on or after December 16, 1986, except for pension plans of nonpublic enterprises consisting of 100 or fewer participants and plans located outside of the United States.

Overview

In connection with the operation of a defined benefit pension plan, FASB-87 (Employers' Accounting for Pensions) provides for the delayed recognition of actuarial gains and losses, prior service costs, and the net obligation or asset that arises at the date of the initial application of FASB-87. As a result, at any given date, an employer's pension plan records may reflect a balance of an (a) unrecognized net gain or loss, (b) unrecognized prior service cost, and/or (c) unrecognized net obligation or net asset. Part or all of these unrecognized balances may be recognized in a settlement or curtailment of a pension plan.

In a settlement of a defined benefit pension plan, the employer or the pension plan is irrevocably released from its primary responsibility for all or part of its pension plan obligation and all significant risks relating to the settlement are eliminated. For example, through the purchase of nonparticipating annuity contracts or cash payments to some or all of the plan participants in exchange for their pension benefits, an employer may be irrevocably released from the pension plan obligation related to the pension benefits involved in the exchange. After the settlement of a pension plan, an employer may continue to provide pension benefits in the same pension plan or a new plan.

The maximum gain or loss recognized at the date of a plan settlement is the total of the unamortized balance of any (a) unrecognized net gain or loss arising after the date of the initial application of FASB-87 and/or (b) unrecognized *net asset* that arose at the date of the initial application of FASB-87. The amount of gain or loss recognized depends on the percentage decrease or increase in the projected benefit obligation resulting from the plan settlement. If the projected benefit obligation is reduced by 40%, only 40% of the gain or loss is recognized. On the other hand, if the projected benefit obligation is completely discharged, 100% of the gain or loss on the plan settlement is recognized.

In a curtailment of a defined benefit pension plan some of the future pension benefits for present employees are significantly reduced, generally resulting in a net decrease (gain) or increase (loss) in the projected benefit obligation. For example, if employees are terminated as a result of a plan curtailment, some or all of their pension benefits based on future compensation levels may cease to be an obligation of the employer or pension plan. In this event, the projected benefit obligation is decreased (a gain) by the amount of the pension benefits that are no longer an obligation of the plan. On the other hand, if terminated employees who are eligible for subsidized early retirement benefits accept the benefits at a date earlier than expected, there is an increase (loss) in the projected benefit obligation. Gain or loss on a plan curtailment is based on the net decrease (gain) or increase (loss) in the projected benefit obligation.

An employer may have to recognize an additional loss that is not included in the gain or loss on a plan curtailment, but is recognized as part of the total effects of a plan curtailment. This loss is equal to the amount of decrease in the unrecognized prior service cost of the pension benefits that are reduced by the plan curtailment. A separate loss computation is necessary for the unrecognized prior service cost of each plan amendment.

The pension benefits that are reduced or eliminated in a plan curtailment may have been granted to some or all of the employees who were working for the employer as of the date of the initial application of FASB-87. For this reason, any unrecognized *net obligation* that arose at the date of the initial application of FASB-87 and that remains unamortized at the date of the plan curtailment is also treated as a separate unrecognized prior service cost.

A pension plan settlement and a pension plan curtailment may occur simultaneously or separately. If the expected years of future service for some employees are reduced but the pension plan continues in existence, a curtailment has occurred but not a settlement. If an employer settles all or a portion of its pension obligation and continues to provide defined benefits to employees for future services, either in the same plan or in a successor plan, a settlement has occurred, but not a curtailment. If an employer terminates its defined benefit pension plan without replacing it with another defined benefit pension plan, and settles its present pension plan obligation in full, a curtailment and settlement has occurred. Under these circumstances, it makes no difference whether or not some or all of the employees continue to work for the employer.

Termination benefits are frequently offered by employers as part of an overall plan to reduce employment levels, to increase productivity, or generally to decrease payroll costs. To induce certain groups of employees to terminate employment, many employers offer attractive termination benefits. This is particularly true for those employees who are close to, or have reached, the early retirement age specified in the employer's existing pension plan. Termination benefits may consist of periodic future payments, lump-sum payments, or a combination of both. The payment of termination benefits may be made from a new or existing employee benefit plan, from the employer's existing assets, or from a combination of these sources.

Under FASB-88, termination benefits are classified either as *special* or *contractual*. Special termination benefits are those that are offered to employees for a short period of time in connection with their termination of employment. Contractual termination benefits are those that are required by the terms of an existing plan or agreement and are provided only on the occurrence of a specified event, such as early retirement or the closing of a facility.

FASB-88 requires that the cost of termination benefits be recognized by an employer as a loss and a corresponding liability. The recognition date depends on whether the benefits are special or contractual.

Updating Pension Plan Records

Before applying the provisions of FASB-88, an employer should bring its defined benefit pension plan records up to date, preferably as of the day before the curtailment and/or settlement of the plan. The effects of the pending curtailment and/or settlement must be ignored in the updating process and all computations including the net periodic pension cost accrual must be consistent with prior periods. The updating process includes the measurement of the fair value of pension plan assets and the computation of the net periodic pension cost accrual.

> **OBSERVATION:** *Neither FASB-87 nor FASB-88 provide any guidance on the appropriate valuation of assets employed in the*

operation of a pension plan in the event such assets are disposed of as part of a curtailment and/or settlement of a plan. Under this circumstance, it appears appropriate to measure these assets at their fair value in spite of the fact that paragraph 51 of FASB-87 requires that such assets be measured, for all purposes, at their cost less accumulated depreciation or amortization.

Settlements of Defined Benefit Pension Plans

Under FASB-88, a settlement of a defined benefit pension plan is an irrevocable transaction that (a) releases the employer or the pension plan from its primary responsibility for the payment of all or a portion of the pension plan obligation and (b) eliminates all of the significant risks associated with the assets and obligations used to effectuate the settlement. A settlement of a defined benefit pension plan does not require that the plan be completely terminated (paragraph 26 of FASB-88).

All or a part of an employer's obligation to provide pension plan benefits to individuals may be effectively transferred to an insurance company by the purchase of annuity contracts. An annuity contract is an irrevocable agreement in which an insurance company unconditionally agrees to provide specific periodic payments or a lump-sum payment to another party in return for a specified premium. For the purposes of FASB-87 and FASB-88, an annuity contract is not considered an annuity contract if the insurance company is a *captive insurer* or there is reasonable doubt that the insurance company will meet its obligation. A captive insurer is one that does business primarily with the employer and its related parties.

An annuity contract may be participating or nonparticipating. In a participating annuity contract the insurance company's investing activities with the funds received for the premium of the annuity contract are generally shared, in the form of dividends, with the purchaser of the contract (the employer or the pension fund). An annuity contract is not considered an annuity contract unless all the risks and rewards associated with the assets and obligations assumed by the insurance company are actually transferred to the insurance company by the employer.

Gain or loss on a plan settlement should be based on pension plan records that have been updated as of the day before the settlement (see above section entitled Updating Pension Plan Records). Under FASB-88, the maximum gain or loss on a settlement of a defined benefit pension plan is equal to the total balance of any (a) unrecognized net gain or loss arising after the date of the initial application of FASB-87 that remains unamortized at the date of the plan settlement, and (b) unrecognized *net asset* that arose at the date of the initial application of FASB-87 that remains unamortized at the date of the plan settlement.

If the total pension plan obligation is settled by the employer, the maximum gain or loss is recognized. If part of the pension benefit obligation is settled, the employer must recognize a pro rata portion of the maximum gain or loss, equal to the percentage reduction in the projected benefit obligation, unless the transaction qualifies as a "small settlement" (discussed below). Thus, if 40% of the pension plan obligation is settled, 40% of the maximum gain or loss on the settlement is recognized, and if 100% of the pension benefit obligation is settled, 100% of the maximum gain or loss is recognized.

If the employer purchases a participating annuity contract to settle a pension obligation, the cost of the contract must be allocated between the cost of the pure annuity feature and the cost of the participation right. The amount of cost allocated to the participation rights reduces gain (but not loss) that would otherwise be recognized on a plan settlement. However, the participation rights do not affect the determination of the amount of loss that is recognized on a plan settlement.

Reporting gain or loss on a plan settlement Gain or loss on a plan settlement is reported as an ordinary gain or loss, unless it meets the criteria of an extraordinary item as specified in APB-30 (paragraph 48 of FASB-88).

> **OBSERVATION:** *SEC Staff Accounting Bulletin No. 52 requires that a gain on the termination of a defined benefit pension plan be reported as an extraordinary item (see discussion below entitled "Conflict with SEC Staff Accounting Bulletin No. 52").*

Small settlement To qualify as a small settlement, the total gain or loss on the plan settlement cannot exceed the sum of the service cost and interest cost components of the net periodic pension cost for the plan for the current year. The gain or loss on a small settlement may be, but is not required to be, reported by the employer; however, the accounting policy adopted for small settlements must be consistently applied from year to year.

> **OBSERVATION:** *If a settlement qualifies as a small settlement, the employer has absolute discretion to decide whether or not to recognize gain or loss, provided only that the accounting policy is followed consistently from year to year.*

Curtailment of Defined Benefit Pension Plans

Under FASB-88, a curtailment of a defined benefit pension plan results from an event in which (a) the expected years of future service arising from a prior plan amendment are *significantly* reduced for present employees who are entitled to receive pension benefits from that prior plan amendment or (b) the accrual of defined pension benefits is eliminated for some or all of the future services of a *significant* number of employees.

The total effects of a plan curtailment consist of (1) the decrease (loss) in the unamortized balance of unrecognized prior service cost (or unrecognized *net obligation*) that results from the significant reduction of the expected years of future service for present employees [see (a) above] and (2) the net decrease (gain) or increase (loss) in the projected benefit obligation that results from the elimination of the accrual of defined pension benefits for some or all of the future services of a significant number of employees [see (b) above]. Each of these two components that comprise the total effects of a plan curtailment are discussed separately below.

Decrease (loss) in unrecognized prior service cost Retroactive pension benefits are sometimes granted by an employer, upon adoption of a plan or through a plan amendment, based on employees' services in prior periods. The costs of these retroactive pension benefits are referred to as prior service costs. Retroactive pension benefits are granted by an employer in expectation of future economic benefits, such as reduced employee turnover and higher productivity. FASB-87 requires that the prior service cost relating to a specific plan amendment be amortized in equal amounts over the expected years of future service of each active employee who is expected to receive benefits from the plan amendment. Periodic amortization for each expected year of future service is calculated by dividing the total expected years of future service into the total amount of unrecognized prior service cost. The total amount of unrecognized prior service cost represents the total cost of pension benefits that have been granted under the provisions of the plan amendment. If the expected years of future service are reduced as a result of a plan curtailment, the related unrecognized prior service cost must also be reduced and recognized as a loss by the employer.

The expected years of future service for present employees may be significantly reduced by the termination or suspension of pension benefits for future services so that employees are no longer allowed to earn additional benefits. In addition, the termination of some of the present employees earlier than expected may also result in a significant reduction in their total expected years of future service. As a result of the significant reduction in the expected years of future service, a loss is incurred by the employer, in the amount of the decrease in the balance of the related unamortized unrecognized prior service cost at the date of the plan curtailment. To compute the loss, the percentage reduction in the total remaining expected years of future service at the date of the plan curtailment must first be calculated (number of expected years of future service that are reduced, divided by, the total number of remaining expected years of future service before reduction). To determine the amount of the loss, the balance of the related unamortized unrecognized prior service cost at the date of the plan curtailment is multiplied by the percentage reduction in the total number of expected years of future service. For example, if the total remaining expected years of future service at the date of the plan curtailment is 1,000, and the number of years of future service that is reduced is 400, the percentage reduction is 40%. The balance of the related unamortized unrecognized prior service cost at the date of the plan curtailment is reduced by 40%, which represents the loss that the employer must recognize as part of the total effects of the plan curtailment.

For the purposes of FASB-88, the balance of any unrecognized *net obligation* that arose at the date of the initial application of FASB-87, which remains unamortized at the date of a subsequent plan curtailment, is also treated as a separate unrecognized prior service cost. Thus, if the expected years of future service are significantly reduced for those employees employed at the date of the initial application of FASB-87, a separate loss must be calculated and recognized by the employer. In this event, the loss is equal to the amount by which the unamortized unrecognized *net obligation* is reduced when multiplied by the percentage reduction resulting from the expected years of future service that are significantly reduced for those employees who were employed at the date of the initial application of FASB-87.

The total of all decreases (losses) in unamortized balances of unrecognized prior service costs and/or unrecognized *net obligation* is included in the total effects of a plan curtailment (illustration 3A of Appendix B of FASB-88), but is not included in the gain or loss on the plan curtailment (paragraph 40 of FASB-88).

The following are the steps necessary to compute each decrease (loss) in the balance of the unamortized unrecognized prior service cost at the date of a plan curtailment arising from a significant reduction in the expected years of employees' future service:

Step 1. Compute the percentage reduction in the total remaining expected years of future service, at the date of the plan curtailment, resulting from the expected years of future service that are significantly reduced. For example, if the expected years of future service that are reduced are 600 and the total remaining expected years of future service at the date of the plan curtailment are 1,000, the percentage reduction is 60%.

Step 2. Multiply the balance of the unamortized unrecognized prior service cost (or unamortized unrecognized *net obligation*) of each plan amendment affected by the plan curtailment by the percentage calculated in Step 1. The result is the amount of loss that must be recognized by the employer as part of the total effects of the plan curtailment. The balance of the unamortized unrecognized prior service cost (or unamortized unrecognized *net obligation*) is also reduced by the same amount.

(From a practical standpoint, the dollar amount of amortization for each expected year of future service can be multiplied by the total number of expected years of future service that are reduced.)

Step 3. The amount of loss recognized on the decrease in the balance of the unamortized unrecognized prior service cost (or unamortized unrecognized *net obligation*) is not part of the gain or loss on the plan curtailment (paragraph 40 of FASB-88), but is included in the total effects of the plan curtailment (illustration 3A of Appendix B of FASB-88).

Decrease (gain) or increase (loss) in the projected benefit obligation A plan curtailment may result in a net decrease (gain) or net increase (loss) in the projected benefit obligation. For example, if employees are terminated as a result of a plan curtailment, some or all of their pension benefits based on future compensation levels may cease to be an obligation of the employer or pension plan. In this event, the projected benefit obligation is decreased (a gain) by the amount of the benefits that are no longer an obligation of the plan. On the other hand, if terminated employees who are eligible for subsidized early retirement benefits accept those benefits at an earlier date than expected, there is usually an increase (loss) in the projected benefit obligation. Gain or loss on a plan curtailment is based on the net decrease (gain) or increase (loss) in the projected benefit obligation.

Pension Plans - Settlements and Curtailments

A plan curtailment may result from the closing of a facility or the disposal of a discontinued business segment. If the event that results in the plan curtailment is related to the disposal of a discontinued business segment, gain or loss on the plan curtailment must be included in the total gain or loss on the disposal of the discontinued business segment (APB-30).

The following steps are necessary to compute the gain or loss on a plan curtailment:

Step 1. Determine the total net gain (decrease) or net loss (increase) in the projected benefit obligation resulting from the plan curtailment. Do not include any increase (loss) in the projected benefit obligation that arises in connection with termination benefits (paragraph 13 of FASB-88, footnote 4).

Step 2. Combine the remaining balance of any unrecognized *net obligation* that arose at the date of the initial application of FASB-87, and that remains unamortized at the date of the plan curtailment, with the balance of any unrecognized net gain or loss that arose after the initial application of FASB-87, and that also remains unamortized at the date of the plan curtailment. (Note: The remaining balance of any unrecognized *net obligation* that arose at the date of the initial application of FASB-87, and that remains unamortized at the date of the plan curtailment is treated as an unrecognized prior service cost.)

The amount of gain or loss on the plan curtailment is determined as follows:

If the change in the projected benefit obligation is a net gain (Step 1) and there is an unrecognized net gain (Step 2) Curtailment gain is recognized in the amount of the net gain in the projected benefit obligation. (The unrecognized net gain computed in Step 2 is not used.)

If the change in the projected benefit obligation is a net gain (Step 1) and there is an unrecognized net loss (Step 2) If the net gain in the projected benefit obligation does not exceed the unrecognized net loss, no curtailment gain or loss is recognized. If the net gain in the projected benefit obligation exceeds the unrecognized net loss, curtailment gain is recognized in the amount of the excess of the net gain in the projected benefit obligation over the unrecognized net loss.

If the change in the projected benefit obligation is a net loss (Step 1) and there is an unrecognized net gain (Step 2) If the net loss in the projected benefit obligation does not exceed the unrecognized net gain, no curtailment gain or loss is recognized. If the net loss in the projected benefit obligation exceeds the unrecognized net gain, curtailment loss is recognized in the amount of the excess of the net loss in the projected benefit obligation over the unrecognized net gain.

If the change in the projected benefit obligation is a net loss (Step 1) and there is an unrecognized net loss (Step 2) Curtailment loss is recognized in the amount of the net loss in the projected benefit obligation. (The unrecognized net loss computed in Step 2 is not used.)

Recognition of the total effects of a plan curtailment As mentioned previously, the total effects of a plan curtailment consist of (a) the decrease (loss) in the unamortized balance of unrecognized prior service cost and/or unrecognized net obligation that arose at the date of initial application of FASB-87, resulting from the significant reduction of the expected years of future service for present employees and (b) the net decrease (gain) or increase (loss) in the projected benefit obligation that results from the elimination of the accrual of defined pension benefits for some or all of the future services of a significant number of employees.

If the total effects of a plan curtailment result in a loss, the loss is recognized when it is *probable* that the curtailment will occur and the effects of the curtailment can be *reasonably estimated*. If the total effects of a plan curtailment result in a gain, the gain is recognized only when the related employees terminate or the plan suspension or amendment is adopted.

Reporting total effects of a plan curtailment Gain or loss on the total effects of a pension plan curtailment is reported as an ordinary gain or loss, unless it meets the criteria of an extraordinary item as specified by APB-30 (paragraph 48 of FASB-88).

> **OBSERVATION:** SEC Staff Accounting Bulletin No. 52 requires that a gain on the termination of a defined benefit pension plan be reported as an extraordinary item (see discussion below - Conflict With Staff Accounting Bulletin No. 52).

Comprehensive illustration The following is a comprehensive illustration of the (a) computation of employees' expected years of future service under a new plan amendment and (b) computation of the loss from the decrease in the balance of the unamortized unrecognized prior service cost related to the expected years of future service that are significantly reduced by the plan curtailment.

Company X had 30 employees who were expected to receive pension benefits under a new pension plan amendment which became effective January 1, 19X1. In the computation of the expected years of future service for each employee who was entitled to receive benefits under the new plan amendment, the company assumed that 10% of the employees would either quit or retire during the next 10 years. The total amount of unrecognized prior service cost arising from the new pension plan amendment was $27,500.

Computation of Expected Years of Future Service and Loss from the Decrease in Unrecognized Prior Service Cost Resulting from the Expected Years of Future Service that Are Significantly Reduced by a Plan Curtailment

Employee Number	Expected Years of Future Service	X1	X2	X3	X4	X5	X6	X7	X8	X9	X10
1-5	5	5									
6-10	10	5	5								
11-15	15	5	5	5							
16-20	20	5	5	5	5						
21-25	25	5	5	5	5	5					
26-30	30	5	5	5	5	5	5				
31-35	35	5	5	5	5	5	5	5			
36-40	40	5	5	5	5	5	5	5	5		
41-45	45	5	5	5	5	5	5	5	5	5	
46-50	50	5	5	5	5	5	5	5	5	5	5
	275										
Service years rendered		50	45	40	35	30	25	20	15	10	5
Amortization fraction		50/275	45/275	40/275	35/275	30/275	25/275	20/275	15/275	10/275	5/275

Amortization for each expected year of future service = $100 ($27,500 unrecognized prior service cost divided by 275 years of expected future service).

If, at the beginning of year 3, ten (10) employees are terminated which results in a reduction of 90 years of expected future service, the percentage reduction is 50% (remaining expected years of future service at the beginning of year 3 is 180 (275 less 50 for year 1 and 45 for year 2 = 180) and the reduction of 90 is equal to 50%). The remaining balance of unrecognized prior service cost relating to the new plan amendment at the beginning of year 3 was $18,000 (180 remaining years of expected future service multiplied by the $100 amortization rate per year). Thus, the pension plan curtailment, relating to the expected years of future service that were significantly reduced by the termination of ten (10) employees, results in a loss of $9,000 (50% of $18,000).

Termination Benefits

Under FASB-88, termination benefits are classified either as *special* or *contractual*. Special termination benefits are those that are offered to employees for a short period of time in connection with the termination of their employment. Contractual termination benefits are those that are required by the terms of an existing plan or agreement, and that are provided only on the occurrence of a specified event, such as early retirement or the closing of a facility.

FASB-88 requires the recognition of the cost of termination benefits as a loss and corresponding liability. The recognition date depends on whether the benefits are special or contractual.

Special termination benefits The recognition date on which the employer records the loss and corresponding liability for special termination benefits occurs when (a) the employees accept the offer of the special termination benefits and (b) the amount of the cost of the benefits can be reasonably estimated. (Note: This represents no change from the accounting specified by FASB-74, which has been superseded by FASB-88).

Contractual termination benefits The recognition date on which the employer records the loss and corresponding liability for contractual termination benefits occurs when (a) it is probable that employees will be entitled to the benefits and (b) the amount of the cost of the benefits can be reasonably estimated.

Reporting a loss on termination benefits A loss on termination benefits is reported as an ordinary loss, unless it meets the criteria of an extraordinary item as specified in APB-30 (paragraph 48 of FASB-88).

Disposal of an Identifiable Business Segment

Under APB-30, severance pay, additional pension costs, and employee relocation expenses are all costs directly associated with the decision to dispose of an identifiable business segment and are properly includable in the total gain or loss on disposal. Gains and losses resulting from the application of FASB-88 that are directly related to the disposal of an identifiable business segment must be accounted for in accordance with APB-30.

The measurement date for determining a gain or loss on the disposal of an identifiable business segment is the date that management commits itself to a formal plan of action to sell or otherwise dispose of the segment. The disposal date is the date of closing in the case of a sale, or the date operations cease in the case of an abandonment.

Determination of gain or loss on disposal of a segment of business should be made as of the measurement date, based on estimates of net realizable values. The estimated loss on the disposal of a segment of business is recognized as of the measurement date. A gain on the disposal of a business segment should not be recognized until it is realized, which is usually the disposal date.

APB-30 specifically requires that a gain or loss on the disposal of an identifiable business segment be reported as an extraordinary item.

Financial Statement Disclosure

An employer must disclose in its financial statements a description of the nature of the events and the amount of gain or loss resulting from the application of the provisions of FASB-88, regardless of whether the gain or loss is directly related to the disposal of a business segment.

Effective Date and Transition

FASB-88 is effective for events that occur in and after the fiscal year in which FASB-87 is first applied. FASB-87 is generally effective for fiscal years beginning on or after December 16, 1986, except for pension plans of nonpublic enterprises consisting of 100 or fewer participants, and plans located outside of the United States.

Retroactive application of the provisions of FASB-88 to previously issued annual financial statements is not permitted. However, if FASB-88 is initially applied in other than the first interim period of a fiscal year, previously issued interim financial statements of the same fiscal year shall be restated.

Asset reversion transactions Some employers are reporting deferred credits on their statements of financial position, resulting from asset reversion transactions in which they received plan assets in excess of plan obligations. Under prior practice, these credit balances have been systematically amortized by entries which reduce the net periodic pension cost of subsequent periods.

Under FASB-88, the entire balance remaining in the deferred credit account at the time of initial application of FASB-87 must be recognized as a gain by the employer, except that the recognized gain may not exceed the balance of any unamortized unrecognized net asset that arose at the date of the initial application of FASB-87. The recognized gain shall be reported in the income statement as a cumulative effect of a change in accounting principle, in accordance with the provisions of APB-20 (Accounting Changes).

Conflict with SEC Staff Accounting Bulletin No. 52

FASB-88 requires the recognition of a *gain,* not only on the complete termination of a pension plan, but also on part settlement of a pension plan, and on a curtailment of a pension plan. Paragraph 25 of FASB-88 states ". . . the present obligation for benefits may be settled without terminating the plan, or a plan may be suspended so that no further benefits will accrue for future services but its obligations are not settled." Furthermore, "... one plan may be divided into two plans, one of which is then terminated, or one-half of the employees in a plan may terminate employment and the obligation for their benefits may be settled."

FASB-88 also requires that the *gain* on all or part of a settlement and/or curtailment of a pension plan be reported as an ordinary gain, unless it meets the criteria specified by APB-30 as an extraordinary item (paragraph 48 of FASB-88).

The above provisions of FASB-88 are in direct conflict with SEC Staff Accounting Bulletin No. 52, which addresses *gains* on the complete termination of a defined benefit pension plan. Staff Accounting Bulletin No. 52 allows recognition of *gain* upon the termination of a pension plan "if all obligations under the terminated plan are fully funded and the substituted employee benefit arrangements are not linked to the prior plan." By contrast, the SEC staff is not likely to approve recognition of *gain* if the present obligation for benefits is settled without terminating the plan, or a plan is suspended so that no further benefits will accrue for future services but its obligations are not settled. Furthermore, the SEC staff is not likely to approve recognition of *gain* if one plan is divided into two plans, one of which is terminated, or one-half of the employees in a plan terminate employment and the obligation for their benefits is settled.

When a *gain* is recognized on the termination of a defined benefit pension plan, SEC Staff Accounting Bulletin No. 52 requires that the *gain* be reported as an extraordinary item in accordance with the provisions of APB-30 (Reporting the Results of Operations). A contrary position is taken by FASB-88, which allows *gain* on the termination of a pension plan to be reported as an extraordinary item, only if the *gain* meets the criteria of an extraordinary item, or the *gain* is realized in connection with the disposal of a segment of a business (paragraph 16 of FASB-88). However, FASB-88 concludes that this type of *gain* does not generally result from the type of unusual and infrequently occurring event or transaction required by APB-30 to be reported as an extraordinary item (paragraph 48 of FASB-88).

Employers who file financial statements with the SEC should ascertain the SEC's position before complying with FASB-88. It is quite possible that the SEC will issue a statement on this issue before FASB-88 becomes effective for any employer. If no SEC statement is available, employers should seek specific guidance from the SEC staff.

Comprehensive Illustration

The following is a comprehensive illustration of a curtailment and settlement of a pension plan.

Complete Termination of a Defined Benefit Pension Plan and the Computation of the Gain or Loss on the Curtailment and Settlement

---

The updated records of a defined benefit pension plan reflect the following:

Pension Plans - Settlements and Curtailments

Vested benefits	$ (30,000)
Nonvested benefits	(50,000)
Accumulated benefit obligation	$ (80,000)
Effects of benefits based on future compensation levels	(20,000)
Projected benefit obligation	$(100,000)
Fair value of plan assets	95,000
Funded status of plan	$ (5,000)
Unrecognized prior service cost	1,000
Unrecognized net (gain) or loss	(1,000)
Unrecognized net obligation or (net asset) at date of initial application of FASB-87	2,000
Accrued pension cost	$ 3,000

Assume that the above plan is completely terminated without a successor plan. Under this circumstance, the effects of the pension benefits that are based on future compensation levels are no longer an obligation of the employer or the plan since all of the plan participants have been terminated. Assume also that the total projected benefit obligation was settled by the purchase of nonparticipating annuity contracts for $80,000, and the excess plan assets in the amount of $15,000 were withdrawn by the employer. The computation of the gain or loss resulting from the curtailment and settlement is as follows:

Computation of the total effects of a plan curtailment The total effects of a plan curtailment consist of (a) the total loss resulting from the decreases in the balances of any unamortized unrecognized prior service costs and/or the unamortized unrecognized *net obligation* that arose at the date of the initial application of FASB-87, relating to the expected years of future service that were significantly reduced for present employees and (b) the net decrease (gain) or increase (loss) in the projected benefit obligation resulting from the elimination of the accrual of defined pension benefits for some or all of the future services of a significant number of employees.

The loss resulting from the decrease in the balance of any unamortized unrecognized prior service costs (or unamortized unrecognized *net obligation*) is computed as follows:

Step 1. The percentage reduction, if any, in the balances of any unamortized unrecognized prior service cost and/or the unamortized unrecognized *net obligation* must be calculated (each loss must be computed separately, unless the pension plan is completely terminated). In the above illustration, the percentage reduction resulting from the significant reduction in the expected years of future service is 100%, because the plan is completely terminated. As a result, no separate computation is necessary.

Step 2. Multiply the unamortized balance of each unrecognized prior service cost and unrecognized *net obligation* by its percentage reduction, if any. In the above illustration, the unamortized balance of the unrecognized prior service cost of $1,000 is multiplied by 100%, and the unamortized balance of the unrecognized net obligation of $2,000 is multiplied by 100%, which results in a total loss of $3,000.

Step 3. The $3,000 computed in Step 2 is treated as an effect of the plan curtailment, not as part of the gain or loss on the plan curtailment.

The net decrease (gain) or increase (loss) in the projected benefit obligation is computed as follows:

Step 4. Calculate the net decrease (gain) or net increase (loss) in the projected benefit obligation resulting from the plan curtailment. Do not include any increase (loss) in the projected benefit obligation that arose in connection with termination benefits (paragraph 13 of FASB-88, footnote 4). In the above illustration, the effects of the pension benefits based on future compensation levels of $20,000 is no longer an obligation of the employer or the plan. This results in a $20,000 net decrease (gain) in the projected benefit obligation, because there are no other decreases or increases.

Step 5. Compute the total of (a) the balance of any unrecognized net gain or loss arising after the initial application of FASB-87 that remains unamortized at the date of the plan curtailment, and (b) the balance of any unrecognized *net asset* that arose at the date of the initial application of FASB-87 that remains unamortized at the date of the plan curtailment. In the above illustration the total is a gain of $1,000 (unrecognized net gain of $1,000 and no unrecognized *net asset*).

Pension Plans - Settlements and Curtailments

Step 6. Compute the gain or loss on the plan curtailment, as follows:

If Step 4 (projected benefit obligation) is a gain and Step 5 is also a gain, curtailment gain is recognized in the amount of Step 4 (the amount of gain in Step 5 is ignored).

If Step 4 (projected benefit obligation) is a loss and Step 5 is also a loss, curtailment loss is recognized in the amount of Step 4 (the amount of loss in Step 5 is ignored).

If Step 4 (projected benefit obligation) is a gain and Step 5 is a loss, curtailment gain is recognized in the amount by which the gain in Step 4 exceeds the loss in Step 5. If Step 5 exceeds Step 4, no gain or loss is recognized.

If Step 4 (projected benefit obligation) is a loss and Step 5 is a gain, curtailment loss is recognized in the amount by which the loss in Step 4 exceeds the gain in Step 5. If Step 5 exceeds Step 4, no gain or loss is recognized.

In the above illustration, the net decrease (gain) in the projected benefit obligation was $20,000 (Step 4) and the total unrecognized net gain or loss is a gain of $1,000 (Step 5). Since Step 4 and Step 5 both result in a gain, a gain on the plan curtailment in the amount of Step 4 is recognized, which is $20,000.

Settlement gain or loss As in Step 5 above, compute the total of (a) the balance of any unrecognized net gain or loss arising after the initial application of FASB-87 that remains unamortized at the date of the plan settlement, and (b) the balance of any unrecognized *net asset* that arose at the date of the initial application of FASB-87 that remains unamortized at the date of the plan settlement.

If part of the pension obligation is settled, the employer must recognize a pro rata portion of the maximum gain or loss, equal to the total of the unrecognized net gain or loss and/or the unrecognized *net asset* multiplied by the percentage reduction in the projected benefit obligation. In the above illustration, there was an unamortized balance of an unrecognized net gain of $1,000 and no unamortized balance of any unrecognized *net asset*. Since the pension plan was terminated, the pension obligation completely settled, and the decrease in the projected benefit obligation was 100%, the pro rata portion that must be recognized is 100%, or $1,000. Thus, the gain on the settlement of the pension plan is $1,000.

Summary The loss on the decrease in the unamortized balance of unrecognized prior service cost and unrecognized *net obligation* is $3,000, which was computed in Step 3. This loss is reported as a "Loss on Effects of Curtailment of Pension Plan." The net gain on the decrease in the projected benefit obligation is $20,000, which was computed in Step 6. This gain is reported as a "Gain on the Curtailment of Pension Plan." The "Gain on the Settlement of Pension Plan" is $1,000, which was computed separately above. Thus, the net gain on the pension plan curtailment and settlement was $18,000 ($3,000 loss, $20,000 gain, and $1,000 gain).

Journal entry The journal entry and suggested financial statement presentation of the net gain on pension plan curtailment and settlement of $18,000 is as follows:

Cash (excess plan assets)	$15,000	
Accrued pension cost	3,000	
Gain from termination of pension plan		$18,000

Suggested financial statement presentation:

Gain on curtailment of pension plan	$20,000
Loss on effects of curtailment of pension plan	3,000
Total effects of plan curtailment	$17,000
Gain on settlement of pension plan	1,000
Net gain on pension plan curtailment and settlement	$18,000

PENSION PLAN FINANCIAL STATEMENTS

Background

Financial reporting for defined benefit plans is covered in FASB Statement-35 (Accounting and Reporting for Defined Benefit Plans). FASB-35 does not require that financial statements be prepared and distributed for defined benefit plans. However, when financial statements of defined benefit plans are prepared and presented, they must comply with the provisions of FASB-35 in order to be in conformity with GAAP.

FASB-75 (Deferral of the Effective Date of Certain Accounting Requirements for Pension Plans of State and Local Governmental Units) supersedes FASB-59 and defers indefinitely the effective date of FASB-35, as it pertains to state and local governmental units.

A defined benefit plan is one that defines the method of determining employee benefits that are expected to be paid on retirement. Based on the benefits that are expected to be paid, the employer's contributions can be actuarially computed. A plan that specifies a fixed rate of employer contributions is considered to be a defined benefit pension plan for the purposes of FASB-35, if the employer's contributions are periodically adjusted to allow for payment of defined benefits which are described in the plan.

FASB-35 apparently covers all defined benefit pension plans including those of state and local governments and those subject to the provisions of the Employee Retirement Income Security Act of 1974 (ERISA). Government sponsored social security plans, temporary plans, and plans that are expected to be terminated are not covered by FASB-35.

Overview

The main objective of financial statements of defined benefit pension plans is to provide financial information that may be utilized to assess the present and future ability of the pension plan to pay benefits as they become due. The financial statements should contain information about (1) the resources of the pension plan, (2) the accumulated plan benefits of participants, (3) the transactions affecting the plan's resources and benefits, and (4) other additional information, as necessary to provide clarity to the financial statement presentation.

FASB-35 requires that the annual financial statements of defined benefit pension plans include:

1. A statement of net assets available for benefits
2. A statement of changes in net assets available for benefits
3. Information on the actuarial present value of accumulated plan benefits
4. Information on the year-to-year changes in the actuarial present value of accumulated plan benefits (if significant)

All financial statements and information should be prepared and presented for the same fiscal or calendar period. Thus, net assets available for benefits and the actuarial present value of accumulated plan benefits must be presented as of the same date and the changes in both should be presented for the same period. Financial statements for the most recent year-end period are preferred by FASB-35. However, if the information on the actuarial present value of accumulated plan benefits is not available or cannot be reasonably determined for the most recent year-end period, then such information shall be presented as of the beginning of the year. In this event, all other financial statements and changes in financial statements must be presented for the same period.

The information concerning the actuarial present value of accumulated plan benefits and its year-to-year changes may be presented on the face of the financial statements, in a footnote thereto, or as a separate statement. However, each category of information must be presented in its entirety in the same location on the financial statements regardless of the format in which it is presented.

> **OBSERVATION:** *FASB-35 was adopted by a four to three vote of the Financial Accounting Standards Board. The basic area of disagreement that led to the three dissenting votes was the perceived accomplishment of including actuarial information in financial statements of pension plans. The affirmative votes believed that better comparability could be achieved among various pension plan financial statements. The dissenting group believed that the CPA's association with actuarial information may lead to an aura of unjustified reliability for financial statement users.*

Reasonable Approximation and Averages

Benefit information may become available during a fiscal year and not at the beginning or end of the year. In this event, FASB-35 allows the use of averages or approximations in determining benefit information at the beginning or end of the fiscal year. However, the method used to estimate benefit information must produce results similar to those required by FASB-35.

Net Assets Available for Benefits

The pension plan's resources should be identified in reasonable detail and presented on the accrual basis of accounting. The following illustrates the type of presentation suggested by FASB-35:

Statement of Net Assets Available for Benefits

	December 31,		Increase
Assets	1981	1980	(Decrease)
Investments at quoted market values (NOTE):			
Federal and state securities	$ 000,000	$0,000,000	$ 00,000
Corporate debt securities	0,000,000	0,000,000	000,000
Preferred stock	000,000	000,000	(0,000)
Common stock	0,000,000	0,000,000	000,000
	$0,000,000	$0,000,000	$ 000,000
Investments at estimated fair value (NOTE):			
Corporate debt securities	$ 000,000	$ 000,000	$ (00,000)
Preferred stock	000,000	000,000	00,000
Mortgages	0,000,000	0,000,000	(000,000)
Real estate	000,000	000,000	0,000
	$0,000,000	$0,000,000	$ 000,000
Deposit administrative contract at contract value (NOTE):	0,000,000	0,000,000	000,000
Total investments	$0,000,000	$0,000,000	$ 000,000
Cash	000,000	000,000	(00,000)
Contributions receivable—employers	000,000	000,000	(00,000)
Accrued interest and dividends	00,000	00,000	00,000
Total assets	$0,000,000	$0,000,000	$ 000,000
Liabilities			
Accounts payable and accrued items	000,000	000,000	(00,000)
Net assets available for benefits	$0,000,000	$0,000,000	$ 000,000

> **OBSERVATION:** *The above illustrated statement and other illustrated statements to follow differ from the illustrations which appear in FASB-35 (Appendix), in the following respects:*
>
> 1. *There is no increase (decrease) column in any of the illustrations in FASB-35.*
> 2. *Comparison of the current year and immediate prior year is used in FASB-35 only when the benefit information date is at the beginning of the current year. Thus, only the current year is shown in the illustration provided in FASB-35 if the benefit information date is at the end of the current year. However, in footnote 1 of FASB-35, it is suggested that comparative financial statements for several plan years are more useful in assessing a plan's ability to provide future benefits.*

Assets that are used in the actual operation of a pension plan should be reported at amortized cost on the financial statements. Thus, buildings, leasehold improvements, furniture, equipment and fixtures which are used in the everyday operation of a pension plan should be presented at historical cost less accumulated depreciation or amortization.

All pension plan investments that are held to provide benefits for the plan's participants, excluding contracts with insurance companies, must be identified in reasonable detail and presented at fair value in the financial statements. Quoted market values, in an active market, should be used as fair value when available. Fair value determined by other methods should be adequately disclosed in the financial statements or footnotes thereto. FASB-35 defines fair value as the amount that could reasonably be expected to be received in a current sale between a willing buyer and willing seller, neither under compulsion to buy or sell. Plan investments include debt or equity securities, real estate, and other types of investments held to provide benefits for the plan's participants.

Contributions receivable from employees, employers, state or federal grants, and other sources should be separately identified in the financial statements. Contributions receivable should be reported on the accrual basis pursuant to actual legal or contractual obligations or formal commitments. The fact that an employer accrues a liability to a pension plan does not, by itself, provide a basis for a pension plan to record a corresponding receivable.

In order for a pension plan to record an employer contribution receivable, the receivable must be supported by a formal commitment or an actual legal or contractual obligation. However, FASB-35 states that evidence of a formal commitment may include (1) the formal approval of a specified contribution, (2) a consistent pattern of payments made after the pension plan's year-end pursuant to an established funding policy that attributes the payments to the preceding plan year, and (3) a federal tax deduction taken for the contribution by the employer for periods ending on or before the reporting date for the pension plan.

> **OBSERVATION:** Many pension plans provide that a company may, at its discretion, discontinue contributions and/or the plan itself. The resulting legal position is that the company has no legal liability for future pension fund contributions, and employees have no rights to any benefits beyond those already provided for in the pension fund. However, the position of promulgated GAAP is one of substance over form and that a business is viewed as an entity which will continue to exist (going-concern concept). Therefore, GAAP require that the "no future legal liability clauses" of a pension plan be ignored for the purposes of determining the annual pension costs of employers.

For the purposes of presenting contracts with insurance companies in the statement of net assets available for benefits, FASB-35 requires that all pension plans, including those not subject to ERISA, shall value such contracts in the same manner as that required by item 13 of the Federal Government's Form 5500 or 5500C (Annual Return/Report of Employee Benefit Plan). Form 5500 is for employee benefit plans with 100 or more participants, and Form 5500C is for employee benefit plans with fewer than 100 participants. Thus, the reader must refer to Form 5500 or 5500C to determine which insurance contracts are included in the presentation required by FASB-35, and which valuation method should be used. The instructions for item 13 of Forms 5500 and 5500C are identical and appear as follows:

---

13 Plan assets and liabilities at the beginning and the end of the plan year (list all assets and liabilities at current value). A fully insured welfare plan or a pension plan with no trust and which is funded entirely by allocated insurance contracts which fully guarantee the amount of benefit payments should check box and not complete this item .... ☐

> **Note:** Include all plan assets and liabilities of a trust or separately maintained fund. (If more than one trust/fund, report on a combined basis.) Include all insurance values except for the value of that portion of an allocated insurance contract which fully

guarantees the amount of benefit payments. Round off amounts to nearest dollar. Trusts with no assets at the beginning and the end of the plan year enter zero on line 13(h).

An allocated insurance contract is one that has been purchased to provide an immediate or deferred annuity for a plan participant. In other words, an insurance company is paid a premium to assume certain specified benefits that must be paid to specified plan participants. An unallocated insurance contract is one that has not been used to purchase specific benefits for specific plan participants. The insurance company accumulates the unallocated funds in the unallocated insurance contract until it is instructed to pay specific benefits from the unallocated funds, or instructed to purchase an annuity to provide specified benefits. Unallocated funds of an unallocated insurance contract may usually be withdrawn and used for other purposes.

The instructions for item 13 of Form 5500 and 5500C affect FASB-35 in two main aspects. The first aspect is that allocated insurance contracts are not included in the financial statements that are required by FASB-35, except for some footnote disclosure. The second aspect is that unallocated insurance contracts (other than pooled separate accounts) must be broken down into (1) unallocated separate accounts, and (2) unallocated other accounts. These accounts should be valued at current value. Forms 5500 and 5500C define current value as the fair market value where available and otherwise as the fair value determined in good faith by a trustee or a named fiduciary pursuant to the terms of the plan, assuming an orderly liquidation at the time of such determination.

> **OBSERVATION:** *The financial information required by Forms 5500 and 5500C must be submitted at current values which is basically what is required by FASB-35. In addition, many of the financial disclosures required by FASB-35 also appear on Forms 5500 and 5500C. Thus, it may be advisable to prepare the Government forms before the financial statements required by FASB-35.*

Changes in Net Assets Available for Benefits

Significant changes in net assets available for benefits should be identified in reasonable detail in the Statement of Changes in Net

Assets Available for Benefits. The following illustrates the type of presentation suggested by FASB-35.

Statement of Changes in Net Assets Available for Benefits
Year Ended December 31

	1981	1980	Increase (Decrease)
Investment Income:			
Interest	$ 00,000	$ 00,000	$ 0,000
Dividend	00,000	00,000	000
Rental	00,000	00,000	(000)
Increase (decrease) in investments at quoted market values (NOTE)	000,000	(00,000)	00,000
Increase (decrease) in investments at estimated fair values (NOTE)	00,000	000,000	$ 0,000
	$ 000,000	$ 000,000	$ 00,000
Less: Investment expenses	00,000	$ 00,000	$ 0,000
	$ 000,000	$ 000,000	$ 000,000
Contributions from employers (NOTE)	000,000	000,000	00,000
Contributions from federal agency	00,000	00,000	(00,000)
Total	$0,000,000	$0,000,000	$ 000,000
Less: direct benefit payments to participants	$ 000,000	$ 000,000	$ 00,000
Less: annuity contracts purchased (NOTE)	000,000	000,000	00,000
Less: expenses of administration	00,000	00,000	0,000
Total	000,000	000,000	00,000
Net increase in net assets	$ 000,000	$ 000,000	$ 00,000
Net assets available for benefits:			
Beginning of year	0,000,000	0,000,000	
End of year	$0,000,000	$0,000,000	

The minimum disclosures required by FASB-35, which should appear in the Statement of Changes in Net Assets Available for Benefits or its related footnotes, are as follows:

1. Investment income other than from realized or unrealized gains or losses on investments, should be separately disclosed in reasonable detail.
2. Realized and unrealized gains or losses on investments presented at quoted market values should be reported separately from those of investments presented at estimated fair value.
3. Contributions from employers, participants, and others, should be reported separately. Cash and noncash contributions from employers should be disclosed. Noncash contributions should be recorded at their fair value on the date of receipt and, if significant, they should be fully described in the financial statements or footnotes thereto.
4. Direct benefit payments to participants should be reported separately.
5. Purchases of insurance contracts that are excluded from the plan's assets should be separately reported. Dividend income on insurance contracts that are excluded from the plan's assets may be netted against the purchase of such contracts. The dividend income policy on insurance contracts should be disclosed in a footnote to the financial statements.
6. Expenses of administrating the plan should be separately reported.

Accumulated Plan Benefits of Participants

FASB-35 requires that certain specified information regarding the actuarial present value of accumulated plan benefits of participants must be disclosed as part and within the financial statements. The present value of the accumulated plan benefits must be determined as at the plan benefit information date. Thus, if the plan benefit information date is the beginning of the year, the present value of the accumulated plan benefits must be determined as at the beginning of the year.

In addition, financial statements as at the beginning of the year must also be included in the presentation. On the other hand, if the plan benefit information is dated as at the end of the year, the present value of the accumulated plan benefits must be determined as at the same date and financial statements as at the end of the year must also be included in the presentation. FASB-35 states a preference for the use of end-of-year benefit information.

FASB-35 allows considerable flexibility in presenting the actuarial present value of accumulated plan benefits and the changes therein from year to year. The following illustrates one type of presentation.

Statement of Accumulated Plan Benefits
December 31,

	1981	1980	Increase (Decrease)
Actuarial present value of accumulated plan benefits (Note):			
Vested benefits			
Participants currently receiving payments	$ 0,000,000	$ 0,000,000	$ 000,000
Other participants	0,000,000	0,000,000	000,000
	$00,000,000	$00,000,000	$0,000,000
Nonvested benefits	0,000,000	0,000,000	000,000
Total actuarial present value of accumulated plan benefits	$00,000,000	$00,000,000	$0,000,000
Net assets available for benefits	$ 0,000,000	$ 0,000,000	

FASB-35 requires that the total actuarial present value of accumulated plan benefits be broken down and presented in at least three categories: (1) vested benefits of participants currently receiving payments, (2) vested benefits of other participants, and (3) nonvested benefits. Vested benefits of participants currently receiving payments should include benefits due and payable as of the benefit information date. Disclosure of the accumulated contributions of present employees, including interest, if any, as of the benefit information date should be made in a footnote to the financial statements. In addition, the rate of interest, if any, should also be disclosed.

For the purposes of FASB-35 it is presumed that a pension plan will continue to exist (going concern concept). The best estimates should be used in each actuarial assumption in order to reflect the pension plan's most likely expectations. The following specific assumptions, which must be applied, appear in FASB-35:

1. Assumed rates of return shall reflect the expected rates of return during the periods for which payment of benefits is deferred and shall be consistent with returns realistically achievable on the types of assets held by the plan and the plan's investment policy. To the extent that assumed rates of return are based on values of existing plan assets, the values used in determining assumed rates of return shall be the values presented in the plan's financial statements pursuant to the requirements of this Statement.
2. Expected rates of inflation assumed in estimating automatic cost-of-living adjustments shall be consistent with the assumed rates of return.
3. Administrative expenses expected to be paid by the plan (not those paid by the sponsor) that are associated with providing accumulated plan benefits shall be reflected either by appropriately adjusting the assumed rates of return or by assigning those expenses to future periods and discounting them to the benefit information date. If the former method is used, the adjustment of the assumed rates of return shall be separately disclosed.

An acceptable alternative in determining the actuarial present value of accumulated plan benefits as of the benefit information date, is to use the same assumptions as an insurance company would use if it were to issue an insurance contract to provide the same accumulated plan benefits to the same participants.

Accumulated plan benefits should be determined at the benefit information date in accordance with the provisions of the pension plan. Accumulated plan benefits should include those expected to be paid to (1) retired or terminated employees or their beneficiaries, (2) beneficiaries of deceased employees, and (3) present employees or their beneficiaries.

Pension plan benefits can usually be determined by reference to the provisions in the plan. In most pension plans, benefits are usually based on each year of service (employment) rendered by the employee. If the benefits are not clearly determinable from the provisions of the plan, FASB-35 requires the following computation to determine the accumulated benefits:

Benefits Includable in Vested Benefits

$$\frac{\text{number of years service completed to the benefit information date}}{\text{number of years service that will have been completed when the benefits will first be fully vested}} \quad \text{EQUALS} \quad \begin{array}{c}\text{Percent}\\\text{of plan benefits}\\\text{accumulated}\end{array}$$

(The above computation is used to determine the amount of plan benefits that have been accumulated to the benefit information date. This computation is used for plan benefits that are classified as vested benefits.)

Benefits Not Includable in Vested Benefits

$$\frac{\text{number of years service completed to the benefit information date}}{\text{estimated number of years service upon anticipated separation from covered employment}} \quad \text{EQUALS} \quad \begin{array}{c}\text{Percent}\\\text{of plan benefits}\\\text{accumulated}\end{array}$$

(The above computation is used to determine the amount of plan benefits that are not includable in vested benefits which have been accumulated to the benefit information date. This type of plan benefit includes death or disability benefits that are payable only if death or disability occurs during active service).

FASB-35 requires that the following procedures be applied in determining accumulated plan benefits:

1. Accumulated plan benefits shall be determined as at the benefit information date based on employees' history of earnings and service, and other appropriate factors.
2. In the case of periodic benefit increases, death benefits, early retirement benefits, and disability benefits, accumulated plan benefits should be based on the employees' projected years of service.
3. All automatic benefit increases that are specified in the plan, such as a cost-of-living-increase, which are expected to occur subsequent to the benefit information date, shall be recognized in determining accumulated plan benefits.
4. Benefits that are covered by allocated insurance contracts which are not included as plan assets (in accordance with FASB-35)

are not included in determining accumulated plan benefits, provided that payment for the allocated insurance contract has been made to the insurance company.
5. Benefits arising from plan amendments adopted subsequent to the benefit information date shall not be included in determining accumulated plan benefits.
6. In computing Social Security benefits, employees' earnings as at the benefit information date shall be used to determine future compensation. Increases in Social Security benefits, or compensation base arising from present or future Social Security laws shall be excluded in determining future compensation.

Changes in Accumulated Plan Benefits

Certain factors that cause changes in the actuarial present value of accumulated plan benefits between the current and prior benefit information dates, if significant either individually or in the aggregation, shall be identified in the financial statements or the footnotes thereto. Significant changes that are caused by individual factors shall be separately identified. The minimum disclosure required by FASB-35 includes the effects of the following factors, if significant:

1. Plan amendments
2. Changes in the nature of the plan, such as a merger with another plan, or a spinoff of a plan
3. Changes in actuarial assumptions

> **OBSERVATION:** *As mentioned previously, an acceptable alternative permitted by FASB-35 to determine the actuarial present value of accumulated plan benefits as of the benefit information date, is to use the same assumptions as an insurance company would use if it were to issue an insurance contract to provide the same accumulated plan benefits to the same participants. If a pension plan uses this method, it should disclose, if practical, the effects of changes in the actuarial present value of accumulated plan benefits which are caused by changes in actuarial assumptions. If the effects cannot be separately disclosed, they should be included in determining accumulated benefits.*

Other factors that result in changes in the actuarial present value of accumulated plan benefits, if significant, may also be identified in the financial statements. Other factors that may cause significant changes in the actuarial present value of accumulated plan benefits are factors that affect (1) the amount of accumulated benefits, (2) the discount period, and (3) the amount of benefits paid. Actuarial gains and losses may be separately disclosed, or included with the effect of additional accumulated benefits.

Amounts paid to an insurance company for the purchase of insurance contracts are included in determining the amount of benefits paid. However, amounts paid by an insurance company for benefits, in accordance with an insurance contract which has been excluded from the plan's assets (in accordance with FASB-35), are not included in determining the amount of benefits paid.

Changes in actuarial assumptions that result from changes in a plan's expected experience, are treated as changes in accounting estimates. Accounting estimates are accounted for in the year of change and, if necessary, future years. Prior years' financial statements are not restated in accounting for a change in an accounting estimate (APB-20).

Changes in the actuarial present value of accumulated plan benefits may be presented in the form of a separate reconciliation statement, or elsewhere in the financial statements. If the reconciliation statement is used, it should reflect the actuarial present value of accumulated plan benefits at both the beginning and the end of the year. The amount of detail between the beginning and end of year depends on whether a full presentation is made, or only the required minimum disclosures. If a full presentation is made, then all changes are identified and disclosed. However, if only the required minimum disclosures are made, it will be necessary to include all other changes on one line to reconcile the beginning and ending balances.

Statement of Changes in Accumulated Plan Benefits

	Year ended December 31, 1980 Increase (Decrease)
Actuarial present value of accumulated plan benefits, at beginning of year	$ 000,000
Plan amendment	00,000
Changes in actuarial assumptions	00,000
Other factors	(0,000)
Actuarial present value of accumulated plan benefits, at the end of the year	$ 000,000

As mentioned previously, the minimum disclosures of changes in the actuarial present value of accumulated plan benefits required by FASB-35 are (1) plan amendments, (2) changes in the nature of the plan, and (3) changes in actuarial assumptions. Thus, when the minimum disclosures are presented in a reconciliation statement, a separate line must be used for all "other" changes in order to balance the statement. When a full presentation is made in a reconciliation statement, all changes are identified and disclosed separately.

If the minimum required disclosures pertaining to the changes in the actuarial present value of accumulated plan benefits are made elsewhere in the financial statements and not in a reconciliation statement format, FASB-35 requires that the actuarial present value of accumulated plan benefits as of the preceding benefit information date, also be disclosed.

Other Financial Statement Disclosures

In addition to the financial statement and footnote disclosures mentioned previously, FASB-35 requires two specific additional footnote disclosures and several other disclosures if they are applicable. The two required footnote disclosures must appear in the footnote disclosures of the pension plan's "significant accounting policies," which is usually the first footnote disclosure (APB-22). They are, as follows:

1. The significant assumptions and method used to determine fair value of investments and the value of reported insurance contracts, must be adequately described.
2. The significant assumptions and method used to determine the actuarial present value of accumulated plan benefits must be adequately described. In addition, any significant changes in assumptions or methods that occur during the reporting period, must also be described.

Other financial statement disclosures that must be made, if applicable are as follows:

1. A brief description of the important provisions of the pension plan agreement. However, if this information is made generally available from sources other than the financial statements, reference to such sources may be made in the financial statements, instead of providing the brief description.
2. Significant amendments to the pension plan that are adopted on or before the latest benefit information date should be described. In the event that significant plan amendments are adopted between the latest benefit information date and the end of the plan's year, disclosure should be made to the effect that the present value of accumulated plan benefits do not include the effects of those amendments.
3. A general description of the order of priority for plan participants' claims to the assets of the plan upon termination of the plan. In addition, a description of any benefits guaranteed by the Pension Benefit Guaranty Corporation (PBGC). Also, a description of the applicability of any PBGC guaranty to any recent plan amendment.

    If the information required in the above paragraph is made generally available from sources other than the financial statements, reference to such sources may be made in the financial statements, providing that the following (or similar) disclosure is made in the financial statements.

    "Should the pension plan terminate at some future time, its net assets generally will not be available on a pro rata basis to provide participants' benefits. Whether a particular participant's accumulated plan benefits will be paid depends on both the priority of those benefits and the level of benefits guaranteed by the Pension Benefit Guaranty Corporation (a Federal Agency) at that time. Some benefits may be fully or partially provided for by the then existing assets and the

Pension Benefit Guaranty Corporation, while other benefits may not be provided for at all".

4. Significant plan administration costs that are being absorbed by the employer should be disclosed, if any.
5. The policy for funding the pension plan and any changes in policy during the plan year should be described. The method for determining participants' contributions, if any, should be described and plans subject to ERISA must disclose whether ERISA minimum funding requirements have been met. The status of minimum funding waivers should be disclosed, if applicable.
6. The pension plan's policy concerning purchased insurance contracts that are excluded from the pension plan's assets should be disclosed.
7. Disclosure of whether or not a favorable "determination letter" has been obtained for federal income tax purposes should be made.
8. Disclosure of any plan investments that represent 5% or more of the net assets available for benefits, should be made.
9. Disclosure of any party-in-interest transactions between the plan and (1) the employer, (2) the sponsor, or (3) the employee organization.
10. The disclosure of unusual or infrequent events and the effects of such events, that occur subsequent to the latest benefit information date, but prior to the issuance of the financial statements, which may significantly affect the plan's present and future ability to pay benefits. In the event that the effects of such events are not reasonably determinable, all substantive reasons should be disclosed.

The following is a comprehensive illustration of many of the footnotes to the financial statements that are required or applicable under the provisions of FASB-35.

FINANCIAL STATEMENT NOTES

Summary of Significant Accounting Policies

Description of Pension Plan This pension plan is called the ABC Company Defined Benefit Pension Plan and covers substantially all of the employees of the ABC Company. The Plan is subject to the provisions of the Employee Retirement Income Security Act of 1974 (ERISA).

Annual pension benefits begin at the normal retirement age (65) for employees with 10 or more years of service to the company. The amount received at age 65 is equal to 1 1/2% of the final five-year average annual compensation for each year of service. Employees may elect to retire early from ages 55 to 64. The portion of the accumulated plan benefits attributable to the Company's contributions to an employee is forfeited if an employee discontinues employment before rendering 10 years of service. Several elections are available to employees for the distribution of pension benefits. Employees may elect to receive their pension benefits in the form of a joint and survivor annuity, single life annuity, or as a lump sum distribution upon termination or retirement. The minimum amount that an employee may receive upon electing a life annuity is the greater of the annuity for five years or the employee's accumulated contributions to the plan, plus interest.

Death benefits are paid to the beneficiary equal to the value of the employee's accumulated pension benefits if the active employee was 55 years or older. Annual disability benefits are paid to an active employee who has become disabled, equal to the normal retirement benefits that have been accumulated at the time of disability. At normal retirement age, the disabled employee would begin receiving normal retirement benefits computed as if he had retired at the date of disability.

Investment Valuation Investments are valued at quoted market prices when available. Securities for which no quoted market price is available are valued at fair value. Fair value is based upon a combination of different factors. In most cases, corporate bonds are valued through comparison of similar securities' yields. Restricted common stock, is usually valued at the quoted price of the issuers unrestricted stock, reduced by a discount to reflect the restriction. If neither a quoted market price is available nor an unrestricted stock of the issuer exists, then a value is determined on a multiple of current earnings reduced by comparison of similar companies' earnings with a quoted price.

Mortgages are valued at their present values based on prevailing interest rates applied to the future principal and interest payments. Real estate leased to third parties is valued at the present value of all future rental receipts and estimated residual values. The interest rate used to discount future values varies with the risks inherent in each real estate investment.

The value of the Plan's deposit administration contract with American Insurance Company is contract value. Contract value is determined by the contributions made plus interest at the rate specified in the contract less funds used to purchase annuities and pay expenses. The Plan's assets do not include those funds used to purchase annuities. When an annuity is purchased, American Insurance Company is required to pay all related pension benefits to a particular employee.

Actuarial Present Value of Accumulated Plan Benefits All future periodic benefit payments, including any lump sum distributions provided for under the provisions of the Plan are included in Accumulated Plan Benefits. Accumulated plan benefits include all benefits which may be paid to present employees or beneficiaries, retired or terminated employees or beneficiaries, and beneficiaries of employees who have died. The plan provides for benefits which are based on the employees compensation during the last five years of eligible service. The basis of the accumulated plan benefits for active employees is the average compensation during the last five years of service. All benefits are included, up to the valuation date, providing that they are related to services rendered by the employee. Any benefits that are provided from assets that are excluded from the Plan's assets, are excluded from accumulated plan benefits.

The actuarial present value for the accumulated plan benefits is computed by American Appraisal Inc. Certain assumptions are utilized to adjust the accumulated plan benefits to reflect the present value of money and the probability of payment. Significant actuarial assumptions utilized in the valuations presented as of December 31, 1980 and December, 1979 are as follows: Participants' life expectancy based on mortality tables (_____), average retirement age of 62.

Termination of the Plan In the event of termination, the net assets of the plan will be allocated, in accordance with ERISA and its related regulations. The order of priority is as follows:

1. Any benefits related to the contributions of the employees.
2. Any annuity benefits that have been received for at least the past three years to former employees or their beneficiaries or that employees eligible to retire for that three year period would have received if they would have retired with benefits under the Plan. The priority amount is the lowest benefit payable or paid during the five year period before termination of the Plan.

3. Insured vested benefits by the Pension Benefit Guaranty Corporation (PBGC) up to certain limitations.
4. All uninsured vested benefits.
5. All nonvested benefits.

NOTE: Annuity contracts for which the American Insurance Company is obligated to pay benefits, are not included in the above priority schedule.

PBGC insurance benefits include most vested normal age retirement benefits, early retirement benefits, and certain disability and survivor's pensions. However, all benefits under the Plan are not guaranteed by PBGC and certain limitations are placed on some of the benefits guaranteed. Vested benefits are guaranteed at the level in effect at the Plan termination date, but are subject to a statutory ceiling which limits individual monthly benefits. The ceiling in 1980 and 1979 was 000,000 and 000,000 respectively for employees who are 65 years old and elect a single life annuity. All other annuitants are subject to a downward adjustment. Benefit improvements as a result of a Plan amendment are not automatically fully guaranteed by PBGC. PBGC guarantees the greater of 20% or $20 for each year following the effective date of an amendment. Thus, the full increase in benefits would be completely guaranteed, within 5 years after an amendment assuming primary ceilings are in effect.

Investments Other Than Insurance Company Contract   All of the Plan's investments are held by a bank-administered trust fund, except for the deposit administration contract. The fair values of those investments for 1980 and 1979 were 000,000 and 000,000 respectively.

Insurance Company Contract   The company entered into a deposit administration contract with the American Insurance Company in 1977. The Plan deposits a minimum of $100,000 annually which is placed in an unallocated fund. American adds interest to the fund at a stated rate of 7%. The interest rate can be changed after 1985, but the different rate only affects deposits made after the date of change. Withdrawals are made from the fund under the direction of the Plan's administration in order to purchase an annuity. American Insurance Company premiums on purchased annuities is fixed for the term of the contract. Periodic dividends, if any, increase the unallocated fund. Dividends received in 1980 and 1979 were 000 and 000 respectively. These dividends are deducted from the purchased annuity contract payments on the Statement of Changes in Net Assets.

Plan Amendment There is an amendment to the plan expected in 1983 which will increase the annual pension benefits for each year of service.

Changes in Accounting Methods In 1980, FASB-35 was issued by the Financial Accounting Standards Board. The financial statements of ABC Defined Benefit Pension Plan comply with this pronouncement. Thus previously reported information pertaining to the years presented has been restated to allow comparability.

PRODUCT FINANCING ARRANGEMENTS

Overview

FASB-49 contains the specialized accounting and reporting principles and practices that were originally published in the AICPA Statement of Position 78-8 (SOP 78-8), entitled "Accounting for Product Financing Arrangements."

FASB-49 indicates that the specialized accounting and reporting principles and practices were extracted from SOP 78-8 without significant change, and that the Financial Accounting Standards Board did not contemplate a comprehensive reconsideration of the accounting issues in SOP 78-8.

Background

Product financing arrangements usually provide for one entity to obtain inventory or product for another entity (the sponsor), which agrees to purchase the inventory or product at specific prices over a specific period. The agreed upon prices to be paid for the inventory or product, by the sponsor, usually include financing and holding costs. The following are a few of the more common types of product financing arrangements:

1. A sponsor sells inventory or product to another entity and in a related arrangement agrees to buy the inventory or product back.
2. Another entity agrees to purchase a product or inventory for a sponsor, who in a related arrangement agrees to buy the product or inventory from the other entity.
3. A sponsor by arrangement controls the product or inventory purchased or held by another entity.

In all of the above arrangements the sponsor agrees to purchase, over a specified period, the product or inventory from the other entity at prearranged prices. The substance of a product financing arrangement, regardless of its legal form, reflects a financing arrangement and not a sale or purchase by the sponsor.

Other factors that frequently, but not always, exist in a product financing arrangement are as follows:

GAAP GUIDE / 31.75

1. The entity that provides the financing arrangement to the sponsor is an existing trust, nonbusiness entity, credit grantor, or was formed for the sole purpose of providing the financing arrangement to the sponsor.
2. Small quantities of the product involved in the financing arrangement may be sold by the financing entity, but most of the product is ultimately used or sold by the sponsor.
3. The product is stored on the sponsor's premises.
4. The sponsor guarantees the debt of the other entity.

For the purposes of FASB-49, unmined or unharvested natural resources and financial instruments are not considered products. Thus, apparently, they are not covered by the provisions of FASB-49.

> **OBSERVATION:** *No mention is made in FASB-49 as to how a product financing arrangement involving unmined or unharvested natural resources should be accounted for. For example, X Company enters into a financing arrangement with Y Company wherein Y Company acquires 10,000 acres of unharvested timberlands for the sole benefit of X Company. X Company guarantees the bank loan that was necessary to acquire the timberlands and agrees to purchase the processed timber from Y Company at specified prices over a specified period. The specified prices include (1) the cost of the timber, (2) processing costs, (3) interest costs on the bank loan, and (4) a small handling fee. Only the standing timber was purchased and not the land.*
>
> *It appears that the provisions of FASB-49 should apply to the above transaction, but FASB-49 expressly does not cover it!*

In a product financing arrangement, the specified prices that the sponsor must pay cannot be subject to change except for fluctuations due to finance and holding costs. The specified prices may be stated or determinable by reference to the substance of the arrangement, such as (1) resale price guarantees, or (2) options which, in substance, compel or require the sponsor to purchase the product. In addition, the cost of the product and related costs to the other entity must be substantially covered by the specified prices that the seller must pay for the product. Related costs include interest, holding costs, and other fees charged by the other entity.

Accounting For Product Financing Arrangements

An arrangement that, in substance, contains the characteristics of a product financing arrangement, shall be accounted for by the sponsor of such an arrangement, as follows:

1. If another entity buys a product from a sponsor and in a related arrangement agrees to sell the product, or a processed product containing the original product, back to the sponsor, no sale should be recorded and the product should remain as an asset on the sponsor's books. Also, the sponsor should record a liability in the amount of the proceeds received from the other entity under the provisions of the product financing arrangement.

    Product financing arrangements are in substance a method of financing a product and should not be recorded as a sale and repurchase by the sponsor.

2. If another entity buys a product for a sponsor's benefit and the sponsor agrees, in a related arrangement, to buy the product, or a processed product containing the original product, back from the other entity, an asset and the related liability should be recorded by the sponsor at the time the other entity acquires the product.

Excluding processing costs, the difference between the regular product cost which the sponsor would have paid if there was no product financing arrangement, and the cost that the sponsor actually pays under the terms of the product financing arrangement, should be accounted for by the sponsor as financing and holding costs. These financing and holding costs should be recorded on the books of the sponsor in accordance with its regular accounting policies for such costs, even though the costs are incurred and paid directly by the other entity.

Separately identified interest costs which the sponsor pays as part of the specified prices may qualify for interest capitalization under FASB-34 (Capitalization of Interest Costs). If not, the separately identified interest costs actually paid by the sponsor would count toward the total interest costs incurred during the period, for the purposes of FASB-34. Under FASB-34, total capitalized interest costs for any particular period may not exceed the total interest costs actually incurred by an enterprise during that particular period.

Effective Date

FASB-49 is effective for product financing arrangements entered into on or after June 16, 1981, and shall be applied to current and/or future periods (prospectively).

QUASI-REORGANIZATIONS

Background

Current promulgated GAAP on quasi-reorganizations appears in ARB-43, Chapter 7A.

A quasi-reorganization is frequently referred to as a corporate readjustment.

Overview

When a business reaches a turnaround point and profitable operations seem likely, a quasi-reorganization may be appropriate to eliminate the accumulated deficit from past unprofitable operations. The resulting financial statements will have more credibility, making it easier for the company to borrow money for its profitable operations. In addition, by eliminating the deficit in retained earnings, the possibility of paying dividends in the future becomes more likely.

Although the corporate entity remains unchanged in a quasi-reorganization, a new basis of accountability is established. Assets are usually restated downward to their fair values, and stockholders' equity is adjusted so that retained earnings has a zero balance. Retained earnings is adjusted to a zero balance by charging the deficit either (1) to capital contributed in excess of par or (2) to capital contributed other than for capital stock (usually donated capital). Obviously, this means that capital accounts (other than for capital stock) must be available to absorb the deficit in retained earnings (after all quasi-reorganization adjustments are made).

Although the capital stock account may not be used to absorb a deficit in retained earnings, it is certainly permissible for a corporation to reduce the par value of its existing capital stock and to transfer the resulting excess to a capital contributed in excess of par account (paid-in capital). As a matter of fact, this procedure is frequently accomplished in a quasi-reorganization.

The following types of situations justify a quasi-reorganization, providing that capital accounts (other than for capital stock) are available to absorb the resulting retained earnings deficit after all adjustments:

1. Historical cost of assets clearly requiring adjustment so that realistic financial reporting is possible.

2. An acceptable alternative to legal proceedings resulting in a reorganization
3. A large deficit from past operations exists

In financial accounting, stockholders' equity is usually made up of:

1. Capital contributed for stock, to the extent of the par or stated value of each class of stock presently outstanding.
2.   a. capital contributed in excess of par or stated value of each class of stock whether as a result of original issues, any subsequent reductions of par or stated value, or transactions by the corporation in its own shares
   b. capital received other than for stock whether from shareholders or others (such as donated capital)
3. Retained earnings (or deficit), which represents the accumulated income or loss of the corporation

Generally, items properly chargeable to current or future years' income accounts may not be charged to capital accounts. An exception to this rule occurs in accounting for quasi-reorganizations.

Accounting and Reporting

If a corporation elects to restate its assets and stockholders' equity through a quasi-reorganization, it must make a clear report of the proposed restatements to its shareholders and obtain their formal consent.

Assets should be written down to their fair values; and if fair values are not readily determinable, conservative estimates may be used. Estimates may also be used to provide for known possible losses prior to the date of the quasi-reorganization, when amounts are indeterminable.

If estimates are used and the amounts are subsequently found to be excessive or insufficient, the difference should be charged or credited to the capital account previously charged or credited, and not to retained earnings.

The steps in the accounting procedure follow:

1. All amounts to be written off should be charged to retained earnings, irrespective of whether retained earnings has or will have a deficit.

2. After all amounts to be written off are recognized and charged to retained earnings, any debit balance in retained earnings may be transferred by journal entry to either (a) capital contributed in excess of par or (b) capital contributed other than for capital stock.

   It makes no difference whether the two capital accounts above were previously existing or were created as a result of the quasi-reorganization.

   It is important to remember that it is improper to increase a credit balance in retained earnings by an accounting or quasi reorganization, but it is acceptable to eliminate a deficit.

3. If a deficit in retained earnings is transferred to an allowable capital account, any subsequent balance sheet must disclose, by dating the retained earnings, that the balance in the retained earnings account has increased since the date of reorganization. For example:

   Retained earnings, since July 1, 19XX $1,234,567

   The dating of retained earnings following a quasi-reorganization would rarely if ever be of significance after a period of 10 years. There may be exceptional circumstances that could justify a period of less than 10 years (ARB-46).

4. New or additional shares of stock may be issued or exchanged for other shares or existing indebtedness. For example, stockholders may agree to subscribe to additional shares, or bondholders may agree to accept capital stock in lieu of interest in arrears, in order to provide new cash for future operations. Accounting entries for these types of transactions are handled in accordance with GAAP.

5. Corporations with subsidiaries should follow the same procedures, so that no credit balance remains in consolidated retained earnings after a quasi-reorganization where losses have been charged to allowable capital accounts.

   In those cases, where losses have been charged to the allowable capital accounts, instead of a credit balance in consolidated retained earnings, the parent company's interest in such retained earnings should be regarded as capitalized by the quasi-reorganization in the same way retained earnings of a subsidiary are capitalized on the date of its acquisition.

6. The effective date of the quasi-reorganization from which income of the corporation is thereafter determined should be as close as possible to the date of formal stockholders' consent and preferably at the start of a new fiscal year.

Under no circumstances should adjustments made pursuant to a quasi-reorganization be included in the determination of net income for any period (APB-9).

If not previously recognized, a tax benefit arising prior to a quasi-reorganization, which is realizable beyond a reasonable doubt, should be recorded as an asset at the date of the reorganization. Such tax benefits may result from the amount of deficit in retained earnings that was applied to paid-in capital as a result of a quasi-reorganization, or from loss carryforwards that arose prior to the quasi-reorganization (APB-11). However, the tax benefit of an unused investment tax credit may never be recorded as an asset (APB-2 and APB-4).

Disclosure

Adequate disclosure of all pertinent information should be made in the financial statements. A new retained earnings account dated as at the date of the quasi-reorganization should be established and reflected in subsequent financial statements. Usually, the dating of the new retained earnings account can be eliminated after 10 years and in unusual circumstances earlier than 10 years (ARB-46).

Comprehensive Illustration

The following example demonstrates the procedures which must be used in accounting for a quasi-reorganization.

The Centrex Company, founded in 1970, has experienced losses in each of its first six years of operation. In May 1976, however, the company acquired two patents on an advanced solar-heating unit, which in several months has become the standard for the industry. The quarter ended September 30, 1976, was extremely profitable, and the patent and accompanying licensing agreements indicate that continuing profitability is quite likely.

The company is closely held, and the stockholders have agreed in principle to a quasi-reorganization. Negotiations have been held with various creditors regarding capitalizing debts.

The balance sheet of the company at December 31, 1976, appeared as follows:

Assets
Cash	$ 25,000
Accounts receivable (net)	410,000
Plant and equipment (net)	1,670,000
Other assets	80,000
Total assets	$2,185,000

Liabilities and Equity
Accounts payable	$ 840,000
Notes payable—other	300,000
Equipment notes payable	240,000
Common stock	500,000
Paid-in capital—common stock	1,017,000
Retained earnings	(712,000)
Total liabilities and equity	$2,185,000

The stockholders and creditors have approved the following plan of informal reorganization effective January 1, 1977:

1. The current shareholders will exchange their 100,000 shares of $5 par stock for 100,000 shares of $1 par stock.
2. The creditors have agreed to accept $300,000 in a 5% preferred stock for $300,000 of accounts payable.
3. The plant and equipment will be written down to its fair value of $1,100,000.
4. $70,000 of accounts receivable will be written off as uncollectible.
5. Other assets will be written down to their fair value of $50,000.

The first step in a quasi-reorganization is to write down all assets to their fair values. In the example the journal entry would be:

Retained earnings	$ 670,000	
Plant and equipment		$ 570,000
Accounts receivable		70,000
Other assets		30,000

Next, the change in the par value of the common stock is recorded:

Common stock	$ 400,000	
Paid-in capital—common stock		$ 400,000

The following journal entry records the new preferred stock issued for $300,000 of accounts payable:

Accounts payable	$ 300,000	
5% preferred stock		$ 300,000

After all the quasi-reorganization adjustments are made, the deficit in retained earnings ($1,382,000) is eliminated against the paid-in capital—common stock, leaving a zero balance in retained earnings:

Paid-in capital—common stock	$1,382,000	
Retained earnings		$1,382,000

The Centrex Company balance sheet after giving effect to the reorganization appears as:

Centrex Company
Assets

Cash	$ 25,000
Accounts receivable (net)	340,000
Plant and equipment (net)	1,100,000
Other assets	50,000
Total assets	$1,515,000

Liabilities and Equity

Accounts payable	$ 540,000
Notes payable—other	300,000
Equipment notes payable	240,000
Common stock ($1 par)	100,000
5% Preferred stock	300,000
Paid-in capital—common stock	35,000
Retained earnings since January 1, 1977	-0-
Total liabilities and equity	$1,515,000

Retained earnings must be dated on the balance sheet after a reorganization.

REAL AND PERSONAL PROPERTY TAXES

Background

ARB-43, Chapter 10A (as amended), provides the existing promulgated GAAP for accounting for real and personal property taxes.

Accounting and Reporting

Although many states have different laws or precedents as to when the legal liability accrues for real and personal property taxes, the general rule is that they accrue on the date they are assessed. However, the exact amount of tax may not be known on the assessment date, and a reasonable estimate must be made. The inability to determine the exact amount of real and personal property taxes is not an acceptable excuse for failure to recognize the existing tax liability. In those cases where the accrued amount is subject to a great deal of uncertainty, the liability should be appropriately described as estimated.

Whether the amount of the accrued tax liability for real and personal property taxes is known or estimated, it should be reported as a current liability in the balance sheet.

A monthly accrual over the fiscal period of the taxing authority is considered the most acceptable basis for recording real and personal property taxes. This will result in the appropriate accrual or prepayment at any closing date.

An adjustment to the estimated tax liability of a prior year will have to be made when the exact amount has been determined. This adjustment is made in the income statement of the period in which the exact amount has been determined, either as an adjustment to the current year's provision or as a separate item on the income statement.

It is sometimes proper to capitalize real estate taxes on property being developed for internal use or sale to customers. However, in most circumstances real and personal property taxes are considered an expense of doing business and are reported in the appropriate income statement (1) as an operating expense, (2) as a deduction from income, or (3) allocated to several expense accounts, such as manufacturing overhead and general and administrative expenses. As a general rule, real and personal property taxes should not be combined with income taxes.

> **OBSERVATION:** *The promulgated GAAP does not describe the criteria for capitalizing or not capitalizing real estate taxes.*

The most important consideration in accounting for real and personal property taxes is consistency. The accounting treatment, and reporting, must be consistently applied from year to year.

RELATED PARTY DISCLOSURES

Overview

FASB-57 establishes the promulgated GAAP for the disclosure of material related party transactions. In general, a related party is one which can exercise control or significant influence over the management or operating policies of another party, to the extent that one of the parties is or may be prevented from fully pursuing its own separate interests.

Background

When an auditor is performing an examination of financial statements, he is responsible for identifying any related party transactions that he encounters during the course of his audit. Related parties include the reporting entity, its affiliates, principal owners, management, and members of their immediate families. Related parties may exist when one entity has the ability to *significantly influence* another entity, through management or otherwise.

Regulation S-X (SEC) requires a prescribed accounting treatment for related parties. However, most transactions between related parties should be accounted for on the same basis as if the parties were not related, unless the *substance* of the transaction is not arm's length. Substance over form is an important consideration when accounting for transactions with related parties.

Under existing generally accepted auditing standards, the independent auditor exercises professional judgment in determining that related party transactions are adequately disclosed in the financial statements. Generally accepted auditing standards (SAS-6) require that significant related party transactions, individually or in the aggregate, be disclosed in the financial statements of the reporting entity. The disclosures should include:

1. The nature of the related party relationship.
2. A description or summarization of the related party transaction, including amounts and other pertinent information.
3. The effects of any change in terms between the related parties from the terms used in prior periods and the dollar amounts of transactions.

4. If not apparent in the financial statements, the terms of related party transactions, the manner of settlement of related party transactions, and amounts due to or from related parties.

Although disclosure of significant related party transactions, based on professional judgment, has been required of auditors for many years, there has been no promulgated GAAP on the subject to guide reporting entities.

Material Related Party Transaction Disclosures

Related parties consist of all affiliates of an enterprise, including (a) its management and their immediate families, (b) its principal owners and their immediate families, (c) its investments accounted for by the equity method, (d) beneficial employee trusts that are managed by the management of the enterprise, and (e) any party that may, or does, deal with the enterprise and has ownership of, control over, or can significantly influence the management or operating policies of another party to the extent that an arm's-length transaction may not be achieved.

FASB-57 requires that material related party transactions which are not eliminated in consolidated or combined financial statements must be disclosed in the financial statements of the reporting entity. However, related party transactions involving compensation arrangements, expense allowances, and similar items incurred in the ordinary course of business do not have to be disclosed.

If separate financial statements of an entity that has been consolidated are presented in a financial report which includes the consolidated financial statements, duplicate disclosure of the related party transactions is not necessary. Thus, disclosure of the material related party transactions in the consolidated statements is all that is required. However, disclosure of related party transactions is required in separate financial statements of (a) a parent company, (b) a subsidiary, (c) a corporate joint venture, or (d) an investee which is 50% or less owned.

The minimum financial statement disclosures required by FASB-57 for material related party transactions that (a) are not eliminated in consolidated or combined financial statements and (b) are not compensation arrangements, expense allowances, or similar items incurred in the ordinary course of business are as follows:

1. The nature of the material related party relationship. In addition, the name of the related party should be disclosed, if it is essential to the understanding of the relationship.

2. A description of the material related party transactions, including amounts and other pertinent information for each period in which an income statement is presented.
   Related party transactions of no or nominal amounts must also be disclosed. In other words, all information that is necessary to an understanding of the effects of the material related party transactions on the financial statements must be disclosed.
3. The effects of any change in terms between the related parties from terms used in prior periods. In addition, the dollar amount of transactions for each period in which an income statement is presented must be disclosed.
4. If not apparent in the financial statements, (a) the terms of related party transactions, (b) the manner of settlement of related party transactions, and (c) the amount due to or from related parties must all be disclosed.
5. If the operating results or financial position of a reporting entity can be altered significantly by the effects of common ownership or management control of the reporting entity and one or more other entities, even if there are no transactions between any of the entities, the nature of the ownership or management control must be disclosed in the financial statements. In other words, if the existence of the control relationship has the potential of producing operating results or financial positions that differ from those that would exist if there were no control relationship, disclosure must be made of the nature of such ownership or management control.

The amount of detail disclosed for related party transactions must be sufficient for the user of the financial statements to be able to understand the related party transaction. Thus, this disclosure of the total amount of a specific type of material related party transaction or of the effects of the relationship between the related parties may be all that is necessary.

One cannot assume that a related party transaction is consummated in the same manner as an arm's-length transaction, since free market competition is not the basis of related party transactions. Disclosures or other representations of a material related party transaction in financial statements should not imply that the transaction was made on the same basis as an arm's-length transaction, unless the disclosures or representations can be substantiated.

FASB-57 is effective for fiscal years ending on or after June 16, 1982, and earlier application of its provisions is encouraged.

RESEARCH AND DEVELOPMENT COSTS

Background

The following pronouncements establish the promulgated GAAP for research and development costs:

FASB-2 – Accounting for Research and Development Costs
FASB-68 – Research and Development Arrangements
FASB-86 – Accounting for the Cost of Computer Software to Be Sold, Leased, or Otherwise Marketed
FASB Interpretation-4 – Applicability of FASB Statement No. 2 to Business Combinations Accounted for by the Purchase Method
FASB Interpretation-6 – Applicability of FASB Statement No. 2 to Computer Software
FASB Technical Bulletin 84-1 – Accounting for Stock Issued to Acquire the Results of a Research and Development Arrangement

FASB-2 is the primary GAAP that addresses the accounting for research and development costs. The following specific activities are not covered by the provisions of FASB-2:

- Activities that are unique to the extractive industries, such as prospecting, exploration, drilling, mining, and similar functions. However, research and development activities which are comparable in nature to other companies not in the extractive industry, such as the development or improvement of techniques and processes, are covered.
- Research and development performed under contract for others, including indirect costs which are specifically reimbursable under a contract.

FASB Interpretation-4 provides guidance in applying the provisions of FASB-2 to research and development costs acquired in a business combination accounted for by the purchase method. FASB Interpretation-6 provides some guidance in applying the provisions of FASB-2 to computer software, but very little text remains in this pronouncement since its amendment by FASB-86.

FASB-68 deals with research and development arrangements which are partially or completely funded by other parties. FASB-68 applies to the party who performs the research and development activities, whether that party is the enterprise, the funding parties, or a third party. FASB-68 does not cover government sponsored research and development projects.

> **OBSERVATION:** FASB Technical Bulletin 84-1 concludes that the acquisition of the results of a research and development arrangement through the issuance of capital stock should be accounted for at the fair value of the stock issued, or at the fair value of the consideration received, whichever is more clearly evident.

FASB-86 establishes accounting and reporting standards for costs incurred for computer software products that are sold, leased, or otherwise marketed by an enterprise. FASB-86 covers the costs incurred for separate computer software products and the costs incurred for integral parts of computer software products or processes, which are either purchased or internally developed and produced by an enterprise. FASB-86 does not cover the costs incurred for computer software that is (a) produced for others by an enterprise under a contractual arrangement or (b) created for the internal use of an enterprise.

Overview

Research is the planned efforts of a company to discover new information that will help create a new product, service, process, or technique, or vastly improve one in current use. Development takes the findings generated by research and formulates a plan to create the desired item or to improve the existing one. Development in the context of this area of GAAP does not include normal improvements in existing operations. The promulgated GAAP does not include market research and testing, because these items specifically relate to the selling and marketing operations of a company. In addition, general and administrative expenses not *directly* related to the R&D activities are also not included in the promulgated GAAP.

The underlying basic principle in accounting for R&D is conservatism, because of the high degree of uncertainty of any resulting future benefit. Since at the time of performing the R&D, there is no possible method of determining any future success, the most conservative approach is to expense the item in the period incurred.

Accounting and Reporting R&D

All R&D costs covered by the promulgated GAAP are expensed when incurred except R&D machinery, equipment, and facilities which have alternative future uses either in R&D activities or otherwise. Machinery, equipment, and facilities, which have alternative future uses, should be capitalized. However, depreciation or amortization on such capitalized R&D machinery, equipment, and facilities is charged to expense. All expenditures in conjunction with an R&D project including personnel costs, materials, equipment, facilities, and intangibles, for which the company has no alternative future use beyond the specific project for which the items were purchased, are expensed. Indirect costs, including general and administrative expenses, which are *directly* related to the R&D are also expensed when incurred.

As mentioned previously, it is important to remember that R&D costs related to market research or testing, and general and administrative expenses that are not directly related to R&D activity, are costs not covered by the promulgated GAAP.

Research and development costs acquired by the purchase method in a business combination shall be assigned their fair values, if any, in accordance with existing promulgated GAAP (APB-16). The subsequent accounting by the acquirer of these R&D costs shall be made in compliance with the promulgated GAAP enumerated herein. Those R&D costs with future alternative use shall be capitalized, and all others expensed (FASB Interpretation-4).

Disclosure

The amount of R&D charged to expense for the period must be disclosed in the financial statements for each period presented.

A company in a regulated industry which defers R&D costs in compliance with the Addendum to APB-2 must disclose the following additional information:

1. Accounting policies in regard to R&D, including the basis for amortization
2. The total amount of R&D that has been expensed, capitalized, or deferred for each period that an income statement is presented

Computer Software To Be Sold, Leased, or Otherwise Marketed

FASB-86 applies only to those costs incurred in purchasing or internally developing and producing computer software products that are sold, leased, or otherwise marketed by an enterprise. The costs covered by FASB-86 may be incurred (a) for separate computer software products or (b) for integral parts of computer software products or processes. FASB-86 does not cover those costs incurred for computer software that is (a) produced by an enterprise for others under a contractual arrangement or (b) created for the internal use of an enterprise.

Under FASB-86, the terms *computer software product, software product,* and *product,* are used interchangeably to mean either (a) a computer software program, (b) a group of programs, or (c) a product enhancement. A product enhancement represents improvement to an existing product that significantly improves the marketability or extends the estimated useful life of the original product. A product enhancement almost always involves a new design or redesign of the original computer software product.

The primary activities that are involved in the creation of a computer software product are the (a) planning function, (b) design function, and (c) production function. The planning function of a computer software product generally includes preliminary product specifications and design and the development of a production and a financial plan for the product. In addition, the planning function should also include a marketing analysis and a marketing plan for the product. The planning function should generate sufficient documentation and detailed information for an enterprise to make a determination of the overall feasibility of the proposed computer software product.

The design function of a computer software product includes the product design and the detail program design. The production of a product master usually begins after the design function. Producing a product master generally involves coding, testing, and the development of training materials. Coding is the process in which the requirements of the detailed program design are converted into a computer language. Testing includes the steps necessary to determine whether the computer software product works in accordance with its design specifications and documentation.

Computer software costs that must be expensed FASB-86 specifies that all costs incurred in establishing the technological feasibility of a computer software product that is sold, leased, or otherwise marketed by an enterprise are research and development costs, which must be accounted for as required by FASB-2 (Accounting for Research and Development Costs). Thus, until technological feasibility is established in accordance with FASB-86 (see below), all costs incurred through the purchase or internal development and production of a computer software product that is sold, leased, or otherwise marketed must be accounted for as research and development costs in accordance with the provisions of FASB-2.

Under the provisions of FASB-2, all research and development costs must be expensed when incurred, except machinery, equipment, and facilities, which have alternative future use in either the research and development activities of an enterprise or otherwise. Market research and testing are not considered research and development activities under the provisions of FASB-2, because these functions specifically relate to the selling and marketing operations of an enterprise. In addition, general and administrative expenses are not considered research and development costs, unless they are *directly* related to the research and development activities of an enterprise. Thus, the development costs of a computer system that improves an enterprise's administrative or selling procedures would not be considered research and development costs. However, all costs incurred for internally developed computer software products used in an enterprise's own research and development activities should be charged to expense when incurred, because the future alternative use test does not apply to such costs (FASB Interpretation-6, Footnote 2).

Under FASB-86, production costs incurred for integral parts of a computer software product or process must be expensed, unless (a) technological feasibility has been established for the computer software product or process and (b) all research and development activities have been completed for the other components of the computer software product or process.

Computer software costs that must be capitalized After technological feasibility has been established, FASB-86 specifies that all costs incurred for a computer software product that is sold, leased, or otherwise marketed by an enterprise shall be capitalized. Thus, the costs of producing product masters for a computer software product, including costs for coding and testing, shall be capitalized, but only after technological feasibility has been established in accordance with FASB-86 (see below).

Production costs for computer software that is to be used as an integral part of a product or process shall be capitalized, but only after (a) technological feasibility has been established for the software and (b) all research and development activities for the other components of the product or process have been completed.

Capitalization of computer software costs shall be discontinued when the computer software product is available to be sold, leased, or otherwise marketed. Costs for maintenance and customer support shall be charged to expense when incurred or when the related revenue is recognized, whichever occurs first.

OBSERVATION: *Under FASB-86, the amount of costs that an enterprise is required to capitalize depends primarily on its choice of production methods. Thus, an enterprise may control the amount of computer software costs that it capitalizes by establishing technological feasibility at a designated time during the production process.*

Establishing technological feasibility Technological feasibility is established when all of the activities that are necessary to substantiate that the computer software product can be produced in accordance with its design specifications have been completed, including functions, features, and technical performance requirements. Thus, all planning, designing, coding, and testing activities that are required to substantiate that the computer software product can be produced to meet its design specifications must be completed before technological feasibility can be established.

Under FASB-86, the method of establishing the technological feasibility of a computer software product depends on whether the process of creating the computer software product includes a detail program design or not. The following are the minimum requirements for establishing the technological feasibility of a computer software product:

Includes Detail Program Design

If the process of creating the computer software product includes a detail program design, an enterprise must comply with the following criteria to establish the technological feasibility of a computer software product.

1. An enterprise must complete the product design and detail program design for the computer software product and establish that it has available the necessary skills, hardware, and software technology to produce the product.
2. An enterprise must substantiate the completeness of the program design and its consistency with the product design by documenting and tracing the detail program design to the product specifications.
3. An enterprise must identify the high-risk development issues in the computer software product through review of the detail program design, and if any uncertainties relating to the high-risk development issues are discovered, they must be resolved through coding and testing. High-risk development issues that

may be encountered in the production of a computer software product may include novel, unique, or unproven functions and features, and/or technological innovations.

Does Not Include Detail Program Design

If the process of creating the computer software product *does not* include a detail program design, an enterprise must comply with the following criteria to establish the technological feasibility of a computer software product.

1. An enterprise must complete a product design and a working model of the computer software product.
2. An enterprise must substantiate the completeness of the working model and its consistency with the product design by testing the model.

Amortization of capitalized computer software costs   Amortization of capitalized computer software costs, on a product-by-product basis, shall begin when the product is available to be sold, leased, or otherwise marketed. Periodic amortization, on a product-by-product basis, shall be equal to the greater of (a) the amount computed by the straight-line method over the estimated useful life of the product or (b) the amount computed by using the ratio that current gross revenues bear to total estimated gross revenues (including current gross revenues).

Inventory costs   Inventory costs shall be capitalized on a unit-specific basis and charged to cost of sales when the related revenue from the sale of those units is recognized. Inventory costs include duplicate copies of the computer software product made from the product master, documentation, training materials, and the costs incurred for packaging the product for distribution.

Periodic evaluation of capitalized computer software costs   Unamortized computer software costs that have been previously capitalized in accordance with FASB-86 are reported at net realizable value on an enterprise's balance sheet. Net realizable value is determined on a product-by-product basis, and is equal to the estimated future gross revenues of a specific product, less estimated future costs of completing and disposing of that specific product, including the costs of performing maintenance and customer support on a product-by-product basis as required by the terms of the sale.

The excess of any unamortized computer software costs over its related net realizable value at a balance sheet date shall be written down. The amount of write-down shall be charged to periodic income. Capitalized costs that have been written down as a charge to income shall not be capitalized again or restored in any future period.

Financial statement disclosures   The total amount of unamortized computer software costs that is included in each balance sheet presented shall be disclosed in the financial statements. The total amount of computer software costs charged to expense shall be disclosed for each income statement presented. The total amount of computer software costs charged to expense shall include amortization expense and amounts written down to net realizable value.

All computer software costs that are classified as research and development costs shall be disclosed as such in accordance with FASB-2 (Accounting for Research and Development Costs). These costs may include the costs of planning, product design, detail program design, and the costs incurred in establishing technological feasibility of a computer software product.

Effective date and transition   FASB-86 is effective for financial statements for fiscal years beginning on or after December 16, 1985, and shall also be applied to all computer software projects in progress at the time of the initial application of FASB-86. Earlier application of the provisions of FASB-86 is permitted in previously unissued annual financial statements.

The amount of capitalized and noncapitalized computer software costs that was incurred prior to the first application of FASB-86 shall not be changed. However, the amortization provisions of FASB-86 shall be applied to any unamortized balance of computer software costs that was capitalized prior to December 16, 1985 (the effective date of FASB-86).

> **OBSERVATION:** *In the period in which FASB-86 is first applied, an enterprise should disclose in its financial statements the effects of the change in accounting principle on income before extraordinary items, net income, and related per share amounts, in accordance with APB-20 (Accounting Changes).*

Research and Development Arrangements

FASB-68 covers research and development arrangements of an enterprise which are partially or completely funded by other parties. In this respect, the typical arrangement is for the parties to set up a limited partnership through which the R&D activities related to a specific project are funded. Although the limited partnership arrangement is used in FASB-68 for illustrative purposes, the legal structure of a R&D arrangement may take a variety of forms and is sometimes influenced by income tax implications and securities regulations.

In a typical R&D arrangement, an enterprise which has the basic technology for a particular project is the general partner and manages the R&D activities. The limited partners, who may or may not be related parties, provide all or part of the funds to complete the project. If the funds are not sufficient, the arrangement may allow or require the general partner to either (a) sell additional limited partnership interests or (b) use its own funds to complete the project. In addition, some funds may be provided in the form of loans or advances to the limited partnership. The repayment of the loans or advances may be guaranteed by the partnership.

The actual R&D activities are usually performed by the enterprise or a related party, under a contract with the limited partnership. The contract price is either fixed or cost plus a fixed or percentage fee and is performed on a "best efforts" basis, with no guarantee of ultimate success. The legal ownership of the results of the project vests with the partnership. Frequently, the enterprise has an option to acquire the partnership's interest in the project or to obtain exclusive use of the results of the project. If the project is a success, the enterprise will no doubt exercise its option to acquire the project. However, under some circumstances, even if the project is unsuccessful, the enterprise may still have reason to acquire the project, in spite of the fact that it is not legally required to do so. For example, the enterprise may want to prevent the final results of the project from falling into the hands of a competitor.

Many of the liabilities and obligations which an enterprise undertakes in a R&D project which is funded by others are specified in the agreements. However, some liabilities and obligations may exist in substance, but may not be reduced to writing. For example, future payments by the enterprise to other parties for royalties or the acquisition of the partnership's interest in the project may, in substance, represent (a) the repayment of a loan or (b) the purchase price of a specific asset.

Nature of R&D arrangement In R&D arrangements that are partially or completely funded by other parties, accounting and reporting for R&D costs depend upon the nature of the obligation that an enterprise incurs in the arrangement. The nature of the obligation in such R&D arrangements can fall into one of the following categories:

1. The obligation is solely to perform contractual services.
2. The obligation represents a liability to repay all of the funds provided by the other parties.
3. The obligation is partly to perform contractual services and partly a liability to repay some, but not all, of the funds provided by the other parties.

No problem arises if the nature of the obligation incurred by an enterprise is solely to perform contractual services. In this event, all R&D costs are charged to "cost of sales." Also, no problem arises if the nature of the obligation represents a liability to repay all of the funds provided by the other parties. In this event, all R&D costs are charged to "expense" when incurred.

If the nature of the obligation incurred by an enterprise is partly a liability and partly the performance of contractual services, R&D costs are charged partly to expense and partly to cost of sales. The portion charged to cost of sales is related to the funds provided by the other parties which do not have to be repaid by the enterprise. The portion charged to expense is related to the funds provided by the other parties which are likely to be repaid by the enterprise. Under FASB-68, the portion charged to expense is referred to as the enterprise's portion of the R&D costs. Under the provisions of FASB-68, an enterprise shall charge its portion of the R&D costs to expense in the same manner as the liability is incurred. Thus, if the liability arises on a pro rata basis, the enterprise's portion of the R&D costs shall be charged to expense in the same manner. If the liability arises as the initial funds are expended, the enterprises's portion of the R&D costs shall be charged to expense in the same manner.

FASB-68 provides guidance in determining the nature of the obligation that an enterprise incurs in R&D arrangements which are partially or completely funded by other parties. FASB-68 requires that an enterprise report in its financial statements the estimated liability, if any, incurred in a R&D arrangement which is partially or completely funded by other parties. The estimated liability shall include any contractually defined obligations and any obligations not contractually defined, but otherwise reasonably evident. A critical factor in determining an enterprise's obligation is whether the financial risks involved in the R&D arrangement have been substantively and genuinely transferred to the other parties. To the extent that an enterprise retains any financial risk, the R&D costs are considered costs incurred by the enterprise on its own behalf and must, therefore, be expensed as incurred. Thus, if an enterprise contractually or otherwise obligates itself to repay any of the funds provided by others, regardless of the outcome of the R&D project, the financial risks have not been transferred and the enterprise's commitment to repay is evident. On the other hand, an enterprise does not undertake any financial risk when it obligates itself to repay the other parties providing that the R&D project results in future economic benefit to the enterprise.

Under the provisions of FASB-68, if significant indications exist that the enterprise is *likely* to repay any funds, it is presumed that a liability has been incurred. This presumption can be overcome only by substantial evidence to the contrary. Circumstances in which significant indications exist that the enterprise is likely to repay funds and a liability is presumed are as follows:

1. Regardless of the success of the R&D project, the enterprise has indicated the intent to repay all or part of the funds provided by other parties.
2. If it failed to repay any of the funds, the enterprise would suffer a "severe economic penalty." Under FASB-68, an economic penalty is "severe" if an enterprise would probably elect, under normal business circumstances, to repay the funds rather than to incur the penalty.
3. At the inception of the R&D arrangement a material related party relationship (FASB-57) exists between the enterprise and any of the parties funding the R&D project.
4. At the inception of the R&D arrangement, the project is substantially complete. Under this circumstance, the financial risks involved in the R&D project are already known to all parties.

Under the provisions of FASB-68, an obligation may represent a liability whether it is payable in cash, securities, or by some other means.

Obligation for contractual services   If substantially all of the financial risks of the R&D project are transferred to the other parties and the enterprise is not committed to repay any of the funds provided by the other parties, the enterprise shall account for its obligation as contractual R&D services. If repayment by the enterprise of any of the funds provided by the other parties depends on the availability of a future economic benefit to the enterprise, the enterprise shall also account for its obligation as contractual R&D services. In these circumstances the financial risks of the R&D arrangement have clearly been transferred to others and the enterprise is only obligated to perform contractual R&D services.

Frequently, an enterprise will make a loan or advance to the other parties, which is designated to be repaid as a reduction of the purchase price for the results of the project, or as a reduction of future royalty payments from the enterprise. In this event, the portion of the loan or advance which is designated to be repaid as a reduction of the purchase price for the results of the project, or as a reduction of future royalties, shall be accounted for by the enterprise as R&D expense, unless it can be attributed to activities other than R&D, such as marketing or advertising.

At or before the completion of the R&D project, the enterprise may elect to exercise its option to purchase the partnership's interest, or to obtain exclusive rights to the results of the project. The enterprise shall account for the purchase of the partnership's interest, or the exclusive rights, in accordance with existing GAAP. Thus, any asset that results from the R&D project shall be assigned its fair value (APB-16), and intangible assets shall be accounted for in accordance with APB-17 (Intangible Assets).

If an enterprise is required to issue warrants or similar instruments in connection with the R&D arrangement, a portion of the funds provided by the other parties shall be recorded as paid-in capital. The amount capitalized as paid-in capital shall be equal to the fair market value of the warrants or other instruments at the date the R&D arrangement is consummated.

Financial statement disclosure   Notes to the financial statements shall include the following disclosures for R&D arrangements which are accounted for as contracts to perform R&D services for others in accordance with FASB-68:

As of the Date of Each Balance Sheet Presented

- The terms of significant agreements relating to the R&D arrangement, including (a) purchase provisions, (b) license agreements, (c) royalty arrangements, and (d) commitments to provide additional funds.

For Each Income Statement Presented

- The amount of R&D costs incurred and compensation earned during the period for such R&D arrangements.

Effective date   FASB-68 is effective for R&D arrangements covered by its provisions that are entered into on or after January 1, 1983.

Earlier application of the provisions of FASB-68 is encouraged in previously unissued financial statements.

Retroactive application of the provisions of FASB-68 to previously issued financial statements is permitted, but not required. If retroactive application is elected, the financial statements of the year of change shall disclose the nature of any restatement and its effects on income before extraordinary items, net income, and related per share amounts, for each year presented.

RESULTS OF OPERATIONS

Background

There are three separate promulgated GAAP in the area of reporting the results of operations, as follows:

    APB-9 (as amended), Reporting the Results of Operations
    APB-30 (as amended), Reporting the Results of Operations—Reporting the Effects of Disposal of a Segment of a Business, and Extraordinary, Unusual, and Infrequently Occuring Events and Transactions
    FASB-16, Prior Period Adjustments
    FASB Interpretation-27, Accounting for a Loss on a Sublease

APB-9 clearly indicates that it applies to general-purpose statements prepared in conformity with GAAP that present the results of operations. Investment companies, insurance companies, and certain nonprofit organizations which have developed special formats for income statements that differ from the typical commercial formats need not comply with the provision of APB-9, which requires that net income be presented as one amount. Otherwise these entities are covered by APB-9. Both APB-30 and FASB-16 are silent in respect to these particular companies, so it is assumed that they must fully comply with these promulgated GAAP.

Overview

Prior to the issuance of APB-9 there were differences in the accounting profession as to what should, or should not, be included in net income. Proponents of the *all-inclusive concept* believe that all items affecting net increases in owners' equity, except dividends and capital transactions, should be included in computing net income. These proponents support their position with the following reasons:

1. Extraordinary items are part of income, and annual income statements over the life of an entity when added together should represent total net income as reported.
2. Omission of extraordinary items will distort the total financial position of an enterprise.

3. Extraordinary items may be manipulated, or possibly overlooked, if they are not included on a regular basis.
4. An income statement that includes all charges or credits arising during the year is simple to prepare, easy to understand, and not subject to variations based on judgment.

Proponents of the *current operating performance concept*, who advocate excluding extraordinary items from net income, maintain the following position:

1. Net income should place emphasis on the normal operations of an enterprise and exclude nonrecurring extraordinary items.
2. The annual income statement's primary purpose is to inform those interested in what an entity was able to earn under the current year's operating conditions.
3. Net income for the year should reflect as clearly as possible what happened under that year's conditions, in order that comparability may be made with prior years and with the performance of other enterprises in the same industry.
4. Readers of financial statements are frequently unable to determine net income from normal operations, when extraordinary items are included in the computation of net income.
5. A material extraordinary item included in net income may be so distorting in its effect as to lead to unsound judgment about the current operating performance of the company.

Although the two schools of thought still exist, present-day GAAP support the *all-inclusive concept*. Net income should include all items of income and loss during a reporting period, except prior-period adjustments, dividends, and capital transactions. All extraordinary items should be segregated and shown separately in the income statement.

APB-9 further describes capital transactions as those:

1. Charges or credits arising from transactions in a company's own capital stock
2. Transfers to and from appropriated retained earnings
3. Adjustments made pursuant to a quasi-reorganization

Extraordinary Items

Extraordinary items are transactions and other events that are (1) material in nature, (2) of a character significantly different from the typical or customary business activities, (3) not expected to recur frequently, and (4) not normally considered in evaluating the ordinary operating results of an enterprise. Extraordinary items must be separately disclosed in the income statement, net of any related income tax effect.

Extraordinary items are usually determined by informed professional judgment, taking into consideration all the facts involved in a particular situation. However, some areas of promulgated GAAP require that an item be treated as extraordinary. The following are the more common items which, if material, should be reported as an extraordinary item:

1. The tax benefit of an operating loss carryforward when recognized in periods subsequent to the year of loss (APB-11)
2. The tax benefit of a loss carryforward when recognized in periods subsequent to the year of loss (APB-11)
3. The profit or loss on disposal of a significant part of the assets, or a separate segment, of the previously separate companies of a business combination, when disposed of within two years after the date of the combination (APB-16)
4. Gains on restructuring payables (FASB-15)
5. Most gains or losses on the extinguishment of debt (FASB-4)
6. Most expropriations of property (APB-30)

The cumulative effect of an accounting change is reflected in the income statement, net of related tax effects, between extraordinary items and net income. On the other hand, a gain or loss on discontinued operations is reflected in the income statement, net of related income tax effects, between income from continuing operations and extraordinary items.

For reporting purposes extraordinary items arising as part of the net income from an investment accounted for by the equity method are combined with extraordinary items of the investor.

If professional judgment dictates individual treatment of a material event or transaction that does not qualify as an extraordinary item, it may be separately reported as a component of income from continuing operations with appropriate footnote disclosure. However, in this event, the separately identified item should not be reported net of its related tax effects.

Prior-Period Adjustments

An SEC staff interpretation of GAAP recently questioned the use of prior-period adjustments to account for certain negotiated settlements of litigation. One criterion for a prior-period adjustment had been that the event which caused the adjustment depended primarily on the determination of persons other than management.

The two most common types of prior-period adjustments had been settlements of litigation and settlements of income taxes. The SEC concluded that management plays a significant role in any negotiated settlement and that these settlements do not meet the criteria for a prior-period adjustment.

Consequently the definition of a prior-period adjustment has been narrowly redefined by FASB-16 as either:

1. A correction of an error in a prior-period statement, or
2. An adjustment for the realization of the tax benefits of the preacquisition operating-loss carryforwards of purchased subsidiaries

All other items of profit and loss (including accruals for loss contingencies) shall be included in the determination of net income for the period. Items which previously had qualified for treatment as prior-period adjustments will now be included in net income and will require disclosure as necessary for conformity with other requirements of GAAP.

Interim-period adjustments An adjustment of prior interim periods of a current fiscal year can include any of the following settlements:

1. Litigation or similar claims
2. Income taxes
3. Renegotiation
4. Utility revenues governed by rate-making processes

In adjusting interim periods of the current year, any adjustment of prior periods is made to the first interim period of the current year. Adjustments to the other interim periods of the current year are related to the interim period affected.

The effects (1) on income from continuous operations, (2) on net income, and (3) on earnings per share of an adjustment to a current interim period must be fully disclosed.

Accounting changes Present promulgated GAAP is unaffected by the new narrow definition of prior-period adjustments.

Accounting changes that will necessitate adjustments of prior periods for reporting purposes are:

1. Reporting a change in an entity
2. An accounting change from the LIFO method to any other method
3. An accounting change in reporting long-term construction contracts
4. A change to or from the full-cost method used in the extractive industries
5. One-time change for closely held corporations in connection with a public offering of its equity securities, or when such a company first issues financial statements for obtaining additional equity capital from outside investors (see APB-20)
6. Change from the retirement-replacement-betterment method of accounting for railroad track structures to the depreciation method of accounting (FASB-73)

In addition, a change in accounting methods of constituents of a pooling of interest to conform with the parent company is still applied retroactively, and financial statements presented for prior periods should be restated.

In those rare material cases when prior-period adjustments are recorded, the resulting effects should be disclosed in the period in which the adjustments are made by *restating the balance of retained earnings at the beginning of such period.*

Both the gross and net effect (of related income taxes) of prior-period adjustments on net income should be disclosed in the year of adjustment and all years presented (APB-9).

Discontinued Operations

Discontinued operations are identifiable segments of a business that have been or will be disposed of.

Identifiable entity Segments of a business are components that represent a major class of a firm's business, usually taking the form of a subsidiary, division, department, or other identifiable entity.

Segments of a business have separate assets and results of operations and activities that can be clearly distinguished for financial reporting purposes.

Facts that indicate there is no separate identity suggest that the form of business should not be classified as a segment of a business.

Measurement date The measurement date of a disposal of a segment of business is the date management commits itself to a formal plan for action to sell or otherwise dispose of the segment.

> **OBSERVATION:** *The plan of disposal should be carried out within one year from the measurement date. If a plan of disposal is estimated to be completed within one year, and subsequently is not, any revision of the net realizable value of the segment should be treated as a change in an accounting estimate and should therefore be made prospectively.*

Disposal date   The disposal date is the date of closing, in the case of a sale, or the date operations cease, in the case of abandonment.

Determination of gain or loss   The estimated loss on disposal of a segment of business should be provided for as of the *measurement date*.

In the case of a gain, it should not be recognized until it is realized (realization principle), which is usually the *disposal date*.

Determination of gain or loss on disposal of a segment of business should be made as of the measurement date, based on estimates of the net realizable value.

Net losses from operations between the measurement date and the expected disposal date should be provided for in the determination of gain or loss.

Estimates should be based on the amounts that can be projected with reasonable accuracy.

> **OBSERVATION:** *Cost, expenses, and other adjustments associated with normal business activities which should have been recognized prior to the measurement date should not be included in the gain or loss on disposal of a segment, but should be included in income (loss) from discontinued operations. Severance pay, additional pension costs, and employee relocation expenses are costs directly associated with the decision to dispose of the segment and are properly includable in the gain or loss on disposal.*

Long-term leases   FASB Interpretation-27 reaffirms that estimated costs and expenses directly associated with a decision to dispose of a business segment should include future rental payments on long-term leases less any future rentals to be received from subleases of the same properties (APB-30). The gain or loss is measured as the difference between the unamortized cost of the leased property (net carrying amount) and the present value of the minimum lease payments which will be received under the terms of the sublease. The gain or loss is included in the overall gain or loss on the disposal of the business segment.

> **OBSERVATION:** *FASB Interpretation-27 is not clear on its coverage of subleases which are classified as operating leases. There is a strong argument that gain or loss on an operating sublease be included as part of the overall gain or loss on disposal of a business segment. APB-30 specifically states that all costs and expenses which are directly associated to the decision to dispose of a business segment be included in the overall gain or loss on the disposal. If a business segment has a long-term operating lease which is subleased and classified as an operating lease as part of the overall disposal of the segment, then any gain or loss would obviously be directly associated with management's decision to dispose of the segment. The gain or loss would be measured as the difference between the present value of the future rental payments which must be paid on the original lease and the present value of the future rental receipts which will be collected on the operating sublease. The journal entry to record a loss would be a debit to the gain or loss account for disposal of the business segment and a credit to a deferred account. The deferred credit account would be amortized each year in an amount which would make up the difference between the payment made on the original lease and the rental collected on the operating sublease.*

Disclosure Notes to the financial statements for the period encompassing the measurement date should include:

1. Identity of the segment of business
2. Expected date of disposal
3. Manner of disposal
4. Description of the remaining assets and liabilities of the segment of business
5. Income and loss from operations and other proceeds from disposal of the segment of business, from the measurement date to the date of the balance sheet

Presentation of Net Income

The following is the preferred method of financial statement presentation of net income:

Income (loss) from continuing operations, before provision for income taxes	$XXXXX	
Provision for income taxes	XXX	
Income (loss) from continuing operations		$XXXXX
Discontinued operations (note ___)		
Income (loss) from operations of discontinued division A (less applicable income taxes $XX)	$ XXXX	
Loss (gain) on disposal of division A, including provision of $XX for operating losses during phase-out period (less applicable income taxes of $XX)	XXX	
Net income (loss) from discontinued operations		XXXX
Net income (loss) before extraordinary items		$XXXXX
Extraordinary items (note ___) (less applicable income taxes of $XX)		XX
Cumulative effect on prior years (to December 31, 19XX) of a change in an accounting principle (less applicable income taxes of $XX).		XXX
Net income		$XXXXX

Earnings per share (EPS) for extraordinary items is not required but is strongly recommended by APB-15 and APB-30. EPS for discontinued operations and the resulting gain or loss on the disposal of the segment may or may not be presented (APB-30).

When common stock equivalents or other dilutive securities cause a dilution in one of the EPS data presented on the face of the income statement, and at the same time cause an antidilution in another EPS data presented on the same income statement, all the EPS data presented should be computed using the common stock equivalents or other dilutive securities (APB-30).

Whenever prior-period adjustments have been recorded during any period included in a five- or ten-year historical financial summary, the reported amounts of net income and components thereof should be appropriately restated.

REVENUE RECOGNITION

Overview

FASB-48 contains the specialized accounting and reporting principles and practices that were originally published in the AICPA Statement of Position 75-1, entitled "Revenue Recognition When Right of Return Exists."

FASB-48 indicates that the specialized accounting and reporting principles and practices were extracted from SOP 75-1, without significant change, and that the Financial Accounting Standards Board did not contemplate a comprehensive reconsideration of the accounting issues covered in SOP 75-1.

FASB-48 does not cover real estate or lease transactions, and does not apply to accounting for revenue of service industries.

> **OBSERVATION:** *FASB-48 covers only sales for which a "right of return exists." Thus, in a sale of $100,000 worth of merchandise, of which 30% can be returned, only $30,000 of the sale is subject to FASB-48. Since the balance of the sale ($70,000) is not subject to a right of return, it is not covered by FASB-48.*

Background

The realization principle requires that revenue be earned before it is recognized. Revenue is usually recognized when the earning process is complete and an exchange has taken place (APB Statement-4). The earning process is not complete until collection of the sales price is reasonably assured (APB-10).

It is common practice in some industries for dealers and distributors of personal property to have the right to return unsold merchandise. The right to return merchandise is usually an industry practice but also occurs as a result of a contractual agreement. The return period can last for a few days, as in the perishable food industry, or can last for several years, which is not infrequent for some types of publishers. The rate of return of some publishers may be as high as 60%, while in other industries such as perishable foods, the rate of return may be insignificant.

As long as a right of return exists and the returns can be significant, the seller is exposed to reacquiring the ownership of the property. In other words, the risks and rewards of ownership are not, in substance, passed on to the buyer.

Since the earning process is not complete until collection of the sales price is reasonably assured, certain accounting problems arise in recognizing revenue when the right to return exists.

Revenue Recognition for Returnable Merchandise

When a buyer has the right to return merchandise purchased, the seller may not recognize income from the sale, unless all of the following conditions are met:

1. The price between the seller and the buyer is substantially fixed, or determinable.
2. The seller has received full payment, or the buyer is indebted to the seller and the indebtedness is not contingent on the resale of the merchandise.
3. Physical destruction, damage, or theft of the merchandise would not change the buyer's obligation to the seller.
4. The buyer has economic substance, and is not a front, straw party, or conduit, existing for the benefit of the seller.
5. No significant obligations exist for the seller to help the buyer resell the merchandise.
6. A reasonable estimate can be made of the amount of future returns.

If all of the above conditions are met, revenue shall be recognized on sales for which a right of return exists, provided that an appropriate provision is made for costs or losses which may occur in connection with the return of merchandise from the buyer. However, if one or more of the conditions prescribed by FASB-48 are not met, revenue cannot be recognized until the right of return privilege has substantially expired, or the provisions of FASB-48 are subsequently met.

> **OBSERVATION:** *An exchange of one item for a similar item of the same quality and value, regardless of size or color, is not considered a "return" for the purposes of FASB-48.*

If all of the conditions of FASB-48 are met, an appropriate provision for costs or losses which may occur in connection with the return of merchandise from the buyer must be made by the seller. The provision for costs or losses must be in accordance with the provisions of FASB-5 (Accounting for Contingencies). Under FASB-5, a determination must be made as to whether the costs or losses are

(1) probable, (2) reasonably possible, or (3) remote. Under FASB-5, a provision for a loss contingency should be accrued, by a charge to income, providing that both of the following conditions exist:

1. It is *probable* that as at the date of the financial statements an asset has been impaired or a liability incurred, based on subsequent available information prior to the issuance of the financial statements.
2. The amount of loss can be reasonably estimated.

The second requirement (above) for the accrual of a loss contingency under FASB-5 will always exist when all of the conditions of FASB-48 are met. This is because condition 6 of FASB-48 requires that a reasonable estimate can be made of the amount of future returns, which also means that the amount of loss on the returns, if any, should be reasonably estimable. Thus, if returns are "probable" and all of the conditions of FASB-48 are met, an accrual is required by FASB-5. This accrual will result in a reduction of sales revenue and related cost of sales in the income statement, which is exactly what FASB-48 requires. However, if returns are "reasonably possible" or "remote" and all of the conditions of FASB-48 are met, an accrual is not required by FASB-5. In this event, FASB-5 requires footnote disclosure only, and not an accrual. If there is no accrual, sales revenue and related cost of sales in the income statement will not be reduced to reflect estimated returns that are reasonably possible or remote. It is highly unlikely that these results were intended by FASB-48.

> **OBSERVATION:** *It certainly seems logical that an accrual be made for returns which meet all of the conditions of FASB-48, and all of the conditions of FASB-5 for the accrual of a loss contingency, except that they are classified as reasonably possible, instead of probable.*

When returns are probable and all of the conditions of FASB-48 are met, sales revenue and related cost of sales of expected returns, along with any estimated losses on reacquiring the returns are, in substance, deferred. During this period of deferral the customer's receivable is overstated because it is unlikely that the customer will pay for merchandise that will probably be returned. Financial statements of the seller during the period of deferral will reflect (1) an overstatement of the customer's receivable, (2) an overstatement of a deferred liability account (provision for expected returns), and (3) an understatement of inventory.

If all of the conditions of FASB-48 are not met, the seller cannot recognize the sales revenue until the right of return privilege has substantially expired or the provisions of FASB-48 are subsequently met. However, FASB-48 is not clear on how the seller should keep track of these types of transactions until they can be recognized. The seller has at least three different alternatives. First, the transaction may not be recorded at all on the books of the seller. Perhaps the seller could maintain a "memorandum account" for these types of transactions. Second, the transaction could be recorded as a debit to a deferred receivable account and a credit to a deferred sales account. Lastly, the seller could handle the transaction as a consignment. In any event, it appears logical that some sort of control be maintained for these types of transactions.

Reasonable Estimates of Returns

Reasonable estimates of returns will depend on individual circumstances. An enterprise must take into consideration its individual customers and the types of merchandise involved in determining the estimated amount of returns that may occur. FASB-48 cites the following factors which tend to decrease the possibility of making a reasonable estimate of returns:

1. Possible technological obsolescence or changes in demand for the merchandise.
2. The length of period that the customer has to exercise the right of return.
3. Little or no past experience in determining returns for specific types of merchandise.
4. Little or no past experience in determining returns for similar types of merchandise.
5. A good chance that future marketing policies of the seller and/or the relationship with its customers will change.

The above factors should be considered in conjunction with the past experience with a specific customer and the individual product involved in the sale. One or more of these factors may or may not impair the ability of an enterprise to make a reasonable estimate of the amount of future returns.

Disclosure and Effective Date

FASB-48 is effective for fiscal years beginning on or after June 16, 1981. As with most promulgated GAAP, earlier application of FASB-48 is encouraged.

> **OBSERVATION:** The Exposure Draft for FASB-48 required that gross sales and related accounting policies be disclosed by an enterprise, if product returns are a significant part of its operation. In spite of the fact that the final draft of FASB-48 makes no mention of this disclosure, it is probably still required by APB-22 (Accounting Policies).

An accounting change which results from the initial application of FASB-48 shall be made, if practical, by retroactive restatement of all comparative financial statements presented. In addition, the financial statements of the year of change shall disclose the nature of any restatement and its effect on sales, income before extraordinary items, net income, and related per share amounts, for each year presented.

> **OBSERVATION:** APB-20 (Accounting Changes) requires some types of accounting changes to be reported in comparative financial statements by the "restatement method," and other types to be reported by the "cumulative effect" method. (Each method is discussed later in this analysis.)
>
> According to APB-20, an accounting change regarding sales when a right of return exists would be reported by the "cumulative effect" method. However, FASB-48 establishes the "restatement" method as the method to be used, if practical, in reporting an accounting change resulting from the initial application of FASB-48. Thus FASB-48 supersedes APB-20 on this particular accounting change. The overriding effect of FASB-48 over APB-20 is in accordance with FASB-16 (Prior Period Adjustments), which permits the FASB to prescribe the manner of reporting accounting changes in new pronouncements, even if they conflict with preexisting GAAP.

If it is impractical to retroactively restate all of the individual financial statements for the comparative years presented, the following procedure must be used:

1. The new accounting principle (FASB-48) is used in determining net income of the year of change (current period).
2. As many consecutive prior years' financial statements as practical (which are presented for comparative purposes) are then retroactively restated.
3. The cumulative effect of the change to FASB-48 is then computed for any remaining prior years.
4. The cumulative effect is then included in determining net income for the earliest year restated.
5. Financial statements presented for years prior to the earliest year restated (which includes the cumulative effect) shall be

presented for comparative purposes as they were originally reported.

> **OBSERVATION:** The "cumulative effect" method and "retroactive restatement" both require exactly the same information. The total effect (direct and indirect) of any change on all prior years must be known. This total effect in a restatement is charged or credited to beginning retained earnings in the year of change. In the cumulative effect method, this total effect appears in the income statement of the year of change, as a separate item immediately above net income.
>
> In order to retroactively restate a particular prior year, the details of any effects on that particular year must be available. If the information is not available, that particular prior year cannot be retroactively restated. In applying the cumulative effect method, the details of any effects on a particular year must also be available to determine the pro forma income statement presentation that is required by APB-20. Thus, if you cannot restate a particular prior year, you cannot determine the pro forma presentation required by APB-20.

In the event that it is impractical to retroactively restate any prior year, FASB-48 requires that the cumulative effect of the change in accounting principle be included in the net income of the year of change, in accordance with APB-20. In any year in which the cumulative effect is used, the effect of the change to FASB-48 on sales, income before extraordinary items, net income, and related per share amounts, shall be disclosed.

> **OBSERVATION:** The above method of accounting for a change in an accounting principle is the one required by APB-20 (Accounting Changes). When using this method, APB-20 requires "regular" and "pro forma" presentation of (1) income before extraordinary items, (2) extraordinary items, (3) cumulative effect of a change in accounting principle, and (4) net income. The "pro forma" presentation discloses the above four income statement items and related per share amounts on the basis that the financial statements presented were retroactively restated.
>
> In addition, the cumulative effect of a change in an accounting principle may be omitted under APB-20, if it is impossible to compute. In this event, the effects of the change, in the year of change, must be disclosed, along with an explanation as to why the cumulative effect was omitted.

In applying the provisions of FASB-48 retroactively, reasonable estimates and approximations may be necessary. Available information on the amount of returns for prior years that have already occurred may be used as a basis for estimates and approximations.

OBSERVATION: Existing GAAP (APB-9) requires that net income include all items of profit and loss recognized during a period, except prior-period adjustments. Prior-period adjustments bypass the income statement and are charged or credited to retained earnings. Retroactive restatement of a financial statement is usually accounted for in the same manner as a prior-period adjustment. Thus, retroactive restatement bypasses the income statement and retained earnings is charged or credited. However, restated financial statements reflect all of the details of the revision.

In order to retroactively restate a financial statement for the effects of a change in an accounting principle, the total effects of the change on all prior years must be determined. Beginning retained earnings of the year in which the change is adopted must be adjusted to the amount it would have been if the change in accounting principle had been used in all prior years. Then, net income of the year of change is determined by using the newly-adopted accounting principle. For example, in a change that results in less depreciation expense (net of taxes) for all prior periods, retained earnings would be increased and accumulated depreciation would be decreased at the beginning of the year of change. In addition, the new depreciation method is used in determining net income of the year of change.

In applying the cumulative effect method, the total effects of the change in accounting principle for all prior periods must also be determined. However, instead of adjusting retained earnings, the total effect (net of taxes) is included in net income of the year of change as a separate item in the income statement. The journal entry is a debit to accumulated depreciation and a credit to an account entitled "cumulative effect of an accounting change," which appears in the income statement directly above net income. In addition, net income of the year of change is determined by applying the new accounting principle.

The cumulative effect method also requires a "regular" and "pro forma" presentation in the income statement of (1) income before extraordinary items, (2) extraordinary items, (3) cumulative effect, and (4) net income. The pro forma presentation is made on the basis that all prior-year financial statements presented are completely restated. However, any detail in the income statement above income before extraordinary items is not reflected. This is the major difference between "restatement" and the "cumulative effect" method. In other words, "restatement" will reflect any change in the financial statements in any particular item, while the "pro forma" presentation reflects the effects of the retroactive restatement only on (1) income before extraordinary items, (2) extraordinary items, (3) cumulative effect of a change in accounting principle, and (4) net income.

Statement of Position 75-1 (*Revenue Recognition When Right of Return Exists*) was issued by the AICPA on January 17, 1975.

Revenue Recognition

> It is probable that most publicly held companies have been complying with its provisions since it was issued. Thus, most publicly held companies are not likely to be subject to the transition provisions of FASB-48.

Comprehensive Illustration

The right to return merchandise to a seller may only apply to a portion of a total sale. For example, X Company sells 100,000 widgets to Y Company on January 1st, for $1 per widget (cost $0.65). In the sales agreement, X Company grants to Y Company the right to return up to a maximum of 30% of the widgets within six months from the date of sale. Under these circumstances, FASB-48 would only apply to the 30% of the widgets that can be returned by Y Company within six months. Assuming that all of the conditions imposed by FASB-48 are met and it is "probable" that one-half (50%) of the widgets subject to return will actually be returned and the estimated cost that the X Company expects to incur in connection with the returns is $1,000, the computations would be as follows:

Total sale	$100,000
Less: Portion of the sale not subject to FASB-48	70,000
Balance of the sale subject to FASB-48	$ 30,000
Less: Provision for estimated returns (50% of $30,000), plus estimated cost to be incurred on reacquiring the returns ($1,000)	16,000
Balance of sale which is recognized	$ 14,000
Balance of sale not subject to FASB-48	70,000
Total revenue recognized at date of sale	$ 84,000
Provision for returnable merchandise	$ 15,000
Provision for related estimated costs	1,000
Total provision for expected merchandise returns and related costs	$ 16,000

Under FASB-48, X Company should report $84,000 of revenue on the date the title to the widgets passes to Y Company. X Company should also set up a provision for returnable merchandise and related costs of $16,000. Sales and related cost of sales should be reported at their gross amounts in the income statement and the sales and related cost of sales for the "probable" returns should be deducted from the gross amounts. After the return period (six months) has substantially expired for Y Company, X Company may recognize as revenue any remaining balance in the provision account. The journal entries to record the transactions on the books of X Company are as follows:

Accounts receivable	$100,000	
Sales		$100,000
To record the gross sales to Y Company		
Cost of sales	$ 65,000	
Inventory		$ 65,000
To record cost of sales for Y Company order		
Sales	$ 15,000	
Deferred cost of sales (65¢ per widget)	9,750	
Deferred cost of reacquiring returns	1,000	
Provision for estimated returns		$ 15,000
Cost of sales		9,750
Provision for cost of reacquiring returns		1,000
To defer sales of $15,000, related cost of sales of $9,750, and estimated cost of $1,000 to reacquire estimated returns (freight $600, handling $300, and insurance $100).		

SEGMENTAL REPORTING

Background

The promulgated GAAP on segmental reporting are:

> FASB-14, Financial Reporting for Segments of a Business Enterprise
>
> FASB-18, Financial Reporting for Segments of a Business Enterprise—Interim Financial Statements
>
> FASB-24, Reporting Segment Information in Financial Statements that are Presented in Another Enterprise's Financial Report

In addition, FASB Technical Bulletins 79-4 and 79-5 have been issued to provide guidance in defining U.S. Territories and the term "customer" for the purposes of FASB-14.

Segmental information for each fiscal year presented is required of all enterprises that issue a complete set of financial statements in conformity with GAAP. However, segmental information is not required (FASB-24) in the following circumstances:

1. If a complete set of financial statements is consolidated or combined in the financial report of another enterprise, then the segmental information does not have to be disclosed in the accompanying separate complete set of financial statements when presented in the same financial report containing the consolidated or combined statements. However, segmental information would have to be disclosed for the consolidated or combined statements.

2. A complete set of financial statements for a foreign investee that is not a subsidiary need not disclose segmental information when presented in the same financial report of a primary reporting enterprise unless the foreign investee's separately issued financial statements already disclose the required segmental data. In other words, if the non-subsidiary foreign investee's financial statements already contain the required segmental information then it must be disclosed when such financial statements are presented in the same financial report of a primary reporting entity.

3. A complete set of financial statements of any enterprise which is presented in the financial report of a nonpublic enterprise

need not disclose segmental information. A non-public enterprise is not required to disclose segmental information (FASB-21—see below).

> **OBSERVATION:** *FASB-24 differentiates between a complete set of financial statements being "presented" and a set which is "consolidated" or "combined." Although the distinction is not clear, it is assumed that being "presented" means that the complete set of financial statements is included in the financial report but not "consolidated" or "combined."*

Disclosure of segmental information is required in a complete set of financial statements of an investment accounted for by the cost or equity method when such statements are presented in the financial report of another enterprise. However, all of the percentage tests required by FASB-14 are computed by excluding the amounts attributable to the investment accounted for by the cost or equity method. For example, the 10% revenue test to determine a reportable segment under FASB-14 must be computed on the total of all the enterprise's industry segments. When determining the same test for an investment accounted for by the cost or equity method, all revenue from such an investment is excluded and the 10% is computed only on the other industry segments of the primary reporting entity. All other percentage tests required by FASB-14 are determined in the same manner (e.g., by excluding the amounts attributable to the investment accounted for by the cost or equity method).

The following definitions are used in segmental reporting (FASB-24):

Segmental information is the information which is required to be disclosed by FASB-14, namely, an enterprise's (1) operations in different industries, (2) foreign operations and export sales, and (3) major customers.

Complete set of financial statements includes financial position, changes in financial position, results of operations, all necessary footnotes and prepared in conformity with GAAP.

Financial report includes one or more complete sets of financial statements and other information (annual reports, SEC filings, etc).

Foreign investee not a subsidiary of the primary reporting enterprise is an entity organized and domiciled in a foreign country of which fifty percent (50%) or more of its voting stock is owned by foreign residents.

Nonpublic Enterprise (FASB-21)

A nonpublic enterprise is an enterprise other than one

1. Whose debt or equity securities are traded in a public market
2. That is required to file financial statements with the SEC

An enterprise loses its status as nonpublic when it issues financial statements in preparation for the sale of any class of securities in a public market.

A public market is a foreign or domestic stock exchange or an over-the-counter market.

A nonpublic enterprise is not required to disclose earnings per share (APB-15) or segment information (FASB-14) in a complete set of separately issued financial statements. The nonpublic enterprise may be a subsidiary, joint venture, or any other investee.

If the nonpublic enterprise elects to disclose earnings per share or segment information, it must comply with the disclosure requirements of GAAP. It may not disclose this information on an arbitrary basis.

Overview

Promulgated GAAP (FASB-14) requires that annual financial statements contain segmental information about a company's operations in (1) different industries, (2) foreign operations and export sales, and (3) major customers.

Financial reporting of segmental information of a business is not required in interim financial statements (FASB-18).

The required financial statement information is basically a disaggregation of the entity's regular financial statements. The accounting principles used in preparing the financial statements should be used for the segment information, *except* that many intercompany transactions that are eliminated in consolidation are included in segmental reporting.

It is not necessary to present segment data regarding unconsolidated subsidiaries or investees. However, identification must be made about the specific industry and geographic area in which these companies operate.

Segmental Reporting

It is important to remember that transactions between the segments of an enterprise are not eliminated, as in consolidation; rather they are reported on a gross basis.

Terminology

The following terminology is used in segmental reporting:

Industry segment   A part of a company that sells primarily to outsiders for a profit. Vertically integrated operations of a company are not considered industry segments.

Reportable segment   Any part of a company for which segment reporting is required by the criteria explained herein.

Revenue   Sales either to outsiders or to other segments of the company. Intersegmental sales should be based on sales or transfer prices used by the company. However, intersegmental sales should not include the cost of shared facilities or other joint costs.

Interest earned on intersegmental trade receivables is included in intersegmental sales, if the receivable or other asset is included in the industry segment's identifiable assets (see below). However, interest on advances or loans between industry segments is not included in intersegmental revenues.

Operating income or loss of an industry segment should include interest on loans or advances between industry segments, if the industry segment's principal operations are financial (banking, insurance, leasing, etc.).

Industry segment's operating profit or loss   Revenue less operating expenses, as defined herein. Operating expenses include those related to intersegmental sales as well as those to unaffiliated customers. Operating expenses incurred by an enterprise that are not directly traceable to a specific industry segment shall be allocated on a reasonable basis to those industry segments for whose benefit the expenses were incurred. Intersegmental purchases are accounted for on the basis of transfer and sales prices used by the company. The operating profit or loss of an industry segment shall not include the following:

1. Revenue not derived from the operation of any industry segment
2. Revenue earned at the corporate level

3. General corporate expenses
4. Interest expense, except for an industry segment whose principal operation is financial
5. Foreign or domestic income taxes
6. Equity in the income or loss from an unconsolidated subsidiary or investee
7. Gain or loss on discontinued operations
8. Extraordinary items
9. Minority interests
10. Cumulative effect of a change in an accounting principle

Operating expenses of industry segments should be determined by their nature and not by the fact that they are recorded as general corporate expenses. If an expense would ordinarily be deducted in computing the operating profit or loss of an industry segment, then it should be so included, regardless of how it was entered on the records. In other words, the nature of the expense should determine its deductibility as an operating expense of an industry segment.

Identifiable assets are either the tangible and intangible assets used exclusively by a segment, or the allocated portion of assets used jointly by more than one segment. General corporate assets are not allocated to segments, and loan and investment accounts are not considered assets unless income from them is included in segment profit or loss.

Goodwill, less any amortization, is included in an industry segment's identifiable assets. An industry segment's identifiable assets should be net of any valuation accounts, such as allowance for doubtful accounts, accumulated depreciation, etc.

Loans and advances between industry segments whose principal operations are financial (banking, leasing, insurance, etc.) and whose income is derived from such loans and advances should be included as an identifiable industry segment asset.

Determining Reportable Segments

There are three steps in determining the reportable segments of an enterprise:

1. Identifying the enterprise's products and services
2. Grouping the products and services into industry segments
3. Selecting the significant industry segments

Grouping Products and Services

Although several systems exist for classifying business activities, the determination of industry segments depends primarily on the judgment of management. Existing profit centers are useful in collecting segment data, unless they cross industry lines.

Industry segmentation of foreign operations should also be performed. However, those foreign operations for which segmentation is impractical should be reported as a single segment, and appropriately disclosed.

Selecting Reportable Segments

10% tests A test is made each fiscal year to determine an enterprise's reportable segments. A reportable segment must satisfy one or more of the following tests:

1. Its revenue (as defined herein to mean revenue both from intercompany and from outsiders) is at least 10% of all the enterprise's industry segments.
2. Its operating profit or loss is 10% or more of the greater of a or b below.
   a. the total of all the enterprise's industry segments that had operating profits
   b. the total of all the enterprise's industry segments that had operating losses
3. Its identifiable assets (as defined herein) are 10% or more of the enterprise's combined industry segments' identifiable assets.

> **OBSERVATION:** To determine criterion 2 above, all losses of industry segments which had operating losses are totaled, and all profits of industry segments which had operating profits are totaled. The greater of the two totals (losses or profits) is then used to apply the 10% test, as follows:
>
> | Segment | Losses | Profits |
> |---------|--------|---------|
> | A | $ 1,000 | |
> | B | | $2,000 |
> | C | | 1,000 |
> | D | 3,000 | |
> | E | 7,000 | |
> | Totals | $11,000 | $3,000 |

Under the 10% rule, the $11,000 is used and the reportable segments are those which have losses or profits in excess of $1,100 (10% of $11,000). Therefore, industry segments B, D, and E qualify as reportable segments for this particular criterion.

In the event that it is impractical to disaggregate part or all of a foreign operation, it should be treated as a single industry segment and should be included in the combined revenue, combined operating profit or loss, and combined identifiable assets of the company's industry segments.

Comparability test   Since the determination of a reportable segment is made each fiscal year, a reportable segment of the immediate prior years may fail to meet the 10% test in the current year. However, if the reportable segment that fails to meet the current year's test is expected to satisfy the 10% test in future years, in order to satisfy the criterion of comparability it would have to be included in the current year, even though it failed to meet the test. On the other hand, if an industry segment that usually never qualifies as a reportable segment happens to qualify because of an unusual event, it may be necessary to exclude the segment on the basis of distorting comparability.

75% test   Combined revenue from sales to outsiders, by all reportable segments, must be at least 75% of the total revenue of all the industry segments of an enterprise. If the 75% test is not met by the reportable segments which passed the 10% and comparability tests, additional industry segments must be added to meet the 75% test. These additional industry segments do not have to pass the 10% or comparability test. Within the framework described above, it is desirable to combine segments as necessary to keep the total number of segments at ten or less.

Dominant Segments

If the revenue, operating profit or loss, and identifiable assets of a segment all exceed 90% of the respective totals for the enterprise, and no other segment meets any 10% test, that segment is considered *dominant*. A dominant segment must be identified, but none of the detailed disclosures applying to multisegment enterprises need be reported.

Information to Be Reported

The enterprise must report revenue, profitability, and identifiable assets for each business segment, total unsegmented foreign operations, and the aggregate of other business which is not by itself significant.

As to revenue, the enterprise should report separately sales to outsiders and intercompany transfers. Transfers should be costed at the rate used by the company for operating purposes, and that basis should be disclosed.

Operating profit or loss of each reportable segment and the amount of expenses allocated to that segment should be disclosed. The methods used to allocate expenses should be consistently applied. In addition to operating profit or loss, the company is free to present some other measure of profitability as long as the methods used in determining the amounts are disclosed.

The aggregate amount of identifiable assets must be disclosed for each segment and in total.

The company must also disclose the types of products and any significant segmental accounting policies not already disclosed in the regular financial statements.

Other disclosures required for each reportable segment include:

1. Depreciation, depletion, and amortization
2. Capital expenditures
3. Equity in unconsolidated but vertically integrated subsidiaries, and the geographic area in which they operate
4. The effect on operating profit of segments due to a change in accounting principle

> **OBSERVATION:** *The pro forma effects of the retroactive application of a change in an accounting principle, and the pro forma supplemental information relating to a business combination accounted for by the purchase method (APB-16), need not be presented for individual reportable segments.*

Reportable segment information may be presented in footnotes to the statements or in separate schedules.

The information presented for revenue, operating profit or loss, and identifiable assets must be reconciled to the related financial statements' amounts for revenue, pretax income, and total assets.

Foreign Operations and Export Sales

Information regarding operations outside the enterprise's home country or which generate revenue from sales or transfers between geographic areas should be included in the financial statements.

> **OBSERVATION:** *For purposes of FASB-14, Puerto Rico and other U.S. Territories are part of the United States and are not considered foreign countries (FASB Technical Bulletin 79-4).*

An enterprise should report segment information for each significant geographic area. A geographic area is a country or a group of countries that is treated as a homogeneous unit for segmental reporting purposes. A geographic area is significant if it meets either of the following tests:

1. Revenue from unaffiliated customers is 10% or more of consolidated revenue.
2. Identifiable assets are 10% or more of consolidated total assets.

The enterprise should disclose revenue, operating profit or loss (or net income or some measure of profitability), and identifiable assets.

When an enterprise has export sales to outsiders which are 10% or more of total sales to outsiders, these amounts should be disclosed.

The enterprise should identify the geographic areas for which it is presenting segment information, and may disclose the information in the statements, footnotes, or a separate schedule.

The amounts shown as revenue, operating profit or loss (or other measure of profitability), and identifiable assets must be reconciled to the related amounts shown in the financial statements for revenue, pretax income, and total assets.

Information about Major Customers

An enterprise that makes 10% or more of its revenue from sales to a single customer or government must disclose such facts. The disclosures required include the identity of the segment, and the amount of revenue involved. Even if the enterprise is not otherwise required to present segment information, it must conform to this requirement.

> **OBSERVATION:** *An insurer who makes payments for patients to a health care facility is not a "customer" for the purposes of FASB-14. The patient is the "customer" because he makes the decision as to the doctor, time and place, and type of service to be received (FASB Technical Bulletin 79-5). However, if the decision as to the doctor, time and place, and type of service is made by the insurer, then the insurer would be considered the "customer" for the purpose of FASB-14. In this respect, some Health Maintenance Organizations (HMO) deny their beneficiaries the choice of doctor (provider) and/or health care facility. Thus, an HMO, while an insurer, may be a "major customer" for the purposes of FASB-14 (Technical Bulletin 79-5).*

Restatement of Previously Reported Segment Information

Since the reporting of segment information is required on a comparative basis, previously reported information must be restated when:

1. The statements of the company have been restated for a change in accounting principle or entity.
2. The company has changed the segment or geographic grouping of its operation, which results in changes in the information presented.

Comprehensive Illustration

The following segmental disclosure appeared in the annual report of Harcourt Brace Jovanovich, Inc.

The principal sources of the company's business are the following:

Segment	Principal Activities
School instructional materials	Publishing textbooks and related learning materials, and distributing supplies to elementary and secondary schools.
University and professional publishing and instruction	Publishing scientific and medical books and journals, college textbooks, reprint editions of scholarly works, books and other materials for use in conducting bar review courses and CPA accreditation courses; distributing professional books; publishing books and journals and conducting seminars for lawyers and other practitioners, including continuing education.
Popular enterprises	Providing instructional entertainment at three marine parks, operating several restaurants and a number of fast-food outlets.
Periodical subscriptions and advertising	Publishing business and professional periodicals and directories, farm mag-

Segment	Principal Activities
	azines and rural-county directories, a magazine for elementary schoolteachers, and magazines that have paid mail subscription or newstand sales or both.
General books	Publishing books of general interest (including children's books) in hardcover, in trade paperback editions, and in mass-market paperback editions; operating book clubs; operating a general bookstore; publishing high-priced illustrated books sold mainly by mail.
Tests and testing services	Publishing tests, and providing scoring services, to assess learning aptitudes and achievements of students and others, and to furnish assessment skills to an executive management service.
Insurance	Selling accident and health and life insurance to individuals, primarily through a farm-magazine subscription sales force, and underwriting and servicing life insurance also generated thereby; acting as general insurance brokers and agents in New York City and its suburbs.

Sales and revenues and income from operations for each of these segments are shown on pages XX and XX. Segment sales and revenues consist of sales and services provided to unaffiliated customers; intersegment sales are not material. Segment income from operations includes segment sales and other publishing income, less operating expenses directly traceable to the segment. General corporate expenses benefiting more than one segment, which include compensation of general corporate officers, certain occupancy costs, stockholder reporting expenses, general insurance, and legal and other corporate consulting fees and expenses, are not allocated to segments.

Consolidated Sales and Revenues By Sources, 19X1–19X5

	19X5		19X4		19X3		19X2		19X1	
	Amount	%	Amount	%	Amount	%	Amount	%	Amount	%
School instructional materials	$109,344,034	29.5	$ 96,746,532	35.8	$ 90,097,760	37.3	$ 77,325,681	37.8	$ 68,831,039	38.9
University and professional publishing and instruction	83,376,749	22.5	73,237,322	27.1	69,630,791	28.9	59,191,248	28.9	48,443,365	27.4
Popular enterprises	60,015,015	16.2	—	—	—	—	—	—	—	—
Periodical subscriptions and advertising	52,137,971	14.0	36,201,794	13.3	30,382,168	12.6	26,702,713	13.1	24,607,403	13.9
General books	31,015,468	8.3	31,584,892	11.7	21,832,971	9.0	13,528,937	6.6	11,571,782	6.5
Tests and testing services	24,925,939	6.7	23,746,824	8.8	21,303,087	8.8	20,814,978	10.2	17,321,338	9.8
Insurance	10,273,504	2.8	8,858,476	3.3	8,099,969	3.4	7,006,332	3.4	6,111,257	3.5
	$371,088,680	100.0%	$270,375,840	100.0%	$241,346,746	100.0%	$204,569,899	100.0%	$176,886,184	100.0%

Consolidated Income from Operations By Sources, 19X1-19X5

	19X5 Amount	%	19X4 Amount	%	19X3 Amount	%	19X2 Amount	%	19X1 Amount	%
School instructional materials	$ 16,202,661	38.6	$ 15,891,954	47.0	$ 16,916,880	54.7	$ 11,998,025	47.2	$ 10,601,534	47.9
University and professional publishing and instruction	11,161,632	26.6	10,355,444	30.6	11,105,255	35.9	8,374,741	33.0	5,282,409	23.9
Popular enterprises	10,409,911	24.8	—	—	—	—	—	—	—	—
Periodical subscriptions and advertising	4,593,876	10.9	3,679,302	10.9	2,731,988	8.8	2,576,287	10.1	2,800,010	12.7
General books	(603,577)	(1.4)	2,199,783	6.5	(1,575,778)	(5.1)	(419,354)	(1.6)	812,751	3.7
Tests and testing services	3,207,615	7.6	4,194,694	12.4	3,673,852	11.9	3,985,873	15.7	3,623,025	16.4
Insurance	2,899,595	6.9	2,626,616	7.8	2,474,197	8.0	2,645,864	10.4	2,413,033	10.9
Unallocated corporate overhead	(5,869,976)	(14.0)	(5,141,580)	(15.2)	(4,415,607)	(14.2)	(3,757,620)	(14.8)	(3,417,347)	(15.5)
	$ 42,001,737	100.0%	$ 33,806,213	100.0%	$ 30,910,787	100.0%	$ 25,403,816	100.0%	$ 22,115,385	100.0%

Note: Income from operations for 19X1–19X4 has been restated to exclude net interest expense.

Segmental Reporting

Identifiable assets, capital expenditures, and depreciation and amortization by segment for the year ended December 31, 19X5, were as follows:

	Assets	Capital Expenditures	Depreciation and Amortization
School instructional materials	$ 74,809,678	$ 4,333,265	$ 2,153,768
University and professional publishing and instruction	59,664,933	7,159,186	3,757,840
Popular enterprises	73,921,849	10,425,400	3,836,850
Periodical subscriptions and advertising	25,361,552	1,282,076	528,510
General books	22,473,489	669,298	578,438
Tests and testing services	8,820,970	457,633	405,675
Insurance	8,923,162	70,740	33,346
General corporate	24,765,184	4,515,250	95,793
	$298,740,817	$28,912,848	$11,390,220

The company's export and foreign subsidiary sales are less than 10% of total revenues, and no single customer, including governmental agencies, accounts for 10% or more of total revenues.

STOCKHOLDERS' EQUITY

Background

This chapter contains promulgated and nonpromulgated GAAP pertaining to items properly included or related to stockholders' equity. The specific promulgated GAAP included herein is:

- ARB-43, Chapter 1A—Capital Surplus
- ARB-43, Chapter 1A—Donated Stock
- ARB-43, Chapter 1A—Treasury Stock
- ARB-43, Chapter 1B—Profits or Losses on Treasury Stock
- ARB-43, Chapter 7B—Stock Dividends and Split-ups
- APB-6, Paragraph 12—Treasury Stock
- APB-10, Paragraphs 10 and 11—Liquidation Preference of Preferred Stock
- APB-12, Paragraphs 9 and 10—Capital Changes

FASB Technical Bulletin 85-6 provides guidance on (a) accounting for treasury shares that are acquired at a price significantly higher than their market price and (b) the income statement classification of costs incurred in consummating a "standstill" agreement and/or in defending against a takeover attempt.

Overview

The various elements constituting stockholders' equity must be clearly classified according to source. Stockholders' equity may be broadly classified into (1) legal capital, (2) paid-in capital, (3) minority interests, and (4) retained earnings.

Legal Capital

Legal (or stated) capital is usually defined by state law. It refers to the amount of capital that must be retained by a corporation for the protection of its creditors. Legal capital may consist of common or preferred shares. Preferred shares may be participating or nonparticipating as to the earnings of the corporation, may be cumulative or noncumulative as to the payment of dividends, may have a claim as to assets on liquidation of the business, and may be callable for redemption at a specified price. Usually, preferred stock does not have voting rights.

Common stock usually has the right to vote, the right to share in earnings, a preemptive right to a proportionate share of any additional common stock issued, and the right to share in assets on liquidation.

Generally, preferred stock is issued at a par value, but common stock may have a par or a no-par value. When no-par common stock is recorded at a particular amount it is called the "stated value."

Any difference between the par value or stated value of stock and the actual price paid is either a discount if issued for less, or a premium if issued for more, than par or stated value.

A corporation's charter contains the types and amounts of stock that it can legally issue, which is called the "authorized capital stock." When part or all of the authorized capital stock is issued, it is called "issued capital stock." Since a corporation may own issued capital stock in the form of "treasury stock," the amount of issued capital stock in the hands of stockholders is called "outstanding capital stock." In summary, capital stock may be (1) authorized, (2) authorized and issued, and (3) authorized, issued, and outstanding.

Frequently, a corporation sells its capital stock by subscriptions. An individual subscriber becomes a stockholder on subscribing to the capital stock, and on full payment of the subscription a stock certificate evidencing ownership in the corporation is issued. When the subscription method is used to sell capital stock a subscription receivable account is debited, and a capital stock subscribed account is credited. On payment of the subscription the subscription receivable account is credited and cash or other assets are debited. On the actual issuance of the stock certificates the capital stock subscribed account is debited and the regular capital stock account is credited. Obviously, if any discount or premium is involved (the difference between the par or stated value and the price received), a separate account must be set up that is usually designated as "premium (discount) on common (preferred) stock." A premium is classified as paid-in capital and a discount is deducted from the capital stock.

Legal Capital—Disclosures

When financial statements are prepared in conformity with GAAP, capital changes must be disclosed in a separate statement(s), or footnote(s) to the financial statement. This requirement is in addition to disclosure of the changes in retained earnings, although all capital changes may be included in one statement. Capital accounts that may have to be disclosed because of changes during the year are capital stock, paid-in capital, retained earnings, treasury stock, and other capital accounts in the particular circumstances (APB-12, paragraphs 9 and 10).

Numerous different types of disclosures pertaining to the components of stockholders' equity are required by GAAP. The more usual disclosures are:

Capital stock   By each different class, the total number of shares authorized, issued, and outstanding; also, the number of shares reserved for stock options outstanding for future grants and the changes during the year. Any unusual voting rights should also be disclosed.

Paid-in capital   The total amount of paid-in capital (capital in excess of par) for each class of security should be disclosed.

Retained earnings   The total appropriated and unappropriated retained earnings.

Restrictions on dividends, participation rights, and liquidation preferences should be fully disclosed, as should the pertinent rights and privileges of the various classes of stockholders.

In the case of options, warrants, and convertible securities, the conversion rates and exercise prices must be disclosed.

Preferred or other senior securities that have preference in involuntary liquidation in excess of their par or stated value must be disclosed as follows (APB-10):

a. Call price per share or in the aggregate at which the security may be called or redeemed through a sinking fund
b. The amount per share and total of all cumulative preferred dividends in arrears

Paid-In Capital

All stockholders' equity that is not classified as legal capital, minority interests, or retained earnings is usually designated as paid-in capital. The common sources of paid-in capital result from:

1. Excess of par or stated value paid for capital stock
2. Sale of treasury stock
3. The issuance of detachable stock purchase warrants (APB-14)
4. Donated assets
5. That created by a corporate readjustment or quasi-reorganization

ARB-43, Chapter 1A, paragraph 6 states the following in reference to donated stock:

> "If capital stock is issued nominally for the acquisition of property and it appears that at about the same time, and pursuant to a previous agreement or understanding, some portion of the stock so issued is donated to the corporation, it is not permissible to treat the par value of the stock nominally issued for the property as the cost of that property. If stock so donated is subsequently sold, it is not permissible to treat the proceeds as a credit to surplus of the corporation."

Charges should not be made to paid-in capital, however created, that are properly chargeable to income accounts of the current or future years (ARB-43, Chapter 1A, paragraph 2).

Minority Interests

The "parent company theory" is used in practice almost exclusively for disclosing minority interests in a consolidated balance sheet. Under the parent company theory, minority interests are *not* considered part of stockholders' equity and are disclosed in the consolidated balance sheet between the liability section and the stockholders' equity section. Where minority interests are insignificant and do not warrant a separate classification in the consolidated balance sheet, some enterprises have seen fit to disclose minority interests among other liabilities. Minority interests in consolidated net income are shown as a deduction of consolidated net income.

Under the "entity theory," minority interests are disclosed within and as part of the consolidated stockholders' equity section of the consolidated balance sheet. Although the entity theory has much theoretical support, it is seldom used in practice, because under GAAP, consolidated financial statements represent the results of operations, changes in financial position, and financial position of a single entity (ARB-51).

Retained Earnings

Appropriated retained earnings should be clearly distinguished from unappropriated retained earnings.

Treasury Stock

Treasury stock is not generally considered an asset, because it is widely held that a corporation cannot own part of itself. When reacquired by a corporation, the status of treasury stock is similar to that of authorized but unissued capital stock. Under no circumstances should a corporation include as income, any dividend on its own treasury shares (Chapter 1A of ARB-43). However, paragraph 4 of Chapter 1A of ARB-43 and paragraph 12b of APB-6 provide that treasury stock may be reported as an asset, under certain circumstances (not described), if adequately disclosed. Accordingly, some corporations in recent years have reported treasury stock as an asset, if the treasury stock was held to liquidate a specific liability which appears on the balance sheet.

> **OBSERVATION:** *Treasury stock should not be classified as an asset under any circumstances. The exception provided by paragraph 4 of Chapter 1A of ARB-43 and paragraph 12b of APB-6 has no foundation, because the definition of a liability, under existing GAAP, is any obligation whose liquidation is reasonably expected to require the use of assets or the creation of other liabilities. Therefore, any obligation that will be liquidated by the use of treasury stock cannot meet the definition of a liability, because of the fact that treasury stock is not an asset.*

Reacquisition of treasury stock If treasury shares are reacquired for a purchase price significantly in excess of their current market price, it is *presumed* that the total purchase price includes amounts for stated or unstated rights or privileges (FASB Technical Bulletin 85-6). Under this circumstance, the total purchase price must be allocated between the cost of the treasury shares and the cost of the rights or privileges that are identified with the purchase of the treasury shares. The allocation of the total purchase price shall be based on the fair value of the rights and/or privileges, or the fair value of the treasury shares, whichever is more clearly evident. Fair value shall be determined as of the date on which the major terms of the purchase agreement were reached. If no rights or privileges can be identified, the entire purchase price shall be allocated to the cost of the treasury shares.

FASB Technical Bulletin 85-6 requires financial statement disclosure of the allocation and accounting treatment of amounts paid in connection with an enterprise's purchase of treasury shares for a price significantly in excess of the current market price.

Greenmail and "standstill" agreements Payments to a shareholder or former shareholder for any agreement in which the shareholder or former shareholder agrees not to purchase additional shares of an enterprise's capital stock should be expensed as incurred, because such payments do not provide any future economic benefits (FASB Technical Bulletin 85-6).

Cost incurred by an enterprise to defend itself against a takeover attempt and costs relating to a standstill agreement do not meet the criteria of extraordinary items (FASB Technical Bulletin 85-6). However, if professional judgment dictates individual treatment of a material transaction that does not qualify as an extraordinary item, it may be separately reported as a component of income from continuing operations with appropriate footnote disclosure.

Accounting and reporting Under GAAP, both the cost method and par value method of accounting for treasury stock are acceptable. Under the cost method, each acquisition of treasury stock is accounted for at cost. In addition, separate records are maintained to reflect the date of purchase of the treasury stock, the number of shares acquired and the reacquisition cost per share. The inventory of treasury stock may be kept on the basis of any acceptable inventory method, such as specific identification, LIFO, FIFO, or average cost basis. Upon the sale or other disposition, the treasury stock account is credited for an amount equal to the number of shares sold multiplied by the reacquisition cost per share. In other words, under the cost method, the amount credited to the treasury stock account upon sale or other disposition is exactly the same as the amount which was debited to the account when the treasury stock was acquired. The cost method of accounting for treasury stock is more commonly used in practice than the par value method.

Under the par value method of accounting for treasury stock, the treasury stock account is debited only for the par or stated value of each share reacquired. Any excess paid per share, over the par or stated value, is debited to additional paid-in capital, but only for the amount per share that was originally credited when the stock was issued. Any excess cost per share remaining over the par or stated value per share and the amount per share originally credited to additional paid-in capital is debited to retained earnings. If the cost per share of treasury stock is less than the par or stated value per share and the amount per share originally credited to additional paid-in capital, the difference is credited to paid-in capital from treasury stock. Under the par value method of accounting for treasury stock, all of the original capital balances related to the shares reacquired are removed from the books.

When treasury stock is acquired with the intent of retiring the stock (whether or not retirement is actually accomplished), the excess of the price paid for the treasury stock over its par or stated value may be allocated between (a) paid-in capital arising from the same class of stock and (b) retained earnings. However, the amount of excess that can be allocated to paid-in capital arising from the same class of stock shall be limited to the sum of (a) any paid-in capital arising from previous retirements and net gains on sales of the same class of treasury stock and (b) the pro rata portion of paid-in capital, voluntary transfers of retained earnings, capitalization of stock dividends, etc., on the same class of stock. For this purpose, any paid-in capital arising from issues of capital stock that are fully retired (formal or constructive) is deemed to be applicable on a pro rata basis to all shares of common stock. As an alternative, the excess of the price paid for the treasury stock over its par or stated value may be charged entirely to retained earnings, based on the fact that a corporation can always capitalize or allocate retained earnings for such a purpose (paragraph 12a(i) of APB-6).

When the price paid for the acquired treasury stock is less than its par or stated value, the difference shall be credited to paid-in capital.

When treasury stock is acquired for purposes other than retirement, it shall be separately disclosed in the balance sheet as a deduction from stockholders' equity; or, as mentioned previously, under certain circumstances the treasury stock may be shown as an asset, provided that it is adequately disclosed.

A gain on the sale of treasury stock acquired for purposes other than retirement shall be credited to paid-in capital from the sale of treasury stock. Losses may be charged to paid-in capital, but only to the extent of available net gains from previous sales or retirements of the same class of stock; otherwise, losses shall be charged to retained earnings.

If a state law prescribes the manner in which a corporation shall account for the acquisition of treasury stock, the state law shall be followed, even if the state law is in variance with existing GAAP (APB-6). Restrictions on the availability of retained earnings for the payment of dividends or any other restrictions required by state law shall be disclosed in the financial statements (APB-6).

If treasury stock is donated to a corporation and then subsequently sold, the entire proceeds shall be credited to paid-in capital from the sale of donated treasury stock.

Dividends

A dividend is a pro rata distribution by a corporation, based on shares of a particular class and usually represents a distribution of earnings.

Cash dividends Cash dividends are the most common type of dividend distribution. Preferred stock usually pays a fixed dividend, expressed in dollars or a percentage.

Three dates are usually involved in a dividend distribution:

1. *Date of declaration:* The date the board of directors formally declares the dividend to the stockholders
2. *Date of record:* The date the board of directors specifies that stockholders of record on a certain date are entitled to the dividend payment
3. *Date of payment:* The date the dividend is actually disbursed by the corporation or its paying agent.

Dividends are recorded on the books of the corporation as a liability (dividends payable) on the date of declaration. Dividends are paid only on authorized, issued, and outstanding shares, thereby eliminating any dividend payment on treasury stock.

Stock dividends A stock dividend is accounted for the same way as a cash dividend, except that since there is no tangible distribution, an amount equal to the fair market value of the stock dividend is transferred from retained earnings to capital stock and, if appropriate, to paid-in capital.

LPS Corporation declares a 5% stock dividend on its 1,000,000 shares of outstanding $10 par common stock (5,000,000 authorized). On the date of declaration, LPS stock is selling for $20 per share.

Total stock dividend (5% of $1,000,000)   50,000 shares
Value of 50,000 shares @ $20 per share (market) $1,000,000

Stockholders' Equity

Journal entry:

Retained earnings	$1,000,000	
Capital stock, $10 par common		$500,000
Paid-in capital, $10 par common		500,000
To record declaration by the board of directors of a 5% stock dividend on the $10 par common capital stock.		

Stock split It is important to differentiate between a stock dividend and a stock split, because the accounting treatment is radically different.

When a stock distribution is more than 20% to 25% of the outstanding shares immediately before the distribution, it is classified as a stock split (ARB-43, Chapter 7B). A straight stock split increases the number of shares of capital stock outstanding and a reverse stock split decreases the number of shares of capital stock outstanding.

In either a straight stock split or reverse stock split, the total dollar amount of stockholders' equity does not change. However, the par or stated value per share of capital stock decreases or increases in proportion with the increase or decrease in the number of shares outstanding. For example, in a straight stock split of 4 for 1 of $40 par value capital stock, the new stock has a par value of $10 and the number of shares outstanding increases to 4 shares for each share of stock previously outstanding. In other words, 1 share of old capital stock is equal to 4 shares of the new capital stock. In a reverse stock split of 1 for 4 of $40 par value capital stock, the new stock has a par value of $160 per share and the number of shares outstanding decreases to 1 share for each 4 shares of stock previously outstanding. In other words, 4 shares of old capital stock are equal to 1 share of the new capital stock.

A straight stock split is used by a corporation to reduce the market price of its capital stock in order to make the market price of the stock more attractive to buyers. Thus, in a 4 for 1 straight stock split, the new shares would probably sell for about one-fourth of the previous market price of the old shares prior to the split. Reverse stock splits are unusual and are used to increase the market price of a corporation's stock. For example, a reverse stock split of 1 for 4 of stock selling for $3 would probably increase the market price of the new shares to about $12 per share.

Stockholders' Equity

No journal entry is required to record a stock split except a memorandum entry in the capital stock account to indicate the new par or stated value of the stock and the number of new shares outstanding after the split.

Stock splits should not be referred to as dividends, and related corporate resolutions, notices, and announcements should use "split effected in the form of a dividend" or avoid the use of the word dividend at all.

Stock Rights

A shareholder's interest in a corporation does not change on account of a stock dividend or a stock split except as to the total number of shares representing his stock interest. The cost of a stockholder's original shares should be reallocated among the new number of shares after a stock dividend or split. Gain or loss is then recognized on the basis of the adjusted cost per share (ARB-43, Chapter 7B). Stock rights should be recorded by the recipient by allocating the original cost of the stock between the stock and the stock right, using the following formula:

$$\frac{\text{Market value of stock right}}{\text{market value of stock right} + \text{market value of stock}} \times \text{cost of stock} = \text{value of right}$$

Original cost of stock is $100. Market value of stock is $90 and the market value of the stock right is $6. At what price should the stock right be recorded?

$$\frac{\$6}{\$6 + \$90} \times \$100 = \$6.25$$

The journal entry to record the stock right is:

Investment in stock right	$6.25	
Investment in stock		$6.25

No accounting entry is necessary for the entity issuing the stock right or warrant, except for detachable stock purchase warrants or similar rights which are accounted for separately and assigned a value (see chapter on Convertible Debt).

When a stock right or warrant is used to purchase the specified security, the cost of the right or warrant is treated as part of the investment in the new security.

STOCK ISSUED TO EMPLOYEES

Background

APB-25 (generally applicable to most stock option plans initiated after December 31, 1972) and ARB-43, Chapter 13B (issued June 1953) establish the current promulgated GAAP for Accounting for Stock Issued to Employees. FASB Interpretation-28, Accounting for Stock Appreciation Rights and Other Variable Stock Option or Award Plans, is an interpretation of APB-15 (Earnings per Share) and APB-25 (Stock Issued to Employees). FASB Interpretation-31, Treatment of Stock Compensation Plans in EPS Computations is also an interpretation of APB-15 and, in addition, modifies FASB Interpretation-28. FASB Interpretation-38 clarifies APB-25 regarding the measurement date for determining compensation cost for stock option, purchase, and award plans involving junior stock. ARB-43 originally established principles and procedures for accounting for "traditional" stock options. APB-25 applies these principles to the various types of stock options and plans that have been developed since the issuance of ARB-43. For instance, it specifies accounting principles for stock options and plans where future events determine the number of shares to be granted the employee and/or the exercise price. APB-25 specifically supersedes ARB-43 in establishing new criteria for measuring a company's compensation cost. APB-25 delineates the income tax treatment originating from any options, purchases, or award plans.

FASB Technical Bulletin 82-2 deals with the accounting implications involved in converting previously issued stock options into the new incentive stock options allowed under the provisions of the Economic Recovery Tax Act of 1981.

Similar to many other areas of accounting, GAAP apply to the substance of an option plan rather than its form. In accounting for an option plan, a company must comply with the GAAP applicable to the option's underlying substance.

A description of the more common types of plans follows:

Typical fixed plan Terms are fixed at the date of grant to determine the number of shares of stock involved and the option price to the employee. Transferability of the stock acquired by the employee is usually restricted and the plan generally provides that the employee must perform current and/or future services.

Stock option and purchase plan An employee is granted the right to purchase a fixed number of shares at a certain price during a specified period.

Stock bonus and award plan An employee is granted a bonus or award in a fixed number of shares or a specified dollar amount which is payable in shares. The employee usually makes no payment to receive the bonus or award of stock.

Shadow or phantom stock plan The employee receives cash, stock, or a combination of both, in an amount equal to a specified increase in the market price of the employer corporation's stock or an amount equal to a specified increase in the dividend distributions of the employer corporation.

Combination and elective plan The employee is granted rights to more than one plan, or the right to select alternatives under one plan. The separate rights may be granted at different intervals or simultaneously and may run concurrently or for different periods. These plans are sometimes referred to as tandem or alternate stock plans.

Overview

A stock option can be compensatory or noncompensatory. A compensatory stock option involves services rendered to the employer corporation and a noncompensatory stock option does not. Accounting for noncompensatory stock options presents few problems. However, when a stock option is compensatory, the compensation costs must be measured, and this may involve some problems.

Noncompensatory Plans

Certain stock options and stock purchase plans are not intended to compensate employees. For example, a corporation's intent may be to raise additional capital or to diversify its ownership to include employees and officers. Usually, the terms of the option will clearly indicate the nature and purpose of the plan.

A plan is noncompensatory if the cash received per share is very close to the amount of cash that would be received if the same deal was offered to all shareholders. In these types of transactions, a company does not generally recognize any compensation costs.

The essential characteristics of noncompensatory stock options or stock purchase plans are:

1. Substantially all full-time employees meeting limited employment qualifications may participate. Excluded are officers and employees who own more than a specific amount of the outstanding stock in the corporation.
2. Stock is offered equally to eligible employees, but the plan may limit the total amount of shares that can be purchased.
3. The time permitted to exercise the rights is limited to a reasonable period.
4. Any discount from the market price is no greater than would be a reasonable offer of stock to shareholders or others.

Plans that do not contain these characteristics are usually classified as compensatory plans. In a compensatory plan, the company receives cash or another asset in addition to an employee's services for the stock it issues.

Compensatory Plans

Stock options may give rise to compensation, usually out of an offer or agreement by a corporation to issue shares to one or more officers or employees (grantees) at a stated price less than the prevailing market. In some instances the grantees' options are exercisable under certain conditions, such as the length of employment of an employee. In other cases, the grantees may agree to take the shares only for investment purposes and not for resale.

Under traditional stock option and stock purchase plans, an employer corporation grants options to purchase shares of its stock, often at a price lower than the prevailing market, making it possible for the individual exercising the option to have at least a potential profit at the moment of acquisition. Most option agreements provide that the purchaser must retain the stock for a minimum period, thus eliminating the possibility of speculation.

Options that give rise to compensation result in compensation expense on the books of the corporation and in compensation income to the recipient. The cost of compensation is measured by the excess of the quoted market price of the stock over the option price on the measurement date.

Stock Issued to Employees

> **OBSERVATION:** *Under the provisions of the Economic Recovery Tax Act of 1981, a corporation can modify existing stock options to conform with the conditions for new incentive stock options. In meeting the pricing requirements of the new incentive stock option plan, an enterprise must increase the exercise price (option price) at the date of grant or last amendment of the exercise price to an amount equal to or in excess of the fair-market value of the underlying stock. This in effect converts the stock option from compensatory to noncompensatory. Thus, any compensation expense and related deferred taxes that an enterprise had previously recorded in connection with the stock option must be adjusted in the period in which the option plan is modified. FASB Technical Bulletin 82-2 provides that this adjustment is accounted for as a change in an accounting estimate, and any compensation expense and related deferred taxes are decreased in the period of change by the amount previously recorded.*

Measurement Date

The quoted market price of the shares granted under an option may vary considerably over the period of the option. This creates a problem in determining a date that may be used to measure the cost of compensation if the shares are offered at less than market. At least six dates can be considered:

1. Date of adoption of the option plan
2. Date on which the option is granted to an employee
3. Date on which the grantee has performed any conditions precedent to the exercise of the option
4. Date on which the grantee may first exercise the option
5. Date on which the option is exercised by the grantee
6. Date on which the grantee disposes of the stock acquired

The measurement date for determining compensation costs in stock options is the first date on which the following is known, which is usually the date the option is granted:

1. *Number of shares an employee is entitled to receive*
2. *Option or purchase price*

Plans that have variable terms which are dependent on events that will occur after the grant date will have a measurement date different from the grant date.

In a stock option for current services, the measurement date may be the end of the fiscal period if the following conditions are met:

1. An established formal plan provides the terms of the award.
2. The plan details how to determine the total dollar amount due to an employee. It is possible that the *actual* amount will be indeterminable at the end of the period because it is dependent on an item, such as net income, which will not be known at that time.
3. The employee is being compensated for services rendered in the current period.

If a company transfers stock to a trustee, agent, or other third party, the measurement date becomes the date of transfer to the trustee if the following items are irrevocable:

1. Transfer of the stock to the trust
2. Terms of the trust agreement
3. Specified employee(s) who will receive the stock

In essence, if all three of the above are met, the company has given up any alternative use of the shares except for the ones specifically stipulated in the stock option agreement.

If treasury stock is distributed in a stock option plan, it is unacceptable to measure compensation costs by the amount paid to reacquire such treasury stock. The only exception to this rule is when a company meets all the conditions in a stock option for current services (above). In this event, the company may elect to measure its compensation costs by the amount paid to reacquire treasury stock, provided the treasury stock is reacquired during the current period in which the award is made and distribution to the employee occurs shortly after the close of the period.

The measurement date for stock options consisting of convertible securities can be determined only after the conversion ratio is known. Compensation is measured on the measurement date by the market price of the convertible security or the security into which it is convertible, *whichever is higher.*

If a company renews a stock option or extends the period during which the recipient can exercise the option, then a new measurement date is established as if a new option had just been granted.

The measurement date does not change merely because the agreement stipulates that termination of employment alters the number of shares an employee will receive.

Variable awards   Under "variable plan awards" the number of shares of stock which an employee can acquire or the exercise price, or both are not determinable until after the date of grant (FASB Interpretation-28). "Variable plan awards" include stock appreciation rights and other variable plans in which the number of shares, exercise price, or both are contingent on a future event.

The vesting period in "variable plan awards" usually runs from the date of grant to the exercise date. For the purposes of GAAP, "variable plan awards" become vested on the date that the employee's right to receive the benefits under the plan are not contingent on any additional services to be performed by the employee (FASB Interpretation-28).

Compensation expense is charged to the "service period" which is the period(s) in which the related services are performed by the employee (FASB Interpretation-28). If the service period cannot be determined by the terms of the plan or otherwise then the service period is presumed to be the same as the vesting period (FASB Interpretation-28). If the variable plan award is for past services, compensation costs are charged as an expense of the period in which the plan was granted.

When the service period of a variable plan award covers more than one fiscal period, compensation costs between the date of grant and the measurement date must be estimated, as follows:

1. In the year of grant or first fiscal period, compensation costs must be measured with whatever information is available. If the number of shares are known but not the exercise price, then an exercise price must be estimated. If the exercise price is known but not the number of shares, then the number of shares must be estimated. If both the number of shares and the exercise price are unknown, then reasonable estimates must be made based upon all information available.
2. Compensation costs are initially measured as the difference between the quoted market price and the option price multiplied by the number of shares involved.
3. In subsequent periods, compensation costs are adjusted, but not below zero, for any increase or decrease in the quoted market price. The adjustment is made to compensation expense of the period in which the change in the quoted market price occurs.
4. The accrued compensation costs for a right which is cancelled or forfeited shall be adjusted by decreasing compensation expense in the period of cancellation or forfeiture. Such adjustments are considered as changes in accounting estimates and are made in the period of change and/or future periods.

5. Accrued compensation costs should be charged to expense over the periods (service period) in which the employee performs the related services.

Junior stock plans Junior stock is a separate class of stock sold to employees for a fraction of the price of the company's regular common stock. The junior stock pays a lower dividend and has less voting rights than the company's common stock and is usually not transferable, except back to the issuing company. The junior stock is convertible into the company's regular common stock if certain performance goals, such as specified levels of sales or profits, are met.

FASB Interpretation-38 requires that all junior stock options be accounted for as variable stock options because at the date of grant of a junior stock option there is no way to determine the number of shares of regular common stock that will ultimately be issued on the date the junior shares are converted by an employee. Thus, under the rules for variable stock options, the date for measuring compensation cost for junior stock plans is the first date on which is known (a) how many shares of regular common stock an employee is entitled to receive in exchange for the junior stock, and (b) the option or purchase price, if any, that the employee pays for the junior stock.

> **OBSERVATION:** Restricted junior stock that is issued to employees and becomes unrestricted when certain performance goals are achieved is also subject to the provisions of FASB Interpretation-38.

Compensation cost is calculated on the measurement date as the difference between (a) the quoted market value of the shares of regular common stock that an employee is entitled to receive upon conversion of the junior stock, and (b) the amount paid or to be paid by the employee for the junior stock. Compensation cost must be charged to expense over the service period specified in the option agreement, which is the period(s) in which the related services are performed by the employee (FASB Interpretation-28). However, in junior stock options, accrual of compensation cost cannot begin until the date it becomes *probable* that the employee will qualify for conversion of the junior stock to regular common stock, through the achievement of performance goals or the occurrence of transactions specified in the plan (FASB Interpretation-38). Once it has become *probable* that an employee will qualify for conversion of junior shares to regular common shares, compensation cost must be accrued. If the plan specifies a period during which performance must occur, the accrual of compensation cost must be allocated to that same period. If no performance period is specified in the plan, compensation cost should be accrued over the period that starts on the date that performance becomes *probable* and ends on the date that performance is *most likely* or when a required service period ends.

> **OBSERVATION:** *As used in FASB Interpretation-38, "probable" has the same meaning as it has in FASB-5 (Contingencies), namely, that it is "likely" that the events will take place. However, the meaning of "most likely" is not clear. Evidently "most likely" is a higher degree of probability, although not explained in either FASB Interpretation-38 or FASB-5.*

If, as a result of vesting provisions, junior stock becomes convertible to regular common stock after the measurement date, compensation cost shall be recognized during the period from (a) the first date that performance becomes *probable* or the date that performance occurs to (b) the date that the junior stock becomes convertible or the end of the service period, whichever occurs first. If cash is paid to the employee to reacquire previously issued junior stock, compensation cost is equal to the excess of the amount of cash paid to the employee, over the amount of cash or other assets received from the employee for the junior stock.

For the purpose of determining earnings per share (APB-15), junior stock options are considered common stock equivalents, to the extent they are convertible into the employer's regular common stock.

FASB Interpretation-38 is effective for grants made to employees on or after March 14, 1984, under stock option, purchase, and award plans involving junior stock. Earlier application in previously unissued financial statements is encouraged, but not required.

Measuring Compensation Costs

The amount of compensation, or the value of the stock option, is the excess of the unadjusted quoted market price of the stock at the measurement date over the amount the employee must pay in cash or other assets. Often, closely held or nonpublic corporation's market quotations are not available and other methods of valuation must be used. No compensation would be recorded if the employee purchases the stock for an amount equal to or greater than the market price.

> **OBSERVATION:** *The value of a stock option may be affected by many factors, such as transferability, and other restrictions. In spite of the recognition of these factors the promulgated GAAP requires (as a practical solution) the use of a quoted market price to measure compensation costs relating to both restricted or unrestricted stock. Only if a quoted market price is not available can an estimate be used.*

Compensation costs related to options for convertible stock are based on the higher market price of either the convertible stock awarded or the underlying security for which the convertible stock can be exchanged.

Cash paid to settle an earlier option right with an employee is the measure of compensation, and the earlier measure of compensation (date the option was granted) should be adjusted.

If a company uses cash to reacquire stock shortly after the stock was issued to an employee through a stock option plan, then the cash paid is used to measure the compensation cost.

If a principal stockholder (one with an interest greater than 10%) establishes a stock option for an employee, the company should recognize compensation costs in accordance with the plan, as long as it derives benefits from the transaction. Stated differently, if the principal stockholder's actions benefit the company by keeping a valuable employee or attempting to improve employee service to the firm, then compensation costs should be recognized in accordance with GAAP. However, if the plan is granted because of a special relationship between an employee and the principal, a prior obligation unrelated to the company, or the company obviously does not benefit, then no compensation costs should be recognized. Obviously, the donated compensation costs by the principal stockholder should be credited to a capital account.

If compensation costs are to be measured at a date in the future, a company must make a reasonable estimate of what the compensation costs will be. Since the measurement date is unknown, the price of the stock at the end of each period should be used. If the number of shares is also unknown, a reasonable estimate, given the known facts, must be made.

> **OBSERVATION:** *Adjustments to estimates in future periods should be made as a change in an accounting estimate. A change in an accounting estimate is made in the period of change and/or in future periods. No restatement of prior financial statements is made.*

When a stock option plan combines two or more plans, compensation cost for each subplan may be measured separately. If the plan gives the employee a choice as to which section of the plan is to be exercised, the measurement at the end of each period should be based on an estimate of which part of the plan the employee is most likely to elect at that point in time.

Related Tax Effects

A company usually realizes a tax deduction for any amount the employee declares as ordinary income. The tax deduction is taken in the year in which the employee includes the benefits from the stock option in his or her gross income. This corporate tax reduction results in a timing difference, because on the company's books the compensation cost is reflected as an expense during the period of related employee service, but is recognized on the tax return in the year the employee includes the benefit in gross income. In such cases deferred taxes should be recorded.

If a tax reduction exists above and beyond that which is recognized as a deferred tax, it should be added to paid-in capital in excess of par in the period of the tax deduction.

It is also possible that recorded compensation cost will be greater than the allowable tax reduction. In such cases a company may deduct the difference from paid-in capital in the period of the tax reduction. This reduction is limited to the amount that the tax reduction for the same plan previously increased paid-in capital.

A company can incur additional compensation costs by reimbursing an employee for the tax benefit derived from the stock option plan. This reimbursement should be recognized as an additional expense against income.

Recognition of Compensation Costs

Compensation costs should be recognized as an expense over the period of employment attributable to the option. If this period is not stated, a reasonable estimate must be made taking into account the circumstances implied by the terms of the agreement.

Stock issued in accordance with a plan for past and future services of an employee must be allocated between expired costs and future costs. Future costs should be charged to the periods in which the employee performs services. In the event stock options are exercised before the related compensation costs are actually incurred, a deferred or prepaid compensation account is set up. Unearned compensation costs should be written off to the period(s) in which they were actually earned, and any balances at a reporting date should be deducted from stockholders' equity.

Recognition of a stock option is made in accordance with the substance of the transaction. Therefore, if an employee gives an employer a nonrecourse note as consideration for stock issued with the stock as collateral, in substance the transaction may be the grant of a stock option. In this event, compensation costs should be measured and the nonrecourse note should be reported as a reduction of stockholders' equity and not as an asset.

Common Stock Equivalents

To the extent that they are payable in common stock, stock options, rights, and other award plans are common stock equivalents for the purposes of determining earnings per share (APB-15). Stock options, rights and other awards which are payable solely in cash are not common stock equivalents.

In applying the treasury stock method to determine the dilutive effect of stock options, rights, and other award plans, the exercise proceeds consist of (1) the exercise price, if any, that the employee must pay, (2) the amount of compensation, if any, to be charged to future periods, and (3) an adjustment, if any, for related tax effects. Under no circumstances should the exercise proceeds include any compensation for past services of an employee (FASB Interpretation-31).

The exercise price that the employee must pay is usually stipulated in the option agreement. Generally, the exercise price must be paid when the employee exercises the options. The amount of compensation to be charged to future periods must be measurable and not have been previously expensed. Measurable compensation to future periods is the difference between the aggregate compensation and the amount of compensation that has been accrued to date. The aggregate compensation is equal to the difference between the market price at the end of the year and the market price at the beginning of the year, multiplied by the number of shares that the employee would be entitled to at the end of the vesting period. The vesting period in "variable plan awards," as mentioned previously, usually runs from the date of grant to the exercise date. For the purposes of GAAP, "variable plan awards" become vested on the date that the employee's right to receive the benefits under the plan are not contingent on any additional services to be performed by the employee (FASB Interpretation-28).

The adjustment, if any, for related tax effects may arise because the tax deduction for compensation expense may be more or less than the compensation expense recognized for financial accounting purposes. If the market price of the stock under option increases from the measurement date to the date on which the tax deduction for compensation expense is determined, a tax benefit will result. The reason why a tax benefit results is that the deduction for compensation expense on the tax return is larger than the deduction for compensation expense that was used for financial accounting purposes. Thus, this tax benefit is included as part of the exercise proceeds (FASB Interpretation-31). When the compensation expense for tax purposes is less than that for financial accounting purposes, the opposite will occur, the exercise proceeds are reduced by the additional tax liability. The tax effects are determined by the "with-and-without" method that is also used to compute deferred income taxes (see chapter on Income Taxes).

For stock appreciation rights and other variable plan awards, the average aggregate compensation and average market price are used to determine the dilutive effect on primary EPS. The dilutive effect on fully diluted EPS is determined in the same manner as for primary EPS except when the ending market price is higher. In this event, the ending market price and the ending aggregate compensation are used (FASB Interpretation-31). Issuable shares must be weighted in the event that stock appreciation rights and other variable plan awards are granted during a current period.

A combination plan usually grants the employee the right to receive either stock or cash for stock appreciation. However, there is a presumption in GAAP that the plan will be paid in stock (FASB Interpretation-31). If past experience or company policy reasonably indicates that payment will be made in cash, the presumption may be overcome. Compensation expense and earnings per share data for a current period must be computed on the same basis. In other words, if it is assumed that an employee will receive stock in a combination plan, then EPS data must be computed on the same basis.

On January 1, 1980, the General Potato Company granted stock appreciation rights to certain employees in tandem with stock options. The rights entitled the employees to the appreciation in the market price of the stock over the market price at the date of grant which was the same as the exercise price ($10.00). The appreciation in market price is payable in stock, cash, or a combination of both, at the election of the employees. Exercise of the stock options automatically cancel the equivalent number of rights, and exercise of the rights cancels the options for an equivalent number of shares of stock. There were 10,000 shares of stock under option which become fully vested in four years (December 31, 1983). The rights and options expire on December 31, 1989, and no related tax effects are expected to arise. The following is a summary of the pertinent data:

Date of grant	January 1, 1980
Vesting period	100% in 1983
Expiration date	December 31, 1989
Number of shares	10,000
Exercise price	$10.00
Quoted market price—grant date	10.00
Market price—December 31, 1980	14.00
Market price—December 31, 1981	16.00
Market price—December 31, 1982	18.00
Market price—December 31, 1983	20.00
Market price—December 31, 1984	22.00

Discussion

At the end of the first year (December 31, 1980) the market price of the stock is $14.00 per share and the market price at the beginning of the year was $10.00 per share. Thus, there has been a $4.00 per share market appreciation, which equals $40,000 for the 10,000 shares under option. The $40,000 would all be compensation expense for 1980, for accounting purposes, if the vesting period was only one year. However, the vesting period is four years and only one-fourth (25%) of the $40,000 should be accrued, for accounting purposes, as compensation expense for the year 1980. The balance of $30,000 is compensation to be charged to future periods. The legal agreement would dictate when the employees could actually exercise the rights or options. However, for accounting purposes, compensation expense is charged to the "service period," which is the period in which the related services are performed by the employee. If the service period cannot be determined by the terms of the plan, the service period is presumed to be the same as the vesting period (FASB Interpretation-28).

Stock Issued to Employees

If the vesting period was 25% each year for four years, instead of 100% in four years, the calculations would differ significantly. Instead of accruing 25% of the stock appreciation ($40,000) in the first year as compensation expense, it would be necessary to accrue 52.08%. The 52.08% in the first year consists of 25% vested in year one; ½ of the 25% (12.5%) vested in year two; ⅓ of the 25% (8.33%) vested in year three; and ¼ of the 25% (6.25%) vested in year four (25 + 12.5 + 8.33 + 6.25 = 52.08). In other words, compensation expense in year one consists of all of the 25% vested in year one; ½ of the 25% vested in year two because it is earned over years one and two; ⅓ of the 25% vested in year three because it is earned over three years; and ¼ of the 25% vested in year four because it is earned over all four years. The following chart illustrates the percentages that should be used when the vesting period is 25% each year for four years, instead of 100% in four years:

Vesting Period	Year One	Year Two (Service Period)	Year Three	Year Four
1	25.00%	25.00%	25.00%	25.00%
2	12.50	25.00	25.00	25.00
3	8.33	16.67	25.00	25.00
4	6.25	12.50	18.75	25.00
Total	52.08%	79.17%	93.75%	100.00%

For earnings per share (EPS) calculation, exercise proceeds are the total of (1) the exercise price, if any, that the employee must pay, (2) the amount of compensation, if any, to be charged to future periods, and (3) an adjustment, if any, for related tax effects. Since the employees are not exercising any rights or options in the first year there are no exercise proceeds for employees. The problem states that there are no related tax effects, so, there are no exercise proceeds from related tax effects. The only exercise proceeds are the $30,000 of compensation that will be charged to future periods. Thus, for both primary and fully diluted EPS, the exercise proceeds are $30,000.

For stock appreciation rights and other variable plan awards, the average aggregate compensation and average market price are used to determine the dilutive effect on primary EPS. The dilutive effects on fully diluted EPS is determined in the same manner as for primary EPS except when the ending market price is higher. In this event, the ending market price and the ending aggregate compensation are used (FASB Interpretation-31). The total aggregate compensation is $40,000, and the average aggregate compensation is $20,000 because this is the first year and the beginning balance of aggregate compensation is zero. ($40,000 + zero, divided by 2 = average for year). The average market price of the stock is $12.00, because at the beginning of the year it was $10.00 per share and at the end of the year it was $14.00 per share ($10.00 + $14.00 = $24.00, divided by 2 = $12.00). The average market price of $12.00 per share is divided into the average aggregate compensation of $20,000 to determine the amount of issuable shares (1,667) for primary EPS.

Under the treasury stock method, the next step is to determine the number of shares that can be reacquired with the exercise proceeds. This is accomplished by dividing the average market price ($12.00) into the average exercise proceeds which is $15,000 (Beginning exercise proceeds are zero and ending exercise proceeds are $30,000.). Thus, the number of shares that can be reacquired for primary EPS with the exercise proceeds is 1,250 ($15,000 divided by $12.00). If we subtract the 1,250 shares that can be reacquired with the exercise proceeds, from the 1,667 issuable shares, the balance of 417 shares must be added to the outstanding shares for primary EPS computations. These shares are called incremental shares.

The dilutive effect on fully diluted EPS is determined in the same manner as for primary EPS except when the ending market price is higher than the average market price for the year, in which case, the ending market price and the ending aggregate compensation are used. The market price is higher ($14.00) at the end of the year than the average market price ($12.00). Thus, the ending market price of $14.00 is divided into the ending aggregate compensation of $40,000 to yield issuable shares of 2,857 for fully diluted EPS. The next step is to determine the number of shares that can be reacquired with the exercise proceeds. This is accomplished by dividing the market price at the end of the year ($14.00) into the end of the year exercise proceeds ($30,000), which results in 2,143 shares. The 2,143 shares that can be reacquired with the exercise proceeds are subtracted from the 2,857 issuable shares which leaves 714 incremental shares that must be added to outstanding shares for computing fully diluted EPS.

All of the above information, along with the remaining years, is summarized in the following illustration:

Computation of Accrued Compensation

Date	Market Price	Aggregate Compensation	% Accrued	Compensation Accrued To Date	Compensation To Be Charged To Future Periods	Exercise Proceeds
1980	$14.00	$40,000	25%	$10,000	$30,000	$30,000
1981	16.00	60,000	50%	30,000	30,000	30,000
1982	18.00	80,000	75%	60,000	20,000	20,000
1983	20.00	100,000	100%	100,000	None	None
1984	22.00	120,000	100%	120,000	None	None

Computation of EPS Data

	Primary EPS			Fully Diluted EPS		
Exercise Proceeds	Issuable Shares	Assumed Repurchased	Incremental Shares	Issuable Shares	Assumed Repurchased	Incremental Shares
$30,000	1,667	1,250	417	2,857	2,143	714
30,000	3,333	2,000	1,333	3,750	1,875	1,875
20,000	4,117	1,470	2,647	4,444	1,111	3,333
None	4,737	526	4,211	5,000	None	5,000
None	5,238	None	5,238	5,454	None	5,454

Explanation of Terminology Used

Aggregate Compensation	= The difference between the market price at the beginning of the year and the market price at the end of the year multiplied by the number of shares that the employee would be entitled to at the end of the vesting period.
% Accrued	= The percentage amount of the aggregate compensation which is vested for the current period.
Compensation Accrued to Date	= The dollar amount of the aggregate compensation which is vested for the current period.
Compensation To Be Charged To Future Periods	= The difference between the aggregate compensation for the period and the amount of aggregate compensation accrued to date.
Exercise Proceeds	= (1) the exercise price, if any, that the employee must pay, (2) the amount of

compensation, if any, to be charged to future periods, and (3) an adjustment, if any, for related tax effects.

PRIMARY EPS

Issuable Shares	= Average aggregate compensation divided by the average market price.
Assumed Repurchased	= Average exercise proceeds divided by the average market price.
Incremental Shares	= The difference between the Issuable Shares and the Assumed Repurchased shares.

FULLY DILUTED EPS

Issuable Shares	= Average aggregate compensation divided by the average market price, UNLESS THE ENDING MARKET PRICE IS HIGHER, in which case, the end of the year aggregate compensation is divided by the end of the year market price.
Assumed Repurchased	= Average exercise proceeds divided by the average market price, UNLESS THE ENDING MARKET PRICE IS HIGHER, in which case, the end of the year exercise proceeds are divided by the end of the year market price.
Incremental Shares	= The difference between the Issuable Shares and the Assumed Repurchased shares.

Note: The above computations are usually done on a more frequent interval than annually (monthly, quarterly, etc.).

Disclosure

When a company issues financial statements, it must adequately disclose the status of all option plans at the end of the period being reported. This disclosure should include:

1. Number of shares covered by each option
2. Exercise price
3. Number of shares that could be exercised
4. Number of shares exercised
5. Option price of exercised shares

Companies filing with the SEC must meet additional disclosure requirements (Regulation SX).

Comprehensive Illustrations

The following examples demonstrate the accounting treatment for stock options.

An officer of a corporation is granted an option to purchase 100 shares of $20 par value stock for $30 when the market price is $40.

Compensation—officers	$1,000	
Outstanding stock options		$1,000

Subsequently, when the stock option is exercised, the journal entry is:

Cash	$3,000	
Outstanding stock options	1,000	
Common stock		$2,000
Paid-in capital		2,000

Outstanding stock options are part of stockholders' equity and are usually classified as paid-in capital until they are exercised.

In more complex situations (such as those where stock options are granted on the basis of performance over a number of years) it becomes necessary to estimate compensation costs for reporting purposes between the date of grant and the measurement date.

Moreover, deferred taxes must be recognized when the corporation expenses the compensation costs for reporting purposes but not for tax purposes. This is because the compensation costs based on a stock option are not usually deductible until the employee exercises the option.

An example of a more complex situation follows.

Stock Issued to Employees

An officer of a corporation is granted an option to purchase up to 1,000 shares of stock ($50 par value) at the end of two years at 80% of the then market price. The amount of the option will be determined by the total net income of the corporation for the two years in accordance with the following schedule:

Number of Shares	Net Income
200	0 to $500,000
500	$500,001 to $1,000,000
700	$1,000,001 to $1,500,000
1,000	above $1,500,000

At the end of the first year assume the following facts:

Market price of stock	$	100
Corporate net income		$700,000
Corporate tax rate		50%

What is the accrual for the compensation costs at the end of the first year?
Compensation costs at the end of the first year are:

500 shares × 20% × market price

or

500 × $20 = $10,000

The journal entry at the end of the first year is:

Deferred taxes	$ 5,000	
Compensation costs	10,000	
Outstanding stock options		$10,000
Income tax expense		5,000

At the end of the second year, corporate net income is $400,000 and the market price of the stock is $110.
The journal entry at the end of the second year to record the stock option is:

Deferred taxes	$ 2,700	
Compensation costs	5,400	
Outstanding stock options		$ 5,400
Income tax expense		2,700

GAAP GUIDE / 39.19

Stock Issued to Employees

The compensation costs and deferred taxes were found by valuing the entire option at the end of two years and subtracting the previous year's compensation costs and related deferred taxes.

The journal entry when the officer exercises the stock option is:

Cash ($110 × 0.80 × 700 shares)	$61,600	
Outstanding stock options	15,400	
Common stock ($50 par × 700 shares)		$35,000
Paid-in capital		42,000

TRANSFER OF RECEIVABLES WITH RECOURSE

Background

FASB-77 establishes the promulgated GAAP for transfers of receivables that are subject to recourse provisions. Transfers of receivables that are subject to recourse must be reported as sales if specified conditions in FASB-77 are met. Otherwise, the proceeds received from a transfer of receivables subject to recourse must be reported by the transferor as a liability. The provisions of FASB-77 cover only the seller's (transferor's) accounting and reporting practices and not the buyer's (transferee's) accounting and reporting practices.

FASB-77 covers the transfer of receivables that are subject to recourse and other comparable transfers of receivables with recourse, including the following:

- Participation agreements in a particular receivable or pool of receivables which provide for recourse
- Factoring agreements with recourse
- Sales or assignments of sales-type and direct financing leases that provide for recourse
- Sales or assignments of property subject to sales-type or direct financing leases that provide for recourse

FASB-77 amends paragraph 20 of FASB-13 (Accounting for Leases), which deals with a lessor's sale or assignment of a lease, or property subject to a lease, that was accounted for as a sales-type or direct financing lease. The thrust of this amendment is that if the sale or assignment is with recourse, it shall be accounted for by the lessor in accordance with the provisions of FASB-77.

FASB-77 is effective for all transfers of receivables subject to recourse, which occur on or after January 1, 1984. Thus, transactions entered into prior to January 1, 1984, that are consummated on or after January 1, 1984, are covered by FASB-77. Earlier application of the provisions of FASB-77 are encouraged in annual or interim financial statements that have not been previously issued.

Overview

Businesses frequently sell receivables to financial institutions and others to raise cash. When receivables are sold on a recourse basis,

Transfer of Receivables With Recourse

the purchaser has a contractual right to demand payment from the seller, in the event of a default by a debtor. Upon receipt of payment for the defaulted receivable, the purchaser returns the defaulted receivable to the seller.

Many different types of arrangements are employed in the sale of receivables. Factoring is a process by which a company can convert its receivables into cash by assigning them to a "factor" either with or without recourse. "With recourse" means that the assignee (buyer) can return the receivable to the assignor (seller) and get back the amount paid if the receivable turns out to be uncollectible. "Without recourse" means that the assignee assumes the risk of any losses incurred on the collection of the receivables. Under factoring arrangements, the customer (debtor) may or may not be notified of the assignment of receivables.

One type of recourse arrangement for the sale of receivables provides for the purchaser to retain a percentage of the total amount paid for the receivables. This safety cushion retained by the purchaser until the receivables are collected is called a "hold back" or "dealer's reserve." The agreement for the sale of receivables may contain a provision for the purchaser to automatically charge defaulted receivables to the "reserve" account. Any amount remaining in the reserve account after all, or a specified percentage, of the receivables have been collected is then remitted to the seller.

Pledging is the process whereby the company uses existing accounts receivable as collateral for a loan. The company retains title to the receivables, but pledges that it will use the proceeds from the receivables to repay the loan.

> **OBSERVATION:** *A sale of receivables subject to recourse is negotiated between the buyer and seller on the basis of (a) the volume of receivables involved, (b) the stated interest rates, service charges, or finance charges on the receivables, (c) the prevailing interest rates at the date of the transaction, (d) the credit rating of the seller, and (e) other similar financial and economic factors.*

The actual process used to dun customers and collect the outstanding receivables is called "servicing." The sales agreement for the receivables should specify whether the seller will continue servicing the receivables or whether the purchaser will assume the servicing function. A "servicing fee" for either the seller or purchaser may be stipulated in the sales agreement. If a servicing fee is not included in the sales agreement, the ultimate price paid for the receivables will, no doubt, include an amount for the additional costs involved in servicing the receivables.

The face amount of a receivable may include amounts for unperformed portions of executory contracts, such as a contract to repair and maintain the property purchased. For example, a $600 receivable for a washing and drying machine may include a $100 contract to provide maintenance of the appliance for a specified period. Unused portions of executory contracts are frequently refundable to the buyer in the event of cancellation or default. Thus, the purchaser of receivables will take executory contracts into consideration when determining the amount that is paid for the related receivables.

Sale or Liability

A transfer of receivables that is subject to recourse must be reported as either a sale or a liability, according to (a) each party's rights and obligations arising from the transfer, and (b) which party controls the future economic benefits of the receivables. The future economic benefits of receivables consist of the rights to exchange or sell the receivables, use the receivables to produce goods or services, or use the receivables to settle liabilities. Legal title or ownership of the receivables does not always include control of the future economic benefits of the receivables. This is especially true where a seller (transferor) of receivables retains the right to repurchase the receivables. Under these circumstances, the seller controls the future economic benefits as a direct result of being able to repurchase the receivables.

FASB-77 requires that a transfer of receivables that are subject to recourse be reported as a sale, if all of the following conditions are met:

1. The seller unequivocally surrenders to the buyer the control of the future economic benefits of the receivables. If the seller has an option to repurchase the receivables from the buyer, control of the future economic benefits of the receivables has not been unequivocally surrendered. However, a right of first refusal, granted to the seller, to reacquire the receivables based on a bona fide offer by an unrelated third party, is not considered an option to repurchase.

2. The seller's remaining obligations to the buyer under the recourse provisions of the transfer agreement must be subject to reasonable estimation on the date of the sale of the receivables. In order to determine the remaining obligations under the recourse provisions of a transfer agreement, the seller will be required to make a reasonable estimate of (a) the amount of bad debts and related costs of collection and repossession,

(b) the amount of prepayments, and (c) the validity of the transferred receivables. If the seller cannot make a reasonable estimate of the collectibility of the transferred receivables and the related costs of collection and repossession, a transfer of receivables shall not be reported as a sale.

3. The seller cannot be required to repurchase the receivables from the buyer except in accordance with the recourse provisions of the transfer agreement. Insignificant repurchases of receivables by the seller in accordance with the recourse provisions of the transfer agreement do not preclude the recognition of a transfer of receivables from being a sale. However, the amount of receivables repurchased by the seller must be minimal.

If all of the above conditions are met, the seller must report the transfer of receivables as a sale. If all of the above conditions for a sale of receivables subject to recourse are not met, the seller shall report the proceeds received from the buyer of the receivables as a liability.

Gain or loss on transfer Gain or loss on the sale of receivables subject to recourse is equal to the difference between the sales price of the receivables (less *probable adjustments*), and the *net receivables*.

Net receivables, for the purposes of FASB-77, does not have the same meaning as is commonly used in accounting literature, which is gross receivables less a provision for doubtful accounts. For the purposes of FASB-77, *net receivables* are equal to gross receivables, including recorded finance and service charges and other fees, less the related amount of unearned finance and service charges and other fees.

Probable adjustments are those which result from (a) the failure of the debtor to make timely payments, such as estimated bad debt losses and related costs of collection and repossessions, (b) the estimated effects of prepayments by debtors, and (c) the defects in the validity of the transferred receivables, such as a defect in the title or ownership of a receivable. For the purposes of FASB-77, all *probable adjustments* that are incurred in connection with a transfer of receivables that qualifies as a sale shall be accrued in accordance with FASB-5. Under FASB-5, a contingency exists, if at the date of its financial statements, an enterprise does not expect to collect the full amount of its accounts receivables. Under this circumstance, an accrual for a loss contingency must be charged to income, if both of the following conditions are met:

- It is *probable* that as of the date of the financial statements an

asset has been impaired or a liability incurred, based on subsequent available information prior to the issuance of the financial statements, and
- The amount of the loss can be *reasonably estimated*

If both of the above conditions are met, an accrual for the estimated amount of uncollectible receivables must be charged to income, even if the uncollectible receivables cannot be specifically identified. An enterprise may base its estimate of uncollectible receivables on its prior experience, the experience of other enterprises in the same industry, the debtor's ability to pay, and an appraisal of current economic conditions. If an enterprise is unable to reasonably estimate the amount of its uncollectible accounts, there may be significant uncertainty as to the ultimate collection of the receivables. If a significant uncertainty exists in the collection of accounts receivable, the installment sales method, cost recovery method, or some other method of revenue recognition should be used (paragraph 12 of APB-10).

> **OBSERVATION:** *FASB-5 requires certain financial statement disclosures for a loss contingency that is reasonably possible, but does not meet both conditions for accrual. However, FASB-77 does not contain any similar disclosure requirement for a probable adjustment that is* reasonably possible *but does not meet both conditions for accrual.*

If the transfer agreement provides for the buyer to service the receivables, no adjustment is necessary. Also, if the transfer agreement requires the seller to service the receivables and provides for a reasonable (normal) servicing fee, no adjustment is necessary. However, if the transfer agreement requires the seller to service the receivables and does *not* provide for a reasonable (normal) servicing fee, the sales price of the transfer of receivables must be adjusted. The amount of adjustment to the sales price is the amount that is required to provide a reasonable (normal) servicing fee. In other words, the amount provided in the transfer agreement for servicing income to the seller, plus the amount of the adjustment shall equal a reasonable servicing fee which shall be amortized over the term of the related receivables. In this event, the seller shall record the total amount provided for a reasonable servicing fee as deferred servicing income, which shall be amortized to income over the servicing period.

Change in interest rates The sales price of a qualified transfer of receivables subject to recourse may be based on a floating interest rate. In this event, the interest rate used to calculate the sales price at the date of transfer shall be determined in accordance with APB-21 (Interest on Receivables and Payables).

> **OBSERVATION:** APB-21 states that there is no predetermined formula for computing an appropriate interest rate for any transaction. However, the objective is to approximate the interest rate that would be negotiated, under the same terms and conditions, by an independent lender. In evaluating the appropriate interest rate to be used, the following guidelines are recommended by APB-21:
>
> a. The credit rating of the borrower
> b. The restrictive covenants or collateral involved
> c. The prevailing interest rates at the date of the transaction
> d. The interest rate at which the debtor could borrow funds
>
> Note: The appropriate interest rate will frequently depend upon a combination of one or more of the above factors.

After the date of transfer of the receivables subject to recourse, a change in interest rates shall be accounted for as a change in accounting estimate (APB-20, Accounting Changes). APB-20 requires that a change in accounting estimate be accounted for prospectively in (a) the period of change, if the change only affects that period, or (b) in the period of change and future periods, if the change affects both periods. Thus, after the date of transfer of the receivables, a change in interest rates is reported in income of the period of change, as an increase or decrease in the original sales price of the receivables.

Financial Statement Disclosures

FASB-77 requires the following disclosures concerning the transfer of receivables subject to recourse which are reported as sales in the transferor's financial statements:

- The amount of proceeds received from the transfer of receivables during each period for which an income statement is presented
- If the information is available, the amount of receivables that remain uncollected at the date of each balance sheet presented

  Note: The disclosure of similar transfers may be aggregated where appropriate.

There may be other disclosures relating to the transfer of receivables subject to recourse that are required by existing GAAP. Some of the more important disclosures required by existing GAAP are discussed below.

FASB-5 (Contingencies)   Even if they have a remote chance of materializing, FASB-5 requires the disclosure of (a) guarantees to repurchase receivables under recourse provisions, (b) guarantees to repurchase the repossessed property underlying the receivables subject to recourse, (c) guarantees of specific yields on the transferred receivables, including "floating interest rate provisions," and (d) assets pledged as security for a loan. Thus, if a transaction involving any transfer of receivables subject to recourse contains any of the aforementioned contingencies, even if they are remote, the following disclosures must be made in the transferor's financial statements or footnotes thereto:

- The specific nature of the contingency
- The amount of the contingency

APB-30 (Reporting Results of Operations)   The nature and financial effects of a material gain or loss on the sale of receivables subject to recourse that occurs infrequently may have to be disclosed as a separate component of income from continuing operations. The disclosure must appear on the face of the income statement, or in a footnote thereto, in accordance with APB-30.

APB-20 (Accounting Changes)   The effects of a change in accounting estimate that covers several future accounting periods, such as a change in interest rates relating to a floating interest rate provision, must be disclosed. In this event, the effect of the change in accounting estimate on income before extraordinary items, net income, and related per share amounts of the current period must be disclosed in the financial statements in accordance with paragraph 33 of APB-20.

FASB-57 (Related Party Disclosures)   A sale of receivables subject to recourse which occurs between related parties must be disclosed in accordance with the provisions of FASB-57. Thus, a transaction between a parent company or an affiliate and an unconsolidated finance subsidiary would have to be disclosed.

TROUBLED DEBT RESTRUCTURING

Background

FASB-15, Accounting by Debtors and Creditors for Troubled Debt Restructuring contains the promulgated GAAP on this subject and supersedes FASB Interpretation-2, Imputing Interest on Debt Arrangements Made under the Federal Bankruptcy Act. FASB Technical Bulletin 82-2 reaffirms that FASB-15 applies to debtors in bankruptcy, as long as most of the debts of the debtor are not "generally restated."

> **OBSERVATION:** *Three FASB Technical Bulletins (79-6, 79-7, and 80-2) have been issued to provide guidance in applying FASB-15. Each Technical Bulletin is covered in its appropriate place in this chapter.*

Early Extinguishment of Debt (APB-26) arising from a troubled debt restructuring is now covered by FASB-15 and excluded from APB-26.

For the purposes of the promulgated GAAP (FASB-15), troubled debt restructiring does not include the following:

1. Changes in lease agreements (FASB-13)
2. Employment-related agreements, such as deferred compensation contracts or pension plans
3. A debtor's failure to pay trade accounts that do not involve a restructure agreement
4. A creditor's legal action to collect accounts that do not involve a restructure agreement

Troubled debt restructuring arranged under any provision of the Federal Bankruptcy Act is covered by the promulgated GAAP unless the debtor generally restates its liabilities, as in the case of a corporate readjustment or quasi-reorganization.

The promulgated GAAP generally establishes standards for accounting and reporting, by both the debtor and creditor, for a troubled debt restructuring.

Troubled Debt Restructuring

Overview

A "troubled" debt restructuring is one in which the creditor allows the debtor certain concessions that he would not normally consider. The concessions *must be* made in light of the debtor's financial difficulty, and the objective of the creditor *must be* to maximize recovery of his investment. Troubled debt restructurings are often the result of legal proceedings or of negotiation between the parties.

FASB Technical Bulletin 81-6 reaffirms that the provisions of FASB-15 are applicable to troubled debt restructurings arranged under any provision of the Federal Bankruptcy Act, except those provisions in which the debtor generally restates most of its liabilities. In other words, if most of a debtor's liablities are being restated, FASB-15 does not apply. A debtor is usually permitted to restate most of its liabilities with the approval of the court and most of its creditors in a quasi-reorganization, corporate readjustment, and similar situations.

A troubled debt restructuring by a debtor in bankruptcy proceedings would be permitted under FASB-15 provided that the restructuring did *not* constitute a "general restatement" of the debtor's liabilities.

Troubled debt restructures include situations in which:

1. The creditor accepts a third-party receivable, or other asset(s) of the debtor, in lieu of his receivable from the debtor.
2. The creditor accepts an equity interest in the debtor in lieu of his receivable. (This is not to be confused with convertible securities, which are *not* troubled debt restructurings.)
3. The creditor accepts modification of the terms of the debt including but not limited to:
   a. reduction in stated interest rate
   b. extension of maturity at a favorable interest rate
   c. reduction in face amount of the debt
   d. reduction in accrued interest

The reductions mentioned in a, c, and d can be either absolute or contingent.

> **OBSERVATION:** *FASB Technical Bulletin 80-2 reaffirms that a debtor and the related creditor in a troubled debt restructuring must independently account for the debt restructure. Thus, a debtor may account for the debt restructure as "troubled," whereas the related creditor may not necessarily account for the debt restructure as "troubled."*

Definition of Terms

A *receivable (or payable)* is defined as a contractual right to receive or pay money that is already recorded on the debtor's or creditor's balance sheet, and includes accrued interest, premiums, discounts, issue costs, and any related valuation allowances. Although transactions affecting these accounts take on a variety of forms, it is the *substance*, not the form, that should govern the accounting.

The *time of restructuring* is defined as the date an agreement to restructure is consummated.

Not all debt restructurings can be considered troubled, even though the debtor is in financial difficulty. Circumstances in which the restructuring is not troubled include:

1. The debtor satisfies the debt by giving fair value of assets or equity that at least equals either:
    a. the creditor's recorded receivable, or
    b. the debtor's carrying amount of the payable
2. The creditor reduces the interest rate primarily in response to changes in market rates.
3. The debtor issues at or near the current market new marketable securities in exchange for the old securities (the fact that the debtor can obtain at similar rates and conditions funds from other sources, is evidence that the restructuring is not troubled).

Accounting and Reporting by Debtors

A debtor accounts for a troubled debt restructuring by the type of restructuring. Types of restructuring include:

1. Transfer of asset(s) in full settlement
2. Granting an equity interest in full settlement
3. Modification of terms of the debt
4. Combinations of the above three types

Transfer of asset(s) The debtor will recognize a gain in the amount of the excess of the carrying amount of the payable (and accrued interest, premiums, etc.) over the fair value of the asset(s) given up. Fair value is, of course, an arm's-length purchase or sale price. The gain, or loss, is reported in net income of the period.

> **OBSERVATION:** Fair value may be determined either by the assets given up or the amount of payable, whichever is more clearly evident. However, in the case of a partial settlement, the value of the asset(s) given up must be used. This eliminates the need to allocate the fair value of the payable between the settled portion and the remaining outstanding balance.

The excess of the carrying amount of the debt over the fair value of the asset(s) given up is the gain on debt restructuring. However, the difference between the fair value and the carrying amount of the asset(s) given up is the gain or loss on the transfer of asset(s), which is included in net income in the period the transfer occurs.

Transfer of equity interest The difference between the fair value of the equity interest and the carrying amount of the payable is recognized as gain or loss. As a practical matter the difference will always be a gain, since it is unlikely the debtor would exchange fair value in *excess* of his obligation to satisfy his creditors.

The difference between the fair value and the carrying amount of the equity interest given up is the gain or loss on the transfer of asset(s), which is included in net income in the period the transfer occurs.

Modification of terms A restructuring that does not involve the transfer of assets or equity will often involve the modification of the terms of the debt. In a modification the debtor accounts for the effects of the restructuring prospectively, and does not change the carrying amount unless the carrying amount exceeds the total future cash payments specified by the new terms. The *total future cash payments* are the principal and any accrued interest at the time of the resturcturing which continues to be payable by the new terms. *Interest expense* is computed by a method which causes a constant effective rate (such as the interest method). The new effective rate of interest is the discount rate at which the carrying amount of the debt is equal to the present value of the future cash payments.

When the total future cash payments are less than the carrying amount, the debtor should reduce the carrying amount accordingly and recognize the difference as a gain. When there are several related accounts (discount, premium, etc.), the reduction may need to be allocated among them. All cash payments after the restructuring go to reduce the carrying amount, and *no* interest expense is recognized after the date of restructure.

When there are indeterminate future payments or anytime the future payments might exceed the carrying amount, the debtor recognizes no gain. The debtor should assume that the future contingent payments will have to be made at least to the extent necessary to obviate any gain.

In estimating future cash payments for any purpose *in this area*, it is assumed that the maximum amount of periods (and interest) is going to occur.

Combination of types   When a restructuring involves combinations of asset or equity transfer and modification of terms, the fair value of any asset or equity is used first to reduce the carrying amount of the payable. The difference between the fair value and the carrying amount of any asset(s) transferred is recognized as gain or loss. No gain on restructuring can be recognized unless the carrying amount exceeds the total future cash payments.

Repossessions and foreclosures shall be accounted for in the same manner as satisfaction by surrender of assets.

All gains on debt restructure are aggregated and included in net income for the period. If substantial, the gains are reported as an extraordinary item (net of tax effects).

Contingently payable accounts   Amounts contingently payable in future periods are recognized as payable and as interest expense in accordance with the treatment of other contingencies. The criteria for contingencies are:

1. Probability that the liability has been incurred
2. The amount must be reasonably estimable

If any contingently payable amounts were included in the total future cash payments, they must now be deducted from the carrying amount of the restructured payable to the extent they originally prevented recognition of a gain at the time of the restructuring.

In estimating future payments subject to fluctuation, estimates should be based on the interest rate in effect at the time of restructure. A change in future rates is treated as a change in an estimate. The accounting for these fluctuations cannot result in an immediate gain. Rather, the future payments will reduce the carrying amount and any residual value shall be considered gain.

Incidental cost of restructure   In an issuance of equity the incidental costs are charged against the equity issued. All other direct costs are either deducted from recognized gains, or, if no gain exists, they are expensed in the period.

Disclosure by debtors   The debtor must disclose the following regarding any debt restructuring during a period:

1. Description of the terms of each restructuring
2. Aggregate gain on restructure and related tax effect
3. Aggregate net gain or loss on asset transfer
4. Per share amount of aggregate gain on restructure, and related tax effect

The debtor should also disclose contingently payable amounts included in the carrying amount of restructured payables, and the total of contingently payable amounts and the conditions under which the amounts become payable or are forgiven.

Accounting by Creditors

The creditor accounts for restructure by the same categories as the debtor. The treatment of each type of restructure is explained below.

Receipt of assets or equity   When the creditor receives either assets or equity as full settlement of a receivable, he should account for these at their fair value at the time of the restructuring. The fair value of the receivable satisfied can be used if it is more clearly determinable than the fair value of the asset or equity acquired. In partial payments the creditor *must* use the fair value of the asset or equity received.

The excess of the recorded receivable over the fair value of the assets received is recognized as a loss. The creditor accounts for these assets as if they were acquired for cash.

Modification of terms   When the creditor accepts a modification of terms, he accounts for the restructuring prospectively and does not change the recorded investment *unless* it exceeds the total future cash payments (as defined in the terms of the new agreement).

The creditor recognizes interest income at a constant rate of effective interest. For the effective rate the creditor uses the discount rate at which the present value of the future cash receipts is equal to the recorded investment.

If the total future cash receipts are less than the recorded investment, the investment should be reduced and a loss is recognized.

All subsequent cash received is applied to reduce the balance of the recorded investment, and none is considered interest.

When the restructured receivable involves indeterminate future cash receipts, the creditor recognizes a loss to the extent that the minimum future cash receipts are less than the recorded investment. As for contingently receivable amounts, the creditor excludes them from the total future cash receipts unless they are *probable* and can be *reasonably estimated*. If exclusion results in a deficiency, it is recognized as a loss. Flexible payments should be estimated on the basis of the minimum allowable length of time.

The provisions of FASB-15 do not affect the requirements of FASB-5 (Contingencies) to provide for probable losses on modified debt restructuring that can be reasonably estimated (FASB Technical Bulletin 79-6).

Naturally, contingently receivable interest should not be recognized until it is earned *and* the contingency has been resolved. However, before these amounts can be recognized as income, they must first be used to reduce the recorded investment *to the extent* that contingent receipts (which were considered receivable) avoided recognition of a loss on restructuring.

> **OBSERVATION:** When future cash receipts exceed the recorded investment in a receivable whose terms have been modified, the excess should be accounted for as interest income. If recognition of excess receipts results in a higher than normal return on investment, the nature of the excess receipts should be disclosed (FASB Technical Bulletin 79-7).

Combination of types   The creditor shall reduce his recorded investment by the fair value of assets received. Any loss recognized is limited to the excess of the remaining recorded investment over the total future cash receipts. Any future interest income is recognized at a constant effective rate of interest (interest method) or other accepted specialized industry practice that is used for receivables.

Related matters   Foreclosures are accounted for in the same manner as the receipt of assets or equity. Losses, to the extent that they were not previously recognized by valuation allowances, enter into net income for the period.

If a loss from a troubled debt restructuring has been previously provided in a valuation allowance account, such a loss shall be deducted from its related valuation allowance and not charged directly to net income.

Fluctuation in interest rates after a restructuring are accounted for as changes in an accounting estimate in the period they occur. A creditor shall recognize a loss and reduce its restructured receivable when fluctuations in interest rates cause the minimum future cash receipts to fall below the recorded investment in the restructured receivable.

Legal fees and other direct costs resulting from a troubled debt restructuring shall be expensed by the creditor when incurred.

Creditor disclosure The creditor shall disclose the following regarding troubled debt restructurings:

1. Restructured receivables, by major category:
    a. aggregate recorded investment
    b. gross interest income that would have been earned if there had been no restructuring
    c. gross interest income on restructured receivables that is included in net income for the period (Modified receivables with a rate of interest greater than or equal to the rate the creditor would require for similar risk receivables need not be included in the disclosures above.)
2. Amount(s) of any commitment(s) to lend additional funds to any debtor who is a party to a restructuring

These disclosures may be made in aggregate by major category.

Substitution of debtors When a restructuring involves the addition of or substitution of a new debtor for the old debtor, the substance of the transaction determines the correct treatment.

Banking and Thrift Institutions

BANKING AND THRIFT INSTITUTIONS

Overview

The specialized industry GAAP for banking and thrift institutions are as follows:

> FASB Interpretation-9—Applying APB Opinion Nos. 16 and 17 When a Savings and Loan Association or a Similar Institution is Acquired in a Business Combination Accounted for by the Purchase Method
> FASB-72—Accounting for Certain Acquisitions of Banking or Thrift Institutions
>
> **OBSERVATION:** *In a special supplement to* The CPA Letter, *dated February 10, 1986, the AICPA Accounting Standards Executive Committee (AcSEC) issued a four-page notice that provides guidance in determining the proper accounting that should be applied to real estate acquisition, development, or construction (ADC) arrangements of financial institutions. This notice applies only to those ADC arrangements in which the lender participates in expected residual profit, which is defined as the amount of profit, whether called interest or another name such as equity kicker, above a reasonable amount of interest and fees expected to be earned by the lender.*
> *A copy of the above AcSEC notice should be obtained by those financial institutions that enter into ADC arrangements.*

FASB Interpretation-9 concludes that the net-spread method should not be used in determining the amount of goodwill or other intangible assets that are acquired in a business combination accounted for by the purchase method. FASB Interpretation-9 also discusses the circumstances in which goodwill recorded in an acquisition of a banking or thrift institution can be amortized by accelerated methods.

FASB-72 is applicable to the acquisition of a troubled banking or thrift institution, and specifically to that portion of goodwill that arises from the excess of the fair value of assumed liabilities over the fair value of acquired identifiable assets. In respect to this portion of goodwill, FASB-72 provides for a different method of amortization from that required by APB-17 (Intangible Assets). Although a shorter period of amortization is generally provided for the portion of goodwill covered by FASB-72, the amortization period can still be as much as 40 years. Any other goodwill that arises in the acquisition of a troubled banking or thrift institution is accounted for in accordance with existing GAAP.

FASB-72 also covers accounting and reporting for financial assistance that may be granted by a regulatory authority in connection with an enterprise's acquisition of a troubled banking or thrift institution.

FASB-72 is applicable to acquisitions of commercial banks, savings and loan associations, mutual savings banks, credit unions, and other similar depository institutions.

FASB-72 is an amendment and interpretation of APB-17 (Intangible Assets), an interpretation of APB-16 (Business Combinations), and an amendment of FASB Interpretation-9 (Applying APB Opinion Nos. 16 and 17 When a Savings and Loan Association or a Similar Institution Is Acquired in a Business Combination Accounted for by the Purchase Method).

> **OBSERVATION:** *A provision in a final rule regarding Delegated Merger Approvals, issued in 1985 by the Federal Home Loan Bank Board states, "Where goodwill has been included in the resulting association's assets (as a consequence of a merger), the applicant must submit an opinion of a certified public accountant..." Apparently, an opinion must be submitted, satisfactory to the principal supervisory agent, that the goodwill's use and value are accounted for in accordance with generally accepted accounting principles. The effective date of the rule is December 23, 1985.*

Background

Current economic and competitive conditions have adversely affected the financial position of many savings and loan associations and mutual savings banks. High interest rates have eroded profit margins and many financial institutions have reported losses in recent years.

The long-term interest-bearing assets of many banking and thrift institutions are presently producing significantly lower interest yields than can be earned under current market conditions. The prevailing high cost of funds to the institution exceeds the lower interest yields on long-term interest-bearing assets, which frequently produces operating losses.

When a troubled banking or thrift institution is acquired and accounted for by the purchase method, the excess of the fair value of the liabilities assumed over the fair value of the individual identifiable assets acquired is accounted for as goodwill (FASB-72). The amount of goodwill recorded by the purchaser is very likely to approximate the discount on the acquired long-term interest-bearing assets.

Under existing GAAP (APB-17, Intangible Assets), goodwill must be amortized over its estimated life, which may not exceed 40 years. In addition, APB-17 requires that the straight-line method be used for amortizing goodwill, unless another systematic and rational method can be justified.

The FASB concluded that goodwill arising in the acquisition of a troubled banking institution should be amortized over a relatively short period because of the uncertainty about the nature and extent of the estimated future benefits related to the goodwill (paragraph 32 of FASB-72). Some of the factors that support this conclusion are:

1. Goodwill has always been related to the excess future profits a business is likely to earn. It is extremely difficult to justify goodwill in the acquisition of a troubled banking institution which has been incurring large losses.
2. FASB Statement of Financial Concepts No. 3 defines an asset as a probable future economic benefit obtained or controlled by an entity as a result of a past transaction or event. It is extremely doubtful whether goodwill resulting from the acquisition of a troubled banking institution can be properly classified as a "probable future economic benefit."

> **OBSERVATION:** *The above factors could lead to the conclusion that any "goodwill" arising in the acquisition of a troubled banking institution should be written off to expense at the time of acquisition. The FASB prefers a special amortization period and method, as a middle ground between the two extremes of (a) complete write-off immediately upon acquisition and (b) 40-year amortization as provided by APB-17.*
>
> *The solution adopted in FASB-72 is characterized by the Board as "a rapid and pragmatic resolution of the problem" (paragraph 31). The Board did not wish, at this time, to reconsider any of the broader issues of business combinations (APB-16) or intangible assets (APB-17).*

Since goodwill is usually related to future excess profits and profitable operations, a more palatable method of accounting for the "goodwill" which arises in the acquisition of a troubled banking or thrift institution may be to treat it as a "preacquisition contingency" (FASB-38).

FASB-38 requires that a portion of the total acquisition cost under the purchase method be allocated to contingent assets, liabilities, and impairments. If it is "probable" that the contingent item existed at the consummation date of the combination and the amount of the contingent item can be "reasonably estimated," FASB-38 requires that it be recognized.

Paragraphs 5 and 6 of FASB-72 are applicable only to acquisitions of banking and thrift institutions in which the fair value of the liabilities assumed exceeds the fair value of all identifiable assets acquired. Paragraphs 5 and 6 provide for a different amortization method for goodwill from the method that is permitted under APB-17. The provisions of paragraphs 4, 7, and 8 through 11 apply to all acquisitions of banking or thrift institutions. Although FASB-72 does not specify, apparently paragraphs 12, 13, 14, and 15 of FASB-72 also apply to all acquisitions of banking and thrift institutions.

Net-Spread Method and Separate-Valuation Method

The two methods available to record the acquisition of a savings and loan association are the net-spread method and the separate-valuation method. Under the net-spread method, the spread between interest paid on deposits and interest received on mortgages is used to evaluate whether the difference is normal, subnormal, or above normal for a particular market area. If the spread is normal, the principal assets and liabilities that are being acquired are recorded at the carrying amounts shown on the financial statements of the association being acquired. If the spread is subnormal or above normal, an adjustment is made to compensate for the difference. In other words, the acquisition is viewed as the purchase of an entire business and not of separate individual assets. The net-spread method is not acceptable for the purposes of GAAP.

The separate-valuation method is based on recording the acquired identifiable assets at fair value at the date of purchase (APB-16), which is the usual method called for by GAAP. Any difference between the fair value of assets acquired less liabilities assumed is recorded as purchased goodwill.

Fair value of assets is influenced by the ability of the assets to generate future income and/or new business within the territory served. Therefore, if the amount paid for the assets to generate future income or new business can be reliably determined, it shall not be recorded as goodwill, but recorded as a separate identifiable intangible asset and amortized over its estimated life. Any portion of the purchase price that cannot be specifically allocated to identifiable tangible or intangible assets shall be recorded as goodwill (FASB Interpretation-9).

Goodwill recorded in an acquisition of a savings and loan association may be amortized by accelerated methods (contrary to the general rule) if both of the following circumstances exist:

1. Included in goodwill is an indeterminable amount for the acquired assets to generate future income or new business, but these factors cannot be separately valued.
2. The expected benefits from such factors are expected to decline over their useful lives.

Acquisitions of Troubled Banking Institutions

At the date of acquisition of a banking or thrift institution, the excess of the fair value of liabilities assumed over the fair value of the acquired identifiable assets shall be classified as goodwill (FASB-72).

> **OBSERVATION:** *Under the purchase method of accounting for a business combination, goodwill is the difference between the cost of the acquisition and the net assets acquired. However, FASB-72 does not necessarily apply to the amount of goodwill computed in this manner. FASB-72 applies only to the excess of the fair value of the liabilities assumed over the fair value of the identifiable tangible and intangible assets acquired.*

Allocating the cost of an acquisition Independent appraisals and/or subsequent sales of acquired assets may provide evidence of fair value (APB-16). Each identifiable tangible and intangible asset acquired is assigned a portion of the acquisition cost, equal to its fair value at the date of acquisition (APB-16). The fair value of a long-term interest-bearing asset is the present value of the amount that will be received, less an allowance for uncollectible accounts (APB-16). The fair value of an assumed liability is its present value at the prevailing interest rates at the date of acquisition (APB-16). A portion of the total acquisition cost must be allocated to contingent assets, contingent liabilities, and contingent impairments of assets, if any, provided that the following conditions are met:

1. It is probable that the contingent item existed at the consummation date of the business combination accounted for by the purchase method.

2. After the consummation date, but prior to the end of the "allocation period," the facts in item 1 above are confirmed.
3. The amount of the asset, liability, or impairment can be reasonably estimated.

If the above conditions are met, the purchase method requires that a portion of the total cost of acquiring a banking institution must be allocated to any contingent items (FASB-38). The allocation period is the period that is required by the purchaser to identify and quantify the acquired assets and assumed liabilities for the purposes of allocating the total cost of the acquisition in accordance with APB-16. The allocation period usually will not exceed one year from the closing date of the purchase transaction (FASB-38).

Identifiable intangible assets Identifiable assets include intangible assets which can be identified and named, including contracts, patents, franchises, customer and supplier lists, and favorable leases, at appraised values (APB-16). Identifiable intangible assets of a banking or thrift institution may include existing depositor or borrower relationships, such as the capacity of existing savings and loan accounts to generate future income and/or additional business or new business (FASB Interpretation-9). The fair value of these types of identifiable intangible assets must be reliably determined on the basis of existing facts at the date of acquisition without regard to future events (FASB-72). If an acquisition of a banking or thrift institution includes any of these types of identifiable intangible assets which can be reliably determined, a portion of the cost of the acquisition should be assigned to such assets and amortized over their estimated useful lives, in accordance with APB-17.

Maximum amortization period The amount of goodwill and the related periodic amortization, computed in accordance with FASB-72, shall be calculated as the date of acquisition. The periodic amortization expense shall not be adjusted in subsequent periods, except as provided by FASB-72 (see below). The maximum period of amortization shall not exceed the lesser of 40 years or the estimated remaining life of the long-term interest-bearing assets with maturities in excess of one year, if any, which were acquired in the transaction. If a significant amount of long-term interest-bearing assets with maturities of over one year is not acquired as part of the acquisition, goodwill shall be amortized over the estimated average remaining life of the acquired existing customer deposit base.

Method of amortization Amortization must be calculated by the use of a constant percentage rate applied to the carrying amount of the long-term interest-bearing assets which is expected to be outstanding at the beginning of each period. The carrying amount that is expected to be outstanding at the beginning of each period shall be determined by reference to the terms of the long-term interest-bearing assets. If any prepayment assumptions are used to calculate the fair value of the acquired long-term interest-bearing assets at the date of acquisition, the same prepayment assumptions must be used to determine the expected carrying amount of long-term interest-bearing assets that will be outstanding in each subsequent period.

> **OBSERVATION:** *The carrying amount of long-term interest-bearing assets is equal to their face amount, increased or decreased by any related unamortized premium or discount (FASB-72).*

Subsequent revision of amortization In periods subsequent to the date of acquisition, an enterprise must continually evaluate the remaining periods of amortization of its unamortized intangible assets to determine whether revision of such amortization periods is necessary (APB-17, paragraph 31). If the remaining amortization period is revised, the unamortized cost of the intangible asset must be allocated to the revised period. However, the total amortization period for an intangible asset can never exceed 40 years from the date of its acquisition. New estimates of value and future benefits may indicate the necessity of reducing significantly the carrying amount of an unamortized intangible asset (APB-17, paragraph 31). Under these circumstances, a charge to net income is made in the year in which the reduction is indicated by the new estimates.

If a significant portion of a segment or separable group of the operating assets of an acquired banking or thrift institution is subsequently sold or otherwise disposed of, a proportionate amount of the unamortized goodwill must be allocated and charged to the cost of the sale (FASB-72). The loss of a significant and valuable customer base of an acquired banking or thrift institution may result from the sale or liquidation of a major portion of the acquired long-term interest-bearing assets, if such assets are not replaced with similar assets. If the estimated value or benefits of the related unamortized goodwill are significantly reduced as a result of such a sale or liquidation, the reduction must be recognized as a charge to income in the year of sale or liquidation.

The amount of goodwill which results from the application of FASB-72 may not be revised upward under any circumstances (FASB-72).

OBSERVATION: *If there is a permanent impairment in the value of an unamortized intangible asset, its carrying amount should be reduced to net realizable value by a charge to income in the year in which the impairment is discovered.*

Additional goodwill   In the acquisition of a banking or thrift institution, the amount of goodwill may exceed the difference between the fair value of the liabilities assumed and the fair value of the assets acquired. In this event, additional goodwill is recognized and accounted for in accordance with the provisions of APB-17.

Accounting for Regulatory Assistance

In connection with the acquisition of a banking or thrift institution, an enterprise may receive financial assistance from a regulatory agency such as the Federal Deposit Insurance Corporation (FDIC) or the Federal Savings and Loan Insurance Corporation (FSLIC). The financial assistance may be immediate, or may be granted in periods subsequent to the date of acquisition of the banking or thrift institution. In addition, as part of the financial assistance, assets and/or liabilities may be transferred to the regulatory agency.

"Additional interest"   A regulatory agency often provides periodic financial assistance which is approximately equal to the difference between the average yield on the long-term interest-bearing assets acquired in the acquisition and the current interest cost of carrying such assets. Under FASB-72, the computation of this type of financial assistance is made as at the date of acquisition and is based on the difference between the average yield on the long-term interest-bearing assets and the current interest cost of carrying such assets. The amount thus computed is treated as additional interest on the long-term interest-bearing assets. The additional interest is included in determining the present value (fair value) of the long-term interest-bearing assets at the date of acquisition. The additional interest is reported in income of the period in which it is accrued. No other adjustment shall be made in the carrying amount of the long-term interest-bearing assets for subsequent changes in the estimated amount of financial assistance.

Long-term interest-bearing assets that the acquiring enterprise intends to sell must be reported at an amount which does not exceed the current market value of such assets.

Other types of financial assistance   Under FASB-72, other types of financial assistance granted by a regulatory agency must be accounted for as part of the combination if (a) the assistance is probable and (b) the amount of assistance can be reasonably estimated. Thus, under the purchase method, assets that are, or will be, received as a result of regulatory financial assistance must be assigned a portion of the total acquisition cost of the banking or thrift institution.

> **OBSERVATION:** FASB-72 does not cover a situation in which the amount of financial assistance by a regulatory agency exceeds the amount of "goodwill" that would otherwise be recorded in the transaction. In this event, the fair value of the assets acquired will exceed the fair value of the liabilities assumed. Under the purchase method, the excess of acquired assets over assumed liabilities shall be accounted for as "negative goodwill." Under APB-16 (Business Combinations), negative goodwill is not recorded unless the fair values of the noncurrent assets acquired, if any, except long-term investments in marketable securities, are proportionately reduced to zero. If a credit still remains after the noncurrent assets have been reduced to zero, the credit should be classified as a *deferred credit* and amortized to income over the period that is expected to benefit, but not to exceed 40 years (APB-17).

Transfer of assets or liabilities   Assets and/or liabilities may be transferred to a regulatory agency as part of the plan of financial assistance. In this event, the fair value of the assets and/or liabilities that are transferred to the regulatory agency shall be excluded from the fair market value of the assets and liabilities acquired in the transaction.

Financial assistance after date of acquisition   Financial assistance may not be recognized at any time, unless (a) it is probable and (b) the amount of assistance can be reasonably estimated. Financial assistance may become probable and the amount reasonably estimable after the date of acquisition of the banking or thrift institution. In this event, the financial assistance must be recognized in the financial statements of the period(s) in which it becomes probable and the amount reasonably estimable. When this occurs, the financial assistance must be reported as a reduction of the balance of the unamortized goodwill; and amortization for subsequent periods must be adjusted proportionately.

> **OBSERVATION:** All types of regulatory financial assistance, except assistance in the form of additional interest, must be "probable" and the amount "reasonably estimable" before such assistance is recognized and reported in the financial statements of an enterprise

(FASB-72). This leads to the conclusion that financial assistance in the form of additional interest is recognized in accordance with existing GAAP and all other types of financial assistance are recognized only if they are "probable" and the amounts are "reasonably estimable."

Under existing GAAP, the accounting recognition of financial assistance depends on the substance of the transaction or the contractual agreement between the parties. Thus, financial assistance may represent (a) a bona fide receivable, (b) a gain contingency, or (c) a contingent asset. A bona fide receivable is recognized when an exchange takes place, collection of the amount is reasonably assured, and the earning process is complete (APB Statement-4). A gain contingency should not be recognized prior to its realization, and financial disclosure is necessary (FASB-5). Under the purchase method of accounting, a contingent asset is allocated a portion of the total acquisition cost if certain conditions are met (FASB-38).

Most technicians will likely agree that the concepts of "probable" and "reasonably estimable" are already embodied in the recognition principles of existing GAAP.

Repayment of financial assistance An enterprise may agree to repay, based on the attainment of future profitability levels, all or part of the financial assistance granted by a regulatory agency. Repayment of financial assistance must be recognized as a liability and a charge to income of the period in which the repayment is probable and the amounts can be reasonably estimated, in accordance with FASB-5 (Accounting for Contingencies).

Disclosure of financial assistance The nature and amount of financial assistance received by an enterprise from a regulatory agency in connection with the acquisition of a banking or thrift institution must be disclosed in the financial statements.

Effective Date

FASB-72 is effective for business combinations initiated on or after October 1, 1982, and earlier application is encouraged. Retroactive application of the provisions of FASB-72 to business combinations initiated prior to October 1, 1982, is permitted but not required.

If financial statements issued prior to March 1, 1983, omit the application of FASB-72 to business combinations initiated and consummated after September 30, 1982, and prior to March 1, 1983, the financial statements in subsequent periods must be restated; or, if not restated, the retained earnings for the subsequent period must be appropriately adjusted.

> **OBSERVATION:** The initiation date of a business combination involving a mutual banking or thrift institution is the date on which notification is given to the board of directors or to the owners. The initiation date of a business combination involving other types of entities is the earlier of:
>
> (a) The date of public announcement, or notification to the shareholders of any one of the combining companies, of the major terms of the plan, including the ratio of exchange or a formula which provides for the ratio of exchange, or
> (b) The date on which shareholders of the company being acquired are notified directly or by newspaper advertisement of the exchange offer (APB Interpretation of APB-16).

Entertainment Industry

BROADCASTERS

Overview

FASB-63 (Financial Reporting by Broadcasters) contains the specialized accounting and reporting principles and practices that were originally published in the AICPA Statement of Position 75-5 (Accounting Practices in the Broadcasting Industry).

FASB-63 defines a "broadcaster" as an entity that transmits radio or television program material. Program material acquired by a license agreement shall be accounted for as a "purchase of rights" by a broadcaster (licensee), provided that certain conditions are met.

A significant change from the specialized accounting principles in SOP 75-5 has been made in FASB-63 concerning the application of APB-21 (Interest on Receivables and Payables) to license agreements for program material rights of broadcasters. Under SOP 75-5, the licensor and licensee were required to apply the provisions of APB-21 to license agreements for program material rights. Under FASB-63, the application of APB-21 is optional.

Background

A broadcasting station may be completely independent or may be affiliated with a network. Independent broadcasters must purchase or otherwise provide for all of their programming, while a network affiliated broadcaster obtains much of its programming from its affiliated network.

Revenues of broadcasters arise from the sale of advertising time. Independent broadcasters must sell all of their advertising time while much of an affiliated broadcaster's advertising time is sold by the network. When the broadcaster airs the sponsor's advertising, revenue is recognized. Network affiliated broadcasters receive revenue from their affiliated networks on a monthly basis. The revenue is based on a formula, and the networks submit weekly reports of revenue to their affiliates.

Advertising rates are usually based on the size of the estimated audience reached by the broadcaster and the quality of the station's programming. Rates vary significantly from market to market. Local and regional rates are generally less than national advertising rates.

Broadcasters

Rate cards that contain the advertising rates of a broadcaster are determined during rating periods in which the size and demographics of the broadcaster's audience are measured along with the quality of the broadcaster's programming. Rate cards are usually broken down into broadcasting time periods and are revised on a regular basis.

A broadcaster may exchange advertising time for services or products. Such barter transactions should not conflict with a broadcaster's regular advertising business.

Programming costs are usually the largest expense of television broadcasters. Independent broadcasters must obtain all of their programming, while network affiliated broadcasters obtain much of their programming from their affiliated networks. Programming costs are generally higher for independent broadcasters than they are for network affiliated broadcasters. Program material for television broadcasters is purchased under television licenses from producers and distributors. These producers and distributors generally package several films and license the broadcaster for one or more exhibitions or for a specified period, at which time the license expires. The license agreement usually provides for installment payments over a period which is almost always less than the license period. Thus, the producer or distributor receives all of its money for the license prior to the expiration of the license.

Many television broadcasters produce some of their programming material either live or on video tape. Local news broadcasts and local interview shows are popular programs produced by television broadcasters.

Television and radio broadcasters are regulated by the Federal Communications Commission (FCC). Broadcasters are licensed periodically to use frequencies in a specific area which are assigned by the FCC. In licensing a broadcaster the FCC may consider the (1) financial position of the broadcaster, (2) advertising policies, (3) quality of the programming, and (4) contribution made to the community in which the broadcaster operates. Advertising rates are not regulated by the FCC, but guidelines have been established for advertising rates by the National Association of Broadcasters.

The major assets of a broadcaster are its FCC license and its network affiliation. Thus, network affiliated broadcasters are usually more valuable than independent broadcasters.

FASB-63 covers three specific aspects of the broadcasting industry: (a) program material license agreements, (b) barter transactions, and (c) intangible assets.

Program Material License Agreements

FASB-63 requires that broadcasters record the assets and liabilities that are involved in a program material license agreement as a purchase of a right or group of rights. The license agreement shall be reported in the financial statements of the licensee when the license period begins and all of the following conditions are met:

1. The cost of each license fee for each program is known or is reasonably determinable.
2. The broadcaster has accepted the program material in accordance with the terms of the license agreement.
3. The licensor can deliver the program material rights and the broadcaster can exercise the rights. Availability of the program material rights exist when they can be shown or telecast by the licensee for the first time under a licensing agreement, regardless of restrictions on the timing of subsequent showings or telecasts.

FASB-63 requires that the balance sheet of broadcasters be classified. Thus, assets and liabilities shall be classified as current or noncurrent based on the normal operating cycle of the enterprise.

> ***OBSERVATION:*** *SOP 75-5 (Accounting Practices in the Broadcasting Industry) specifies that one year should be used as the normal operating cycle in the broadcasting industry. Thus, program material rights should be classified as current if they are expected to be used within one year. Liabilities should be classified as current if they are expected to be paid within one year.*

The asset and liability that arise from the purchase of program material rights shall be reported by the licensee or licensor at either (a) the gross amount of the liability or (b) the present value of the liability computed in accordance with APB-21 (Interest on Receivables and Payables). Under the provisions of APB-21, the present value of the liability (over one year) is reported as an asset, and the difference between the present value and the face amount of the liability is reported as deferred interest expense. The deferred interest expense is amortized to income in proportion to the payments made on the liability.

> ***OBSERVATION:*** *The thrust of APB-21 is to require the imputation of interest on liabilities (over one year) that bear an unreasonable rate of interest or no interest at all. Thus, if a reasonable*

> rate of interest is charged on a liability, the provisions of APB-21 would not apply and the liability would be recorded at its gross amount. In addition, APB-21 does not apply to receivables or payables with terms of less than one year.
>
> APB-21 was based on the pervasive principle of "substance over form." Allowing the licensee or licensor to report the liability or receivable either "gross" or at "present value" is equivalent to permitting the licensee or licensor to report either the "substance" or the "form" of the transaction.
>
> In addition, FASB-63 represents an amendment of APB-21, in that it provides an exemption from compliance with APB-21 for receivables and payables arising from licensing agreements involving program material rights.

Amortization of program material rights shall be computed on the estimated number of times that the program will be aired by the broadcaster. An accelerated method of amortization must be used when the first broadcast of a program is more valuable than its reruns, which is usually the case. Thus, the straight-line method of amortization shall be used only when each broadcast is expected to produce approximately the same amount of revenue.

Feature programs shall be amortized on an individual basis. However, series programs shall be amortized on a series basis. Program rights purchased for unlimited broadcasts shall be amortized over the term of the license agreement. The cost of rights to a package of programs shall be allocated to each program right in the package, based on the relative value of each program right to the broadcaster.

Unamortized program rights shall not exceed their net realizable value. In the event that program rights do exceed their net realizable value, they shall be written down to net realizable value by a charge to current income. Program rights shall be reported in the balance sheet at the lower of their unamortized cost or their estimated net realizable value.

Barter Transactions

FASB-63 requires that all barter transactions be recorded in accordance with existing GAAP (APB-29, Accounting for Nonmonetary Transactions). The transaction shall be reported at the time the broadcaster airs the commercial. If the services or products have not been received at the date the commercial is aired, a receivable shall be reported. On the other hand, if services or products are received before the date the commercial is aired, a liability shall be reported.

APB-29 requires that nonmonetary exchanges be accounted for at the fair value of the assets or services received or surrendered, whichever is more clearly evident. If fair value is indeterminable, the only valuation available may be the recorded book value of the nonmonetary assets exchanged. When barter revenue is significant, SOP 75-5 suggests that it be disclosed in the financial statements or footnotes thereto.

A broadcaster that is affiliated with a network does not usually record barter transactions consummated by the affiliated network. Compensation to the broadcaster, if any, on these types of barter transactions is usually included in the periodic report from the affiliated network.

Intangible Assets

FASB-63 requires that intangible assets in the broadcasting industry shall be accounted for in accordance with existing GAAP (APB-17, Intangible Assets). Thus, intangible assets in the broadcasting industry must be amortized by the straight-line method over a period not to exceed forty years.

If a network affiliation is terminated, any unamortized network affiliation costs shall be charged to expense unless a replacement agreement exists. In this event, if the fair value of the replacement agreement exceeds the unamortized network affiliation cost of the terminated agreement, no gain is recognized. However, if the fair value of the replacement agreement is less than the unamortized network affiliation cost of the terminated agreement, a loss is recognized to the extent of the difference.

Under the provisions of APB-17, a company shall record as assets the cost of intangible assets acquired from other enterprises or individuals. Costs of developing, maintaining, or restoring intangible assets that are not specifically identifiable, have indeterminate lives, or are inherent in a continuing business and related to an enterprise as a whole, such as goodwill, shall be deducted from income when incurred.

> **OBSERVATION:** SOP 75-5 states that a change in network affiliation is not, by itself, justification to support a change in the amortization method used by a broadcaster. FASB-63 is silent on this point.

Disclosure and Effective Date

Unrecorded program material license agreements that have been executed and do not meet the criteria of FASB-63 must be disclosed in the notes to the financial statements.

> *OBSERVATION:* FASB-63 is silent on the extent of footnote disclosure that is necessary for unrecorded license agreements that have been executed but do not meet the criteria of FASB-63. However, it appears that the provisions of FASB-47 (Disclosure of Long-Term Obligations) may apply to some unrecorded license agreements that have been executed. FASB-47 requires that unrecorded unconditional purchase obligations that (a) are substantially non-cancellable, (b) are related to the costs of the specific goods or services in the contract, or are part of the financing arrangement for the facilities that will provide the specified goods or services in the contract, and (c) are for a remaining term in excess of one year must be disclosed by footnote in the purchaser's financial statements. The disclosures include:
>
> 1. A description of the nature and term of the obligation.
> 2. The total determinable amount of unrecorded unconditional purchase obligations as of the latest balance sheet date, and the total determinable amount of unrecorded unconditional purchase obligations for each of the five years after the latest balance sheet date.
> 3. A description of the nature of any variable component of the unrecorded unconditional purchase obligations.
> 4. For each income statement presented, the amounts actually purchased under the unconditional purchase obligations.

FASB-63 is effective for fiscal years beginning on or after December 16, 1982, and earlier application is encouraged. Retroactive restatement of previously issued annual financial statements is permitted but not required. If retroactive restatement of previously issued annual financial statements, which are presented for comparative purposes, is not elected by an entity, the cumulative effect of the change to FASB-63 shall be included in net income of the year of change in accordance with the provisions of APB-20 (Accounting Changes). In this event, the effect of the change to FASB-63 on income before extraordinary items, net income, and related per share amounts shall be disclosed in the financial statements of the period in which the change occurs.

If retroactive restatement of all comparative financial statements presented is elected by an entity, the financial statements of the year of change shall disclose the nature of any restatement and its effects on income before extraordinary items, net income, and related per share amounts, for each year presented.

If it is impractical to retroactively restate all of the individual financial statements for the comparative years presented, the following procedure must be used:

1. The new accounting principle (FASB-63) is used in determining net income of the year of change (current period).
2. As many consecutive prior years' financial statements as practical (which are presented for comparative purposes) are then retroactively restated.
3. The cumulative effect of the change to FASB-63 is then computed for any remaining prior years.
4. The cumulative effect is then included in determining net income for the earliest year restated.
5. Financial statements presented for years prior to the earliest year restated (which includes the cumulative effect) shall be presented for comparative purposes as they were originally reported.

> **OBSERVATION:** *Simply put, an enterprise has a choice in reporting the effects of the accounting change arising from FASB-63. An enterprise may report the effects of the change by the "cumulative effect method" or by the "retroactive restatement method."*

CABLE TELEVISION COMPANIES

Overview

FASB-51 (Financial Reporting by Cable Television Companies) contains the specialized accounting and reporting principles and practices that were originally published in the AICPA Statement of Position 79-2 (Accounting by Cable Television Companies).

Background

CATV systems are organized and built to provide uninterrupted program entertainment, usually not available on regular commercial television. The distribution of the television programs by a CATV system is usually made over coaxial cables or satellites to a defined area. A CATV system network may cover a small community or a major metropolitan area.

Ordinarily, a cable TV company obtains a franchise from a local governmental authority which permits the distribution of CATV programs in a specified area. The franchise agreement usually provides for payment of fees to the granting authority and contains, among other provisions, the maximum fees that the company can charge a subscriber. In addition, franchise agreements may include many provisions pertaining to the type and quality of service that must be provided, number of TV channels, type of construction, and duration of the franchise. If all of the terms of the franchise agreement are not met, the governmental authority may retain the right to terminate the contract with the cable TV company.

The operation of a CATV system begins with the purchase of program entertainment from a cable service company or a production company. Program entertainment is usually acquired on a long-term contract with one or more cable service companies. The transmission signals of the cable service company are picked up by the CATV system by microwave relay, antennas, or satellite, then amplified and distributed to subscribers via coaxial cables. The subscriber usually pays an initial hookup charge and thereafter, a monthly subscription fee.

The size of the franchise area and the density of the population will usually determine the construction period required to install a CATV system. However, the type of system being built may also affect the period of construction. For example, if the coaxial cables must be installed underground rather than on utility poles, the period of construction will likely take longer. The construction period is completed when all of the equipment used to receive transmissions (head-end equipment) is installed, all main (head-end) and distribution cables are in place, and most subscriber drops (installation hardware) are installed. The CATV system is "energized" when the first transmission is made to subscribers. It is not unusual to "energize" part of a CATV system before the entire system is built because large CATV systems are generally built in sections over several years. When this occurs, a "prematurity period" is established. A prematurity period begins when the first subscriber's revenue is earned and ends when construction of the system is completed or when the first major stage of construction is completed. The prematurity period will vary in direct relation to the size of the franchise and the density of the population.

The capital investment that is necessary, even for a small CATV system, is quite substantial. The acquisition of a franchise and the cost of the physical facilities are expensive and the operating overhead during the construction period requires a great deal of working capital. Space on utility poles or underground ducts is usually leased from utility companies.

Generally accepted accounting principles which have been promulgated for commercial companies are also used in reporting on cable television companies. However, FASB-51 contains the specialized methods of applying existing GAAP to cable TV companies.

Initial Recording of Assets

In the construction of a cable TV company the *prematurity period* begins on the date that subscribers' revenue is earned, and ends on the date that the construction of the CATV system is completed or when the first major stage of construction is completed. However, some cable TV companies have determined that the prematurity period begins on the date that subscribers' revenue is earned and ends on the date that a predetermined number of subscribers is reached.

The prematurity period must be determined by management prior to the recognition of any earned revenue from the first subscriber. Generally, the prematurity period will rarely exceed two years, except in large major market areas. FASB-51 contains a presumption that the prematurity period usually should not exceed two years. Unless very unusual circumstances arise, a prematurity period shall not be changed after it is established by management.

A clearly identifiable portion of a cable TV system which is in a prematurity period should be accounted for separately from the rest of the system. A clearly identifiable portion of a system is distinct from the rest of the system in that it meets most of the following conditions:

1. It is a separate franchise area or different geographic area.
2. It has separate equipment or facilities.
3. It has a separate construction period, break-even point, and/or separate accountability.
4. It has a separate budget and/or separate accountability.

FASB-51 distinguishes between capitalized costs attributable to the main cable television plant and other related capitalized costs of a fully operational system, such as the cost of leases on utility poles or underground ducts, leases on satellite or microwave installations, property taxes, and capitalized interest costs. FASB-51 requires that these other related capitalized costs of a fully operational system be amortized over the same period used to depreciate the main cable television plant.

All costs of constructing the physical facilities of a CATV system should be capitalized. However, during the prematurity period some subscribers are receiving service while construction continues on the system. Thus, during the prematurity period a distinction must be made between costs related to (1) the current period, (2) future periods, and (3) both current and future periods.

Costs related to current period   Selling, marketing, and administrative expenses and all costs related to current subscribers should be accounted for as period costs.

Costs related to future periods   During the prematurity period all costs of constructing the physical facilities of the CATV system should continue to be capitalized.

Costs related to both current and future periods   Tangible and intangible costs which are incurred and capitalized or deferred during the prematurity period are related to both current and future periods. Capitalized costs of the main cable television plant and other related capitalized costs of a fully operational system (such as the cost of leases on utility poles or underground ducts, leases on satellite or microwave installations, property taxes, and capitalized interest costs) must be amortized or depreciated over their estimated useful lives or the life of the franchise, whichever is less.

Thus, during the prematurity period a portion of these costs must be "matched" with current revenue from subscribers.

FASB-51 requires that during the prematuritγ period charges for capitalized costs, other than those of the main cable television plant, should be allocated to both current and future periods based on a fraction. The denominator of the fraction is the total expected subscribers at the end of the prematurity period; the numerator of the fraction is the estimated number of subscribers at the end of each month of the prematurity period. The fraction results in the amount of amortization which is charged to expense in the current period.

During the prematurity period, depreciation of the cost of the main cable television plant of the CATV system should also be allocated by the same fraction. However, instead of computing depreciation on the costs incurred to date, the total depreciable base of the main cable television plant is estimated, and the total amount of depreciation is determined by applying the depreciation method normally used by the company. After the total amount of depreciation is computed, the fraction described in the previous paragraph is applied to arrive at the amount of depreciation expense that should be charged to the current period.

Under the provisions of FASB-34 (Capitalization of Interest Cost) certain interest costs, if material, must be capitalized and added to the acquisition cost of assets that require a period of time to get ready for their intended use. The cost of assets to which capitalized interest should be allocated includes the cost of both those assets acquired for a company's own use and those acquired for sale in the ordinary course of business.

FASB-34 does not allow the capitalization of interest for (1) assets that are ready for their intended use or are actually being used in the earning activities of a business and (2) assets that are not being used in the earning activities of a business and that are not undergoing the activities required to get them ready for use.

The interest capitalization period commences with the first expenditure for the asset and continues through the acquisition period. Interest is not capitalized during delays or interruptions, other than brief, which occur during the acquisition or development stage of the qualifying asset. When the qualifying asset is substantially complete and ready for its intended use, the capitalization of interest ceases.

Total capitalized interest costs for any particular period may not exceed the total interest costs actually incurred by an enterprise during that particular period. In consolidated financial statements, this limitation on the total amount of interest costs which may be capitalized in a period should be applied on a consolidated basis.

Capitalized interest costs for a particular period are determined by applying an interest rate to the average amount of accumulated expenditures during the period for the qualifying asset. The interest rate paid on borrowings during a particular period should be used to determine the amount of interest costs which should be capitalized for the period. Where a qualifying asset is related to a specific new borrowing, the allocated interest cost is equal to the amount of interest incurred on the new borrowing. However, if the average accumulated expenditures outstanding for the period exceed the amount of the related specific new borrowing, interest cost should be computed on the excess. The interest rate that should be used on the excess is the weighted average interest rate for other borrowings of the company.

Thus, interest cost must be capitalized during the prematurity period on that portion of the CATV system which is undergoing activities to get it ready for its intended use and is not being used in the earning activities of the system.

Hookup Revenue and Franchise Costs

Hookup revenue should be included in current revenue, but only to the extent of direct selling costs. Direct selling costs include those costs which are incurred in obtaining and processing new subscribers. Hookup revenue in excess of direct selling costs should be deferred and amortized to revenue over the estimated average subscription period.

Initial hookup costs for subscribers should be capitalized and subsequent disconnects and connects shall be charged to expense as incurred. The depreciation period for initial hookup costs for subscribers should not exceed the depreciation period of the main cable television plant.

Usually, a CATV company makes a formal franchise application to a local governmental unit to provide cable television service in its geographical area. The costs associated with any successful application may be significant and are accounted for in accordance with APB-17 (Intangible Assets). These successful franchise costs are capitalized and amortized to income over the lesser of their estimated useful life or the life of the franchise, but in no event longer than 40 years (APB-17). The straight-line method is used for amortization purposes unless a different method can be justified.

The costs associated with unsuccessful franchise applications and abandoned franchises are charged to expense in the period in which it is determined that they cannot benefit any future period.

Periodic Review of Recoverability

Capitalized assets not only benefit a future period, but their costs should be recoverable from expected future revenue. Thus, a periodic review of the capitalized costs of a cable TV company must be made to determine whether the costs are recoverable through future successful operations or future sale of the assets. Capitalized costs shall be written down to recoverable values by the use of a contra account. Thus, the asset account should be debited with all additions, and the contra account, when deducted from the asset account, will equal the recoverable value of the asset.

Effective Date

FASB-51 is effective for fiscal years beginning on or after December 16, 1981, and earlier application is allowed, but not required. In addition, FASB-51 states that its provisions may be, but are not required to be, applied retroactively. Thus, comparative financial statements presented for prior years may be, but are not required to be, restated. Actual historical subscriber data may be used for restatement purposes if estimates of subscribers are not available.

MOTION PICTURE FILMS

Overview

FASB-53 contains the specialized accounting and reporting principles and practices that were originally published in the AICPA industry accounting guide entitled "Accounting for Motion Picture Films" and the AICPA Statement of Position 79-4 (Accounting for Motion Picture Films). The specialized accounting and reporting principles and practices are directed primarily to licensors of motion picture films. In addition, a licensor should account for a license agreement as a sale of a right or a group of rights.

FASB-53 indicates that the specialized accounting and reporting principles and practices were extracted from the AICPA publications without significant change.

Background

The exhibition rights to a film are usually licensed by the licensor who may be the original producer of the film or a distributor of the film. The rights licensed may be for one showing of the film or for multiple showings of the film over a specified period. Generally, only one first-run telecast of a film is licensed in a given market at a given time.

A film starts with the acquisition of a story property (book, stage play, original screenplay, etc.), goes through the various stages of film production, and is then distributed for exhibition. The production-to-distribution cycle can be as short as a few months and sometimes exceeds three years, depending on the nature and length of the film. Films can be produced for television or theaters, or eventually they can be exhibited in both medias.

Revenue Recognition

Revenue for motion picture film rights is recognized in accordance with the basic realization principle embodied in GAAP. However, FASB-53 requires that certain events occur before revenue may be recognized. Revenue recognition from theatrical exhibitions is discussed separately from television exhibitions.

Motion Picture Films

Theatrical exhibitions In larger markets, exhibition rights are sold on a percentage of box office receipts, sometimes with a nonrefundable guarantee. In smaller markets, the film rights are usually sold on a flat-fee basis. In foreign markets, nonrefundable guarantees are generally considered outright sales because additional revenues based on percentage of box office receipts are seldom, if ever, remitted to the licensor. This is particularly true in foreign markets where the licensor has no control over distribution. Thus, nonrefundable guarantees, which are essentially outright sales, should be recognized as revenue on the execution of a noncancellable agreement.

Under normal conditions, revenue should be recognized for percentage and flat-fee contracts on the date the film is exhibited by the licensee. Normal nonrefundable guarantees against a percentage of box office receipts should be deferred and recognized as revenue on the date of the exhibition of the film.

Television exhibitions Exhibition contracts of film rights for television usually provide for more than one exhibition over a specific period. In addition, most television contracts include a package of several films. These types of contracts expire on the date of the last authorized telecast, or on a specific date, if it occurs sooner. Payment for the contract is usually made in installments over a period which is shorter than that of the licensing agreement. Under FASB-53, revenue can be recognized on a television exhibition contract, when the license period begins and all of the following conditions are met:

1. The license fee for each film is known.
2. The cost of each film can be reasonably determined.
3. Collection of the full contract is reasonably assured.
4. The licensee has accepted the film in accordance with the conditions of the license agreement.
5. Availability of the film exists. The licensor can deliver the right and the licensee can exercise the right. Availability of the film exists when a film may be shown for the first time under a licensing agreement.

Revenue recognition should be postponed if an option or any other condition creates a doubt as to the ability or obligation of both parties to perform.

If a receivable from the sale of film rights extends over a long period and is either noninterest bearing or has an unreasonable rate of interest, the provisions of APB-21 (Interest on Receivables and

Payables) should be applied. Thus, the present value of the long-term receivable will be recorded as a sale, and the difference between the present value and face amount of the receivable will be recorded as deferred interest income.

Costs and Expenses

The production costs of motion picture films usually consist of (1) costs for acquisition of story rights, (2) pre-production costs, (3) principal photography costs, and (4) post-production costs. Production costs are generally accounted for on a film-by-film basis. Production costs include all items that are required and necessary to complete a film. Production overhead is part of completing a film and should be allocated on a systematic and rational basis in accordance with GAAP.

Motion picture film talent is sometimes compensated, in part or all, by participation in the revenues produced by the film. A percentage amount from all or from specific revenues or profits is the usual arrangement. The total participation is estimated and then amortized in the same manner as the amortization of production costs (see below).

A film may have a primary and secondary market. The first market in which the film is exhibited is the primary market and is probably the market for which the film was produced.

Amortization of production costs and other amortizable amounts should commence with the release of the film for exhibition purposes. FASB-53 recommends the "Individual Film Forecast Computation Method" for amortizing film production costs. This method amortizes the costs in the same ratio that current revenues bear to total estimated gross revenues. The computation is similar to the percentage-of-completion method used in long-term construction-type contracts. The following formula does not appear in FASB-53, but may be used:

$$\frac{\text{Total Revenue to Date}}{\text{Total Estimated Gross Revenues}} \times \text{Total Amortizable Amount} - \text{Prior Period Amortization} = \text{Current Amortization}$$

Care must be exercised in determining the "total estimated gross revenues" because long-term noninterest bearing revenues can only be included to the extent of their present values (APB-21). Thus, the difference between the present value of the estimated long-term gross revenue and its face amount is recorded as deferred interest income at the inception of the contract. The "total revenues to date" in the fraction (numerator) must also exclude any interest income collected to date. In other words, both the numerator and denominator of the fraction do not include any imputed interest.

Periodic reviews should be made of the total estimated gross revenue, and appropriate revisions made when current information dictates. Revisions should be made prospectively as a change in accounting estimate (APB-20).

FASB-53 states that periodic table computations may be used to determine amortization providing that the results approximate those computed under the "Individual Film Forecast Computation Method."

Inventory Adjustments

The inventory of motion picture films consists of the unamortized production and other properly capitalized costs. A periodic review must be made of each individual film to determine whether the total estimated gross revenues for the film are enough to recover the unamortized costs, talent participation percentages, and all direct distribution expenses. When total estimated gross revenues are insufficient, an inventory write-down to net realizable value is necessary.

If the estimate of future gross revenues for a particular film is subsequently increased during the same fiscal period in which the film was written down to net realizable value, the film may be written back up in an amount that does not exceed the current year write-down. Any film costs that have been reduced to net realizable value at the end of a fiscal period may not be written back up in subsequent fiscal periods.

It may become necessary to reduce unfinished and/or unreleased films to their net realizable value. This can occur in situations where the film costs have significantly exceeded budgeted costs, or where major downward revisions of estimated gross revenue are required because of existing circumstances.

The inventory of story costs (rights to books, stage plays, etc.) must be reviewed periodically to determine whether they will be used in the production of a motion picture film. Industry practices dictate that story costs held for more than three years, which have not been set for production of a film, should be charged off to current production overhead. After being charged off, story costs should not be reinstated even if they are set for production.

Loans and Interest Costs

Loans, guarantees, and advances by motion picture companies to independent producers should be recorded to reflect the substance of the transaction. Loans and/or advances to independent producers for the production of motion picture films should be recorded as film cost inventory by the motion picture film company. All other items of revenue and expense should be accounted for in accordance with the provisions of FASB-53.

> *OBSERVATION:* Although the original AICPA industry accounting guide specifically covers the interest costs incurred in the production of a motion picture film, FASB-53 does not. However, FASB-34 (Capitalization of Interest Cost) does allow the capitalization of interest costs for qualifying assets which require a period of time to be completed for their intended use. The cost of assets to which capitalized interest may be allocated includes the cost of both those assets acquired for a company's own use and those acquired for sale in the ordinary course of business. Thus, interest costs may be capitalized in the production of motion picture films that qualify under the provision of FASB-34.

Financial Statements

FASB-53 allows a motion picture company to use a classified or unclassified balance sheet for reporting purposes. Motion picture companies that segregate assets and liabilities between current and noncurrent classifications (classified balance sheet) should use the following guidelines:

1. Unamortized film inventory in release to a primary market; completed films not released, reduced by secondary market allocations, if any; and television films in production that are under contract for sale should all be classified as current assets.
2. Secondary market allocations of films which will not be realized within 12 months and all related film production costs should be classified as noncurrent.
3. Production costs that are allocated to secondary television markets should be classified as noncurrent. These costs should be amortized as revenues are recorded from secondary television markets. (*Note:* This treatment of production costs allocated to secondary television markets is expected to avoid reclassification of items, back and forth, between current and noncurrent classifications.)

4. Liabilities should be recorded in accordance with existing GAAP. Thus, current liabilities are obligations whose liquidation is reasonably expected to require the use of current assets or the creation of other current liabilities (ARB-43).
5. From the time of execution to the time of revenue recognition, license agreements for the sale of television film rights are to be considered as executory and should not be reported on the balance sheet until revenues are recognized. Amounts received on such agreements should be reported as advance payments and be classified as current or noncurrent according to the circumstances.

Home Market

Motion picture films licensed for use at home on video cassettes, video disks, or through cable television should be accounted for in accordance with the provision of FASB-53.

Disclosure and Effective Date

FASB-53 requires disclosure of film inventories, including films (1) released, (2) completed but not released, and (3) in process. In addition, the amount of story rights should also be disclosed.

> **OBSERVATION:** *The industry accounting guide entitled "Accounting for Motion Picture Films" required that accounting policies peculiar to the industry be disclosed in accordance with APB-22 (Accounting Policies); it also required that a description of the amortization methods of film costs used by a company be disclosed in accordance with APB-17 (Intangible Assets). Although FASB-53 makes no mention of these disclosures, it is apparent that they are still required by existing GAAP.*

FASB-53 is effective for fiscal years beginning after December 15, 1981, and earlier application is encouraged. In addition, FASB-53 encourages entities to apply its provisions retroactively. Thus, comparative financial statements presented for prior years may be restated.

RECORD AND MUSIC

Overview

FASB-50 (Financial Reporting in the Record and Music Industry) contains the specialized accounting and reporting principles and practices that were originally published in the AICPA Statement of Position 76-1 (Accounting Practices in the Record and Music Industry).

Background

Music publishers usually control the copyright on their music and are frequently owned by an artist-composer. On the other hand, record companies must usually depend on an artist who is employed under a personal service contract to produce the record master that is used in manufacturing the ultimate product. As a general rule, the caliber and reputation of the recording artist has a direct effect on the success of any album or individual record.

The more successful recording artists are paid a nonrefundable advance against future royalties. Lesser known recording artists are not paid any advance and frequently must bear some of the cost of producing the record master.

A record master is produced by an expert sound engineer. Each instrument and voice is first recorded separately on magnetic tape. The sound engineer then combines each instrument and voice, emphasizing and deemphasizing as he deems appropriate. This process is called mixing and is probably the most important phase of manufacturing a record. The mixing process produces a record master, which is used to make acetate discs that are coated with metal. The metal coated disc is used to produce the mold that is eventually used to make the final product. Record masters are also utilized to produce tapes for the manufacturer of tape cartridges and cassettes. The following costs are usually incurred in the production of a record master:

  a. Costs for the recording studio
  b. Costs for engineers, mixing experts, directors, and other technical talent
  c. Costs for musicians, arrangers, vocal background, and other similar talent
  d. Costs for producing the record master itself

Music publishers usually license others, on a royalty basis, to use their music. Additional sources of income for music publishers include royalties from public performances, revenue from the music used in motion picture films, and revenue from the sale of sheet music.

Music publishers are usually members of ASCAP (American Society of Composers, Authors, and Publishers) or some other society or association. These organizations act as collection agencies for music publishers and composers by monitoring radio and TV stations and live performances. Copyright laws provide that each time that music is played publicly, the publisher and/or composer are entitled to a minimum royalty. By monitoring radio and TV stations and live performances, ASCAP collects the royalties due to various publishers and/or composers. After collecting the royalties, ASCAP makes periodic remittances to the publisher and/or composer.

One of the major accounting problems in the record and music industry is the timing of the recognition of a sale. This is because of the return privileges that manufacturers and distributors must make to their customers. In addition, some manufacturers create discounts by including a certain number of free records in proportion to the size of the order.

> **OBSERVATION:** *Accounting and reporting for revenue when a right of return exists is covered by FASB-48.*

Licensor Accounting

Owners of music copyrights or record masters usually enter into license agreements based on a minimum guarantee, which is generally paid in advance by the licensee. The licensor should record the receipt of a minimum license guarantee as deferred income (liability), which should be recognized as it is earned in accordance with the license agreement. If the license agreement is unclear as to when the guarantee is earned, the only alternative may be to recognize the guarantee over the term of the license agreement.

Fees that are not fixed in amount by the terms of the license agreement cannot be recognized as revenue by the licensor until a reasonable estimate can be made of such fees or the license agreement expires.

A license agreement must be examined carefully to determine whether an outright sale was consummated or a license was granted. An outright sale of specific rights must be distinguished from a minimum license agreement. When a licensee receives from the licensor a noncancelable contract for a specified fee granting specific rights to the licensee, who may use these rights at any time without restriction, an outright sale has been consummated. In this event, the earning process is complete and revenue should be recognized if collectibility of the balance of the fee, if any, is reasonably assured.

> **OBSERVATION:** Promulgated GAAP prohibits accounting for revenue by any form of installment accounting except under exceptional circumstances where collectibility cannot be reasonably assured. In such cases, a company can use either the cost recovery method or the installment sales method of accounting (APB-10).

Royalties paid to artists should be accounted for on the accrual basis of accounting. Thus, royalty advances should be recorded as prepaid royalties when evidence is available that such advances will be recouped from future earned royalties.

Future royalty guarantees and commitments, if material, should be disclosed in the financial statements.

The cost of a record master should be recorded as an asset if it is reasonably assured that such cost will be recovered from expected future revenue. The cost of a record master should be amortized to income in proportion to the net revenue that is expected to be realized.

Any portion of the cost of a record master which is recoverable from the artist should be accounted for appropriately. Any portion of the cost of a record master that is recorded as an asset shall be disclosed separately in the financial statements.

Licensee Accounting

As mentioned previously, license agreements are usually based on a minimum guarantee that is generally paid in advance to the licensor by the licensee. The licensee should record this minimum payment as a deferred charge. The deferred charge should be amortized to income over the periods that are benefited, which is usually the term of the license agreement.

The last sentence of paragraph 15 of FASB-50 requires that fees not fixed in amount by the terms of the license agreement before the agreement expires "shall be estimated and accrued on a license-by-license basis by the licensee."

Effective Date

FASB-50 is effective for fiscal years beginning on or after December 16, 1981, and earlier application is encouraged. The provisions of FASB-50 are to be applied retroactively. Thus, financial statements presented for prior periods shall be restated to reflect the provisions of FASB-50.

Franchise Fee Revenue

FRANCHISE FEE REVENUE

Overview

FASB-45 (Accounting for Franchise Fee Revenue) contains the specialized accounting and reporting principles and practices that were originally published in an AICPA industry accounting guide entitled "Accounting for Franchise Fee Revenue." This industry accounting guide was published in 1973 and is devoted solely to the accounting problems of the party granting the franchise (franchisor).

FASB-45 indicates that the specialized accounting and reporting principles and practices were extracted from the franchise fee revenue guide, and that the FASB did not contemplate a comprehensive reconsideration of the accounting issues covered in the guide.

Background

In brief, a franchise agreement usually transfers certain rights (the franchise), which are owned by the franchisor, to a franchisee. The rights transferred for a specified period may include the use of patents, secret processes, trademarks and trade names. Payment for the franchise rights may include an initial franchise fee and/or continuing fees or royalties. The agreement should also provide for any continuing services which are to be rendered by the franchisor, and any inventory or purchases which may be required of the franchisee. In addition, the franchise agreement should clearly set forth the procedure for cancellation, resale, or reacquisition of the franchise by the franchisor.

Conventional accounting practices and methods, including existing promulgated GAAP should be used in accounting for franchise revenue. However, the timing and classification of franchise revenues and the association of franchise costs to related franchise revenues, may create unique accounting problems.

Revenue Recognition—Individual Franchise Fees

The two major accounting problems in revenue recognition of initial franchise fees are (1) the time the fee is properly regarded as earned, and (2) the assurance of collectibility of any receivable resulting from unpaid portions of the initial fee.

> **OBSERVATION:** *These accounting problems are not unique to franchise accounting and merely represent a rehash of the basic realization of revenue principle. The realization principle requires that revenue be earned before it is recorded. GAAP require that the realization of revenue be recognized in the accounting period in which the earning process is substantially completed and an exchange has taken place (APB Statement 4). In addition, revenue is usually recognized at the amount established by the parties to the exchange except for transactions in which collection of the receivable is not reasonably assured (APB Statement 4). In the event that collection of the receivable is not reasonably assured, the installment method or cost recovery method may be used (APB-10).*

FASB-45 requires that revenue on individual franchise fees be recognized on the consummation of the transaction, which occurs when all material conditions of the sale have been substantially performed. Substantial performance by the franchisor occurs when the following conditions are met:

1. The franchisor is not obligated in any way (trade practice, law, intent, or agreement) to excuse payment of any unpaid notes or to refund any cash already received.
2. The initial services required of the franchisor by contract or otherwise, have been substantially performed.
3. All other conditions have been met which affect the consummation of the sale.

It is presumed that substantial performance does not usually occur prior to the commencement of operations by the franchisee. In other words, the earliest that substantial performance is presumed to occur under FASB-45 is when the franchisee actually commences operations of the franchise. However, this presumption may be overcome if the franchisor can demonstrate that substantial performance occurs at an earlier date.

Another accounting problem involved in the recognition of individual franchise fees is the collectibility of any receivable resulting from unpaid portions of the initial franchise fee. An adequate provision for estimated uncollectible amounts from individual franchise fees must be established, if necessary. If the collection of long-term receivables from individual franchise fees is not reasonably assured, the cost recovery or installment sale accounting methods should be used to recognize revenue.

Cost recovery method The cost recovery method, also known as the sunk-cost theory, is used in situations where recovery of cost is undeterminable or extremely questionable. The procedure is simply that all cost is recovered before any gain is recognized. Once all cost has been recovered, any other collections are recognized as revenue. The only expenses remaining to be charged against such revenue are those relating to the collection process. For example, if a company sells for $100 an item that cost $40, and receives no down payment, the first $20 collected, regardless of the year collected, would be considered recovery of one-half the cost. The next $20 collected would be recovery of the balance of the cost, regardless of the year collected. The remaining $60 (all gross profit) would be recognized as income when received. The only additional expenses that could be charged against the remaining $60 would be those directly related to the collection process.

Installment sales method   Under the installment sales method of accounting, each payment collected consists of part recovery of cost and part recovery of gross profit, in the same ratio that these two elements existed in the original sale. For example, assume that a furniture dealer sells for $100 a chair that cost him $70. The gross profit percentage for this sale is 30%. The dealer would recognize 70% of any payment as a recovery of cost and 30% as realized gross profit.

Continuing franchise fees   In the event that the continuing franchise fees appear to be insufficient to cover the costs and reasonable profit of the franchisor for the continuing services required by the franchise agreement, a portion of the initial franchise fee, if any, should be deferred as appropriate, and amortized over the term of the franchise. The amount deferred should be sufficient to cover all the costs of the continuing services plus a reasonable profit.

> **OBSERVATION:** *Apparently, FASB-45 assumes that continuing services required by the franchisor always coincide with the term of the franchise and amortization should be based on the term of the franchise. A more realistic approach would be to relate the amortization period to the period in which the continuing services will be provided by the franchisor, which may not necessarily be the entire term of the franchise.*
>
> *Also, it may be desirable to replace "reasonable profit" with "normal profit." Normal profit for a product, service or industry, is more precise and determinable than a "reasonable profit."*

Revenue Recognition—Area Franchise Fees

Revenue recognition from an area franchise is accounted for exactly the same as that for individual franchise fees. The only difference is that substantial performance of the franchisor may be more difficult to determine. The terms of the franchise agreement must be used to determine when substantial performance has occurred. In addition, it may be necessary to use the percentage-of-completion method of recognizing revenue in some franchise agreements. For example, an area franchise agreement may require the franchisor to provide specific initial services to any franchise opened in the area. In this event, the franchisor should reasonably estimate the number of franchises that are expected to be opened in the area and should recognize a portion of the total area franchise fee as substantial performance occurs for each franchise in the area. Thus, it is necessary to determine the cost of servicing each individual franchise within the area and the total cost of all individual franchises that are expected to be opened in the area. The next step is to determine the percent of costs that have been substantially performed to the total costs of all individual franchises that are expected to be opened in the area. The resulting percent is applied to the total initial area franchise revenue to determine the amount of area franchise revenue that can be recognized.

> **OBSERVATION:** *The percentage-of-completion method of recognizing revenue should only be used in those situations in which costs can be reasonably estimated with some degree of reliability.*

Estimates of the number of franchises that are expected to be opened in an area franchise should be determined by reference to the significant terms and conditions of the franchise agreement.

If the franchisor's substantial performance under the terms of the franchise agreement is related to the area franchise, and not to the individual franchises within the area, revenue recognition occurs when all material services and conditions relating to the area franchise have been substantially performed. Thus, this type of area franchise is treated similarly to an individual franchise.

Any portion of the franchise revenue that is related to unperformed future services which may have to be refunded shall not be recognized by the franchisor until the right to refund has expired.

Franchisee and Franchisor—Unusual Relationships

Unusual relationships may exist between the franchisee and franchisor, besides those created by the franchise agreement. The franchisor may guarantee debt of the franchisee, or contractually control the franchisee's operations to the extent that an affiliation exists. In all these circumstances, FASB-45 requires that all material services and conditions relating to the franchise be substantially performed by the franchisor before revenue is recognized.

> **OBSERVATION:** *The above requirements for unusual relationships between the franchisee and franchisor are no different than those for an individual or area franchise. That is, substantial performance must occur before the franchisor may recognize any revenue.*

> **OBSERVATION:** *The conclusions reached by FASB-45 relating to unusual relationships between the franchisee and franchisor are not in complete agreement with the conclusions reached in the industry accounting guide entitled "Accounting for Franchise Fee Revenue." The guide's conclusions are that, "Revenue should not be recognized if these relationships overcome the concepts of revenue recognition referred to above." In other words, the guide's position is that if the unusual relationships overcome the concepts of recognizing revenue when substantial performance occurs, revenue should not be recognized. Thus, the substance of the franchise transaction must be viewed in the context of the unusual relationships between the franchisee and the franchisor, before revenue can be recognized.*

According to FASB-45, the initial franchise fee shall be deferred if it is probable that the franchisor will acquire the franchise back from the franchisee because of an option, or other understanding. In this event, the deferred amount is accounted for as a reduction of the cost of reacquiring the franchise when the option or understanding is exercised.

Tangible Assets Included in the Franchise Fee

Besides the initial services of the franchisor, the initial franchise fee may include the sale of specific tangible property, such as inventory, signs, equipment, or real property. Thus, a portion of the initial franchise fee must be allocated to such tangible property. FASB-45 requires that the amount allocated shall be the fair value of the property. The fair value of the tangible property shall be recognized as revenue when title to such property passes to the franchisee, even though substantial performance has not occurred for other services included in the franchise agreement.

> **OBSERVATION:** *FASB-45 does not mention the date on which fair value of the tangible property must be determined. It is assumed that the fair value should be determined as at the date of the franchise agreement, which ordinarily establishes the date of the sale.*

Franchise Fee Revenue

The franchise agreement may also allocate a portion of the initial franchise fee to specific services that the franchisor will provide. If the various services that the franchisor will provide are interrelated to the extent that objective segregation is impossible, FASB-45 prohibits the recognition of revenue for any specific service until all the services required under the franchise agreement have been substantially performed. However, if actual prices are available for a specific service, through recent sales of the specific service, FASB-45 does permit recognition of revenue based on substantial performance of the specific service. In other words, if the franchisor has established objective prices for specific services, a portion of the total franchise fee may be recognized on completion of substantial performance of the specific services.

Continuing Franchise Fees

Continuing franchise fees are consideration for the continuing rights granted by the franchise agreement and for general and specific services during the life of the franchise agreement. Continuing franchise fees are recognized as revenue when actually earned and receivable from the franchisee. This is true, even if the continuing franchise fee is designated for a specific purpose. However, if an agency relationship is established by the franchise agreement and a designated portion of the continuing franchise fee is required to be segregated for a specific purpose, the designated amounts shall be recorded as a liability. Any costs incurred for the specific purpose would be charged against the liability. All other costs relating to continuing franchise fees are expensed as incurred.

> **OBSERVATION:** *There is apparently a conflict between paragraphs 14 and 17 of FASB-45. Paragraph 14 (second sentence) indicates that all direct and indirect costs relating to continuing franchise fees be expensed as incurred. Paragraph 17 (first sentence) indicates that direct costs related to all franchise sales be deferred and recognized at the time that the related revenue is recognized.*
>
> *The industry accounting guide entitled "Accounting for Franchise Fee Revenue" (page 15) clearly indicates, in the first paragraph under Continuing Franchise Fees, that expenses related to such fees be recorded on the accrual basis. However, the third paragraph does indicate that costs which are related to a portion of a continuing franchise fee that has been designated for a particular purpose, be expensed as they are incurred.*

Continuing Product Sales

If the terms of the franchise agreement allow the franchisee to obtain equipment and supplies from the franchisor at bargain purchase prices, a portion of the initial franchise fee must be deferred. The portion of the initial franchise fee that must be deferred is either: (1) the difference between the normal selling price of the equipment and supplies and the bargain purchase price, or (2) an amount which will enable the franchisor to recover all costs and provide a normal profit. The deferred amount is accounted for as an adjustment of the initial franchise fee and an adjustment of the selling price of the bargain purchase items.

> **OBSERVATION:** *The sale of equipment and supplies by the franchisor at normal selling prices, which should include a reasonable profit for the franchisor, is accounted for at the time that the sale is complete. The amount of sale is found by reference to the franchise agreement and the cost of the sale is the cost of the equipment or supplies to the franchisor. If it is apparent that the franchisor is not making a reasonable profit on the equipment or supplies, then the rules for "bargain purchases" must be followed.*

Agency Sales

Some franchise arrangements in substance establish an agency relationship between the franchisor and the franchisee. The franchisor acts as agent for the franchisee by reselling inventory, equipment, and supplies at no profit. In other words, the franchisor orders items for the franchisee and then resells the same items to the franchisee at no profit. FASB-45 requires that these transactions be accounted for on the franchisor's books as receivables and payables, and not as profit or loss items.

Matching of Revenue and Costs

Direct franchising costs should be matched to their related franchise revenue in accordance with the accrual basis of accounting. This may necessitate the deferral of direct costs incurred prior to revenue recognition and the accrual of direct costs, if any, not yet incurred through the date on which revenue is recognized.

Total direct costs that are deferred or accrued must not exceed their estimated related revenue.

Selling, general, administrative, and other indirect costs that occur on regular basis regardless of the sales volume, are required by FASB-45 to be expensed when incurred.

Repossessed Franchises

In repossessing a franchise, the franchisor may, or may not, refund the consideration previously paid by the franchisee. If a refund is paid by the franchisor, the accounting treatment is equivalent to a cancellation of the original sale. Any revenue previously recognized is treated as a reduction of the revenue of the current period in which the franchise is reacquired.

> **OBSERVATION:** Since substantial performance is required before any revenue may be recognized, it is unlikely that a franchisor would grant a refund in the event that the revenue had already been recognized. Instead, it is more likely that the franchisor would enforce collection of any balance due rather than cancel the sale.

If a refund is not paid by the franchisor, the transaction is not considered a cancellation of the sale and no adjustment is made to the previously recorded revenue. However, if a balance is still owed by the franchisee, it may be necessary to review the allowance for uncollectible amounts for the transaction. Also, any deferred revenue on the original sale should now be recognized in full.

Business Combinations

When a franchisor acquires the operations of one of its own franchisees, in an arms-length transaction, FASB-45 requires that the acquisition be accounted for in accordance with APB-16 (Business Combinations).

Pooling-of-interests method If the acquisition of one of its own franchisees is accounted for as a pooling-of-interests, the financial statements of the two entities are combined as of the beginning of the year and all intercompany transactions are eliminated in the combined financial statements. Thus, the original sale of the franchise and any other sales of products or services do not appear on the combined financial statements. In addition, any prior years' financial statements which are presented would have to be retroactively restated to reflect the business combination.

Franchise Fee Revenue

Purchase method If the acquisition of one of it own franchisees is accounted for as a purchase, the financial statements of the two entities are combined as of the date of the acquisition and no prior intercompany accounts are eliminated in the combined financial statements. In addition, details of the results of operations for each separate company, prior to the date of combination, that are included in the current combined net income, must be disclosed by footnote.

Disclosures

FASB-45 requires that the following disclosures be made in the financial statements or footnotes thereto:

1. The nature of all significant commitments and obligations of the franchisor, including a description of the services that have not been substantially performed.
2. If the installment or cost recovery method is being used to account for franchise fee revenue, the following must be disclosed:
    a. the sales price of franchises being reported on the installment or cost recovery method
    b. the revenue and related deferred costs (currently and cumulative)
    c. the periods in which the franchise fees become payable
    d. the total revenue that was originally deferred because of uncertainties and then subsequently collected because the uncertainties were resolved
3. If significant, separate disclosure for (a) initial franchise fees, and (b) other franchise fee revenue.
4. Revenue and costs related to non-owned franchises as opposed to franchises owned and operated by the franchisor.
5. If significant changes in the ownership of franchises occurs during the period, the following shall be disclosed:
    a. the number of franchises sold during the period
    b. the number of franchises purchased during the period
    c. the number of franchised outlets in operation during the period
    d. the number of franchisor-owned outlets in operation during the period

The following disclosures, while not required, are considered desirable:

1. A statement of whether initial franchise fee revenue will probably decline in the future because sales will reach a saturation point.
2. If not apparent in the financial statements, the relative contribution to net income of initial franchise fee revenue.

Effective Date

FASB-45 is effective for fiscal years beginning on or after June 16, 1981, and earlier application is encouraged. Financial statements presented for prior periods shall be restated to reflect the provisions of FASB-45.

Insurance Industry

INSURANCE ENTERPRISES

Overview

FASB-60 contains the specialized accounting and reporting principles and practices that were originally published in the following AICPA publications:

- Audits of Stock Life Insurance Companies
- Audits of Fire and Casualty Insurance Companies
- Statement of Position 79-3 (Accounting for Investments of Stock Life Insurance Companies)
- Statement of Position 80-1 (Accounting for Title Insurance Companies)

The provisions of FASB-60 cover general purpose financial statements for stock life insurance companies and property and liability insurance companies (stock and mutual), including reciprocal or inter-insurance exchanges. Title insurance companies are also covered by FASB-60, with the exception of accounting for a *title plant*, which is covered by FASB-61 (Accounting for a Title Plant). In addition, mortgage guaranty insurance companies are covered by FASB-60, except for premium revenue recognition, claim costs, and acquisition costs. Mutual life insurance companies, assessment enterprises, and fraternal benefit societies are expressly excluded from the provisions of FASB-60.

BACKGROUND

Property and Liability Insurance Companies

Property and liability companies are very similar to life insurance companies. The big difference is that property and liability insurance companies cover risks incurred on property or liability and life insurance companies cover risks involving the death or disability of the insured. Both types of insurance companies collect premiums and usually pay commissions to agents or sales personnel. In addition, both types of insurance companies have underwriting departments and utilize other insurance companies to spread excess or specialized risks (reinsurance).

A property and liability insurance company may be organized as (1) a stock company, (2) a mutual company, or (3) a reciprocal or inter-insurance exchange.

A stock property and liability insurance company is owned by its stockholders and is organized as a corporation. Because of the corporate form, stockholders' liability is usually limited to the amount of their investment in capital stock.

In a mutual property and liability insurance company the current policyholders are the owners at any given time and they share in the earnings and have the right to vote for the members of the board of directors. Upon liquidation of a mutual company, the current policyholders receive any remaining assets after payment of all liabilities. Most mutual companies issue nonassessable insurance policies that limit the liability of the policyholders in the event of bankruptcy or lack of capital.

A reciprocal insurance exchange is comprised of subscribers who sign subscribers' agreements. The subscribers' agreements provide, among other things, for an attorney-in-fact who has the power to underwrite insurance for the subscribers. However, each subscriber's liability is several and not joint. Thus, the liability of each subscriber is limited by the amount stated in the subscriber's agreement. Subscribers may be individuals, corporations, trusts, or partnerships. Compensation is paid to the attorney-in-fact based either on a percentage of premium income, or some other appropriate method.

A property and liability insurance company may underwrite one line of insurance business, or may be licensed to sell multiple lines of insurance. The lines of property and liability insurance are usually grouped as (1) fire and similar perils, (2) general liability, (3) marine perils, (4) automobile liability and property damage, (5) homeowners' insurance, (6) accident and health, (7) workmen's compensation, (8) fidelity, (9) theft, (10) glass, (11) surety, (12) boiler and equipment, and other miscellaneous commercial insurance.

From an economic standpoint, insurance is a method which is used to spread a specific risk among policyholders. The insurance company assumes the specific risk and charges a premium based on past loss experiences for the specific risk. The premiums collected by the insurance company are used to pay current losses and operational costs, and the balance is invested. Thus, the two main sources of income for a property and liability insurance company are (1) premiums and (2) investment income.

An owner of an insurance contract must have an insurable interest in the subject matter of the policy in order for the contract to be valid. An insurable interest in life insurance need only exist at the time the policy is issued, while an insurable interest in property insurance must exist at the time of the loss.

An insurable interest is a test of financial relationship. A wife may insure the life of her husband, an employer the life of an employee, a creditor the life of his debtor, and a partner the life of his copartners. In life insurance the insurable interest must exist only at the time the policy is issued and if subsequently the relationship is broken (divorce of a marriage, dissolution of a partnership) the owner may still collect the benefits of the insurance contract.

A landlord may insure his property and a homeowner his home. However, in property insurance the insurable interest must exist at the time a loss is incurred. If a landlord sells his property, he has no further insurable interest and is not entitled to collect for any losses on the property sold.

The departmental functions of a typical property and liability insurance company would usually consist of (1) an agency department, (2) an underwriting department, (3) a policy service department, and (4) an investment department.

The agency department is responsible for the marketing functions of the insurance company. Supervision and training of sales personnel, sales promotion, and other selling activities are handled by the agency department.

The underwriting department is responsible for evaluating the risks which are undertaken by the insurance company, and also controls the issuance of all policies. Premium rates are determined by past loss experiences for specific types of risks. In addition, the underwriting department determines all reinsurance arrangements.

The policy service department is responsible for the bookkeeping activities, such as premium notices and collection, changes in address, beneficiary and similar changes, and the payment of loss claims.

The insurance company's investments are managed by the investment department.

Usually, insurance companies keep their general ledgers on a cash basis, because this is exactly how they do business. Another reason why the cash basis is used is that some reports required by regulatory agencies must be prepared on a cash basis, particularly details of income and expense. Assets that have been recorded on the books of an insurance company are called *ledger assets*. Assets that are not recorded on the books are called *nonledger assets*. Nonledger assets arise from the adjusting journal entries which are necessary to convert the cash basis trial balance to the accrual basis. Liabilities are referred to in the same manner, so that those that are recorded on the books are called *ledger liabilities*, and those not recorded on the books are called *nonledger liabilities*.

Because insurance companies use the cash basis, very few liabilities are recorded, and consequently most liabilities are nonledger. However, most assets arise from cash transactions, and, thus, an insurance company will have few nonledger assets.

When adjusting journal entries are made for workpapers, to convert the cash basis trial balance to the accrual basis, they are not posted to the books. Therefore, the books of insurance companies are always on the cash basis. This procedure makes it necessary for the insurance company to keep certain other records, such as a *claims register*, so that information is available to adjust easily to the accrual basis. The claims register keeps track of claims pending, paid, negotiated, and rejected, while the cash basis trial balance will only reflect the claims actually paid. The claims register is used to prepare some of the necessary adjusting journal entries for conversion to the accrual basis.

All insurance companies theoretically have a maximum financial capacity or limit as to the amount of insurance they should underwrite. In addition, many insurance companies set their own limit on the amount of risk they are willing to undertake and thus, the amount of insurance they will underwrite. However, even if an insurance company has reached its theoretical financial capacity or self-imposed limit, the company can still write additional business and utilize reinsurance to keep within its established limits. Reinsurance is the transfer of one or more policies from one insurance company (the ceding company) to another (the reinsurer). The reinsurer charges the ceding company a premium for the amount of risk it has assumed and agrees to pay its share of any losses. In practice, some insurance companies have entered into agreements with other insurance companies for automatic reinsurance. Automatic reinsurance means that a specific portion or percentage of the total business written by the ceding company is automatically reinsured by one or more insurance companies. On the other hand, *facultative reinsurance* means that the ceding company submits each individual risk or portion of risk to the reinsurer, who then has the choice of accepting or rejecting each individual risk.

Another form of reinsurance occurs when one insurance company sells all or part of its insurance in force to another insurance company. However, this form of reinsurance almost always includes the transfer of policy service responsibilities to the assuming company. Thus, the assuming company takes over the actual bookkeeping responsibilities, such as premium notices and collections.

Frequently, a sale of insurance policies in force will require the approval of local regulatory agencies.

Every state has statutory laws governing the insurance industry. The insurance department of each state is charged with the responsibility of making sure that insurance companies remain solvent and deal fairly with policyholders. In addition, most states require some sort of periodic uniform financial report from insurance companies. Insurance companies are also restricted as to the types of investments that they can make.

The National Association of Insurance Commissioners (NAIC) is an organization comprised of the insurance commissioners from each state. The NAIC meets semi-annually and makes recommendations for new rules and procedures which are almost always adopted by all of the states. The NAIC is very concerned with financial reporting and auditing of insurance companies. The results have been the establishment of uniform annual reports and the development of an examiner's manual which is written in the form of an audit program for insurance companies.

Property and liability insurance companies obtain their business through (1) direct writing, (2) brokers, (3) local and regional agents, and (4) general agents. In obtaining its business through direct writing, an insurance company usually has salaried or commission sales personnel who do not have the power to bind the company on any insurance risks. The sales personnel who work directly for the company must submit all policies sold to a branch or home office for approval. Insurance brokers are usually independent agents who represent many insurance companies. Brokers can submit policies which they have sold to any insurance company they wish and the insurance company may accept or reject the broker's business as they see fit. Local and regional agents usually report to a branch or home office and are appointed on a nonexclusive territory basis. They are generally paid a commission based on a percentage of the premiums they produce. General agents are also compensated on a percentage of the premiums that they produce. However, the percentage is almost always higher for a general agent than for any other type of insurance solicitor. General agents usually sign contracts with the insurance company, and agree to maintain a sales force and promote the insurance company's business. In addition, a general agent agrees to pay its own expenses and often agrees to obtain subagents. In exchange, the insurance company usually grants an exclusive territory to the general agent.

Many property and liability insurance companies handle their own policy claims through salaried employees. These employees often investigate a claim and propose a settlement with the claimant. However, in most cases, settlements must be approved by the home office.

Another method used by insurance companies to investigate, adjust, and settle policy claims is through an adjustment bureau. Adjustment bureaus consist of several insurance companies which are all members of the adjustment bureau. The expenses of a bureau are paid by the members, usually based on the number of claims handled or the dollar value of the claims. The right of final approval of all settlements made by an adjustment bureau is usually exercised by the insurance company. Members are not obligated to use the bureau.

Independent insurance adjustors, who work on a fee basis, are another alternative an insurance company may use to investigate, adjust, and settle policy claims.

Most of the accounting and statistical data used by a property and liability insurance company appear in the *daily reports*. A daily report is a copy of a section of the insurance policy that was sold, and it contains practically all of the accounting and statistical data necessary to record the transaction. Copies of the daily reports are distributed to several departments at the home office of the insurance company. The underwriting department receives a copy of the daily report from which the correct premium for the policy is computed.

Stock Life Insurance Companies

The proceeds of a life insurance policy usually provide some degree of financial security to one or more beneficiaries named in the policy. Upon death of the insured, the insurance company pays the face amount of the policy, less any outstanding indebtedness, to the beneficiary. However, the proceeds of the insurance policy are not always paid in a lump sum at the time of death of the insured. Many different choices are available as to how the proceeds will be paid. For example, an election can be made for the insurance company to pay certain periodic amounts to the beneficiary, or to pay the proceeds when the beneficiary reaches a specified age. In this event, the proceeds are held by the insurance company and will usually earn interest. Almost any type of arrangement can be made with a life insurance company for the payment of a policy's proceeds.

An owner of an insurance contract must have an insurable interest in the subject matter of the policy in order for the contract to be valid. An insurable interest in life insurance need only exist at the time the policy is issued, while an insurable interest in casualty insurance must exist at the time of the loss.

From an economic standpoint, insurance is a method which is used to spread a specific risk among many individuals. The insurance company assumes the specific risk, such as death, and charges a premium based on actuarial calculations. In the case of death, mortality tables have been established which take into consideration the frequency of deaths among individuals in various age groups. The premiums collected by the insurance company are used to pay current benefits and costs and the balance is invested to yield investment income. Theoretically, if an individual dies in the year that the mortality tables predict, the accumulated net premiums collected by the insurance company, plus the investment earned on the accumulated premiums, should be sufficient to pay the face amount of the policy and still leave a profit. These accumulated premiums and investment income are reflected on the balance sheet of an insurance company as *policy reserves.*

An annuity insurance policy is one that the insured does not have to die to collect. It is more like a fixed compulsory saving plan. The insured pays premiums for a stated period, after which the insurance company makes fixed payments to the insured either for a specified time or for the balance of the insured's life.

Accident and health insurance policies are issued on an individual or group basis. In these types of policies the insurance company pays for hospital and medical care, and sometimes for the loss of income during periods that the insured is incapacitated.

The important thing to remember is that revenues of an insurance company are usually derived from premiums and investment income.

The two most common types of insurance companies are (1) stock companies and (2) mutual companies. Stock companies are formed to earn profit for their shareholders. A stock life insurance company may issue participating and nonparticipating insurance policies. Participating policyholders share in the earnings created by their policies. These earnings, if any, are returned to the participating policyholders in the form of dividends. Nonparticipating policyholders do not share in any earnings of the company.

As a general rule, mutual insurance companies issue only participating policies. Thus, all of the policyholders share in the earnings and all have the right to vote for the members of the board of directors.

The departments of a typical life insurance company would include (1) an agency department, (2) an underwriting department, (3) a policy service department, (4) an actuarial department, and (5) an investment department.

The agency department is responsible for the marketing functions of the insurance company. Supervision and training of sales personnel, sales promotion, and other selling activities are handled by the agency department.

The underwriting department is responsible for evaluating the risks which are undertaken by the insurance company and also controls the issuance of all policies.

Determining premium rates and calculating the dividends on participating policies are functions of the actuarial department. Long range planning and the calculation of the adequacy of policy reserves are also the responsibility of the actuarial department.

The policy service department is responsible for the bookkeeping activities, such as premium notices and collection; changes in address, beneficiary and similar changes; and the payment of claims or benefits.

The insurance company's investments are managed by the investment department.

Generally, life insurance companies are exempt from registration under the Securities Exchange Act of 1934. However, many insurance companies have established holding companies, which are not considered life insurance companies and, thus, must be registered under the 1934 Act. In addition, some insurance companies have registered their shares under the 1934 Act so that the shares can be listed and traded on a national stock exchange. Public offerings of life insurance companies' stock must be registered under the Securities Act of 1933.

If an insurance company has registered under either of the securities acts, it must comply with annual and periodic reporting requirements and proxy solicitation rules.

An insurance company receives its revenues from premiums and investment income. Premium income may be derived directly from the owner of the policy or from reinsurance agreements with other insurance companies. Investment income is regulated by insurance statutes which set forth the types of investments that may be made.

Life insurance companies generally sell (1) life insurance, (2) annuity contracts, and (3) accident and health contracts. There are many different types of life insurance coverage; the more common are discussed below.

Whole-life policies Benefits are paid upon death of the insured. Benefits are usually equal to the face amount of the policy, less loans or indebtedness owed to the insurance company. Whole-life policies usually accumulate a cash surrender value which increases as each year passes. The owner of the policy can usually borrow from the insurance company or a bank using the cash surrender value as collateral.

Premiums for whole-life insurance are generally level, that is, they are the same amount each year. They are payable annually but more frequent payments can be made by payment of a small service fee. A whole-life policy can be paid in one lump-sum payment at the beginning of the policy term, but this is an exception, as most policies are paid either quarterly, semi-annually, or annually. A *straight-life* policy (also called *ordinary life*) requires that premiums be paid during the entire life of the insured. A limited-payment policy requires that premiums be paid over a specified period, which is usually ten, twenty, or thirty years. As a result, the premiums on a limited-payment policy are always higher than those of a straight-life policy, but the total cost of the policy is usually less.

Term insurance policies   are issued for a specific period and death benefits are paid only if the insured dies during the specified period. Benefits are usually equal to the face amount of the policy. Term insurance policies generally do not accumulate any cash surrender value, and thus, no loans can be made against them.

Term insurance policies are written for short periods, usually one to five years. However, in most cases the policyholder is granted the right to renew a term insurance policy up to a maximum age (60 or 65) without having to submit additional evidence of insurability. The term policy may also grant the right to the policyholder to convert the term insurance to whole-life or some other type of coverage.

Premiums for term insurance policies usually increase with the age of the insured. Payment must be made annually, but may be made at interim periods during the year for an additional service charge.

Since term insurance does not usually accumulate any cash value, the premiums constitute payment for insurance protection only. Thus, most people feel that term insurance is best in those cases where protection is sought.

Besides individual term policies, an insurance company may issue group term life insurance policies. A group term policy insures a specific group of individuals under a single master contract, usually for one year. Premiums are calculated on the basis of the ages of the individuals in the group.

Endowment insurance policies   are issued for a specific time, called the *endowment period*, and have a maturity date on which the insured receives the face amount of the policy, less any indebtedness owed to the insurance company. However, if the insured dies during the endowment period the insurance company pays the face amount, less any indebtedness, to the beneficiary of the policy. Thus, the insured has insurance protection during the endowment period and, if living at the maturity date, receives the face amount of the policy, less any indebtedness due to the insurance company. Endowment policies accumulate a cash value which increases with time. The cash value may be used as collateral for a loan.

Premiums for endowment policies can be on a single lump-sum payment or on a limited-payment basis, but are generally payable over the endowment period specified in the policy.

Basic insurance policies can be expanded by the use of riders which are attached to, and made part of, the insurance contract. A nonforfeiture rider can be attached to a policy which provides that in the event the policyholder fails to make a premium payment, the insurance company may use the cash value of the policy to make the premium payment. Another type of nonforfeiture rider provides for the entire policy to be converted to a term insurance policy in the event that a premium payment is not made on time. Thus, the policyholder is given extended protection instead of having the insurance protection lapse.

Still another type of common rider provides for the waiver of all premiums during periods of disability that the insured might experience. An accidental death benefit rider (double indemnity) provides that the insurance company will pay twice the face amount of the policy, if the insured dies by accidental means.

Obviously, each rider has its price which increases the overall premium on the insurance policy.

In an annuity contract, the insurance company guarantees to pay the annuitant for as long as he lives a periodic sum of money. The annuity can begin immediately or at some specified future date. Annuity contracts can be issued on an individual or group basis and group annuities are often utilized to fulfill a company's pension plan obligations. Premiums for annuities are based on the amount of the periodic payment, the date the payments begin, and the age of the annuitant.

Straight-life annuity The annuitant receives guaranteed periodic payments as long as he or she lives. No further payments are made by the insurance company after the date of death of the annuitant.

Life annuity—period certain exactly the same as a straight-life annuity except that the insurance company agrees to make the guaranteed payments for a specified time. Thus, if the annuitant dies before the end of the specified time, the annuitant's beneficiary continues to receive the guaranteed payments until the specified time comes to an end.

Joint and survivorship annuity   involves two or more annuitants and provides for guaranteed periodic payments to any surviving annuitant.

Variable annuity   The periodic annuity payment varies in accordance with investment experience. Investments for variable annuities are kept in a separate fund and the amount of the periodic annuity is based on the performance of the investments. Variable annuities may or may not include a minimum death benefit during the accumulation period.

There are many types of accident and health insurance policies available today. However, most of the coverage is provided by group contracts. The more common types provide for reimbursement of medical expenses and for loss of income during periods of partial or total disability. Medical coverage is frequently broken down into hospital expenses and reimbursement for doctor bills. Health insurance policies almost always contain a *deductible clause,* which requires that the insured pay a stipulated amount of losses before the coverage is effective.

Title Insurance Companies

The main business activity of a title insurance company is to issue title insurance policies. Title insurance provides protection against loss or damage that results from liens or defects in the ownership document to a parcel of real estate. Thus, if a buyer obtains title insurance on real estate that is being purchased and subsequently a loss is incurred because of a lien or defect in the title to the property, the title insurance company will pay any loss or damage. Generally, every mortgage lender will require a title insurance policy on the property being purchased before they will lend any funds as a mortgage.

A title insurance policy is very unique inasmuch as the premiums are usually not refundable and the term of the policy is indefinite. However, the amount of title insurance and the date of title search are stated in the policy. Thus, any loss in excess of the amount of title insurance and any loss which occurs because of a lien or defect that did not exist up to the date of the title search will not be covered by the policy.

When an application for title insurance is received by the insurance company a title search is made. A title search consists of reviewing and scrutinizing the chain of ownership of the property being insured up to the date of the title search. Some title searches may go back several hundred years. Each change of ownership is examined to make sure it was properly made and that no unpaid liens or defects exist against the title to the property. If a lien or defect is discovered, the title insurance policy is still usually issued but the discovered lien or defect is cited in the policy and not covered. In this event, the buyer may be able to cancel the purchase of the property or compel the seller to take care of the existing lien or defect. Most contracts for the sale of real property contain a provision to the effect that the property is being sold free of any liens and/or defects, and that the buyer has a specified period to determine whether any liens or defects do exist against the property being purchased.

The records that a title insurance company uses to search the chain or ownership of a parcel of real estate is called the *title plant*. The title plant consists of the public records of a specific geographic area (town, city, county, etc.) that have been appropriately indexed and integrated so that an individual parcel of real property may be easily located. From the title plant, the insurance company can prepare an abstract on any piece of real estate in the particular geographic area. An abstract is a short summary of the ownership history of a specified parcel of real property.

A title plant is usually kept up-to-date on a daily basis. A well maintained title plant will usually increase in value over time and seldom, if ever, decreases in value. In addition, the estimated useful life of a title plant is generaly indefinite. These unusual characteristics make a title plant quite unique.

CLASSIFICATION OF INSURANCE CONTRACTS

FASB-60 requires that insurance policies be classified as either short-duration contracts or long-duration contracts. A short-duration contract is not expected to cover an extended period and a long-duration contract is expected to cover an extended period. In a short-duration contract, the insurance carrier primarily provides insurance protection, while in a long-duration contract the insurance company provides other services and functions in addition to insurance protection. Other services and functions that an insurance company may provide to a policyholder include loans secured by the insurance policy and various options for the payment of policy benefits.

In determining whether an insurance contract is of short duration or long duration, FASB-60 requires that the following factors be considered.

Short-duration contracts   The amount of premiums charged, the amount of coverage provided, or other provisions of the contract can be adjusted or canceled by the insurance company at the end of any contract period. A short-duration insurance contract provides insurance protection and is issued for a short, fixed period.

Long-duration contract   The contract is usually noncancelable, guaranteed renewable, or otherwise not subject to unilateral changes in its provisions. A long-duration insurance contract provides insurance protection for an extended period and includes other services and functions which must be performed.

Most property and liability insurance contracts and some specialized short-term life insurance contracts are classified as short-duration contracts. Most life insurance contracts and title insurance contracts are classified as long-duration contracts. Accident and heatlh insurance contracts may be of short duration or long duration, according to their expected term of coverage.

PREMIUM REVENUE RECOGNITION

As mentioned previously, FASB-60 requires that insurance policies be classified as either short-duration contracts or long-duration contracts according to whether or not the coverage is for an extended period. Premium revenue recognition is based on whether the insurance policy is classified as a short-duration contract or a long-duration contract, as follows:

Short-duration contracts   FASB-60 requires that premium revenue from short-duration contracts be periodically recognized in proportion to the insurance company's performance under the contract. The insurance company's performance under the contract is the coverage of the risks that are insured. Thus, in those insurance policies in which coverage is provided evenly over the term of the insurance, the premiums should be recognized evenly over the term of the insurance. However, if the period of coverage (risk) is different from the term of the insurance contract, then the premium should be recognized over the period of coverage. In other words, the premium income must be "matched" to the period of risk (coverage) during which the insurance company is exposed to potential loss. In the event the amount of insurance declines over the term of the insurance, the premium should be recognized in proportion to the amount of insurance over the term of the insurance.

In some types of insurance, such as workmen's compensation, the final premium is not determined until after the term of the insurance contract because the premium is based on the total amount of compensation paid to employees. The insurance company receives a premium deposit at the inception of the policy and after the term of the insurance, a premium adjustment is made. In this event, an estimate of the final premium adjustment is necessary in order to recognize the total premium revenue over the term of insurance coverage. If the final total premium cannot be reasonably estimated, the cost recovery method or the deposit method of accounting may be used until the final total premium is known.

Over the term of an insurance policy, the premiums are expected to pay for losses, if any, and operational expenses and still provide the insurance company with a profit. The amount of losses that a single insurance policy may incur is based on the law of averages. In other words, the possible loss that a single policy may incur is based on the loss experience of many policies. As long as an insurance policy is outstanding, there may be a claim for a loss. Thus, the unearned portion of a premium, at any time, should be sufficient to pay losses, operational expenses and a margin for profit. Statutory laws, in most states, provide that insurance companies must maintain reserves for possible losses equal to the unearned premiums of all insurance policies outstanding. The most common method used to determine unearned premiums is the "monthly pro rata fractional basis." This method assumes that the same dollar amount of insurance business is written each day of every month. Thus, the mean of all insurance business written in any month is the middle of the month. One year is divided into 24 periods, and a fraction is assigned to each month as follows: January 1/24, February 3/24, March 5/24, April 7/24, May 9/24, June 11/24, and so forth. The appropriate fraction is then applied to the total original premium to determine the amount of earned and unearned premium.

Most state statutes require that insurance companies maintain their records in a manner in which a determination can be made annually on December 31 of the (1) premiums in force on direct insurance business and any reinsurance business and the (2) premiums in force on insurance business that has been ceded on a reinsurance basis to other insurance companies.

Long-duration contracts   FASB-60 requires that premium revenue from long-duration contracts be recognized when due from the policyholder. Thus, premiums for whole-life, endowment, renewable term, and other long-duration contracts are recognized as revenue when the premiums are due from the policyholders.

Title insurance premiums are considered due from policyholders and recognized as revenue when the title insurance company is legally or contractually entitled to the premium. Either the effective date of the title insurance policy or the date of the binder is the likely date on which the title insurance company is legally or contractually entitled to collect the premium.

> **OBSERVATION:** *The reasoning behind recognizing the entire title insurance premium on the effective date of the policy is because the insurance company has performed all of the acts necessary to earn the revenue. If a subsequent loss occurs, it will be because the insurance company did not uncover the cause of the loss at the time of the title search.*

CLAIM COSTS AND FUTURE POLICY BENEFITS

Property and liability insurance companies must pay claims to policyholders who incur losses which have been insured. At any given time, claims may (1) be reported to the insurance company and be in the process of settlement or (2) be incurred but not reported to the insurance company.

As mentioned previously, a title insurance company insures ownership to real property. The title company scrutinizes the chain of title to uncover any defects. Presumably, if a title company does its job properly, there should be no claims for losses. In practice, however, claims do occur and the title company does incur losses.

Life insurance companies also incur costs in the form of policy benefits that are paid to the beneficiary in accordance with the terms of the insurance policy.

FASB-60 contains specific promulgated GAAP for claim costs and future policy benefits, as follows:

Claim Costs

Title insurance companies should accrue estimated claim costs at the time the related insurance premiums are recognized as revenue. Claim costs for other types of insurance contracts shall be accrued as they occur. Thus, a provision for claim costs (liability) should include (1) reported losses in the process of settlement and (2) estimated losses incurred but not reported. The provision for reported claims in the process of settlement may be made by estimating each reported claim on an individual basis. However, because of their large number, smaller reported claims may be estimated by an average dollar loss per claim. Thus, the provision for smaller claims is frequently made by multiplying the number of smaller claims by the estimated average loss per claim.

Claims incurred but not reported are more difficult to determine and are usually estimated on a formula basis. Formulas are usually determined on the basis of statistics on actual claim experience for prior years, which is then adjusted for current trends and other factors. This is usually accomplished by examining specific types of insurance policies for a selected period and then relating the loss experience to the premiums in force for the specific type of insurance policies. Formulas are only used for normal losses which are expected to recur. Large losses resulting from catastrophies are not included in the statistics used in determining formulas, but are estimated separately, usually on the basis of judgment. Thus, a formula will usually consist of the loss experience determined for a prior period, adjusted for current trends, and a factor for large catastrophic losses.

Statutory Formula Reserves are required by most states for bodily injury, liability, and workmen's compensation insurance. In addition, several states require minimum reserves for unreported losses incurred on surety and fidelity insurance policies.

FASB-60 requires that a liability be accrued in the financial statements for reported losses in the process of settlement and unreported losses incurred but not reported. The liability for unpaid losses should include the effects of inflation and other economic factors, and should be based on the best estimate of the cost of settlement, arrived at by using past loss experience adjusted for current trends. The cost of settlement may be reduced by an estimated salvage and/or subrogation expected to be recovered from the claim. Amounts of salvage and/or subrogation should be deducted from the liability for unpaid losses in the balance sheet and the amount deducted should be disclosed in a footnote to the financial statements.

Differences in and adjustments to estimates and actual claim payments, which result from periodic reviews, shall be recognized in net income of the period in which the differences or adjustments occur.

> **OBSERVATION:** *An insurance company may elect to report its liability for unpaid claims and the related claim adjustment expense for short-duration contracts at their present value. In this event, the amount of the effects of such a presentation must be disclosed in the financial statements (see "Disclosures").*

Title insurance companies and mortgage guaranty companies sometimes acquire real property as a result of settling a claim. Real property acquired in settlement of a claim should be reported at estimated fair value. Subsequent adjustments to the reported fair value and realized gain or loss on the final disposition of the real property shall be reported in the financial statements as an increase or decrease of claim costs. Real property acquired in settling a claim should not be classified as an investment, but should be reported separately in the balance sheet.

Claim adjustment expense Figuring the liability for reported claims in the process of settlement and for claims incurred but not reported involves the calculation of the amount of claim that will be paid to the policyholder. The claims adjustment expense represents the estimated expenses that are related to, and will be incurred in, settling the claims of policyholders. Claims adjustment expense may be classified as allocated or unallocated. *Allocated claims adjustment expenses* are those that can be directly associated with a specific claim. *Unallocated claims adjustment expenses* are those that cannot be associated with a specific claim and include indirect salaries, stationery, postage, rent, travel, and other similar expenses of the claims department.

The liability for the claims adjustment expense is generally determined by a formula based on expenses incurred in the settlement of claims in prior periods. In other words, the formula is based on past experience which may be adjusted for current trends.

FASB-60 requires that a liability for claims adjustment expense for short-duration contracts be accrued for all reported claims in the process of settlement and all claims incurred but not reported.

Future Policy Benefits

An insurance company pools the risks of many individuals and businesses. Thus, the undertaking of risks is the primary business of an insurance company. However, the real risk that an insurance company takes is that actual experience will be worse than the actuarial assumptions used in calculating the premium. When this occurs, the insurance company loses money. Thus, it is important that insurance companies be reasonably conservative in their basic assumptions, which should include a provision for the "risk of adverse deviation."

The normal costs of an insurance company include the payment of policy benefits and the expenses of doing business. These costs must be matched to their related premium revenue.

FASB-60 requires that a liability for future policy benefits on long-duration insurance contracts be accrued at the time that premium revenue is recognized. The liability includes the present value of future policy benefits and related expenses, less the present value of related future net premiums. Stated another way, the liability for future policy benefits for a particular group of insurance contracts is the excess of the total amount of net premiums collected over the total amount of related policy benefits paid to date. *Gross premium* is the total cost of the insurance contract to the policyholder. When accumulated with investment income, the gross premium is supposed to create a fund which will be sufficient to pay all policy benefits and related costs and expenses and provide a profit for the insurance company. *Net premium* is that portion of the gross premium which is necessary to cover all policy benefits and related costs and expenses. In other words, net premium is supposed to represent the gross premium, less a profit for the insurance company.

Future policy benefits and related expenses are calculated by the use of actuarial assumptions, such as investment yields, mortality and morbidity rates, and estimated terminations or withdrawals. The liability for future policy benefits and related expenses is based on actuarial assumptions existing at the time the insurance contract is consummated, and is presented in the balance sheet at its present value. The liability for future policy benefits should include a provision for unfavorable deviations from the original actuarial assumptions. This provision is referred to as the *risk of adverse deviation*. Changes in the original actuarial assumptions in subsequent periods are recognized in net income of the period of change.

OTHER COSTS

Since the matching concept is applied to the recognition of premium revenue, it is only logical that the same principal be used in accounting for the costs incurred in obtaining the premium revenue. Thus, variable acquisition costs that are directly or indirectly related to the production of new or renewal premium revenue, should be deferred and amortized as a charge against income as the related premium revenue is earned. Acquisition costs that are directly related to the production of insurance business include all direct costs and indirect costs, such as underwriting and policy issuance expenses. Collection expenses, professional fees, depreciation, and general and administrative expenses are not directly related to, nor do they vary directly with, the production of new or renewal insurance business, and should be expensed as incurred.

Deferred acquisition costs should be amortized as a charge to income in the same manner as the related premium revenue is earned. The method of amortization should be consistently applied from year to year. Unamortized acquisition costs are classified in the balance sheet as assets.

Actual acquisition expenses for long-duration contracts should be compared to those used in the actuarial assumptions and, when possible, the actual acquisition expenses should be used in the actuarial assumptions instead of estimates. When estimates are used to determine the acquisition expenses which should be deferred, it is necessary to adjust such estimates to actual amounts if the differences are significant.

> **OBSERVATION:** *Under regulatory accounting practices, all acquisition expenses are charged against income in the period incurred. Thus, a significant difference between regulatory accounting practices and GAAP is the deferral and amortization of acquisition expenses. This difference is reflected in stockholders' equity and net income determined under regulatory accounting practices, and stockholders' equity and net income determined under GAAP.*

Other expenses of insurance companies are treated in accordance with existing GAAP. Thus, if an expenditure benefits future periods, it may be deferred and charged to the periods benefited. However, all other expenses, such as policy maintenance, investment expenses, and general overhead, which are not directly related to the production of new or renewal insurance business should be charged to operations in the period incurred.

DEFICIENCY IN PREMIUMS OR LIABILITY FOR FUTURE POLICY BENEFITS

Insurance companies may incur losses on short-duration and long-duration contracts. For the purposes of FASB-60, premium deficiencies shall be determined by reasonable grouping of similar insurance policies which is consistent with a company's usual system of acquiring, servicing, and measuring profitability for its insurance business. Each of these types of deficiencies is discussed separately below.

Short-Duration Contracts

Premium revenue is supposed to be sufficient to cover expected claim costs, claim adjustment expenses, acquisition costs, policy maintenance costs, and estimated dividends to policyholders and provide a margin of profit for the insurance company. Whenever unearned premiums are less than (1) the related liability for unpaid claim costs and claim adjustment expenses, (2) related unamortized acquisition costs, (3) related estimated policy maintenance costs, and (4) related dividends to policyholders, a premium deficiency exists.

Premium deficiencies should be recognized in the financial statements. Recognition should be made by reducing unamortized deferred acquisition costs by a change to income in the amount of the deficiency. If the unamortized deferred acquisition costs are smaller than the amount of premium deficiency, all of the unamortized deferred acquisition costs should be charged to income, and an additional separate liability for the balance of the premium deficiency should be recorded by a charge to income.

> *OBSERVATION: A provision for anticipated premium deficiencies should be provided when unearned premiums are insufficient to cover all related costs and expenses. Related costs and expenses should include expected claims and claims adjustment expenses, expected policyholder dividends, unamortized deferred acquisition costs, and any anticipated expenses that are expected to be incurred*

subsequent to the inception date of the policy. If a cost, subsequent to the inception date of the policy, is direct or can be attributed to maintaining the policy in force, it should be included in the determination of the premium deficiency.

If an insurance company includes anticipated investment income in the determination of a premium deficiency, FASB-60 requires that the effects, and the amount of the effects on the financial statements, be disclosed.

Long-Duration Contracts

As mentioned previously, FASB-60 requires that the liability for future policy benefits for long-duration contracts be accrued at the time that the premium revenue is recognized. The liability is based on actuarial assumptions at the time the insurance contracts are consummated, and is presented in the balance sheet at present value. In subsequent periods, changes in the original actuarial assumptions which result in changes in future policy benefits or related costs and expenses are recognized in net income of the period of change.

The liability for future policy benefits consists of the present value of future policy benefits and related expenses, less the present value of related future net premiums. Net premium is that portion of the gross premium which is necessary to cover future payment of all policy benefits and related costs and expenses. Gross premium is the amount the policyholder pays, and is equal to the net premium plus the profit made by the insurance company.

At any given time, the present value of future gross premiums for a particular group of insurance contracts may be insufficient to cover (1) the present value of future policy benefits and related expenses and (2) the remaining unamortized acquisition costs. In this event, a gross premium deficiency occurs. The gross premium deficiency is usually the result of significant changes in the original actuarial assumptions. The procedure to determine a gross premium deficiency is as follows:

1. Compute the present value of future policy benefits and related settlement and maintenance expenses using revised assumptions and updated experience.
2. Compute the present value of future gross premiums using revised assumptions and updated experience.
3. Subtract 1 from 2 to arrive at the new liability for future policy benefits based on revised assumptions and updated experience.

4. Compare the new liability for future policy benefits determined in 3 with the actual recorded liability for future policy benefits, reduced by the actual remaining unamortized acquisition costs. A deficiency exists if the newly computed liability exceeds the actual liability, reduced by the actual remaining unamortized acquisition costs.

A deficiency in the liability for future policy benefits must be recognized in net income by either increasing the liability for future policy benefits, or by decreasing unamortized acquisition costs. The revised assumptions and updated experience shall be used subsequently to determine changes in the liability for future policy benefits. Under no circumstances should a deficiency be reported if its effect is to create income in future periods.

A deficiency in the liability for future policy benefits is usually determined by groups or blocks of similar insurance policies. However, if a group or block of insurance contracts does not indicate a deficiency, but the aggregate liability for an entire line of insurance business does indicate a deficiency, the deficiency should be recognized.

REINSURANCE

When one insurance company reinsures part or all of an outstanding policy, with one or more other insurance companies, it is called *reinsurance*. If a loss is incurred on a policy that has been reinsured, the reinsurers will have to pay their proportionate share of the settlement. Thus, amounts recoverable from reinsurers should be included in the determination of (1) the liability for unpaid claims in the process of settlement, (2) the liability for unpaid claims incurred but not reported, and (3) the liability for claim adjustment expenses.

FASB-60 requires that amounts recoverable from reinsurers be reported as follows:

1. Amounts recoverable for claims and claim adjustment expenses that have already been paid should be accounted for as a receivable (asset) from the reinsurers.
2. Amounts recoverable for claims and claim adjustment expenses that have not been paid should be deducted from the liability for unpaid claims and claim adjustment expenses.
3. Collectible premiums that have been ceded to a reinsurer are not considered receivables, and they should be netted against their related unearned premiums.

4. Receivables and payables to the same reinsurer should be offset against each other.
5. Premiums ceded to a reinsurer should be deducted from the related earned premiums in the income statement.
6. Recovery of claims from reinsurers should be deducted from the related incurred claims in the income statement.

A liability for estimated future servicing costs shall be accrued if a ceding insurance company agrees to service, without reasonable compensation, insurance contracts that have been ceded to a reinsurer. If a reinsurance contract does not shift the risk of loss to the reinsurer, the ceding insurance company shall account for the premiums paid by the insured, less the premium paid to the reinsurer, as a deposit.

POLICYHOLDER DIVIDENDS

Policyholder dividends must be accrued and reported in the financial statements. If the amount is not known, the use of reasonable estimates is required by FASB-60.

The amount of current income which is allocated to participating insurance contracts must be excluded from stockholders' equity by a charge to current operations and a credit to a liability account. The liability account is reduced when dividends are subsequently declared or paid. Dividends declared or paid to participating insurance contracts in excess of the liability should also be charged to current operations.

Life insurance companies do not usually pay or declare dividends on participating insurance policies during the first two years, because of the high initial policy acquisition costs. In determining the amount of dividends on participating insurance policies, consideration must be given to any restrictions on such amounts which may be imposed by the terms of the insurance contract, governing law, or company policy. Where participating policy dividends are specified in the policy or projected at the time the policy is issued, they should be accrued ratably over the periods in which premiums are collected.

CONTINGENT COMMISSIONS

Insurance companies usually agree to pay additional commissions to their brokers and agents if the business they generate results in a favorable loss experience. Therefore, these additional commissions are contingent on whether or not a favorable loss experience occurs.

FASB-60 requires that contingent commissions (receivable or payable) be appropriately accrued and appear in the income statement of the periods in which the related profits are recognized.

INVESTMENTS

FASB-60 contains specific guidance in the valuation of investments of insurance companies.

Bonds If the insurance company has the ability and intent to keep bonds to maturity, the bonds should be carried at amortized cost, providing that there has been no permanent decline in the market value of the bonds below amortized cost. Bonds held for speculation should be carried at market value, and unrealized gains or losses should be periodically recognized.

Common and nonredeemable preferred stock Common and nonredeemable preferred stock should be carried at market value. If the insurance company has the ability and intent to keep redeemable preferred stock until redemption, the preferred stock should be carried at amortized cost, providing that there has been no permanent decline in the market value of the preferred stock below amortized cost.

Mortgages Mortgages should be carried at the balance of the unpaid principal. Mortgages purchased at a discount or premium should be carried at amortized cost. An allowance for estimated uncollectible mortgage loans should be used, if necessary, and changes in the allowance account should be included in realized gains and losses.

Real estate investments Real estate investments should be carried at depreciated cost. Amortization, depreciation, and other related costs or credits should be included in the determination of investment income.

Commitment fees Commitment fees for mortgage loans which exceed those fees that are currently being charged in the industry should be accounted for as an adjustment of the effective rate of the permanent financing. Thus, commitment fees in excess of those charged currently are capitalized and amortized to income over the term of the related mortgage loans. Normal commitment fees, less direct costs and related expenses, should be recognized as income over the commitment period. Unamortized commitment fees should be included in income in the period in which the company's obligation no longer exists.

Realized gains and losses All realized gains and losses on all assets held for investment should appear, net of related taxes, in the income statement below operating income. Realized gains and losses applicable to property used in business should be included as part of operating income.

Unrealized investment gains and losses should not be included in the determination of net income, but are recognized, net of related taxes, as an addition to, or reduction of, stockholders' equity.

Permanent declines in security investments, below cost or amortized cost, should be recognized as realized losses. These security investments should be written down to their net realizable values, which subsequently become their new cost basis. Recovery in market value above the new cost basis shall not be recognized until sale, maturity, or other disposition of the security.

REAL ESTATE USED IN BUSINESS AND SEPARATE ACCOUNTS

Real estate should be classified in accordance with its predominant use as either property used in business or as an investment. Real estate operating expenses, including depreciation, should be classified in a manner consistent with the related asset, as either investment expenses or operating expenses. Real estate that is used in business by the insurance company should not be accounted for as investment income with a corresponding charge to operations for rental expense. In other words, an insurance company cannot include rental income in its financial statements for property it uses in the regular course of business.

> **OBSERVATION:** *Real estate is always classified as an investment, for regulatory accounting purposes, regardless of its use. Rental expense is charged to operations, and rental income is included in investment income for real estate used by the insurance company in its own business.*

As a fiduciary, an insurance company may maintain assets and liabilities in separate accounts for the purposes of funding fixed-benefit plans. In this capacity, the insurance company usually receives a fee and does not assume any investment risk. Except for long-term separate accounts in which the insurance company has guaranteed a specific investment return, investments in separate accounts shall be valued at market. Long-term separate accounts with guaranteed returns shall be valued in the same manner as any other investment of the insurance company. Assets and liabilities of separate accounts shall be reported in the financial statements in summary totals.

DEFERRED INCOME TAXES

The Life Insurance Company Act of 1959 covers the taxation of life insurance companies for federal tax purposes. For the purposes of GAAP, life insurance companies must comply with existing promulgated pronouncements, and thus must determine deferred income taxes when appropriate.

If circumstances indicate that the current tax effects of a timing difference will not reverse in subsequent periods, an insurance company does not have to accrue deferred income taxes. However, deferred taxes shall be accrued if the reversal of the timing difference cannot be reasonably determined. Deferred income taxes shall be accrued in accordance with existing GAAP (APB-11), and the *with-and-without* method should be used to determine the tax effects of timing differences.

Once a determination is made as to whether deferred income taxes should or should not be provided on the tax effects of timing differences, circumstances may change. In this event, if deferred taxes have not previously been provided, they should be accrued and reported as an income tax expense in the period of correction. Deferred taxes accrued under these circumstances should not be reported as an extraordinary item. Regardless of whether the gross change or net change method is used, previously accrued deferred income taxes should be included in income as the related timing differences reverse, if the previously determined tax effects are expected to be different from those originally anticipated.

Policyholders' surplus of stock life insurance companies that create a difference between taxable income and pretax financial accounting income are usually considered permanent differences, because the company controls the events that create the tax consequence. However, if circumstances dictate that income taxes will be paid because of a reduction in policyholders' surplus, an income tax expense should be accrued on such reductions in the period in which they occur. In effect, these reductions do create a timing difference when they occur, and they should not be accounted for as an extraordinary item.

> **OBSERVATION:** The Tax Reform Act of 1984 requires life insurance enterprises with assets of $100 million or more to recompute their policy reserves as of the beginning of the first taxable year beginning after December 31, 1983. Insurance companies with assets of less than $100 million may make a special election not to have their reserves recomputed. The computation of the new policy reserves, as of the beginning of the first taxable year beginning after December 31, 1983, shall be based on the recomputation of each existing insurance contract, as if the provisions of the Act had applied to the contract when it was issued.
>
> If an insurance enterprise changes its method of accounting, solely for the purpose of complying with the Act, the change will not be treated as a change in the method of accounting under the provisions of the Internal Revenue Code. Furthermore, any change in the method of accounting for policy reserves will not be treated as such, if the change is made solely to comply with the provisions of the Act. A change in the method of accounting and/or a change in the method of computing policy reserves, between an insurance company's first taxable year beginning after December 31, 1983, and the preceding year, shall not give rise to any taxable income or loss, if the change is made solely to comply with the provisions of the Act. This provision of the Act is referred to as the "fresh start adjustment," because it is likely that most insurance companies will permanently escape taxation on the decrease in the amount of their policy reserves.
>
> If the recomputation required by the Act results in a decrease in the amount of policy reserves, deferred income taxes that have been recorded on the books by an insurance enterprise will have to be adjusted. FASB Technical Bulletin 84-3 provides that the adjustment to deferred taxes should be recognized as a reduction of income tax expense, in one interim period of the current year. The effect of the adjustment on income tax expense should be disclosed and may be shown as a separate component of income tax expense.
>
> FASB Technical Bulletin 84-3 is effective for financial statements and interim financial information issued after September 30, 1984, for fiscal years ending after July 18, 1984 (the enactment date of the Tax Reform Act of 1984). Earlier application is permitted, but not required. Interim financial information issued after September 30, 1984, for fiscal years ending after July 18, 1984, should be retroactively restated, if necessary.

Insurance Enterprises

DISCLOSURE

FASB-60 requires specific disclosures in the financial statements of insurance companies. These disclosures are listed below.

1. The basis for estimating:
    a. The liability for unpaid claims
    b. The liability for claim adjustment expenses
2. The methods and assumptions used in calculating the liability for future policy benefits. In addition, FASB-60 encourages, but does not require, the disclosure of the average rate of assumed investment yields that are in effect for the current period.
3. Capitalized acquisition costs:
    a. The nature of such costs
    b. The method of amortizing such costs
    c. The amount of amortization of such costs for the current period
4. If the liabilities for unpaid claims and claim adjustment expenses for short-duration contracts are reported at their present values in the financial statements:
    a. The carrying amount of those liabilities
    b. The range of interest rates used to discount those liabilities
5. If estimated investment income is used in calculating a premium deficiency for short-duration contracts:
    a. If yes, a statement disclosing that fact
    b. If no, no disclosure necessary
6. Reinsurance transactions of an insurance company:
    a. The nature and significance of such transactions
    b. Estimated amounts recoverable from reinsurers that are related to unpaid claims and claim adjustment expenses
7. Participating insurance of an insurance company:
    a. The relative percentage of participating insurance
    b. The method of accounting for participating insurance policyholder dividends
    c. The amount of such dividends
    d. The amount of any additional income allocated to participating insurance policyholders
8. Stockholders' equity, statutory capital, and surplus:
    a. The amount of statutory capital and surplus

b. The amount of statutory capital and surplus required for regulatory purposes, if significant to the enterprise's total statutory capital and surplus
c. The nature of statutory restrictions on dividends and the amount of retained earnings not available for dividends to stockholders
9. Policyholders' surplus of life insurance companies (when an insurance company is consolidated or accounted for by the equity method, these disclosures also apply to the parent company):
    a. The treatment of the policyholders' surplus under the provisions of the Internal Revenue Code.
    b. The fact that income taxes may become payable if the company takes specific action, which should be appropriately disclosed
    c. The total amount of policyholders' surplus for which income taxes have not been provided
10. If no current or deferred federal income taxes have been provided by a life insurance company for any retained earnings in excess of policyholders' surplus:
    a. The amount of such retained earnings
    b. The reasons for not accruing deferred federal income taxes

OBSERVATION: *SEC reporting companies should refer to Accounting Series Release 301 (October 21, 1981) for a complete list of disclosures required by the SEC for insurance companies.*

AMENDMENTS TO EXISTING GAAP

As a result of the promulgation of FASB-60, the following amendments are made to existing GAAP:

1. All of the AICPA publications from which the specialized accounting principles and practices have been extracted and included in FASB-60 are deleted from Exhibits A and B of FASB-32 (Specialized Accounting and Reporting Principles and Practices in AICPA Statements of Position and Guides on Accounting and Auditing Matters).
2. The references to AICPA insurance industry guides in footnote 8 of APB-30 (Reporting the Results of Operations) is

changed to refer to FASB-60 (Accounting and Reporting by Insurance Enterprises).
3. The reference to AICPA insurance industry guides in paragraph 41 of FASB-5 (Accounting for Contingencies) is changed to refer to FASB-60 (Accounting and Reporting by Insurance Enterprises).
4. Paragraphs 26 through 30 of APB-23 (Accounting for Income Taxes—Special Areas) are deleted. The provisions of these paragraphs, which discuss policyholders' surplus of life insurance companies, have been included without reconsideration in FASB-60 (Accounting and Reporting by Insurance Enterprises).
5. The following footnote is added to the end of paragraph 6 of APB-11 (Accounting for Income Taxes):

For life insurance companies, also refer to paragraphs 55–59 and subparagraphs 60(h) and (i) of FASB Statement No. 60, Accounting and Reporting by Insurance Enterprises.

EFFECTIVE DATE AND TRANSITION

FASB-60 is effective for fiscal years beginning on or after December 16, 1982. As with most promulgated GAAP, earlier application of FASB-60 is encouraged.

An accounting change which results from the initial application of FASB-60 shall be made, if practical, by retroactive restatement of all comparative financial statements presented. In addition, the financial statements of the year of change shall disclose the nature of any restatement and its effect on income before extraordinary items, net income, and related per share amounts, for each year restated. The individual effects of changing to conform with FASB-60 must also be disclosed.

If it is impractical to retroactively restate all of the individual financial statements for the comparative years presented, the following procedure must be used:

1. The new accounting principles (FASB-60) are used in determining net income of the year of change (current period).
2. As many consecutive prior years' financial statements as prac-

tical (which are presented for comparative purposes) are then retroactively restated.
3. The cumulative effect of the change to FASB-60 is then computed for any remaining prior years.
4. The cumulative effect is then included in determining net income for the earliest year restated.
5. Financial statements presented for years prior to the earliest year restated (which includes the cumulative effect) shall be presented for comparative purposes as they were originally reported.

In the event that it is impractical to retroactively restate any prior year, FASB-60 requires that the cumulative effect of the change in accounting principle be included in the net income of the year of change, in accordance with APB-20 (Accounting Changes). In any year in which the cumulative effect is used, the effect of the change to FASB-60 on income before extraordinary items, net income, and related per share amounts shall be disclosed.

> **OBSERVATION:** The specialized accounting principles and practices which have been extracted from various AICPA insurance publications and which are included in FASB-60 have been in effect for several years. As a result, it is highly unlikely that many insurance companies will be subject to the transition provisions of FASB-60, because they have probably been applying the specialized accounting principles and practices since they were promulgated by the AICPA.
>
> In addition, the cumulative effect of a change in an accounting principle may be omitted under APB-20 if it is impossible to compute. In this event, the effects of the change, in the year of change, must be disclosed, along with an explanation as to why the cumulative effect was omitted.

OTHER SIGNIFICANT INFORMATION

There are significant differences in accounting principles and practices used in reporting to insurance regulatory agencies and generally accepted accounting principles. The following are some of the more important exceptions to GAAP which are used in regulatory accounting practices:

1. Increasing the "policy reserves" account by a direct debit to

unassigned surplus (retained earnings) instead of a charge to income.
2. Charging unassigned surplus with prior service costs of pension plans instead of a charge to income.
3. Netting liabilities against related assets.
4. Debiting unassigned surplus for only the par value of certain stock dividends.

Mandatory securities valuation reserve   In most states, a Mandatory Securities Valuation Reserve (MSVR) must be established in accordance with a formula. Unassigned surplus is debited and a reserve account is credited. This procedure is unacceptable under GAAP.

Under GAAP the MSVR represents an appropriation of retained earnings (surplus) which should be included in the equity section of the balance sheet.

Nonadmitted assets   It is not permitted to show certain assets on the balance sheet of an insurance company under regulatory accounting practices. Nonadmitted assets are charged to surplus and thus eliminated from the regulatory balance sheet. The following is a list of the more common nonadmitted assets.

1. Furniture and equipment
2. Automobiles
3. Prepaid and deferred expenses
4. Goodwill and other intangible assets
5. Unauthorized investments
6. Investments in excess of authorized amounts
7. Receivables from agents (debit balances)
8. Receivables from employees and officers
9. Accrued income on investments in default
10. Receivables from unauthorized reinsurers

Nonadmitted assets must be restored in presenting financial statements in conformity with GAAP. This is accomplished by debiting the various assets and crediting retained earnings (surplus). However, care must be exercised in determining the collectibility of receivables which are restored.

Stockholder's equity It may be necessary to reclassify an insurance company's equity accounts for the purposes of financial statements presented in conformity with GAAP. As mentioned previously, nonadmitted assets must be restored by a credit to retained earnings. If an insurance company has increased its policy reserves by a direct charge to surplus, the transaction will have to be redone to be in conformity with GAAP. Care must also be exercised in segregating appropriated surplus from unassigned surplus for financial statement purposes.

TITLE PLANT

Overview

FASB-61 contains the specialized accounting principles and practices for title plants that were originally published in the AICPA Statement of Position 80-1 (Accounting for Title Insurance Companies).

The provisions of FASB-61 are directed to companies that utilize title plants in their operations, such as title abstract companies, title agents, and title insurance companies.

Background

The main business activity of a title insurance company is to issue title insurance policies. Title insurance provides protection against loss or damage to a parcel of real estate that results from liens or defects in the ownership document. Thus, if a buyer obtains title insurance on real estate that is being purchased and subsequently a loss is incurred because of a lien or defect in the title to the property, the title insurance company will pay any loss or damage. Generally, every mortgage lender will require a title insurance policy on the property being purchased before they will lend any funds as a mortgage.

A title insurance policy is unique inasmuch as the premiums are usually not refundable and the term of the policy is indefinite. However, the amount of title insurance and the date of title search are stated in the policy. Thus, any loss in excess of the amount of title insurance and any loss which occurs because of a lien or defect that did not exist up to the date of the title search will not be covered by the policy.

When an application for title insurance is received by the insurance company, a title search is made. A title search consists of reviewing and scrutinizing the chain of ownership of the property being insured up to the date of the title search. Some title searches may go back several hundred years. Each change of ownership is examined to make sure it was properly made and that no unpaid liens or defects exist against the title to the property. If a lien or defect is discovered, the title insurance policy is still usually issued but the discovered lien or defect is cited in the policy and not covered. In this event, the buyer may be able to cancel the purchase

GAAP GUIDE / **66.01**

of the property or compel the seller to take care of the existing lien or defect. Most contracts for the sale of real property contain a provision to the effect that the property is being sold free of any liens and/or defects, and that the buyer has a specified period to determine whether any liens or defects do exist against the property being purchased.

The records that a title insurance company uses to search the chain of ownership of a parcel of real estate are called the *title plant*. The title plant consists of the public records of a specific geographic area (town, city, county, etc.) that have been appropriately indexed and integrated so that an individual parcel of real property may be easily located. From the title plant the insurance company can prepare an abstract on any piece of real estate in the particular geographic area. An abstract is a short summary of the ownership history of a specific parcel of real property.

A title plant is usually kept up-to-date on a daily basis. A well maintained title plant will usually increase in value over time and seldom, if ever, decrease in value. In addition, the estimated useful life of a title plant is generally indefinite. These unusual characteristics make a title plant unique.

Capitalization of Title Plant

Up until the time that a title plant is ready for its intended use, all direct costs incurred to acquire, organize, or construct the title plant shall be capitalized.

> **OBSERVATION:** *A title plant may be constructed or purchased by an enterprise. In either case, costs directly identified with the title plant are capitalized. A purchase may consist of (a) a copy of the title plant, (b) an undivided interest in the title plant, or (c) the exclusive ownership (outright purchase) of the title plant. In any event, the costs directly related to the title plant are capitalized.*

A title plant that is constructed or otherwise acquired will cover a definite period of time. For example, an enterprise may purchase a title plant of a particular geographic area, which covers the period January 1, 1940, through December 31, 1981. Subsequently, the enterprise may construct or otherwise acquire a title plant for the same geographic area which covers the period from January 1, 1900, through December 31, 1939. This type of title plant is sometimes referred to as an *antecedent title plant* or *backplant*. The same rules for capitalization of direct costs apply to this type of title plant. Thus, costs incurred to construct or otherwise acquire a backplant are capitalized if they can be directly identified to the acquisition of the backplant.

FASB-61 expressly states that capitalized costs of a title plant should not ordinarily be depreciated or otherwise charged to income. Thus, unless there is an impairment in the carrying amount of the title plant, the undepreciated capitalized costs are reported as an asset indefinitely on the balance sheet. The impairment of a title plant below its carrying amount is recognized in the income of the period in which the impairment is discovered.

The carrying amount of a title plant may become impaired if any of the following conditions exist:

1. The title plant is not properly maintained on a current basis.
2. The title plant may become partially or completely obsolete.
3. The title plant may be abandoned or severely neglected.
4. Economics, competition, or legal factors may result in a decline in the value of the title plant.

Maintenance and Operating Expenses

Costs incurred to modernize or modify a title plant may be expensed or separately deferred, but may not be added to the carrying amount of the title plant. If such costs are separately deferred, they should be amortized over their estimated useful lives in a systematic manner.

FASB-61 requires that all title plant maintenance and operational costs be expensed in the period incurred. Thus, the cost to update or maintain the title plant on a current basis and the cost of performing title searches to issue title policies are expensed as they are incurred.

Sale of Title Plant

A sale of a title plant may consist of (a) an outright sale, (b) a sale of an undivided interest, or (c) a sale of a copy, or the right to use, the title plant. FASB-61 requires that gain or loss on any sale of a title plant be reported separately in the financial statements.

Gain or loss on the sale of a title plant depends on the type of sale consummated by the seller. In the event of an outright sale of the title plant, gain or loss is the difference between the selling price and the net carrying amount of the title plant on the date of sale. In the event of the sale of an undivided interest in a title plant, gain or loss is the difference between the selling price and the pro rata portion of the title plant which is attributable to the sale of the undivided interest. However, in a sale of a copy, or the right to use the title plant, no cost is allocated to the sale unless the value of the title plant decreases as a result of the sale. Thus, in the sale of a copy or the right to use the title plant, the sales price usually represents the gain on the sale.

Effective Date

FASB-61 is effective for fiscal years beginning on or after December 16, 1982. As with most promulgated GAAP, earlier application of FASB-61 is encouraged.

An accounting change which results from the initial application of FASB-61 shall be made, if practical, by retroactive restatement of all comparative financial statements. In addition, the financial statements of the year of change shall disclose the nature of any restatement and its effect on income before extraordinary items, net income, and related per share amounts, for each year presented.

If it is impractical to retroactively restate all of the individual financial statements for the comparative years presented, the following procedure must be used:

1. The new accounting principle (FASB-61) is used in determining net income of the year of change (current period).
2. As many consecutive prior years' financial statements (which are presented for comparative purposes) are then retroactively restated.
3. The cumulative effect of the change to FASB-61 is then computed for any remaining years in accordance with APB-20 (Accounting Changes).
4. The cumulative effect is then included in determining net income for the earliest year restated.
5. Financial statements presented for years prior to the earliest year restated (which include the cumulative effect) shall be presented for comparative purposes as they were originally reported.

In the event that it is impractical to retroactively restate any prior year, FASB-61 requires that the cumulative effect of the change in accounting principle be included in the net income of the year of change, in accordance with APB-20. In any year in which the cumulative effect is used, the effect of the change to FASB-61 on income before extraordinary items, net income, and related per share amounts shall be disclosed.

> **OBSERVATION:** *The cumulative effect of a change in an accounting principle may be omitted under APB-20 if it is impossible to compute. In this event, the effects of the change, in the year of change, must be disclosed, along with an explanation as to why the cumulative effect was omitted.*

Mortgage Banking Industry

MORTGAGE BANKING INDUSTRY

Overview

FASB-65 contains the specialized accounting and reporting principles and practices that were originally published in the AICPA Statement of Position 74-12 (Accounting Practices in the Mortgage Banking Industry) and Statement of Position 76-2 (Accounting for Origination Costs and Loan and Commitment Fees in the Mortgage Banking Industry). FASB Technical Bulletin 85-2 (Accounting for Collateralized Mortgage Obligations (CMOs) is discussed at the end of this chapter.

FASB-65 establishes the promulgated GAAP for (a) an enterprise or (b) that portion of an enterprise's operations engaged primarily in originating, marketing, and servicing mortgage loans for other than its own account. Thus, a financial institution or other enterprise that has operations which consist of originating, marketing, and servicing mortgage loans for others must apply the provisions of FASB-65 to those operations.

Accounting for Mortgage Loans

One of the more difficult problems in accounting for mortgage loans receivable and mortgage-backed securities of an enterprise engaged in mortgage banking activity is their valuation for reporting purposes. The valuation of mortgage loans receivable and mortgage-backed securities depends upon whether they are held for sale or for long-term investment. However, it should be noted that most mortgage loans and mortgage-backed securities are usually held for sale in the ordinary course of the business of a mortgage banker. Valuation of mortgage loans receivable and mortgage-backed securities for reporting purposes shall be determined as of the balance sheet date.

Held for long-term investment Before a mortgage loan or a mortgage-backed security can be classified as a long-term investment, the intent and ability of an enterprise to hold the loan to maturity or for an extended period must exist. When a mortgage loan receivable or security held for sale is reclassified as a long-term investment, the transfer must be made at the lower of cost or market on the date of transfer. In the event of a permanent impairment in the value of a mortgage loan or security classified as a long-term investment, its carrying value shall be further reduced to net realizable value. The amount of reduction shall be reported in net income of the period in which the impairment is discovered. In subsequent periods, any market recovery from the net realizable value shall be realized only at the time of sale, maturity, or other disposition of the mortgage loan or security.

Any difference between the carrying value of a mortgage loan or mortgaged-backed security held as a long-term investment and its par value shall be amortized to income by the interest method over the estimated life of the loan.

> **OBSERVATION:** SOP 74-12 (*Accounting Practices in the Mortgage Banking Industry*) requires that mortgage loans and mortgage-backed securities held for long-term investment be reported at cost for financial statement purposes. FASB-65 does not specify or indicate the basis of valuation which should be used to record mortgage loans or mortgage-backed securities that are held for long-term investment. There is no apparent explanation for this omission.
>
> In addition, SOP 74-12 requires a number of conditions to exist at the time a mortgage loan or mortgage-backed security is classified as a long-term investment, so as to substantiate the intent and ability of the enterprise. The conditions spelled out in SOP 74-12 are:
>
> a. The accounting records and financial reports of the enterprise must reflect these mortgage loans and mortgage-backed securities separately as long-term investments.
>
> b. Documentary evidence should exist, such as a corporate resolution, that these mortgage loans and mortgage-backed securities will be held for an extended period of time or to maturity.
>
> c. In classified balance sheets of the enterprise, if any, the mortgage loans and mortgage-backed securities will be reflected as noncurrent assets.
>
> d. Evidence of financial strength of the enterprise should exist to substantiate that the mortgage loans and mortgage-backed securities can be held for an extended period or until maturity.
>
> Only the last of the above conditions is mentioned in FASB-65. There is no apparent explanation for the omission of the other three conditions. Since FASB-65 purports to extract the specialized accounting principles from SOP 74-12 without significant change, the unexplained omission of (a) a valuation basis for reporting long-term investments in mortgage loans and mortgage-backed securities and (b) the other three conditions which substantiate the intent and ability of the enterprise causes uncertainty as to whether these omitted provisions of SOP 74-12 are still applicable.

Held for sale All mortgage loans receivable and mortgage-backed securities held for sale shall be valued at the lower of cost or market as defined by FASB-65, according to the type of mortgage loan or mortgage-backed security. Write-downs of a mortgage loan or mortgage-backed security to the lower of cost or market shall be included in net income of the period in which the adjustment occurs. After write-down, write-ups to market values in subsequent periods shall be recorded, but total recorded market value may not exceed cost. The journal entry to record the recovery of market value is a debit to mortgage loans or mortgage-backed securities and a credit to an income account.

For the purposes of disclosure, mortgage loans and mortgage-backed securities shall be classified in at least the following two categories: (a) residential (one to four units) and (b) commercial. Lower of cost or market can be determined on the total of all mortgage loans in a particular category or for each individual mortgage loan or mortgage-backed security.

Discounts resulting from the purchase of mortgage loans that are held for sale shall not be realized as income until the loans are actually sold.

Lower of cost or market shall be determined in accordance with the type of mortgage loan receivable or mortgage-backed security, as follows:

Loans and Securities Covered by Commitments

Mortgage loans and mortgage-backed securities that are covered by commitments shall be valued as specified in the commitment, in other words, the actual prices specified in the commitments. The reason for this is that the mortgage banker is, at least, guaranteed those prices agreed on in the commitments.

Mortgage loans and mortgage-backed securities that do not conform to the required specifications in the commitments must be classified as loans and securities *not* covered by commitments.

Loans Not Covered by Commitments

Market value for loans not covered by commitments is the market value of the loans as determined by reference to the normal market in which the mortgage banker operates.

Quotations supplied by GNMA or the FNMA Free Market System or other public markets should be used when appropriate. If no established market quotations are available, market prices should be determined by the enterprise's normal market outlets.

Mortgage-Backed Securities Not Covered by Commitments

GNMA Mortgage-Backed Securities may be held by a mortgage banker for the purpose of trading on the open market. The current market value of the underlying mortgage loans which are pledged by the mortgage banker as collateral for the GNMA securities is usually the same as the current market value of the securities themselves. In other words, the market value of the mortgage loans held in trust as collateral for the GNMA securities should certainly be approximately the same as the value at which the GNMA securities are being traded.

Market value for GNMA Mortgage-Backed Securities for the purposes of lower of cost or market depends upon whether the trust agreement which covers the mortgage banker's underlying mortgage loans can be terminated on short notice and the mortgage loans sold on the open market. In this event, market value for the GNMA securities is either the current market value of the GNMA securities or the current market value of the underlying mortgage loans. The choice of which current market to use should be based on whether or not the mortgage banker intends to terminate the trust. If the mortgage banker does not intend to terminate the trust, market value for the purposes of lower of cost or market should be current market value of the GNMA securities. If the mortgage banker intends to terminate the trust, market value for the purposes of lower of cost or market should be the current market value of the underlying mortgage loans.

If the trust cannot be terminated on short notice by the mortgage banker, market value of the GNMA securities for the purposes of lower of cost or market should be based on the published GNMA securities yield.

Block purchases of mortgage loans   Block purchases of mortgage loans have been made by mortgage bankers from GNMA or other investors. As discussed later, certain costs incurred in block purchases of mortgage loans which can be associated with future servicing income are capitalized and amortized over the estimated average term of the mortgage loans. When these costs are appropriately capitalized in accordance with FASB-65, they shall be added to the valuation of the loans, after cost or the lower of cost or market is determined. However, if the costs have been inappropriately capitalized they must be included as part of cost, or the lower of cost or market, of the mortgage loans.

Repurchase agreements   Frequently, a mortgage banking enterprise will enter into formal or informal repurchase agreements (repos) with a lending institution. In a repurchase agreement the mortgage banking enterprise will give the lending institution a block of mortgage loans and/or mortgage-backed securities as collateral for a loan. On the surface, the transaction may appear as a sale of the mortgage loans and/or mortgage-backed securities to the lending institution, with an agreement, formal or otherwise, that the mortgage banking enterprise will repurchase the loans and/or securities at an agreed upon price, which usually is equal to the amount of the loan. If the mortgage banking enterprise fails to repurchase the mortgage loans and/or mortgage-backed securities in accordance with the agreement, the lending institution exercises ownership of the loans and/or securities. The mortgage banking enterprise pays an agreed upon rate of interest for the use of the funds.

Formal and informal repurchase agreements shall be accounted for by the mortgage banking enterprise as a financing, and no sale shall be recorded.

Historically, short-term interest rates have always been less than long-term interest rates. Thus, when a mortgage banker paid interest on short-term warehouse loans, the interest received on the pledged mortgage loans always exceeded the amount paid to carry them on a short-term basis. The difference between the short-term and long-term interest rates creates a "positive spread" for the mortgage banker. However, sometimes interest rates reverse, and short-term rates exceed long-term rates. This results in a "negative spread" in interest rates for the mortgage banker. Since the cost of warehousing mortgage loans by a mortgage banker is primarily a financing activity, negative spreads in interest rates should be charged to current operations as they are incurred.

Mortgage servicing fees   All types of mortgage loans must be serviced. The process of collecting, sending notices, maintaining mortgage records, and other related chores are referred to as "servicing." The owner of a loan or portfolio of loans may perform the "servicing function," or it may engage someone else to perform such services. An entity which performs the servicing for mortgage loans usually charges a fee based on a percentage of the unpaid principal balance of the loans. Servicing revenue can be quite substantial.

As a general rule, most mortgage bankers service their own outstanding loans, and they may also service a large number of mortgage loans for others.

A problem may arise when a mortgage banker sells a loan or a portfolio of loans and agrees to continue servicing the loans at a fee which is significantly different from prevailing servicing rates.

Ordinarily, when a loan or portfolio of loans is sold and the buyer assumes the servicing function, no problem arises. Gain or loss on the sale of loans is the difference between the sales price and the net carrying amount of the loans. However, when loans are sold and the seller continues the servicing function for the buyer, a problem arises if the servicing fee charged is significantly different from prevailing service rates and the result is expected to materially affect current or future operating results. In this event, gain or loss on the sale of the mortgage loans must be increased or decreased to provide a normal profit on future servicing income, based on estimated prevailing servicing fee rates. The amount of adjustment shall be calculated on the date of sale and is equal to the difference between total servicing fee income based on the current prevailing servicing fee rate and total servicing fee income based on the contractually agreed upon servicing fee rate. In the event that the contractually agreed upon servicing fee rate is significantly lower than the current prevailing rate, the journal entry to record the adjustment is a debit to the gain or loss on the sale of mortgage loans and a credit to deferred servicing fee revenue. The deferred servicing fee revenue is amortized to income over the life of the related loans, so that each future period will include servicing fee revenue equal to the prevailing servicing fee rate at the date of sale of the mortgage loans.

Occasionally, estimated servicing costs may be expected to exceed normal servicing income over the estimated life of the related mortgage loans. In this event, the resulting loss shall be accrued on the date of sale or the date on which the loss is discovered.

It is important to note that the adjustment of future servicing fees is only made when (a) the agreed upon servicing fee rate at the date of sale is materially different than the current prevailing servicing fee rate, and (b) the agreed upon servicing fee rate is expected to significantly affect current or future operating results.

Transactions with affiliates In separate financial statements of mortgage banking enterprises, special treatment is afforded sales of mortgage loans and/or mortgage-backed securities which are made to affiliated enterprises. The selling affiliate must first adjust the carrying amount of the mortgage loans and/or mortgage-backed securities to the lower of cost or market before computing gain or loss on the sale. Any adjustment is charged or credited to income by the selling affiliate. Thus, the gain or loss on the sale of mortgage loans and/or mortgage-backed securities to an affiliated enterprise is the difference between the sales price and the lower of cost or market of the loans and/or securities.

Gain or loss on the sale of mortgage loans and/or mortgage-backed securities is determined as of the measurement date. The measurement date is the first date that management decides that the sale shall take place. The measurement date must be supported by formal approval of the sale by the purchasing affiliate and the issuance of a binding commitment. The binding commitment must be approved and accepted by the selling mortgage banker.

A mortgage banker may act in the capacity of an agent for an affiliated company. In the capacity of an agent the mortgage banker will originate certain specified types of loans for the affiliated company. Under these circumstances the mortgage banker may charge an origination fee for services rendered in acquiring the loans. However, all risks of ownership must be assumed by the affiliated company in order to constitute an agency relationship. The affiliated company should record the loans acquired at the mortgage banker's acquisition cost.

Agreements, or arrangements which do not bind the affiliated company to purchase the loans originated by the affiliated mortgage banker, such as "right of first refusal" contracts, do not establish an agency relationship.

> **OBSERVATION:** *This section on "transactions with affiliates" is only applicable to the separate financial statements of mortgage banking enterprises. Also, in separate financial statements of mortgage banking enterprises, material "transactions with affiliates" are subject to the disclosure provisions of FASB-57 (Related Party Disclosures).*

> **OBSERVATION:** *SOP 74-12 states that in the sale of mortgages from an affiliated mortgage banker to another affiliated enterprise, there is a presumption that the purchasing affiliate is acquiring the mortgage loans for long-term purposes. Thus, if a repurchase or similar agreement exists between the affiliated mortgage banker and the affiliated purchaser, the presumption that the mortgage loans are being acquired for long-term investment purposes cannot be supported. In this event, the transaction between the two affiliates may have to be accounted for as an intercompany loan, collateralized by the mortgage loans. FASB-65 does not cover this point.*

In-house origination costs   In-house origination costs incurred in obtaining mortgage loans for direct borrowers usually consist of direct personnel costs and other direct costs such as appraisals and site inspection fees. However, many mortgage banking enterprises include general and administrative expenses and costs of short-term financing (warehousing mortgage loans in process) in the category of origination costs.

Identifying origination costs to specific loans is almost impossible, and the cost to do so is usually prohibitive.

For the purposes of GAAP, FASB-65 requires that all costs incurred in originating in-house mortgage loans of a mortgage banker must be charged to current operations. Origination costs should include general and administrative expenses and short-term financing costs which are incurred during the origination of in-house mortgage loans. The deferral of any origination costs for in-house mortgage loans is not acceptable under GAAP.

Issuance costs for GNMA securities A mortgage banking enterprise may use either the concurrent dates method (15 days) or the internal reserve method (45 days) to pay the holder(s) of GNMA Mortgage-Backed Securities. Under the internal reserve method the mortgage banking enterprise is required to deposit one month's interest on the mortgage loans with a trustee. These is no such requirement under the concurrent dates method.

Under the provisions of FASB-65 the one month's interest required by the internal reserve method shall be capitalized and amortized by a mortgage banking enterprise. Amortization of any amount deferred must be over the period of, and in proportion to, the estimated net servicing income expected to be earned from the related underlying mortgage loans.

The total amount deferred by a mortgage banking enterprise for issuance costs or under any other provision of FASB-65 may not exceed the present value of the future net servicing income. Future net servicing income is the difference between estimated future servicing revenue and the estimated future related servicing costs.

Accounting for Servicing Rights

Mortgage banking enterprises sometimes acquire blocks of mortgages in bulk purchases from GNMA, FNMA, and others. Part of the purchase price may be attributable to the right to receive future servicing income. In addition, in a business combination, part of the purchase price may be properly allocable to the right to receive future servicing income. In either event, the amount directly attributable to the right to receive future servicing income shall be deferred with certain limitations. The first limitation is that the amount deferred for the right to receive future servicing income shall not be more than the difference between the market value (excluding servicing rights) of the mortgage loans at the date of purchase and the total purchase price paid for the loans, plus transfer fees, if any. Market value of the mortgage loans at the date of purchase must be determined in accordance with the provisions of FASB-65 (lower of cost or market), which have been discussed earlier. In addition, the following conditions must be met:

1. Prior to the date of purchase, the mortgage banker must have obtained commitments from investors to purchase the mortgage loans or related mortgage-backed securities, or obtains such a commitment no later than 30 days after the date of the purchase. The commitments must provide for the mortgage banker to continue servicing the mortgage loans.
2. If the sales price to the permanent investors exceeds the market value of the mortgage loans at the date of purchase, the difference must be applied to reduce any amount deferred for the right to receive future servicing income.
3. Other than those costs identified above, no other costs relating to the purchase of mortgage loans can be deferred.

> **OBSERVATION:** *If the above conditions are not met, the cost of the right to receive future servicing income is usually included as part of the cost of the mortgage loans for the purposes of determining lower of cost or market.*

The second limitation is that under no circumstances shall the amount allocated to the right to receive future servicing income, exceed the present value of the estimated future *net* servicing income. A long-term interest rate is considered appropriate in calculating the present value of the estimated future *net* servicing income. The future *net* servicing income is the difference between the estimated future servicing revenue and the estimated future servicing costs. Probable late charges and other ancillary revenue shall be included in the estimated future servicing revenue, and direct costs and appropriate allocations of other costs related to the servicing function shall be included in the estimated future servicing costs. Servicing costs may be determined on an incremental cost basis.

The amortization of the right to receive future servicing income shall be made over the period of, and in proportion to, the estimated future *net* servicing income.

Origination, Placement, and Commitment Fees

Origination, placement, and commitment fees represent a primary source of revenue to a mortgage banking enterprise. In addition, a mortgage banker may pay a fee to a permanent investor for a commitment by a permanent investor to purchase certain specified mortgage loans from the mortgage banker during a specific term.

All fees received by a mortgage banking enterprise for services rendered, such as site inspection or appraisals, shall be recognized as revenue in the period in which the services are rendered.

Loan Held for Sale

A loan origination fee is usually charged to a prospective borrower to reimburse the mortgage banker for the costs involved in processing a loan application. Loan origination costs (underwriting costs) include direct loan personnel salaries, appraisals, site inspections, loan processing costs, and other direct related costs. A portion of a loan origination fee, equal to the underwriting costs of the loan, shall be recognized as revenue when the loan is made by the mortgage banking enterprise. Loan origination fees in excess of the underwriting costs of the loan shall be recognized as revenue when the mortgage loan is sold to a permanent investor.

The task of attributing direct underwriting costs to a specific loan is very difficult. If underwriting costs cannot be identified to specific loans, a mortgage banking enterprise shall estimate underwriting costs as an amount that does not exceed the current allowable VA or FHA rates for origination fees.

A loan commitment is usually a written representation from the mortgage banker to a borrower to lend funds for a specific purpose and term. A commitment term may be for as little as one week or possibly as much as one year or longer. A "floating rate commitment" is one in which the interest rate to be charged on the loan is determined by the prevailing rate of interest at the time the loan is drawn upon. A "fixed rate commitment" is one in which the interest rate is specified in the commitment.

The recognition of revenue from loan commitment fees varies with the type and substance of the commitment. Obviously, income is recognized on all commitments if the loan is not made and the term of the commitment expires. In this event, the mortgage banker has no obligation to perform, and the loan commitment fee is earned.

All commitment fees received or paid by a mortgage banker for the purpose of funding a residential or commercial loan which is held for sale by the mortgage banker shall be deferred and recognized as revenue on completion of the sale of the mortgage loan to permanent investors. In the case of commitment fees received or paid for blocks of mortgage loans, the mortgage banker shall recognize as revenue only that portion of the fee attributable to those individual mortgage loans which have been completed.

Loans Not Held for Sale

The recognition of commitment fees is different for mortgage loans that are not held for sale by a mortgage banking enterprise. These commitment fees usually involve land acquisition, development, and construction and include both a commitment period and a loan period. All commitment fees relating to mortgage loans that are not held for sale are recognized as revenue over the estimated period of both the commitment and the mortgage loan. The estimated period of both the commitment and the mortgage loan presumably depends upon how long the mortgage banking enterprise intends to retain the loan. During the commitment period, the straight-line method is used to recognize revenue from the commitment fee. During the loan period, the interest method is used to recognize revenue from the balance of the commitment fee. However, the straight-line method may also be used during the loan period if circumstances make it impractical to apply the interest method. If the original commitment period is materially revised, any additional fees received and any balance of the original commitment fee at the date of revision shall be recognized as revenue over the revised period.

Standby and gap loan commitment fees are recognized as revenue over the combined commitment and loan period. During the commitment period, the straight-line method is used to recognize revenue from the commitment fee. During the loan period, the interest method is used to recognize revenue from the remaining balance of the commitment fee. However, the straight-line method may also be used during the loan period if circumstances make it impractical to apply the interest method. If additional fees are received by the mortgage banking enterprise when the loan is funded, they are recognized as revenue over the loan period.

Financial Statement Disclosure

Balance sheet presentations of mortgage banking enterprises for reporting purposes may be classified or unclassified. In other words, segregation between current and noncurrent items is optional. However, mortgage loans receivable and mortgage-backed securities must be separately disclosed as to (a) those held for sale and

(b) those held for long-term investment. In addition, disclosure must be made of the method used to determine the lower of cost or market value of mortgage loans receivable and mortgage-backed securities.

In connection with the capitalization of any "servicing rights" acquired by purchase during the period, the following disclosures must be made:

1. The amount capitalized.
2. The method of amortization used.
3. The amount of amortization.

> **OBSERVATION:** Under FASB-65, the above disclosures pertain only to "servicing rights" acquired by bulk purchases made during the current period. Since "servicing rights" are intangible assets, they are subject to the provisions of APB-17 (Intangible Assets). Thus, "servicing rights" acquired during the current period in a business combination and all "servicing rights" acquired in prior periods must be disclosed, if material, in accordance with APB-17. APB-17 generally requires that a description of intangible assets, method of amortization, and estimated useful lives be appropriately disclosed in the financial statements or in footnotes. In the event that a large part or all of the amortized cost of an intangible asset is included as an extraordinary charge in the determination of current net income, APB-17 requires that the reasons for the extraordinary deduction be fully disclosed.

The provisions of FASB-65 relating to (a) lower of cost or market (paragraph 4) and (b) disclosures (paragraphs 28, 29, and 30) are effective for fiscal years beginning on or after December 16, 1982, and earlier application is encouraged. All other provisions of FASB-65 shall be applied prospectively to transactions entered into on or after January 1, 1983, and earlier application is also encouraged.

ACCOUNTING FOR COLLATERALIZED MORTGAGE OBLIGATIONS (CMOs)

Overview

FASB Technical Bulletin 85-2 (FASB:TB 85-2), issued on March 18, 1985, provides guidance on the issuer's accounting for certain types of bonds that are collateralized by pools of real estate mortgages, and are commonly referred to as collateralized mortgage obligations (CMOs).

Background

A security whose payment is guaranteed by a specific pool of real estate mortgages is referred to as a mortgage-backed security. Generally, a mortgage-backed security is issued either as a pass-through certificate or a fixed-rate bond, which is commonly referred to as a *collateralized mortgage obligation*.

In addition to its payment being guaranteed by a specific pool of mortgages, the payment of a mortgage-backed security may also be guaranteed by the Government National Mortgage Association (GNMA), an agency of the United States Government. GNMA guarantees, with the full faith and credit of the United States Government, the timely payment of principal and interest to the registered holders of the securities.

A mortgage lender must apply to GNMA for approval to become an issuer of GNMA mortgage-backed securities and for a commitment for GNMA to guarantee a particular mortgage-backed security. An approved GNMA mortgage lender originates or acquires government insured or guaranteed mortgages (VA and FHA) and assembles them into a specific pool or loan package of mortgages. The mortgages within a specific pool must be of the same type, have similar maturities, be less than 12 months old and, in the case of GNMA I pools, all have the same interest rate. Mortgages in a GNMA II pool may have interest rates that vary within a one-percent range. The minimum pool size is typically one million dollars.

GNMA reviews the documents submitted by the issuer and authorizes its transfer agent to prepare and deliver securities to investors. The issuer is fully responsible for the marketing and administration of the securities. In the GNMA I program the issuer makes the monthly payment of principal and interest directly to the investors. In the GNMA II program, the issuer remits the principal and interest payments to GNMA's central paying agent, which in turn pays the holders of the securities. The issuer in both programs carries out mortgage servicing and prepares periodic reports to GNMA.

GNMA securities are modified pass-through securities. This means that holders of the securities receive monthly pass-through payments of interest, at the rate shown on the securities, plus principal as scheduled on the pooled mortgages, whether or not such payments are made by the mortgagors. Holders of securities also receive pass-throughs of any early (unscheduled) recoveries of principal and, ultimately, the full repayment, at par, of all principal outstanding on the securities. All of these payments are guaranteed to the issuer by GNMA.

The Federal National Mortgage Association (Fannie Mae) and the Federal Home Loan Mortgage Corporation (Freddie Mac) are quasi-government agencies which issue securities backed by "conventional" mortgages that are not government insured or guaranteed. Fannie Mae and Freddie Mac securities are not backed by the full faith and credit of the United States government, but usually carry an AAA bond rating.

The irregular flow of income from a pass-through certificate does not appeal to all investors. Some Wall Street brokerage firms have responded with the *collateralized mortgage obligation* (CMO), which provides a more predictable cash flow. A CMO consists of a series of bonds that mature in approximately five, ten, twenty, and thirty years and that are collateralized by a specific pool of real estate mortgages. Maturity dates are approximate because they depend on how promptly the mortgagors make their mortgage payments and the number of mortgages that are paid off before their maturity dates. Each series of bonds is periodically paid a fixed rate of interest, usually every one, three, or six months. As they are collected, all principal payments received from the mortgagors are deposited in an escrow account. The funds in the escrow account are used to retire the principal amount of the bonds in the order of their maturity. Thus, the principal amounts of the five-year bonds are paid off first, then the ten-year bonds, and so forth.

As a conduit for marketing the CMOs, one or more sponsors form a special purpose corporation, which is usually minimally capitalized. The special purpose corporation originates or acquires the mortgages, which are then pledged to an independent trustee, under the terms of the bond indenture. The obligations of the special purpose corporation are enumerated in the bond indenture.

If an enterprise has issued mortgage-backed securities and the amount is material, disclosure of the amount, type, interest rate, and all other pertinent facts should be made in the financial statements or footnotes thereto (FASB-65).

Accounting for CMOs

Under FASB Technical Bulletin 85-2, collateralized mortgage obligations (CMOs) are presumed to be borrowing transactions and should be recorded as liabilities in the financial statements of the issuer. However, a CMO shall not be accounted for as a borrowing transaction if (a) all but a nominal portion of the future economic benefits inherent in the associated collateral have been irrevocably passed to the investor and (b) no affiliate of the issuer can be required to make any future payments with respect to the obligation.

If each of the following conditions exists at the issuance date of the CMOs, they would generally indicate that the borrowing presumption has been overcome, and the obligation and its related collateral should be eliminated from the financial statements of the issuer:

1. The future economic benefits in the collateral securing the obligation are irrevocably surrendered by the issuer and/or its affiliates.
    a. The right or obligation to substitute or reacquire the collateral is irrevocably surrendered by the issuer and/or its affiliates. (Under FASB:TB 85-2, the CMO may contain a "call" provision, provided that the amount of reacquired collateral is expected to be minor.)
    b. The expected residual interest, if any, in the collateral is nominal. (This condition would not be met if an affiliate of the issuer retained a partial ownership interest in the CMO or its related collateral.
        The expected residual interest in the collateral is equal to the present value of all amounts expected to revert to the issuer or its affiliates, including reinvestment earnings and servicing fees in excess of normal servicing fees.)
2. No affiliate of the issuer can be required to make any future payments with respect to the obligation. (Under FASB:TB 85-2, an affiliate of the issuer may retain the servicing rights to the pooled mortgages.)
    a. The investor agrees to look solely to the segregated assets of the issuer, insurers, guarantors, or other third parties for repayment of the obligation, and the issuer's sponsor or affiliates cannot be secondarily liable for the payment of the obligation.
    b. The issuer and its affiliates cannot be required to redeem the obligation prior to its maturity date.

If the above conditions are met, the borrowings for the CMOs and the related collateral should be eliminated from the issuer's financial statements, and all other costs associated with the offering transaction should be charged to expense. The expected residual interest in the collateral, if any, should not be recorded until it accrues to the benefit of the issuer or its affiliates.

Servicing rights If the servicing rights are retained by an affiliate of the issuer, and the servicing fee rate is less than the prevailing market servicing fee rates, the proceeds from an offering of collateralized mortgage obligations must be adjusted to provide a normal profit on future servicing income. The amount of adjustment shall be calculated on the issuance date of the CMOs, and is equal to the difference between the total servicing fee income based on the current prevailing service fee rate and the total servicing fee income based upon the contractually agreed upon servicing fee rate. In the event that the contractually agreed upon servicing fee rate is significantly lower than the current prevailing rate, the journal entry to record the adjustment is a debit to the gain or loss on the CMO offering and a credit to deferred servicing fee revenue. The deferred servicing fee revenue is amortized to income over the life of the related mortgages, so that each future period will include servicing fee income equal to the prevailing market servicing fee rate on the issuance date of the CMOs.

Consolidated statements Usually the issuer of the CMO is a minimally capitalized special-purpose corporation that has been established by one or more sponsors. FASB:TB 85-2 concludes that since the majority-owned special-purpose corporation simply acts as a conduit for the sponsor, the financial statements of the special-purpose corporation should be consolidated with those of the sponsor in order to present more meaningful information.

Offsetting As a general rule, the offsetting of assets and liabilities in the balance sheet is unacceptable unless a right of offset exists.

Collateralized mortgage obligations that do not meet the conditions of FASB:TB 85-2 shall be recorded as liabilities in the financial statements of the issuer. In respect to those CMOs, the pledging of collateral against the related liability is not equivalent to prepayment as described in paragraph 7 of APB-10. Thus, CMOs do not qualify as an exception to APB-10, and offsetting the associated collateral against the liability in the issuer's financial statements is not appropriate.

Effective date and transition The provisions of FASB:TB 85-2 are effective for collateralized mortgage obligations issued after March 31, 1985. Earlier application is encouraged, but not required, for interim or annual financial statements that have not been previously issued. The provisions of FASB:TB 85-2 may be retroactively applied to financial statements that have been previously issued.

Oil and Gas Producing Companies

OIL AND GAS PRODUCING COMPANIES

Background

The promulgated GAAP on Accounting and Reporting by Oil and Gas Producing Companies is FASB-19, which superseded FASB-9, and was to be effective for fiscal years beginning after December 15, 1978. Because the SEC rejected the successful efforts accounting method embodied in FASB-19 for a current value method, FASB-19 was subsequently amended in February 1979 by FASB-25 (see Effects of FASB-25, below). Nonpromulgated GAAP, in the form of industry practices, exists for alternative methods (full-costing, current-value, and discovery-value accounting methods).

FASB-69 establishes comprehensive financial statement disclosures for oil and gas producing companies. Portions of the disclosure requirements in FASB-69 appeared in FASB-19 (Financial Accounting and Reporting by Oil and Gas Producing Companies), as amended by FASB-25 (Suspension of Certain Accounting Requirements for Oil and Gas Producing Companies). FASB-69 supersedes the disclosure requirements of both FASB-19 and FASB-25, and also incorporates some of the disclosure requirements for oil and gas producing activities which are required by the SEC.

As a result of the issuance of FASB-69, an enterprise is not required to present the supplementary current cost information mandated by FASB-33, unless it has significant holdings of inventory and property, plant and equipment apart from oil and gas producing activities or certain other specialized assets. In this respect, FASB-69 also permits an enterprise to substitute historical cost/constant dollar information for the current cost supplementary information which is required by FASB-33.

The promulgated GAAP (FASB-19) covers only producing activities and specifically excludes the transporting, refining, and marketing of oil and/or gas. In addition, the promulgated GAAP does not cover the following:

1. Production of other wasting (nonregenerative) natural resources
2. Production of geothermal steam
3. Extraction of hydrocarbons as a by-product of the production of geothermal steam (Geothermal Steam Act of 1970)
4. Extraction of hydrocarbons from shale, tar sands, or coal
5. Accounting for interest on funds borrowed to finance oil and/or gas producing activities.

Effects of FASB-25

The effective date of the promulgated GAAP on Oil and Gas Producing Companies (FASB-19) has been suspended indefinitely insofar as it requires the use of the successful efforts method of accounting (FASB-25). In other respects, the effective date of FASB-19 has been changed to fiscal years ending after December 25, 1979, although earlier application is encouraged.

The definitions of reserves used in FASB-19 were completely rescinded by FASB-25. The definitions that shall be used are those adopted by the SEC for its reporting purposes and which are in effect on the date reserve disclosures are made. Revision of previously reported reserves do not have to be made in the event the SEC changes its definitions of reserves.

Other disclosures required by FASB-25 have since been superseded by the comprehensive disclosure requirements of FASB-69.

Furthermore, FASB-25 specifically states that for the purposes of the promulgated GAAP on Accounting Changes (APB-20) the provisions of FASB-19 pertaining to the successful efforts method remain in effect. Since FASB-19 expresses a preference for the successful efforts method of accounting and rejects other methods, an enterprise that changes to any method other than the successful efforts will have the burden of justifying such change (APB-20).

The income tax allocation requirements of FASB-19 were not changed by FASB-25 and therefore remain in effect.

Overview

The promulgated GAAP supports and advocates the traditional historical cost accounting approach. The major problem is in understanding the activities and related terminology pertaining to the oil and gas producing industry.

Properties   includes any ownership in, or an interest representing the right to, or the participation in, the extraction of oil and/or gas. Includes also nonoperating interests, such as a royalty interest, or production interest payable in oil and/or gas. Properties exclude contracts representing the right to purchase oil and/or gas (supply contracts).

Reservoir   refers to a separate confined underground formation containing a natural accumulation of producible oil and/or gas.

Field   refers to one or more reservoirs related to the same individual geological structural feature and/or stratigraphic condition.

Proved area   is that part of the property in which proved reserves have been specifically attributed.

Proved reserves   The following definitions of proved reserves are those adopted by the SEC on December 19, 1978 (ASR-257) and were current at the date of publication. These definitions were developed by the Department of Energy for its financial reporting purposes.

Proved oil and gas reserves.   Proved oil and gas reserves are the estimated quantities of crude oil, natural gas, and natural gas liquids which geological and engineering data demonstrate with reasonable certainty to be recoverable in future years from known reservoirs under existing economic and operating conditions, i.e., prices and costs as of the date the estimate is made. Prices include consideration of changes in existing prices provided only by contractual arrangements, but not on escalations based upon future conditions.

1. Reservoirs are considered proved if economic producibility is supported by either actual production or conclusive formation test. The area of a reservoir considered proved includes (a) that portion delineated by drilling and defined by gas-oil and/or oil-water contacts, if any, and (b) the immediately adjoining portions not yet drilled, but which can be reasonably judged as economically productive on the basis of available geological and engineering data. In the absence of information on fluid contacts, the lowest known structural occurrence of hydrocarbons controls the lower proved limit of the reservoir.
2. Reserves which can be produced economically through application of improved recovery techniques (such as fluid injection) are included in the "proved" classification when successful testing by a pilot project, or the operation of an installed program in the reservoir, provides support for the engineering analysis on which the project or program was based.
3. Estimates of proved reserves do not include the following: (a) oil that may become available from known reservoirs but is classified separately as "indicated additional reserves;" (b) crude oil, natural gas, and natural gas liquids, the recovery of which is subject to reasonable doubt because of uncertainty as to

geology, reservoir characteristics, or economic factors; (c) crude oil, natural gas, and natural gas liquids, that may occur in undrilled prospects; and (d) crude oil, natural gas, and natural gas liquids, that may be recovered from oil shales, coal, gilsonite and other such sources.

Proved developed oil and gas reserves. Proved developed oil and gas reserves are reserves that can be expected to be recovered through existing wells with existing equipment and operating methods. Additional oil and gas expected to be obtained through the application of fluid injection or other improved recovery techniques for supplementing the natural forces and mechanisms of primary recovery should be included as "proved developed reserves" only after testing by a pilot project or after the operation of an installed program has confirmed through production response that increased recovery will be achieved.

Proved undeveloped reserves. Proved undeveloped oil and gas reserves are reserves that are expected to be recovered from new wells on undrilled acreage, or from existing wells where a relatively major expenditure is required for recompletion. Reserves on undrilled acreage shall be limited to those drilling units offsetting productive units that are reasonably certain of production when drilled. Proved reserves for other undrilled units can be claimed only where it can be demonstrated with certainty that there is continuity of production from the existing productive formation. Under no circumstances should estimates for proved undeveloped reserves be attributable to any acreage for which an application of fluid injection or other improved recovery technique is contemplated, unless such techniques have been proved effective by actual tests in the area and in the same reservoir.

Wells, related equipment and facilities includes the cost of drilling and equipping *completed* wells, access to proved reserves, and facilities for extracting, treating, gathering, and storing the oil and/or gas.

Uncompleted wells, equipment and facilities includes the costs of all uncompleted wells, equipment and facilities.

Support equipment and facilities includes the cost of support equipment and facilities used in producing oil and/or gas. Examples are construction and grading equipment, seismic equipment, vehicles, repair shops, warehouses, camps, and division, district, or field offices.

Stratigraphic test wells (expendable wells) are generally drilled without the intention of being completed for production, and are a geological drilling effort to gather information about specific geologic conditions. Core tests and other expendable holes are classified as stratigraphic test wells.

A stratigraphic test well drilled in a proved area is called a *development-type stratigraphic test well*. When drilled on an unproved area, these wells are called exploratory-type stratigraphic test wells.

Service wells are wells drilled to service or support production in an existing field. Examples are injection wells (gas, water, steam, air, etc.) and observation wells.

Development wells are wells drilled for producing oil and/or gas in a proved area known to be productive.

Exploratory wells are wells drilled for exploration or discovery, usually on unproved areas. If a well is classified as a development, service, or stratigraphic test well, it cannot be an exploratory well.

Supply agreements are long-term contracts or similar agreements that represent the right to purchase oil and/or gas, including those with foreign governments.

Discovery-value accounting refers to estimated methods used to determine the value of oil and/or gas reserves, either when discovered or at a later date when developed. The most common estimated valuation methods are:

1. <u>Current cost</u>—the amount of cash that currently would have to be paid to acquire the same asset. Similar to current reproduction cost or current replacement cost.
2. <u>Current exit value in orderly liquidation</u>—the net amount of cash that would be received in the current orderly liquidation of the asset.
3. <u>Expected exit value in due course of business</u>—the nondiscounted amount of cash the asset is expected to bring in the due course of business, less any direct costs incurred in its disposal (net realizable value). Under this method the oil and/or gas reserves would be valued at an amount equal to the estimated net cash flow from the reserves.
4. <u>Present value of expected cash flow</u>—the present value of the expected cash inflows from the reserves, less the present value of the expected related cash outflows to produce the cash

inflows. Various different discount rates have been recommended, such as the prime rate, company's cost of capital, and the rate on long-term government bonds.

Under the discovery-value accounting method, property acquisition and other prediscovery expenditures would be deferred and written off when the areas to which the costs apply have been explored and the reserves, if any, determined and valued.

Under the promulgated GAAP (FASB-19), the discovery-value accounting method is unacceptable.

Current-value accounting   One of the four valuation methods mentioned above in discovery-value accounting is applied on a continuous basis, and oil and/or gas reserves are revalued at each financial statement date using the most current information available. Property acquisition and other prediscovery expenditures are deferred and written off when the areas to which the costs apply have been explored and the oil and/or gas reserves, if any, determined and valued.

The uncertainties and inherent unreliability in using estimates to value oil and/or gas reserves renders the discovery-value and current-value methods as undesirable.

Under the promulgated GAAP (FASB-19), both the discovery-value and current-value methods are unacceptable.

Full-costing accounting   considers all costs of unsuccessful and successful property acquisition and exploration activities as a cost of discovering reserves. Thus, all costs are considered an integral part of the acquisition, discovery, and development of oil and/or gas reserves, and costs that cannot be directly related to the discovery of specific reserves are nonetheless capitalized.

In full costing, a country is usually selected as a cost center, and all costs incurred within the cost center are capitalized and subsequently amortized against the oil and/or gas reserves produced within the cost center. There is a limitation that capitalized costs of a cost center should not exceed the value of the oil and/or gas reserves of the same cost center.

Under the promulgated GAAP (FASB-19), the full-costing accounting method is unacceptable.

Successful-efforts costing   a cause-and-effect relationship between costs incurred and the discovery of specific reserves is required. The incurrence of a cost with no identifiable future benefit is usually expensed under the successful-efforts methods.

The two major variations in the successful-efforts costing method are (1) the use of a small "area of interest" cost center, or (2) the accounting treatment of an item is determined by its nature. When a small "area of interest" cost center, such as a field, lease, or reservoir, is used, costs relating to the cost center are capitalized and subsequently amortized against the oil and/or gas reserves discovered within the cost center. When the nature of the expenditure is used as the method for capitalizing or expensing an expenditure, the nature of the expenditure determines its treatment. As a result, geological and geophysical costs and unsuccessful exploratory wells (dry holes) are immediately charged to expense. In addition, some companies use a combination of both variations to determine whether an expenditure is capitalized or expensed.

Under successful-efforts costing, all property acquisition costs are capitalized when incurred, though different methods may subsequently be used to dispose of these costs.

Under present tax law, intangible drilling costs are generally deductible as an expense in the year incurred.

The promulgated GAAP (FASB-19) is generally based on the successful-efforts costing method.

Background Information

In 1975, the Energy Policy and Conservation Act, public law 94-163, was enacted by Congress. Title V, Section 503, of the act grants the following powers to the Securities and Exchange Commission:

> to prescribe rules applicable to persons engaged in the production of crude oil or natural gas, or make effective by recognition, or by other appropriate means indicating a determination to rely on, accounting practices developed by the Financial Accounting Standards Board, if the Securities and Exchange Commission is assured that such practice will be observed by persons engaged in the production of crude oil or natural gas to the same extent as would result if the Securities and Exchange Commission had prescribed such practices by rule.

In addition, the Energy Policy and Conservation Act of 1975 requires that certain information about national energy be compiled for both domestic and foreign operations, and consist of the following data:

(1) The separate calculation of capital, revenue, and operating cost information pertaining to—

(a) prospecting,
(b) acquisition,
(c) exploration,
(d) development, and
(e) production,

including geological and geophysical costs, carrying costs, unsuccessful exploratory drilling costs, intangible drilling and development costs on productive wells, the cost of unsuccessful development wells, and the cost of acquiring oil and gas reserves by means other than development. Any such calculation shall take into account disposition of capitalized costs, contractual arrangements involving special conveyance of rights and joint operations, differences between book and tax income, and prices used in the transfer of products or other assets from one person to any other person, including a person controlled by, controlling, or under common control with such person.

(2) The full presentation of the financial information of persons engaged in the production of crude oil or natural gas, including—

(a) disclosure of reserves and operating activities, both domestic and foreign, to facilitate evaluation of financial effort and result; and

(b) classification of financial information by function to facilitate correlation with reserve and operating statistics, both domestic and foreign.

(3) Such other information, projections, and relationships of collected data as shall be necessary to facilitate the compilation of such data base.

Securities Act Release No. 5706, issued on May 12, 1976, requires that certain information relating to oil and/or gas properties, reserves, and production be disclosed in registration statements, proxy statements, and reports filed with the Commission.

Securities Act Release No. 5801, issued on January 31, 1977, states that the Commission, consistent with its policy established in Accounting Series Release No. 150, will look to the FASB to provide leadership in setting forth accounting standards and principles for the producers of oil and/or gas.

Securities Act Release No. 5837, issued on June 30, 1977, solicits comments from interested parties with respect to the Commission's responsibility under the Energy Policy and Conservation Act of 1975. The release also states that the Commission will attempt to coordinate the reporting requirements promulgated by the FASB in its own disclosure and reporting requirements.

Securities Release No. 5861 and Securities Release No. 5877, issued on August 31, 1977, and October 26, 1977, respectively, generally adopt as a Commission regulation the accounting standards and disclosures that are contained in FASB-19. These releases apply to filings with the SEC and to reports filed with the Department of Energy.

Securities Release No. 5878, also issued on October 26, 1977, deals with replacement cost information (ASR 190) for certain registrants. In lieu of replacement cost information the release requires the disclosure of the present value of future net revenues estimated to be received in the future from the production of proved oil and/or gas reserves. This release becomes effective for filings covering fiscal year ending after December 24, 1978.

On August 31, 1978, the SEC issued ASR-253 which included the following:

1. Adopted the successful-efforts accounting method and disclosure requirements of FASB-19.
2. Indicated that a form of full cost accounting for oil and gas producing companies will be developed by the SEC as an acceptable reportable alternative for the SEC.
3. Concluded that the full cost and successful-efforts method based upon historical costs fails to provide sufficient information for gas and oil producing companies and that the SEC would take steps to develop an accounting method based on current valuation of proved oil and gas reserves.
4. Adopted disclosure rules for certain information regardless of the accounting method used.
5. Adopted the definition of proved reserves which differed from those prescribed by FASB-19.

On December 19, 1978, the SEC issued ASR-257 and ASR-258 which included the following:

1. Reaffirmed the conclusions the SEC prescribed in ASR-253 (enumerated above).
2. Adopted definitions of proved reserves developed by the Department of Energy for its reporting purposes.
3. Described the form of full cost accounting for gas and oil producing companies that would be acceptable as an alternative to the successful-efforts method for reporting to the SEC.

Accounting Principles—Basic Concepts

The promulgated GAAP (FASB-19) does not address itself to the transporting, refining, and marketing aspects of oil and/or gas production. The functions covered by the promulgated GAAP are (1) acquisition of properties, (2) exploration, (3) development, and (4) production.

Generally, the incurrence of a cost that results in the acquisition of an asset is capitalized and subsequently amortized, unless the asset becomes impaired or worthless, in which case it is reduced in value or written off. Costs that do not result in the acquisition of an asset, such as carrying costs of undeveloped properties, geological and geophysical (G&G) costs, and the costs of drilling exploratory wells that do not find proved reserves, are charged to expense when incurred.

Costs incurred to operate and maintain producing wells, related equipment and facilities, become part of the total production costs (also known as lifting costs). The other part of production costs comprise depreciation, depletion, and amortization of the costs capitalized as property acquisition, exploration, and development costs.

Before the accounting treatment of a cost can be determined, it must be first classified as a cost of acquiring properties, exploring, developing, or producing. For example, support equipment and labor can be classified as any of the functional activities in the oil and gas industry. Labor used in developing a producing well is capitalized and subsequently amortized, whereas labor costs incurred in operating producing wells become part of production costs.

The following is a brief discussion of the accounting principles and basic concepts involved in each function of the oil and gas industry:

Acquisition of properties includes all costs to purchase, lease, or otherwise acquire a proved or unproved property, including broker's, legal, and recording fees, and other costs incurred in acquiring properties. The acquisition of properties may include the transfer of all or part of the rights and responsibilities of operating the properties (operating interest) or none of the rights or responsibilities of operating (nonoperating interest).

If the interest in the property acquired is of substance a borrowing repayable in cash or its equivalent, it should be treated as a borrowing and not as the acquisition of an interest in the property.

If part or all of an interest in a property is sold and substantial uncertainty exists in the recovery of the applicable costs involved, or if the seller has a substantial future performance obligation to drill a well or to operate the property without reimbursement, no gain should be recognized on these types of conveyances.

As in all nonmonetary exchanges of like property, gain or loss is recognized only to the extent of any "boot" received, as follows:

1. Exchange of assets used in oil and gas producing activities for other assets used in oil and gas producing activities
2. A joint pooling of assets to find, develop, or produce oil and/or gas from a particular property

Unproved properties should be reclassified to proved properties when proved reserves are attributed to the property. Periodic assessment of unproved properties should be made to determine whether they have been impaired. Impairment is likely if a dry hole has been drilled and there are no future plans to continue drilling, or if the end of a lease approaches and drilling has not commenced on the property. Losses for impairment of unproved properties are made by a charge to income and a credit to a valuation account in the year the impairment occurs.

If an unproved property is abandoned or becomes worthless, all related capitalized costs should be charged first against any related allowance for impairment account, and any excess charged to income of the period that the unproved property is abandoned or becomes worthless. If only a small portion of an amortization base is abandoned or becomes worthless, then that portion should be considered fully amortized and its cost charged to the accumulated depreciation, depletion, or amortization account, and no gain or loss is recognized.

The unit-of-production method is used to amortize (deplete) all capitalized property acquisition costs of proved properties. As stated previously, this amortization (depletion) becomes part of the production costs (lifting costs). Amortization rates should be reviewed at least annually and revisions should be accounted for prospectively as changes in accounting estimates (APB-20).

In proved properties that contain both oil and gas reserves, a common unit of measure based on the approximate relative energy content of the oil and gas should be used as the unit of production in the current period. Amortization is then based on the converted common unit of measure. In the event that either oil or gas dominates the content of both reserves and current production, unit-of-production amortization may be computed on the dominant mineral only.

Exploration includes all costs relating to the search for oil and/or gas reserves, including depreciation and applicable costs of support equipment and facilities, drilling exploratory wells, and exploratory-type stratigraphic test wells. Exploration costs may be incurred before the actual acquisition of the property, and in this sense they are sometimes referred to as prospecting costs.

Some exploration costs do not represent the acquisition of an identifiable asset, and are therefore charged directly to expense when incurred. The cost of carrying and maintaining undeveloped properties is an expense, because such costs do not increase the potential that the properties will contain proved reserves. Examples of these types of expenses are delay rentals, taxes on properties, legal costs, and land maintenance.

Geological, topographical, and geophysical studies (G&G costs) and related salary and other expenses are also expensed, because they do not represent the acquisition of an identifiable asset. The studies are frequently made before the acquisition of the property and represent research or information costs. More frequently than not, G&G costs are incurred and the properties are never acquired.

Pending the determination of whether a well has proved reserves, all costs of drilling exploratory wells are capitalized and are classified as uncompleted wells, equipment and facilities. The disposition of exploratory wells and their related costs is usually made shortly after completion, and if the well has proved reserves, the costs are capitalized and reclassified as wells, related equipment and facilities. However, if no proved reserves are found, the capitalized costs of drilling the well, less any salvage value, is charged to expense.

Sometimes an exploratory well cannot be classified as having found proved reserves on completion of drilling, because justification for major capital expenditures, such as a trunk pipeline, must be made, which may depend on the success of additional exploratory wells in the same area. In this event, the exploratory well and its related costs may be carried on the books as an asset for a period not exceeding one year, providing both of the following conditions are met:

1. A sufficient quantity of reserves was found to justify the completion as a producing well if the required capital expenditures are made.
2. Drilling of other exploratory wells has commenced or is firmly planned for the near future.

If the above conditions are not met, the exploratory well and all its related costs are charged to expense.

Costs incurred for an exploratory well or stratigraphic test well, net of salvage value, shall be charged to expense for the period, if the following conditions exist:

1. The well is in progress (uncompleted) at the end of the period.
2. A determination has been made prior to the issuance of the financial statements that the well has not located any proved reserves. In other words, the well has proved to be dry.

FASB Interpretation-36 requires that only the costs incurred through the end of the reporting period, net of any salvage value, need be charged to expense. The amount charged to expense should include costs incurred during the current period, as well as costs that were incurred and capitalized in prior periods. Thus, estimated costs to complete the uncompleted "dry well," if necessary, should not be accrued, since they will be charged to expense when incurred in subsequent periods.

The unit-of-production method is used to amortize all capitalized exploration costs, including support equipment and facilities. As stated previously, this amortization becomes part of the cost of production (lifting costs).

Development includes all costs incurred in creating a production system of wells, related equipment and facilities, on proved reserves so that the oil and/or gas can be lifted (produced). Development costs are associated with specific proved reserves; exploration costs are associated with unproved reserves. The cost of building a road to gain access to proved reserves is a development cost, as is the cost of providing facilities for extracting, treating, gathering, and storing the oil and/or gas. Development costs also include depreciation and operating costs of support equipment and facilities used in development activities.

Development costs are associated with previously discovered proved reserves with known future benefits. Therefore, under the promulgated GAAP, unsuccessful development wells (dry holes) are capitalized as a cost of creating the overall production system for proved reserves.

The unit-of-production method is used to amortize (deplete) all capitalized development costs. As stated previously, this amortization (depletion) becomes part of the production costs (lifting costs). Amortization rates should be reviewed at least annually, and revisions should be accounted for prospectively as changes in accounting estimates (APB-20).

In proved properties that contain both oil and gas, a common unit of measure based on the approximate relative energy content of the oil and gas should be used as the unit of production for the purpose of determining the number of units produced in the current period. Amortization is then based on the converted common unit of measure. In the event that either oil or gas dominates the content of both reserves and current production, unit-of-production amortization may be computed on the dominant mineral only.

Production includes all costs incurred in lifting the oil and/or gas to the surface, and gathering, treating, field processing, and field storage. The promulgated GAAP provides that the production function terminate at the outlet valve on the leased property or the field production storage tank, or under unusual circumstances, at the first point at which the oil and/or gas is delivered to a main pipeline, refinery, marine terminal, or a common carrier.

Production costs include labor, fuel, and supplies needed to operate the developed wells and related equipment, repairs, property taxes, and insurance on proved properties, and wells, related equipment and facilities.

Costs incurred to operate and maintain the production system become part of the total production costs (lifting costs). The other part of the production costs consists of the depreciation, depletion, and amortization of the costs capitalized as acquisition of properties, exploration, and development costs.

Support Equipment and Facilities

Costs for support equipment and facilities may be incurred for exploration, development, or production activities. Generally, these costs are capitalized and depreciated over their estimated useful lives or the life of the lease, whichever is appropriate. The depreciation expense and related costs of operating the support equipment and facilities is charged to the related activity (exploration, development, or production). When support equipment and facilities are utilized for more than one activity, the depreciation expense and operating costs should be allocated between the activities on a reasonable basis.

Residual salvage values and estimated costs of dismantlement, restoration, and abandonment should be considered in determining depreciation and amortization rates.

Balance Sheet—Subsequent Information

The promulgated GAAP requires that information that becomes available subsequent to the balance sheet date and prior to the issuance of the financial statements should be taken into consideration in determining conditions that existed at the balance sheet date. The determination at the balance sheet date of whether an exploratory well has found proved reserves, the impairment of unproved properties, and similar conditions may be based on information that becomes available subsequent to the balance sheet date and prior to the issuance of the financial statements.

Income Tax Considerations

Comprehensive interperiod income tax allocation (APB-11) should be applied for items that enter into the determination of pretax accounting income and taxable income in different periods (timing differences). However, a future tax benefit arising from an excess of statutory depletion over cost depletion is not treated as a timing difference but is accounted for as a permanent difference in the period in which it is allowed as a deduction for income tax purposes.

Segmental Reporting

Segmental reporting (FASB-14) is not necessary for oil and/or gas producing companies, because the functional activities of property acquisition, exploration, development, and production are not considered industry segments. However, the promulgated GAAP does require some disclosure information based on geographic areas.

DISCLOSURES (FASB-69)

Most of the disclosure requirements of FASB-69 pertain to "publicly held enterprises," as that term is defined in FASB-33 (Financial Reporting and Changing Prices). FASB-33 defines a public enterprise as "a business enterprise (a) whose debt or equity securities are traded in a public market on a domestic stock exchange or in a domestic over-the-counter market (including securities quoted only locally or regionally), or (b) that is required to file financial statements with the Securities and Exchange Commission. An enterprise is considered to be a public enterprise as soon as its financial statements are issued in preparation for the sale of any class of securities in a domestic market."

General Disclosures

Interim financial reports are not required to contain the disclosures mandated by FASB-69. However, interim financial reports are required to contain disclosure of favorable or adverse events concerning an enterprise's proved oil and gas reserves. A major oil or gas discovery is the type of favorable event that must be disclosed in interim financial reports. A major accident, such as a fire, that consumes significant quantities of proved oil and gas reserves is the type of adverse event that must be disclosed in interim financial reports.

> *OBSERVATION: APB-28 (Interim Financial Reporting) encourages the disclosure of significant events which affect the interim financial results.*

The method of accounting for costs incurred in oil and gas producing activities and the manner of disposing of capitalized costs must be fully disclosed by both public and nonpublic enterprises that are engaged in oil and gas producing activities..

> *OBSERVATION: Disclosure of accounting policies is required by APB-22 which states a preference for the presentation of disclosing accounting policies in the first footnote to the financial statements under the caption "Summary of Significant Accounting Policies."*
>
> *Under APB-22, both the accounting principle and the method of applying the principle should be disclosed, but accounting principles and their methods of application in the following areas are considered particularly important:*
>
> *(a) A selection from existing acceptable alternatives*
> *(b) The areas that are peculiar to a specific industry in which the entity operates*
> *(c) Unusual and innovative applications of GAAP*

When a complete set of annual financial statements is presented, publicly held enterprises that have significant oil and gas producing activities shall also disclose, as supplementary information to the financial statements, the following information relating to gas and oil producing activities:

a. Proved oil and gas reserve quantities
b. Capitalized costs
c. Costs incurred for property acquisition, exploration, and development activities
d. Results of operations
e. A standardized measure of discounted future net cash flows

The above supplementary information shall be disclosed in complete sets of annual financial statements by publicly traded enterprises that have significant oil and gas producing activities. The test of whether an enterprise has significant oil and gas producing activities must be applied separately for each year that a complete set of annual financial statements is presented.

Generally, an enterprise has significant oil and gas producing activities if its oil and gas producing activities qualify as an industry segment under the provisions of FASB-14 (Segmental Reporting). Thus, if an enterprise satisfies one or more of the following tests, it is considered as having significant oil and gas producing activities:

1. Its revenue from oil and gas producing activities (defined below) is at least 10% of the total revenue from all of the enterprise's industry segments (defined below).
2. Its operating profit from oil and gas producing activities is at least 10% of the total operating profit of all of the enterprise's industry segments which reflect operating profits.
3. Its operating loss from oil and gas producing activities is at least 10% of the total operating losses of all of the enterprise's industry segments which reflect operating losses.
4. Its identifiable assets (defined below) relating to oil and gas producing activities are at least 10% of all of the identifiable assets of all of the enterprise's industry segments.

The following definitions are used in applying the above tests for significant oil and gas producing activities:

Revenues shall include sales to unaffiliated organizations in connection with (a) net working interests, (b) royalty interests, (c) oil payment interests, and (d) net profit interests of the reporting enterprise. Intercompany sales or transfers shall also be included as revenue, based on appropriate market prices which are equivalent to an arm's length transaction at the point of delivery from the producing unit. Excluded from gross revenue are (a) royalty payments and (b) net profit disbursements. Production or severance taxes are included as part of production costs and shall not be deducted in determining gross revenue.

Industry segment is a component of an enterprise that sells its products or services primarily to outsiders for a profit.

Identifiable assets are tangible and intangible assets used exclusively by a segment of an enterprise, or the allocated portion of assets used jointly by more than one segment. General corporate assets are not allocated to segments and loan and investment accounts are not considered assets unless income from them is included in segment profit or loss.

Goodwill, less any amortization, is included in an industry segment's identifiable assets. An industry segment's identifiable assets are computed net of any valuation account, such as allowance for doubtful accounts, accumulated depreciation, etc.

Loans and advances between industry segments whose principal operations are financial (banking, leasing, insurance, etc.) and whose income is derived from such loans and advances, should be included as an identifiable industry segment asset.

Disclosures—Proved Oil and Gas Reserve Quantities

Publicly held enterprises shall disclose as supplementary information to each of their annual financial statements presented, the net quantities of proved reserves and proved developed reserves of crude oil and natural gas.

The net quantities of crude oil which includes condensate and natural gas liquids should be stated in barrels. The net quantities of natural gas should be stated in cubic feet. Net quantities of crude oil and gas, if significant, should be reported for the company's home country and each foreign geographic area (country or group of countries) in which significant reserves are located.

In determining net quantities the following rules shall apply:

1. Net quantities shall exclude oil and gas subject to purchase under long-term supply, purchase, or similar agreements, including those with governments. However, if the company participates in the operation of the oil and/or gas producing properties or otherwise acts as a producer, this information is reported separately (see below).
2. Companies issuing consolidated financial statements shall include all the net quantities attributable to the parent company and all the net quantities attributable to the consolidated subsidiaries whether or not wholly owned.

    A significant portion of the net quantities at the end of the year may be attributable to a consolidated subsidiary that has a significant minority interest. In this event, disclosure of these facts and the approximate portion attributable to the consolidated subsidiary is required by FASB-69.

3. Net quantities of investments that are proportionately consolidated shall include the proportionate share of the investee's net quantities of oil and gas reserves.
4. Net quantities of investments that are accounted for by the equity method shall be excluded. (This information is separately reported; see below.)
5. Net quantities shall include any from royalty interests owned if the information is available. If the information is not available, a statement of that fact must be made and net quantities *produced* attributable to the royalty interest must be disclosed for each period presented.
6. Net quantities include operating and nonoperating interest in properties.
7. Net quantities shall not include interests of others in properties.

Beginning and ending net quantities in proved reserves and proved developed reserves of crude oil (including condensate and natural gas liquids) and natural gas and net changes during the year must be reported at the end of each year in which a complete set of financial statements is presented.

The following chart illustrates the method of disclosing net quantities recommended in the promulgated GAAP:

	Total Worldwide		United States		Foreign Geographic Area A		Foreign Geographic Area B		Other Foreign Geographic Areas	
	Oil	Gas	Oil	Gas	Oil	Gas	Oil	Gas	Oil	Gas
Proved developed and undeveloped reserves:										
1. Beginning of year	X	X	X	X	X	X	X	X	X	X
2. Revisions of previous estimates	X	X	X	X	X	X	X	X	X	X
3. Improved recovery	X	X	X	X	X	X	X	X	X	X
4. Purchases of minerals-in-place	X	X	X	X	X	X	X	X	X	X
5. Extensions, discoveries, and other additions	X	X	X	X	X	X	X	X	X	X
6. Production	(X)	(X)	(X)	(X)	(X)	(X)	(X)	(X)	(X)	(X)
7. Sales of minerals-in-place	(X)	(X)	(X)	(X)	(X)	(X)	(X)	(X)	(X)	(X)
8. End of year	X	X	X	X	X	X	X	X	X	X
9. Proved developed reserves:										
Beginning of year	X	X	X	X	X	X	X	X	X	X
End of year	X	X	X	X	X	X	X	X	X	X

Oil and Gas Producing Companies

	Total Worldwide		United States		Foreign Geographic Area A		Foreign Geographic Area B		Other Foreign Geographic Areas	
	Oil	Gas	Oil	Gas	Oil	Gas	Oil	Gas	Oil	Gas
Oil and gas applicable to long-term supply agreements with foreign governments or authorities in which the company acts as producer:										
10. Proved reserves at end of year	X	X	X		X	X	X	X	X	X
11. Received during the year	X	X	X		X	X	X	X	X	X
12. Company's proportional interest in reserves of investees accounted for by the equity method, end of year	X	X	X		X	X	X	X	X	X

An explanation of each item in the chart follows:

1. *Beginning of year*—the total net quantities at the beginning of the year
2. *Revisions of previous estimates*—upward or downward revision of proved reserves resulting from new information or changes in economic factors
3. *Improved recovery*—changes during the year resulting from new recovery techniques
4. *Purchases of minerals-in-place*—purchases during the year of proved developed and undeveloped reserves
5. *Extensions, discoveries, and other additions*—proved reserves resulting from the extension of previously discovered reservoirs, discovery of new fields or new reservoirs in old fields, and other additions
6. *Production*—the total amount of net quantities produced for the year
7. *Sales of minerals-in-place*—sales during the year of proved developed and undeveloped reserves
8. *End of year*—the total net quantities at the end of the year (All items above this item should add up to this item.)
9. *Proved developed reserves*—net quantities of proved developed reserves only for the beginning and ending of the year. Proved developed reserves include oil and/or gas expected to be

recovered through existing wells using existing equipment and operation methods. Proved undeveloped reserves are those where oil and/or gas is expected to be recovered from new wells on undrilled acreage or from existing wells that require major expenditures for completion.

Net quantities subject to purchase under long-term supply agreements with governments or authorities and net quantities received during the year under such agreements must be separately disclosed as indicated in items 10 and 11.

An investor's share of net quantities of an investment accounted for by the equity method shall be separately disclosed at the end of the year (as indicated in item 12).

If important economic factors or significant uncertainties are involved in any of the net quantities reported by an enterprise, an explanatory note should accompany the supplementary oil and gas information. Important economic factors or significant uncertainties would include (a) exceptionally high future development or lifting expenditures, and (b) contractual obligations requiring the enterprise to sell significant quantities of oil or gas at substantially lower prices than the expected market price at the time of production.

If a government restricts or prohibits the disclosure of any of the net quantities of oil and gas reserves required by FASB-69, or requires disclosure of a different nature than required by FASB-69, an enterprise must disclose the fact that (a) the net quantity reserves from that particular country are excluded from the supplementary information, or (b) the net quantity reserves from that particular country are not reported in accordance with the FASB-69.

Disclosures—Capitalized Costs

Publicly held enterprises shall disclose in each of their annual financial statements presented, the total amount of capitalized costs and related accumulated depreciation (depletion) (amortization) and valuation allowances relating to oil and gas producing activities. Under FASB-19, capitalized costs are classified as follows:

1. Mineral interests in properties which must be classified as (a) proved properties or (b) unproved properties
2. Wells, related equipment and facilities
3. Support equipment and facilities used in oil and gas producing activities
4. Uncompleted wells, equipment and facilities

Existing GAAP (APB-12) require that the balances of major classes of depreciable assets, by nature or function, be disclosed in the financial statements of an enterprise. Thus, to comply with existing GAAP, it would appear appropriate to use the above classifications for capitalized costs relating to oil and gas producing activities. However, FASB-69 states that it often may be appropriate to combine one or more, or two or more, of the classifications of capitalized costs and offers the following illustration:

	Total
Unproved oil and gas properties	$XXX,XXX
Proved oil and gas properties	XXX,XXX
	$XXX,XXX
Less: Accumulated depreciation, depletion, amortization, and valuation allowances	XX,XXX
Net capitalized costs	$XXX,XXX
Proportionate share of capitalized costs of investments accounted for by the equity method	$ XX,XXX

FASB-69 expressly requires that capitalized costs of unproved properties, if significant, be separately disclosed.

Under the provisions of FASB-69, capitalized costs of support equipment and facilities may be disclosed separately or included as appropriate with capitalized costs of proved and unproved properties.

An enterprise's proportionate share of the total capitalized costs relating to oil and gas producing activities of an investment accounted for by the equity method must be separately disclosed in each annual financial statement presented.

Disclosures—Incurred Functional Costs

Publicly held enterprises shall disclose in each of their annual financial statements presented, the total capitalized or expensed costs for the following functional activities of oil and gas producing companies:

1. Property acquisition costs
2. Exploration costs
3. Development costs

Exploration and development costs shall include the depreciation expense of support equipment and facilities, but exclude the expenditures to acquire such equipment and facilities. Any of these functional costs which are incurred in a foreign country shall be separately disclosed by geographic areas in the same manner that net quantities of oil and gas are disclosed.

An enterprise's proportionate share of the total property acquisition, exploration, and development costs relating to oil and gas producing activities of an investment accounted for by the equity method must be separately disclosed, in total and by geographic area, in each annual financial statement presented.

The following illustrates the disclosure of the property acquisition, exploration, and development costs required by FASB-69:

	Total Worldwide		United States		Foreign Geographic Area A		Foreign Geographic Area B		Other Foreign Geographic Areas	
	Oil	Gas	Oil	Gas	Oil	Gas	Oil	Gas	Oil	Gas
Property acquisition costs	X	X	X	X	X	X	X	X	X	X
Exploration costs	X	X	X	X	X	X	X	X	X	X
Development costs	X	X	X	X	X	X	X	X	X	X
Proportionate share of the property, acquisition, exploration, and development costs from investments accounted for by the equity method	X	X	X	X	X	X	X	X	X	X

If costs to acquire mineral interests in proved reserves are significant, FASB-69 requires that they be separately disclosed apart from costs to acquire interests in unproved reserves.

Disclosures—Results of Operations

Publicly held enterprises shall disclose in each of their annual financial statements presented, the results of operations (as defined below) for oil and gas producing activities. However, if the enterprise is subject to the segmentation provisions of FASB-14 (Segmental Reporting), the results of operations shall be included with the other segment information required by FASB-14.

Results of operations shall include an enterprise's interests in proved oil and gas reserves and oil and gas subject to purchase under long-term supply contracts and similar agreements.

Under FASB-69, results of operations for oil and gas producing activities shall be disclosed in total and for each geographic area for which related reserve quantities are disclosed.

The following information shall be disclosed for results of operations for oil and gas producing activities:

Revenues shall include sales to unaffiliated organizations in connection with (a) net working interests, (b) royalty interests, (c) oil payment interests, and (d) net profit interests of the reporting enterprise.

Intercompany sales or transfers shall also be included as revenue, based on appropriate market prices which are equivalent to arm's-length transactions at the point of delivery from the producing unit.

Excluded from gross revenue are royalty payments and net profit disbursements. Production or severance taxes are included as part of production costs and shall not be deducted in determining gross revenue.

Production includes all costs incurred in lifting the oil and/or gas to the surface, and gathering, treating, field processing, and field storage. The production function terminates at the outlet valve on the leased property or the field production storage tank, or under unusual circumstances, at the first point at which the oil and/or gas is delivered to a main pipeline, refinery, marine terminal, or a common carrier.

Production costs include labor, fuel, and supplies needed to operate the developed wells and related equipment, repairs, property taxes, and insurance on proved properties, and wells, related equipment and facilities.

Costs incurred to operate and maintain the production system become part of the total production costs (lifting costs).

Depreciation, depletion, amortization, and valuation allowances related to capitalized costs are excluded from production costs and disclosed under a separate caption (see below).

Exploration includes all costs relating to the search for oil and/or gas reserves, including applicable costs of support equipment and facilities, drilling exploratory wells, and exploratory-type stratigraphic test wells. Exploration costs may be incurred before the actual acquisition of the property, and in this sense they are sometimes referred to as prospecting costs.

Some exploration costs do not represent the acquisition of an identifiable asset, and are therefore charged directly to expense when incurred. The cost of carrying and maintaining undeveloped properties is an expense, because such costs do not increase the potential that the properties will contain proved reserves. Examples of these types of expenses are delay rentals, taxes on properties, legal costs, and land maintenance.

Geological, topographical, and geophysical studies (G&G costs) and related salary and other expenses are also expensed, because they do not represent the acquisition of an identifiable asset. The studies are frequently made before the acquisition of the property and represent research or information costs. More frequently than not, G&G costs are incurred and the properties are never acquired.

Depreciation, depletion, amortization, and valuation allowances related to capitalized costs are excluded from exploration expenses and disclosed under a separate caption (see below).

> *OBSERVATION: Enterprises using methods of accounting other than the "successful efforts" method will usually have no exploration costs to disclose. In this event, all exploration costs are usually capitalized and subsequently charged to net income as depreciation, depletion, amortization, and valuation allowances.*

Depreciation, depletion, amortization, and valuation allowances related to oil and gas producing activities, except that which is part of general corporate overhead and financing costs, are disclosed separately under this caption.

> *OBSERVATION: Interest capitalized under the provisions of FASB-34, on qualifying assets used in oil and gas producing activities, will be charged to net income as depreciation, depletion, or amortization of the cost of the related asset.*

Income tax expense The statutory tax rate for the period shall be applied to the results of operations (as defined herein) to determine the income tax expense for the period. The determination of income tax expense shall reflect any permanent differences relating to oil and gas activities, provided that such permanent differences are appropriately reflected in the enterprise's consolidated income tax expense for the period.

Results of operations are equal to revenues, less (a) production costs, (b) exploration expenses, (c) depreciation, depletion, amortization, and valuation allowances, and (d) income tax expense. Results of operations for oil and gas producing activities shall not include general corporate overhead and financing costs. However, corporate overhead or expenses incurred at a central administrative office may include operating expenses of oil and gas producing activities and should be accounted for as such. In determining whether an expenditure is or is not an operating expense of oil and gas producing activities, the nature of the expense governs. The location in which the expense is recorded or paid is irrelevant.

Oil and Gas Producing Companies

Results of operations do not include an enterprise's proportionate share of the results of operations (as defined herein) of oil and gas producing activities from investments accounted for by the equity method. An enterprise's proportionate share of the results of operations (as defined herein) from an investment accounted for by the equity method must be separately disclosed, in total and by geographic area, in each annual financial statement presented.

The following illustrates the disclosure of results of operations (as defined herein):

	Total Worldwide	United States	Foreign Geographic Area A	Foreign Geographic Area B	Other Foreign Geographic Areas
Revenues	$ X	$ X	$ X	$ X	$ X
Production costs	(X)	(X)	(X)	(X)	(X)
Exploration expenses	(X)	(X)	(X)	(X)	(X)
Depreciation, depletion, and amortization, and valuation provisions	(X)	(X)	(X)	(X)	(X)
	X	X	X	X	X
Income tax expense	(X)	(X)	(X)	(X)	(X)
Results of operations for producing activities (excluding corporate overhead and financing costs)	$ X	$ X	$ X	$ X	$ X
Enterprise's share of equity method investees' results of operations for producing activities (excluding corporate overhead and financing costs)	$ X	$ X	$ X	$ X	$ X

Disclosures—Discounted Future Net Cash Flows

Publicly held enterprises shall disclose, in each of their annual financial statements presented, a statement of the present value of future net cash flows, in total and by geographic area, from (a) the net quantities of proved reserves and proved developed reserves of crude oil and natural gas, and (b) the net quantities of oil and gas subject to purchase under long-term supply contracts and similar agreements, and contracts in which the enterprise participates in the operation of the oil or gas producing properties or otherwise acts as a producer. Items (a) and (b) may be combined into one statement of the present value of future net cash flows.

Under the provisions of FASB-69, a standardized measure of discounted future net cash flows is achieved by utilizing a 10% discount rate. The statement of the present value of future net cash flows must include the following detail:

Future cash inflows are calculated by multiplying the current year-end net quantities of oil and gas reserves (items (a) and (b) above) by their respective current year-end prices. Future price changes shall be considered, but only to the extent of existing contractual agreements. In other words, prices that appear in existing agreements may be used, but only to the extent of the quantities involved in the agreement.

Future development and production costs are estimated expenditures which should be incurred in producing the future cash inflows. Future development and production costs shall be estimated based on current year-end costs and existing economic environment. If significant, future development costs shall be separately disclosed.

Future income tax expenses are calculated by applying the current year-end statutory income tax rates to the total pretax future cash flows from the net quantities of oil and gas reserves, less (a) the tax basis of the properties involved and (b) the tax effects of any permanent differences, such as investment tax credits and the excess of statutory depletion over the tax basis.

Future tax rates should be used if legislated before issuance of the financial statements.

Future net cash flows are calculated by deducting future development and production costs and future income tax expenses from the future cash inflows.

Discount is calculated by applying a standardized 10% rate per year, which shall reflect the timing of the receipts of the future net cash flows from the net quantities of oil and gas reserves.

Standardized measure of discounted future net cash flows is calculated by deducting the discount from the future net cash flows.

A significant portion of the consolidated standardized measure of discounted future net cash flows may be attributable to a consolidated subsidiary that has a significant minority interest. In this event, disclosure of these facts and the approximate portion attributed to the consolidated subsidiary is required by FASB-69.

The standardized measure of discounted future net cash flows does not include an enterprise's proportionate share of the standardized measure of discounted future net cash flows from investments accounted for by the equity method. An enterprise's proportionate share of the standardized measure of discounted future net cash flows from investments accounted for by the equity method must be separately disclosed, in total and by geographic area, in each annual financial statement presented.

An enterprise shall disclose in each of its annual financial statements presented a statement of the changes in the standardized measure of discounted future net cash flows, in total and by geographic area. The factors which cause the changes in the standardized measure of discounted future net cash flows shall be separately disclosed, if significant, under the following categories:

1. Sales and transfers of oil and gas produced during the period, net of production costs.
2. Net changes in sales and transfer prices, and changes in future development and production (lifting) costs.
3. Previously estimated future development costs incurred during the period.
4. Net changes for extensions, discoveries, additions, and improved recovery, less related future development and production costs.
5. Net changes for revisions in quantity estimates.
6. Net changes due to purchases and sales of minerals in place.
7. Accretion of discount.
8. Net changes in income taxes.
9. Other (including the effect of changes in estimated rates of production).

> **OBSERVATION:** Accretion of discount *(item 7 above) is a term used by the SEC, which refers to the annual amount of imputed interest that is calculated on the standardized measure of discounted future net cash flows (see illustration below).*

A newly formed oil company spends $200,000 to drill for oil and discovers a commercially exploitable well. At year-end it is estimated that this well will produce 10,000 barrels of oil for the next three years, or a total of 30,000 barrels. The year-end price of oil is $35 per barrel and future development and production costs and future income tax expenses are estimated at year-end prices to be $5 per barrel. The standardized measure of discounted future net cash flows (present value) at 10% is $30 ($35 − $5) × 10,000 = $300,000 × 2.48685 = $746,055. The amortization table for the three-year period is as follows:

Year	Present Value (A)	Interest (B)	Total	Net Cash Flow	Present Value Balance
1	$746,055	$74,606	$820,661	$300,000	$520,661
2	520,661	52,066	572,727	300,000	272,727
3	272,727	27,273	300,000	300,000	0

(A) = Standardized measure of discounted future net cash flows
(B) = Accretion of discount

In computing the changes in the standardized measure of discounted future net cash flows, the effects of price changes shall be calculated before the effects of quantity changes, so that the latter will be priced at year-end prices. The effect of changes in income taxes shall include the effect of the income taxes incurred during the period and the effect of changes in future income tax expenses. All other changes except the accretion of discount and income taxes shall be reported pretax.

Footnotes shall be provided for any additional information which is necessary to prevent the disclosures from being misleading.

> **OBSERVATION:** FASB-19 requires information that becomes available after the balance sheet date and before the issuance of the financial statements to be taken into consideration in determining conditions that existed at the balance sheet date. The determination at the balance sheet date of whether an exploratory well contains proved reserves, the impairment of unproved properties, and similar factors may be based on information that becomes available after the balance sheet date and before the issuance of the financial statements.
>
> A four to three vote of the FASB adopted paragraphs 30-34 of this Statement, "Disclosure of a Standardized Measure of Discounted Future Net Cash Flows Relating to Proved Oil and Gas Reserves." The three dissenting Board members described this measurement as "completely lacking in reliability."

Oil and Gas Producing Companies

The following is an illustration of the disclosure of the standardized measure of discounted future net cash flows and changes therein:

	Total	United States	Foreign Geographic Area A	Foreign Geographic Area B	Other Foreign Geographic Areas
Future cash inflows*	$ X	$ X	$ X	$ X	$ X
Future production and development costs*	(X)	(X)	(X)	(X)	(X)
Future income tax expenses*	(X)	(X)	(X)	(X)	(X)
Future net cash flows	X	X	X	X	X
10% annual discount for estimated timing of cash flows	(X)	(X)	(X)	(X)	(X)
Standardized measure of discounted future net cash flows relating to proved oil and gas reserves	$ X	$ X	$ X	$ X	$ X
Enterprise's share of equity method investees' standardized measure of discounted future net cash flows relating to proved oil and gas reserves	$ X	$ X	$ X	$ X	$ X
Beginning of year	$ X	$ X	$ X	$ X	$ X
Changes resulting from:					
Sales and transfers of oil and gas produced, net of production costs	(X)	(X)	(X)	(X)	(X)
Net changes in prices, and development and production costs	X	X	X	X	X
Extensions, discoveries, additions, and improved recovery, less related costs	X	X	X	X	X
Development costs incurred during the period	X	X	X	X	X
Revisions of previous quantity estimates	X	X	X	X	X
Net change in purchases and sales of minerals in place	X	X	X	X	X
Accretion of discount	X	X	X	X	X
Net change in income taxes	X	X	X	X	X
Other	X	X	X	X	X
End of year	$ X	$ X	$ X	$ X	$ X

*Future net cash flows were computed using year-end prices and costs, and year-end statutory tax rates (adjusted for permanent differences) that relate to existing proved oil and gas reserves in which the enterprise has mineral interests, or for which the enterprise has long-term supply, purchase, or similar agreements where the enterprise serves as the producer of the reserves.

Disclosures—Current Cost Information

FASB-33 (Financial Reporting and Changing Prices), as amended by FASB-39, requires that oil and gas producing enterprises disclose certain supplementary information on a constant dollar basis and also on a current cost basis. FASB-69 amends FASB-33 and FASB-39, as follows:

1. The supplementary current cost information need be presented only if an enterprise's inventory and property, plant and equipment which are not used in oil and gas producing activities are significant in amount.
2. An oil and gas producing enterprise may substitute historical cost/constant dollar information for the current cost supplementary information which is required by FASB-33. However, the current cost supplementary information disclosure is required for mining mineral resource assets and related expenses.

Real Estate Transactions

REAL ESTATE COSTS AND INITIAL RENTAL OPERATIONS

Overview

FASB-67 contains the specialized accounting and reporting principles and practices that were originally published in the following AICPA publications:

- Statement of Position 78-3 (Accounting for Costs to Sell and Rent, and Initial Rental Operations of Real Estate Projects)
- Statement of Position 80-3 (Accounting for Real Estate Acquisition, Development, and Construction Costs)

In addition, FASB-67 includes those portions of the industry accounting guide entitled "Accounting for Retail Land Sales," which cover costs of real estate projects.

FASB-67 establishes the promulgated GAAP for the acquisition, development, construction, and selling and rental costs, which are related to real estate projects. In addition, FASB-67 covers (a) accounting for initial rental operations and (b) the rules for ascertaining when a real estate project is substantially completed and available for occupancy.

The following items are expressly excluded from the provisions of FASB-67:

1. Real estate projects that are not for sale or rent and are developed by an entity for its own use. This includes real estate reported in consolidated financial statements that was developed by one affiliated member of the group for the use in the operations of another member of the group.
2. Initial direct costs of leases (FASB-17).
3. Direct costs that are related to commercial activities such as manufacturing, merchandising, or service orientated activities.
4. Real estate rental periods of less than one month in duration.

Background

Real estate acquisition costs may be broken down into (a) preacquisition costs and (b) postacquisition costs. Preacquisition costs are those which are incurred prior to the acquisition of the property, such as appraisals, surveys, legal fees, travel expenses, and costs to acquire options to purchase the property. Postacquisition costs are those which are incurred after the property has been acquired, such as development and construction costs. Postacquisition costs may be further broken down into (a) direct costs, (b) indirect costs, (c) costs of amenities, and (d) incidental operational costs.

Direct costs are those that can be directly identified with the real estate project. Indirect costs may, or may not, be related to a specific real estate project. Indirect costs of several real estate projects may be allocated to each project on a reasonable allocation basis.

Golf courses, swimming pools, tennis courts, clubhouses, and other amenities are frequently included in the overall plans of a real estate project. Ownership of these types of amenities may be retained by the real estate developer, or may be included in the sale of individual units within the project. When the ownership of an amenity is included in the individual sales within a real estate project, the net cost of the amenity is considered a common cost of the project. Common costs of a real estate project are allocated on a reasonable basis to the individual components within the project. The net cost of an amenity is equal to the total cost of the amenity, less any anticipated proceeds. When a developer retains ownership of an amenity for resale or operations, the cost of the amenity is capitalized in an amount not to exceed its estimated fair value at the date of substantial completion of the amenity. Costs in excess of the estimated fair value of the amenity at the date of substantial completion are accounted for as common costs of the real estate project. After it is substantially completed and ready for its intended use, the cost of the amenity should not be revised.

Incidental operations of a real estate project occur during the development stage of the project and are intended to reduce the cost of the real estate project. Incidental operations do not include activities that result in a profit or return on the use of the real property. If the incremental revenues from incidental operations exceed the incremental costs, they are accounted for as a reduction of the capitalized costs of the project. However, if the incremental costs of incidental operations exceed the incremental revenue, they are charged to expense as incurred.

Capitalized costs of a real estate project must be allocated to the individual components within the project. The allocation is usually accomplished by the specific identification method, if the individual components within the project can be specifically identified. If specific identification is not possible, capitalized land cost and all other common costs, including common costs of amenities, shall be allocated on the basis of the relative fair value of each land parcel benefited prior to any construction. Capitalized construction costs are allocated on the basis of the relative sales value of each individual component within the real estate project. Individual components of a real estate project may consist of lots, acres, or some other identifiable unit.

Estimates are used extensively in the acquisition, development, and construction of a real estate project. As a result, revisions of estimated costs occur frequently and past, present, and future accounting periods may be affected by the revisions.

Revisions of estimates that occur in the acquisition, development, and construction stages of a real estate project are accounted for as changes in accounting estimates (APB-20). The effects of a change in accounting estimates should be accounted for (a) in the period of change, if the change affects only that period or (b) in the period of change and future periods, if the change affects both. A change in an accounting estimate caused in part or in whole by a change in accounting principle should be reported as a change in accounting estimate (APB-20). APB-20 (Accounting Changes) requires that disclosure be made in current period financial statements of the effects of a change in an accounting estimate on (a) income before extraordinary items, (b) net income, and (c) related per share data.

Ordinary accounting estimates for uncollectible accounts or inventory adjustments, made each period, do not have to be disclosed, unless they are material.

Sometimes there is a significant change in the use of the property in a real estate project, or the project is completely abandoned. In the event that the project is abandoned, all capitalized costs of the project should be expensed immediately. Under no circumstances should capitalized costs of an abandoned real estate project be allocated to other real estate projects. In addition, if a portion of a real estate project is abandoned, the related capitalized costs should be expensed and not allocated to other portions of the same or other projects which are not abandoned.

The cost of land donated to governmental units should not be classified as abandoned if the donated land benefits part or all of the real estate project. Under these circumstances, the donated land shall be accounted for as a common cost of the real estate project.

Capitalized costs incurred prior to the change in use of all or part of the property in a real estate project are charged to expense, except in the following circumstances:

1. The change in use of all or part of the property in the real estate project is supported by a formal plan which indicates that a higher economic yield will result from the change in

use. In this event, the capitalized costs incurred prior to the change and the estimated capitalized costs expected to be incurred to substantially complete the project are capitalized to the extent that the total capitalized costs do not exceed the estimated value of the completed revised project. Capitalized costs in excess of the estimated value of the completed revised project, if any, are charged to expense.
2. The change in use of all or part of the property in the real estate project is *not* supported by a formal plan, but the change in use is expected to produce a higher economic yield for the project. In this event, capitalized costs incurred prior to the change are capitalized to the extent that they do not exceed the net realizable value of the project based on the assumption that the property will be sold "as is," in its present condition.

Costs incurred to sell real estate projects may be accounted for as (a) project costs, (b) prepaid expenses, or (c) period costs, according to the accounting periods which are benefited.

Costs to rent real estate projects under operating leases are either chargeable to future periods, or chargeable to the current period, according to whether their recovery is reasonably expected from future rental revenue.

Initial rental operations commence at the time a real estate project is substantially completed and available for occupancy. A real estate rental project is considered substantially completed and available for occupancy when tenant improvements have been completed by the developer, but in no event later than one year after major construction activity has been completed, excluding routine maintenance and clean-up.

Some portions of a real estate rental project may still require major construction for completion and other portions of the same project may be substantially completed and available for occupancy. In this event, each portion should be accounted for as a separate project.

Suspension of major construction activity may occur because of a decline in rental demand. In this event, the carrying costs of the real estate project may be permanently impaired and a provision for losses may be required. Impairment of the carrying cost of a real estate project may occur from insufficient rental demand even if construction is not suspended.

Once a real estate rental project is substantially completed and available for occupancy, depreciation on the entire project should be appropriately recorded.

Preacquisition Costs of Real Property

Frequently, costs are incurred prior to the actual date on which a parcel of real property is acquired. These costs are referred to by FASB-67 as preacquisition costs. Practically any type of cost may be classified as a preacquisition cost if it is incurred prior to the date of acquisition of a parcel of real property. The cost of an option to purchase real property at a future date is a preacquisition cost and is usually capitalized. However, if the option is not exercised on or before its expiration date, the option becomes worthless and should be expensed.

All other types of preacquisition costs are expensed when incurred, unless they can be specifically identified to the real property being acquired, and:

1. They would be capitalized if the property was acquired, and,
2. The acquisition of the property is likely to occur.

> **OBSERVATION:** *Likely to occur* implies that the property is available for sale, the purchaser is currently trying to acquire the property, and the necessary financing is apparently available.

Thus, preacquisition costs of a real estate project consist of (a) unexpired options to purchase real property and (b) other costs which meet all of the above conditions. Preacquisition costs that do not qualify for capitalization should be expensed when incurred.

After a parcel of real property is acquired, preacquisition costs should be reclassified as project costs. In the event that the property is not acquired, capitalized preacquisition costs shall not exceed the amount recoverable, if any, from the sale of options, developmental plans, and other proceeds. Capitalized preacquisition costs in excess of recoverable amounts shall be charged to expense.

Taxes and Insurance on Real Property

FASB-67 requires that property taxes and insurance be capitalized as project costs only during periods in which activities necessary to get the property ready for its intended use are in progress.

> **OBSERVATION:** Frequently, a land company will purchase a tract of land that will not be developed for several years. Apparently, under the provisions of FASB-67, real estate taxes, insurance, and interest related to the tract of land cannot be capitalized

unless activities necessary to get the property ready for its intended use are in progress. However, this position apparently differs from the AICPA industry accounting guide entitled "Accounting for Retail Land Sales." Paragraph 51 of this guide states that "Costs directly related to inventories of unimproved land . . . are properly capitalizable until a salable condition is reached." Paragraph 51 further states that "Those costs would include interest, real estate taxes, and other direct costs incurred during the inventory and improvement periods."

FASB-67 requires that property taxes and insurance costs be expensed as incurred, if the real property is not undergoing activities necessary to get it ready for its intended use.

> **OBSERVATION:** Obviously, FASB-67 requires that the cost of a three-year insurance policy on a tract of land be expensed when incurred, if the land is not undergoing activities necessary to get it ready for its intended use. However, the accrual basis for accounting would require that the insurance policy be capitalized and amortized over the periods benefited.

After real property is substantially completed and ready for its intended use, FASB-67 also requires that property taxes and insurance costs be expensed as incurred.

Project Costs of Real Property

Project costs of real estate projects may be direct or indirect. Direct costs that are related to the acquisition, development, and construction of a real estate project shall be capitalized as project costs.

Indirect costs of real estate projects that can be clearly identified to specific projects under development or construction shall be capitalized as project costs. Indirect costs that are accumulated in one account, but clearly relate to several real estate projects under development or construction, should be allocated on a reasonable basis to each of the projects.

Indirect costs on real estate projects not under development or construction must be expensed as incurred. In addition, indirect costs that cannot be clearly identified with specific projects such as general and administrative expenses should be charged to expense when incurred.

Amenity Costs of Real Property

Golf courses, swimming pools, tennis courts, clubhouses, and other types of amenities are frequently included in the overall plans of a real estate project. However, the ultimate disposition of an amenity may vary from one real estate project to another. Thus, accounting for the costs of amenities is based on the developer's (management) ultimate plans for the disposition of the amenity. In this respect, a developer may decide to retain ownership of the amenity and to either (a) operate the amenity, or (b) eventually sell the amenity. On the other hand, the developer may be required under the terms of the individual sales agreements to sell, or otherwise transfer ownership of the amenity to the purchasers of the individual components within the project. In this event, the purchasers of the individual components within the project usually form an "association" for the purposes of taking title to the amenity and to operate the amenity for the common benefit of all owners of individual components within the project.

Accounting for the costs of amenities under the provisions of FASB-67, is as follows:

Ownership Not Retained by Developer

When the ownership of an amenity is to be transferred to the individual components within the real estate project, the net cost of the amenity is accounted for by the developer as a capitalized common cost of the project. The capitalized common cost of an amenity is allocated to the individual components within the project which are expected to benefit from the use of the amenity. Thus, the total cost of each individual component in the project which benefits from the amenity will include a proportionate share of the costs of the amenity.

The developer's net cost or gain that is accounted for as a common cost (reduction) of the real estate project may include the sales price, if any, and all other proceeds, if any, from the transfer of the amenity, less the following items:

1. Direct costs that are clearly identifiable to the amenity
2. Indirect costs that are clearly related to the amenity
3. The developer's cost of operating the amenity until the amenity is transferred to the individual components in the project

in accordance with the sales or other contractual agreement, and
4. Common costs of the project that are appropriately allocated to the amenity

If an amenity clearly benefits specific individual components within a real estate project, the common cost (reduction) of the amenity should be allocated only to those specific individual components.

Ownership Retained by Developer

When a developer retains ownership of an amenity, the total cost of the amenity is capitalized as a separate asset. The total cost of an amenity includes direct costs, indirect costs, and the allocation of common costs, including operating results of the amenity prior to its date of substantial completion and availability for its intended use. However, under FASB-67 the amount capitalized cannot exceed the estimated fair value of the amenity at its expected date of substantial completion. Any costs in excess of the estimated fair value of the amenity at the expected date of its substantial completion are accounted for as common costs of the real estate project.

After it is substantially completed and ready for its intended use, further revision of the final capitalized cost of an amenity not in excess of its estimated fair value is not permitted. This cost becomes the basis of the amenity for any future sale. The subsequent basis for determining gain or loss on the sale of the amenity is the capitalized cost of the amenity not in excess of its estimated fair value at its date of substantial completion, less any allowable depreciation to the date of the sale.

After its date of substantial completion and availability for its intended use, the operational results of an amenity that is owned by the developer shall be included in the developer's current net income.

Incidental Operations of Real Property

Incidental operations of a real estate project usually occur during the holding or development stage of the project and are intended to reduce the cost of the project. Incidental operations do not include activities that result in a profit or return from the proposed development of the real property. For example, revenue received from billboard advertisements placed on the property or miscellaneous concession income would be classified as incidental operations.

If the incremental revenue received from incidental operations exceeds the related incremental costs, the difference is accounted for as a reduction of the capitalized costs of the real estate project. Thus, when incidental operations of a real estate project result in a profit, the capitalized costs of the project are reduced by the amount of profit. However, under FASB-67 the same does not hold true if the incidental operations result in a loss. Under FASB-67, if the incremental costs of incidental operations exceed the related incremental revenue, the difference is charged to expense when incurred.

Allocation of Capitalized Costs

All capitalized costs of a real estate project must be allocated to the individual components within the project. If practicable, FASB-67 requires that capitalized costs be allocated by the specific identification method. Under this method, capitalized costs are specifically identified with the individual components within the real estate project. However, if it is impractical to use the specific identification method to allocate capitalized costs, FASB-67 requires that allocation be made, as follows:

Land Costs

Only capitalized costs associated with the land prior to any construction are allocated as land costs. Land costs prior to any construction include capitalized land costs and other preconstruction common costs related to the land, including preconstruction common costs of amenities.

Total capitalized land costs are allocated on the basis of the relative fair value of each land parcel prior to any construction. A land parcel may be identified as a lot, an acre, acreage, a unit, or a tract.

Construction Costs

Capitalized construction costs are allocated on the basis of the relative sales value of each individual structure or unit located on a parcel of land. In the event capitalized costs of a real estate project cannot be allocated by the specific identification method or the relative sales value method, the capitalized cost shall be allocated on area methods or other methods appropriate under the circumstances.

Revisions of Estimates

Estimates are used extensively in the acquisition, development, and construction of a real estate project. As a result, revisions of estimated costs occur frequently and past, present, and future accounting periods may be affected by the revisions.

Revisions of estimates that occur in the acquisition, development, and construction stages of a real estate project are accounted for as changes in accounting estimates (APB-20). The effects of a change in accounting estimates should be accounted for (a) in the period of change, if the change affects only that period, or (b) in the period of change and future periods, if the change affects both. A change in an accounting estimate caused in part or in whole by a change in accounting principle should be reported as a change in accounting estimate (APB-20). APB-20 (Accounting Changes) requires that disclosure be made in current period financial statements of the effects of a change in an accounting estimate on (a) income before extraordinary items, (b) net income, and (c) related per share data. However, ordinary accounting estimates for uncollectible accounts or inventory adjustments, made each period, do not have to be disclosed, unless they are material.

Abandonments and Changes in Use

Occasionally a real estate project is partially or completely abandoned, or there is a significant change in the use of the property in the project. Under the provisions of FASB-67, if part or all of a real estate project is abandoned, the related capitalized costs must be expensed immediately. Under no circumstances should the capitalized costs of an abandoned real estate project be allocated to other real estate projects.

The cost of land donated to a governmental authority should not be accounted for as abandoned. Under these circumstances, the cost of the donated land should be accounted for as common costs of acquiring the project. Thus, the cost of the donated land is allocated to the other land in the project, based on the relative fair value of each parcel of land prior to construction of any buildings or structures.

After significant development and construction costs have been capitalized in a real estate project, there may be a change in the use of part or all of the land within the project. Under the provisions of FASB-67, capitalized costs incurred prior to a change in use of all or part of the land within a real estate project are charged to expense, except in the following circumstances:

1. The enterprise has developed a formal plan which indicates that the change in use of the land will result in a higher economic yield than was originally anticipated. In this event, the maximum costs that can be capitalized must not exceed the estimated value of the revised project at the date of substantial completion and availability for its intended use. Capitalized costs in excess of the estimated value of the revised project when substantially completed, if any, are charged to expense.
2. The enterprise has not developed a formal plan, but the change in use of the land is expected to yield a higher economic return than was originally anticipated. In this event, the maximum cost that can be capitalized at the date of change in use cannot exceed the net realizable value of the project based on the assumption that the property will be sold "as is," in its present condition. Capitalized costs incurred prior to the change in use which exceed the net realizable value must be expensed.

Selling Costs of Real Estate Projects

Costs incurred to sell real estate projects should be accounted for as either (a) project costs, (b) prepaid expenses, or (c) period costs.

Project costs are capitalized as part of the construction costs of the real estate project provided that both of the following conditions are met:

1. They are incurred for tangible assets which are used as marketing aids during the marketing period of the real estate project, or for services performed in obtaining regulatory approval for real estate sales in the project.
2. The costs incurred are reasonably expected to be recovered from sales.

Costs to sell real estate that qualify as project costs, less recoverable amounts from incidental operations or salvage value, include legal fees for prospectuses, sales offices, and model units, with or without furnishings.

Costs to sell real estate projects that qualify as project costs become part of the capitalized cost of the project and are allocated to the individual components of the project as common costs.

Prepaid expenses   which are sometimes called "deferred charges," are capitalized and amortized over the period that is expected to benefit from the expenditure. However, if the prepaid item can be identified with certain future revenue, it should be amortized to the periods in which the future revenue is earned. Costs incurred as prepaid expenses to sell real estate projects must meet the following conditions:

1. They do not qualify as project costs.
2. They are incurred for goods or services that will be used in future periods.

Advances on commissions, future advertising costs, and unused sales brochures are examples of costs to sell real estate projects which qualify as prepaid expenses.

Period costs   are charged to expense in the period incurred because they do not meet the criteria for project costs or prepaid expenses. Costs to sell real estate projects which do not benefit future periods should be expensed in the period incurred, as period costs. Grand opening expenses, sales salaries, sales overhead, and used advertising costs are examples of period costs.

Rental Costs of Real Estate Projects

Costs incurred to rent real estate projects under operating leases are either chargeable to future periods or chargeable to the current period.

Chargeable to future periods   If the costs can be identified to, and reasonably expected to be recovered from specific revenue, such costs should be capitalized and amortized to the periods in which the specific revenue is earned. If the costs are for goods not used or services not received, such costs should be charged to the future periods in which the goods are used or services are received.

If deferred rental costs can be associated with the revenue from a specific operating lease, such costs should be amortized over the lease term. The amortization period commences when the rental project is substantially completed and available for occupancy. (See

Initial Rental Operations for definition.) On the other hand, if deferred rental costs cannot be identified with the revenue from a specific operating lease, such costs should be amortized over the periods benefited. The amortization period commences when the rental project is substantially completed and available for occupancy.

Unamortized rental costs that subsequently become unrecoverable from future operations should be expensed when they are determined to be unrecoverable. For example, unamortized rental costs related to specific leases which have, or will be, terminated should be charged to expense.

Chargeable to the current period If the costs to rent real estate projects under operating leases do not qualify as chargeable to future periods, they should be accounted for as period costs and expensed as incurred.

Initial Rental Operations

Initial rental operations commence at the time when a real estate project is substantially completed and available for occupancy. A real estate project is considered substantially completed and available for occupancy when tenant improvements have been completed by the developer, but in no event later than one year after major construction activity has been completed, excluding routine maintenance and clean-up.

The actual rental operation of a real estate project shall commence at the time the project is substantially completed and available for occupancy. At this time rental revenues and related operating costs shall be recognized on an accrual basis. Operating costs shall include amortization of deferred rental costs, if any, and depreciation expense.

Some portions of a real estate rental project may still require major construction for completion and other portions of the same project may be substantially completed and available for occupancy. In this event, each portion should be accounted for as a separate project.

Recoverability

Under the provisions of FASB-67, the net carrying amount of a real estate project under development or held for sale shall not exceed its estimated net realizable value. In the event that the net carrying amount of a real estate project exceeds its estimated net realizable value, a provision to reduce the net carrying amount to its estimated net realizable value shall be established in the books of account. The difference between the net carrying amount of the project and the provision, or allowance account, should equal the estimated net realizable value of the real estate project. Each individual project shall be separately analyzed to determine whether its net carrying amount exceeds its estimated net realizable value. An individual project is considered to consist of similar components within the real estate project, such as (a) individual residences, (b) individual apartments or condominiums, or (c) individual lots, acres, or tracts. Thus, a real estate project which includes 50 individual residences, 10 condominium buildings, 20 multifamily buildings, and 100 residential lots would be considered four separate projects for the purposes of determining net realizable values. The net carrying amount of the 100 residential lots may exceed their net realizable value, while the individual net carrying values of the 50 individual residences, 10 condominium buildings, and 20 multifamily buildings may not exceed their individual estimated net realizable values.

Suspension of major construction activity may occur because of a decline in rental demand. In this event, the carrying costs of the real estate rental project may be permanently impaired and a provision for losses may be required. Impairment of the net carrying amount of a real estate project may occur from insufficient rental demand even if construction is not suspended.

Amendments and Effective Data

FASB-32 (Specialized Accounting and Reporting Principles and Practices in AICPA Statements of Position and Guides on Accounting and Auditing Matters) is amended by FASB-67, by deleting Statement of Position 78-3 from Appendix A, and deleting Statement of Position 80-3 from Appendix B.

FASB-67 is effective for costs of real estate projects incurred in fiscal years beginning on or after January 1, 1983. Earlier application of the provisions of FASB-67 are not required, but is encouraged.

REAL ESTATE—RECOGNITION OF SALES

Overview

FASB-66 contains the specialized accounting and reporting principles and practices that were originally published in the following AICPA publications:

- Industry Accounting Guide (Accounting for Profit Recognition on Sales of Real Estate)
- Industry Accounting Guide (Accounting for Retail Land Sales)
- SOP 75-6 (Questions Concerning Profit Recognition of Sales of Real Estate)
- SOP 78-4 (Application of the Deposit, Installment, and Cost Recovery Methods in Accounting for Sales of Real Estate)

FASB-66 does not include those portions of the industry accounting guide entitled "Accounting for Retail Land Sales," which cover costs of real estate projects. These costs of real estate projects are covered in FASB-67 (Accounting for Costs and Initial Rental Operations of Real Estate Projects).

FASB-66 establishes the promulgated GAAP for the recognition of profit on all real estate transactions for any type of accounting entity. In this respect, FASB-66 provides separate criteria for the recognition of profit on (a) all real estate transactions, except retail land sales, and (b) retail land sales. The following items are expressly excluded from the provisions of FASB-66:

1. Exchanges of real estate for other real estate
2. Sales and leasebacks

In extracting the specialized accounting principles and practices from the various AICPA publications, the FASB has made the following changes:

1. Sales of "Time-Sharing Interests in Real Estate" that represent fee simple ownership, or are sales-type leases under FASB-13, are accounted for as sales of real estate and are included in the provisions of FASB-66.

2. The discount rate which is applied to the total contract price of a retail land sale has been changed to a rate that produces an amount at which the receivable could be sold on a volume basis without recourse to the seller.
3. The disclosure requirements of the Retail Land Sales Guide have been condensed and certain disclosures omitted because of duplication with other existing GAAP.

Background

The "matching" concept requires that revenue and related costs be "matched" in determining net income for a specific period. If revenue is deferred to a future period, the associated costs of that revenue must also be deferred. Frequently, it is necessary to estimate revenue and/or costs in order to achieve a proper "matching." The result of using the matching concept in determining income or loss is called the earning process. When the earning process is complete and an exchange has taken place, only then is the realization of revenue recognized. The realization principle requires that revenue be earned before it is recorded.

GAAP require that the realization of revenue be recognized in the accounting period in which the earning process is substantially completed and an exchange has taken place (APB-4). In addition, revenue is usually recognized at the amount established by the parties to the exchange except for transactions in which collection of the receivable is not reasonably assured (APB-4). In the event that collection of the receivable is not reasonably assured, the installment method or cost recovery method may be used (APB-10). Alternatively, collections may be properly recorded as deposits in the event that considerable uncertainty exists as to their eventual collectibility.

Under the provisions of FASB-66, real estate transactions are broken down into (a) all real estate transactions, except retail land sales, and (b) retail land sales.

All real estate transactions, except retail land sales More often than not, in a real estate sale, a significant portion of the sales price is represented by a long-term receivable which is not backed by the full faith and credit of the buyer. Usually, the seller can only recover the property in the event of default by the buyer. Another unusual facet of real estate sales is the possible continuing involvement in the property by the seller. For instance, the seller may be legally bound to make certain improvements to the property or to adjacent property.

In order to assure the collection of the long-term receivable which is usually part of a real estate transaction, FASB-66 requires minimum down payments for all real estate sales before a seller may recognize a profit. FASB-66 emphasizes the timing of the recognition of profits but does not cover other aspects of real estate accounting.

Real estate transactions that are not considered "retail land sales" include the following:

1. Sales of homes, buildings, and parcels of land
2. Sales of lots to builders
3. Sale of corporate stock, or a partnership interest where the economic substance of the transaction is actually a sale of real estate
4. Sales of options to acquire real estate
5. Sale of time-sharing interests in real estate

Retail land sales The development of a large tract of land usually over several years is typical of a company in the retail land sales industry. Master plans are drawn for the improvement of the property which may include amenities, and all necessary regulatory approvals are obtained. Large advertising campaigns are held at an early stage which frequently result in substantial sales prior to significant development of the property. In most retail land sales, a substantial portion of the sales price is financed by the seller in the form of a long-term receivable secured by the property. Interest and principal are paid by the buyer over an extended number of years. In the event of default, the buyer usually loses his entire equity and the property reverts back to the seller. Frequently, the retail land sales contract or existing state law provides for a period in which the purchaser may receive a refund of all or part of any payments made. In addition, the seller may be unable to obtain a deficiency judgment against the buyer because of operation of the law. Finally, many project-wide improvements and amenities are deferred until the later stages of development when the seller may be faced with financial difficulties.

Because of the small down payments, frequent cancellations and refunds, and the possibility that the retail land sales company may not be financially able to complete the project, certain specific conditions must be met before a sale can be recognized.

REAL ESTATE SALES, EXCEPT RETAIL LAND SALES

In order for a seller to report the total profit on a sale of real estate by the full accrual method, FASB-66 requires that the transaction meet specific criteria. The criteria are as follows:

1. A sale must be completed (consummated).
2. The initial and continuing payments (investment) made by the buyer must be adequate.
3. The seller's receivable shall not be subject to future subordination, except to (a) a primary lien on the property existing at the date of sale, or (b) a future loan, or existing permanent loan commitment of which the proceeds must first be applied to the payment of the seller's receivable.
4. All of the benefits and risks of ownership in the property must be substantially transferred to the buyer by the seller.
5. The seller must not have a substantial continued involvement with the property after the sale.

If a sale of real estate, other than a retail land sale, meets all of the above criteria, the seller must recognize the entire profit on the sale in accordance with the full accrual method of accounting. In the event a real estate sale fails to meet all of the above criteria, profit on the sale must be recognized by either (a) the deposit method, (b) the installment sales method, (c) the cost recovery method, or (d) the reduced profit method. The method that must be used for profit recognition is determined by the specific circumstances of each real estate sale.

First, FASB-66 reviews in detail each of the specific criteria that must be present if the full accrual method is to be used.

When a Real Estate Sale Is Consummated

FASB-66 contains four criteria that must be met for a sale of real estate to be considered "consummated." The criteria are as follows:

1. The contracting parties are legally bound by the contract.
2. All consideration required by the terms of the contract has been paid.
3. If the seller is responsible by the terms of the contract to obtain permanent financing for the buyer, the seller must have arranged for such financing.

4. The seller has performed all of the acts required by the contract to earn the revenue.

Under FASB-66, all of the above criteria must be met before the sale of real estate is considered "consummated." As a general rule, the above criteria are met at the time of, or after, the closing of the real estate sale. These criteria are rarely met prior to closing or at the time a sales agreement is executed.

An exception to the "consummation rule" may occur if, after the date of sale, the seller has continued involvement with the property to construct office buildings, condominiums, shopping centers, or other similar improvements on the land which take a long time to complete. As will be discussed later, FASB-66 permits some profit recognition under certain circumstances even if the seller has this type of substantial continued involvement with the property.

Buyer's Initial and Continuing Investment

In determining whether the buyer's minimum initial investment (down payment) is adequate under the provisions of FASB-66, the *sales value* of the property is used and not the stated sales price in the contract. The *sales value* is defined as the stated sales price of the property, increased or decreased for other considerations included in the sale that clearly represent more or less proceeds to the seller on the sale. Thus, any payments made by the buyer that are not included in the stated sales price in the contract and which represent additional proceeds to the seller should be included as part of the buyer's minimum investment. These additional proceeds enter into the determination of both the buyer's minimum investment and the *sales value* of the property. Examples of additional proceeds to the seller are (a) the exercise price of a real estate option to purchase the property, (b) management fees, (c) points to obtain financing, (d) prepaid interest and principal payments, (e) payments by the buyer to third parties which reduce previously existing indebtedness on the property, and (f) any payments made by the buyer to the seller which will be applied at a future date against amounts due the seller. However, payments by the buyer to third parties for improvements to the property or payments which are not verifiable cannot be considered as additional proceeds to the seller.

Decreases in the stated sales price that are necessary to arrive at the *sales value* of the property may include, but are not limited to, the following:

1. The amount of discount, if any, necessary to reduce the buyer's receivable to its present value. Thus, if the buyer's receivable

does not bear interest or the rate of interest is less than the prevailing rate, a discount would be required to reduce it to its present value (APB-21).
2. The present value of services that the seller agrees to perform without compensation or, if the seller agrees to perform services at less than prevailing rates, the difference between (a) the present value of the services at prevailing rates and (b) the present value of the agreed upon compensation.

The effects of an underlying land lease must also be included in computing the *sales value* of the property. If a seller sells improvements to a buyer to be built on property subject to an underlying land lease, the present value of the lease payments must be included in the *sales value* of the property. The present value of the lease payments should be computed over the actual term of the primary indebtedness of the improvements, if any, or over the usual term of primary indebtedness for the type of improvements involved. The present value of the land lease payments is tantamount to additional indebtedness on the property. If the land lease is not subordinated, the discount rate to determine the present value of the land lease payments should be comparable to interest rates on primary debt of the same nature. However, if the land lease is subordinated, a higher discount rate, comparable to secondary debt of the same nature, should be used.

XYZ, Inc. agrees to build improvements for ABC Company for a total price of $1,750,000. The improvements are to be built on land leased by ABC from a third party. The payments on the land lease are $18,000 per year, payable monthly in advance, and the lease term is for 45 years. ABC Company will pay for the improvements as follows:

Cash down payment	$ 250,000
10% unsecured note payable in five annual payments of $20,000 plus interest	100,000
Primary loan from insurance company secured by improvements to the property, payable in equal monthly payments over 28 years at 8½% interest	1,400,000
Total Stated Sales Price of Improvements	$1,750,000

The computation of the *sales value*, as required by FASB-66, is as follows:

Present value of land lease payments for 28 years, payable $1,500 monthly, discounted at 8½% interest	$ 193,361
Primary loan from insurance company	1,400,000
Total equivalent primary debt	$1,593,361
Unsecured note from buyer to seller	100,000
Cash down payment	250,000
Sales Value*	$1,943,361

*The adequacy of the buyer's minimum initial investment in the property is based on the *sales value* of the property and not on the stated sales price.

If a land lease exists between the buyer and a third party, its effects on the sales value of the property are used only to determine the adequacy of the buyer's initial investment. However, when the seller of the improvements is also the lessor of the land lease, the computation of the profit on the sale of the improvements is also affected. Since it is impossible to separate the profits on the improvements from the profits on the underlying lease, FASB-66 requires a special computation limiting the amount of profit that can be recognized. The amount of profit which can be recognized on the improvements is equal to the *sales value* of the property less the cost of improvements and the cost of the land. However, the present value of the lease payments in the sales value may not exceed the actual cost of the land.

The result of the limitation on the amount of profit which can be recognized on the sale of improvements is to defer any residual profit on the land from being recognized until the land is sold or the future rental payments are actually received.

If a land lease between a buyer and a seller of improvements on the land is for a term of less than 20 years or does not substantially cover the economic life of the improvements being made to the property, the transaction should be accounted for as a single lease of land and improvements.

The buyer's minimum initial investment must be made at or before the time of sale in cash or cash equivalency. A buyer's note does not qualify for the minimum initial investment unless payment of the note is unconditionally guaranteed by an irrevocable letter of credit from an established unrelated lending institution. A permanent loan commitment by an independent third party to replace a loan made by the seller shall not be included in the buyer's initial investment. Any funds that have been loaned or will be loaned, directly or indirectly, to the buyer by the seller must be deducted from the buyer's initial investment (down payment) to determine whether the required minimum has been met. For the purposes of this provision, the seller must be exposed to a potential loss as a result of the funds loaned to the buyer. For example, if a buyer made an initial cash investment of $200,000 in a real estate transaction, $25,000 of which was a loan from the seller, the buyer's minimum initial investment under the provisions of FASB-66 would be $175,000. However, if an unrelated reputable banking institution unconditionally guaranteed the timely repayment of the $25,000 to the seller, the entire $200,000 would be eligible as the buyer's initial investment.

There is a direct relationship between the amount of the buyer's initial investment (down payment) and the probability that the seller will eventually collect the balance due. The larger the down payment, the more likely the buyer will pay the balance due. A reasonable basis for establishing the amount of a buyer's initial investment is the prevailing practices of independent lending institutions. Thus, the difference between the amount of primary mortgage an independent lending institution would lend on a particular parcel of real estate and the *sales value* of the property is a realistic guide as to the amount of the buyer's initial investment.

In order to apply the full accrual method of accounting to a real estate transaction (other than a retail land sale), FASB-66 provides that the minimum initial investment (down payment) of the buyer should be the greater of 1 or 2 below:

1. The percentage of the sales value of the property as indicated on the following table:

	Minimum Down Payment (% of Sales Value)
Land:	
Held for commercial, industrial, or residential development to commence within two years after sale	20%
Held for commercial, industrial, or residential development after two years	25%

Commercial and Industrial Property:
  Office and industrial buildings, shopping centers, etc.:
    Properties subject to lease on a long-term lease basis to parties having satisfactory credit rating; cash flow currently sufficient to service all indebtedness — 10%
    Single tenancy properties sold to a user having a satisfactory credit rating — 15%
    All other — 20%

Other Income-Producing Properties (hotels, motels, marinas, mobile home parks, etc.):
    Cash flow currently sufficient to service all indebtedness — 15%
    Start-up situations or current deficiencies in cash flow — 25%

Multi-Family Residential Property:
  Primary residence:
    Cash flow currently sufficient to service all indebtedness — 10%
    Start-up situations or current deficiencies in cash flow — 15%
  Secondary or recreational residence:
    Cash flow currently sufficient to service all indebtedness — 15%
    Start-up situations or current deficiencies in cash flow — 25%

Single Family Residential Property (including condominium or cooperative housing):
    Primary residence of the buyer — 5%*
    Secondary or recreational residence — 10%*

*If collectibility of the remaining portion of the sales price cannot be supported by reliable evidence of collection experience, a higher down payment is indicated and should not be less than 60% of the difference between the sales value and the financing available from loans guaranteed by regulatory bodies, such as FHA or VA, or from independent financial institutions. This 60% test applies when independent first mortgage financing is not utilized and the seller takes a receivable from the buyer for the difference between the sales value and the initial investment. When independent first mortgage financing is utilized, the adequacy of the initial investment on sales of single family residential property should be determined in accordance with FASB-66.

2. The lesser of the following:
    a. The difference between the *sales value* of the property and 115% of the maximum permanent mortgage loan or commitment on the property recently obtained from a primary independent lending institution, OR
    b. Twenty-five percent (25%) of the *sales value* of the property

Real Estate—Recognition of Sales

The following illustrates how the buyer's minimum initial investment (down payment) is determined in accordance with FASB-66.

The *sales value* of property being sold is $200,000, and the maximum permanent mortgage loan recently placed on the property from an independent lending institution is $150,000. The property being sold is commercial land, which will be developed by the buyer within two years after the date of sale. In order to apply the full accrual method of accounting to this real estate transaction, FASB-66 provides that the minimum initial investment (down payment) of the buyer should be the greater of 1 or 2 below:

1. The percentage of the *sales value* of the property as indicated on the table is $40,000 (20% of $200,000),
2. a. The difference between the *sales value* of the property and 115% of the recently placed permanent mortgage loan is $27,500 (115% of $150,000 = $172,500 and the difference between $200,000 [sales value] and $172,500 is $27,500).

    b. 25% of the sales value ($200,000) is $50,000.

The lesser amount between 2a ($27,500) and 2b ($50,000) = $27,500
The greater amount between 2a ($27,500) and 1 ($40,000) = $40,000

Thus, the minimum down payment of the buyer is $40,000.

OBSERVATION: *The above method of determining the buyer's initial minimum investment (down payment) is described differently in the AICPA industry accounting guide entitled "Accounting for Profit Recognition of Sales of Real Estate." The AICPA Guide permits the use of two independent methods to determine the minimum initial investment (down payment) of the buyer. The first and by far the simplest is that the minimum initial investment of the buyer be not less than 25% of the sales value of the property. The other method is that the minimum initial investment of the buyer be the greater of:*

1. *The difference between the* sales value *of the property and 115% of the primary permanent commitment or loan on the property, or*
2. *The percentage of the* sales value *of the property as indicated on the table*

Apparently, in extracting the specialized accounting principles from the AICPA Guide, the FASB concluded that the method promulgated in FASB-66 either (a) is a better method than that in the Guide or (b) produces the same results as the method described in the AICPA Guide.

Even if the required minimum initial investment is made by the buyer, a separate assessment must be made to determine the collectibility of the receivable. In other words, there must be reasonable assurance that the receivable will be collected after the minimum initial investment is received by the seller, and if not, the sale should not be recorded by the full accrual method. The minimum initial investment must be made by the buyer, and the seller must be reasonably assured that the balance of the sales price will be collected before the real estate sale is recorded and any profits are recognized. The assessment of the receivable by the seller should include credit reports on the buyer and an evaluation of the adequacy of the cash flow from the property.

In addition to an adequate initial investment, FASB-66 also requires that the buyer maintain a continuing investment in the property by increasing his investment each year. The buyer's total indebtedness for the purchase price of the property must be reduced each year in equal amounts which will extinguish the entire indebtedness (interest and principal) over a specified maximum period. The specified maximum period for land transactions is twenty (20) years. The specified maximum period for all other real estate transactions is no more than that offered at the time of sale for first mortgages by independent financial institutions.

The buyer's commitment to pay the full amount of his indebtedness to the seller becomes doubtful if the total indebtedness is not to be paid within the specified maximum period.

A buyer's payments on his indebtedness must be in cash or cash equivalency. Funds provided directly or indirectly by the seller cannot be used in determining the buyer's continuing investment in the property.

Release Provisions

Real estate agreements involving land frequently provide for the periodic release of part of the land to the buyer. The buyer obtains the released land free of any liens. The conditions for the release usually require that sufficient funds have previously been paid by the buyer to cover the sales price of the released land and often an additional sum is required to effectuate the release. In these types of transactions involving released land, the requirements for a buyer's initial and continuing investment must be determined on the basis of the *sales value* of property not released or not subject to release. In other words, for a seller to recognize profit at the time of sale, a buyer's investment must be enough to pay any amounts for the release of land and still meet the specified initial and continued investment required by the provisions of FASB-66. If the buyer's initial and continuing investment is not sufficient, then each release of land should be treated as a separate sale and profit recognized at that time.

Future Subordination

If, at the time of sale, a seller's receivable is subject to future subordination, other than (a) to a primary lien on the property existing at the date of sale or (b) to a future loan, or existing permanent loan commitment, the proceeds of which must first be applied to the payment of the seller's receivable, no profit should be recognized because the effect of future subordination on the collectibility of a receivable cannot be reasonably evaluated. The cost recovery method should be used to recognize profit at the time of sale if the seller's receivable is subject to future subordination, other than the two exceptions noted above.

Nontransfer of Ownership and Seller's Continued Involvement

Real estate transactions must be carefully analyzed to determine their economic substance. Frequently, the economic substance of a real estate sale is no more than a management fee arrangement or an indication that the risks and benefits of ownership have not really been transferred in the agreement. Therefore, accounting for a real estate transaction can become quite complicated because of the many types of continuing relations that can exist between a buyer and a seller. The substance of the real estate transaction should dictate the accounting method which should be used.

As a general rule, before a profit may be recognized, a sale must occur, collectibility of the receivable must be reasonably assured, and the seller must perform all of the acts required by the contract to earn the revenue. Profit may also be recognized, at the time of the sale, on contracts which provide for the continued involvement of the seller if the maximum potential loss of the seller is expressly limited and defined by the terms of the contract. In this event, the total profit on the sale, less the maximum potential loss which could occur because of the seller's involvement, is recognized at the time of the sale.

The two most important factors in evaluating the economic substance of a real estate sale are (1) the transfer of the usual risks and rewards of ownership in the property and (2) the full performance by the seller of all acts required by the contract to earn the revenue. Generally, both of these factors must be accomplished before full profit may be recognized on the sale of real estate. The more common types of real estate transactions and how they should be accounted for are discussed in the following paragraphs.

Profit Recognition Other Than Full Accrual Basis

As mentioned previously, in order for a seller to report the total profit on a sale of real estate by the full accrual method of accounting, FASB-66 requires that all of the following criteria be met:

1. A sale is consummated.
2. The initial and continuing payments (investment) made by the buyer must be adequate.
3. The seller's receivable shall not be subject to future subordination, except to (a) a primary lien on the property existing at the date of sale, or (b) a future loan, or existing permanent loan commitment of which the proceeds must first be applied to the payment of the seller's receivable.
4. All of the benefits and risks of ownership in the property must be substantially transferred to the buyer by the seller.
5. The seller must not have a substantial continued involvement with the property after the date of sale.

If a sale of real estate, other than a retail land sale, meets all of the above criteria, the seller must recognize the entire profit on the sale in accordance with the full accrual basis of accounting.

When one or more of the above criteria is not met in a real estate sale, an alternative method of recognizing revenue from the sale must be used. The alternative method selected may be required by FASB-66 or may be a matter of professional judgment. The four accounting methods recommended by FASB-66 are (a) the deposit method, (b) the cost recovery method, (c) the installment sales method, and (d) the reduced profit method.

Deposit accounting The uncertainty about the collectibility of the sales price in a real estate transaction may be so great that the effective date of the sale should be deferred and any cash received by the seller should be accounted for as a deposit. However, cash received that is designated by contract as nonrefundable interest may be applied as an offset to existing carrying charges on the property, such as property taxes and interest, instead of being accounted for as a deposit.

All cash received except that appropriately used as an offset to the carrying charges of the property must be reflected in the seller's balance sheet as a liability (deposit on a contract for the sale of real estate). No change is made in accounting for the property subject to the contract and its related mortgage debt, if any. However, the seller's financial statements should disclose that these items are subject to a sales contract. Depreciation expense should continue as a period cost, in spite of the fact that the property has been legally sold. Until the requirements of FASB-66 are met for profit recognition, the seller does not report a sale and continues to report all cash received either as a deposit or in the case of nonrefundable interest, as an offset to the carrying charges of the property involved. In the event that the buyer forfeits a nonrefundable deposit, or defaults on the contract, the seller should reduce the deposit account appropriately and include such amounts in income of the period.

Cost recovery method If a seller's receivable is subject to subordination which cannot be reasonably evaluated, or uncertainty exists as to the recovery of the seller's cost on default by the buyer, the cost recovery method should be used. Even if cost has been recovered by the seller but additional collections are highly doubtful, the cost recovery method would be appropriate. Frequently, the cost recovery method is initially used for transactions which would also qualify for the installment sales method.

> **OBSERVATION:** *The cost recovery and installment sales methods both defer the recognition of profit on the sale until collections are actually received.*

Under the cost recovery method, all collections are applied first to the recovery of the cost of the property, and only after full cost has been received is any profit recognized. The only expenses remaining to be charged against the profit are those relating to the collection process. When the cost recovery method is used, the total sales value is included in the income statement for the period in which the sale is made. From the total sales value in the income statement, the total cost of the sale and the deferred gross profit on the sale are deducted. On the balance sheet the deferred gross profit is reflected as a reduction of the related receivable. Until full cost is recovered, principal payments received are applied to reduce the related receivable and interest payments received are added to the deferred gross profit. At any given time, the related receivable less the deferred gross profit equals the remaining cost which must be recovered. After all cost is recovered, subsequent collections reduce the deferred gross profit and appear as a separate item of revenue on the income statement.

Installment sales method   Promulgated GAAP prohibit accounting for sales by any form of installment accounting except under exceptional circumstances where collectibility cannot be reasonably estimated or assured. The doubtfulness of collectibility can be caused by the length of an extended collection period or because no basis of estimation can be established. In such cases a company can use either the cost recovery method or the installment sales method of accounting (APB-10).

The installment sales method is frequently more appropriate for real estate transactions in which collectibility of the receivable from the buyer cannot be reasonably assured because defaults on loans secured by real estate usually result in the recovery of the property sold.

Under the installment sales method of accounting, each payment collected consists of part recovery of cost and part recovery of gross profit, in the same ratio that these two elements existed in the original sale. In a real estate transaction, the original sale is equal to the *sales value* of the property. Thus, under the installment sales method, profit is recognized on cash payments made by the buyer to the holder of the primary debt assumed, and cash payments to the seller. The profit recognized on the cash payments is based on the percentage of total profit to total *sales value*.

Jones Company sells real property to Smith for $2,000,000. Smith will assume an existing $1,200,000 first mortgage and pay $300,000 in cash as a down payment. The balance of $500,000 will be in the form of a 12% second mortgage to Jones Company payable in equal payments of principal and interest over a ten-year period. The cost of the property to Jones is $1,200,000.

Real Estate—Recognition of Sales

Computation of Sales Value and Gross Profit

Cash	$ 300,000
Second mortgage	500,000
First mortgage	1,200,000
Total Sales Value (which happens to be the same as the stated sales price)	$2,000,000
Less: Cost of property sold	1,200,000
Total gross profit on sale	$ 800,000
Gross profit percentage	40.0%
Profit to be recognized on down payment (40% of $300,000)	$ 120,000

Assuming that the $300,000 down payment is insufficient to meet the requirements of full profit recognition on the sale (accrual basis of accounting), Jones would recognize $120,000 gross profit at the time of sale. Assume that several months later Smith makes a cash payment of $100,000 on the first mortgage and $50,000 on the second mortgage. The amount of gross profit which Jones would recognize on these payments would be as follows:

Payment of first mortgage	$100,000
Payment of second mortgage	50,000
Total cash payments	$150,000
Gross profit realized (40% of $150,000)	$ 60,000

The point is that even though Jones does not receive any cash on the payment of the first mortgage by Smith, gross profit is still realized because the gross profit percentage was based on the total *sales value* which included the first mortgage liability.

When the installment sales method is used, the total sales value is included in the income statement of the period in which the sale is made. From the total sales value in the income statement, the total cost of the sale and the deferred gross profit are deducted. On the balance sheet the deferred gross profit on the sale is deducted from the related receivable. As cash payments are received, the portion allocated to realized gross profit is presented as a separate item of revenue on the income statement and deferred gross profit is reduced by the same amount. At any given time, the related receivable less the deferred gross profit represents the remaining cost of the property sold. Since realized gross profit is recognized as a portion of each cash collection, a percentage relationship will always exist between the long-term receivable and its related deferred gross profit. This percentage relationship will be the same as the gross profit ratio on the initial sales value.

Reduced profit method   The buyer's receivable is discounted to the present value of the lowest level of annual payments required by the sales contract. The discount period is the maximum allowed under the provisions of FASB-66, and all lump sum payments are excluded in the calculation. The discount rate cannot be less than that stated in the sales contract, if any, or the prevailing interest rate in accordance with existing GAAP (APB-21). The buyer's receivable discounted as described above is used in determining the profit on the sale of real estate and usually results in a "reduced profit" from that which would be obtained under normal accounting procedures. Lump sum and other payments are recognized as profit when they are received by the seller.

Change to full accrual method   After the cost recovery or installment sales method is adopted for a real estate transaction, a periodic evaluation should be made of the collectibility of the receivable. When it becomes apparent that the seller's receivable is reasonably assured of being collected, a change to the full accrual accounting method should be made by the seller. The change is not a change in an accounting principle (Statement of Position 78-4). When the change to the full accrual accounting method is made, any remaining deferred gross profit is recognized in full in the period in which the change is made. If the change creates a material effect on the seller's financial statements, full disclosure of the effects and the reason for the change should be appropriately made in the financial statements or footnotes thereto (Statement of Position 78-4).

Profit Recognition When Sale Is Not Consummated

If a real estate sale has not been consummated in accordance with the provisions of FASB-66, the deposit method of accounting shall be used until the sale is consummated.

As mentioned previously, an exception to the "consummation rule" occurs if the terms of the contract require the seller to sell a parcel of land and also construct on the same parcel a building which takes an extended period to complete. In other words, the seller is still involved with the property after the sale because he must construct the building. In most jurisdictions a "certificate of occupancy" must be obtained for a building or other structure. The certificate of occupancy indicates that the building has been constructed in accordance with the local building regulations and is ready for occupancy. Thus, a certificate of occupancy is usually necessary to consummate the real estate transaction. However, FASB-66 contains a special provision for profit recognition when a sale of real estate requires the seller to develop the property in the future. If the seller has contracted (a) for future development of the land, (b) to construct buildings, amenities, or other facilities on the land, or (c) to provide offsite improvements, partial recognition of profit may be recognized if future costs of development can be reasonably estimated at the time of sale. In this event, profit can be recognized for any work performed and finished by the seller when (a) the sale of the land is consummated and (b) the initial and continuing investments of the buyer are adequate. In other words, if the sale of the land meets the first two criteria for the use of the full accrual method of accounting, any profit allocable to (a) the work performed prior to the sale of the land and (b) the sale of the land can be recognized by the percentage-of-completion method. Thus, the total profit on the sale may be allocated to work performed prior to the sale of the land and to future construction and development work. The allocation of the total profit is based on the estimated costs for each activity using a uniform rate of gross profit for all activities. However, if significant uncertainties exist or costs and profits cannot be reasonably estimated, the completed contract method should be used.

If a buyer has the right to defer until completion payments due for developmental and construction work, or if the buyer is financially unable to pay these amounts as they come due, care should be exercised in recognizing any profits until completion or satisfactory payment.

The terms of a real estate transaction accounted for by the deposit method may indicate that the carrying amount of the property involved is more than the sales value in the contract and that a loss has been incurred. Since the seller is using the deposit method, no sale is recorded and thus no loss. However, the information indicates an impairment of an asset which should be appropriately recorded by the seller in the period of discovery by a charge to income and the creation of a valuation allowance account for the property involved.

Profit Recognition When Buyer's Investment Is Inadequate

If all of the criteria for the full accrual method of accounting are met except that the buyer's initial investment is inadequate, the seller shall account for the sale by the installment sales method, provided that the seller is reasonably assured of recovering the cost of the property if the buyer defaults. If the seller is not reasonably assured of recovering the cost of the property upon default by the buyer, or if cost recovery has been made but future collections are uncertain, the cost recovery method or the deposit method shall be used by the seller to account for the sale.

If all of the criteria for the full accrual method of accounting are met, except that the buyer's continuing investment is inadequate, the seller shall account for the sale by the reduced profit method, provided that the buyer's periodic payments cover both of the following items:

1. Amortization of principal and interest based on the maximum primary mortgage that could be obtained on the property.
2. Interest, at an appropriate rate, on the excess amount, if any, of the total actual debt on the property over the maximum primary mortgage that could be obtained on the property.

If both of the above conditions are not met, the reduced profit method shall not be used by the seller. In this event, the seller should account for the sale either by the installment sales method or the cost recovery method, whichever is more appropriate under the specific circumstances.

Profit Recognition—Subordinated Receivable

As mentioned previously, the cost recovery method shall be used to recognize profit at the time of sale if the seller's receivable is subject to future subordination, except in the following situations:

1. Subordinated to a primary lien on the property existing at the date of sale.
2. Subordinated to a future loan, or existing permanent loan commitment, the proceeds of which must first be applied to the payment of the seller's receivable.

Profit Recognition—Seller's Continued Involvement

In some real estate transactions the seller does not transfer the benefits and risks of ownership to the buyer, or the seller maintains a substantial continued involvement with the property after the date of sale. These types of real estate transactions require careful examination to determine the appropriate method of accounting that should be applied.

In legal form a real estate transaction may be a sale, but in substance the contract may be a profit-sharing, financing, or leasing arrangement. If in substance the transaction is a profit-sharing, financing, or leasing arrangement, no sale or profit is recognized. If a real estate contract contains any of the following provisions, it should be accounted for as a profit-sharing, financing, or leasing arrangement:

1. The return of the buyer's investment in the property is guaranteed by the seller.
2. The buyer can compel the seller to repurchase the property.
3. An option or obligation exists for the seller to repurchase the property.
4. The seller is required to operate the property at its own risk for an extended period.
5. The seller, as general partner, holds a receivable from the limited partnership as a result of a real estate sale. The collection of the receivable depends on the successful operation of the limited partnership by the general partner who is also the seller and holder of the receivable.
6. A specific return on the buyer's investment is guaranteed by the seller for an extended period of time.

In real estate transactions in which the seller guarantees for a limited period (a) to return the buyer's investment or (b) a specific rate of return to the buyer, the seller shall account for the sale by the deposit method of accounting. After the operations of the property become profitable, the seller may recognize profit on the basis of performance. After the limited period has expired and all of the criteria for the full accrual method of accounting are met in accordance with FASB-66, the seller may recognize in full any remaining profit on the sale of real estate.

Initiating and supporting operations As part of a real estate transaction, the seller may be required to initiate or support the operations of the property for a stated period of time or until a certain level of operations has been achieved. In other words, the seller may agree to operate the property for a certain period or until a certain level of rental income has been reached.

Even if there is no agreement, there is a presumption that a seller has an obligation to initiate and support operations of the property he has sold in any of the following circumstances:

1. An interest in property is sold by the seller to a limited partnership in which he is a general partner.
2. An equity interest in the property sold is retained by the seller.
3. There is a management contract between the buyer and seller which provides for compensation that is significantly higher or lower than comparable prevailing rates and which cannot be terminated by either the buyer or the seller.
4. The collection of the receivable from the sale held by the seller is dependent on the operations of the property and represents a significant portion of the sales price. A significant receivable is defined as one in excess of 15% of the maximum primary financing that could have been obtained from an established lending institution.

If the seller has agreed to the initiating and supporting operations for a limited period, the seller may recognize profit on the sale on the basis of the performance of the required services. The measurement of performance shall be related to the cost incurred to date, and the total estimated costs to be incurred for the services. However, profit recognition may not start until there is reasonable assurance that estimated future rent receipts will cover (a) all operating costs, (b) debt service, and (c) any payments due the seller under the terms of the contract. For this purpose, the estimated future rent receipts shall not exceed the greater of (a) leases actually executed or (b) two thirds of the estimated future rent receipts. The difference between the estimated future rent receipts and the greater of (a) the signed leases or (b) two thirds of the estimated rent receipts shall be reserved as a safety factor.

In the event the sales contract does not specify the period for which the seller must initiate and support operations of the property, a two-year period shall be presumed. The two-year period shall commence at the time of initial rental, unless rent receipts cover all operating cost, debt service, and other commitments before the time of initial rental.

Services without compensation As part of the contract for the sale of real estate, the seller may be required to perform services related to the property sold without compensation or at a reduced rate. In determining profit to be recognized at the time of sale, a value should be placed on such services at the prevailing rates and deducted from the sales price of the property sold. The value of the compensation should then be recognized over the period in which the services are to be performed by the seller.

Sale of real estate options Proceeds from the sale of real estate options shall be accounted for by the deposit method. If the option is not exercised by its expiration date, the seller of the option shall recognize profit at that time. If an option is sold by the owner of the land and subsequently exercised, the proceeds from the sale of the option are included in determining the *sales value* of the property sold.

Sales of partial interests in property A seller may continue to be involved in property sold by retaining an interest in the property and by giving the buyer preference as to profits, cash flow, return on investment, or some other similar arrangement. In this event, if the transaction is in substance a sale, the seller shall recognize profit to the extent that the sale proceeds, including receivables, exceed the seller's total cost in the property.

A seller may retain a partial interest in the property sold, such as an undivided interest or some other form of equity. If a seller sells a partial interest in real estate property and the sale meets all of the criteria for the full accrual method, except for the seller's continued involvement related to the partial interest in the property, the seller shall recognize the proportionate share of the profit that is attributable to the outside interests in the property. However, if the seller controls the buyer, profit on the sale shall not be recognized until realized from transactions with outside individuals, or through the sale of the property to outside parties.

A seller may sell single-family units or time-sharing interests in a condominium project. If the units or interests are sold individually, the seller shall recognize profit on the sales by the percentage-of-completion method, provided that all of the following conditions are met:

1. Construction has progressed beyond the preliminary stage, which means that the engineering and design work, execution of construction contracts, site clearance and preparation, and excavation or completion of the building foundation have all been completed.

2. The buyer cannot obtain a refund, except for nondelivery.
3. The property will not revert to rental property as evidenced by the number of units or interests that have been sold. In determining the sufficiency of the number of units or interests sold, reference shall be made to local and state laws, the provisions of the condominium or time-sharing contract, and the terms of the financing agreements.
4. Total sales and costs can be reasonably estimated in accordance with the percentage-of-completion method of accounting.

Until all of the above conditions are met, the seller shall account for the sales proceeds from the single-family units or time-sharing interests by the deposit method of accounting.

Disclosures FASB-66 does not contain any specific disclosure requirements for the sale of real estate, other than retail land sales. However, professional judgment may require that a significant sale of real estate be appropriately disclosed in the financial statements.

If interest is imputed on a receivable arising out of a real estate sale, certain disclosures are required by APB-21 (Interest on Receivables and Payables). In addition, if commitments or contingencies arise in a real estate sale, disclosure may be required by FASB-5 (Contingencies).

RETAIL LAND SALES

Profit Recognition

FASB-66 requires that profit on all retail land sales within a project shall be recognized by a single accounting method. As conditions change for the entire project, the method of profit recognition shall change in accordance with the provisions of FASB-66. The provisions of FASB-66 require that the profits on a retail land sales project be recognized either (a) by the full accrual method, (b) by the percentage-of-completion method, (c) by the installment sales method, or (d) by the deposit method. FASB-66 contains specific criteria which must be met before a particular profit recognition method can be used.

A retail land sales project is defined as "a homogeneous, reasonably contiguous area of land that may, for development or marketing, be subdivided in accordance with a master plan."

Profit Recognition—Full Accrual Method

All of the following conditions must be met for the entire retail land sales project before the full accrual method of accounting can be used for the recognition of profit on retail land sales:

1. The down payment and all subsequent payments have been made by the buyer, through and including any period of cancellation, and all periods for any refund have expired.
2. The buyer has paid a total of 10% or more in principal or interest of the total contract sales price.
3. The seller's collection experience for the project or prior projects indicates that 90% of the receivables in force for six months after the sale is recorded will be collected in full. A down payment of 20% or more is an acceptable substitute for this experience test.

   > **OBSERVATION:** *Profit may be recognized before the end of six months if collection experience is based on a prior project. The six-month period is an eligibility test for the full accrual method of accounting.*

   The collection experience of a prior project may be used if (a) the prior project was similar in characteristics to the new project and (b) the collection period was long enough to determine collectibility of receivables to maturity dates.
4. The seller's receivable for the property sold is not subject to subordination of new loans. However, subordination is allowed for construction of a residence providing the project's collection experience for such subordinated receivables is approximately the same as that for those receivables which are not subordinated.
5. The seller is not obligated to construct amenities or other facilities, or complete any improvements for lots which have been sold.

If all of the above conditions are met for the entire retail land sales project, the seller shall recognize profits by the full accrual method of accounting.

The actual procedures that must be used to record retail land sales under the full accrual method of accounting are as follows:

1. The total contract price of the retail land sale, before any deductions, is recorded as a gross sale. The total contract price includes the total amount of principal and interest which is expected to be received from the sale.
2. The down payment on the sale is recorded. The difference between the total contract price of the retail land sale and the down payment is the gross receivable.
3. The gross receivable is discounted at the date of sale to yield an amount at which it could be sold on a volume basis without recourse to the seller. The discount on the gross receivable is referred to as a "valuation discount."
4. The valuation discount is amortized to income over the life of the retail land sales contract. The interest method should be used to produce a constant rate of amortization.
5. An allowance for contract cancellations is established based on estimates of contracts that are not expected to be collected in subsequent periods. Cancelled contracts are charged directly to the allowance account.

    For the purpose of determining the adequacy of the allowance for contract cancellations in subsequent periods, all receivables which do not conform to the criteria in the following table shall be considered uncollectible and the allowance account shall be appropriately adjusted:

Percent of contract price paid	Delinquency period
Less than 25%	90 days
25% but less than 50%	120 days
50% and over	150 days

    If a buyer is willing to assume personal liability for his debt and apparently has the means and ability to complete all payments, the delinquency periods in the above table may be extended.
6. The following items represent deductions from the gross sale to arrive at net sales for the period:
    a. Valuation discount
    b. Allowance for contract cancellations
    c. Deferred portion of gross sale (to be matched with future work or performance of the seller)
7. Cost of sales should be computed on net sales for the period.
8. A sale which is made and cancelled in the same reporting

period should be included in and also deducted from gross sales or appropriately disclosed in some other manner.
9. The unamortized valuation discount (discount on receivables) and the allowance for contract cancellations are shown on the balance sheet as deductions from the related receivables.
10. Deferred revenue, less any related costs, is shown on the balance sheet as a liability. Deferred revenue should be recognized in future periods as the work is performed by the seller.

Profit Recognition—Percentage-of-Completion Method

If the first four criteria for applying the full accrual method of accounting are met for the entire retail land sales project and the fifth criterion is not met, the seller shall recognize profits by the percentage-of-completion method of accounting, provided that the following additional criteria are met for the entire project:

1. Progress on the entire project has passed the preliminary stages and tangible evidence exists to indicate that the project will be completed according to plans. Tangible evidence of such progress includes the following:
   a. Expenditure of funds has actually been made.
   b. Work on project improvements has been initiated.
   c. Engineering plans and construction commitments pertaining to lots that have been sold are in existence.
   d. There has been substantial completion of access roads and amenities.
   e. There is no evidence of any significant delay to the project and dependable estimates of costs to complete the project and extent of progress are reasonable.
2. At the end of the normal payment period it is reasonably expected that the property will clearly be useful for its intended purposes as represented by the seller at the time of sale.

If the above criteria are met for the entire project and the first four criteria for applying the full accrual method of accounting are met for the entire project, the seller shall recognize profits on retail land sales by the percentage-of-completion method.

Profit Recognition—Installment Sales Method

If the first two criteria for applying the full accrual method of accounting are met for the entire project and the other three criteria are not met, the seller shall recognize profits by the installment sales method, provided that the following additional criteria are met for the entire project:

1. The current and prospective financial capabilities of the retail land sales company (seller) must reflect with reasonable assurance that the company is capable of completing all of its obligations under the sales contract and master plan.
2. Indications of the seller's financial capabilities include (a) the sufficiency of equity capital, (b) borrowing capacity, and (c) positive cash flow from present operations.

If the above criteria are met for the entire project and the first two criteria for applying the full accrual method of accounting are met for the entire project, the seller shall recognize profits on retail land sales by the installment sales method.

Profit Recognition—Deposit Accounting Method

If the criteria for the full accrual method, percentage-of-completion method, or installment sales method are not met, the seller shall account for all proceeds from retail land sales by the deposit method of accounting. Under the deposit method of accounting, the effective date of the sale is deferred and all funds received, including principal and interest, are recorded as deposits on retail land sales.

Change in Accounting Method

If a retail land sales entity has been reporting sales for the entire project by the deposit method and subsequently the criteria for the installment sales method, percentage-of-completion method, or the full accrual method are met for the entire project, the change to the new method shall be accounted for as a change in accounting estimate. Thus, the effects of the change shall be accounted for prospectively in accordance with APB-20 (Accounting Changes). If the effects of the change in an accounting estimate are significant, disclosure of the effects on (a) income before extraordinary items, (b) net income, and (c) the related per share data should be made in the financial statements of the period of change.

Retail land sales may initially be accounted for by the installment sales method and subsequently the criteria for the percentage-of-completion method may be met for the entire project. In this event, the percentage-of-completion method may be adopted for the entire project. The effects of the change to the percentage-of-completion method are accounted for as a change in accounting estimate and, if material, disclosure of the effects on (a) income before extraordinary items, (b) net income, and (c) related per share data should be made in the financial statements of the period of change.

In reporting the change from the installment sales method to the percentage-of-completion method, the following procedures should be observed:

1. If required, the receivables should be discounted to their present values at the date of change in accordance with APB-21.
2. The liability for the remaining future performance of the seller should be discounted to its present value at the date of the change.
3. The amount of discount, if any, on the receivables and the amount of discount, if any, on the liability for remaining future performance by the seller are deducted from the unrealized gross profit on installment sales at the date of the change to arrive at the net credit to income resulting from the change.

Disclosure—Retail Land Sales

Retail land sales companies, diversified entities with significant retail land sales operations, and investors who derive a significant portion of their income from investments involved in retail land sales must comply with specific financial statement disclosures, as follows:

1. The maturities of the receivables from retail land sales for each of the five years following the date of the financial statements.
2. The amount of delinquent receivables and the method used to determine delinquency.
3. The weighted average and range of stated interest rates on receivables from retail land sales.
4. Estimated total costs and anticipated expenditures to improve major areas of the project from which sales are being made, for each of the five years following the date of the financial statements.

5. The amount of recorded obligations for improvements.

> **OBSERVATION:** Although FASB-66 is silent on the subject, the AICPA industry accounting guide entitled "Accounting for Retail Land Sales" contains a discussion on the statement of changes in financial position for retail land sales companies.
> The financial statements of a retail land sales company typically reflect (1) long-term receivables, (2) deferred revenue, and (3) deferral of income recognition. Because of these factors, a statement of changes in financial position based on working capital may be misleading. Therefore, the preferable accounting principles in the Retail Land Sales Guide consider a statement of changes in financial position which reflects sources and uses of cash more meaningful and thus, preferable. The statement of changes in financial position based on sources and uses of cash should be provided for all periods presented whenever earnings information is reported.
> If a statement of changes in financial position is presented on a working capital basis, then only long-term receivables maturing within one year and expenditures expected to be expended within one year for improvements and accrued commissions should be included in working capital.

Amendments to Existing GAAP

The references to the following AICPA publications in FASB-32 (Specialized Accounting and Reporting Principles and Practices in AICPA Statements of Position and Guides on Accounting and Auditing Matters) are deleted from Appendix A:

- Accounting for Profit Recognition on Sales of Real Estate (An Industry Accounting Guide)
- Accounting for Retail Land Sales (An Industry Accounting Guide)
- Questions Concerning Profit Recognition on Sales of Real Estate (Statement of Position 75-6)
- Application of the Deposit, Installment, and Cost Recovery Methods in Accounting for Sales of Real Estate (Statement of Position 78-4)

In addition, the references to the Industry Accounting Guide entitled "Accounting for Profit Recognition on Sales of Real Estate" in a footnote to FASB-26 (Profit Recognition of Sales-Type Leases of Real Estate), and in paragraphs 23-25 of FASB-28 (Accounting for Sales with Leasebacks), are changed to refer to FASB-66 (Accounting for Sales of Real Estate).

Effective Date

FASB-66 is effective for all real estate sales transactions entered into and for all accounting changes that result from such transactions, on or after January 1, 1983. Financial statements for accounting periods ending on or after December 16, 1982, must contain the disclosures required by FASB-66 for retail land sales. Earlier application of the provisions of FASB-66 is not required but is encouraged.

Regulated Industries

REGULATED INDUSTRIES

Overview

FASB-71 establishes new promulgated GAAP for an enterprise that is regulated by a regulator who approves and/or regulates the rates that an enterprise can charge to its customers for its services or products. For the purposes of FASB-71, a regulator may be an independent third party, or may be a governing board of the regulated enterprise that has been empowered by statute or contract. FASB-71 supersedes the Addendum to APB-2 (Accounting Principles for Regulated Industries), and amends APB-30 (Reporting the Results of Operations).

> **OBSERVATION:** In order to provide the accounting profession with adequate information, amendments to existing GAAP should appear in a visable location. One would be hard pressed to locate the amendment to APB-30 which appears in paragraph 108 of FASB-71.
>
> FASB-71 amends APB-30 to provide that utility refunds to customers be disclosed net of their tax effects, as a separate line item in the income statement. APB-30 generally prohibits net-of-tax disclosure of unusual or infrequently occurring items that do not qualify as extraordinary items.

FASB-71 does not change the fact that companies in regulated industries must comply with all existing and future authoritative accounting pronouncements. However, if a conflict arises between an authoritative accounting pronouncement and FASB-71, a regulated enterprise shall apply the provisions of FASB-71 instead of the conflicting pronouncement. The following conditions govern the application of FASB-71:

1. FASB-71 applies only to financial statements issued for external general purposes. Thus, FASB-71 does not apply to financial statements submitted to a regulatory agency.

   > **OBSERVATION:** FASB-71 is silent as to whether its provisions apply to financial statements for other than annual periods. Thus, it is unclear whether or not FASB-71 must be applied to interim financial statements.

2. FASB-71 shall be applied only to regulated enterprises or those portions of the operations of a regulated enterprise which meet the specific criteria established by FASB-71.
3. FASB-71 does not apply to emergency governmental actions that are imposed under unusual circumstances, such as price controls during periods of high inflation.

Background

Over the years, regulatory agencies have been established by governmental authorities to regulate certain industries that provide essential services to the general public, such as public utilities, railroads, insurance companies, airlines, and so forth. One of the primary functions of most regulatory agencies is to establish the rates that the regulated enterprise can charge its customers for its services or products. In connection with their regulatory authority, most agencies prescribe the types of accounting records and reports that the regulated enterprise must maintain. Frequently, the accounting rules prescribed by these regulatory agencies conflict with GAAP.

The Addendum to APB-2 (Accounting Principles for Regulated Industries) required that financial statements of a regulated business intended for public use should be based on existing GAAP, with appropriate recognition given to the rate-making process established by the regulatory agency. Under GAAS, an independent auditor must comply with the first standard of reporting, which requires that financial statements be presented in accordance with GAAP.

Many different methods are used by regulatory agencies to set rates for regulated enterprises. However, the many different methods can be classified into (a) individual cost-of-service, (b) group rate-setting, and (c) a combination of both individual cost-of-service and group rate-setting.

Under the individual cost-of-service method of rate setting, the "allowable costs" that an enterprise is usually permitted to recover are all actual and/or estimated costs that are required to provide the service to the public, including a return on investment to compensate sources of long-term debt and equity capital. The rate or rates charged to different classes of customers are designed, but not guaranteed, to produce total revenue for the enterprise equal to the allowable costs. The individual cost-of-service method is usually used in setting rates for public utilities. An enterprise is more assured of cost recovery under the individual cost-of-service method than any other method.

Under the group rate-setting method, the allowable costs that an enterprise may recover are based on rates established on an industrywide, areawide, or some other aggregate basis. Group rate-setting is usually utilized in more competitive industries than those in which the individual cost-of-service method is used, such as airlines, motor carriers, railroads, insurance companies.

Under the combination of individual cost-of-service and group rate-setting methods, the allowable costs that an enterprise can recover are based on some combination of both methods. However, under the combination method, allowable costs do not usually include a provision for a return on investment, but may include an allowance for inflation or working capital.

Through the regulatory process, an enterprise is substantially assured of recovering its allowable costs by the collection of revenue from its customers. It is important to bear in mind that under some methods of rate-setting, allowable costs include a return on investment for the regulated enterprise. The economic effect of regulation is the substantiation that an asset exists or does not exist. Thus, as allowable costs are incurred by a regulated enterprise they should be capitalized as assets. On the other hand, costs that are not allowable under the regulatory process are not substantially assured of being recovered and should be expensed as incurred.

FASB-71 contains the criteria that an enterprise must meet to be classified as a "regulated enterprise" and also establishes the promulgated GAAP for the capitalization of allowable costs.

Criteria for Regulated Operations

FASB-71 applies to financial statements that are issued for general purposes by an enterprise which has regulated operations and meets all of the following criteria:

1. An independent third party regulator or a governing board of the regulated enterprise that has been empowered by statute or contract establishes or approves the rates the enterprise can charge its customers for its services or products.
2. The established or approved rates of the independent third party regulator or governing board of the regulated enterprise are intended to recover the specific costs of the regulated services or products.
3. The rates set by the independent third party regulator or governing board of the regulated enterprise to recover the costs of the regulated enterprise are reasonable and likely to be col-

lected. In applying this criterion, consideration must be given to the demand for the services or products and the level of direct and indirect competition.

The thrust of FASB-71 is that the regulatory process can provide a basis for the regulated enterprise to recognize a specific asset. In this respect, FASB-71 requires that the following conditions be met for a regulated enterprise to recognize an incurred cost as a specific asset:

1. It must be clear that the regulator's intent is to provide recovery of a specific incurred cost.
2. On the basis of available evidence, it is expected that the regulated rates will produce revenue about equal to the specific incurred cost.

Thus, first an enterprise must qualify as a regulated enterprise by meeting the specified criteria of FASB-71, and then both of the above conditions must be met before an incurred cost can be capitalized as an asset.

FASB-71 does not identify any specific industry as "regulated." Instead, the focus of FASB-71 is on the nature of regulation and its resulting financial effects on a specific enterprise. Thus, any enterprise in any industry which meets all of the criteria of FASB-71 must comply with its provisions.

The essence of the first criterion in FASB-71 is the existence of a regulator that can approve and/or regulate the rates that the enterprise can charge its customers for its services or products. The regulator may be an independent third party or a governing board of the enterprise empowered by statute or contract to approve and/or regulate the rates that the enterprise can charge its customers for its services or products. A contractual arrangement between an enterprise and its sole or principal customer may create the appearance of "regulation." However, the sole or principal customer of the enterprise is also responsible for payment of the services or products and thus is not, in a strict sense, an independent third party regulator or governing board empowered by statute or contract. Therefore, Medicare, Medicaid, and similar contractual arrangements are excluded from the scope of FASB-71.

The principal economic effect of the regulatory process covered by FASB-71 is that it can provide substantiation that an asset does or does not exist at the time a regulated enterprise incurs costs to provide services or products.

OBSERVATION: *FASB-71 reaches this conclusion by reasoning that the essence of an asset is its potential for future economic benefit. Some Financial Accounting Standards Board members disagree with the notion that regulatory action can create an asset.*

Under the provisions of FASB-71 the regulated rates must be designed to recover the specific costs of the regulated services or products. This is usually best accomplished by the individual cost-of-service method of rate-setting. Thus, the second criterion of FASB-71 requires that there be a cause-and-effect relationship between costs and revenues. A cause-and-effect relationship does not usually exist if regulated rates are based on industrywide costs. However, the cause-and-effect relationship is intended to be applied to the substance of the regulation and not the form of the regulation. Thus, if regulated rates are based on the costs of a particular group of companies and there is a dominant company within the group, the costs of the dominant company may represent the costs of the entire group. In this event, the second criterion of FASB-71 would be met.

The third criterion of FASB-71 requires that the regulated rates which are sufficient to recover incurred costs are reasonable to the ultimate consumer and likely to be collected.

If the regulatory process is based on the recovery of future costs and not on specific incurred costs, the provisions of FASB-71 are not met. If a "rate order" authorizing regulated rates for an enterprise does not clearly specify the recovery of specific incurred costs, the provisions of FASB-71 are not met. In other words, the rate order must clearly indicate the specific incurred costs that are designated for recovery. These specific incurred costs that are designated for recovery are referred to as allowable costs.

Sometimes the nature of an incurred cost, such as the abandonment of part or all of a particular facility, cannot be anticipated by the regulated enterprise or the regulator. Under these circumstances, the intent of the regulator may be inferred based on available evidence, and, as a result, it may be probable that the future rate increases will be provided by the regulator for the specific recovery of the unanticipated future cost.

On the other hand, the regulatory process may indicate the reduction or elimination of an existing asset or substantiate the existence of a new liability. If a cost or related asset is not classified as an allowable cost by the regulator, it will not produce future revenue through the regulatory process. In this event, the cost or related asset must be accounted for under existing GAAP which are applied to other enterprises in general.

OBSERVATION: *If the regulatory process can create an asset, it appears that deregulation may result in the permanent impairment of an asset that owes its existence to regulation. This conclusion is consistent with FASB-44 (Accounting for Intangible Assets of Motor Carriers).*

A regulated enterprise may be required by the regulator to refund revenue that was collected in prior periods; or the regulator may include in its regulated rates amounts that are intended to recover specific costs that may be incurred in the future, with the understanding that if the costs are not incurred, an adjustment will be made to future regulated rates. In either instance, the regulator has substantiated the existence of a liability. In the event of customer refunds, FASB-71 requires that they be recorded as liabilities if they can be reasonably estimated and either (a) ordered by the regulator and are unpaid or (b) are likely to occur and are not yet recorded. In the event that the regulator includes in its regulated rates amounts that are intended to recover expected future costs which must be accounted for, a liability is created equal to the amount of revenue collected for the expected future costs.

The amount of revenue collected for the expected future costs is recorded as unearned revenue until the expected future costs are actually incurred or an adjustment is made by the regulator. For example, a regulator may include in its regulated rates an amount for expected future uninsured storm damages. In this respect, the regulator may require that any amounts not actually incurred in the future for storm damages must be refunded to customers in the form of a future adjustment in the regulated rates. As the revenue attributable to the future storm damage is collected, FASB-71 requires that it be recorded as a liability and included in income only when the actual storm damage costs are incurred.

A regulator can substantiate the existence of another type of liability by requiring the regulated enterprise to credit customers over a future period for gains or other reductions of net allowable costs. The gains or other reductions in net allowable costs would usually be amortized over the related future periods by a corresponding reduction in the approved regulated rates. In this event, FASB-71 requires that a liability be recorded in the amount of the future amortization.

If a liability is recorded because of the regulatory process, it can only be reduced or eliminated by the regulatory process. In other words, if a liability is created and recorded by the actions of the regulator, it can only be reduced or eliminated through the same process.

An enterprise subject to FASB-71 must comply with all of its provisions. If there is a conflict between FASB-71 and existing GAAP, the provisions of FASB-71 must be applied. However, in all other circumstances existing GAAP must be followed and applied by a regulated enterprise. Thus, if a regulated enterprise is required by court order to capitalize and amortize a particular cost and the cost does not qualify for capitalization under existing GAAP or FASB-71, the regulated enterprise cannot capitalize the cost in financial statements purported to be presented in accordance with GAAP. In other words, the capitalized cost would not be in conformity with GAAP.

Specific Standards for Regulated Enterprises

Regulated enterprises subject to the provisions of FASB-71 must comply with the following specific standards.

Capitalization of interest In the construction or acquisition of plant and equipment, a regulator may require a regulated enterprise to capitalize certain interest as part of the cost of the asset. The capitalized interest usually includes interest costs on borrowing, or interest costs on a designated portion of equity funds, or on both. The cost of the plant and equipment is increased by the amount of capitalized interest; and, for regulatory purposes, subsequent depreciation expense is based on the total cost of the asset. In other words, the depreciation is classified as an allowable cost. Under these circumstances, a regulated enterprise shall capitalize the amount of interest that the regulator requires and not the amount of capitalized interest which would be required by FASB-34 (Capitalization of Interest Cost). Under any other circumstances, the regulated enterprise shall comply with the provisions of FASB-34.

The amount of interest that is required to be capitalized by the regulator shall be included in the income statement of the regulated enterprise as either (a) an item of other income, (b) a reduction of interest expense, or (c) as both an item of other income and a reduction of interest expense. In addition, the income statement shall indicate the basis for the amount of capitalized interest.

Intercompany profits Under existing GAAP, 100% of any intercompany profits must be eliminated in consolidated financial statements (ARB-51) and investments accounted for by the equity method (APB-18). However, under the provisions of FASB-71, a regulated enterprise shall not eliminate intercompany profits on sales to regulated affiliates if the following conditions are met:

1. The sales price is reasonable, as evidenced by the acceptance of the sales price by the enterprise's regulator, or in light of the specific circumstances, and
2. It is expected, based on available evidence, that the approximate sales price which resulted in the intercompany profit will be recovered as an allowable cost.

If the above conditions are met, the realization of the intercompany profits are reasonably substantiated by the regulatory process. Thus, the intercompany profits shall not be eliminated because they are reasonably assured of being realized.

Deferred income taxes Comprehensive interperiod income tax allocation includes the effects of timing differences in computing income tax expense for a period. Timing differences are transactions that do not appear in financial accounting income (books) and taxable income (tax return) in the same reporting period. Timing differences always reverse themselves in one or more future periods.

Frequently, a regulator will include income tax expense as an allowable cost only in the period in which the income tax is actually paid. In other words, the regulator includes the tax effects of a timing difference as an allowable cost only in the period in which the timing difference reverses and the income taxes become payable. Under the provisions of FASB-71, deferred income taxes shall not be recorded as required by APB-11 (Accounting for Income Taxes) if it is likely that a regulator will include income tax expense as an allowable cost in the period in which the income tax is actually paid. In this event, FASB-71 requires the disclosure of the net cumulative amount of timing differences for which no deferred taxes have been recorded.

In all other circumstances, regulated enterprises must comply with the provisions of APB-11.

Disclosure of customer refunds Disclosure shall be made of any refunds that have a material effect on net income and which are not recognized in the same period as the related revenue. Disclosure shall include the effect on net income and indicate the years that the related revenue was recognized. The material effect on net income, net of related income taxes, may be disclosed as a separate line item in the income statement, but may not be presented as an extraordinary item.

Disclosure of certain unamortized costs Generally, a regulated enterprise recovers its allowable costs through a rate base established by a regulator. The rate base usually includes an amount for recovery of specific incurred costs plus a return based on the net equity of the regulated enterprise. Once the rate base is established, it is converted into specific prices that the regulated enterprise can charge for its services, such as X dollars per kilowatt hour.

A regulator may allow the recovery of a specific cost over the current and future periods, but not allow a return on equity for the same specific cost. In other words, a regulator may exclude a specific cost in calculating the return on equity for a regulated enterprise, but may allow recovery of the actual cost over the current and future periods. For example, severe storm damage may be incurred for which the regulator allows the recovery over the current and future periods. However, the storm damage is not allowed to be included in determining the rate of return on equity for the regulated enterprise. Thus, the regulator allows recovery of the actual cost, but no profit is made on the incurred storm damage cost. The following disclosures are required by FASB-71 for major costs that do not provide a return on investment and are required to be amortized over the current and future periods:

1. The unamortized amount of such costs
2. The remaining period of amortization

> **OBSERVATION:** *The thrust of the above disclosure requirements of FASB-71 is that if a cost is recoverable over an extended period and the regulator does not allow a return on investment (profit) for that specific cost, the unamortized balance of such costs must be disclosed along with the remaining amortization period.*

Amendments to Existing GAAP

As mentioned previously, FASB-71 supersedes the Addendum to APB-2 (Accounting Principles for Regulated Industries). FASB-71 specifically amends all existing GAAP in which reference is made to the Addendum to APB-2. Thus, the reference to the Addendum to APB-2 in all existing GAAP is deleted by FASB-71.

Effective Date

FASB-71 is generally effective for fiscal years beginning on or after December 16, 1983, with earlier application encouraged. Except for refunds and leases, the provisions of FASB-71 shall be retroactively applied, if practicable.

Changes in accounting for refunds which result from the initial application of FASB-71 shall not be made by retroactive restatement of previously issued financial statements.

> **OBSERVATION:** *The two methods for recognizing a change in accounting principle are the (a) retroactive restatement method and (b) the cumulative effect method. Since FASB-71 prohibits the use of the retroactive restatement method for changes in accounting that result from the initial application of FASB-71, the cumulative effect method should be applied to account for the change.*

Commencing with the initial application of FASB-71, leases with inception dates subsequent of December 31, 1982, shall be classified in accordance with FASB-13. Leases with inception dates prior to January 1, 1983, can either be classified in accordance with FASB-13 or classified as they would have been prior to the issuance of FASB-71. However, FASB-71 requires that for fiscal years beginning on or after December 16, 1986, leases must be either:

1. Retroactively reclassified in the financial statements in accordance with FASB-13, or
2. Disclosure must be made in the financial statements of the amount of additional capitalized leased assets and lease obligations that would result from the retroactive reclassification made in accordance with FASB-13.

All other accounting changes which result from the initial application of FASB-71 shall be made, if practical, by retroactive restatement of all comparative financial statements presented. In addition, the financial statements of the year of change shall disclose the nature of any restatement and its effect on income before extraordinary items, net income, and related per share amounts for each year presented. However, related per share amounts need not be disclosed if an enterprise does not disclose earnings per share.

If it is impractical to retroactively restate all of the individual financial statements for the comparative years presented, the following procedure must be used:

1. The new accounting principle (FASB-71) is used in determining net income of the year of change (current period).
2. As many consecutive prior years' financial statements as practical (which are presented for comparative purposes) are then retroactively restated.

3. The cumulative effect of the change to FASB-71 is then computed for any remaining prior years.
4. The cumulative effect is then included in determining net income for the earliest year restated.
5. Financial statements presented for years prior to the earliest year restated (which includes the cumulative effect) shall be presented for comparative purposes as they were originally reported.

In the event that it is impractical to retroactively restate any prior year, FASB-71 requires that the cumulative effect of the change in accounting principle be included in the net income of the year of change in accordance with APB-20 (Accounting Changes). In any year in which the cumulative effect is used, the effect of the change to FASB-71 on income before extraordinary items, net income, and related per share amounts shall be disclosed. However, related per share amounts need not be disclosed if an enterprise does not disclose earnings per share.

> **OBSERVATION:** *The cumulative effect of a change in an accounting principle may be omitted under the provisions of APB-20 if it is impossible to compute. In this event, the effects of the change, in the year of change, must be disclosed, along with an explanation as to why the cumulative effect was omitted.*

Discontinuing Application of FASB-71

The following article appeared early in 1986 in *The CPA Letter*, which is published by the AICPA:

> "At its February 5 meeting, the FASB agreed to provide guidance on how to report the accounting change that results from discontinuing application of FASB Statement no. 71, *Accounting for the Effects of Certain Types of Regulation*.
>
> The board tentatively concluded that, ideally, the accounting entry that results from discontinuing application of Statement no. 71 should result in a balance sheet, at the date of the change, that reflects assets, liabilities and shareholders' equity as they would be if Statement no. 71 had never been applied. The board also tentatively agreed that the net effect of the change should be included in net income as an extraordinary item in the period of change."

Enterprises that are discontinuing the application of FASB-71 should determine whether or not the above information is still effective.

Disclosure Index

DISCLOSURE INDEX

This Disclosure Index contains both required and recommended disclosures that are currently in use. Although the utmost care has been exercised in the preparation of this Index, it is not meant to be a substitute for professional judgment. There are circumstances in which disclosure is not required or recommended, but because of special factors, professional judgment may dictate that disclosure is necessary for a fair presentation.

This Disclosure Index has been designed to assist the preparer or reviewer of financial statements in determining whether necessary disclosures have been made. Its proper use can expedite the preparation or review of financial statements.

BALANCE SHEET

Cash

1. Withdrawal restrictions on funds
2. Segregation of funds to be used for specific purposes

Marketable Securities

1. Specialized industry practices
2. Method of valuation
3. Aggregate cost and market for current portfolio and noncurrent portfolio
4. Carrying value of each portfolio
5. Gross unrealized gains and losses for each portfolio
6. Net realized gain or loss included in determining net income of the period
7. Amount of change in valuation allowances
8. Significant net realized and unrealized gains and losses subsequent to the balance sheet date

Disclosure Index

9. Significant net realized and unrealized gains and losses occurring between a parent company and a subsidiary with different balance sheet dates
10. Investments accounted for by the equity method should not be combined with current or noncurrent portfolios of marketable securities
11. Financial statements that contain entities which have specialized industry practices and which do not have specialized industry practices must include the necessary disclosure of FASB-12 for both circumstances
12. Investments accounted for by the equity method may not be combined with current or noncurrent portfolios of marketable securities
13. Investments in affiliated companies should be separately identified
14. It may be desirable to identify government securities separately
15. Futures contracts:
    a. the nature of the items that are hedged or related to futures contracts
    b. the accounting method(s) used for futures contracts
    c. a description of the events or transactions that will result in recognition in income of changes in value of the futures contracts

Notes Receivable

1. Trade notes receivable
2. Nontrade segregated by type:
   a. from subsidiaries or affiliates
   b. from officers or employees
3. Installment notes receivable
4. Equity in accounts sold
5. Due from factors
6. Pledged as collateral
7. Face amount of notes
8. Effective interest rates
9. Notes discounted—contingent liability
10. Repayment terms and dates
11. Amounts of unearned income, discounts, premiums, finance charges, and interest deducted from related notes receivable

12. Allowance for possible losses
13. Noncurrent portions properly classified
14. Significant balances with one customer
15. Government contracts (CPFF) properly disclosed

Imputed Interest on Notes Receivable (Payable)

1. Description of note
2. Effective interest rate
3. Face amount of note
4. Value of any rights or privileges exchanged
5. Fair value of nonmonetary transaction except in those cases in which the earning process is not culminated
6. Unearned interest and finance charges deducted from related notes

Accounts Receivable

1. Trade accounts receivable
2. Nontrade segregated by type:
    a. from subsidiaries or affiliates
    b. from officers or employees
    c. tax refunds
    d. claims against government contracts (CPFF)
3. Allowance for uncollectible accounts
4. Accounts sold (contingent liability)
5. Equity retained in accounts sold
6. Accounts receivable—discounted
7. Accounts receivable—pledged
8. Accounts receivable—factored
9. Significantly large balances
10. Unbilled receivables shown separately from billed receivables
11. Possible provision for sales returns, allowances, or discounts
12. Amounts from affiliates or subsidiaries properly classified as current or noncurrent

Disclosure Index

Inventories

1. Basis of valuation and method of costing
2. Significant changes and effect on net income
3. Amounts by major categories
4. Amounts pledged as collateral
5. Amounts valued in excess of cost, such as precious metals, minerals, etc.
6. Substantial or unusual losses separately disclosed
7. Losses on firm purchase commitments
8. Principles particular to a given industry
9. Replacement cost and effect on net income of depleted LIFO layer
10. SEC filings—current replacement costs
11. Oil and gas producing companies must comply with special disclosure requirements
12. Consignments
13. Product financing arrangements

Prepaid Items

1. Segregated into types
2. Properly classified as current or noncurrent

Depreciable Assets and Depreciation

1. Basis for valuation
2. Balances of major classes of depreciable assets by nature or function
3. Accumulated depreciation, either by major classes or in total
4. Description of depreciation methods used by major classes
5. Depreciation expense for the period
6. Significant commitments for depreciable assets
7. Significant sale-and-leasebacks
8. Segregation of depreciable assets not used in trade or business (idle facilities, investments, etc.)
9. Pledged as collateral

10. Estimated costs of completion for depreciable assets being constructed
11. Regulated companies subject to the rate-making process must disclose the nonrecognition of deferred income taxes resulting from the use of the declining-balance method of depreciation

Unconsolidated Investments

1. Name of each investment
2. Percentage of ownership
3. Accounting policies with respect to each investment
4. Differences between the carrying value and underlying equity in net assets and the treatment of such difference
5. Quoted market value of each investment (not required for subsidiaries)
6. Summary of assets, liabilities, and results of operation for each significant investment
7. Effect on the investor of any outstanding conversions or dilutive securities of the investee
8. If investment is 20% or more and the equity method is not used, the reason(s) must be disclosed
9. If investment is less than 20% and the cost method is not used, the reason(s) must be disclosed
10. Changes in the status of an investment
11. Declaration of intent to reinvest the undistributed earnings of a subsidiary (nonaccrual of income taxes)
12. Declaration of intent that undistributed earnings will be in the form of a tax-free liquidation (nonaccrual of income taxes)
13. The cumulative amount of undistributed earnings on which a parent company or investor has not recognized income taxes
14. Significant tax credits and deductions resulting from investments

Intangible Assets

1. Method of amortization and estimated useful life

Disclosure Index

2. Carrying basis of intangibles
3. Explanation of the nonamortization of pre-11/1/70 intangibles
4. Intangible assets of motor carriers

Deferred Income Taxes

1. Segregated between net current amount and net noncurrent amount
2. Operating-loss carryforwards not used, including expiration dates
3. Significant other unused tax credits or deductions including expiration dates
4. Reason(s) for significant differences in the customary relationship between income tax expense and pretax accounting income
5. Nature of significant differences between pretax accounting income and taxable income
6. Components of income tax expense for the period (intraperiod tax allocation)
7. Tax effects of adjustments to prior periods
8. Amount of operating-loss carryback applied during the period

Leases—Lessee

1. Description of lessee's leasing arrangements:
   a. basis of contingent payments
   b. renewal or purchase options
   c. escalation clauses
   d. restrictions on dividends, further leasing, additional debt, etc.
2. Capital leases:
   a. Gross amount of assets by major classes under capital leases in accordance with their nature and/or function
   b. Aggregate future minimum lease payments for the period and for each of the five succeeding fiscal years, less executory costs (including profit thereon) included in the minimum lease payments
   c. Amount of imputed interest necessary to reduce the net minimum lease payments to its present value

d. Total minimum sublease rentals to be received under noncancelable subleases
e. Total amount of contingent rentals actually incurred during each period presented
3. Operating leases:
   a. Aggregate future minimum rental payments for the period and for the next succeeding five fiscal years
   b. Total minimum rentals to be received under noncancelable subleases
   c. Total rental expense for each period presented

Leases—Lessor

Where leasing, excluding leveraged leases, is a significant portion of a lessor's business in terms of net assets, revenue, or net income, the following is required for both sales-type and direct financing leases:

1. The components of the net investment in leases, including:
   a. future minimum lease payments less executory costs (and profits thereon) included in the minimum lease payments
   b. accumulated allowance for uncollectible minimum lease payments
   c. unguaranteed residual values accruing to the lessor
   d. unearned income
2. Future minimum lease payments to be received for each of the five succeeding fiscal years
3. Total contingent rentals included in income for each period presented
4. For direct-financing leases only: the amount of unearned income used to offset initial direct costs charged to income for each period presented
5. For operating leases:
   a. by major classes of property on lease or held for lease and according to nature or function; (1) cost, (2) carrying amount, and (3) accumulated depreciation in total
   b. minimum future rentals on noncancelable leases in the aggregate and for each of the five succeeding fiscal years

Disclosure Index

      c. Total contingent rentals included in income for each period presented

  6. General description of the lessor's usual leasing arrangements

Leveraged Leases

1. Deferred taxes related to leveraged leases should be separately disclosed
2. A separate presentation of pretax income from leveraged leases should be made in the income statement or footnote thereto to include (1) pretax income, (2) the tax effect on pretax income, and (3) the amount of investment tax credit recognized during the period
3. When leveraged leasing constitutes a significant portion of a lessor's business activity in terms of assets, revenue, or net income, the following components of the net investment balance in leveraged leases should be disclosed by footnote:
   a. rentals receivable, net of rentals applicable to principal and interest on nonrecourse debt
   b. estimated residual value of the leased property
   c. unearned or deferred income, including (1) estimated pretax lease income less initial direct costs and (2) investment tax credit remaining to be allocated to income over the lease term
   d. the amount, if any, remaining to be collected for the investment tax credit realized on the transaction

Unbilled Costs

1. Expenditures billable to customers
2. Unreimbursed costs and fees (CPFF contracts)
3. Costs and estimated earnings in excess of billings on uncompleted contracts

Notes Payable

1. Description of note
2. Amount of note
3. Effective interest rate
4. Segregation of type of notes:
   a. trade
   b. banks

        c. items collateralized
        d. related parties—stockholders, directors, officers, or employees
        e. intercompany
   5. Nonmonetary transaction:
        a. imputed interest
        b. premium or discount
        c. face amount
        d. effective interest rate
        e. valuation of rights or privileges

Accounts Payable

1. Segregation by types:
    a. trade
    b. nontrade
    c. related parties
    d. intercompany
2. Accounts collateralized

Income Taxes Payable

1. Segregated between current and deferred
2. Amounts in dispute

Other Current Liabilities

1. Current accruals
2. Current portion of long-term obligations
3. Customers' advances or deposits
4. Guarantees, warranties, etc.
5. Billings in excess of costs and estimated earnings on uncompleted contracts
6. Compensated absences

Long-Term Obligations

1. Description of terms and interest rates
2. Assets pledged, restrictions on dividends or retained earnings, sinking fund requirements, etc.
3. Current portions shown as current

Disclosure Index

    4. Capitalized lease obligations
    5. Convertibility
    6. Nonmonetary transactions:
        a. imputed interest
        b. premium or discount
        c. face amount
        d. effective interest rates
        e. valuation of rights and privileges
    7. Unrecorded unconditional purchase obligations
    8. Other unconditional obligations
    9. Product financing arrangements

Unrealized Gross Profits on Installment Sales

Stockholders' Equity

    1. Common stock:
        a. title of each class
        b. par or stated value
        c. number of shares authorized, issued, and outstanding
        d. reserved shares and purpose
    2. Preferred stock:
        a. title of each class
        b. par or stated value
        c. number of shares authorized, issued, and outstanding
        d. reserved shares and purpose
        e. convertibility
        f. call price
        g. cumulative or noncumulative
        h. dividends in arrears
        i. participating or nonparticipating
        j. preference in liquidation
    3. Stock subscriptions:
        a. description
        b. details of amounts

4. Additional capital:
    a. segregated by source
    b. restrictions
5. Retained earnings:
    a. appropriated and unappropriated
    b. dividend restrictions
    c. stock dividends
    d. treasury stock restrictions where required by charter or state law
    e. dated, in case of a quasi-reorganization
6. Treasury stock:
    a. number of shares
    b. basis of valuation
    c. reserved shares and purpose

STATEMENT OF CAPITAL CHANGES

A statement of changes in the separate accounts of stockholders' equity, including retained earnings, is necessary when financial position, changes in financial position, and results of operations are presented in conformity with GAAP. This disclosure may be presented as a separate statement, as part of the basic financial statements, or in footnotes thereto.

STATEMENT OF CHANGES IN FINANCIAL POSITION

A statement of changes in financial position is required for presentations that purport to present both financial position and results of operations in conformity with GAAP.

1. Prepared on a broad concept that discloses all significant financing and investing activities of the enterprise
2. Working capital provided from or used in operations
3. Total increase (decrease) in working capital
4. Schedule of changes in each element of working capital

Disclosure Index

5. Prepared on a gross basis except for normal trade-ins to replace equipment
6. Isolated statistics of working capital should not be shown

INCOME STATEMENT

1. Substantial sales to one customer or a few customers
2. Method of recognizing long-term construction-type contracts
3. Method of reporting revenues for cost reimbursement contracts
4. Method of reporting income from leases
5. Proportionate share of income from investees
6. Depreciation expense separately shown
7. Significant interest income or expense
8. Amount of investment tax credit, accounting method, and carryovers
9. Method of foreign exchange conversion
10. Gain or loss on foreign exchange
11. Significant losses on firm purchase commitments
12. Unusual or infrequently occurring items other than extraordinary should be separately shown
13. Research and development costs
14. Bad debt reserves of savings and loan associations
15. Policyholders' surplus of stock life insurance companies
16. Pension plan expense
17. Discontinued operations
18. Gain or loss from extinguishment of debt
19. Cumulative effect of an accounting change
20. Extraordinary items
21. Intraperiod income tax allocation
22. Reasons for significant variations between income tax expense and pretax accounting income
23. Material differences between pretax accounting income and taxable income
24. Earnings per share (primary and fully diluted for complex capital structures)

Disclosure Index

GENERAL

Accounting Policies

1. Description of all significant accounting policies (Summary of Significant Accounting Policies)
2. Methods of applying accounting principles:
    a. selection of acceptable alternatives
    b. peculiar to a particular industry
    c. unusual application of GAAP

Accounting Changes

1. Description of change
2. Nature and justification
3. Effect of change:
    a. cumulative effect
    b. restatement of financials
4. Reason for omitting cumulative effect and *pro forma* information
5. Change in method of amortizing new assets:
    a. nature of change and method
    b. effect on net income in period of change
    c. related per share data
6. Change in reporting entity (restatement)
7. Correction of error in previous financial statements:
    a. nature of error
    b. effect on components of net income
    c. related per share data

Business Combinations

1. Purchase method:
    a. name, description, and total cost of acquisition
    b. method of accounting (purchase)

c. period in which results of operations are included
d. amortization of goodwill
e. other pertinent information
f. contingent payments
g. *pro forma* results for current period as if acquisition had been combined from the beginning of fiscal year, and comparative year, if presented

   Disclosure g. above is not required for a nonpublic enterprise as described in FASB-79.

2. Pooling of interests:
   a. name and brief description of companies combined
   b. basis of presentation in current period and restatements of prior periods
   c. method of accounting (pooling)
   d. description and amount of shares issued
   e. separate results of operation for each combining company
   f. nature of adjustments to net assets of each combining company in order to adopt the same accounting policies
   g. change in fiscal year
   h. reconciliation of revenue and earnings previously reported by acquiring company with combined amounts presented in the financial statements
   i. *pro forma* information of proposed pooling to stockholders
   j. gain or loss on disposal of significant portions of the assets or segments of combining companies
   k. pooling consummated after balance sheet date but before issuance of financial statements
   l. earnings of separate companies where new corporation is formed to effectuate combination

Commitments and Contingencies

1. Probable and reasonably possible losses where liability can be ascertained
2. Nature and range of loss
3. Remote losses on guarantees and similar items
4. Pending litigation
5. Guarantees of subsidiaries or affiliates
6. Tax contingencies

7. Accounts sold with recourse
8. Renegotiation of governmental contracts
9. Losses after balance sheet date but before issuance of financial statements
10. All material commitments
11. Gain contingencies that are not misleading as to likelihood of realization
12. Unused letters of credit
13. Information on noncancelable leases which are not capitalized
14. Indirect guarantees of indebtedness of others
15. Franchise commitments and obligations

Development Stage Enterprises

1. Cumulative net losses
2. Cumulative income statement
3. Cumulative statement of changes in financial position
4. Date and number of shares of stock issued for cash or other consideration
5. Nature and valuation of noncash consideration received for stock issued
6. Description of development stage enterprises

Extraordinary Items

1. Nature and amount of each item with related tax effects
2. Unamortized cost of intangible assets included as extraordinary charge
3. Tax benefit of any operating-loss carryforward reported as an extraordinary item in the period realized
4. Investor's share of investee's extraordinary items
5. Extinguishment of debt

Extinguishment of Debt

1. Description of extinguishment
2. Gain or loss
3. Related tax effects

4. Assets placed in an irrevocable trust:
    a. a general description of the transaction
    b. the total amount of debt outstanding at the end of the period
    c. the total amount of debt that is considered extinguished at the end of the period

Foreign Currency Exchange

1. Aggregate transaction gain or loss
2. Analysis of changes in separate component of stockholders' equity which must include
    a. beginning and ending cumulative balances
    b. aggregate increase or decrease for the period from translation adjustments and gains and losses from (i) hedges of a net investment in a foreign entity and (ii) long-term intercompany transactions
    c. amount of income taxes allocated to translation adjustments
    d. amount of translation adjustment of a sale or substantial liquidation of a foreign investment
3. Exchange rate changes and effects on foreign currency transactions subsequent to balance sheet date, if material

Government Contracts

1. Advance payments as offsets
2. Inability to provide for renegotiation
3. Significant portion of a company's business
4. Basis of provision for renegotiations
5. Reasonable estimate of termination not possible
6. Material termination claims
7. Controversial items
8. Claims against government segregated

Interest Costs Capitalized

1. The total amount of interest costs incurred and charged to expense during the period

2. The amount of interest costs that have been capitalized during the period

Interim Financial Reporting

1. Interim inventory cost method
2. Material contingencies
3. Significant seasonable variations in revenue
4. Disposal of a segment
5. Changes in accounting principle or estimate
6. Significant variations between income tax expense and pretax accounting income

Pension Plans—Employers

1. A full description of the plan, including the employees covered.
2. A full description of the accounting and funding policies.
3. The pension plan expense for the current period, and other periods presented.
4. The nature and effect of all items affecting comparability for all periods presented.
5. The following information determined in accordance with FASB-35 shall also be disclosed for plans with 100 or more participants:
    a. The actuarial present value of accumulated plan benefits that are vested.
    b. The actuarial present value of accumulated plan benefits that are not vested.
    c. The net assets of the pension plan that are available for benefits. Any excess of accrued pension liability on the balance sheet of the employer as of the benefit information date, over the plan's contribution receivable from the employer on the same date, should be added to the net assets of the pension plan that are available for benefits.
    d. The assumed rates of return that are used to determine the actuarial present values of vested and nonvested benefits in a and b above.
    e. The benefit information date.

For pension plans with less than 100 participants, the following is substituted for item 5:

5. The excess (deficit) of the total present value of vested benefits over amounts that have been provided for them (the pension fund, plus balance sheet accruals, minus balance sheet prepayments and deferrals.)

Pension Plan—Financial Statements

1. Statement of net assets available for benefits
2. Statement of changes in net assets available for benefits
3. Actuarial present value of accumulated plan benefits
4. Year-to-year changes in the actuarial present value of accumulated plan benefits (if significant)

Quasi-Reorganizations

1. Disclose all pertinent information
2. Date retained earnings accounts

Related Party Disclosures

1. The nature of the material related party relationship. In addition, the name of the related party should be disclosed, if it is essential to the understanding of the relationship.
2. A description of the material related party transactions, including amounts and other pertinent information for each period in which an income statement is presented.
   Related party transactions of no, or nominal, amounts must also be disclosed.
3. The effects of any change in terms between the related parties from terms used in prior periods. In addition, the dollar amount of transactions for each period in which an income statement is presented must be disclosed.
4. If not apparent in the financial statements, (a) the terms of related party transactions, (b) the manner of settlement of related party transactions, and (c) the amount due to, or from, related parties, must all be disclosed.

5. If the operating results or financial position of a reporting entity can be altered significantly by the effects of common ownership or management control of the reporting entity and one or more other entities, even if there are no transactions between any of the entities, the nature of the ownership or management control must be disclosed in the financial statements.

Segmental Reporting

1. Nonpublic companies are not required to disclose EPS data and segmental information
2. Industry segments and foreign operations
3. Sales and revenue:
    a. to unaffiliated customers
    b. to intercompany segments
    c. types of products
    d. revenue of each reportable segment
    e. accounting policies
4. Operating profit or loss:
    a. allocation of common operating costs and expenses
    b. exclude revenue not derived from operations
    c. exclude general corporate overhead, interest expense, income taxes, earnings from unconsolidated subsidiaries, discontinued operations, minority interests, extraordinary items, and cumulative effect of a change in an accounting principle
5. Other measures of profitability may be used
6. Tangible and intangible identifiable assets:
    a. by industry segments or foreign operations
    b. exclude assets for general corporate use which are not used in any reportable segment
7. Other reportable segment information (by industry segments):
    a. depreciation, depletion, or amortization
    b. capital expenditures
    c. net income from unconsolidated subsidiaries and investees whose operations are vertically integrated
    d. nature and amount of unusual or infrequently occurring items included in the operating profit or loss of a reportable segment

Disclosure Index

      e. effect on a reportable segment's operating profit or loss of a change in an accounting principle
      f. method(s) used to allocate common costs between reportable segments
  8. Export sales
  9. Significant sales to one customer
 10. Significant sales to governments if they exceed 10% of consolidated sales
 11. All segmental information reconciled to financial statements

Stock Options

1. Status of all option plans:
   a. number of shares covered by each option and date of grant
   b. exercise price
   c. number of shares that can be exercised
   d. number of shares exercised
   e. option price of exercised shares
   f. expiration dates
2. All pertinent information about stock option plan, etc.

Short-Term Obligations Expected to Be Refinanced

1. General description of irrevocable financing agreement
2. Terms of new obligation or details of equity securities to be issued
3. Amount excluded from current liabilities as a result of refinancing

Supplementary Information on Changing Prices

1. Income from continuing operations, on a constant dollar and current cost basis
2. Purchasing power gain or loss on net monetary items
3. Current cost amounts of inventory and property, plant, and equipment

4. Increases or decreases in current cost amounts of inventory and property, plant, and equipment, net of inflation
   5. Five year summary of financial data, including:
      a. income
      b. sales and other operating revenues
      c. net assets
      d. dividends per common share
      e. market price per share
   6. Timberlands, growing timber, mineral ore bodies, proved oil and gas reserves, income producing real estate, and motion picture films are classified as specialized assets. The disclosures for specialized assets are similar to other assets, except that specific information based on "fair value" is required for certain disclosures

Tax Examinations

   1. Examination or litigation in progress
   2. All pertinent information
   3. Settlement of examination or litigation

Transfers of Receivables With Recourse

   1. the amount of proceeds received from the transfer
   2. if the information is available, the amount of receivables that remain uncollected

Troubled Debt Restructuring

   1. Debtor's troubled debt restructuring:
      a. description of terms of restructuring
      b. aggregate gain and related tax effect
      c. aggregate gain or loss on transfer of assets
      d. per share data on aggregate gain on restructure (net of related tax)
      e. contingent payable amounts with description of terms
   2. Creditor's troubled debt restructuring:
      a. restructured receivables by major categories

       b. aggregate recorded investment
       c. gross interest income not earned as a result of debt restructuring
       d. gross interest income on restructured receivables included in current net income
       e. commitments to lend additional funds to debtor

AUDITOR'S REPORT

Scope Limitation

1. Time constraints
2. Insufficient competent evidence:
    a. inability to observe inventory
    b. inability to confirm receivables
    c. client restrictions
    d. restrictions on the use of audit procedures
3. Inadequate records

Other Auditor's Report

1. Report being based in part on another auditor's report
2. Sharing of responsibility

Departure from GAAP

1. Lack of conformity to GAAP
2. Material departure
3. Inadequate disclosure

Consistency

1. Exception to change in accounting principle
2. Inconsistency in accounting principles

Uncertainties

1. Recurring losses (going concern principle)
2. Deficiency in working capital

3. Inability to obtain financing
4. Failure to comply with loan agreement

SPECIALIZED INDUSTRY DISCLOSURES

Entertainment Industry

Broadcasters

1. Unrecorded program material license agreements that have been executed not meeting the criteria for recording in the financial statements

Motion Picture Films

1. Film inventories, including films released, completed and in process
2. Amount of story rights

Franchises

1. Nature of franchise agreement
2. Initial franchise fee
3. Other franchise fee revenue
4. Changes in ownership of franchises

Insurance Industry

1. The basis for estimating:
   a. The liability for unpaid claims
   b. The liability for claim adjustment expenses
2. The methods and assumptions used in calculating the liability for future policy benefits. In addition, FASB-60 encourages, but does not require, the disclosure of the average rate of assumed investment yields that are in effect for the current period.
3. Capitalized acquisition costs:
   a. The nature of such costs

Disclosure Index

      b. The method of amortizing such costs

      c. The amount of amortization of such costs for the current period

4. If the liabilities for unpaid claims and claim adjustment expenses for short-duration contracts are reported at their present values in the financial statements:

      a. The carrying amount of those liabilities

      b. The range of interest rates used to discount those liabilities

5. If estimated investment income is used in calculating a premium deficiency for short-duration contracts:

      a. If yes, a statement disclosing that fact

      b. If no, no disclosure necessary

6. Reinsurance transactions of an insurance company:

      a. The nature and significance of such transactions

      b. Estimated amounts recoverable from reinsurers that are related to unpaid claims and claim adjustment expenses

7. Participating insurance of an insurance company:

      a. The relative percentage of participating insurance

      b. The method of accounting for participating insurance policyholder dividends

      c. The amount of such dividends

      d. The amount of any additional income allocated to participating insurance policyholders

8. Stockholders' equity, statutory capital, and surplus:

      a. The amount of statutory capital and surplus

      b. The amount of statutory capital and surplus required for regulatory purposes, if significant to the enterprise's total statutory capital and surplus

      c. The nature of statutory restrictions on dividends and the amount of retained earnings not available for dividends to stockholders

9. Policyholders' surplus of life insurance companies (when an insurance company is consolidated or accounted for by the equity method, these disclosures also apply to the parent company):

      a. The treatment of the policyholders' surplus under the provisions of the Internal Revenue Code

b. The fact that income taxes may become payable if the company takes specific action, which should be appropriately disclosed
  c. The total amount of policyholders' surplus for which income taxes have not been provided
10. If no current or deferred federal income taxes have been provided by a life insurance company for any retained earnings in excess of policyholders' surplus:
   a. The amount of such retained earnings
   b. The reasons for not accruing deferred federal income taxes

Mortgage Banking Industry

1. Mortgage loans receivable and mortgage backed securities must be separately disclosed as those held for sale and those held for investment
2. Method used to determine lower of cost or market value of mortgage loans receivable and mortgage backed securities
3. The amount of capitalized servicing rights including method and amount of amortization

Oil and Gas Producing Companies

1. Reserves and operating activities—domestic and foreign
2. Oil and gas properties, reserves, and production
3. Present value of future net revenues from production of proved oil and gas reserves
4. Quantities of crude oil and natural gas
5. Proportionate share of investee's quantities
6. Quantities from royalties
7. Long-term supply agreements with foreign governments
8. Capitalized costs, related depreciation, depletion, amortization, and valuation allowances:
   a. mineral interests in property
   b. wells, related equipment and facilities

    c. support equipment and facilities
    d. uncompleted wells, equipment and facilities
 9. Functional costs:
    a. property acquisitions
    b. exploration
    c. development
    d. production
 10. Economic factors and significant uncertainties for proved reserves

Topical Index

TOPICAL INDEX

ACCOUNTING CHANGES
Background **1.01**
  Coverage of GAAP **1.01**
Changes in an accounting estimate **1.15**
  Causes of change in estimate **1.15**
Changes in accounting principles **1.02**
  Change in composition of inventory costs **1.04**
  Change in estimate as a result of change in principle **1.02**
  Examples of changes in principles **1.04**
  Exceptions **1.06**
  Newly promulgated GAAP **1.02**
  Rule of preferability **1.03**
Comprehensive illustration **1.17**
Cumulative effect vs retroactive restatement **1.13**
  Cumulative effect method **1.13**
  Retroactive restatement **1.13**
Financial summaries **1.16**
  Presentation of accounting changes **1.16**
  Calculation of effect impossible **1.06**
  Pro forma presentation **1.08**
Oil and gas producing companies **1.01**
Reporting accounting changes—interim periods **1.11**
  Cumulative effect **1.11**
  Cumulative effect cannot be calculated **1.11**
  Disclosures **1.12**
  Nature and justification **1.12**
  Pro forma effects **1.12**
  Publicly traded companies **1.12**
Reporting a change in accounting estimate **1.14**
  Disclosures **1.15**
  Procedures **1.14**
Reporting a change in accounting principle **1.05**
  Changes requiring restatement **1.06**
  Cumulative effect **1.05**
    Presentation in income statement **1.05**
  Direct effects **1.06**
  Earnings per share data **1.06**
  Nondiscretionary effects **1.06**
Reporting a change in an entity **1.15**
  Disclosures **1.15**
  Procedures **1.15**
Reporting corrections of errors **1.15**
  Definition of prior period adjustment **1.15**
  Disclosures **1.16**
Types of accounting changes **1.02**

ACCOUNTING POLICIES
Background **2.01**

Coverage of GAAP **2.01**
Unaudited reports **2.01**
Comprehensive illustration **2.02**
Disclosure **2.02**
Overview **2.01**
Significant accounting policies **2.01**
  Compliance with GAAP **2.01**
  Method of applying such principles **2.02**
  Preferable presentation of disclosure **2.01**

ACCOUNTS RECEIVABLE
Allowance for uncollectibles **8.05**
Current assets and liabilities **8.05**
Factoring **8.07**
Installment sales **20.04**
Pledging **8.07**

ACID-TEST RATIO
Current assets and liabilities **8.04**

ACTUARIAL ASSUMPTIONS
Pension plans—employers **30.04**

ACTUARIAL GAINS OR LOSSES
Pension plans—employers **30.05**

ACTUARIAL VALUATION
Pension plans—employers **31.03**

ALL-INCLUSIVE CONCEPT
Results of operations **36.01**

ALLOWANCE FOR BAD DEBTS
Allowance method **8.06**
Direct write-off method **8.06**

AMORTIZATION
Goodwill **21.03**
Intangible assets **21.02**
Interest on receivables and payables **22.02**
Investment tax credit **25.01**
Leases **26.14**
Negative goodwill **21.04**
Pension plans—employers **31.01**
  Total prior service cost **30.18–30.19**
  Unrecognized net obligation/asset **30.27**
  Unrecognized prior service cost **30.18**
Pension plans—settlements and curtailments **31.06**

ANNUITY CONTRACTS
Pension plans—employers **30.34**
Pension plans—settlements and curtailments **31.04**

ANTIDILUTION
Earnings per share **13.07**

APPRAISAL VALUES
Business combinations **3.02**
Depreciable assets and depreciation **11.03**
Depreciation of appraisal values **11.03**

GAAP GUIDE / 96.01

Topical Index

BAD DEBTS
  Current—assets and liabilities **8.04**

BANKING AND THRIFT INSTITUTIONS
  Accounting for regulatory assistance **45.08**
    Additional interest **45.08**
    Disclosure **45.10**
    Financial assistance after acquisition **45.09**
    Other types of assistance **45.08**
    Repayment of assistance **45.10**
    Transfer of assets/liabilities **45.09**
  Acquisitions of troubled banking institutions **45.05**
    Additional goodwill **45.08**
    Allocating the cost **45.05**
    Identifiable intangible assets **45.06**
    Maximum amortization period **45.06**
    Method of amortization **45.07**
    Subsequent revision of amortization **45.07**
  Background **45.02**
  Effective date **45.10**
  Net-spread method **45.04**
  Overview **45.01**
  Separate-valuation method **45.03**

BARGAIN PURCHASE OPTION
  Leases **26.04**

BARGAIN RENEWAL OPTION
  Leases **26.04**

BASE STOCK METHOD
  Inventory pricing and methods **24.14**

BROADCASTERS
  Background **50.01**
    Advertising rates **50.01**
    Programming costs **50.02**
    Regulation **50.02**
    Revenue **50.01**
  Barter transactions **50.04**
  Disclosure **50.06**
  Effective date **50.06**
  Intangible assets **50.05**
  Overview **50.01**
    Definition of broadcaster **50.01**
  Program material license arrangements **50.03**
    Amortization of program rights **50.04**
    Asset and liability **50.03**
    Classified balance sheet **50.03**
    Conditions necessary **50.03**
    Unamortized program rights **50.04**

BUSINESS COMBINATIONS
  Acquisition of stock directly from subsidiary **3.16**
    Determining acquirer's stock interest **3.16**
  Application of pooling-of-interests method **3.26**
    Accounting prior to consummation date **3.27**
    Accounts combined at cost **3.27**
    Disposal of significant portion of assets **3.27**
    Expenses of combination **3.27**
    Foreign currency translation **16.07**
    Intercorporate investments **3.27**
    Reporting in period of combination **3.27**
    Restatement of prior years' statements **3.27**
    Treasury stock **3.27**
  Background **3.01**
    Coverage of GAAP **3.01**
  Conditions for pooling of interests **3.19**
    Acquisition of 90% or more of voting stock **3.21**
      Determining independence **3.22**
      Equivalent number of shares **3.22**
      Shares excluded from 90% determination **3.22**
      Transfer of net assets **3.23**
    Autonomy **3.19**
      Initiation date **3.19**
    Completion of plan **3.21**
    Equity interest changes **3.25**
    Inconsistent transaction **3.26**
    Independence **3.20**
      Downstream mergers **3.21**
    Proportionate voting stock interest **3.26**
      Completion of plan **3.26**
      Same voting rights **3.26**
    Reacquisition of voting stock **3.25**
  Different classes of capital stock **3.14**
    Guidelines for preferred stock issues **3.14**
    Computing parent's investment **3.14**
  Disclosure for pooling of interests **3.28**
    Adjustments to net assets **3.28**
    Amount of shares issued **3.28**
    Change in fiscal year **3.28**
    Description of companies **3.28**
    Method of accounting **3.28**
    Reconciliation of revenue and earnings **3.28**
    Results for each separate company **3.28**
    Unconsummated plans **3.28**
  Disclosure for purchase method **3.08**
    Basic disclosures **3.08**
    Supplemental disclosures **3.08**
  Earnings per share **13.22**
  Franchise fee revenue **60.08**
  Inventory in business combinations **24.17**
  Investment tax credit **25.12**
  Leases **26.44**
  Overview **3.01**
    Definition of business combinations **3.01**
    Pooling **3.02**
    Pooling-of-interests method **3.19**
    Purchase **3.01**
  Purchase method **3.02**
    Acquisition of pension plan assets and liabilities **3.06**
    Allocating cost **3.05**
    Contingent assets and liabilities **3.07**
    Determination of cost **3.02**
    Fair value **3.02**

Purchase versus pooling of interests **3.09**
  Goodwill **3.09**
  Negative goodwill **3.09**
  Purchase of assets **3.09**
  Purchase of stock interest **3.11**
Step-by-step acquisition **3.17**
Stock exchanges **3.18**

CABLE TELEVISION COMPANIES
Background **51.01**
  Construction period **51.01**
  Franchise **51.01**
  Prematurity period **51.02**
  Program entertainment **51.01**
Effective date **51.06**
Hookup revenue and franchise costs **51.05**
Initial recording of assets **51.02**
  Capitalized costs **51.03**
    Costs related to both current and future period **51.03**
    Costs related to current period **51.03**
    Costs related to future period **51.03**
  Clearly identifiable portion **51.02**
  Prematurity period **51.02**
Overview **51.01**
  Coverage of GAAP **51.01**
Review of recoverability **51.06**

CAPITAL CHANGES
Equity method **14.02**
Stockholders' equity **38.01**

CAPITAL LEASE
Leases **26.02**

CAPITAL STRUCTURE
Complex capital structures **13.09**
  Fully diluted EPS **13.10**
  Presentation of EPS **13.10**
  Primary EPS **13.10**
Earnings per share **13.09**
Simple capital structures **13.09**
  Presentation of EPS **13.09**

CARRYBACK LOSSES
Income taxes **19.04**

CARRYFORWARD LOSSES
Income taxes **19.04**

CASH SURRENDER VALUE OF LIFE INSURANCE
Current assets and liabilities **8.07**

CHANGES IN FINANCIAL POSITION
Background **4.01**
  Existing GAAP **4.01**
  Statements issued for internal use only **4.01**
  Unclassified balance sheets **4.01**
Cash format **4.04**
  Cash provided (used) in operations **4.04**
  Changes in current accounts **4.04**
  Increase (decrease) in cash **4.04**
  No separate schedule of changes **4.04**
Comprehensive illustration **4.05**
Concept of funds **4.02**
  All financial resources **4.02**
  Cash **4.02**
  Cash and marketable securities **4.02**
  Cash basis **4.02**
  Changes in working capital **4.03**
    Each element **4.03**
    Increase (decrease) in working capital **4.03**
  Funds provided (used) in operations **4.03**
  Net quick assets **4.02**
  Net working capital **4.04**
  Statement format **4.03**
  Unclassified balance sheets **4.03**
Gross basis **4.02**
  Conflict with FASB-12 **4.02**
  Normal trade-ins **4.02**
Overview **4.01**
  All changes in financial position **4.01**
  Broad concept **4.01**
  Exception book entries **4.01**
  Financing and investing activities **4.01**
  Working capital—operations **4.01**
    Net changes in **4.01**
Per share amounts **4.04**
  Isolated statistics **4.04**
  Per share information **4.04**

COMBINED FINANCIAL STATEMENTS
Consolidated financial statements **5.04**

COMMON STOCK
Marketable securities **28.01**
Stockholders' equity **38.02**
  Authorized issued, outstanding **38.02**
  Legal capital **38.01**
  Subscriptions **38.02**
  Treasury stock **38.05**

COMMON STOCK EQUIVALENTS (CSE)
Convertible debt **13.04**
Definition **13.03**
Determination of CSE **13.03**
Dilution **13.03**
Earnings per share **13.07**
Materiality (3% rule) **13.08**
Security becoming a CSE after issuance **13.04**
Substance over form **13.03**
Types of CSE **13.04**
  Contingent shares **13.06**
  Covertible debt **13.04**
  Covertible stock **13.04**
  Participating securities **13.06**
  Stock options, warrants, etc. **13.04**

COMPARABILITY
Comparative financial statements **5.04**

Topical Index

COMPARABILITY (continued)
Consistency **5.04**
COMPENSATED ABSENCES
Current assets and current liabilities **8.16**
COMPENSATORY PLANS
Stock issued to employees **39.01**
COMPLETED-CONTRACT METHOD
Long-term contracts **27.01**
COMPREHENSIVE ILLUSTRATIONS
Accounting changes **1.17**
Accounting policies **2.02**
Changes in financial position **4.05**
Completed-contract method **27.04**
Cost method **14.13**
Cost to equity method **14.15**
Current value accounting **9.04**
Deferred compensation contracts **10.02**
Earnings per share **13.24**
Equity method **14.14**
Extinguishment of debt **15.04**
Financial reporting and changing prices **15.67**
Foreign operations and exchange **16.26**
General price-level changes **17.08**
Intangible assets **21.08**
Interest costs capitalized **22.62**
Interest on receivables and payables **22.03**
Interest method **22.03**
Inventory pricing and methods **24.21**
Average method **24.22**
FIFO method **24.21**
LIFO method **24.22**
Leases **26.44**
Marketable securities **28.09**
Pension plan financial statements **31.66**
Pension plans—employers **30.23**
Pension plans—settlements and curtailments **31.11, 31.15**
Computation of total effects of plan curtailment **31.15**
Decrease/increase in projected benefit obligation **31.11**
Percentage-of-completion method **27.04**
Presentation of net income **36.08**
Purchase method **3.03**
Quasi-reorganization **32.04**
Revenue recognition **36.58**
Segmental reporting **37.10**
Stock issued to employees **39.16**
CONSISTENCY
Comparability **5.04**
Comparative financial statements **5.04**
CONSOLIDATED FINANCIAL STATEMENTS
Accounting and reporting **5.01**
Disclosures when cost method is used **5.03**
Disposal of a subsidiary **5.03**

Exclusion of a subsidiary **5.02**
Minority interest **5.03**
Purchase of net assets **5.02**
Retained earnings of a subsidiary **5.01**
Step-by-step acquisition **5.02**
Subsidiary with different fiscal years **5.01**
Use of cost method **5.03**
Use of equity method **5.03**
Background **5.01**
Coverage of GAAP **5.01**
Combined financial statements **5.04**
Justification—consolidated statements **5.04**
Comparative financial statements **5.04**
Comparability **5.04**
Consistency **5.04**
Consolidated work papers **5.05**
Compared with regular work papers **5.05**
Consolidation versus equity method **5.04**
One-line consolidation **5.05**
Disclosure **5.15**
Consolidation policy **5.15**
Entity theory **5.15**
Income tax considerations **5.13**
Deferred income taxes **5.13**
Intercompany transactions **5.05**
Intercompany bond holdings **5.09**
Intercompany dividends **5.13**
Intercompany stock holdings **5.13**
Receivables and payables **5.05**
Unrealized profits in inventory **5.06**
Unrealized profits in long-lived assets **5.07**
Minority interests **5.13**
Father-son-grandson affiliation **5.13**
In net income **5.14**
Balance sheet presentation **5.14**
Overview **5.01**
When consolidated statements should be prepared **5.01**
CONSTANT DOLLAR DISCLOSURES
Financial reporting and changing prices **15.60**
CONTINGENCIES
Accounting and reporting a loss contingency **6.02**
Requirements **6.02**
Background **6.01**
Coverage of GAAP **6.01**
Classification of contingencies **6.02**
How a loss contingency may arise **6.02**
Types **6.02**
Contingency reserves **6.08**
Establishment of reserve **6.08**
Types **6.08**
Use of reserves **6.08**
Disclosure of noninsurance **6.07**
Disclosure of reasonably possible losses **6.03**
Disclosure of remote losses **6.05**
Indirect guarantees of indebtedness of others **6.06**

Topical Index

Gain contingencies **6.08**
  Disclosure requirements **6.08**
No accrual of loss contingency **6.02**
  Accrual of loss—range of losses **6.03**
  Disclosure requirements **6.03**
Overview **6.01**
  Definition of contingency **6.01**
  Preacquisition of contingencies **6.08**
  Unasserted claims **6.05**
    Disclosure not required **6.05**

CONVERTIBLE DEBT
Applying the provisions of FASB-84 **7.12**
Background **7.01**
  Induced conversion **7.01**
  Substance of transaction **7.01**
  Time of issuance **7.01**
Calculation of incremental consideration **7.07**
  Market value of securities based on inducement **7.08**
  Market value of securities based on original terms **7.08**
Critique of FASB-84 **7.09**
  Conversion accounting **7.09**
  Extinguishment accounting **7.09**
Induced conversion of convertible debt **7.06**
  Changes in original conversion terms **7.06**
  Incremental consideration **7.07**
Overview **7.01**
  Convertible debt–characteristics **7.01**
    Callable **7.01**
  Conversion feature–exercise **7.03**
    Inseparable **7.04**
    Separable **7.03**
  Conversion feature–issuance **7.02**
    Inseparable **7.04**
    Separable **7.03**
  Extinguishment of debt **7.05**
    Conversion of debt **7.05**
    Troubled debt restructuring **7.05**
  Inducements to convert **7.05**
    Issuer exercises call provision **7.06**
    Issuer offers inducement exceeding original terms **7.06**

CORPORATE READJUSTMENT
Quasi-reorganization **32.01**

COST METHOD
Equity method **14.05**

COST-PLUS-FIXED-FEE CONTRACTS
Disclosure **18.02**
Government contracts **18.01**
Renegotiation **18.02**
Termination claims **18.02**
Typical provisions **18.01**

COST RECOVERY METHOD
Depreciable assets and depreciation **11.08**
Franchise fee recognition **60.02**
Installment method of accounting **20.01**

CUMULATIVE EFFECT
Accounting changes **1.05**
Calculation not possible **1.06**
Reporting in interim periods **1.11**

CURRENT ASSETS AND CURRENT LIABILITIES
Background **8.01**
  Coverage of GAAP **8.01**
Cash surrender value of life insurance **8.07**
  Accounting for purchases of life insurance **8.08**
  Insurable interest **8.08**
Classification of callable obligations **8.13**
Compensated absences **8.16**
Computing life insurance expenses **8.10**
Current assets **8.02**
  Categories **8.02**
  Definition **8.02**
Current liabilities **8.03**
  Definition **8.02**
  Recorded at present values **8.03**
  Types **8.03**
Current obligations expected to be refinanced **8.10**
  Alternative financing sources **8.12**
    Revolving credit agreements **8.12**
  Amount which can be excluded **8.11**
  Conditions for exclusion **8.11**
  Coverage of GAAP **8.10**
  Disclosure **8.12**
  Prerequisites for reclassification **8.10**
Disclosures **8.10**
Factoring **8.07**
Operating cycle **8.01**
  Definition **8.01**
  Determination of current—assets and liabilities **8.01**
  Natural business year **8.02**
Pledging **8.07**
Receivables **8.05**
Working capital **8.03**
  Acid-test ratio (quick ratio) **8.04**
  Changes in elements of working capital **8.04**
  Current ratio (working capital ratio) **8.04**
  Definition **8.03**
  Statement of changes in financial position **8.03**

CURRENT COST DISCLOSURES
Financial reporting and changing prices **15.56**
Specialized assets **15.64**

CURRENT OBLIGATIONS EXPECTED TO BE REFINANCED
Current assets and current liabilities **8.10**

CURRENT OPERATING INCOME
Current value accounting **9.03**

Topical Index

CURRENT OPERATING PERFORMANCE CONCEPT
Results of operations **36.02**
CURRENT RATIO
Current assets and current liabilities **8.04**
CURRENT VALUE ACCOUNTING
Background **9.01**
Comprehensive illustration **9.04**
Current value income **9.03**
  Current operating income **9.03**
  Realized income **9.03**
Current value methods **9.01**
  Entry value system **9.01**
  Exit value system **9.01**
Financial reporting and changing prices **15.51**
Holding gains **9.02**
  Realized **9.02**
  Unrealized **9.02**
Monetary and nonmonetary items **9.02**
  Monetary items **9.02**
  Nonmonetary items **9.02**
Overview **9.01**
CURRENT VALUE INCOME
Current value accounting **9.03**
CURTAILMENT OF DEFINED BENEFIT PENSION PLAN
Pension plans—settlements and curtailments **31.04**

DEBT ISSUED WITH STOCK PURCHASE WARRANTS
Convertible debt–characteristics **7.01**
DEFERRAL METHOD
Investment tax credit **25.01**
DEFERRED COMPENSATION CONTRACTS
Background **10.01**
  Compensation contracts treated like pension plans **10.01**
  Coverage of GAAP **10.01**
Comprehensive illustration **10.02**
Overview **10.01**
  Basis of accounting **10.01**
  Determination of total liability **10.01**
  Periodic accruals **10.01**
Pension plans **10.01**
Postretirement benefits **10.02**
  Financial statement disclosures **10.03**
DEFERRED INCOME TAXES
Consolidated financial statements **5.13**
Deferred tax method **19.10**
Foreign operations and exchange **16.20**

Income taxes **19.10**
Installment method of accounting **20.03**
DEFERRED PROFIT-SHARING PLAN
Pension plans—employers **31.03**
DEFERRED TAX METHOD
Computation **19.10**
Consistent application **19.14**
Definition of taxable income **19.10**
Gross change method **19.14**
Income taxes **19.10**
Individual method **19.14**
Net amount on balance sheet **19.14**
Net change method **19.14**
Permanent differences **19.10**
Short-cut approach **19.14**
Tax expense **19.10**
Tax liability **19.11**
DEFINED BENEFIT PLAN
Pension plans—employers **30.02**
Pension plans—curtailments **31.06**
Pension plans—settlements **31.04**
DEFINED CONTRIBUTION PLAN
Pension plans—employers **30.35**
DEPARTURE FROM COST BASIS
Inventory pricing and methods **24.03**
DEPLETION
Annual depletion expense **11.09**
Cost depletion **11.09**
Depletion rate per unit **11.09**
Depreciable assets and depreciation **11.09**
Disclosure **11.09**
Recoverable units **11.09**
DEPRECIABLE ASSETS AND DEPRECIATION
Asset cost **11.01**
  Capitalized **11.01**
  Normal expenditures **11.01**
  Razing and removal costs **11.01**
  Unnecessary expenditures **11.01**
Background **11.01**
  Coverage of GAAP **11.01**
Depletion **11.09**
  Annual depletion expense **11.09**
  Cost depletion **11.09**
    Depletion rate per unit **11.09**
    Recoverable units **11.09**
Depreciation methods **11.04**
  Cost recovery **11.08**
  Declining balance **11.07**
  Inflation and depreciation **11.09**
  Matching concept **11.04**
  Other types of depreciation **11.08**
    Present value **11.08**
    Replacement **11.08**
    Retirement **11.08**
  Straight line **11.04**
  Sum-of-the-years'-digits **11.05**
  Systematic and rational allocation **11.08**

Topical Index

Timing differences **11.08**
Units of production **11.05**
Disclosure **11.09**
  Accumulated allowances **11.09**
  Deducted from related asset **11.09**
  Depreciation and depletion **11.09**
  Depreciation expense for period **11.09**
  Major classes of assets **11.10**
  Method used **11.10**
Estimated useful life **11.02**
  Longevity **11.02**
  Maintenance policy **11.02**
  Physical life **11.02**
  Service life **11.02**
Improvement of depreciable assets **11.03**
Write-up of assets **11.03**
  Depreciation of appraisal values **11.03**
  GAAP prohibits **11.03**

DEPRECIATION
Cost recovery method **11.08**
Declining balance **11.07**
Deducted from related assets **11.09**
Depreciable assets and depreciation **11.04**
Disclosure **11.09**
Functional depreciation **11.04**
Matching concept **11.04**
Physical depreciation **11.04**
Present value **11.08**
Replacement depreciation **11.08**
Retirement depreciation **11.08**
Straight line **11.04**
Sum-of-the-years'-digits **11.05**
Units of production **11.05**

DEVELOPMENT STAGE ENTERPRISES
Accounting and reporting **12.01**
Basic financial statements **12.01**
  Conformity with GAAP **12.01**
Background **12.01**
  Current promulgated GAAP **12.01**
  Established operating companies **12.01**
  Extractive industries **12.01**
  Real estate properties **12.01**
Disclosure **12.02**
  Accumulated losses **12.02**
  Cumulative changes in financial position **12.02**
  New accounting principle **12.02**
  No longer in development stage **12.03**
  Statement of stockholders' equity **12.02**
    Noncash consideration **12.02**
    Number of shares **12.02**
Overview **12.01**
  Development stage **12.01**
    Establishing a new business **12.01**
    Principal operations **12.01**

DIRECT EFFECTS
Accounting change **1.06**

DIRECT FINANCING LEASES
Leases **26.03**

DISCLOSURES
Accounting changes in interim periods **1.12**
Accounting estimates **1.15**
Accounting policies **2.02**
Broadcasters **50.06**
Business combinations—pooling of interests **3.24**
Business combinations—purchase method **3.02**
Change in an entity **1.16**
Consolidation policy **5.15**
Correction of prior-period errors **1.16**
Current assets and current liabilities **8.10**
Current obligations expected to be refinanced **8.09**
Depletion **11.09**
Depreciation methods **11.09**
Development stage enterprises **12.02**
Earnings per share **13.23**
Equity method **14.08**
Extinguishment of debt **15.04**
Financial reporting and changing prices **15.51**
  Current cost disclosure **15.56**
Foreign operations and exchanges **16.23**
Franchise fee revenue **60.09**
Gain contingency **6.05**
Government contracts **18.02**
Income taxes **19.23**
  Balance sheet classification of deferred income taxes **19.24**
  Claims for refund **19.25**
  Components of tax expense **19.25**
  Deferred charges and credits **19.23**
  Indefinite reversal criteria **19.26**
  Operating loss carryforward **19.26**
  Prior period adjustments **19.26**
  Significant unused credits and deductions **19.25**
Installment method of accounting **20.04**
Insurance enterprises **65.27**
Intangible assets **21.06**
  Amortization **21.06**
  Estimated useful life **21.06**
  Goodwill **21.05**
  Negative goodwill **21.04**
Interest costs capitalized **22.61**
Interest on receivables and payables **22.03**
Interim financial reporting **23.01**
Inventory pricing and method **24.15**
Investment tax credit **25.14**
Lessee's disclosures **26.17**
Lessor's disclosures **26.27**
Long-term contracts **27.04**
Long-term obligations **27.54**
Loss contingencies **6.03**
Marketable securities **28.05**
  Nonspecialized industries **28.05**
  Specialized industries **28.08**
Mortgage banking **70.11**
Motion picture industry **52.06**

Topical Index

DISCLOSURES (continued)
Noninsurance **6.06**
Nonmonetary transactions **29.06**
Oil and gas producing companies **75.15**
Pension plan financial statements **31.64**
Pension plans—employers **30.32**
Postretirement benefits **10.03**
Quasi-reorganization **32.04**
Reasonably possible losses **6.03**
Remote losses **6.03**
Research and development costs **35.03**
Results of operations **36.07**
Revenue recognition **36.54**
Segmental reporting **37.08**
Stockholders' equity **38.02**
   Legal capital **38.02**
      Capital stock **38.03**
      Paid-in capital **38.03**
      Retained earnings **38.03**
Stock issued to employees **39.16**
Troubled debt restructuring **40.05**
   Creditors **40.08**
   Debtors **40.06**

DISCONTINUED OPERATIONS
Income taxes **19.19**
Inventory pricing and methods **24.16**
   Loss on write-down **24.16**
Results of operations **36.05**
   Disposal date **36.06**
   Gain or loss **36.06**
   Identifiable entity **36.05**
   Measurement date **36.05**

DISCOUNTED NOTES RECEIVABLE
Current assets and current liabilities **8.06**

DISCOUNTED TAX ALLOCATION
Income taxes **19.16**

DISCOVERY VALUE ACCOUNTING
Oil and gas producing companies **75.05**

DISPOSAL OF A SEGMENT
Results of operations **36.05**
Segmental reporting **37.05**

DIVIDENDS
Stockholders' equity **38.08**
   Cash dividend **38.08**
   Stock dividend **38.08**
   Stock split **38.09**

DOLLAR-VALUE LIFO
Inventory pricing and methods **24.07**

DOMINANT SEGMENTS
Segmental reporting **37.07**

DONATED STOCK
Stockholders' equity **38.01**

EARNINGS PER SHARE
Antidilution **13.09**

Definition **13.09**
Background **13.01**
   Coverage of GAAP **13.01**
   Special purpose statements **13.01**
Business combinations **13.23**
   Pooling method **13.23**
   Purchase method **13.23**
Common stock equivalents **13.03**
   Contingent shares **13.06**
      Certain level of earnings **13.07**
      Contingent on future market price **13.07**
      Future earnings and future market price **13.07**
   Definition **13.03**
   Determination of CSE **13.03**
   Dilution **13.03**
   EPS computation for subsidiary—parent **13.07**
   Future conversion of CSE **13.07**
   Materiality **13.08**
   Presentation of stock dividend **13.08**
   Security becoming a CSE after issuance **13.04**
   Stock issued to employees **39.09**
   Substance over form **13.03**
   Type of CSE **13.04**
      Contingent shares **13.06**
      Convertible debt and convertible preferred stock **13.04**
      Participating securities **13.06**
      Stock options, warrants, and similar instruments **13.04**
Complex capital structures **13.11**
   Exclusion of antidilutive securities **13.11**
   Fully diluted earnings **13.11**
   Primary earnings **13.12**
   Primary EPS vs. fully diluted EPS **13.13**
   Securities in fully diluted EPS **13.13**
Comprehensive illustration **13.24**
Disclosures **13.24**
   All rights and privileges of the various security holders **13.24**
   Bases on which primary and fully diluted EPS have been calculated **13.24**
   Effects of recapitalization **13.24**
   Other specific disclosures **13.24**
Dual presentation of net income **13.11**
   Definition **13.11**
If-converted method **13.20**
   Adjustments to net income **13.20**
   Assumptions **13.20**
   Objectives **13.20**
   Summary of steps necessary **13.22**
   When used **13.20**
Loss per share **13.23**
Modified treasury stock method **13.17**
   Adjustments to net income **13.17**
   Procedures **13.18**
   Summary of steps necessary **13.19**
   When used **13.17**

Topical Index

Nonpublic enterprise **13.01**
   Definition **13.01**
   Suspension of disclosure requirement **13.01**
  Overview **13.02**
   Accounting changes **13.02**
   Dilution effect ignored **13.02**
   Dual presentation **13.02**
   Prior period adjustments **13.02**
   Prominent presentation of EPS **13.02**
   Subsequent events affecting EPS **13.03**
  Simple capital structures **13.10**
   Definition **13.10**
   Presentation of EPS **13.10**
  Treasury stock method **13.14**
   Procedures **13.16**
   Theory behind treasury stock method **13.17**
   When used **13.14**
  Two-class method **13.23**
   Procedures **13.23**
   When used **13.23**
  Weighted averaged shares **13.12**

ENTITY THEORY
  Disclosure of minority interests **5.15**

ENTRY VALUE SYSTEMS
  Current value accounting **9.01**

EQUITY METHOD
  Adjustments **14.06**
   Capital transactions **14.06**
   Definition of outstanding shares **14.07**
   Discontinuance of equity method **14.07**
   Dissimilar investments **14.08**
   Intercompany profits and losses **14.06**
   Investment account **14.06**
   Ownership decreases below 20% **14.07**
   Ownership increases above 20% **14.07**
   Permanent declines in investment **14.07**
   Preferred stock dividends **14.07**
   Restricted foreign investments **14.08**
   Sale of investment **14.06**
   Temporary investments **14.08**
   Underlying equity **14.06**
   Untimely financial reports **14.06**
  Background **14.01**
   Corporate joint ventures **14.01**
   Exclusions **14.01**
   Leasing subsidiaries **14.01**
  Comprehensive illustrations **14.13**
   Cost method **14.13**
   Cost to equity method **14.15**
   Equity method **14.14**
  Conclusion **14.12**
  Cost method **14.05**
   Continuing operating losses **14.06**
   Dividends are income **14.05**
   Original investment **14.05**
   Ownership of less than 20% **14.05**
  Disclosure **14.08**

   Accounting policies **14.08**
   Carrying value **14.08**
   Convertible securities **14.08**
   Description of investment **14.08**
   Equity method not used **14.08**
   Extent of disclosure **14.09**
   Percentage of ownership **14.08**
   Quoted market prices **14.08**
    Summary **14.09**
    Assets **14.09**
    Liabilities **14.09**
    Results of operations **14.09**
  Equity method **14.06**
   Dividends not income **14.06**
   Investor's share of earnings **14.06**
   One-line consolidation **14.06**
   Original investment **14.06**
  Overview **14.01**
   Consolidation more meaningful **14.02**
   Control less than majority **14.01**
   Dividends received **14.02**
   Effect of equity method **14.02**
   Less than 20% **14.02**
   Proportionate share of net income **14.02**
   Significant influence **14.01**
    More than 20% **14.02**
   Presumption of significant influence **14.02**
   Unincorporated real estate ventures **14.09**
    Accounting for losses **14.10**
    Capital transactions **14.11**
    Purchased goodwill **14.11**

ESTIMATED RESIDUAL VALUE
  Leases **26.04**

ESTIMATED USEFUL LIFE
  Depreciable assets and depreciation **11.02**
  Intangible assets **21.03**
  Physical life **11.02**
  Service life **11.02**

EXCHANGE RATE
  Foreign operations and exchanges **16.22**

EXECUTORY COSTS
  Leases **26.04**

EXIT VALUE SYSTEMS
  Current value accounting **9.01**

EXPORT SALES
  Segmental reporting **37.08**

EXTINGUISHMENT OF DEBT
  Accounting for extinguishments of debt **15.04**
   Computation of gain or loss **15.04**
   Exchange of securities **15.05**
   Method of accounting **15.04**
   Net carrying amount **15.05**
   Reacquisition price **15.04**
   Treatment for other extinguishments **15.04**
  Background **15.01**
   Coverage of GAAP **15.01**
   Comprehensive illustration **15.11**

Topical Index

EXTINGUISHMENT OF DEBT (continued)
Critique of FASB-84 **7.09**
Disclosure **15.11**
  Description of transaction **15.11**
  Gain or loss **15.11**
  Gain or loss per share **15.11**
  Tax effect **15.11**
Gain or loss **15.09**
  Reported as extraordinary item **15.09**
Overview **15.02**
  Call provision **15.02**
  Defeasance provision **15.02**
  Definition **15.02**
  Instantaneous in-substance defeasance **15.03**
Refunding of tax exempt debt **15.10**
When debt is extinguished **15.05**

EXTRACTIVE INDUSTRIES
Development stage enterprises **12.01**

EXTRAORDINARY ITEMS
Carryforwards **36.03**
Changes in financial position **4.03**
Criteria **36.03**
Extinguishment of debt **15.02**
Income taxes **19.19**
Interim period **23.03**
Results of operations **36.03**

FACTORING
Current assets and current liabilities **8.07**

FINANCIAL ACCOUNTING INCOME
Income taxes **19.01**

FINANCIAL REPORTING AND CHANGING PRICES
Additional disclosures for the current year **15.62**
Current cost or lower recoverable amount at end of current year of inventory and property, plant, equipment **15.64**
Depreciation methods, useful lives, and salvage values **15.64**
Income for current year/current cost basis **15.62**
Increase/decrease in current cost or lower recoverable amount before and after adjusting for effects of inflation of inventory and property, plant, equipment **15.64**
Principal types and sources of information to calculate current cost for current year **15.64**
Background **15.51**
Coverage of GAAP **15.51**
Comprehensive illustration **15.67**
Current cost accounting **15.55**
  Definition **15.56**

Disclosure—selected financial data **15.56**
Functional currency **15.55**
Determining current costs **15.56**
  Definition **15.56**
  Depreciation methods **15.57**
  Income tax expense **15.57**
  Net realizable value **15.57**
  Recoverable amounts **15.57**
  Value in use **15.57**
Minimum supplementary information **15.57**
  Aggregate foreign currency translation adjustment **15.60**
  Average level of CPI-U **15.61**
  Cash dividends declared per common share **15.61**
  Explanatory disclosures **15.61**
  Five-year summary **15.57**
  Income from continuing operations **15.58**
  Income per common share/current cost basis **15.61**
  Increase/decrease in inventory and property, plant, equipment **15.60**
  Market price per common share at year end **15.61**
  Net sales and other operating revenue **15.58**
  Purchasing power gain or loss **15.59**
Monetary assets and liabilities **15.53**
Net monetary position **15.54**
  Table of monetary-nonmonetary classified **15.55**
Nonmonetary assets and liabilities **15.53**
Scope and applicability of FASB-33 **15.52**
  Publicly held enterprises **15.52**
  Required supplementary information **15.52**
Specialized assets—current costs **15.64**
  Income producing real estate **15.65**
  Mineral resource assets **15.65**
    Probable mineral reserves other than oil and gas **15.68**
    Proved mineral reserves other than oil and gas **15.68**
  Motion picture films **15.65**
  Timberlands and growing timber **15.65**

FIRM PURCHASE COMMITMENTS
Inventory pricing and methods **24.15**

FIRST-IN, FIRST-OUT (FIFO)
Inventory pricing and methods **24.06**

FLOW OF COST FACTORS
Inventory pricing and methods **24.05**

FLOW-THROUGH METHOD
Investment tax credit **25.01**

FOREIGN OPERATIONS AND EXCHANGE
Average or approximations **16.23**
Background **16.01**
  Foreign currency transaction **16.02**
  Summary of FASB-52 **16.02**
  Translation of financial statements **16.02**

Topical Index

Comprehensive illustration **16.26**
Deferred foreign currency transactions **16.17**
   Classification **16.18**
   Differences between FASB-8 and FASB-52 **16.20**
   Forward exchange contracts **16.16**
   Intercompany transactions **16.19**
Deferred taxes **16.20**
Disclosures **16.23**
Effective date and transition **16.24**
Elimination of intercompany profits **16.22**
Exchange rates **16.22**
Foreign currency transactions **16.15**
   Different treatment for some transactions **16.15**
   Gain and loss **16.15**
Forward exchange contracts **16.16**
Definition **16.16**
Discount or premium **16.17**
   All other contracts **16.17**
   Hedge of net investment **16.17**
   Identifiable hedge **16.17**
Gains and losses **16.18**
   Hedge contracts **16.17**
   Speculative contracts **16.17**
Functional currency **16.04**
   Component operation of parent **16.04**
   Gain or loss from remeasurement **16.07**
   Guidelines for determining functional currency **16.05**
      Cash flow **16.05**
      Expense **16.05**
      Financing **16.06**
      Intercompany transactions **16.06**
      Sales market **16.05**
      Sale price **16.05**
   Remeasurement process **16.07**
Inflationary economics **16.11**
   Remeasurement process **16.11**
Overview **16.01**
   Coverage of GAAP **16.01**
Realization of separate component of equity **16.14**
   Sources **16.15**
Translation objectives **16.03**
Translation of foreign currency statements **16.12**
   Assets and liabilities **16.13**
   Gains and losses **16.13**
   Revenues and expenses **16.13**
   Translation process **16.14**

FORWARD EXCHANGE CONTRACTS
Definition **16.16**
Discount or premium **16.17**
Foreign operations and exchange **16.01**
Gain or loss **16.18**

FRANCHISE FEE REVENUE
Agency sales **60.07**
Background **60.01**

Coverage of GAAP **60.01**
Business combinations **60.08**
   Pooling-of-interests **60.08**
   Purchase method **60.09**
Continuing franchise fee **60.06**
   Agency relationship **60.06**
   Recognized **60.06**
Continuing product sales **60.07**
   Deferred franchise fee **60.07**
Disclosures **60.09**
Franchisee and franchisor—unusual relationships **60.04**
   Contractual control **60.04**
   Guaranteed debt **60.02**
Matching of revenue and costs **60.07**
Overview **60.01**
   Definition of franchise **60.01**
Repossessed franchises **60.08**
   Refund of consideration **60.08**
Revenue recognition—area franchise fees **60.03**
   Determination of substantial performance **60.03**
   Example **60.04**
Revenue recognition—individual franchise fees **60.01**
   Continuing franchise fees **60.03**
   Cost recovery method **60.02**
   Initial fee recognition **60.01**
      Collectibility **60.01**
      Earned **60.01**
   Installment sales method **60.03**
   Tangible assets **60.05**
      Allocation of franchise fee **60.05**
      Specific services **60.06**
      Tangible property **60.05**

FULL-COSTING ACCOUNTING
Interest costs capitalized **22.60**
Oil and gas producing companies **75.06**

FULLY DILUTED EARNINGS
Earnings per share **13.10**

FUNCTIONAL CURRENCY
Component operation of parent **16.03**
Gain or loss from remeasurement **16.07**
Guidelines for determining functional currency **16.05**
   Cash flow **16.05**
   Expense **16.05**
   Financing **16.06**
   Intercompany transactions **16.06**
   Sales market **16.05**
   Sales price **16.05**
Remeasurement process **16.07**

GAIN CONTINGENCIES
Contingencies **6.05**

Topical Index

GENERAL PRICE-LEVEL CHANGES
  Advantages of restatement **17.06**
  Background **17.01**
    Coverage of GAAP **17.01**
  Comprehensive illustration **17.08**
  Disadvantages of restatement **17.06**
  Financial reporting and changing prices **15.51**
  General **17.01**
    Basis of price-level statements **17.01**
  General price-level financial statements **17.07**
    Rules for preparation **17.07**
  General price-level gain or loss **17.04**
    Individual items **17.05**
    Percentage change in price index **17.03**
    Restating net monetary position **17.03**
  Inventories—general price level **24.18**
  Monetary assets and liabilities **17.02**
    Changes in purchasing power **17.02**
    Definition **17.02**
  Net monetary position **17.03**
    Definition **17.03**
    Determination of monetary or nonmonetary **17.03**
    Negative **17.03**
    Positive **17.03**
  Nonmonetary assets and liabilities **17.02**
    Definition **17.02**
    Restatement **17.02**
  Overview **17.01**
    What price-level statements represent **17.01**
  Price indexes **17.03**
    Formula for restatement **17.04**
  Schedule of price-level gain or loss **17.06**
    Procedure **17.06**
    When loss or gain occurs **17.06**

GOLD
  Inventory pricing and methods **24.05**

GOODWILL
  Amortization **21.03**
  Intangible assets **21.02**
  Purchase method **3.02**
  Recording **21.02**
  Step-by-step acquisition **3.15**

GOVERNMENT CONTRACTS
  Background **18.01**
    Coverage of GAAP **18.01**
  CPFF contracts **18.01**
    Advance payments **18.02**
    Recognition of profits **18.01**
    Typical provisions **18.01**
  Overview **18.01**
    Cost-plus-fixed-fee arrangement **18.01**
  Renegotiation **18.02**
    Adjustment of original selling price **18.02**
    Collection not reasonably assured **18.02**
    Disclosure **18.02**
    Provision for renegotiation **18.02**
  Terminated war and defense contracts **18.02**
    Determination of profit or loss **18.03**
    Disclosure **18.03**
    Disposal credits **18.03**
    Termination claims **18.03**

GROSS PROFIT METHOD
  Inventory pricing and methods **24.16**

HOLDING GAINS
  Current value accounting **9.02**
  Realized **9.02**
  Unrealized **9.02**

IF-CONVERTED METHOD
  Earnings per share **13.19**

INCOME TAXES
  Background **19.01**
    Coverage of GAAP **19.01**
    Regulated industries **19.01**
  Changes in investment **19.08**
    Deferred taxes resulting from **19.08**
    Investment becomes a subsidiary **19.08**
    Investment falls below 20% **19.09**
    Subsidiary relationship **19.08**
  Deferred tax method **19.10**
    Computation of deferred tax **19.11**
    Consistent application **19.11**
    Definition of taxable income **19.10**
    Gross change method **19.14**
    Individual method **19.14**
    Net amount on balance sheet **19.14**
    Net change method **19.14**
    Permanent differences **19.10**
    Short-cut approach **19.14**
    Tax expense **19.11**
    Tax liability **19.11**
    With and without method **19.10**
  Disclosure **19.23**
    Balance sheet classification of deferred income taxes **19.24**
    Claim for refunds and offsets **19.25**
    Components of tax expense **19.26**
    Deferred charges and credits **19.24**
    Differences between taxable income and pretax accounting income **19.26**
    Indefinite reversal criteria **19.26**
    Operating-loss carryforward **19.26**
    Prior-period adjustments **19.26**
    Significant unused credits or deductions **19.25**
  Discounting tax allocation accounts **19.16**
  Glossary **19.27**
    Deferred taxes **19.27**

Topical Index

Income taxes **19.27**
Income tax expense **19.27**
Income tax liability **19.27**
Indefinite reversal criteria **19.27**
Interperiod tax allocation **19.27**
Intraperiod tax allocation **19.27**
Net of tax presentation **19.27**
Permanent differences **19.27**
Pretax accounting income **19.28**
Taxable income **19.28**
Tax carrybacks and carryforwards **19.28**
Tax effects **19.28**
Timing differences **19.28**
Income taxes—interim periods **19.16**
Adjustment to net deferred credits **19.17**
Determination of interim period tax **19.17**
Discontinued operations **19.19**
Effect of change—accounting principle **19.22**
Estimated annual effective tax rate **19.17**
Extraordinary items **19.19**
Realization of tax benefit **19.19**
Recognition of tax benefit of prior years' operating loss **19.22**
Required by GAAP **19.16**
Tax in more than one jurisdiction **19.22**
Exceptions **19.23**
Use of actual effective tax rate **19.18**
Indefinite reversal criteria **19.07**
Controlling interests **19.08**
Specific plan **19.07**
Intraperiod tax allocation **19.16**
Relationship between income tax expense and other items **19.16**
Matching concept **19.15**
Interperiod tax allocation—principles **19.15**
Undistributed earnings of investees **19.15**
Measuring timing differences **19.09**
Determining if undistributed earnings will be realized in dividends **19.09**
Use of estimates and assumptions **19.09**
Offsetting—taxes payable **19.16**
Operating losses **19.04**
Carrybacks **19.04**
Carryforwards **19.05**
Extraordinary items **19.05**
Purchased subsidiary **19.05**
Quasi-reorganization **19.05**
Realizable beyond any reasonable doubt **19.05**
Tax benefits **19.05**
Overview **19.01**
Financial accounting income **19.01**
Going concern concept **19.01**
Taxable income **19.01**
Timing differences **19.02**
Permanent differences **19.03**
Bad debt allowances—S&L associations **19.04**

Policyholders' surplus—stock life insurance **19.04**
Types **19.03**
Railroad gradings and tunnel bores **19.09**
Tax allocation must be made **19.09**
Timing differences **19.02**
Timing differences—special areas **19.06**
Investment in common stock—equity method **19.06**
Losses of a subsidiary **19.07**
Undistributed earnings of a subsidiary **19.06**
Transactions that cause timing differences **19.02**
Four basic causes **19.02**
United Kingdom Tax Benefits **19.26**
U.S. steamship companies **19.09**

INDEFINITE REVERSAL CRITERIA
Income taxes **19.07**

INDUSTRY SEGMENT
Segmental reporting **37.04**

INFLATION ACCOUNTING
Financial reporting and changing prices **15.51**

INITIAL DIRECT COSTS
Leases **26.06**

INSTALLMENT METHOD OF ACCOUNTING
Background **20.01**
Existing GAAP **20.01**
Cost recovery method **20.01**
Expenses of collection **20.01**
Recover cost first **20.01**
Recovery of cost doubtful **20.01**
Revenue recognition **20.01**
Sunk-cost theory **20.01**
Deferred income taxes **20.03**
Installment sales for tax purposes **20.03**
Normal accrual accounting **20.04**
Timing difference **20.04**
Disclosure **20.04**
Balance sheet presentation **20.04**
Classification as current asset **20.04**
Percentage relationship **20.04**
Unrealized gross profit **20.04**
Franchise fee revenue **60.03**
Overview **20.01**
Collectibility **20.01**
Extended collection period **20.01**
Recording installment sales **20.01**
Different products and departments **20.02**
Gross profit ratio **20.02**
Part recovery cost **20.01**
Part recovery profit **20.01**
Realized gross profit **20.02**
Repossessed goods **20.02**
Selling and administrative costs **20.02**
Separate records **20.02**

INSTALLMENT METHOD OF ACCOUNTING (continued)
- Title to goods **20.02**
- Unrealized gross profit **20.02**
- Value of repossessed goods **20.03**

INSURANCE ENTERPRISES
- Amendments to existing GAAP **65.28**
- Background **65.01**
  - Property and liability insurance companies **65.01**
  - Claims **65.06**
    - Departmental functions **65.03**
    - Facultative reinsurance **65.03**
    - General ledger **65.03**
    - Insurable interest **65.02**
    - Insurance laws **65.05**
    - Limit of insurance **65.04**
    - Mutual companies **65.02**
    - Reciprocal **65.02**
    - Stock companies **65.02**
  - Stock life insurance companies **65.06**
    - Annuity policy **65.07**
    - Departmental functions **65.07**
    - Endowment policies **65.09**
    - Insurable interest **65.06**
    - Joint and survivorship annuity **65.11**
    - Life annuity **65.10**
    - Straight-life annuity **65.10**
    - Term policies **65.09**
    - Variable annuity **65.11**
    - Whole life policies **65.08**
  - Title insurance companies **65.11**
    - Title plant **65.12**
    - Title search **65.11**
- Claim costs and future policy benefits **65.15**
  - Claim adjustment expense **65.17**
  - Claim costs **65.16**
    - Estimates **65.16**
    - Formulas **65.16**
  - Future policy benefits **65.18**
- Classification of insurance contracts **65.12**
  - Long duration contracts **65.12**
  - Short duration contracts **65.12**
- Contingent commissions **65.23**
- Deferred income taxes **65.26**
- Deficiency in premiums or liability for future policy benefits **65.20**
  - Long duration contracts **65.21**
  - Short duration contracts **65.20**
- Disclosure **65.27**
- Effective date and transition **65.29**
- Investments **65.24**
  - Bonds **65.24**
  - Commitment fees **65.24**
  - Mortgages **65.24**
  - Real estate **65.24**
  - Realized gains and losses **65.25**
  - Stock **65.24**
- Other costs **65.19**
  - Acquisition costs **65.19**
- Collection expense **65.19**
- Other significant information **65.30**
  - Mandatory securities valuation reserve **65.31**
  - Nonadmitted assets **65.31**
  - Stockholders' equity **65.32**
- Overview **65.01**
  - Coverage of GAAP **65.01**
- Policyholder dividends **65.23**
- Premium—revenue recognition **65.13**
  - Long duration contracts **65.15**
  - Short duration contracts **65.13**
- Real estate used in business and separate accounts **65.25**
- Reinsurance **65.22**
  - Reporting requirements **65.22**

INTANGIBLE ASSETS
- Amortization **21.03**
  - Amortization period **21.03**
  - Income tax effect **21.04**
  - Method **21.03**
- Background **21.01**
  - Coverage of GAAP **21.01**
- Broadcasters **50.05**
- Comprehensive illustrations **21.08**
- Cost of intangibles **21.02**
  - Measurement of cost **21.03**
- Disclosure **21.06**
- Disposal of goodwill **21.04**
- Intangible assets of motor carriers **21.06**
- Negative goodwill **21.04**
  - Amortization **21.03**
  - Reduction of noncurrent assets **21.04**
- Overview **21.02**
  - Definition of intangible asset **21.02**
  - Identifiability **21.02**
  - Life **21.02**
  - Manner of acquisition **21.02**
  - Transferability **21.02**
- Savings and loan associations **21.01**
  - Net-spread method **21.01**
  - Separate-valuation method **21.01**
- Step-by-step acquisitions **21.05**

INTERCOMPANY BOND HOLDINGS
- Consolidated financial statements **5.09**

INTERCOMPANY DIVIDENDS
- Consolidated financial statements **5.13**

INTERCOMPANY STOCK HOLDINGS
- Consolidated financial statements **5.13**

INTERCOMPANY TRANSACTIONS
- Bonds **5.09**
- Dividends **5.13**
- Receivables and payables **5.05**
- Sales and purchases **5.05**
- Stock **5.13**
- Unrealized profit in inventory **5.06**
- Unrealized profits—long lived assets **5.07**

INTEREST COST COMPONENT
Pension plans—employers **30.17**
INTEREST COSTS CAPITALIZED
Amount of interest costs to be capitalized **22.54**
Background **22.52**
Capitalization of interest cost—general **22.52**
Capitalization period **22.56**
Comprehensive illustration **22.62**
Disclosure **22.61**
Disposition of capitalized interest **22.60**
Full cost method in extractive industries **22.61**
Investor's qualifying assets **22.56**
Overview **22.51**
   Coverage of GAAP **22.51**
Qualifying assets—acquisition period **22.53**
Qualifying assets—intended use **22.54**
Tax exempt borrowings, gifts and grants **22.58**
   Restricted grants and gifts **22.59**
INTEREST METHOD
Leases **26.14**
Receivables and payables **22.03**
INTEREST ON RECEIVABLES AND PAYABLES
Amortization of discount or premium **22.02**
   Conditions for discount or premium **22.02**
   Interest method **22.03**
Background **22.01**
   Coverage of GAAP **22.01**
   Exclusion **22.01**
Comprehensive illustrations **22.03**
Determining present value **22.02**
   Guidelines **22.02**
   Objective **22.02**
Disclosure **22.03**
Overview **22.01**
   Recorded at present value **22.01**
   Rights and privileges attached **22.01**
   Valuation in noncash transactions **22.02**
Statement presentation—discount or premium **22.03**
INTEREST RATE IMPLICIT
Leases **26.05**
INTERIM FINANCIAL REPORTING
Accounting and reporting **23.01**
   Disclosure of material contingencies **23.03**
   Income taxes **23.03**
   Product costs **23.02**
   Recognition of revenues **23.01**
   Rules for other costs and expenses **23.02**
Background **23.01**
   Coverage of GAAP **23.01**
Inventory for interim financial reporting **23.02**
   Inventory losses **23.02**
   LIFO method **23.02**
   Standard costs **23.02**
   Use of estimated gross profit **23.02**
Oil and gas producing companies **75.16**
Overview **23.01**
   Discussion of interim reports **23.01**
Summarized interim financial statements **23.03**
   Disclosures—fourth quarter results **23.04**
   Information to be included **23.03**
INTERPERIOD TAX ALLOCATION
Income taxes **19.16**
Oil and gas producing companies **75.15**
INTRAPERIOD TAX ALLOCATION
Income taxes **19.16**
INVENTORY PRICING AND METHODS
Background **24.01**
   Coverage of GAAP **24.01**
Base stock method **24.14**
Comprehensive illustrations **24.21**
Conclusion **24.19**
Cost methods **24.05**
   Assumptions **24.05**
   Flow of cost factors **24.05**
   Inventory identification **24.05**
   Objective **24.05**
Costs **24.03**
Departure from cost basis **24.03**
Disclosure **24.15**
Dollar-value LIFO **24.07**
Firm purchase commitments **24.15**
First-in, first-out method (FIFO) **24.06**
Inventories—accounting change **24.18**
Inventories—construction-type contracts **24.18**
Inventories—general price-level changes **24.18**
Inventories in business combinations **24.17**
   Valuation **24.17**
Inventories in foreign currency **24.18**
Inventories—intercompany profits **24.18**
Inventories—interim reporting **24.16**
   Inventory losses **24.16**
   LIFO method **24.16**
   Standard costs **24.17**
   Use of estimated gross profit **24.16**
Inventories—nonmonetary exchanges **24.19**
Inventories—research and development **24.17**
Inventories—tax allocation **24.18**
Inventory for terminated contracts **24.17**
Inventory of discontinued segments **24.16**
   Loss on write-down **24.16**
Inventory profits **24.19**
Inventory systems **24.01**
   Periodic **24.01**
   Perpetual **24.02**
Last-in, first-out method (LIFO) **24.06**
   Disclosures **24.07**
   LIFO layers **24.06**

Topical Index

INVENTORY PRICING AND METHODS (continued)
Lower of cost or market **24.03**
  Exceptions **24.05**
  Market **24.03**
  Maximum **24.03**
  Minimum **24.03**
  Reasons for maximum and minimum **24.04**
Moving-average method **24.08**
Overview **24.01**
  Classification of inventories **24.01**
  What inventories include **24.01**
Relative sales value costing **24.14**
Retail inventory method **24.09**
  Computing cost-to-retail ratio **24.09**
  Cost-to-retail ratio **24.09**
  LIFO application **24.12**
    Computing cost-to-retail ratio **24.13**
    Differences from conventional method **24.12**
  Purpose **24.11**
Standard costs **24.06**
  Use of standards **24.06**
  Variations from standards **24.06**
Title of goods **24.02**
  Terminology **24.02**
  When title to goods passes to buyer **24.02**
Weighted-average method **24.08**

INVESTMENT TAX CREDIT
Accounting for investment tax credit **25.04**
  Business combinations **25.12**
  Carryback and carryforward **25.06**
  Example **25.06**
  Offset of deferred tax credits **25.05**
  Percentage limitation **25.04**
  Unused investment tax credit **25.04**
Background **25.01**
  Coverage of GAAP **25.01**
Conflict in GAAP **25.14**
Disclosure **25.14**
IRC provisions **25.02**
  Carryback or carryforward **25.05**
  Maximum investment tax credit **25.02**
  Other than recovery property **25.03**
  Recovery property **25.02**
  Section 38 property **25.03**
Other considerations **25.13**
Overview **25.01**
  Deferral method **25.01**
  Flow-through method **25.01**
  Methods of recognition **25.01**
  SEC statement (ASR 96) **25.01**

LAST-IN, FIRST-OUT METHOD (LIFO)
Inventory pricing and methods **24.06**
  LIFO layers **24.06**

LEASES
Accounting and reporting by lessees **26.11**
  Amortization **26.14**
  Initial recording **26.11**
  Interest expense: interest method **26.14**
  Leases with escalation clauses **26.12**
Accounting and reporting by lessors **26.20**
Accounting and reporting for leveraged leases **26.42**
  Amount of net income recognized **26.43**
  Characteristics of leveraged leases **26.42**
  Computation of periodic net income **26.43**
  Disclosure **26.44**
  Initial and continuing investment **26.42**
Accounting for lease changes—lessee **26.15**
  Change in classification **26.15**
  Change in lease term **26.16**
  Change in minimum lease payments **26.15**
  Inoperative guarantee or penalty **26.15**
Accounting for lease changes—lessor **26.24**
  Change to direct financing lease **26.24**
  Change to operating lease **26.25**
  Change to sales-type lease **26.24**
  No change in classification **26.24**
Annual review of residual values—lessor **26.24**
Background **26.01**
  Coverage of GAAP **26.01**
Balance sheet classifications—lessor **26.24**
Business combinations **26.44**
  Change in lease classification **26.44**
Changing a provision of a lease **26.10**
  Reclassification of lease agreement **26.10**
  Refundings of tax-exempt debt **26.10**
Classification of leases by lessees **26.09**
  Four criteria for classification **26.09**
  Lessee's discount rate **26.09**
  Lessor's discount rate **26.09**
Classification of leases by lessors **26.09**
  Additional criteria for classification **26.09**
Comprehensive illustration—capital lease **26.44**
Effective date and transition **26.44**
Leases involving government units **26.35**
Leases involving real estate **26.31**
  Leases involving land and building **26.32**
    Fair value of land is less than 25% **26.32**
    Fair value of land is more than 25% **26.33**
  Leases involving land, building, equipment **26.34**
  Leases involving land only **26.31**
  Leases involving only part of building **26.34**
  Review of classifications **26.31**
Lease term **26.06**
  Duration of lease term **26.06**
  Noncancelable lease term **26.07**
Lessee's minimum lease payment **26.07**
  Bargain purchase option **26.07**

Topical Index

Normal minimum lease payments **26.07**
Lessee's operating leases **26.16**
   Contingent rental expense **26.16**
   Scheduled rent increases/decreases **26.17**
Lessee's statement disclosure **26.17**
   Capital leases **26.17**
   General disclosure **26.17**
   Illustrations **26.18**
   Operating leases **26.17**
Lessor's minimum lease payments **26.08**
Lessor's operating leases **26.25**
   Amortization of rental income **26.26**
   Contingent rental income **26.26**
   Scheduled rent increases/decreases **26.26**
Lessor's statement disclosure **26.28**
   General disclosure **26.28**
   Illustration **26.29**
   Operating leases **26.28**
   Sales-type and direct financing leases **26.28**
Recording leases by lessors **26.21**
   Direct financing leases **26.21**
   Lessor's gross investment **26.20**
   Other methods **26.22**
   Sales-type leases **26.21**
   Sales-type leases involving real estate **26.22**
Related party leases **26.35**
Sale-leaseback transactions **26.34**
   Accounting for certain losses on sale-leasebacks **26.39**
   Accounting for sale-leasebacks **26.36**
     Minor **26.37**
     More than minor but less than substantially all **26.38**
     Substantially all **26.37**
   Terminology **26.36**
     Profit or loss on the sale **26.36**
     Purchaser-lessor **26.36**
     Sale-leaseback **26.36**
     Substantially all or minor **26.36**
Sale or assignment to third parties **26.27**
   Nonsubstantial risk of the seller **26.27**
   Recognition of profit or loss **26.27**
   Sale recorded as a borrowing **26.27**
   Substantial risk of the seller **26.27**
Sales-type vs. direct financing leases **26.03**
   Bargain purchase option **26.04**
   Bargain renewal option **26.04**
   Dealer's profit or loss **26.04**
   Estimated residual value **26.05**
   Executory costs **26.04**
Subleases and similar transactions **26.39**
   Capital leases **26.39**
   Operating leases **26.39**
     Original lessee is obligated **26.39**
   Recognition of loss **26.40**
Substance over form **26.02**
   Criteria for transfer of ownership **26.02**
Termination of a capital lease—lessee **26.16**

Termination of a lease—lessor **26.25**
Terminology **26.03**
   Capital lease **26.03**
   Direct financing lease **26.03**
   Sale-type lease **26.03**

LESSEE'S INCREMENTAL BORROWING RATE
Leases **26.05**

LESSOR'S IMPLICIT INTEREST RATE
Leases **26.05**

LEVERAGED LEASES
Leases **26.42**

LONG-TERM CONSTRUCTION CONTRACTS
Accounting—completed-contracts **27.02**
   Important points **27.02**
Accounting—percentage-of-completion **27.04**
   Important points **27.04**
Background **27.01**
   Coverage of GAAP **27.01**
Choice of method **27.04**
Completed-contract method **27.01**
   Advantages and disadvantages **27.02**
   Allocation of G&A expenses **27.02**
   Balance sheet classifications **27.02**
   Provision for expected loss **27.02**
   Recognition of income **27.02**
Comprehensive illustration **27.04**
Disclosure **27.04**
Overview **27.01**
   Methods for long-term contracts **27.01**
Percentage-of-completion method **27.03**
   Advantages and disadvantages **27.03**
   Provision for expected loss **27.03**
   Recognition of income **27.03**

LONG-TERM OBLIGATIONS
Background **27.51**
   Conditional right or obligation **27.51**
   Disclosure in accordance with GAAP **27.52**
   Recognition of asset or liability **27.52**
   Unconditional right or obligation **27.51**
Disclosure of other unconditional obligations **27.56**
   Specific balance sheet disclosures **27.56**
   Illustrations **27.56**
Disclosure of unrecorded unconditional purchase obligations **27.54**
   Disclosure of present values **27.55**
     Examples **27.55**
   Necessary disclosures **27.55**
Overview **27.51**
   Coverage of GAAP **27.51**
Product financing arrangements **27.59**
   Accounting for take or pay contracts versus financing arrangements **27.59**
Unconditional purchase obligations **27.52**
   Criteria of obligations **27.53**
   Definition of unconditional obligation **27.52**

GAAP GUIDE / 96.17

Topical Index

LOSS CONTINGENCIES
  Contingencies **6.02**
LOWER OF COST OR MARKET
  Foreign operations and exchange **16.10**
    Translation **16.10**
  Inventory pricing and methods **24.03**
  Marketable securities **28.06**

MARKETABLE SECURITIES
  Accounting for futures contracts **28.11**
    Accounting for hedges **28.16**
    Accounting for speculative futures contracts **28.15**
    Background **28.13**
    Hedge criteria **28.15**
    Overview **28.12**
  Background **28.01**
    Coverage of promulgated GAAP **28.01**
      Employee benefit plans **28.01**
      Investments—equity method **28.01**
      Mutual life insurance companies **28.01**
      Nonmarketable securities **28.01**
      Nonprofit organizations **28.01**
      Nonspecialized industry practices **28.01**
      Personal financial statements **28.01**
      Specialized industry practices **28.01**
  Comprehensive illustration **28.10**
  Income tax effects **28.10**
  Industries having specialized practices **28.06**
    Brokers and dealers **28.06**
    Casualty insurance companies **28.06**
    Compliance with promulgated GAAP **28.06**
      Accounting change **28.06**
      Aggregate cost or market **28.07**
      Appraised value **28.06**
      Broader definition for market **28.07**
      Conforming to a parent's practices **28.07**
      Current group **28.07**
      Fair value **28.06**
      Investments—equity method **28.07**
      Lower of cost or market **28.06**
      Noncurrent group **28.07**
      Unclassified balance sheets **28.07**
      Valuation accounts **28.07**
    Disclosure—specialized industry practices **28.08**
      Changes in net unrealized gains or losses **28.08**
      Consolidated balance sheets **28.08**
        Nonspecialized industry practices **28.08**
        Specialized industry practices **28.08**
      Gross unrealized gains and losses **28.08**
      Inclusion of unrealized gains and losses **28.08**
        Stockholders' equity **28.08**
      Subsequent events **28.08**

    Industries not having specialized practices **28.03**
      Accounting procedures **28.03**
        Current group **28.03**
        Lower of cost or market **28.03**
        Noncurrent group **28.03**
        Total cost and total market **28.03**
        Unclassified balance sheet **28.03**
      Consolidation **28.04**
        Aggregate cost or market **28.04**
        Different balance sheet dates **28.04**
        Investment—equity method **28.05**
      Disclosure **28.05**
        Change in valuation account **28.06**
        Consolidated balance sheets **28.06**
        Cost basis **28.06**
        Gross unrealized gains **28.06**
        Gross unrealized losses **28.06**
        Net realized gains or losses **28.06**
        Subsequent events **28.06**
        Total cost and market value **28.05**
        Unclassified balance sheets **28.06**
      Reclassification **28.04**
        Date of transfer **28.04**
        Lower of cost or market **28.04**
        New cost basis **28.04**
      Sale of a security **28.04**
        Basis—original cost **28.04**
        Realized gain or loss **28.04**
        Reported in net income **28.04**
      Subsequent gains or losses **28.04**
        Adjustment of allowance account **28.04**
        Not to exceed original cost **28.04**
      Unrealized losses **28.03**
        Allowance account **28.04**
        Current group **28.03**
        Noncurrent group **28.03**
  Marketability **28.02**
    Determination of marketability **28.02**
      Balance sheet date **28.02**
      Foreign stock markets **28.02**
      Lack of market **28.02**
      Restricted or legend stock **28.02**
    Evidence of marketability **28.02**
      Current "bid" and "ask" **28.02**
      Over-the-counter securities **28.02**
  Other than temporary declines—noncurrent group **28.02**
    Decline in market—other than temporary **28.08**
    Determination of permanent decline **28.09**
      Subsequent recoveries **28.09**
    New cost basis **28.09**
    Recognize a realized loss **28.09**
    Subsequent increases **28.09**
  Overview **28.01**
    Definition of a marketable security **28.01**
      Common stock **28.02**
      Convertible bonds **28.02**
      Preferred stock **28.02**

Puts and calls **28.02**
Stock options **28.02**
Stock rights **28.02**
Stock warrants **28.02**
Treasury stock **28.02**
Realized gain or loss **28.02**
Unrealized gain or loss **28.02**
MATCHING CONCEPT
Depreciable assets and depreciation **11.04**
Depreciation method **11.04**
Franchise fee revenue **60.07**
Income taxes **19.15**
Percentage-of-completion method **27.01**
MINORITY INTERESTS
Consolidated financial statements **5.13**
Equity method **14.01**
Father-son-grandson affiliation **5.13**
In net income **5.13**
Presentation on balance sheet **5.15**
Stockholders' equity **38.04**
MODIFIED TREASURY STOCK METHOD
Earnings per share **13.16**
MONETARY AND NONMONETARY ITEMS
Current value accounting **9.02**
Table of monetary-nonmonetary classified **15.55**
General price-level changes **17.02**
Changes in purchasing power **17.02**
Definition **17.02**
Net monetary position **17.03**
Nonmonetary transactions **29.01**
MORTGAGE BANKING INDUSTRY
Accounting for collateralized mortgage obligations **70.12**
Accounting for CMOs **70.14**
Borrowing transactions **70.14**
Exceptions **70.15**
Background **70.13**
Collateralized mortgage obligation **70.13**
Federal Home Loan Mortgage Corporation **70.14**
Federal National Mortgage Association **70.14**
Government National Mortgage Association **70.13**
Mortgage-backed security **70.13**
Consolidated statements **70.16**
Effective date **70.16**
Offsetting **70.16**
Overview **70.01**
Coverage of GAAP **70.12**
Servicing rights **70.16**
Accounting for mortgage loans **70.01**
Block purchases of mortgage loans **70.04**
Held for long-term investment **70.01**
Held for sale **70.03**
In-house origination costs **70.07**
Issuance costs for GNMA securities **70.08**
Mortgage servicing fees **70.05**
Repurchase agreements **70.05**
Transactions with affiliates **70.06**
Accounting for servicing rights **70.08**
Financial statement disclosure **70.11**
Origination, placement and commitment fees **70.09**
Loans held for sale **70.10**
Loans not held for sale **70.11**
Overview **70.01**
Coverage of GAAP **70.01**
MORTGAGE LOANS
Block purchases of mortgage loans **70.04**
Collateralized mortgage obligations **70.12**
Held for long-term investment **70.01**
Held for sale **70.03**
In-house origination costs **70.07**
Issuance costs for GNMA securities **70.08**
Mortgage servicing fees **70.05**
Repurchase agreements **70.05**
Transactions with affiliates **70.06**
MOTION PICTURE FILMS
Background **52.01**
Costs and expenses **52.03**
Amortization **52.03**
Disclosure **52.06**
Effective date **52.06**
Financial statements **52.05**
Guidelines **52.05**
Home market **52.06**
Inventory adjustments **52.04**
Loans and interest costs **52.05**
Overview **52.01**
Coverage of GAAP **52.01**
Revenue recognition **52.01**
Television exhibitions **52.02**
Theatrical exhibitions **52.02**
MOVING-AVERAGE METHOD
Inventory pricing and methods **24.08**

NATURAL BUSINESS YEAR
Current assets and current liabilities **8.02**
NEGATIVE GOODWILL
Intangible assets **21.04**
Purchase method **3.02**
NET CARRYING AMOUNT
Extinguishment of debt **15.02**
NET PERIODIC PENSION COST
Pension plans—employers **30.10**
NET REALIZABLE VALUE
Current assets **8.02**
Financial reporting and changing prices **15.66**
Inventory pricing and methods **24.03**

Topical Index

NONCOMPENSATORY PLANS
Stock issued to employees **39.02**
  Characteristics **39.02**
  Definition **39.02**

NONDISCRETIONARY EFFECTS
Accounting change **1.05**

NONMONETARY TRANSACTIONS
Background **29.01**
  Coverage of GAAP **29.01**
Conclusion **29.08**
  Interperiod tax allocation **29.08**
Disclosure **29.06**
Earning process not complete **29.05**
  Basis of monetary consideration **29.04**
  Formula for recognition of gain or loss **29.06**
  Payor of monetary consideration **29.06**
  Recipient of monetary consideration **29.05**
Exchange (reciprocal transfer) **29.02**
Fair value **29.02**
Fair value not determinable **29.03**
Gain or loss **29.07**
Involuntary conversion **29.07**
Monetary assets or liabilities **29.01**
Nonmonetary assets or liabilities **29.01**
Nonreciprocal transfer **29.02**
Nonreciprocal transfers to owners **29.03**
  FHLMC participating preferred stock **29.03**

NONPUBLIC ENTERPRISES
Definition **13.01**
Earnings per share **13.01**
Segmental reporting **37.03**
Suspension of disclosure requirements **13.01**

NONRECIPROCAL TRANSFER
Nonmonetary transactions **29.03**

OFFSETTING-TAXES PAYABLE
Income taxes **19.16**

OIL AND GAS PRODUCING COMPANIES
Accounting principles—basic concepts **75.10**
  Acquisition of properties **75.10**
  Amortization **75.11**
  Costs **75.10**
  Nonmonetary exchange **75.11**
  Sale of an interest in property **75.10**
Development **75.13**
  Amortization **75.13**
  Costs **75.13**
Exploration **75.12**
  Amortization **75.13**
  Conditions for carrying exploratory well as an asset **75.12**
  Costs **75.13**
  Exploratory wells **75.12**
Production **75.14**
  Costs **75.14**
  Lifting costs **75.14**
Background **75.01**
  Coverage of GAAP **75.01**
Background information **75.07**
  Accounting Series Release 253 **75.09**
  Accounting Series Release 257 **75.09**
  Accounting Series Release 258 **75.09**
  Energy Policy and Conservation Act of 1975 **75.07**
  Securities Act Release No. 5706 **75.08**
  Securities Act Release No. 5801 **75.08**
  Securities Act Release No. 5837 **75.08**
  Securities Act Release No. 5861 **75.09**
  Securities Act Release No. 5877 **75.09**
  Securities Act Release No. 5878 **75.09**
Balance sheet—subsequent information **75.14**
Disclosure **75.15**
  Capitalized costs **75.16**
  Functional costs **75.22**
  Illustration of net quantities **75.18**
  Interim financial statement **75.16**
  Net quantities of crude oil and gas **75.18**
  Rules for determining net quantities **75.18**
Effects of FASB-25 **75.02**
  Accounting changes **75.02**
  Definition of reserves **75.02**
  Disclosure **75.02**
Income tax considerations **75.15**
  Interperiod tax allocation **75.15**
Overview **75.02**
  Current value accounting **75.06**
  Development well **75.05**
  Discovery value accounting **75.05**
    Current costs **75.05**
    Current exit value in liquidation **75.05**
    Expected exit value **75.05**
    Present value of expected cash flow **75.05**
  Exploratory well **75.05**
  Field **75.03**
  Full-costing accounting **75.06**
  Properties **75.02**
  Proved area **75.03**
  Proved reserves **75.03**
    Proved developed reserves **75.04**
    Proved undeveloped reserves **75.04**
  Reservoir **75.02**
  Service well **75.05**
  Stratigraphic test well **75.05**
    Development—type test well **75.05**
  Successful efforts costing **75.06**
  Supply agreements **75.05**
  Support equipment and facilities **75.04**
  Uncompleted wells, equipment and facilities **75.04**
  Wells, related equipment and facilities **75.04**
Segmental reporting **75.15**
Support equipment and facilities **75.14**

Topical Index

ONE-LINE CONSOLIDATION
Consolidated financial statements **5.05**
Equity method **14.02**
OPERATING CYCLE
Current assets and current liabilities **8.01**
OPERATING LEASES
Leases **26.16**
OPERATING LOSSES
Carrybacks **19.04**
Carryforwards **19.05**
Extraordinary items **19.05**
Income taxes **19.04**
Tax benefits **19.05**

PAID-IN CAPITAL
Stockholders' equity **38.03**
Definition **38.03**
Sources **38.03**
PAST-SERVICE COSTS
Pension plans—employers **30.18**
Pension plans—settlements and curtailments **31.06**
PAY-AS-YOU-GO METHOD
Pension plans—employers **31.06**
PENSION PLAN FINANCIAL STATEMENTS
Accumulated plan benefits of participants **31.58**
Background **31.51**
Changes in accumulated plan benefits **31.62**
Changes in net assets available for benefits **31.57**
Financial statement note **31.66**
Net assets available for benefits **31.53**
Other financial statement disclosures **31.64**
Overview **31.51**
Reasonable approximations and averages **31.52**
PENSION PLANS—EMPLOYERS
Actual return on plan assets component **30.17**
Fair value of assets **30.17**
Pension benefit payments made **30.17**
Realized/unrealized gains and losses **30.18**
Recognition **30.17**
Actuarial assumptions **30.04**
Actuarial gain or loss **30.05**
Discount rates **30.05**
Going-concern concept **30.05**
Amortization of unrecognized net obligation or net asset (initial application of FASB-87) **30.27**
Amortization **30.27**
Defined contribution plan **30.27**
Inactive participants **30.27**
Funded status of plan **30.27**
Unrecognized net obligation/asset definition **30.27**
Amortization of unrecognized prior service cost component **30.18**
Amortization of total prior service cost **30.18–30.19**
Active participants **30.18**
Alternative amortization approach **30.19**
Inactive participants **30.18**
Amount includable in net periodic pension cost **30.18**
Plan amendment **30.19**
Prior service cost **30.18**
Annuity contracts **30.34**
Cost of participation rights **30.34, 30.35**
Date of purchase **30.35**
Subsequent to date of purchase **30.35**
Currently earned benefits cost **30.34**
Definition **30.34**
Captive insurer **30.34**
Risks and rewards transferred **30.34**
Other contracts with insurance companies **30.35**
Participating or nonparticipating **30.34**
Dividends **30.34**
Background **30.01**
Coverage of GAAP **30.01**
Deferred compensation plans **30.01**
Postemployment/postretirement benefits **30.02**
Business combinations—purchase method **30.38**
Single-employer pension plan acquired **30.38**
Initial recognition of asset or liability **30.38**
Subsequent recognition of asset or liability **30.38**
Capsule analysis of FASB-87 **30.06**
Journal entries **30.06**
Reconciling funded status of plan illustration **30.07**
Accrued/prepaid pension cost **30.10**
Accumulated benefit obligation **30.08**
Fair value of plan assets **30.08**
Funded status of plan **30.08**
Projected benefit obligation **30.07**
Unrecognized net gain or loss **30.09**
Unrecognized net obligation/asset **30.09**
Unrecognized prior service cost **30.08**
Change in accounting principle **30.40**
Defined contribution plans **30.35**
Definition **30.35**
One or more plans' disclosures **30.36**
Participants' individual accounts **30.35**
Determination of contribution **30.35**
Net periodic pension cost **30.36**
Pension benefits available **30.35**
Target benefit plans **30.36**
Unrecognized net obligation or asset **30.36**
Amortization **30.36**

GAAP GUIDE / 96.21

Topical Index

PENSION PLANS—EMPLOYERS (continued)
Employers with two or more pension plans **30.33**
  Disclosures **30.36**
  Plans outside U.S. **30.33**
  Separate application of FASB-87 **30.33**
Financial statement disclosure **30.32**
  Amounts and types of securities **30.33**
  Description of plan **30.32**
  Funded status of plan reconciliation **30.32**
  Net periodic pension cost **30.32**
  Rate of compensation increases used to determine projected benefit obligation **30.33**
  Weighted-average assumed discount rate used to determine projected benefit obligation **30.33**
  Weighted-average expected long-term rate of return on plan assets **30.33**
Gains and losses component **30.19**
  Actual return on plan assets **30.20**
  Actuarial gain or loss **30.20**
  Amortization **30.23**
    Unrecognized net gain or loss **30.23**
  Change in fair value of plan assets **30.20**
  Change in projected benefit obligation **30.20**
  Comprehensive illustration **30.23**
  Defined **30.19**
  Expected long-term rate of return **30.20**
  Expected return on plan assets **30.21**
  Fair value of plan assets **30.20**
  Market-related value of plan assets **30.21**
    Actual fair value **30.21**
    Calculated value **30.21**
    Illustration **30.21**
  Net assets gain or loss **30.20**
    Included in net periodic pension cost component **30.20, 30.22**
Interest cost component **30.17**
  Probability of benefit payment **30.17**
  Recognition **30.17**
  Time value of money **30.17**
Measurement dates **30.31**
  Additional minimum liability **30.32**
  Net periodic pension cost **30.32**
  Plan assets and obligations **30.32**
Measurement of plan assets **30.31**
  Held as investment **30.31**
  Used in plan operation **30.31**
Multiemployer plans **30.36**
  Assets contributed **30.37**
  Disclosures **30.37**
  Multiple-employer plans **30.37**
  Net periodic pension cost **30.37**
  Withdrawing employer **30.37**
Net periodic pension cost **30.10**
  Actuarial assumption **30.11**
  Adjustments (actuarial gain or loss) **30.11**

Components **30.11**
Employers' worksheet records **30.11**
Estimate of at beginning of period **30.11**
Illustration **30.12**
  Explanation of changes in accounts **30.13**
  Journal entry **30.12**
Plan amendment **30.11**
Recognition on trustee books **30.11**
Non U.S. pension plans **30.38**
  Effective date **30.38**
Overview **30.02**
  Accrual basis of accounting **30.02**
  Accrued/prepaid pension cost **30.02**
  Contributory/noncontributory **30.02**
  Funded/unfunded **30.02**
  Net periodic pension cost **30.02**
  Pension plan accounting **30.03**
    Trust account **30.03**
    Withdrawal of plan assets **30.03**
Pension plan assets **30.05**
  Measurement **30.05**
    Held as investment **30.05**
    Used in operation **30.05**
  Reduced by liabilities **30.05**
  Restricted **30.05**
Recognition of liabilities and assets **30.27**
  Accumulated benefit obligation **30.28**
  Additional minimum liability **30.28**
    Calculation **30.29**
    Intangible assets **30.29**
    Recognition **30.28**
  Prepaid pension cost **30.28**
  Projected benefit obligation **30.28**
  Unfunded accrued pension cost **30.28**
  Unfunded accumulated benefit obligation **30.28**
Scope and applicability of FASB-87 **30.03**
  Arrangement similar to pension plan **30.04**
  Defined benefit pension plan **30.03**
  Defined contribution pension plan **30.03**
  Postemployment health care/life insurance benefits **30.03**
  Settlement/curtailment of pension plan **30.04**
  Target benefit plans **30.03**
  Use of estimates, averages, computational shortcuts **30.04**
Service cost component **30.14**
  Definition **30.15**
  Estimated future compensation levels **30.15**
  Nonvested benefit **30.16**
  Pension benefit formula **30.14**
    Attribution **30.14**
  Plan amendment **30.15**
    Employer's substantive commitment **30.15**
  Total future value of pension benefits **30.15**
  Total projected benefit **30.16**

96.22 / GAAP GUIDE

Topical Index

Benefit included in vested benefits **30.16**
Benefit not included in vested benefits **30.16**
  Vested benefit **30.16**
Transition and effective date **30.39**
  Nonpublic enterprise **30.39**
  Recognition of unrecognized net obligation or asset **30.39**
  Retroactive application **30.39**

PENSION PLANS—SETTLEMENTS AND CURTAILMENTS

Background **31.01**
  Coverage of GAAP **31.01**
Comprehensive illustration **31.15**
  Computation of total effects of plan curtailment **31.16**
  Journal entry **31.19**
  Settlement gain or loss **31.18**
Conflict with SEC Staff Accounting Bulletin-52 **31.14**
Curtailment of defined benefit pension plans **31.06**
  Decrease/increase in projected benefit obligation **31.08**
    Comprehensive illustration **31.11**
    Computation steps on plan curtailment **31.09**
    Determination of gain/loss **31.09**
    Disposal of discontinued business segment **31.09**
    Recognition of total effects of plan curtailment **31.10**
    Reporting total effects of plan curtailment **31.10**
  Decrease in unrecognized prior service cost **31.06**
    Amortization **31.06**
    Computation steps **31.07**
    Expected years of future service **31.06**
    Included in total effects of plan curtailment **31.07**
    Unrecognized net obligation **31.07**
  Definition **31.06**
Disposal of identifiable business segment **31.13**
  Determination of gain/loss **31.13**
    Measurement date **31.13**
  Disposal date **31.13**
  Extraordinary item **31.13**
Effective date and transition **31.13**
  Asset reversion transaction **31.14**
Overview **30.02**
  Curtailment of plan **31.02**
  Settlement of plan **31.01**
  Termination benefits **31.03**
    Contractual **31.03**
    Special **31.03**
Settlements of defined benefit pension plans **31.04**
  Annuity contract **31.04**

Definition **31.04**
Maximum gain or loss recognition **31.04**
Participating annuity contract **31.05**
Reporting gain or loss **31.05**
Small settlement **31.05**
Transfer of obligation **31.04**
Updating records **31.03**
Termination benefits **31.12**
  Contractual **31.12**
  Reporting loss **31.12**
  Special **31.12**
Updating pension plan records **31.03**

PERCENTAGE-OF-COMPLETION METHOD
Long-term contracts **27.03**

PERIODIC INVENTORY SYSTEM
Inventory pricing and methods **24.01**

PERMANENT DIFFERENCES
Bad debts—savings and loan associations **19.04**
Income taxes **19.03**
Indefinite reversal criteria **19.07**
Policyholders' surplus—stock life insurance co. **19.04**
Types **19.03**

PERPETUAL INVENTORY SYSTEM
Inventory pricing and methods **24.02**

PLEDGING
Current—assets and liabilities **8.07**

POOLING-OF-INTERESTS METHOD
Business combinations **3.02**
Conditions for pooling **3.19**
Disclosures **3.28**
Disposal of significant portion of assets **3.27**
Effective date of consummation **3.20**
Expenses of combination **3.27**
Inconsistent transactions **3.26**
Intercorporate investments **3.27**
Reacquisition of voting stock **3.25**
Restatement of prior years **3.27**
Treasury stock **3.27**

PREFERRED STOCK
Marketable securities **28.01**
Stockholders' equity **38.01**

PRICE INDEXES
General price-level changes **17.03**

PRICE-LEVEL CHANGES
Financial reporting and changing prices **15.51**
General price-level changes **17.01**

PRIMARY EARNINGS PER SHARE
Earnings per share **13.10**

PRIOR-PERIOD ADJUSTMENTS
Earnings per share **13.02**
Income taxes **19.02**
Results of operations **36.03**

GAAP GUIDE / 96.23

PRIOR-PERIOD ADJUSTMENTS (continued)
Accounting changes **36.04**
Definition **36.04**
Interim **36.04**

PRIOR-SERVICE COSTS
Pension plans—employers **30.18**
Pension plans—settlements and curtailments **31.06**

PRODUCT FINANCING ARRANGEMENTS
Accounting for product financing arrangements **31.77**
Accounting by sponsor **31.77**
Background **31.75**
Definition of financing arrangement **31.75**
Examples **31.75**
Other factors **31.76**
Long-term obligations **27.59**
Overview **31.75**
Coverage of GAAP **31.75**

PROFIT-SHARING PLANS
Pension plans—employers **31.02**

PROJECTED BENEFIT OBLIGATION
Pension plans—employers **30.07**
Change in **30.20**
Recognition of liabilities/assets **30.28**
Total projected benefit **30.16**
Pension plans—settlements and curtailments **31.08**

PROPERTY AND LIABILITY INSURANCE COMPANIES
Claims **65.05**
Departmental functions **65.03**
Facultative reinsurance **65.04**
General ledger **65.03**
Insurable interest **65.02**
Insurance laws **65.05**
Limit of insurance **65.04**
Mutual companies **65.02**
Reciprocal **65.02**
Stock companies **65.02**

PUBLICLY TRADED COMPANIES
Accounting changes—interim periods **1.11**
Interim financial reporting **23.03**
Summarized interim reports **23.03**

PURCHASE METHOD
Acquisition of pension plan assets/liabilities **3.06**
Allocating cost **3.05**
Amortization of goodwill **3.09**
Business combinations **3.01**
Contingent assets/liabilities **3.07**
Contingent consideration **3.03**
Determination of cost **3.02**
Direct expenses **3.06**
Disclosures **3.08**

Fair value **3.02**
Goodwill **3.11**
Indirect expenses **3.06**
Net-spread method **3.04**
Purchase vs. pooling **3.09**
Registration and issuing costs **3.03**
Separate-valuation method **3.04**

QUASI-REORGANIZATIONS
Accounting and reporting **32.02**
Accounting procedure **32.02**
Charge to retained earnings **32.02**
Dating retained earnings **32.03**
Effective date **32.03**
New or additional shares **32.03**
Parent and subsidiary **32.03**
Write-offs **32.02**
Fair values **32.02**
Formal consent **32.03**
Provide for all losses **32.02**
Report to stockholders **32.02**
Tax benefits **32.04**
Background **32.01**
Corporate readjustment **32.01**
Coverage of GAAP **32.01**
Comprehensive illustration **32.04**
Disclosure **32.04**
Dating retained earnings **32.04**
New retained earnings account **32.04**
Overview **32.01**
Accumulated deficit **32.02**
Justification for reorganization **32.01**
Alternative to legal steps **32.02**
Assets require adjustment **32.02**
Eliminate large deficit **32.02**
New basis of accountability **32.01**
Reduction of par value **32.01**
Stockholders' equity **32.01**
Turnaround point **32.01**

RAILROAD GRADINGS AND TUNNEL BORES
Income taxes **19.09**

RAILROAD TRACK STRUCTURES
Accounting changes **1.01**

RAZING AND REMOVAL COSTS
Depreciable assets and depreciation **11.01**

REACQUISITION PRICE
Extinguishment of debt **15.02**

REAL AND PERSONAL PROPERTY TAXES
Accounting and reporting **33.01**
Adjustment to tax liability **33.01**
Assessment date **33.01**
Capitalization of real estate taxes **33.01**

Topical Index

Consistent application **33.02**
Recognition of tax liability **33.01**
Reporting taxes in the income statement **33.01**
Background **33.01**

REAL ESTATE COSTS AND INITIAL RENTAL OPERATIONS
Abandonment and changes in use **80.10**
Allocation of capitalized costs **80.09**
Amenity costs **80.07**
Background **80.01**
Direct costs **80.06**
Incidental operations **80.08**
Indirect costs **80.06**
Initial rental operations **80.13**
Overview **80.01**
   Coverage of GAAP **80.01**
Preacquisition costs **80.05**
   Other costs **80.05**
   Unexpired options **80.05**
Recoverability **80.13**
Rental costs **80.12**
   Current period **80.13**
   Future periods **80.12**
Revisions of estimates **80.10**
Selling costs **80.11**
   Period costs **80.12**
   Prepaid expenses **80.12**
   Project costs **80.11**

REAL ESTATE—RECOGNITION OF SALES
Background **81.02**
Overview **81.01**
   Coverage of GAAP **81.01**
Real estate sales, except retail land sales **81.04**
   Buyer's initial and continuing investment **81.05**
      Continuing investment **81.11**
      Minimum initial investment **81.07**
      Sales value **81.05**
   Buyer's investment inadequate **81.19**
   Disclosure **81.23**
   Nontransferability of ownership **81.12**
   Profit recognition other than full accrual **81.13**
   Sales not consummated **81.17**
   Seller's continued involvement **81.20**
   When a sale is consummated **81.04**
Retail land sales **81.23**
   Change in accounting method **81.27**
   Deposit accounting **81.27**
   Disclosure **81.28**
   Full accrual **81.24**
   Installment sales **81.27**
   Percentage of completion **81.26**
   Profit recognition **81.23**

REALIZED GROSS PROFIT
Installment method of accounting **20.02**

REALIZED INCOME
Current value accounting **9.03**

RECORD AND MUSIC
Background **53.01**
Costs **53.01**
   Record making process **53.01**
Effective date **53.03**
Licensee accounting **53.03**
Licensor accounting **53.02**
Overview **53.01**

REDUCTION OF TAX BASIS IN PROPERTY
Investment tax credit **25.01**

REGULATED INDUSTRIES
Accounting principles **85.01**

RELATED PARTIES
Leases **26.35**

RELATED PARTY DISCLOSURES
Background **34.01**
   Definition of related party **34.01**
   Disclosures **34.01**
Material related party disclosures **34.02**
   Description of disclosures **34.02**
   Detail necessary **34.03**
   Examples of related parties **34.02**
Overview **34.01**
   Coverage of GAAP **34.01**

RELATIVE SALES VALUE COSTING
Inventory pricing and methods **24.14**

RENEGOTIATION
Adjustment of selling price **18.02**
Disclosure **18.02**
Government contracts **18.02**
Provision for renegotiation **18.02**

REPORTABLE SEGMENT
Segmental reporting **37.04**

REPOSSESSED GOODS
Franchises repossessed **60.08**
Installment method of accounting **20.02**

RESEARCH AND DEVELOPMENT
Accounting and reporting **35.02**
   Acquired by purchase method–business combination **35.03**
   Exceptions **35.02**
   Expensed when incurred **35.02**
   Inventories—research and development **24.17**
Background **35.01**
   Coverage of promulgated GAAP **35.01**
   Exclusions **35.01**
Computer software to be sold, leased, or otherwise marketed **35.03**
   Amortization of capitalized computer software costs **35.07**
   Costs that must be capitalized **35.05**
      Costs incurred after technological feasibility established **35.05**

RESEARCH AND DEVELOPMENT (continued)

Costs that must be expensed **35.04**
  Costs incurred to establish technological feasibility **35.04**
  Exceptions **35.05**
  Production costs incurred for integral parts of computer software product/process **35.05**
Discontinuance of capitalizing computer software costs **35.05**
Effective date **35.08**
Establishing technological feasibility **35.06**
  Includes detail program design **35.06**
  Does not include detail program design **35.07**
Financial statement disclosure **35.08**
Inventory costs **35.07**
Periodic evaluation of capitalized computer software costs **35.07**
Primary activities **35.04**
Purchasing or internally developing and producing **35.03**
  Integral parts **35.03**
  Separate products **35.03**
Disclosure **35.03**
  Amount charged to expense **35.03**
  Regulated industries **35.03**
    Accounting policies **35.03**
    Total amount expensed, capitalized, or deferred **35.03**
Overview **35.02**
  Conservatism **35.02**
  Definition of development **35.02**
  Definition of research **35.02**
  General and administrative **35.02**
  Market research and testing **35.02**
  Uncertainty of future benefits **35.02**
R & D arrangements **35.08**
  Nature of arrangement **35.09**
  Obligation for contractual services **35.11**
  Financial statement disclosure **35.12**
  Effective date **35.13**

RESIDUAL VALUE
Depreciable assets and depreciation **11.02**

RESTRICTED OR LEGEND STOCK
Marketable securities **28.02**

RESTRUCTURING OF DEBT
Troubled debt restructuring **40.01**

RESULTS OF OPERATIONS
Background **36.01**
  Coverage of GAAP **36.01**
Disclosure **36.07**
Discontinued operations **36.05**
  Determination of gain or loss **36.06**
  Disposal date **36.06**
  Identifiable entity **36.05**
  Long-term leases **36.06**
  Measurement date **36.05**
Extraordinary items **36.02**
  Characteristics **36.02**
  Items which are extraordinary **36.03**
  Items which are not extraordinary **36.03**
Overview **36.01**
  All-inclusive concept **36.01**
  Capital transactions **36.02**
  Current operating performance **36.02**
Presentation of net income **36.08**
  EPS presentation **36.08**
Prior-period adjustments **36.03**
  Accounting changes **36.04**
  Definition **36.03**
  Interim-period adjustments **36.04**

RETAIL INVENTORY METHOD
Cost-to-retail ratio **24.09**
Inventory pricing and methods **24.09**
LIFO application **24.12**

RETAIL LAND SALES
Change in accounting method **81.27**
Deposit accounting method **81.27**
Disclosure **81.26**
Full accrual **81.24**
Installment sales **81.27**
Percentage of completion **81.26**
Profit recognition **81.23**

RETAINED EARNINGS
Stockholders equity **38.03**

REVENUE RECOGNITION
Background **36.51**
  Realization principle **36.51**
  Right to return **36.51**
Comprehensive illustration **36.58**
Disclosures **36.54**
  Accounting change **36.55**
    Cumulative effect **36.56**
    Retroactive restatement **36.55**
Franchise fee revenue **60.03**
Overview **36.51**
  Coverage of GAAP **36.51**
Reasonable estimates of returns **36.54**
  Factors affecting estimates **36.54**
Revenue recognition for returnable merchandise **36.52**
  Conditions for income recognition **36.52**
  Provision for costs or losses **36.52**
    Loss contingency **36.53**

RULE OF PREFERABILITY
Accounting changes **1.02**

SALE-LEASEBACK TRANSACTIONS
Leases **26.35**

SALES-TYPE LEASE
Leases **26.03**

SALVAGE
Depreciable assets and depreciation **11.02**

Topical Index

SAVINGS AND LOAN ASSOCIATIONS
Intangible assets **21.01**
   Net-spread method **21.02**
   Separate-valuation method **21.02**

SEGMENTAL REPORTING
Background **37.01**
   Coverage of GAAP **37.01**
Comprehensive illustration **37.10**
Determining reportable segments **37.05**
Dominant segments **37.07**
Foreign operations and export sales **37.08**
   Geographic areas **37.09**
Grouping products and services **37.06**
Information about major customers **37.09**
Information to be reported **37.08**
   Identifiable assets **37.08**
   Operating profit or loss **37.08**
   Other disclosure **37.08**
   Revenue **37.08**
Nonpublic enterprise **37.03**
   Definition **37.03**
   Suspension of disclosure **37.03**
Oil and gas producing companies **75.15**
Overview **37.03**
Restatement of previously reported segment information **37.10**
Segment information not required **37.01**
Selecting reportable segments **37.06**
   Comparability test **37.07**
   75% test **37.07**
   10% test **37.06**
Terminology **37.04**
   Complete set of financial statements **37.02**
   Financial report **37.02**
   Foreign investee **37.02**
   Identifiable assets **37.05**
   Industry segment **37.04**
   Industry segment's operating profit **37.04**
   Interest on intersegmental receivables **37.04**
   Operating expenses of industry segments **37.04**
   Operating income of industry segments **37.04**
   Reportable segments **37.04**
   Revenue **37.04**
   Segmental information **37.02**

SELF-CONSTRUCTED FIXED ASSETS
Depreciable assets and depreciation **11.03**
Interest costs capitalized **22.51**

SETTLEMENTS OF DEFINED BENEFIT PENSION PLANS
Pension plans—settlements and curtailments **31.04**

SPECIAL TERMINATION BENEFITS PAID TO EMPLOYEES
Pension plans—employers **31.01**

Pension plans—settlements and curtailments **31.12**

STANDARD COSTS
Inventory pricing and methods **24.06**
   Use of standards **24.06**
   Variations from standard **24.06**

STEP-BY-STEP ACQUISITION
Consolidated financial statements **5.02**
Intangible assets **21.05**
Purchase method **3.15**

STOCK DIVIDEND
Stockholders' equity **38.08**

STOCKHOLDERS' EQUITY
Background **38.01**
   Coverage of GAAP **38.01**
Dividends **38.08**
   Cash dividends **38.08**
      Date of declaration **38.08**
      Date of payment **38.08**
      Date of record **38.08**
   Stock dividends **38.08**
Legal capital **38.01**
   Capital stock—authorized, issued, outstanding **38.02**
   Common stock characteristics **38.02**
   Preferred stock characteristics **38.01**
   Subscription method **38.02**
Legal capital—disclosures **38.02**
   Capital stock **38.03**
   Paid-in capital **38.03**
   Retained earnings **38.03**
Minority interests **38.04**
Overview **38.01**
Paid-in capital **38.03**
   Definition **38.03**
   Sources **38.03**
Retained earnings **38.04**
Stock rights **38.09**
   Accounting for issuer **38.09**
   Accounting for recipient **38.09**
Stock split **38.09**
   Difference from stock dividend **38.09**
Treasury stock **38.05**
   Accounting and reporting **38.06**
      Cost method **38.06**
      Par value method **38.06**
      Retirement **38.07**
   Greenmail and standstill agreements **38.06**
   Reacquisition **38.05**

STOCK ISSUED TO EMPLOYEES
Background **39.01**
   Coverage of GAAP **39.01**
Common stock equivalents **39.11**
   Determining dilutive effects **39.11**
   Illustration **39.12**
Compensatory plans **39.03**
   Basic provisions **39.03**
   Comprehensive illustration **39.18**
   Disclosure **39.16**

Topical Index

STOCK ISSUED TO EMPLOYEES (continued)
Measurement date **39.04**
  Distribution of treasury stock **39.05**
  Junior stock plans **39.07**
  Renewal of stock option **39.05**
  Stock option for current services **39.04**
  Stock options of convertible securities **39.05**
  Transfer of stock to a trustee **39.05**
  Variable awards **39.05**
  When the measurement date is **39.04**
Measuring compensation costs **39.08**
  Combination of two or more plans **39.08**
  Future compensation costs **39.08**
  Option in convertible stock **39.08**
  Payment of cash to settle an earlier option **39.07**
  Reacquisition of stock issued **39.07**
  Stock option plan by principal stockholder **39.07**
Noncompensatory plans **39.02**
  Characteristics **39.02**
  Definition **39.02**
Overview **39.02**
  Compensatory stock option **39.02**
  Noncompensatory stock option **39.02**
Recognition of compensation costs **39.10**
  Periods over which costs are recognized **39.10**
  Plans with past and future services **39.10**
  Substance of transaction **39.10**
  Unearned compensation costs **39.10**
Related tax effects **39.10**
  Additional compensation costs **39.10**
  Tax deduction taken by company **39.10**
  Timing difference **39.10**
Types of plans **39.01**
  Combination and elective **39.02**
  Shadow or phantom stock **39.02**
  Stock bonus and award **39.02**
  Stock option and purchase **39.02**
  Typical fixed **39.01**

STOCK LIFE INSURANCE COMPANIES
Annuity policy **65.07**
Departmental functions **65.07**
Endowment policies **65.09**
Insurable interest **65.06**
Joint and survivorship annuity **65.11**
Life annuity **65.10**
Straight-life annuity **65.10**
Term policies **65.09**
Variable annuity **65.11**
Whole-life policies **65.08**

STOCK OPTIONS AND WARRANTS
Convertible debt—characteristics **7.01**
Earnings per share **13.04**
Marketable securities **28.01**

STOCK RIGHTS
Stockholders' equity **38.09**

STOCK SPLIT
Stockholders' equity **38.09**
Difference from a stock dividend **38.09**

STOCK SUBSCRIPTIONS
Stockholders' equity **38.02**

SUBSTANCE OVER FORM
Common stock equivalents **13.03**
Earnings per share **13.04**
Leases **26.02**
Receivables and payables **22.01**

SUCCESSFUL-EFFORTS COSTING
Oil and gas producing companies **75.06**

SUPPORT EQUIPMENT AND FACILITIES
Oil and gas producing companies **75.04**

SYSTEMATIC AND RATIONAL ALLOCATION
Depreciable assets and depreciation **11.04**
Depreciation methods **11.04**
Intangible assets **21.03**

TAXABLE INCOME
Income taxes **19.28**

TERMINATION CLAIMS
Determination of profit or loss **18.03**
Disclosure **18.03**
Disposal credits **18.03**
Government contracts **18.03**
Inventory for terminated contracts **24.17**

TIMING DIFFERENCES
Deferred tax method **19.10**
Depreciation **11.08**
Foreign operations and exchange **16.06**
Income taxes **19.02**
Indefinite reversal criteria **19.07**
Losses of a subsidiary **19.07**
Marketable securities **28.08**
Measuring timing differences **19.03**
Railroad gradings and tunnel bores **19.09**
Stock issued to employees **39.01**
Undistributed earnings of a subsidiary **19.06**
U.S. steamship companies **19.09**

TITLE INSURANCE COMPANIES
Title plant **65.12**
Title search **65.11**

TITLE PLANT
Background **66.01**
  Title insurance **66.01**
Capitalization of title plant **66.02**
  Carrying amount **66.02**
Effective date **66.04**
Maintenance and operating expenses **66.03**
Overview **66.01**
Sale of title plant **66.03**

Topical Index

TRANSFER OF RECEIVABLES WITH RECOURSE
Background **39.51**
Financial statement disclosures **39.51**
Overview **39.51**
Sale or liability **39.53**
TREASURY STOCK
Business combination **3.27**
Marketable securities **28.02**
Stockholders' equity **38.04**
  Accounting and reporting **38.06**
  Greenmail and standstill agreements **38.06**
  Profits or losses **38.06**
  Reacquisition **38.05**
  Stock issued to employees **39.05**
TREASURY STOCK METHOD
Earnings per share **13.13**
TROUBLED DEBT RESTRUCTURING
Accounting and reporting by debtors **40.03**
  Combination of types **40.05**
  Contingently payable amounts **40.05**
    Criteria **40.05**
  Disclosure by debtors **40.06**
  Incidental cost of restructure **40.05**
  Modification of terms **40.04**
  Transfer of assets **40.03**
  Transfer of equity interest **40.04**
Accounting by creditors **40.06**
  Combination of types **40.07**
  Creditor disclosure **40.08**
  Modification of terms **40.06**
  Receipt of assets or equity **40.06**
  Related matters **40.07**
  Substitution of debtors **40.08**
Background **40.01**
  Coverage of GAAP **40.01**
  Definition **40.01**
  Situation of troubled debt **40.01**
Definition of terms **40.03**
  Receivable (or payable) **40.03**
  Situations not troubled debt **40.03**
  Time of restructuring **40.03**
Overview **40.02**
TWO-CLASS METHOD
Earnings per share **13.22**

UNAMORTIZED DISCOUNT OF PREMIUM
Interest on receivables or payables **22.02**
UNAMORTIZED POLICY ACQUISITION COSTS
Foreign operations and exchange **16.05**

Translation—stock life insurance companies **16.05**
UNASSERTED CLAIMS
Contingencies **6.03**
UNAUDITED FINANCIAL STATEMENTS
Accounting policies **2.01**
UNCLASSIFIED BALANCE SHEETS
Changes in financial position **4.01**
Concept of funds **4.02**
Marketable securities **28.07**
UNCONDITIONAL PURCHASE OBLIGATIONS
Long-term obligations **27.52**
UNREALIZED GROSS PROFIT
Installment method of accounting **20.04**
UNREALIZED PROFITS IN INVENTORY
Consolidated financial statements **5.06**
Inventory pricing and methods **24.19**
UNREALIZED PROFITS IN LONG-LIVED ASSETS
Consolidated financial statements **5.08**
UNITED KINGDOM TAX BENEFITS
Income tax **19.26**
U.S. STEAMSHIP COMPANIES
Income taxes **19.09**

VALUATION OF ASSETS
Depreciable assets and depreciation **11.02**
Goodwill **3.07**
Historical cost **11.02**
Intangible assets **21.02**
Inventory in business combinations **24.17**
Present value **11.03**
Price-level restatement **17.01**
Replacement cost **11.02**
VESTED BENEFITS
Pension plans—employers **30.16**

WEIGHTED-AVERAGE METHOD
Inventory pricing and methods **24.08**
WEIGHTED-AVERAGE SHARES
Earnings per share **13.10**
WORKING CAPITAL
Acid-test ratio **8.04**
Changes in each element **8.04**
Current ratio **8.04**
Definition **8.03**
Changes in financial position **4.01**

OTHER PROFESSIONAL PUBLICATIONS OF INTEREST

MILLER COMPREHENSIVE 1987 GAAS GUIDE®

Since its publication in June of 1982, the *Miller Comprehensive GAAS Guide®* has won the acceptance of thousands of accounting professionals. Here, in one handy volume, are all the promulgated and many of the nonpromulgated standards, practices, and procedures which an independent auditor or accountant must apply in the performance of any type of professional engagement. Over 1,300 pages. Paperback—$32.00. Deluxe hardcover edition—$42.00

MILLER COMPREHENSIVE 1987 GOVERNMENTAL GAAP GUIDE™

In this new volume, Larry Bailey, co-author of the *Miller Comprehensive GAAS Guide,*® has analyzed and condensed all official governmental accounting pronouncements in one volume—the *Miller Comprehensive Governmental GAAP Guide,*™ the basic governmental accounting reference for your professional library. Paperback—$35.00. Deluxe hardcover edition—$45.00

MILLER ACCOUNTING UPDATE SERVICES

Subscribers to Miller Accounting Update Services can count on keeping up with changes in GAAP and/or governmental GAAP. Within weeks of any official FASB or GASB pronouncement you will receive your Update Bulletin—a complete restatement and analysis of the new pronouncement. With your subscription, you receive one copy of the *GAAP Guide* or the *Governmental GAAP Guide,* or both guides if you subscribe to both Updates. Save 10% on an order of 3 or more subscriptions. Each 1-year Subscription $110. Each 2-year Subscription $200.

STANDING ORDER PLAN... allows you to automatically receive one or all of our Miller Accounting Guides each year. Standing orders may be canceled at any time. Free shipping included.

SAVE 10%... when you purchase sets of our Guides. Call our toll-free number for more information.

QUANTITY DISCOUNT... of 23% on all orders for 25 or more copies.

TOLL-FREE ORDERING AND INFORMATION
Call **1-800-543-1918**. In CA and AK, call collect **619-699-6335**.

HBJ   MILLER ACCOUNTING PUBLICATIONS, INC.
A subsidiary of Harcourt Brace Jovanovich, Inc.
1250 Sixth Ave., San Diego, CA 92101-9803

Prices subject to change without notice.
(Offer restricted to continental U.S. and Canada.)   Printed in U.S.A.